Wissenschaftliche Untersuchungen
zum Neuen Testament · 2. Reihe

Herausgeber / Editor
Jörg Frey (Zürich)

Mitherausgeber / Associate Editors
Friedrich Avemarie (Marburg)
Markus Bockmuehl (Oxford)
James A. Kelhoffer (Uppsala)
Hans-Josef Klauck (Chicago, IL)

311

Stephen E. Young

Jesus Tradition in the Apostolic Fathers

Their Explicit Appeals to the Words of Jesus in Light of
Orality Studies

Mohr Siebeck

STEPHEN E. YOUNG, born 1965; 2010 PhD in Theology from Fuller Theological Seminary in Pasadena, CA; currently teaches at Fuller as Affiliate Instructor of New Testament.

ISBN 978-3-16-151010-6
ISSN 0340-9570 (Wissenschaftliche Untersuchungen zum Neuen Testament, 2. Reihe)

Die Deutsche Nationalbibliothek lists this publication in the Deutsche Nationalbibliographie; detailed bibliographic data are available on the Internet at *http://dnb.d-nb.de*.

The book was printed by Laupp & Göbel in Nehren on non-aging paper and bound by Buchbinderei Nädele in Nehren.

Printed in Germany.

To Susan and Berto

*for the joy of
who you are*

Preface

This monograph is a slightly revised version of my Ph.D. thesis, submitted in June 2010 to the faculty of the School of Theology at Fuller Theological Seminary. I have become indebted to many during my years at Fuller. I would like to thank Dr. Richard Beaton, who walked with me as I narrowed down my dissertation topic, and provided guidance and encouragement in my work. I also thank Dr. Marianne Meye Thompson, who read an early draft of Chapter 3 and made many helpful suggestions. I owe Dr. Donald A. Hagner a special debt of gratitude: he has always made time to discuss my work, and to provide valuable feedback as needed. His interest has not been limited to my academic pursuits, as he has ever been concerned also with my well-being and that of my family. His friendship has been a constant source of encouragement, strength, and inspiration throughout my doctoral program and after. For all of this I am deeply grateful. I am also grateful to Dr. Andrew Gregory of the University of Oxford for his insightful and relevant criticism. His feedback, informed by his deep familiarity with my subject matter (I cite him frequently in the pages that follow), proved uniquely helpful during the final revision process. I also thank Susan Wood in Faculty Publications at Fuller for her advice on technical matters related to my manuscript. I am, of course, fully responsible for any and all shortcomings that remain.

It has been a pleasure to work with the editors and staff at Mohr Siebeck, who have been not only efficient and professional, but also personable and gracious. I warmly thank Professor Jörg Frey and Dr. Henning Ziebritzki for accepting this work for publication in the second series of Wissenschaftliche Untersuchungen zum Neuen Testament. I also thank Anna Krüger for her excellent editorial advice and her assistance with several technical matters that were quite over my head.

I deeply appreciate the assistance received from many other people during the long process that led to the completion of this project. Among them I would like to thank Dr. Richard Erickson, Dr. Seyoon Kim, Dr. Charles Scalise, and Dr. Pamela Scalise, former professors who I am fortunate to count among my friends. Each of them has not only taught me much, but also affirmed and encouraged me in various ways, for all of which I am grateful. My previous forays into the subject matter of this monograph took the form of papers written for a masters-level course on Christology taught by Dr. Bryan Burton in Winter 2002, and for a doctoral seminar on the Apostolic Fathers taught by Dr. David M. Scholer in Fall 2004. I thank Dr. Burton for his feedback, which encouraged me to further pursue this topic. I wish I could also thank Dr. Scholer, who was ever supportive even in the midst of a lengthy battle with cancer. Unfortunately, however, he eventually lost that battle and passed away in 2008.

It has been a pleasure to work with the staff at Fuller's David Allan Hubbard Library. I thank Gail Frederick of the InterLibrary Loan department who cheerfully and efficiently tracked down many important resources. I also thank Associate Provost for Library Services Dr. David Bundy, and Assistant Provost for Library and Information Technology Michael Murray, for acquiring a number of volumes for the Library that were important for my research.

It would have been impossible for me to complete my program without financial assistance from several quarters. I thank the Center for Advanced Theological Studies (CATS) Committee at Fuller, for the Fellowships the Center provided from 2003 through 2007, and for a Dissertation Writing Award in 2008. I am grateful also to Dr. Charles E. Carlston for generously funding a New Testament Scholarship through CATS, from which I benefited in 2005–2006. I also thank the New Testament department in the School of Theology for giving me the opportunity to teach while engaged in my doctoral work. In this connection I wish to thank as well Jeannette Scholer, Dr. Linda Peacore, Christine Cervantes, Catherine Kelly and others at the Academic Programs office, and also Dr. Juan Martinez at Fuller's Center for the Study of Hispanic Church and Community. This teaching experience provided an opportunity for me to engage with the wonderful student body at Fuller, and also contributed significantly to meeting my financial needs.

Last in order, but first in affection, I thank my wife Susan and our son Alberto for much love and support during these years of research and writing. It was a challenge for Susan and I to leave the many comforts that came with a caring community and two secure jobs in Seattle, to embark on a journey into many unknowns, with our then four-month-old son (now 8 years old!). I am deeply grateful to Susan, given that without her many sacrifices and ongoing encouragement it would have been impossible for me to complete my program. However, I am even more grateful to both her and Alberto for that love that creates home, and that gives meaning to sacrifices and accomplishments. It is to the two of them that I dedicate this book.

Pasadena, August 1, 2011   Stephen E. Young

Table of Contents

Abbreviations

The following abbreviations are used in addition to those found in P. H. Alexander, ed., *The SBL Handbook of Style: For Ancient Near Eastern, Biblical, and Early Christian Studies* (Peabody: Hendrickson, 1999), with full bibliographical detail given in the Bibliography:

//	Parallel(s)
AcBib	Academia Biblica (Society of Biblical Literature)
AmAn	*American Antiquity*
ApFa	Apostolic Fathers
Apoc	*Apocrypha: Revue Internationalle des Littératures Apocryphes/International Journal of Apocryphal Literatures*
ARS	*Annual Review of Sociology*
ASBT	Acadia Studies in Bible and Theology (Baker Academic)
AV	Die Apostolischen Väter (Mohr Siebeck)
AYB	The Anchor Yale Bible (Yale University Press)
BECNT	Baker Exegetical Commentary on the New Testament (Baker Academic)
BibSem	Biblical Seminar (Sheffield)
BNE	Biblioteca para la nueva evangelización (Caparrós Editores)
BPC	Biblical Performance Criticism (Cascade)
CCR	Cambridge Companions to Religion
CCWJCW	Cambridge Commentaries on Writings of the Jewish and Christian World 200 BC to AD 200
CJA	Christianity and Judaism in Antiquity (Notre Dame)
ClAnt	*Classical Antiquity*
ContRev	*Contemporary Review*
CSOLC	Cambridge Studies in Oral and Literate Culture
CTL	Crown Theological Library (G. P. Putnam's Sons/Williams & Norgate)
DBI	*Dictionary of Biblical Interpretation*. Ed. John H. Hayes. 2 vols. Nashville: Abingdon, 1999
DJG	*Dictionary of Jesus and the Gospels*. Ed. Joel B. Green, Scot McKnight, and I. Howard Marshall. Downers Grove: InterVarsity, 1992
ECC	Early Christianity in Context (T&T Clark)
EHJ	*Encyclopedia of the Historical Jesus*. Ed. Craig A. Evans. New York and London: Routledge, 2008
ERPWLA	*Encyclopedia of Religious and Philosophical Writings in Late Antiquity: Pagan, Judaic, Christian*. Ed. in Chief Jacob Neusner and Alan J. Avery-Peck. Consulting Ed. William Scott Green. Leiden: Brill, 2007
ETSSS	Evangelical Theological Society Studies Series (Baker and Apollos)
FonC	Fontes Christiani (Herder)
FPat	Fuentes Patrísticas (Ciudad Nueva)

FSC	Faith and Scholarship Colloquies (Trinity Press International)
FTMT	Fortress Texts in Modern Theology (Fortress)
GBSNTS	Guides to Biblical Scholarship: New Testament Series (Fortress)
GFB	Garland Folklore Bibliographies
GRLH	Garland Reference Library of the Humanities
HHM	Harvard Historical Monographs (Harvard University Press)
HJ	*Historisches Jahrbuch*
HSHJ	*Handbook for the Study of the Historical Jesus*. Ed. Tom Holmén and Stanley E. Porter. 4 vols. Leiden: Brill, 2011
HTCNT	Herder's Theological Commentary on the New Testament
JGGPÖ	*Jahrbuch der Gesellschaft für die Geschichte des Protestantismus in Österreich*
JJTP	*The Journal of Jewish Thought and Philosophy*
JSHJ	*Journal for the Study of the Historical Jesus*
KTAH	Key Themes in Ancient History (Cambridge)
LBS	Linguistic Biblical Studies (Brill)
LJS	Lives of Jesus Series (Fortress)
LkR	Lukan Redaction
LTT	Library of Theological Translations (James Clarke)
MattR	Matthean Redaction
MnS	Supplements to Mnemosyne (Brill)
NAl	Nueva Alianza (Ediciones Sígueme)
NC	Narrative Commentaries (Trinity Press International)
NGC	*New German Critique*
NGS	New Gospel Studies (Mercer)
NLH	*New Literary History*
NTAF	*The New Testament in the Apostolic Fathers*. By a Committee of the Oxford Society of Historical Theology. Oxford: Clarendon, 1905
NTAF	The New Testament and the Apostolic Fathers (Oxford)
ODCC	*The Oxford Dictionary of the Christian Church*. Ed. F. L. Cross and E. A. Livingstone. 3rd ed., revised. Oxford: Oxford University Press, 2005
OLAG	Orality and Literacy in Ancient Greece (Brill)
OrTr	*Oral Tradition*
PFLUS	Publications de la Faculté des Lettres de l'Université de Strasbourg (Ophrys)
PillNTC	Pillar New Testament Commentary
PSCE	Princeton Series of Collected Essays
RCatT	*Revista Catalana de Teologia*
RPP	*Religion Past and Present: Encyclopedia of Theology and Religion*. Ed. Hans Dieter Betz, Don S. Browning, Bernd Janowski, and Eberhard Jüngel. Leiden: Brill, 2007–
SBEC	Studies in the Bible and Early Christianity (Edwin Mellen)
SchU	Schriften des Urchristentums (Wissenschaftliche Buchgesellschaft)
SD	Scripta et documenta (Abadia di Montserrat)
SH	Scripture and Hermeneutics (Paternoster and Zondervan)
SHBC	Smyth & Helwys Bible Commentary (Smyth & Helwys)
SLFCS	Studies in Literacy, Family, Culture and the State (Cambridge)
SM	Scripta Minora (Gleerup)
SNTW	Studies in the New Testament and Its World (T&T Clark)
SocTh	*Sociological Theory*

SST	Schleiermacher: Studies and Translations (Edwin Mellen)
STAR	Studies in Theology and Religion (Deo)
StBibLit	Studies in Biblical Literature (Peter Lang)
T&TCBS	T&T Clark Biblical Studies
TICP	Travaux de l'Institut Catholique de Paris (Bloud & Gay)
TSS	Themes in the Social Sciences (Cambridge)
TUMSR	Trinity University Monograph Series in Religion
UCL	Universitas Catholica Lovaniensis Series
VCSup	Supplements to Vigiliae Christianae (Brill)
VetChr	*Vetera Christianorum*
VPT	Voices in Performance and Text (Indiana University Press)

Chapter 1

Orality and the Study of Early Christianity

"… notwithstanding its stunning accomplishments, [historical biblical scholarship] is empowered by an inadequate theory of the art of communication in the ancient world."
– Werner H. Kelber, *The Oral and the Written Gospel*, xxviii

1.1 Introduction

Early Christianity arose and spread within cultures that were predominantly oral.[1] The full implications of this basic insight are just beginning to be worked out within the field of New Testament studies. Not that oral tradition is a new concept; on the contrary, New Testament scholars have appealed to it for centuries in debating such topics as the sources and historical reliability of the canonical Gospels.

In the modern period, scholars began to give serious attention to the place of oral tradition in the composition of the canonical Gospels in reaction to Hermann Samuel Reimarus (1694–1768). In the Wolfenbütel Fragments (1774–78), Reimarus held that the disciples fabricated much of the Gospels' history and doctrine; see his "Concerning the Intention of Jesus and His Teaching," in *Reimarus: Fragments* (ed. C. H. Talbert; trans. R. S. Fraser; LJS; Philadelphia: Fortress, 1970), 59–269. The reactionary appeal to oral tradition in support of the reliability of the Gospels is traceable through the works of Gotthold Lessing (1729–1781), Johann Gottfried Herder (1744–1803), Johann Gieseler (1792–1854), and Brooke Foss Westcott (1825–1901); see Lessing, "New Hypothesis Concerning the Evangelists Regarded as Merely Human Historians," in *Lessing's Theological Writings* (ed. and trans. H. Chadwick; LMRT; Stanford: Stanford University Press, 1956), 65–81; J. G. Herder, *Against Pure Reason* (FTM; ed. and trans. M. Bunge; Minneapolis: Fortress, 1993); Westcott, *An Introduction to the Study of the Gospels* (7th ed.; London: Macmillan, 1888), 166–71; on Gieseler see W. G. Kümmel, *The New Testament: The History of the Investigation of its Problems* (trans. S. M. Gilmour and H. C.

---

[1] "Predominantly oral" here and below is used in reference to societies with a literate minority in which most of daily life is conducted (even for the literate minority) on the basis of orality. In these societies one cannot make the distinction between "oral" and "literate" individuals, in that even those who have gained the skill of writing and reading use them for very limited activities, while relying on orality in most social contexts; see D. Tannen, "The Oral/Literate Continuum in Discourse," in *Spoken and Written Language: Exploring Orality and Literacy* (ed. D. Tannen; Norwood, N.J.: Ablex, 1982), 1–16, and the other essays in the same volume, and further ch. 3 below.

Kee; Nashville: Abingdon, 1972), 83; W. Baird, *History of New Testament Research*, Vol. 1: *From Deism to Tübingen* (Minneapolis: Fortress, 1992), 296–7.

A different trajectory, anticipating and including the form-critical view of oral tradition as fragmentary and open to constant innovation and invention on the part of the early church, runs through Friedrich Schleiermacher (1768–1834), David Friedrich Strauss (1808–1874), Julius Wellhausen (1844–1918), William Wrede (1859–1906), Hermann Gunkel (1862–1932), Karl Ludwig Schmidt (1891–1956), Martin Dibelius (1883–1947), and Rudolf Bultmann (1884–1976); see Schleiermacher, *Luke: A Critical Study* (trans. C. Thrilwall; SST 13; Lewiston: Edwin Mellen, 1993), 7–15; Strauss, "Hermann Samuel Reimarus and His Apology," in *Reimarus: Fragments* (ed. Talbert), 44–57; idem, *The Life of Jesus Critically Examined* (ed. P. C. Hodgson; trans. G. Eliot; LJS; Philadelphia: Fortress, 1974), 58, 73–4, 82–6, 467. On the importance of Wrede, Wellhausen, Schmidt, and Gunkel for the form-critical perspective see R. Bultmann, "The New Approach to the Synoptic Problem," in *Existence and Faith* (selected and trans. S. M. Ogden; Cleveland: World, 1960), 35–40, who gives a brief history of the scholarship that led to the development of his own approach. See also P. C. Hodgson, Introduction and editorial note in Strauss, *Life of Jesus*, xvii–xviii, 786 (n. 74); Kümmel, *History*, 84, 282, 328; Baird, *History*, 1:215–17; idem, *History of New Testament Research,* Vol. 2: *From Jonathan Edwards to Rudolf Bultmann* (Minneapolis: Fortress, 2003), 156. We will return to the topic of form criticism and the work of Dibelius and Bultmann below.

Relatively new, however, are the numerous insights into the inner workings of oral tradition developed by a number of scholars in the wake of the pioneering work of Milman Parry and Albert Lord.[2] Notable among these scholars for the purposes of the present study are John Miles Foley,[3] Jack

---

[2] M. Parry's publications have been conveniently collected in *The Making of Homeric Verse: The Collected Papers of Milman Parry* (ed. A. Parry; Oxford: Clarendon, 1971). Parry's work, which was cut short by his early accidental death in 1935 at the age of 33 (see A. Parry, Introduction to ibid., ix–x) was carried on by his assistant, Albert Lord. The most important works of the latter for the present monograph include *The Singer of Tales* (HSCL 24; Cambridge, Mass.: Harvard University Press, 1960); "The Gospels as Oral Traditional Literature," in *The Relationships Among the Gospels: An Interdisciplinary Dialogue* (ed. W. O. Walker, Jr.; TUMSR 5; San Antonio: Trinity University Press, 1978), 33–91; "Memory, Fixity, and Genre in Oral Traditional Poetries," in *Oral Traditional Literature: A Festschrift for Albert Bates Lord* (ed. J. M. Foley; Columbus: Slavica, 1981), 451–61; "Perspectives on Recent Work on the Oral Traditional Formula," *OrTr* 1 (1986): 467–503; "Characteristics of Orality," *OrTr* 2, no. 1 [FS for W. J. Ong] (1987): 54–72; "The Nature of Oral Poetry," in *Comparative Research on Oral Traditions: A Memorial for Milman Parry* (ed. J. M. Foley; Columbus: Slavica, 1987), 313–49; *The Singer Resumes the Tale* (ed. M. L. Lord; Ithaca and London: Cornell University Press, 1995). For a bibliography of Lord's publications see M. E. Grey, M. L. Lord, and J. M. Foley, "A Bibliography of Publications by Albert Bates Lord," *OrTr* 25 (2010): 497–504. On both Parry and Lord see further sec. 3.3 below, under the subtitle "Markers of Orality: Oral Indicators in an Oral Medium."

[3] See J. M. Foley, "The Oral Theory in Context," in *Oral Traditional Literature* (ed. Foley), 27–122; idem, "Tradition-Dependent and -Independent Features in Oral Literature: A Comparative View of the Formula," in *Oral Traditional Literature* (ed. Foley), 262–81; idem, *The Theory of Oral Composition: History and Methodology* (Bloomington

R. Goody,[4] Eric A. Havelock,[5] and Walter J. Ong.[6] The insights of these and other scholars have the potential to greatly impact our understanding of early Christian writings, both in terms of the interrelationships among them and of the nature of their sources.[7]

---

and Indianapolis: Indiana University Press, 1988); idem, *Traditional Oral Epic: The Odyssey, Beowulf, and the Serbo-Croatian Return Song* (Berkeley and Los Angeles: University of California Press, 1990); idem, *Immanent Art: From Structure to Meaning in Traditional Oral Epic* (Bloomington and Indianapolis: Indiana University Press, 1991); idem, *The Singer of Tales in Performance* (VPT; Bloomington and Indianapolis: Indiana University Press, 1995); idem, *Homer's Traditional Art* (University Park: Pennsylvania State University Press, 1999); idem, "What's In a Sign?," in *Signs of Orality: The Oral Tradition and its Influence in the Greek and Roman Worlds* (ed. E. A. Mackay; MnS 188; Leiden: Brill, 1999), 1–27; idem, *How to Read an Oral Poem* (Urbana: University of Illinois Press, 2002); idem, "Memory in Oral Tradition," in *Performing the Gospel: Orality, Memory, and Mark: Essays Dedicated to Werner Kelber* (ed. R. A. Horsley, J. A. Draper, and J. M. Foley; Minneapolis: Fortress, 2006), 83–96. Foley has also made an important contribution through the volumes he has edited, two of which were already mentioned above: *Oral Traditional Literature: A Festschrift for Albert Bates Lord* and *Comparative Research on Oral Traditions: A Memorial for Milman Parry*, and see further idem, ed., *Oral Tradition in Literature: Interpretation in Context* (Columbia: University of Missouri Press, 1986); idem, ed., *Teaching Oral Traditions* (New York: Modern Language Association, 1998).

[4] J. Goody and I. Watt wrote the seminal essay "The Consequences of Literacy," in *Literacy in Traditional Societies* (ed. J. R. Goody; Cambridge: Cambridge University Press, 1968), 27–68; see further J. R. Goody, *The Domestication of the Savage Mind* (TSS; Cambridge: Cambridge University Press, 1977); idem, *The Logic of Writing and the Organization of Society* (SLFCS; Cambridge: Cambridge University Press, 1986); idem, *The Interface between the Written and the Oral* (SLFCS; Cambridge: Cambridge University Press, 1987).

[5] Among the works by E. A. Havelock see especially *Preface to Plato* (Cambridge, Mass. and London: Belknap Press of Harvard University Press, 1963); idem, *The Literate Revolution in Greece and Its Cultural Consequences* (PSCE; Princeton: Princeton University Press, 1982); idem, *The Muse Learns to Write: Reflections on Orality and Literacy from Antiquity to the Present* (New Haven and London: Yale University Press, 1986).

[6] Among his many works, see especially W. J. Ong, *The Presence of the Word: Some Prolegomena for Cultural and Religious History* (Terry Lectures; New Haven and London: Yale University Press, 1967); idem, *Interfaces of the Word: Studies in the Evolution of Consciousness and Culture* (Ithaca and London: Cornell University Press, 1977); and (one of the writings that provided the initial impetus for this book) idem, *Orality and Literacy: The Technologizing of the Word* (New Accents; London and New York: Methuen, 1982; many reprints since 1988 by London and New York: Routledge). For a selected bibliography of Ong's works up to 1987 see R. F. Lumpp, "Walter Jackson Ong, S.J.: A Selected Bibliography," *OrTr* 2 [FS W. J. Ong] (1987): 19–30. I am indebted to many other authors as well, but those mentioned above are not only (after Parry and Lord) pioneers in the field or contemporary orality studies, but also have exerted the most influence upon the thought process that led to the present study.

[7] The best guide to the expanding literature on oral tradition is J. M. Foley, *Oral-Formulaic Theory and Research: An Introduction and Annotated Bibliography* (GFB 6;

Some of this impact is already being felt, as exemplified by the presidential address delivered by James Dunn at the 57th Annual Meeting of Studiorum Novi Testamenti Societas in 2002, entitled, "Altering the Default Setting: Re-envisaging the Early Transmission of the Jesus Tradition."[8] Dunn's address was a call for the New Testament guild to recognize that members of ancient oral cultures operated very differently than scholars in today's Western cultures. Western scholars' "default setting" – Dunn's image for "an established mindset, an unconscious bias or *Tendenz*, an instinctive reflex response"[9] – is literary. Due to this literary mindset, Dunn argued, they naturally propose literary answers for problems in Christian antiquity that, given the insights into oral tradition provided by those who have built upon Parry and Lord's research, are better solved using the presuppositions of an oral mindset.[10]

Dunn devoted a large part of his address to discussing how one might "alter the default setting" in relation to various aspects of the reigning solution to the Synoptic Problem, the Two-Source Theory. Though we cannot cover all of Dunn's arguments here, we will give an example to illustrate his point. First, a brief introduction to place Dunn's comments in context: according to the Two-Source Theory Mark wrote first, and Mat-

---

GRLH 400; New York: Garland, 1985), together with its updates by various authors in *OrTr* 1 (1986): 767–808; 3 (1988): 191–228; 12 (1997): 366–484 (complete back issues available at http://journal.oraltradition.org/; accessed 03/11/2011).

[8] Published in *NTS* 49 (2003): 139–75, and reprinted as an appendix in Dunn's *A New Perspective on Jesus: What the Quest for the Historical Jesus Missed* (ASBT; Grand Rapids: Baker Academic, 2005), 79–125; see further idem, *New Perspective on Jesus*, 35–56; idem, *Christianity in the Making,* Vol. 1: *Jesus Remembered* (Grand Rapids: Eerdmans, 2003), 173–254; idem, *Christianity in the Making,* Vol. 2: *Beginning from Jerusalem* (Grand Rapids: Eerdmans, 2009), 111–27; idem, "Reappreciating the Oral Jesus Tradition," *SEÅ* 74 (2009), 1–17; idem, "Remembering Jesus: How the Quest of the Historical Jesus Lost Its Way," in *Handbook for the Study of the Historical Jesus* (ed. T. Holmén and S. E. Porter; Leiden: Brill, 2011), 183–205.

[9] Dunn, "Altering," 141.

[10] In addition to Parry and Lord, Dunn makes special reference to the work of J. Vansina, *Oral Tradition as History* (Madison: University of Wisconsin Press and London: Currey, 1985), the comparative work of R. Finnegan, *Oral Literature in Africa* (Oxford: Clarendon, 1970) and I. Okpewho, *African Oral Literature: Backgrounds, Character and Continuity* (Bloomington and Indianapolis: Indiana University Press, 1992), as well as "the 30 years' personal, albeit anecdotal, experience of [K. E.] Bailey in the Middle East" as reflected in Bailey's "Informal Controlled Oral Tradition and the Synoptic Gospels," *AJT* 5 (1991): 34–54; idem, "Middle Eastern Oral Tradition and the Synoptic Gospels," *ExpTim* 106 (1994–95): 363–67 (quote from Dunn, "Altering," 150). In the course of his discussion Dunn also refers to R. Finnegan, *Oral Poetry: Its Nature, Significance, and Social Context* (Bloomington: Indiana University Press, 1992); Foley, *Immanent Art*; idem, *Singer*; Havelock, *Muse*; Ong, *Orality and Literacy*, as well as other works that apply the insights of orality studies to Jesus tradition and the Gospels.

thew and Luke depended on Mark. In addition, Matthew and Luke followed a second main source, commonly called Q, discernible behind the
double tradition (material common to Matthew and Luke but not found in
Mark). Dunn saw no problem with this general hypothesis. He did see a
problem, however, with the way Western scholars – given their literary
mindset – envision Q as a written document that can be clearly delineated
in terms of extent, content, redactional layers, and so on.

In order to fit the theory to the evidence, e.g., scholars hypothesize that
Matthew and Luke had access to two different Q documents, Q^M and Q^L,
that reflected the redaction to which Q was subject during the time that in-
tervened between its use by each evangelist. The theory of a Q^M and Q^L,
however, built on the *differences* between Matthew and Luke, calls into
question the basic theory of Q's existence, which is predicated on the *similarities* between Matthew and Luke in the double tradition. Dunn argued
that taking seriously the insight that much of the Jesus tradition was transmitted early on by word of mouth entails recognizing, among other things,
that the variations and agreements between Matthew and Luke in certain
cases are best understood as reflecting the combination of fixity and flexibility, or stability and diversity, characteristic of oral tradition.[11] To put it
in general terms, certain variations among the Gospels are best understood
as arising neither from different versions of their written source, nor from
the literary redaction of the evangelists, but from the very nature of their
source(s) as oral tradition.

1.2 Thesis

Dunn's address was necessarily limited in scope, dealing primarily with
the topic of the interrelations of the Synoptic Gospels. The need to "re-
envisage the early transmission of the Jesus tradition" in light of ongoing
revisions to our understanding of orality is not limited, however, to the
study of the Gospels. It also carries over to the study of Jesus tradition in
other early Christian literature, such as the NT epistles, the Apostolic Fathers, and the Nag Hammadi texts.[12]

---

[11] Dunn's examples are the pericopes on turning the other cheek (Mt 5:39b–42//Lk
6:29–30), dividing families (Mt 10:34–38//Lk 12:51–53, 14:26–27), and forgiving sin
seven times (Mt 18:15, 21–22//Lk 17:3–4); see ibid., 163–64.

[12] The words in quotation marks reflect the sub-title of Dunn's "Altering." Dunn
himself notes that the study of the Jesus tradition outside the Gospels, in documents such
as the NT epistles, the Apostolic Fathers, and the Nag Hammadi texts, "has been seriously flawed by overdependence on the literary paradigm" (ibid., 169–70), which in essence constitutes a call to investigate this literature afresh from the perspective of orality.

Some of this re-envisaging has been taking place over the past three decades, spurred on especially by the publication in 1983 of Werner Kelber's groundbreaking work entitled *The Oral and the Written Gospel: The Hermeneutics of Speaking and Writing in the Synoptic Tradition, Mark, Paul, and Q.*[13] Kelber, Dunn and others have examined a variety of early Christian writings from the perspective of orality: a number of studies have been conducted on the double tradition or Q,[14] as well as the synoptic tradition in general (including the implications of orality studies for the Synoptic Problem),[15] and also on the Gospel of Matthew,[16] the Gospel of

---

[13] Philadelphia: Fortress, 1983. In his introduction to a *Festschrift* in Kelber's honor, R. A. Horsley gives credit to Kelber as "the first to recognize that the Gospels were composed and received in a world dominated by oral communication," and goes on to state that Kelber has also "patiently explained the implications to other scholars still stubbornly faithful to the typographical assumptions of the modern western study of sacred texts" (Horsley, introduction to *Performing the Gospel* [ed. Horsley, Draper, and Foley], viii).

[14] J. D. G. Dunn, "Q[1] as Oral Tradition," in *The Written Gospel [FS for Graham Stanton]* (ed. M. Bockmuehl and D. A. Hagner; Cambridge: Cambridge University Press, 2005), 45–69; R. A. Horsley with J. A. Draper, *Whoever Hears You Hears Me: Prophets, Performance, and Tradition in Q* (Harrisburg: Trinity Press International, 1999); R. A. Horsley, ed., *Oral Performance, Popular Tradition, and Hidden Transcript in Q* (SBL SemeiaSt 60; Atlanta: Society of Biblical Literature, 2006).

[15] A. D. Baum, *Der mündliche Faktor und seine Bedeutung für die synoptische Frage: Analogien aus der antiken Literatur, der Experimentalpsychologie, der Oral Poetry-Forschung und dem rabbinischen Traditionswesen* (TANZ 49; Tübingen: Francke, 2008); Dunn, *Jesus Remembered*, 173–254; idem, *New Perspective on Jesus*, 35–56; idem, "Reappreciating the Oral Jesus Tradition," 1–17; idem, "Remembering Jesus," 183–205; W. H. Kelber, *The Oral and the Written Gospel: The Hermeneutics of Speaking and Writing in the Synoptic Tradition, Mark, Paul, and Q* (repr. with a new intro. by the author and a foreword by W. J. Ong; Bloomington and Indianapolis: Indiana University Press, 1997); T. C. Mournet, *Oral Tradition and Literary Dependency: Variability and Stability in the Synoptic Tradition and Q* (WUNT 2.195; Tübingen: Mohr Siebeck, 2005); idem, "The Jesus Tradition as Oral Tradition," in *Jesus in Memory: Traditions in Oral and Scribal Practices* (ed. W. H. Kelber and S. Byrskog; Waco, Tex.: Baylor University Press, 2009), 39–61. We might also include here Bailey, "Informal" and idem, "Middle Eastern," who charts a path of his own. For a survey of research conducted during the last three decades on oral tradition and the Gospels, see K. R. Iverson, "Orality and the Gospels: A Survey of Recent Research," *Currents in Biblical Research* 8 (2009): 71–106.

[16] A. D. Baum, "Matthew's Sources – Oral or Written? A Rabbinic Analogy and Empirical Insights," in *Built Upon the Rock: Studies in the Gospel of Matthew* (ed. D. M. Gurtner and J. Nolland; Grand Rapids: Eerdmans, 2008), 1–23; R. Beaton, "How Matthew Writes," in *Written Gospel* (ed. Bockmuehl and Hagner), 116–34; S. I. Wright, "Debtors, Laborers and Virgins: The Voice of Jesus and the Voice of Matthew in Three Parables," in *Jesus and Paul: Global Perspectives in Honor of James D. G. Dunn for His 70th Birthday* (ed. B. J. Oropeza, C. K. Robertson, and Douglas C. Mohrmann; LNTS 414; London and New York: T&T Clark International, 2009).

Mark[17] and the Gospel of John,[18] the Pauline literature,[19] the Apocalypse of John,[20] and the New Testament in general.[21] Non-canonical writings have

---

[17] P. J. J. Botha, "Mark's Story as Oral Traditional Literature: Rethinking the Transmission of Some Traditions about Jesus," *HvTSt* 47 (1991): 304–31; J. Dewey, "Oral Methods of Structuring Narrative in Mark," *Int* 43 (1989): 32–44; idem, "Mark as Interwoven Tapestry: Forecasts and Echoes for a Listening Audience," *CBQ* 53 (1991): 221–36; idem, "Mark as Aural Narrative: Structures as Clues to Understanding," *STRev* 36 (1992): 45–56; idem, "The Gospel of Mark as an Oral-Aural Event: Implications for Interpretation," in *The New Literary Criticism and the New Testament* (ed. E. V. McKnight and E. S. Malbon; JSNTSup 109; Sheffield: JSOT Press, 1994), 145–63; idem, "The Survival of Mark's Gospel: A Good Story?," *JBL* 123 (2004), 495–507; idem, "The Gospel of Mark as Oral Hermeneutic," in *Jesus, the Voice, and the Text: Beyond The Oral and the Written Gospel* (ed. T. Thatcher; Waco: Baylor University Press, 2008), 71–87; R. A. Horsley, *Hearing the Whole Story: The Politics of Plot in Mark's Gospel* (Louisville: Westminster John Knox, 2001), 53–78 and passim; idem, "Oral and Written Aspects of the Emergence of the Gospel of Mark as Scripture," *OrTr* 25 (2010): 93–114; idem, "Oral Performance and Mark: Some Implications of The Oral and the Written Gospel, Twenty-Five Years Later," in *Jesus, the Voice, and the Text* (ed. Thatcher), 45–70; idem, "A Prophet Like Moses and Elijah: Popular Memory and Cultural Patterns in Mark," in *Performing the Gospel* (ed. Horsley, Draper, and Foley), 166–90; W. H. Kelber, "Mark and Oral Tradition," in *Perspectives on Mark's Gospel* (ed. N. R. Petersen; *Semeia* 16; Missoula: Society of Biblical Literature/Scholars, 1979), 7–55; idem, *Oral and Written*, 44–139; Y.-M. Park, *Mark's Memory Resources and the Controversy Stories (Mark 2:1–3:6): An Application of the Frame Theory of Cognitive Science to the Markan Oral-Aural Narrative* (LBS 2; Leiden: Brill, 2010); V. K. Robbins, "Interfaces of Orality and Literature in the Gospel of Mark," in *Performing the Gospel* (ed. Horsley, Draper, and Foley), 125–46; W. Shiner, *Proclaiming the Gospel: First Century Performance of Mark* (Harrisburg: Trinity Press International, 2003); idem, "Memory Technology and the Composition of Mark," in *Performing the Gospel* (ed. Horsley, Draper, and Foley), 147–65; contrast B. W. Henaut, *Oral Tradition and the Gospels: The Problem of Mark 4* (JSNTSup 82; Sheffield: JSOT Press, 1993), which is based on the literary "default setting."

[18] J. D. G. Dunn, "John and the Oral Gospel Tradition," in *Jesus and the Oral Gospel Tradition* (ed. H. Wansbrough; JSNTSup 64; Sheffield: JSOT Press, 1991), 351–79; see also T. Thatcher, *The Riddles of Jesus in John: A Study in Tradition and Folklore* (SBLMS 53; Atlanta: Society of Biblical Literature, 2000).

[19] J. Dewey, "Textuality in an Oral Culture: A Survey of the Pauline Traditions," in *Orality and Textuality in Early Christian Literature* (ed. J. Dewey; *Semeia* 65; Atlanta: Society of Biblical Literature/Scholars, 1994), 37–65; J. D. Harvey, *Listening to the Text: Oral Patterning in Paul's Letters* (ETSSS; Grand Rapids: Baker/Leicester: Apollos, 1998); T. Holtz, "Paul and the Oral Gospel Tradition," in *Jesus and the Oral Gospel* (ed. Wansbrough), 380–93; Kelber, *Oral and Written*, 140–83; S. Tsang, "Are We 'Misreading' Paul?: Oral Phenomena and Their Implication for the Exegesis of Paul's Letters," *OrTr* 24 (2009): 205–25; see also D. E. Aune, "Jesus Tradition and the Pauline Letters," in *Jesus in Memory* (ed. Kelber and Byrskog), 63–86.

[20] D. Barr, "The Apocalypse of John as Oral Enactment," *Int* 40 (1986): 243–56.

[21] P. J. Achtemeier, *"Omne Verbum Sonat:* The New Testament and the Oral Environment of Late Western Antiquity," *JBL* 109 (1990): 3–27; C. B. Amphoux, "Le style

also been the focus of orality studies, including the Gospel of Thomas,[22] the *Didache*,[23] the *Shepherd* of Hermas,[24] and the *Acts of Peter*,[25] among others.[26] All of these studies together – and the above list is meant to be illustrative rather than exhaustive – are moving New Testament studies in a new direction, one that increasingly recognizes the impact of orality upon early Christianity and its writings.

The present work is envisioned as a contribution along the above lines: its purpose is to reevaluate the tradition of Jesus' sayings in the Apostolic Fathers from the perspective of orality. No full-scale study of the Apostolic Fathers has been published which takes into account the new insights into oral tradition in Christian antiquity that have been gained over the last

---

oral dans le Nouveau Testament," *ETR* 63 (1988): 379–84; W. H. Kelber, "New Testament Texts: Rhetoric and Discourse," in *Teaching Oral Traditions* (ed. Foley), 330–8.

[22] A. D. DeConick, *Recovering the Original Gospel of Thomas: A History of the Gospel and its Growth* (LNTS 286; ECC; New York: T&T Clark International, 2005); idem, "The Gospel of Thomas," *ExpTim* 118 (2007): 469–79; R. Uro, "*Thomas* and Oral Gospel Tradition," in *Thomas at the Crossroads: Essays on the Gospel of Thomas* (ed. R. Uro; SNTW; Edinburgh: T&T Clark, 1998), 8–32.

[23] J. A. Draper, "Vice Catalogues as Oral-Mnemonic Cues: A Comparative Study of the Two-Ways Tradition in the *Didache* and Parallels from the Perspective of Oral Tradition," in *Jesus, the Voice, and the Text* (ed. Thatcher), 111–33; W. Rordorf, "Does the Didache Contain Jesus Tradition Independently of the Synoptic Gospels?," in *Jesus and the Oral Gospel* (ed. Wansbrough), 394–423; A. Milavec, *The Didache: Faith, Hope, and Life of the Earliest Christian Communities, 50–70 C.E.* (New York and Mahwah: Newman, 2003), esp. xxxii–xxxiii and also passim; idem, "Synoptic Tradition in the *Didache* Revisited," *JECS* 11 (2003): 443–80.

[24] C. Osiek, "The Oral World of Early Christianity in Rome: The Case of Hermas," in *Judaism and Christianity in First-Century Rome* (ed. K. P. Donfried and P. Richardson; Grand Rapids: Eerdmans, 1998), 151–72.

[25] C. M. Thomas, "Word and Deed: The *Acts of Peter* and Orality," *Apoc* 3 (1992): 125–64.

[26] See other essays and bibliographies in Dewey, ed., *Orality and Textuality*; Horsley, Draper, and Foley, eds., *Performing the Gospel*; L. H. Silberman, ed., *Orality, Aurality and Biblical Narrative* (*Semeia* 39; Decatur: Society of Biblical Literature/Scholars 1987); Thatcher, ed., *Jesus, the Voice, and the Text*; Wansbrough, *Jesus and the Oral Gospel*; see also L. C. A. Alexander, "The Living Voice: Scepticism towards the Written Word in Early Christian and in Graeco-Roman Texts," in *The Bible in Three Dimensions: Essays in Celebration of Forty Years of Biblical Studies in the University of Sheffield* (ed. D. J. A. Clines, S. E. Fowl, and S. E. Porter; JSOTSup 87; Sheffield: JSOT Press, 1990), 221–47; F. G. Downing, "A bas les aristos: The Relevance of Higher Literature for the Understanding of the Earliest Christian Writings," *NovT* 30 (1988): 212–30; T. J. Farrell, "Early Christian Creeds and Controversies in the Light of the Orality-Literacy Hypothesis," *OrTr* 2 (1987): 132–49; J. Halverson, "Oral and Written Gospel: A Critique of Werner Kelber," *NTS* 40 (1994): 180–95.

four decades following the pioneering work of Parry and Lord.[27] It is this lack that the present study seeks to address.

The thesis that will guide this work is that an oral-traditional source best explains the form and content of the explicit appeals to Jesus tradition in the Apostolic Fathers that predate *2 Clement*. It will argue further that there is no unequivocal evidence for the use of any of the canonical Gospels by any of the Apostolic Fathers. Rather, much of the evidence that has been brought forward in the past in support of the Apostolic Fathers' use of the canonical Gospels points to the independent use of common or related sources by the Apostolic Fathers and the gospel writers. While it is possible that *2 Clement* marks the beginning of the appeal to written sources that will characterize Christian literature after Irenaeus, this is also open to other interpretations, and is therefore not conclusive.

1.3 Problems

A danger inherent in much historical research is that one's method and presuppositions too often predetermine the outcome of one's work. Previous studies of the Jesus tradition in the Apostolic Fathers have tended to err on the side of hypothesizing an unwarranted degree of dependence on the canonical Gospels, a trend that is often traceable to the presuppositions and method that under-girded these studies.[28] Similarly, the presuppositions and method applied in the present work could lead to hypothesizing an unwarranted degree of dependence on oral tradition. This is a risk worth taking, however, in order to test the limits of the theory that a large percentage of the Jesus tradition in the Apostolic Fathers *can* be understood as having derived from oral tradition. If this work succeeds in showing that this understanding is truly feasible, then the way is open to ask the further question of which of the two paradigms best accounts for all of the evidence: dependence on literary or oral sources.

Inherent in the task of comparing variations of a saying of Jesus to each other is the problem that one can often not be certain that the variations

---

[27] H. Köster (hereafter Koester to be consistent with his later publications) gives an important place to oral tradition in his monograph *Synoptische Überlieferung bei den apostolischen Vätern* (TU 65; Berlin: Akademie-Verlag, 1957). His understanding of oral tradition, however, is derived from the presuppositions of form criticism, which leave much to be desired; on the form-critical perspective on oral tradition see sec. 1.4.1 below, under the sub-title "Form Criticism." Koester will be a valuable conversation partner throughout the present work.

[28] For a full discussion see ch. 2 below entitled "A Brief History of Scholarship on the Sources of the Jesus Tradition in the Apostolic Fathers."

being compared are of the same saying, let alone of the same utterance. In identifying parallels to consider, materials that are similar to each other will be chosen for comparison, but similarity may arise not from a shared origin in a single speaking event, but from Jesus having said similar things on different occasions. Jesus probably repeated the same stories and sayings not twice but *many* times, in many different contexts, before many audiences, and in different versions, with various applications, as suited both to the parabolic nature of much of his teaching and to his itinerant career.[29] Even though this brings an element of unknown to investigations such as the one undertaken here, one can only proceed, as the alternative would be paralysis.

One of the inevitable problems involved in the type of work attempted here is that one only has access to the oral Jesus tradition from antiquity as it has been captured in written sources.[30] In the form the oral Jesus tradition has come down to us, it is no longer "oral" in the most basic sense of the term. As will be developed more fully in chapter 3, however, the fluid relationship between writing and reading in antiquity means that to classify materials primarily on the basis of whether they are found in a written or oral medium is to make a somewhat superficial distinction. A more appropriate distinction is based on the *conception* both of the discourse in the sources and of the process in which it was put into writing. In other words, did the discourse originate as, and therefore follow the norms associated with, a spoken interaction or a written text? How was the discourse put into writing? Was it composed in writing or transcribed?[31]

In the final analysis it is not possible to prove that any particular saying or tradition in any given document was derived from oral tradition. It is not, however, a matter of proof, but of identifying which approach to the material under consideration best accounts for all of the evidence in light of what we know of Christian antiquity. This is where the two main alter-

---

[29] W. H. Kelber, "Jesus and Tradition: Words in Time, Words in Space," in *Orality and Textuality* (ed. Dewey), 146, 148–51; idem, "The Works of Memory: Christian Origins as Mnemohistory – a Response," in *Memory, Tradition, and Text: Uses of the Past in Early Christianity* (ed. A. Kirk and T. Thatcher; SBL SemeiaSt 52; Atlanta: Society of Biblical Literature, 2005), 237–8; N. T. Wright, *Christian Origins and the Question of God,* Vol. 1: *The New Testament and the People of God* (Minneapolis: Fortress, 1992), 422–23; idem, *Christian Origins and the Question of God,* Vol. 2: *Jesus and the Victory of God* (Minneapolis: Fortress, 1996), 136, n. 32; 170–71; 181. Other factors may also produce variables, such as the process of translation from Aramaic to Greek; see Dunn, "Altering," 171.

[30] This problem is frequently noted; see, e.g., Ø. Andersen, "Oral Tradition," in *Jesus and the Oral Gospel* (ed. Wansbrough), 30.

[31] See further the discussion in sec. 3.1 below, under the subtitle "Orality in Oral-Derived Texts," which is based in large part on the work of Egbert Bakker. I have left the citation of Bakker's works for ch. 3, to avoid cluttering up the footnotes unnecessarily here.

natives to the approach to oral tradition taken in the present work, i.e., form criticism and the rabbinic model developed by Birger Gerhardsson, have fallen short. We will consider why this is the case in what follows.

1.4 An Alternative to Form Criticism and the Rabbinic Model

In the introductory remarks to this chapter we noted that oral tradition is not a new topic of discussion in New Testament studies. Here we turn to address the question of why the approach to oral tradition used in the present work was chosen over those offered by form criticism and by Birger Gerhardsson, what we will call the "rabbinic model."

1.4.1 Form Criticism

Form criticism, especially the pioneering work of R. Bultmann and M. Dibelius in the 1920s, did a great service to New Testament studies in drawing attention to the importance of oral tradition for understanding the background of the Gospels.[32] According to Bultmann (and here he agrees

---

[32] The three classic form-critical texts are K. L. Schmidt, *Der Rahmen der Geschichte Jesu* (Berlin: Trowitzsch, 1919); M. Dibelius, *From Tradition to Gospel* (LTT; Cambridge: James Clarke, 1971 [1st German ed. 1919]), and R. Bultmann, *The History of the Synoptic Tradition* (3rd ed.; Oxford: Blackwell, 1972 [1st German ed. 1921]). The following assessment of form criticism is perforce brief. For fuller treatments see R. Bauckham, *Jesus and the Eyewitnesses: The Gospels as Eyewitness Testimony* (Grand Rapids: Eerdmans, 2006), 241–49; K. Berger, "Form Criticism, New Testament," *DBI* 1:413–17; C. L. Blomberg, "Form Criticism," *DJG* 243–50; D. L. Bock, "Form Criticism," in *Interpreting the New Testament: Essays on Methods and Issues* (ed. D. A. Black and D. S. Dockery; Nashville: Broadman & Holman, 2001), 106–27; S. Byrskog, review of R. Bultmann, *History of the Synoptic Tradition*, *JBL* 122 (2003): 549–55; D. R. Catchpole, "Source, Form and Redaction Criticism of the New Testament," in *Handbook to Exegesis of the New Testament* (ed. S. E. Porter; NTTS 25; Leiden: Brill, 1997), 167–88; C. A. Evans, "Source, Form and Redaction Criticism: The 'Traditional' Methods of Synoptic Interpretation," in *Approaches to New Testament Study* (ed. S. E. Porter and D. Tombs; JSNTSup 120; Sheffield: Sheffield Academic, 1995), 27–32; idem, "Form Criticism," in *Encyclopedia of the Historical Jesus* (ed. C. A. Evans; New York and London: Routledge, 2008), 204–8; Kelber, *Oral and Written*, 2–14; idem, "The Oral-Scribal-Memorial Arts of Communication in Early Christianity," in *Jesus, the Voice, and the Text* (ed. Thatcher), 243–46; Mournet, *Oral Tradition*, 55–63; V. K. Robbins, "Form Criticism: New Testament," *ABD* 2:841–44; K. L. Sparks, "Form Criticism," *DBCI* 111–4; S. H. Travis, "Form Criticism," in *New Testament Interpretation: Essays on Principles and Methods* (ed. I. H. Marshall; Grand Rapids: Eerdmans, 1977), 153–64; C. Tuckett, "Form Criticism," in *Jesus in Memory* (ed. Kelber and Byrskog), 21–38. For a full introduction see E. V. McKnight, *What is Form Criticism?* (GBSNT; Philadelphia: Fortress, 1969), and for extensive critiques see E. Güttgemanns, *Candid Questions Concerning Gospel Form Criticism: A Methodological Sketch of the Fundamental Problematics of Form and*

with Dibelius), the ultimate goal of form criticism is "to rediscover the origin and the history of the particular units [of Jesus tradition] and thereby to throw some light on the history of the tradition before it took literary form."[33] The influence of Bultmann, Dibelius and other form critics upon New Testament studies was such that their view of the tradition's oral period became dominant for over half a century. As a result it has become almost axiomatic to recognize that there was a period prior to the formation of the Gospels during which the Jesus tradition was transmitted primarily in oral form.[34] In this regard not only the present work but also the entire field of gospels studies stands in debt to the form critics.

The basic problem with the form critical approach, however, is that it was not based upon an informed model of how oral tradition functioned in antiquity. Instead, it was based upon the form critics' understanding of the needs of the early church. In an important work dedicated to examining the form-critical approach to Jesus tradition,[35] E. P. Sanders explains this problem as follows: given that the early form critics appealed to analogies to the Jesus tradition such as folk tradition, one would expect that they would have based their understanding of how oral tradition worked in early Christianity upon these analogies. Instead, Sanders notes, the early form critics turned to the church's *motive* for spreading the early Jesus tradition, and upon this basis fashioned "laws" that governed the tradition. For example, for Dibelius the sermon was one of the essential ways in which the early church spread the Jesus tradition, given the motive to further the mission of the church. Dibelius identified the "paradigm" as the form in which the words and deeds of Jesus were passed on in keeping with the requirements of the sermon. He then explained the presence of elements in paradigmatic Jesus sayings that did not conform to the needs of the sermon as arising out of the church's changed situation (*Sitz im Leben*), and thus as later developments. Sanders concludes, "So we see that, for Dibelius, the laws of the development of the Christian tradition are not derived from ob-

---

Redaction Criticism (trans. W. G. Doty; PTMS 26; Pittsburgh: Pickwick, 1979) and E. P. Sanders, *The Tendencies of the Synoptic Tradition* (SNTSMS 9; Cambridge: Cambridge University Press, 1969).

[33] Bultmann, *Synoptic Tradition*, 4.

[34] As stated by E. P. Sanders and M. Davies, "Everyone accepts oral transmission at the early stages of the gospel tradition. ... The problem is that we do not know how to imagine the oral period, neither how long it lasted not how oral transmission actually functioned" (*Studying the Synoptic Gospels* [London: SCM/Philadelphia: Trinity Press International, 1989], 141.

[35] On what follows see Sanders, *Tendencies*, 10–14.

serving the development of other folk traditions, but by analyzing the needs and activities of the Christian communities."[36]

Due to their lack of a solid theoretical foundation in the topic of orality in antiquity, for the most part form critics simply assumed that certain things were true of the Jesus tradition in its oral stage, that upon closer scrutiny have been shown to be unfounded. For example, one of Bultmann's basic tenets was that oral tradition by its very nature tended to grow and expand: brief sayings were enlarged; different but similar sayings were combined; sayings already in circulation occasioned others by analogy, accrued introductory or concluding material derived from their context, or were enhanced with dialogue; unspecified characters were given names and descriptions; stories were developed out of sayings or parables; secular proverbs or folk stories were added to the tradition when the Church began to use them as sayings of or stories about Jesus; separate small units were gathered into "speeches" or even "catechisms"; and so on.[37] In short, the Jesus tradition moved inexorably from the simple to the complex, leading up to the written Gospels.[38] As (once again) E. P. Sanders has shown, however, in the synoptic tradition there is movement *both* from the simple to the complex *and* from the complex to the simple.[39] That Bultmann was mistaken in this regard calls into question much of his form-critical work that was built upon this basic premise.

Many of the other basic presuppositions of form criticism have been either refuted or seriously called into question: that the pre-gospel Jesus tradition existed in pure forms, and that one can trace the history of the tradition by studying the corruption of these forms; that oral sayings floated freely in isolation from each other; that each form of the Jesus tradition can be assigned to a unique *Sitz im Leben* in the early church; that for those transmitting the tradition there was a sharp discontinuity between

---

[36] Sanders, *Tendencies*, 14. Bultmann appeals to analogies in rabbinic stories and sayings, Hellenistic stories, proverbs, anecdotes and folk-tales, and "the history of the Jakata collection of the Buddhist canon," and adds "Fairy stories are instructive in many respects, and in some ways folk-songs are even more so, because the characteristics of primitive story telling are even more firmly preserved in their set form" (*Synoptic Tradition*, 6–7). Yet, as Sanders notes, his laws of the transmission of the Jesus tradition are not based on these analogies at all, but on observing the interrelations of the written Gospels (*Tendencies*, 15–20).

[37] Bultmann, *Synoptic Tradition*, 51–54, 67–69, 81–93, 102–8, 148–50; 230–31, 322–28. This list is not exhaustive, but only the result of glancing through Bultmann's work following the list provided in Kelber, *Oral and Written*, 4.

[38] Not that Bultmann did not allow for exceptions; e.g., he was willing to admit that "occasionally a saying has been abridged" and give several examples (*Synoptic Tradition*, 84).

[39] Sanders, *Tendencies*, 24, 68, 272–75.

the Jesus of history and the Christ of faith, so that they had no interest in preserving the reliability of tradition that spoke about the past of Jesus; that the tradition was transmitted by anonymous communities; that the early Christian communities played a large role not only in transmitting the tradition but also in freely creating and modifying much of it (e.g., by not distinguishing between sayings of the earthly Jesus and sayings from the present, risen Lord received by early Christian prophets), and that therefore the Jesus tradition says more about these communities than about Jesus himself; that the Gospels are essentially non-literary "folk" productions (*Kleinliteratur*), implying that the evangelists were mere collectors of tradition; and finally, that there was a clear distinction between (early) Palestinian and (later) Hellenistic tradition.[40]

In sum, the work of the form critics was not informed by an understanding of predominantly oral cultures or the inner workings of oral tradition, and instead applied models derived from a literary paradigm to the study of a predominantly oral context.[41] Most of the presuppositions that guided form criticism as a discipline have been shown to be unfounded. Given that the form-critical paradigm does not fit the reality of what we have come to know regarding early Christianity, it is now time to shape a new paradigm.[42]

The present work seeks to contribute to such a new paradigm. It represents a departure from the standard form-critical perspective in that it seeks to apply insights provided by orality studies to the study of the early Jesus tradition. It will thus not address standard form-critical issues such as the age of a particular tradition, its place (*Sitz im Leben*) in the life of the early church, the circumstances surrounding its origin, or how one could arrive

---

[40] These and other problems with the form-critical model are often noted in the literature; see the items by Bauckham, Berger, Blomberg, Bock, Evans, Robbins, Sparks, Travis, and Tuckett listed in n. 32 on p. 11 above, and also Dunn, "Altering," 144; idem, *Jesus Remembered*, 194–95; idem, "Reappreciating," 12–14; M. D. Hooker, "On Using the Wrong Tool," *Theology* 75 (1972): 570–81; W. H. Kelber, "The Case of the Gospels: Memory's Desire and the Limits of Historical Criticism," *OrTr* 17 (2002): 62–65. Not all form critics based their work on these presuppositions. Vincent Taylor, the leading form critic in the English-speaking world, called a number of these presuppositions into question; see his *The Formation of the Gospel Tradition* (2nd ed.; London: Macmillan, 1935 [1st ed. 1933]).

[41] Bauckham, *Eyewitnesses*, 244–45; Dunn, "Altering," 144; idem, *Jesus Remembered*, 194–95, 248–49; idem, *New Perspective on Jesus*, 39; Kelber, *Oral and Written*, 2–8; Robbins, "Form Criticism," 842.

[42] Here I agree with R. Bauckham when he states, "the form critical paradigm has now been comprehensively disproved, and it is time we adopted another paradigm for understanding how the Gospel traditions were preserved in the predominantly oral period prior to the written Gospels" ("The Transmission of the Gospel Traditions," *RCatT* 32 [2008]: 378).

at its "original" or "pure" form. Instead, the present study will focus on the dynamics surrounding why oral traditions were preserved, how they were retained and transmitted (i.e., how a memory specialist or "traditionist" acquired and performed traditions), their compositional elements, and how an audience was impacted by their performance.[43]

1.4.2 The Rabbinic Model

Birger Gerhardsson's work represents a conscious departure from form criticism. In his view, form critics have not paid sufficient attention to how "holy, authoritative tradition" was transmitted in New Testament times within Jewish circles in Palestine and elsewhere.[44] Fittingly, Gerhardsson takes as his starting point the rabbinic corpus, since it both contains considerable evidence of techniques of teaching and transmission of tradition (or "pedagogics"[45]), and illumines the historical Jewish context of the Gospels.[46]

---

[43] See further ch. 3 below.

[44] B. Gerhardsson, *The Reliability of the Gospel Tradition* (Peabody, Mass.: Hendrickson, 2001), 2; for further critiques of form criticism see ibid., 29–35, 82–86; idem, *Tradition and Interpretation in Early Christianity* (trans. E. J. Sharpe; ConBNT 20; Lund: Gleerup/Copenhagen: Munksgaard, 1964), 6; idem, *Memory and Manuscript: Oral Tradition and Written Transmission in Rabbinic Judaism and Early Christianity* (trans. E. J. Sharpe; ASNU 22; Lund: Gleerup/Copenhagen: Munksgaard, 1961), 9–15; latter two works repr. as *Memory and Manuscript: Oral Tradition and Written Transmission in Rabbinic Judaism and Early Christianity,* with *Tradition and Interpretation in Early Christianity* (BRS; Grand Rapids: Eerdmans/Livonia: Dove, 1998).

[45] Gerhardsson uses the term "pedagogics" as "a simplified substitute for 'technique of teaching and transmission'" (*Tradition*, 11, n. 18).

[46] Gerhardsson, *Memory*, 15, 19–189, 193–335; idem, *Tradition*, 11–12, 47, n. 115. Gerhardsson studies the transmission of early Jesus tradition in two steps: he first tries to "gain a concrete historical picture of the techniques of teaching and transmission [or pedagogics] used by Jesus and the early Church," and having laid this groundwork, then analyses the Gospel material to see if in fact it shows evidence of the application of such a pedagogics (see his *Tradition*, 8, 11 [quote from p. 11] and *Memory*, 9–11): Gerhardsson carries out the first step primarily in his *Memory* and *Tradition*, and the second step primarily in the essays collected in *Reliability* and a number of other works: *The Testing of God's Son* (ConBNT 2.1; Lund: Gleerup, 1966); idem, *The Mighty Acts of Jesus According to Matthew* (SM 1978–79 5; Lund: Gleerup, 1979); idem, "If We Do Not Cut the Parables out of Their Frames," *NTS* 37 (1991): 321–35; idem, "Illuminating the Kingdom: Narrative Meshalim in the Synoptic Gospels," in *Jesus and the Oral Gospel* (ed. Wansbrough), 266–309; idem, "The Narrative Meshalim in the OT Books and in the Synoptic Gospels," in *To Touch the Text: Biblical and Related Studies in Honor of Joseph A. Fitzmyer* (ed. M. Horgan and P. Kobelski; New York: Crossroad, 1989), 289–304; see also idem, "The Secret of the Transmission of the Unwritten Jesus Tradition," *NTS* 51 (2005): 1–18.

Gerhardsson begins by tracing a consistent approach to pedagogics from the Rabbinic period back through first-century Palestine and further still to the time of the OT. This approach was founded upon memorization techniques for learning large blocks of tradition,[47] and included,

> the learning by heart of the basic texts; the principle that 'learning comes before under-standing'; the attempt to memorize the teacher's *ipsissima verba*; the condensation of material into short, pregnant texts; the use of mnemonic technique …; the use of note-books and secret scrolls; the frequent repetition of memorized material, aloud and with melodic inflexion; the retention of knowledge by these methods – not to mention the idea of the teacher as 'pattern' and the pupil as 'imitator.'[48]

According to Gerhardsson this approach to pedagogics was present in first-century Palestinian culture not only in Pharisaic circles – the precursor to the Rabbinic movement – but also in the wider spheres of the home, the congregation, and the elementary system of education.[49]

Applying his findings to the early church, Gerhardsson reasons that since Jesus and his followers taught, and the sources show no evidence that they developed a new pedagogics, their pedagogics "must for the most part have resembled those used by other teachers in the same milieu."[50] Jesus "must have made his disciples learn certain sayings off by heart; if he taught, he must have required his disciples to memorize."[51] Jesus' status as Messiah and *only* teacher for the early Christian community would have increased the authority and sanctity of his words and works, which were "stamped on the memories of [his] disciples."[52] Given that in the apostle's eyes Jesus' words and works were "a higher equivalent of the oral Torah," they had special reason to safeguard the integrity of the tradition.[53]

Gerhardsson pictures the leading disciples forming a species of *col-legium*, similar to the Rabbinic body that made decisions over traditional and doctrinal matters. In this *collegium* the Twelve and other authoritative teachers "worked on the Scriptures, and on the Christ-tradition (which was originally oral): they gathered, formulated (narrative tradition), interpreted,

---

[47] See Gerhardsson, *Tradition*, 11–17; idem, *Memory*, 19–189; idem, *Reliability*, 71–73, 97–101.

[48] Gerhardsson, *Tradition*, 17, summarizing his *Memory*, 181–89; see also idem, *Reliability*, 9–14.

[49] Gerhardsson, *Tradition*, 21.

[50] Gerhardsson, *Tradition*, 22; see also ibid., 22–31; idem, *Memory*, 326–33; idem, *Reliability*, 36–37.

[51] Gerhardsson, *Memory*, 328; similarly idem, "Illuminating," 305–6; idem, "Secret," 9.

[52] Gerhardsson, *Memory*, 329.

[53] Gerhardsson, *Memory*, 325–34, quote from p. 334; see also idem, *Tradition*, 41, 44; idem, *Reliability*, 27–29, 32–35, 39–40, 49, 73, 106–7, 130–32; idem, "Secret," 14–15.

adapted, developed, complemented and put together collections for various definite purposes."[54] The disciples remembered what Jesus did on certain occasions, and applied this to specific questions as they arose, not *creating* material about Jesus' life and teaching, but rather *bringing it to bear* on these situations.[55] The evangelists in their turn depended on this authoritative Jesus tradition, "a fixed, distinct tradition from, and about, Jesus – a tradition that was partly memorized and partly written down in notebooks and private scrolls."[56]

Gerhardsson is to be commended for seeking to understand the transmission of the early Jesus tradition within its historical context. His early publications especially provided a timely corrective to form criticism, and his work overall has greatly impacted the study of the Jesus tradition.[57] Unfortunately, however, though the historical scenario Gerhardsson pictures is very attractive, it also has its problems. Due to space considerations we will focus here only on three main problems that relate directly to the present work.[58]

---

[54] Gerhardsson, *Tradition*, 40; see also idem, *Memory*, 332; idem, *Reliability*, 50–51. Gerhardsson reasserts his commitment to this formulation in his "Secret," 18, citing his own words quoted here.

[55] Gerhardsson, *Memory*, 332; here Gerhardsson is countering assumptions of the form critics; see also idem, *Tradition*, 42–43.

[56] Gerhardsson, *Memory*, 335.

[57] For an in-depth analysis of Gerhardsson's lasting impact on NT studies see essays in Kelber and Byrskog, eds., *Jesus in Memory*, including a summary of Gerhardsson's contributions to NT scholarship by his student S. Byrskog ("Introduction," pp. 1–20). Byrskog's work on Jesus tradition in itself is one area of Gerhardsson's lasting impact; see Byrskog's *Jesus the Only Teacher: Didactic Authority and Transmission in Ancient Israel, Ancient Judaism and the Matthean Community* (CBNTS 24; Stockholm: Almqvist & Wiksell, 1994); idem, *Story as History – History as Story: The Gospel Tradition in the Context of Ancient Oral History* (WUNT 123; Tübingen: Mohr Siebeck, 2000; repr. Leiden: Brill, 2002); idem, "When Eyewitness Testimony and Oral Tradition Become Written Text," *SEÅ* 74 (2009): 41–53; idem, "A New Perspective on the Jesus Tradition: Reflections on James D. G. Dunn's *Jesus Remembered*," in *Memories of Jesus: A Critical Appraisal of James D. G. Dunn's* Jesus Remembered (ed. R. B. Stewart and G. R. Habermas; Nashville: B&H Publishing Group, 2010), 59–78.

[58] For other assessments of Gerhardsson's model see Sanders, *Tendencies*, 294–96; Mournet, *Oral Tradition*, 63–66; Kelber, *Oral and Written*, 8–14; idem, "Memory's Desire," 59–61; Sanders and Davies, *Studying*, 129–45. While what follows will deal primarily with Gerhardsson's treatment of the gospel tradition, there are also problems with his understanding of Rabbinic pedagogics, on which see P. H. Davids, "The Gospels and Jewish Tradition: Twenty Years after Gerhardsson," in *Gospel Perspectives: Studies of History and Tradition in the Four Gospels* (ed. R. T. France and D. Wenham; Sheffield: JSOT Press, 1980), 1:75–99; E. S. Alexander, "The Orality of Rabbinic Writing," in *The Cambridge Companion to the Talmud and Rabbinic Literature* (ed. C. E. Fonrobert and M. S. Jaffee; CCR; Cambridge: Cambridge University Press, 2007), 38–57.

(1) There is little historical evidence to support Gerhardsson's hypothesis of an exclusive *collegium* of apostles in Jerusalem carefully editing, adding to, and guarding the integrity of the Jesus tradition.[59] The evidence that Gerhardsson musters in its favor turns out upon close scrutiny to point elsewhere.[60] While there are sources that place the apostles in Jerusalem,[61] e.g., and some mention that they dealt with doctrinal issues,[62] the distance between this historical information and the picture of their detailed and extensive work with Jesus tradition that Gerhardsson envisions is immense.[63]

The activities of the Twelve according to the Book of Acts centered on prayer (probably to be understood as including the liturgy)[64] and preach-

---

[59] See C. K. Barrett, *Jesus and the Gospel Tradition* (Philadelphia: Fortress, 1968), 10–11; Davids, "Gospels and Jewish Tradition," 87–88; Kelber, *Oral and Written*, 14; Tuckett, "Form Criticism," 26; S. J. Patterson, "Can You Trust a Gospel? A Review of Richard Bauckham's *Jesus and the Eyewitnesses*," *JSHJ* 6 (2008): 194–210, esp. 205–9 (though in these pages Patterson is primarily in conversation with Bauckham, *Jesus and the Eyewitnesses*, 264–89, he also critiques Gerhardsson's theory under consideration here).

[60] For Gerhardsson, a weighty argument in favor of his historical reconstruction is that "Paul, a former proto-rabbinic disciple, mentions that he has himself both received and handed over early Christian tradition … with the same quasi-technical terminology as what we find in the gospels about the Pharisaic tradition: παράδοσις, παραλαμβάνειν, etc." ("Secret," 18, see also ibid., 9; idem, *Memory*, 288–306; idem, *Reliability*, 14–25). Paul's statements are important in that they *do* witness to a conscious activity within early Christianity of preserving and passing on tradition. For Paul to speak of receiving and handing on tradition says nothing, however, regarding the source of that tradition. In spite of Gerhardsson's assertions that Paul had received the tradition in 1 Cor 15:3ff "undoubtedly from Jerusalem" (*Memory*, 280) and that Paul believed that the eucharistic tradition he included in 1 Cor 11 was "derived from Jesus via the college of Apostles" (ibid., 321) (I am indebted for this insight to Kelber, *Oral and Written*, 12), Paul never appealed to the authority of the apostles as those from whom he received the tradition. One cannot ultimately prove or disprove that the Apostles were (or were not) Paul's direct source for the Jesus tradition, since the sources are silent on this point. This silence, however, does not justify the central place of the apostolic *collegium* in Gerhardsson's model.

[61] The Book of Acts consistently places the Twelve in Jerusalem, even after the persecution broke out against the Christians (Acts 8:1), at least as their center of operations from where they travel elsewhere (8:4, 14, 25; 9:32).

[62] E.g., Acts 11:1–18; 15:2–30; 16:4; 21:25; Gal 2:1–10.

[63] Gerhardsson presents the apostolic gathering described in Acts 15 as an example of the traditioning work of the *collegium* (*Memory*, 245–61), but in so doing far overreaches what the evidence can support; see the comments by C. K. Barrett, *A Critical and Exegetical Commentary on the Acts of the Apostles* (2 vols.; ICC; Edinburgh: T&T Clark, 1994, 1998), 1:313.

[64] Acts 1:13–14; 6:4; see also 8:15; on "prayer" and the liturgy see F. F. Bruce, *The Acts of the Apostles: The Greek Text with Introduction and Commentary* (3rd rev. and enl. ed.; Grand Rapids: Eerdmans/Leicester: Apollos, 1990), 183; J. A. Fitzmyer, *The Acts of the Apostles: A New Translation with Introduction and Commentary* (AB 31; New

ing.[65] In this light, the "ministry of the word" to which the apostles were devoted according to Acts 6:4 should be understood not as the traditioning activity that Gerhardsson portrays, but as their preaching activity.[66] While it is sensible to hold that the apostles were important among the traditionists of the early Christian movement, there is nothing in the sources to suggest that the traditioning activity centered exclusively (or even primarily) on them; one should not discount the involvement of teachers and prophets and many others in passing on the tradition from and about Jesus, especially given that the number of churches would have soon grown beyond the capability of the apostles to be present at each.[67]

(2) A second problem with Gerhardsson's model is his supposition that Jesus as a teacher "must have made his disciples learn certain sayings off by heart ... he must have required his disciples to memorize,"[68] so that Jesus' words and works were "stamped on the memories of [his] disciples."[69] That the Gospels are full of memorable sayings and material that bears the marks of memorization only implies that these materials were probably memorized, not necessarily that the impetus for that memorization came from Jesus himself. It is to be expected that if the material in the Gospels derived primarily from oral tradition then it would show evidence of mne-

---

York: Doubleday, 1998), 349; B. Witherington, III, *The Acts of the Apostles: A Socio-Rhetorical Commentary* (Grand Rapids: Eerdmans/Carlisle: Paternoster, 1998), 250. In E. Haenchen's view it refers to the Jewish times of prayer as well as prayer "as a meritorious work of piety" (*The Acts of the Apostles: A Commentary* [trans. B. Noble and G. Shinn; rev. and updated by R. McL. Wilson; Philadelphia: Westminster, 1971], 263).

[65] Acts 2:14–36; 3:12–26; 4:8–12, 29; 5:20–21, 42; 8:12, 25, 40. The apostles' activity also often included the working of miracles, but this is attendant to their work of proclamation rather than central in itself; see Acts 3:1–11; 4:30; 5:15; 9:40–41; 10:34–43.

[66] *Pace* Gerhardsson, *Memory*, 234–45. This is the standard understanding among commentators; see, e.g., Barrett, *Acts of the Apostles*, 1:311, 313; Bruce, *Acts of the Apostles: Greek Text*, 183; J. D. G. Dunn, *The Acts of the Apostles* (NC; Valley Forge: Trinity Press International, 1996); 83; Fitzmyer, *Acts of the Apostles*, 349 ("proclamation of the Christian message"); D. G. Peterson, *The Acts of the Apostles* (PillNTC; Grand Rapids: Eerdmans/Nottingham: Apollos, 2009), 234; Witherington, *Acts of the Apostles*, 250. L. T. Johnson notes that "Luke can use 'word of God' for the entire mission (4:31; 6:2, 7; 8:14; 11:1; 12:24; 19:20), so the 'service' here probably means more than simply preaching" (*The Acts of the Apostles* [SP 5; Collegeville: Liturgical, 1992], 106).

[67] See J. D. G. Dunn, "On History, Memory and Eyewitnesses: In Response to Bengt Holmberg and Samuel Byrskog," *JSNT* 26 (2004): 482–85, who makes this argument regarding "the original disciples (not just the twelve)" (p. 483); idem, "Eyewitnesses and the Oral Jesus Tradition," *JSHJ* 6 (2008): 98–99, 105. See further Kelber, *Oral and Written*, 21, and cf. R. J. Bauckham, "The Eyewitnesses in the Gospel of Mark," *SEÅ* 74 (2009): 19–20, 29–33.

[68] Gerhardsson, *Memory*, 328, and further 334–35; similarly idem, "Secret," 9.

[69] Gerhardsson, *Memory*, 329.

monic techniques, an insight fully in keeping with the approach to oral tradition that under-girds the present work.[70] This need not also imply, however, that *Jesus required* memorization (he is never portrayed as doing so
in the Gospels[71]), or that the *disciples* were those who put a mnemonic
stamp on the tradition.[72] The present critique could be viewed as an argument from silence, but silence does not imply the truth of any given hypothesis, whether it be that Jesus required his disciples to memorize or that
he did not. At issue, then, is whether the silence in the sources is enough to
support the weight of the tenet that Jesus required his disciples to memorize, given the central place of this tenet in Gerhardsson's model.

The lack of evidence to show that Jesus required his disciples to memorize his words is important because it relates directly to one of the main
characteristics (not a rule, but a characteristic) of orality: the evanescent
nature of the spoken word. While written texts last beyond the moment in
which they are written, spoken words vanish after they are uttered except
for what remains in the memory of their hearers.[73] Written texts have
originals against which copies can be checked for accuracy, but this is not
true of spoken words: a moment (a minute, an hour, a day?) after they are
spoken, one is left to re-present as faithfully as possible what was said

---

[70] See sec. 3.3.9 below, and the similar statements in Kelber, "Memory's Desire," 60;
idem, "The Generative Force of Memory: Early Christian Traditions as Process of Remembering," *BTB* 36 (2006): 16–17, 20.

[71] Dunn, *Jesus Remembered*, 198; M. Hengel, *The Charismatic Leader and His Followers* (ed. John Riches, trans., J. C. G. Greig; Edinburgh: T&T Clark, 1996), 80–81;
Wright, *New Testament and the People of God*, 423–24.

[72] E.g., to say that Jesus' sayings "consist of brief, laconic, well-rounded texts, of
pointed statements with a clear profile, rich in content and artistic in form" so that Jesus
is creating an "object" with his sayings that could be "passed on" to his hearers and by
them to others (Gerhardsson, *Reliability*, 42, 77–78) is more of a reflection on the *text of
the Gospels*, than on the words of Jesus. We do not have direct access to the words of
Jesus, to know whether the "objects" in the Gospels, including their memorizable form,
reflect Jesus' teaching techniques or the mnemonic techniques of a traditionist. The
changing form of the sayings, and the many mnemonic techniques that become apparent
upon examining the various Jesus sayings and their parallels in the following chapters,
would suggest that the mnemonic form was superimposed on the material by the traditionists. This critique applies also to the similar perspective developed in great detail by
R. Riesner in *Jesus als Lehrer: Eine Untersuchung zum Ursprung der Evangelien-
Überlieferung* (3rd. expanded ed; WUNT 2.7; Tübingen: Mohr Siebeck, 1988 [especially
pp. 392–404, 516–18]; 4th rev. ed. to appear in 2011), summarized in idem, "From the
Messianic Teacher to the Gospels of Jesus Christ," *HSHJ*, 1.405–46; see also idem, "Jesus as Preacher and Teacher," in *Jesus and the Oral Gospel* (ed. Wansbrough), 185–210,
esp. pp. 202–8.

[73] Kelber, "Jesus and Tradition," 147, 150–51; see further idem, *Oral and Written*,
30; idem, "Generative Force of Memory," 17; idem, "Works of Memory," 231, 236–37;
Dunn, *New Perspective on Jesus*, 46–47.

from the recollection of the hearer(s).[74] The exception would be a case in which a speaker repeats the same lines over and over with no variation, so as to drum them into the head of the hearer(s). Gerhardsson's model pictures Jesus as doing precisely this,[75] but also precisely this is being called into question here (among other things) due to the lack of evidence for this kind of activity among Jesus' followers, either in the Gospels or in other early Christian sources.[76]

(3) A third problem with Gerhardsson's model is that, even though it has been instrumental in drawing scholarly attention to issues related to oral transmission of tradition, it requires too high a level of literacy from those who handled the tradition.[77] This is where the present study departs most fundamentally from Gerhardsson. Given both the evanescent nature of the spoken word, and the lack of evidence for Jesus making the disciples learn his teaching by rote memorization (both discussed above), the disciples simply could not have done the things Gerhardsson describes without

---

[74] For further discussion of this characteristic of oral tradition see secs. 3.3.5 and 3.3.10 below.

[75] See Gerhardsson, *Memory*, 328; idem, "Illuminating," 305–6; idem, "Secret," 9.

[76] Two statements by Kelber are apropos here: "One searches the synoptic gospels in vain for so much as a glimpse of authoritative memorization by means of continual repetition. None of the canonical gospels depicts Jesus as being insistent on verbatim learning of his words. Nor is there any indication that apostles, teachers, prophets, or ordinary people were trained in what Gerhardsson considered to be a Rabbinic tradition of memorization" (*Oral and Written*, 21); and, "Is it in fact imaginable that Jesus expounded his message with rote regularity and pedantic repetitiveness, and without any regard for the diversity of audiences and circumstances?" ("Memory's Desire," 66). See also Kelber's critique of Gerhardsson's understanding of "cold" memory in light of the views on "hot" memory found in more recent studies of social memory, in his "Works of Memory," 231–32; cf. Barrett, *Jesus*, 8–12; Dunn, *Jesus Remembered*, 198.

[77] On what follows see the more extensive discussion in Kelber, *Oral and Written*, 9–32, and A. Kirk, "Memory," in *Jesus in Memory* (ed. Kelber and Byrskog), 161–66. It should come as no surprise that Gerhardsson's model requires literacy, as the rabbinic model upon which it is based – as noted by Kelber and Kirk – was at its core a model for memorizing written texts. On this see especially E. S. Alexander, *Transmitting Mishnah: The Shaping Influence of Oral Tradition* (Cambridge: Cambridge University Press, 2006), 1–29; M. S. Jaffee, "Figuring Early Rabbinic Literary Culture: Thoughts Occasioned by Boomershine and Dewey," in *Orality and Textuality* (ed. Dewey), 67–72, and his book-length treatment, *Torah in the Mouth: Writing and Oral Tradition in Palestinian Judaism 200 BCE – 400 CE* (Oxford: Oxford University Press, 2001). One could summarize one of the main point of Jaffee's book with his phrase, "*rabbinic disciples encountered as oral tradition the performative embodiment of memorized rabbinic manuscript*" (p. 124, emphasis original; this section of Jaffee's book is a revision of his earlier article, "Writing and Rabbinic Oral Tradition: On Mishnaic Narrative, Lists and Mnemonics," *JJTP* 4 [1994]: 123–46). Jaffee's work serves as a corrective not only to Gerhardsson's approach, but also to that of his student S. Byrskog in his treatment of the rabbinic oral torah in, e.g., *Jesus the Only Teacher*, 156–160, 171–75.

the aid of written texts. His model does not simply *allow* for the presence of written texts that antedate the Gospels (as does the model used in the present work), it *relies* on the existence and use of these texts by the apostles.[78] In addition, it requires the involvement of highly literate individuals not just at the point of producing the written Gospels, but also for the thirty to forty years leading up to that, in order to preserve the integrity of the tradition.[79]

This dependence on literacy provides the context within which to understand Gerhardsson's statement that "Jesus and his disciples did not move within an oral society."[80] Strictly speaking Gerhardsson is correct, in that the distinction that used to be made between pure oral societies and

---

[78] This statement is, again, based on both the evanescent nature of the spoken word and the lack of evidence for Jesus making the disciples learn his teaching by rote memorization. Without texts, and without Jesus making the disciples learn his words by rote memorization, the disciples could not carry out the work that Gerhardsson envisions when he states that they "worked on the ... Christ-tradition (which was originally oral): they gathered, formulated (narrative tradition), interpreted, adapted, developed, complemented and put together collections for various definite purposes" (Gerhardsson, *Tradition*, 40; see also idem, *Memory*, 332; idem, *Reliability*, 50–51; idem, "Secret," 18).

[79] For Gerhardsson the transition from oral tradition to written texts was "certainly a drawn-out and involved process," materials were committed to writing first in private notebooks, then blocks of tradition were brought together, until the need for a full written Gospel arose (*Reliability*, 48).

[80] Gerhardsson, "Secret," 13; he states similarly on p. 14 that "I cannot ... see that the Israel of NT times can be characterized as an oral society." Some of the distance between Gerhardsson's perception of literacy and orality in early Christianity and the approach taken here is due to different valuations of orality. Gerhardsson's valuation of orality is clear from the following statements: "To assume that the leading representatives of the gospel tradition were illiterate is certainly to underestimate them. They were not children of an undeveloped, oral culture" (ibid., 14). Two things must be noted: (1) From the perspective of orality, to consider people illiterate does not imply underestimating them; such an implication is, however, at home within the presuppositions of literate, Western culture. It is anachronistic to impose present-day views of illiteracy upon the members of ancient predominantly oral societies, whose recourse to oral means did not place them at a disadvantage in handing down tradition when compared to members of predominantly literate societies. Their methods were different, but not inferior. This understanding depends on the prior recognition that the canons of accuracy and fidelity in handing on tradition are different for predominantly oral societies than for predominantly literate societies. (2) Similarly, to equate "undeveloped" with "oral" (as does Gerhardsson) is only natural from the perspective of Western literate cultures. In contrast, the approach taken in this book recognizes that members of predominantly oral societies in antiquity were not deficient in literacy, but proficient in orality. Ø. Andersen rightly states, "[an oral culture] should be interpreted in terms of what it has, that is, orality, and not in terms of what others have, that is, literacy" ("Oral Tradition," 21); on this point see further ch. 3 below.

pure literary societies was an oversimplification.[81] Yet, as will be covered in more depth in chapter 3 below, evidence shows that literacy among Jews in Israel in the first century *at most* might have been slightly higher than 3%, and mostly limited to the scribal elite.[82] One can therefore speak of Jewish society in first-century Palestine as predominantly oral.[83] In addition, there is nothing in the Gospels to indicate that Jesus chose his disciples from the literate 3% minority, and many indications to the contrary.[84] Gerhardsson's model is coherent if one presupposes that the disciples were fully literate, and ceases to be so if their literacy is questioned. In sum, popular movements within predominantly oral societies, such as earliest Christianity in first-century Palestine, simply do not depend upon literate individuals and written texts in the manner that Gerhardsson's model envisions.[85] All of this justifies the examination of the preservation and transmission of the Jesus tradition from the perspectives on orality adopted in the present work.

---

[81] See R. Finnegan, *Literacy and Orality: Studies in the Technology of Communication* (Oxford: Blackwell, 1988), 62; J. M. Foley, "The Bard's Audience Is Always More Than a Fiction," in *Time, Memory, and the Verbal Arts: Essays on the Thought of Walter Ong* (ed. D. L. Weeks and J. Hoogestraat; Selinsgrove: Susquehanna University Press/London: Associated University Presses, 1998), 95–96; idem, *Homer's Traditional Art*, 3; idem, "What's In a Sign," 3; R. Thomas, *Literacy and Orality in Ancient Greece* (KTAH; Cambridge: Cambridge University Press, 1992), 4.

[82] See sec. 3.2 below, entitled "Orality and Literacy in the Ancient Mediterranean World," and M. Bar-Ilan, "Illiteracy in the Land of Israel in the First Centuries C.E," in *Essays in the Social Scientific Study of Judaism and Jewish Society* (ed. S. Fishbane, S. Schoenfeld, and A. Goldschläger; Hoboken: KTAV, 1992), 46–61, esp. 56, who concludes that it was lower than 3%. Two book-length studies, C. Hezser's *Jewish Literacy in Roman Palestine* (TSAJ 81; Tübingen: Mohr Siebeck, 2001) and Jaffee's, *Torah in the Mouth* (15–27) generally support Bar-Ilan's findings, though Hezser leaves open the possibility that the literacy rate might have been slightly higher than 3% (p. 496). Section 3.2 below includes a discussion of the work of two scholars who posit a higher level of literacy in Palestine but without appeal to secure evidence: A. Millard, *Reading and Writing in the Time of Jesus* (BibSem 69; Sheffield: Sheffield Academic, 2000), 154–58 and L. Hurtado, "Greco-Roman Textuality and the Gospel of Mark: A Critical Assessment of Werner Kelber's *The Oral and the Written Gospel*," *BBR* 7 (1997): 93–97.

[83] See footnote 1 at the beginning of the present chapter.

[84] See further Kelber, *Oral and Written*, 21; Mournet, *Oral Tradition*, 65; also C. Hezser, "Oral and Written Communication and Transmission of Knowledge in Ancient Judaism and Christianity," *OrTr* 25 (2010): 77–80.

[85] For the application of this insight to theories regarding the composition of Mark's Gospel see Horsley, "Oral Performance and Mark," 60–63.

1.5 Parameters

The two main parameters that limit the material in the present work are its focus upon the Apostolic Fathers, and explicit appeals to Jesus tradition. We will address the rationale for each of these below.

1.5.1 Apostolic Fathers

The term "Apostolic Fathers" has been used since the last decade of the 17th century to refer to a group of early Christian documents that were written shortly after the close of the New Testament age.[86] Standard editions of the corpus usually include *1 Clement*, *2 Clement*, the *Didache*, the *Epistle of Barnabas*, the seven letters of Ignatius of Antioch, Polycarp of Smyrna's *Letter to the Philippians*, the letter from the church at Smyrna to the church at Philomelium, usually referred to as the *Martyrdom of Polycarp*, the *Shepherd* of Hermas, the *Epistle to Diognetus*, and the fragments of Papias and Quadratus. The writings of the Apostolic Fathers are rather heterogeneous, in that they not only include letters (*1 Clement*, Ignatius, Polycarp, the *Martyrdom of Polycarp*), but also a church order (the *Didache*), a homily (*2 Clement*), an apocalypse (*Shepherd* of Hermas), a didactic treatise (*Barnabas*), a collection of Jesus tradition (the original form of Papias), and two apologetic texts (*Diognetus* and Quadratus). These texts were probably gathered into one corpus based on two main criteria: their early date – they were probably all written between the late first century and the middle of the second century[87] – and the traditional view that

---

[86] The origin of the title "Apostolic Fathers" is usually traced to J. B. Cotelier (1627–86), *SS. Patrum qui Temporibus Apostolicis floruerunt, Barnabae, Clementis, Hermae, Ignatii, Polycarpi opera edita et inedita, vera, et suppositicia; una cum Clementis, Ignatii, Polycarpi actis atque martyriis* (2 vols; Paris: Petri Le Petit, 1672). H. J. de Jonge has argued, however, that William Wake (1657–1737) may have been as influential as Cotelier in the origin of the title, given that he is the first to use the expression "Apostolical Fathers" not only in the title of a book dedicated to these writings but also often in the introductory "discourse" to the same work: W. Wake, *The genuine epistles of the Apostolical fathers S. Barnabas, S. Clement, S. Ignatius, S. Polycarp: The Shepherd of Hermas, and the Martyrdoms of St. Ignatius and St. Polycarp ...: Translated and published with a large preliminary discourse* (London: Printed for Richard Sare at Grays-Inn Gate in Holbourn, 1693); see H. J. d. Jonge, "On the Origin of the Term 'Apostolic Fathers,'" *JTS* n.s. 29 (1978): 503–5, and further J. A. Fischer, "Die ältesten Ausgaben der Patres Apostolici: Ein Beitrag zu Begriff und Begrenzung der Apostolischen Väter," *HJ* 94 (1974): 157–90; 95 (1975): 88–119.

[87] The composition of certain documents may fall outside of this timeframe; the most likely to be earlier is the *Didache*, possibly written closer to the middle of the first century (as argued, e.g., by J. A. T. Robinson, *Redating the New Testament* [London and Philadelphia: SCM and Westminster, 1976], 322–27, esp. 327 [A.D. 40–60]; Milavec, *Didache: Faith, Hope, and Life*, xii–xiii; idem, "When, Why, and for Whom Was the

their authors either knew, or were discipled by somebody who had known, one of the twelve apostles.[88]

The late-first- to mid-second-century dating for the Apostolic Fathers carries implications for the Jesus tradition they contain. This was a time of transition prior to the closing of the New Testament canon,[89] thus antedating the widespread appeal to the canonical Gospels that will characterize Christian literature after Irenaeus.[90] It is also a time in which the oral tradition that informed the Gospels (and other writings) was still in use among the churches.[91] This is, in part, why the Apostolic Fathers were chosen as the focus of the present work that has oral Jesus tradition as its subject matter.

1.5.2 Explicit Appeals to Jesus Tradition

One of the methodological features distinguishing the current study from the standard works published on the topic is its focus on sayings *explicitly* attributed to Jesus by the Apostolic Fathers. This approach was chosen as the most suitable for a study that assigns a central place to oral Jesus tradition, as it provides a reliable criterion for identifying material that was recognized and used *as* Jesus tradition by these writers. The alternative of including implicit sayings has inherent problems, in that it might lead one to (a) build a methodological bias in favor of a source one uses for comparative purposes, or (b) include in one's pool of Jesus tradition sayings (and/or other material) that were not even attributed to him in any given Apostolic Father's milieu, which would almost certainly skew the results of one's investigation. Following is a brief explanation of these two problems:

Didache Created?: Insights into the Social and Historical Setting of the Didache Communities," in *Matthew and the Didache: Two Documents from the Same Jewish-Christian Milieu?* [ed. H. Van de Sandt; Assen: Van Gorcum/Philadelphia: Fortress, 2005], 63–84 [ca. A.D. 50]), the most likely to be later is *Diognetus*, as some would date it as late as the early fourth century (see T. H. Olbricht, "Apostolic Fathers," *DNTB* 85). A majority of scholars, however, would place all the writings of the Apostolic Fathers, including the *Didache* and *Diognetus*, within the late first to the mid-second centuries.

[88] See further Olbricht, "Apostolic Fathers," 81–85; A. Lindemann, "Apostolic Fathers," *RPP* 1:335.

[89] See B. M. Metzger, *The Canon of the New Testament: Its Origin, Development, and Significance* (Oxford: Clarendon/New York: Oxford University Press, 1987), 39–73.

[90] As G. Stanton states, "When Irenaeus set out the earliest defence of the church's fourfold Gospel in about A.D. 180, he almost certainly did so on the basis of his use of codices that contained all four Gospels" ("Jesus Traditions," *DLNTD* 577).

[91] One of the lasting insights of form criticism corroborated by many of the studies cited throughout the present work; for a classic statement see H. von Campenhausen, *The Formation of the Christian Bible* (trans. J. A. Baker; Philadelphia Fortress, 1972), 121.

(a) Studies that seek to recognize implicit Jesus tradition in the Apostolic Fathers on the basis of its similarity to material contained *in any given extant document* will tend to be biased in favor of said document in assigning an origin to the tradition. This criticism has often been leveled, for example, at the work of É. Massaux and W.-D. Köhler, who after identifying Matthew-like material in the Apostolic Fathers, conclude that a vast majority of this material is dependent at least indirectly upon Matthew.[92] In these studies, the method largely predetermines the outcome.[93] Of particular relevance to the present work, studies such as those of Massaux and Köhler tend to neglect oral tradition as a possible source for the sayings they consider, due in part to the bias built into their method. Oral tradition becomes a last resort, catch-all category for material that cannot be assigned with certainty to an identifiable written source.

(b) One can never be certain whether or not every so-called "implicit reference to Jesus tradition" was actually known and appealed to *as* Jesus tradition by the author in whose work it is found.[94] If an Apostolic Father explicitly cites a tradition as coming from Jesus, it is legitimate to use this material to study the origin and use of Jesus tradition in the Apostolic Fathers. If, however, an Apostolic Father only seems to cite such a tradition,

---

[92] É. Massaux, *The Influence of the Gospel of Saint Matthew on Christian Literature before Saint Irenaeus* (trans. N. J. Belval and S. Hecht; ed. A. J. Bellinzoni; NGS 5; 3 vols.; Leuven: Peeters/Macon: Mercer University Press, 1990–93); W.-D. Köhler, *Die Rezeption des Matthäusevangeliums in der Zeit vor Irenäus* (WUNT 2.24; Tübingen: Mohr Siebeck, 1987).

[93] Koester's remarks regarding Köhler's treatment of *1 Clem.* 16.17 are pertinent here, "It is typical for the methodological weakness of Köhler's approach that he points out that the 'yoke of grace' is the 'yoke of Jesus' and finds 'great nearness to Matthew'; therefore, this 'passage can be reconciled with the assumption of the dependence (of *1 Clement*) upon Matthew', although he admits that it cannot carry the burden of proof (*Rezeption des Matthäusevangeliums*, 60). Unfortunately, Köhler never considers seriously the existence of the oral tradition or of early collections of sayings" (H. Koester, *Ancient Christian Gospels: Their History and Development* [London: SCM/Philadelphia: Trinity Press International, 1990], 71, n. 1).

[94] This is not the same as arguing that one cannot recognize whether or not a particular saying originated with Jesus – for the latter, one can apply to these implicit sayings the same criteria that are used in determining the authenticity of other Jesus sayings. Even when an Apostolic Father explicitly attributes a saying to Jesus this attribution may be mistaken. The latter does not present much of a problem in the earlier Apostolic Fathers, in that the sayings they quote find clear parallels in other documents of the period that contain Jesus tradition. The criterion of multiple attestation thus makes it quite likely that the sayings in question go back to Jesus himself. The situation changes, however, with the later Apostolic Fathers such as *2 Clement* and Papias. There we find sayings that have no clear parallel in other Jesus tradition, but at times are paralleled in other (e.g., Jewish) sources; see further ch. 9 and "Appendix: The Fragments of Papias," below.

it is more difficult to justify using this implicit material in the same way.[95] Sources other than Jesus tradition could account for such a saying, in which case its inclusion in a study of Jesus tradition would negatively affect the study's results.

For example, the saying in *Barnabas* 4.14, ὡς γέγραπται, πολλοὶ κλητοί, ὀλίγοι δὲ ἐκλεκτοὶ εὑρεθῶμεν is not explicitly identified as a saying of Jesus, though it finds a parallel in Mt 22:14: πολλοὶ γάρ εἰσιν κλητοί, ὀλίγοι δὲ ἐκλεκτοί. Scholars continue to debate whether the author of *Barnabas*, (a) mistakenly cites Jesus tradition as if it came from the Jewish Scriptures, since the formula ὡς γέγραπται is used regularly in the Apostolic Fathers for quoting OT materials, and similar formulas are also used elsewhere in *Barnabas* in reference to the OT or Jewish documents that held authoritative status for the writer; (b) cites from a non-extant Jewish source that may also inform such passages as 4 Ezra 8:3 ("Many have been created, but few will be saved"), 9:15 ("There are more who perish than those who will be saved") and 10:57 ("For you are more blessed than many, and you have been called before the Most High, as but few have been");[96] or (c) cites Mt 22:14, and in so doing perhaps attaches scriptural status to the Gospel of Matthew (again, because of the introduction ὡς γέγραπται).[97] We need not resolve here the ongoing debate regarding the source of the saying in *Barn.* 4.14. Rather, what is important for the point being made is that if Barnabas is citing, e.g., a non-extant Jewish source (option 'b') rather than a source of Jesus tradition, any conclusions drawn from the study of *Barn.* 4.14 *as Jesus tradition* would skew the results of an investigation.

One must also take into account that the language of a community of followers of Jesus can be expected to reflect to some extent the language of their founder. When one encounters so-called "implicit Jesus sayings" in any given writing, these may be nothing more than a reflection of the language current in the early Christian community in which the writing originated. If "implicit sayings" are in reality simply the common language of the community, it is fruitless to examine them in order to learn how the

---

[95] I am indebted for this formulation of the problem to C. M. Tuckett's similar remarks regarding Jesus tradition in Paul; see his "Synoptic Tradition in 1 Thessalonians?," in *The Thessalonian Correspondence* (ed. R. F. Collins; BETL 87; Leuven: Leuven University Press and Peeters, 1990), 162.

[96] Citations are from B. M. Metzger, "The Fourth Book of Ezra," in *OTP* 542, 545, 548.

[97] For a recent overview of the discussion of this passage and other Jesus tradition in *Barnabas* see J. Carleton Paget, "The *Epistle of Barnabas* and the Writings that later Formed the New Testament," in *The Reception of the New Testament in the Apostolic Fathers* (ed. A. Gregory and C. M. Tuckett; NTAF 1; Oxford: Oxford University Press, 2005), 232–39, 249.

community used Jesus tradition, whether Jesus tradition was given any more respect or held more authority than other materials, or to ascertain the care with which it was transmitted, or lack thereof.[98] In short, if one cannot determine whether or not any given saying functioned *as* Jesus tradition, then one cannot use it to arrive at certain conclusions *regarding* Jesus tradition.

One further point deserves mention: the focus on tradition explicitly attributed to Jesus in the Apostolic Fathers will result in a fairly small sample of material, which is of benefit rather than detriment to our study. A. Gregory and C. M. Tuckett articulate this methodological point well when they state, "Given that we know so little about the early transmission of the gospels in general, and given that so much of early Christian literature is lost, it may be the case that a small sample of quite secure evidence may be of more value than a larger sample of less secure evidence."[99]

In sum, the value of focusing upon material that is explicitly attributed to Jesus in the sources is threefold: (i) it lessens the likelihood that one's study will be methodologically biased in favor of any given document as the source of the sayings under consideration; (ii) it enables one to arrive at conclusions specifically about *Jesus tradition*; and (iii) it provides a small, fairly secure sample of tradition upon which to base one's study. All of this is not meant to detract from the importance of studying implicit say-

---

[98] Any given Apostolic Father may adapt, paraphrase or otherwise alter material that he does not consider Jesus tradition in ways that might not be true if he regarded it as the words of Jesus. Such material, if included in a study of the use of Jesus tradition by the author, might lead the researcher to assume that Jesus tradition was treated with more freedom than may have actually been the case.

[99] A. Gregory and C. M. Tuckett, "Reflections on Method: What Constitutes the Use of the Writings that later Formed the New Testament in the Apostolic Fathers?," in *Reception* (ed. Gregory and Tuckett), 75. The value of the present approach is analogous to that of a series of studies by Tuckett and Gregory: while their aim was to arrive at a minimum of sayings that (in their view) show clear dependence upon the written Gospels of Matthew and Luke, the present approach aims to provide the bare minimum of material within the ApFa that can be identified with certainty as originating with Jesus. See C. M. Tuckett, "Synoptic Tradition in the *Didache*," in *The Didache in Modern Research* (ed. J. A. Draper; AGJU 37; Leiden: Brill, 1996), 92–128; ibid., "The *Didache* and the Synoptics Once More: A Response to Aaron Milavec," *JECS* 13 (2005): 509–18; ibid., "The *Didache* and the Writings that later Formed the New Testament," in *Reception* (ed. Gregory and Tuckett), 83–127; A. Gregory, *The Reception of Luke and Acts in the Period before Irenaeus: Looking for Luke in the Second Century* (WUNT 2.169; Tübingen: Mohr Siebeck, 2003); ibid., "Looking for Luke in the Second Century: A Dialogue with François Bovon," in *Reading Luke: Interpretation, Reflection, Formation* (ed. C. G. Bartholomew, J. B. Green, and A. C. Thiselton; SH 6; Milton Keynes: Paternoster/Grand Rapids: Zondervan, 2005), 401–15.

ings, which also has its place,[100] but only to explain the centrality of explicit sayings to this study.[101]

The above parameters limit the Apostolic Fathers that will be included in this study, as only five of them appeal explicitly to Jesus tradition: Clement of Rome (*1 Clem.* 13.2; 46.7–8), Polycarp (*Phil.* 2.3), Ignatius (*Smyrn.* 4.2a), the *Didache* (8.2; 9.5), and Pseudo-Clement (*2 Clem.* 2.4; 3.2; 4.2, 5; 5.2–4; 6.1–2; 8.5; 9.11; 12.2, 6; 13.4).[102]

1.6 Definition of "Oral Jesus Tradition"

The present work is concerned primarily with oral Jesus tradition. It is thus helpful before proceeding to define oral tradition in contradistinction to other forms of orality. The transmission of *oral tradition* can be distinguished from the more general *oral communication* in that it implies something – a tradition – in existence before the oral communication takes

---

[100] Part of the power of referring *implicitly* to a Jesus tradition that was held in common would have been the creation of an "insider language," enabling the ability to communicate to other members of the Christian community through veiled allusions and implied connections to which an outsider would remain oblivious (see J. D. G. Dunn, "Jesus Tradition in Paul," in *Studying the Historical Jesus: Evaluations of the State of Current Research* [ed. B. Chilton and C. A. Evans; NTTS 19; Leiden: Brill, 1994], 155–78, here pp. 176–78; repr. in *The Christ and the Spirit: Collected Essays of James D. G. Dunn*, Vol. 1: *Christology* [Grand Rapids: Eerdmans, 1998], 169–89, here pp. 187–89; idem, *Jesus Remembered*, 183).

[101] The sheer number of possible implicit allusions to Jesus' sayings in the Apostolic Fathers is also a factor to be taken into consideration, as covering them thoroughly would call for a separate study of each book. A number of studies have been conducted on the use of the NT as a whole by an individual early Christian writer, such as P. Hartog, *Polycarp and the New Testament: The Occasion, Rhetoric, Theme, and Unity of the Epistle to the Philippians an its Allusions to New Testament Literature* (WUNT 2.134; Tübingen: Mohr Siebeck, 2002); K. Berding, *Polycarp and Paul: An Analysis of their Literary and Theological Relationship in Light of Polycarp's Use of Biblical and Extra-Biblical Literature* (VCSup 62; Leiden: Brill, 2002). Other studies have been written on the reception of a specific NT book or writer by a number of Patristic writers, such as Massaux, *Influence*; Köhler, *Rezeption*; Gregory, *Reception of Luke and Acts*. Due to constraints of space only monographs have been mentioned above. Of the many important articles written on these topics, special attention is due to those collected in the two volumes edited by A. Gregory and C. Tuckett, *Reception of the New Testament in the Apostolic Fathers* and *Trajectories through the New Testament and the Apostolic Fathers* (NTAF 1 and 2; Oxford: Oxford University Press, 2005).

[102] The fragments of Papias will be dealt with separately below in an appendix (for reasons that will be explained there; see "Appendix: The Fragments of Papias"). Fragments containing explicit appeals to Jesus tradition that are usually attributed to Papias include 1.1b–5 (Iren. *Adv. Haer.*, 5.33,3–4) and 13.2 (George Hamartolos, *Chronicon*).

place.[103] It can be distinguished from both *oral history* and *oral testimony* (which also imply something in existence before the communication takes place), in that while these are based on the "verbal memoirs of firsthand observers," oral tradition is not first hand, but has been passed on in a traditioning process.[104] Having defined oral tradition negatively against these other forms of orality, we now turn to define oral tradition in its own right.

For the purposes of this study "oral Jesus tradition" can be defined as discourse material that is both (a) attributed to and/or (b) about the person of Jesus of Nazareth, material that originated in a spoken venue and was transmitted primarily by oral means from the past, and was the common property of the Jesus movement in the first and second centuries.[105]

This definition is intended to emphasize all three components of the designation "oral / Jesus / tradition." Six main elements merit highlighting in this regard:

(1) That the tradition is both *attributed to* and *about* Jesus implies the inclusion not only of discourse material containing the tradition of Jesus' *words*, but also tradition that narrated his *deeds*; both are necessary for a complete definition.[106] While the present work will deal primarily with Jesus' words (which predominate in the texts under consideration), it will also touch upon the tradition about his deeds (particularly in discussing *2 Clement*).

(2) That the tradition is "oral" implies that it originated and was (primarily) transmitted in a spoken and heard venue. Since we will further elaborate on this element in chapter 3, for now it is sufficient to say that while we only have access to the discourse that will be the focus of this

---

[103] Andersen, "Oral Tradition," 26.

[104] Citation from R. C. Echo-Hawk, "Oral history is best defined as the verbal memoirs of firsthand observers, while oral traditions are verbal memoirs that firsthand observers have passed along to others" ("Ancient History in the New World: Integrating Oral Traditions and the Archaeological Record in Deep Time," *AmAn* 65 [2000]: 270); see also Andersen, "Oral Tradition," 27. According to D. Henige, oral history is "the study of the recent past by means of life histories or personal recollections, where informants speak about their own experiences," and is to be distinguished from oral traditions that are "recollections of the past that are commonly or universally known in a given culture" and "must have been handed down for at least a few generations" (*Oral Historiography* [New York: Longman, 1982], 2).

[105] This definition was crafted primarily in conversation with Andersen, "Oral Tradition," 25–27; S. Byrskog, *Jesus the Only Teacher*, 20–24; idem, "Eyewitness Testimony and Oral Tradition," 42–43; Henige, *Oral Historiography*, 2; idem, "Oral, but Oral What? The Nomenclatures of Orality and Their Implications," *OrTr* 3 (1988): 231–38; C. Nogueira, "Oral Tradition: A Definition," *OrTr* 18.2 (2003): 164–65; and Vansina, *Oral Tradition*, 27–28.

[106] See Gerhardsson, *Memory*, 328. As Byrskog notes, "the constant focus on Jesus was *the* characteristic feature of the Jesus tradition" (*Jesus the Only Teacher*, 21).

study from written sources, what is important is not the context in which they are *found*, but the context in which they *originated* and were *transmitted* prior to being set to writing.[107] In the case of the Jesus tradition one cannot exclude the possible use of written notes, but these would have served more as aids to memorization than as repositories of the tradition.

(3) That the Jesus material is "tradition" implies an element of continuity involving repeated instances of performance of the oral discourse over time, by various traditionists, and in a variety of contexts. This continuity is captured in D. Henige's criterion that oral traditional materials "should have been transmitted over several generations."[108] It is not necessary, however, for several generations to have gone by for materials to become traditional. The Jesus discourse would have become "tradition" by nature of its repeated performances over a shorter time frame, as a result of its transmission from traditionist to traditionist, accompanying the spread of the early Jesus movement from Palestine into the wider Greco-Roman world. It would not cease to be tradition simply because it became incorporated into the writings of the Apostolic Fathers within a single generation, or only one generation removed, from the time of Jesus.[109]

(4) That the tradition was not only *about* the past of Jesus but *was transmitted from* the past by a succession of performers implies a certain

---

[107] On the nuances of defining oral vs. literate discourse and transcription vs. composition, see E. J. Bakker, "How Oral is Oral Composition?," in *Signs of Orality* (ed. Mackay), 30–31.

[108] Henige, "Oral What," 233.

[109] Cf. E. Tonkin, *Narrating our Pasts: The Social Construction of Oral History* (CSOLC 22; Cambridge: Cambridge University Press, 1992), 87. Jan Vansina's definition is closer to my own in this respect, in that his criterion is "beyond the present generation" (*Oral Tradition*, 27). S. Byrskog's definition becomes too broad when he states that "The observation of an eyewitness becomes, in a sense, tradition as soon as it is communicated from one person to another" ("Eyewitness Testimony and Oral Tradition," 42 [on pp. 42–43 he qualifies this statement somewhat], and see the similar statement in ibid., "The Eyewitnesses as Interpreters of the Past: Reflections on Richard Bauckham's, *Jesus and the Eyewitnesses*," *JSHS* 6 [2008], 159, where he also speaks of an "interaction and even fusion of oral history and oral tradition" [p. 160]); this is to confuse "tradition" with "testimony" (see point 5 that follows). There is a similar problem with Byrskog's statement, "It even happens that a teacher deliberately formulates sayings to serve as traditions from the beginning. In such cases, a tradition is at hand as soon as a saying is received by the first pupil(s) in accordance with the teacher's intention" (*Jesus the Only Teacher*, 20; see the similar statement in his "The Transmission of the Jesus Tradition," in *HSHJ*, 2.1477); this is to confuse "tradition" with "teaching." The teacher may *intend* that it become tradition, but it remains only a teaching until it has been *accorded* the status of tradition by taking on, as it were, a life of its own separate from the teacher via repeated transmission; i.e., if the pupil(s) to whom Byrskog refers do(es) not preserve and pass on the teaching, then simply having received it from the teacher does not make it tradition, even if that was the teacher's intention.

autonomous tie to the past that transcends the individuality of the tradition-ists.[110] This is important to distinguish oral *tradition* from other forms of oral communication. Along these lines Øivind Andersen rightly refers to tradition as "not personal but *transpersonal*," and adds, "Tradition stems from others, and if the message has weight, it is not by virtue of the trans-mitter, but by coming from somewhere else."[111]

(5) That the tradition was "the common property of the Jesus move-ment in the first and second centuries" serves to further differentiate "tra-dition" from "testimony." David Henige observes that "testimony" is more appropriate as a reference to information that is "the property of a few in-dividuals," as opposed to the "widespread belief and common acceptance" implied by the term "tradition."[112] Though perhaps originating in "testi-mony," the Jesus material that is the focus of this study has grown beyond that and become "tradition" as it became the property of the growing Jesus movement.[113]

(6) Finally, that the oral Jesus tradition was "the common property of the Jesus movement" also indicates that the gathering of the early Jesus communities, including traditionists/performers (including apostles, teach-ers, evangelists, missionaries, prophets, but also many others) and their audiences, provided the context within which the oral Jesus tradition found the continuity of reception necessary for its survival.[114] This continuity of

---

[110] "Performers" in the sense that they would conduct an "oral performance" of the tradition, understood as "verbalization which has no direct connection with writing" (Ong, *Presence*, 22); see further ch. 3 below.

[111] Andersen, "Oral Tradition," 26, emphasis his; cf. Gerhardsson, *Reliability*, 25–27.

[112] See Henige, "Oral What," 232; idem, *Oral Historiography*, 2–3; cf. Byrskog, *Jesus the Only Teacher*, 21; Havelock, *Muse*, 54–59.

[113] For further discussion see Andersen, "Oral Tradition," 26.

[114] On the responsibility of the audience in maintaining the "continuity of reception" necessary for the survival of a tradition see Foley, "Bard's Audience," 92–108, esp. 104; idem, *Immanent Art*, 6–13, 42–45; idem, *Singer*, 42–59; idem, "Memory"; see also Dunn, *New Perspective on Jesus*, 48–49; idem, "Remembering Jesus," 196; Vansina, *Oral Tradition*, 41–42. On the participation of audiences in oral performances see S. O. Iyasere, "African Oral Tradition – Criticism as a Performance: A Ritual," in *African Literature Today,* No. 11: *Myth and History* (ed. E. D. Jones; London: Heinemann/New York: Afri-cana, 1980), 169–74; D. Rhoads, "Biblical Performance Criticism: Performance as Re-search," *OrTr* 25 (2010): 162–63, 165–66; Shiner, *Proclaiming*, 143–52; idem, "Oral Performance in the New Testament World," in *The Bible in Ancient and Modern Media: Story and Performance* (ed. H. E. Hearon and P. Ruge-Jones; BPC 1; Eugene, Ore.: Cas-cade, 2009), 60–62; Vansina, *Oral Tradition*, 34–36. To speak of the oral Jesus tradition as "the common property of the Jesus movement" is not to deny the role of individuals; only individuals remember, and traditionists were, after all, individuals (see Vansina, *Oral Tradition*, 36–39; J. K. Olick, "Collective Memory: The Two Cultures," *SocTh* 17 [1999], 338, 346). Their individual role, however, was carried out within the context of community, as described above – otherwise we are no longer speaking of "tradition"; as

reception was guaranteed because the oral Jesus tradition was central to the identity of the early Jesus communities. There was a symbiotic relationship between tradition and community: the tradition both engendered the community (e.g., as essential to the proclamation that gave it birth) and shaped it (e.g., as essential to its catechetical and didactic activity),[115] as the community both preserved the tradition (through its retelling and application) and in turn also shaped it (e.g., by interpreting it and bringing out those aspects of it that were most relevant to the community's present).[116]

That the early Jesus communities were responsible for the ongoing preservation and performance of the Jesus tradition gave the tradition *con-*

Dunn states succinctly, "it is not really possible to speak of *tradition* except as community tradition" ("On History, Memory and Eyewitnesses," 482; emphasis his; see further Vansina, *Oral Tradition*, 147–60). One should not confuse the individual nature of the traditionist's role with the individual nature of personal recollections by eyewitnesses – the latter constitutes "testimony" rather than "tradition" if it has not become the common property of the community via the role of the traditionist(s); cf. S. Byrskog, "A New Quest for the *Sitz im Leben*: Social Memory, the Jesus Tradition and the Gospel of Matthew," *NTS* 52 (2006): 324–25.

[115] This is one of Dunn's main emphases in *Jesus Remembered*, which can be summarized in his statement, "it was the realization that the impact [Jesus] made on individuals was shared by others which drew disciple groups and then churches together; and ... what gave them their continuing identity as disciples was that shared memory and the continuing sharing of these memories, that is, the oral traditions that bound them together as one" ("On History, Memory and Eyewitnesses," 481). On the importance of *practicing* the teaching contained in a tradition for its preservation see Byrskog, *Jesus the Only Teacher*, 324–331; also briefly idem, "Transmission of the Jesus Tradition," 1467–68.

[116] In speaking of the interrelation between group identity and preserved memory, J. Olick comments that "It is not just that we remember as members of groups, but that we constitute those groups and their members simultaneously in the act (thus re-membering)," and refers to the work of R. Bellah in stating further that "genuine communities [are] communities of memory" (Olick, "Collective Memory," 342; see R. N. Bellah et al., *Habits of the Heart: Individualism and Commitment in American Life* [Berkeley: University of California Press, 1985], 153). The interplay between remembered past, present concerns, and group identity is greatly informed by the field of social memory studies, pioneered by M. Halbwachs in *Les cadres sociaux de la mémoire* (Paris: F. Alcan, 1925; new ed. Paris: Presses Universitaires de France, 1952) and *La topographie légendaire des évangiles en terre sainte: Etude de mémoire collective* (Paris: Presses Universitaires de France, 1941); most of the former and the conclusions of the latter were translated in *On Collective Memory* (ed., trans., and intro. by L. A. Coser; Chicago: University of Chicago Press, 1992). Halbwach's *La mémoire collective* (published posthumously; Paris: Presses Universitaires de France, 1950) has been translated as *The Collective Memory* (trans. F. J. Ditter, Jr. and V. Y. Ditter; New York: Harper & Row, 1980). Among recent contributions to the study of social memory see especially the two works by J. Assmann, *Das kulturelle Gedächtnis: Schrift, Erinnerung und politische Identität in frühen Hochkulturen* (Munich: C. H. Beck, 1992) and *Religion and Cultural Memory: Ten Studies* (Stanford, Calif.: Stanford University Press, 2006). We will further address social memory in relation to Jesus tradition in chapter 3 (esp. sec. 3.3.10) below.

tinuity of context. This continuity of context was indispensable in (a) informing the meaning not just of the words of the tradition, but also of its gestures and symbols (e.g., anointing, washing, a kiss; bread, wine, oil, water),[117] and in (b) maintaining the values and communal memories within which the tradition was to be understood.[118] This continuity thus served to render the tradition into an insider language with a set of associations, institutionalized references, and expectations that were fully perceived only by a "competent audience" well versed in the tradition: those who belonged to the early Jesus communities.[119]

1.7 Presuppositions and Assumptions

In using male pronouns in referring to the authors of the writings of the Apostolic Fathers and of the Synoptic Gospels throughout the present work, I do so based on the assumption that the authors of these documents were men; to my knowledge no cogent argument to the contrary has been offered in relation to any of the writings in question.

Certain portions of the investigation that follows will depend on insights provided by source and redaction criticism. In the course of the discussion it will become clear that one of the basic presuppositions of the present work is that the Two Source Hypothesis – that Mark wrote first, and was used by both Matthew and Luke, both of whom also used Q – remains the best solution for the Synoptic Problem.[120] My agreement with this Hypothesis, however, does not extend to viewing all of Q as a written document. As will become clear in the course of our investigation, one must leave open the possibility that Matthew and Luke were familiar with certain portions of what is commonly called Q *as oral tradition*, particularly the Sermon on the Mount/Plain. To fully investigate this topic as it relates to the whole Sermon on the Mount/Plain, let alone the entirety of what is usually designated as Q, lies outside of the scope of our investigation. Certain conclusions arrived at in this study, however, will inform the wider discussion of Q.

---

[117] These aspects of the tradition are often investigated in liturgical studies, but are not limited to the liturgy.

[118] Cf. Nogueira, "Oral Tradition," 164.

[119] See Foley, *Singer*, 29–59, especially his discussion of "Performance Arena," "Register," and "Communicative Economy" on pp. 47–56, and cf. the notions of "reenactment" and "preservation" developed by E. J. Bakker in "Activation and Preservation: The Interdependence of Text and Performance in an Oral Tradition," *OrTr* 8 (1993): 10–15; also Vansina, *Oral Tradition*, 137–46.

[120] See comments on the synoptic problem in sec. 1.1 above.

1.8 Procedure

The discussion that follows will unfold in four main steps: First, chapter 2 will provide a brief history of the scholarly treatment of the Jesus tradition in the Apostolic Fathers. In this survey particular attention will be given to presuppositions and issues of method, and the impact of these on the findings of various scholars. Second, chapter 3 will deal with some preliminary matters regarding orality and literacy in antiquity (orality in written texts; the place of orality in first-century Mediterranean societies), followed by a description of the method to be applied in studying the Jesus tradition in the present work. It will conclude with two methodological caveats related to the limits of comparative studies and the need to give scribality its fair due even in a study centered on orality. Third, in chapters 4 through 9, which constitute the bulk of the present work, the method described in chapter 3 will be applied to a series of texts from the Apostolic Fathers. Chapters 4 through 7 will each deal with a single text, chosen for treatment in order of decreasing complexity. The rationale behind this order is that the more complex texts allow for a more in-depth application of the method upon which the present work is based. The text chosen for consideration in chapter 4 (*1 Clem.* 13.2) contains the greatest number of sayings as well as the most parallels in other early Christian literature, making it the ideal candidate for a full initial exploration. Much of what is developed in chapter 4 will be presupposed in later chapters. Chapter 8 differs from the four that precede it in that three different texts will be considered briefly in rather quick succession. This format was chosen primarily because the isolated, short proverbial sayings contained in these texts do not lend themselves to extended analysis. Chapter 9 is reserved for the problem child, the Jesus tradition in *2 Clement*. The sheer amount of texts that contain Jesus tradition (ten in all), the variety of introductory formulas, and the diverse genre of Jesus material in *2 Clement*, among other things, contribute to making the study of the Jesus tradition in this book a particular challenge. Fourth, a brief concluding section will summarize some key points from chapters 4 through 9, relate them back to the thesis statement included in this introduction, and draw out some implications for further study of the Jesus tradition. Though not the focus of the present work, elements of our discussion will inform larger issues such as the reliability of the tradition that was used in the canonical Gospels, and the use of texts within early Christian communities. These issues will also be addressed in the concluding section. An appendix will treat the Jesus tradition in the fragments of Papias.

Chapter 2

A Brief History of Scholarship on the Sources of the Jesus Tradition in the Apostolic Fathers

2.1 Introduction

The purpose of this chapter is to provide a general overview of some of the roads that have been traversed by scholars in the study of the Jesus tradition in the Apostolic Fathers. It will not be possible to survey all of the relevant literature, since the sheer number of ancient documents involved causes scholarship to splinter into too many subtopics. For example, the topic of the Jesus and/or gospel tradition in the *Didache* alone has generated a considerable body of secondary literature in its own right.[1] The sur-

---

[1] Besides the relevant sections in the major commentaries (J. P. Audet, *La Didachè: Instructions des Apôtres* [EBib; Paris: Lecoffre, 1958]; R. A. Kraft, *Barnabas and the Didache* [ApFa 3; New York: Thomas Nelson & Sons, 1965]; K. Niederwimmer, *The Didache: A Commentary* [ed. H. W. Attridge; trans. L. M. Maloney; Hermeneia; Minneapolis: Fortress, 1998]; W. Rordorf and A. Tuilier, *La Doctrine des Douze Apôtres [Didaché]* [2nd rev. and expanded ed.; SC 248 bis; Paris: Cerf, 1998]; K. Wengst, *Didache [Apostellehre], Barnabasbrief, Zweiter Clemensbrief, Schrift an Diognet* [SchU 2; Darmstadt: Wissenschaftliche Buchgesellschaft, 1984]), see V. Balabanski, *Eschatology in the Making: Mark, Matthew and the Didache* (SNTSMS 97; Cambridge: Cambridge University Press, 1997); B. C. Butler, "The Literary Relations of Didache, Ch. XVI," *JTS* n.s. 11 (1960): 265–83; J. M. Court, "The Didache and St. Matthew's Gospel," *SJT* 34 (1981): 109–20; J. A Draper, "The Jesus Tradition in the Didache," in *Gospel Perspectives*, Vol. 5: *The Jesus Tradition Outside the Gospels* (ed. D. Wenham; Sheffield: JSOT Press, 1985), 269–87, rev. ed. in *The* Didache *in Modern Research* (ed. J. A. Draper; AGJU 37; Leiden: Brill, 1996), 72–91, references below are to the 1996 ed.; idem, "Lactantius and the Jesus Tradition in the Didache," *JTS* n.s. 40 (1989): 112–16; idem, "Torah and Troublesome Apostles in the *Didache* Community," in Didache *in Modern Research* (ed. Draper), 340–63; and also idem, "First-fruits and the Support of Prophets, Teachers, and the Poor in *Didache* 13 in Relation to New Testament Parallels," in *Trajectories* (ed. Gregory and Tuckett), 223–43; A. J. P. Garrow, *The Gospel of Matthew's Dependence on the Didache* (JSNTSup 254; London and New York: T&T Clark International, 2004); R. Glover, "The Didache's Quotations and the Synoptic Gospels," *NTS* 5 (1958–59): 12–29; C. N. Jefford, *The Sayings of Jesus in the Teaching of the Twelve Apostles* (VCSup 11; Leiden: Brill, 1989); I. H. Henderson, "Didache and Orality in Synoptic Comparison," *JBL* 111 (1992): 283–306; idem, "Style-Switching in the *Didache:* Fingerprint or Argument?," in *The* Didache *in Context: Essays on Its Text, History and Transmission* (ed. C.

vey that follows will therefore be built around the major works that deal with the corpus of the Apostolic Fathers as a whole, supplemented by some additional works that have been influential in the ongoing discussion. Other contributions will not be ignored, but interaction with them will be limited to brief comments, primarily in the footnotes.

The period of scholarship most relevant for the present study begins with the early twentieth century. At the beginning of this period scholars made the first serious attempt to challenge the widely held assumption that (what would become)[2] the canonical Gospels were the main source of the Jesus tradition in the Apostolic Fathers.[3] Since then much of scholarship

---

N. Jefford; NovTSup 77; Leiden: Brill, 1995), 177–209; J. S. Kloppenborg, "Didache 16 6–8 and Special Matthaean Tradition," *ZNW* 70 (1979): 54–67; idem, "The Use of the Synoptics or Q in *Did.* 1:3b–2:1," in *Matthew and the Didache* (ed. van de Sandt), 105–29; B. Layton, "The Sources, Date and Transmission of *Didache* 1.3b–2.1," *HTR* 61 (1968): 343–83; T. Löfstedt, "A Message for the Last Days: Didache 16.1–8 and the New Testament Traditions," *EstBib* 60 (2002): 351–80; Milavec, "Synoptic Tradition"; idem, "A Rejoinder [to C. M. Tuckett]," *JECS* 13 (2005): 519–23; J. A. Robinson, "The Epistle of Barnabas and the Didache," *JTS* 35 (1934): 225–48; W. Rordorf, "Le problème de la transmission textuelle de *Didachè* 1, 3b.–2, 1," in *Überlieferungsgeschichtliche Unter-suchungen* (ed. F. Paschke; TU 125; Berlin: Akademie-Velag, 1981), 499–513, repr. in *Liturgie, foi et vie des premiers Chrétiens: Études Patristiques* (ThH 75; Paris: Beauchesne, 1986), 139–53, references below are to the reprint; idem, "Does the Di-dache"; H. van de Sandt, "'Do Not Give what Is Holy to the Dogs' (Did 9:5d and Matt 7:6a): The Eucharistic Food of the Didache in its Jewish Purity Setting," *VC* 56 (2002): 223–46; idem, "Matthew and the *Didache*," in *Matthew and His Christian Contemporar-ies* (ed. D. C. Sim and B. Repschinski; LNTS [JSNTSup] 333; London and New York: T&T Clark, 2008), 123–38; Tuckett, "Tradition in the *Didache*"; idem, "*Didache* and the Synoptics"; idem, "*Didache* and the Writings"; A. Tuilier, "La Didaché et le probléme synoptique," in Didache *in Context* (ed. Jefford), 110–30. To this list could be added nu-merous other items that touch at some point on the topic without it being central, and see also the other articles in van de Sandt, ed., *Matthew and the Didache* and H. van de Sandt and D. Flusser, *The Didache: Its Jewish Sources and its Place in Early Judaism and Christianity* (CRINT 3.5; Assen: Van Gorcum/Minneapolis: Fortress, 2002); H. van de Sandt and J. K. Zangenberg, eds., *Matthew, James, and Didache: Three Related Docu-ments in Their Jewish and Christian Settings* (SBLSymS 45; Atlanta: Society of Biblical Literature, 2008).

[2] All of the works of the Apostolic Fathers in this study were written before the close of the NT canon. Therefore in speaking of their use or non-use of "canonical Gospels" in what follows we are referring to gospels that only later became part of the canon. For ease of reference, however, in the current study we will simply use "canonical Gospels" (or "canonical Matthew," etc.) to refer to the four that were later incorporated into the NT canon.

[3] There were others who challenged this view prior to the twentieth century, but by assertion rather than by argument based on a close analysis of the sources. See, e.g., B. F. Westcott, *A General Survey of the History of the Canon of the New Testament* (7th ed.; London and New York: Macmillan, 1896), 47–63 (esp. 60–63), who concludes among other things that "No Evangelic reference in the Apostolic Fathers can be referred cer-

has been concerned with the issue of whether or not one can show conclusively that any given Apostolic Father used any given canonical gospel. Criteria toward that end have been developed and refined, and arguments exchanged on both sides of the issue, which has led among other things to an increasing recognition of the ambiguity of the ancient sources. In this ongoing process, theoretical studies of how oral tradition functioned in antiquity have played a surprisingly minor role. Surprising, because most scholars are at least open to the possibility that the Jesus or gospel tradition that is the focus of their study may have derived from oral sources. Certain studies give a prominent place to oral tradition as one of the sources of Jesus' sayings in the Apostolic Fathers, but even these have rarely included any extended discussion of the theoretical underpinnings of how oral tradition functioned in antiquity,[4] or have been limited to the study of a single book, so that it is not clear whether and how their findings might apply to the corpus of the Apostolic Fathers as a whole.[5] What follows will seek to bring out the place given to oral tradition in the history of scholarship, partly in order to show the need for a fresh approach to the topic.

---

tainly to a written record," and that "It appears most probable from the form of the quotations that they were derived from oral tradition" (ibid., 63).

[4] The work of D. A. Hagner might constitute an exception: an important study that includes the entire corpus of the ApFa and concludes that most of the Jesus tradition it contains can be traced to oral tradition is his article "The Sayings of Jesus in the Apostolic Fathers and Justin Martyr," in *Jesus Tradition* (ed. Wenham), 233–68. Hagner includes a brief discussion of the nature and workings of oral tradition in antiquity (ibid., 255–57) that is much indebted to the work of B. Gerhardsson (on Gerhardsson see sec. 1.4.2 above), to which one can add Hagner's earlier, fuller treatment in *The Use of the Old and New Testaments in Clement of Rome* (NovTSup 34; Leiden: Brill, 1973), 303–12; on this see further below. A classic study that assigns a significant role to oral tradition, and that includes the whole corpus of the Apostolic Fathers in its scope, is Koester, *Synoptische Überlieferung*. Though it is interspersed with brief discussions of the oral sources used by various Apostolic Fathers, however, Koester's study did not include an extended treatment of how oral tradition functioned in antiquity. One is left to gather from indications here and there that the theoretical underpinnings of his study are derived from his training in form criticism (also addressed further below).

[5] Many studies have concluded, e.g., that much of the Jesus tradition in the *Didache* is derived from oral tradition. In addition to the commentaries by Audet (*Didachè*, 166–86), Niederwimmer (*Didache*, 46–51) and Rordorf and Tuillier (*Doctrine*, 83–91), see Draper, "Jesus Tradition"; Hagner, "Sayings," 240–42; Kloppenborg, "Didache 16"; Milavec, *Didache: Faith, Hope, and Life*, esp. pp. xxxii–xxxiii; and idem, "Synoptic Tradition," esp. pp. 466–71, among others.

2.2 Foundation for a New Approach (1905)

Prior to the turn of the 20th century it was commonly assumed that the Apostolic Fathers had depended on the canonical Gospels when quoting or alluding to Jesus tradition.[6] This assumption was challenged in 1905 with the publication of *The New Testament in the Apostolic Fathers*, written by a Committee of the Oxford Society of Historical Theology.[7] In preparation for the volume, the members of the Committee examined every passage in the Apostolic Fathers that had been taken to indicate acquaintance with the canonical Gospels.[8] In each case they considered the possibility that the passage might be derived from the canonical Gospels, and weighed the evidence in favor of a direct quotation, free allusion, or faulty quotation from memory. They also considered in each case, however, the possibility that the passage might not be derived from the canonical Gospels at all, but from oral tradition or a non-canonical written source. The general conclusions of the members of the Committee were rather surprising, given the noted prevalent view.[9] Most notably, the Committee did not find a single case in which they were able to decide with "no reasonable doubt" that an

---

[6] This assumption provided the basis for the appeals to the Apostolic Fathers in arguing for a *terminus ad quem* for the writing of the canonical Gospels. Constantin von Tischendorf wrote the classic treatment, *Wann wurden unsere Evangelien verfaßt?* 4th ed. (Leipzig: Hinrichs, 1880), ET: *When were Our Gospels Written? An Argument* (London: Religious Tract Society, 1896), while Theodor Zahn wrote what may be considered the definitive study in terms of comprehensiveness: *Geschichte des neutestamentlichen Kanons* (2 vols.; Erlangen and Leipzig: A. Deicheret, 1888–90); see H. Koester, "The Text of the Synoptic Gospels in the Second Century," in *Gospel Traditions in the Second Century: Origins, Recensions, Text, and Transmission* (ed. W. L. Petersen; CJA 3; Notre Dame: University of Notre Dame Press, 1989), 26.

[7] *The New Testament in the Apostolic Fathers*, by a Committee of the Oxford Society of Historical Theology (Oxford: Clarendon, 1905), hereafter *NTAF*. The contributors to this volume were J. V. Bartlet, K. Lake, A. J. Carlyle, W. R. Inge, P. V. M. Benecke, and J. Drummond. The writings included under the rubric of "Apostolic Fathers" were *Barnabas*, the *Didache*, *1 and 2 Clement*, the letters of Ignatius, the *Epistle of Polycarp*, and the *Shepherd* of Hermas.

[8] *NTAF*, iii. The work covered not just perceived references to the Gospels, but also to the other NT writings; we will only address the former here, however, as most pertinent to Jesus tradition. The Committee examined many more passages than those which ultimately were included in their volume, but these were "not mentioned because the Committee came to the conclusion that there was no serious ground for arguing that they showed the influence of the New Testament" (ibid., iv).

[9] For guidelines on the following categorization see *NTAF*, iii–iv, and for a chart showing the conclusions reached by the Committee (which was the primary source for what follows) see ibid., 137.

Apostolic Father had used any given canonical gospel.[10] Only in one case did they view it as "highly probable" that an Apostolic Father had used one or more of the Gospels.[11] In a number of cases they allowed for "a lower degree of probability" that certain writings of the Apostolic Fathers might show use of the Gospels.[12] Finally, there were a number of cases in which they considered dependence upon the Gospels as possible, but for which "the evidence appeared too uncertain to allow any reliance to be placed upon it."[13]

The implication of the above is that the possibility that a non-canonical source (written or oral) lies behind any given passage rises in inverse proportion as the degree of probability for a canonical source decreases. In keeping with this, the Committee often suggests (as options among others) sources that are either (a) written, such as an apocryphal work,[14] an early harmony of the Gospels,[15] or an early written Christian catechism,[16] or (b) oral, such as a well-known maxim,[17] an early Christian liturgy[18] or oral

---

[10] This does not include cases in which the Committee found clear dependence on synoptic *tradition*, but without being able to identify a particular gospel, e.g., Herm. *Sim.* IX.20.2 (Herm. 97.2) and Mt 19:23//Mk 10:23//Lk 18:24, on which they conclude, "We can hardly doubt that this is a quotation" (*NTAF*, 121). These cases, however, are quite rare in the volume.

[11] With Ignatius' use of Matthew and John. Elsewhere in the volume the Committee concludes, "Ignatius was certainly acquainted either with our Matthew, or with the source of our Matthew, or with a Gospel very closely akin to it. In the present uncertain state of the Synoptic Problem, it would be rash to express any confident opinion ; but the indications on the whole favour the hypothesis that he used our Greek Matthew is something like its present shape" and also "Ignatius's use of the Fourth Gospel is highly probable, but falls some way short of certainty" (*NTAF*, 79, 83).

[12] The use of John in Polycarp's *Philippians*, the use of Matthew and Mark in the *Shepherd* of Hermas, and the use of Matthew in *2 Clement*.

[13] The use of Matthew in *Barnabas*, of Luke in the *Didache*, of Mark and Luke by Ignatius, of Luke and John in the *Shepherd* of Hermas, and of Luke in *2 Clement* (the use of Matthew in the *Didache* fell between this category and the previous one).

[14] E.g., *Barn.* 4.14; *Did.* 1.2; Ign. *Smyrn.* 3.2; *2 Clem.* 5.2–4; 8.5; 12.2; 13.4 (*NTAF*, 18–19, 26, 79–80, 124–25, 132–33, 135–36), and possibly *Did.* 1.3, 4–5; *2 Clem.* 2.4, 5, 7; 4.5 (ibid., 34–35, 35–36, 132, 133, 135). On Poly. *Phil.* 7.2 they suggest the possibility that it might have arisen from "a document akin to our Gospels, though not necessarily those Gospels themselves" (ibid., 103; cf. the similar statements regarding *2 Clem.* 3.2; 4.3; in ibid., 130–31).

[15] E.g., *Did.* 1.3, 4–6 (ibid., 34–35, 35–36).

[16] E.g., *1 Clem.* 13.1–2 (ibid., 59–61), possibly *1 Clem.* 46. 7, 8 (unclear whether it is written or oral; ibid., 61–62).

[17] E.g., *Barn.* 5.9; *Did.* 1.5; 9.5; 11.7; 13.1; Ign. *Eph.* 5.2 (ibid., 19, 27, 29, 30, 34, 77).

[18] E.g., *Did.* 7.1; 8.1–2 (ibid., 27, 28–29).

catechism,[19] or streams of tradition parallel to those that were incorporated into the canonical Gospels.[20] At times they consider the possibility that a passage may have originated from a written gospel, while its form is to be explained as due to faulty quotation from memory.[21]

Unfortunately, the Committee did not include any extended discussion of the method they had applied in their volume, nor (of importance to us here) of their views on how oral tradition functioned in antiquity. The reader is simply reassured with the following lines: "The editors are quite aware that their judgements may not command universal assent ; but they may claim at least that these judgements have been carefully formed, sometimes after considerable hesitation, by men who are not without prac- tice in this kind of investigation."[22] Despite this lack, the work of the Ox- ford Committee served to raise many of the questions regarding the sources of the Jesus tradition in the Apostolic Fathers that were to engage scholarship for much of the following century. One of the abiding strengths of *The New Testament in the Apostolic Fathers* is the nuanced discussion brought to bear on each passage by the members of the Com- mittee.[23]

---

[19] E.g., *1 Clem.* 13.1–2 (ibid., 59–61), possibly *1 Clem.* 46. 7, 8 (unclear whether it is written or oral; ibid., 61–62).

[20] *Did.* 1.3, 4–6; 16.3–5, 6; Poly. *Phil.* 7.2; *2 Clem.* 4.2 (ibid., 32, 32–33, 34–35, 35– 36, 103, 130–31), and possibly *Barn.* 7:9; *Did.* 9.2 (ibid., 21, 30; cf. the treatment of *Did.* 7.2 and 9.3 in ibid., 30). On Poly. *Phil.* 2.3 they state (ibid., 102; cf. their treatment of Poly. *Phil.* 12.3; ibid., 103), "Polycarp assumes that a body of teaching, oral or written, similar to the Sermon on the Mount, was familiar to the Philippian church," but beyond that they do not arrive at a more definite conclusion. At other times the members of the Committee are rather vague, as when they conclude that *Barn.* 7.3 and Mt 27:14 "seem to represent independent traditions influenced by Ps. 68," but do not specify what type of traditions, or that "in general, Barnabas's handling of the Passion ... seems parallel to, rather than dependent on, Matthew's narrative," but without specifying in what form that parallel material might have been preserved (ibid., 18). Many more similar instances could be listed.

[21] E.g., *1 Clem.* 13.1–2, 46.7, 8, in which cases they conclude against this possibility (ibid., 58–61, 61–62), and a number of passages in Ignatius, in which cases they appear to conclude in its favor (ibid., 76–81, read in light of their comments in ibid., 64 and 79, "Ignatius always quotes from memory" and "the indications on the whole favour the hy- pothesis that he used our Greek Matthew in something like its present shape"). The latter is possibly also the case with their understanding of the Jesus tradition in Poly. *Phil.*, of which they state that "The quotations have the appearance of having been made from memory ; rarely, if ever, from a book" (ibid., 84) – it is unclear here whether they imply that a written document played no role in the material being transmitted, or if they only intend to say that a written document was not quoted directly.

[22] Ibid., iii.

[23] Though much of this nuance is lost in such a brief summary as that given above, we will have occasion to interact with some of it in detail in the chapters that follow.

2.3 Establishing the Scholarly Agenda: Massaux and Koester (1950s)

Building upon the careful scholarship of the Oxford Committee, and representing divergent responses to the Committee's conclusions, two works published in the 1950s were to set the agenda for the following decades of scholarly discussion on the Apostolic Fathers' use of Jesus tradition. These two works were Édouard Massaux's *Influence de l'Évangile de saint Matthieu sur la littérature chrétienne avant saint Irénée* (1950),[24] and Helmut Koester's *Synoptische Überlieferung bei den apostolischen Vätern* (1957).[25]

2.3.1 Édouard Massaux

Massaux concurred with many of the Committee's insights, citing them frequently in support of a number of his own points.[26] He differed fundamentally from the Committee, however, when it came to positing sources

---

[24] Édouard Massaux, *Influence de l'Évangile de saint Matthieu sur la littérature chrétienne avant saint Irénée* (UCL 2.42; Leuven, 1950). A 2nd ed., with new bibliographical supplement 1950–1985 by B. Dehandschutter, was published as BETL 75; Leuven: Leuven University Press and Peeters, 1986; E.T.: *Influence*. References given below are to the English translation. Despite what one might be led to believe from the title of his work, Massaux did not limit his discussion only to the use of Matthew in the literature he covered, but analyzed the use of all the documents that were to become part of the NT.

[25] Koester's (Köster's) *Synoptische Überlieferung* was published in 1957 but was completed four years earlier, in 1953; see H. Koester, "Written Gospels or Oral Tradition?," *JBL* 113 (1994): 295–96. The importance of the above two works by Massaux and Koester in setting the agenda for subsequent scholarly discussion is widely acknowledged; see F. Neirynck, "Preface to the Reprint" in Massaux, *Influence*, 1:xiv–xviii (Neirynck's "Preface" is found in all 3 vols., though with different pagination); O. Knoch, "Kenntnis und Verwendung des Matthäus-Evangeliums bei den Apostolischen Vätern," in *Studien zum Matthäusevangelium: Festschrift für Wilhelm Pesch* (ed. L. Schenke; SBS; Stuttgart: Katholisches Bibelwerk, 1988), 159–60; Köhler, *Rezeption*, 2–6; W. R. Schoedel, Review of Massaux, *Influence* and Köhler, *Rezeption*, *CBQ* 51 (1989): 562–64; A. J. Bellinzoni, "The Gospel of Matthew in the Second Century," *SecCent* 9 (1992): 199–201, 215–16, and passim; ibid., "The Gospel of Luke in the Apostolic Fathers: An Overview," in *Trajectories* (ed. Gregory and Tuckett), 51–52; Gregory, *Reception of Luke and Acts*, 7–8; much of Gregory's discussion can also be found, with some changes, in Gregory and Tuckett, "Reflections on Method," 70–78. I am especially indebted to Gregory (and Tuckett) for some of the following insights.

[26] See, e.g., Massaux, *Influence*, 1:64, 88, 89, 93 (where, however the reference to *NTAF* is given mistakenly as p. 77 rather than p. 78, and it is questionable whether or not the Committee is actually in agreement with Massaux, despite his claim to that effect), 94, 95, 99 (where the reference should be to *NTAF* p. 80, not p. 79), 106, 110, 112, 117; 2:35, 37, 39, 112, 114, 121, 123, 125, 132, 135, 146–47, 154, 160; 3:166.

outside of the canonical Gospels for the Jesus tradition used by the Apostolic Fathers. Illustrative of this difference is Massaux's response to the Committee's suggestion that the dominical saying in Pol. *Phil.* 7.2 may not derive from the Gospels themselves, but from oral tradition or a document that was similar to the Gospels. Massaux states, "I do not see the need to multiply hypotheses unnecessarily, since the text of Mt. was within reach .... Why then turn to an oral tradition or to a parent document of the gospels, whose existence is hypothetical?"[27] Massaux did occasionally suggest oral tradition or an apocryphal document as a possible source used by the Apostolic Fathers, but one is left with the impression that he did so only as a last resort, when he found no basis upon which to tie a passage in the Apostolic Fathers to one of the canonical Gospels. At times his language captures this reticence: e.g., following his discussion of *Barn.* 7.11b he states, "No other solution arises, except to think of a saying of Christ taken from the oral tradition."[28] Similarly, after considering the possible depend-

---

[27] Massaux, *Influence*, 2:32 (cf. the similar statement on *2 Clem.* 2.4 in ibid., 2:5–6, and on the *Didache* in general in ibid., 3:176, though the latter two are not related to his reading of *NTAF*). It bears noting that the Committee had not suggested "a parent document" but a document "akin to our Gospels" (*NTAF*, 103). Elsewhere Massaux also recognizes his basic disagreement with the Committee in the above regard, e.g., "The Oxford Committee, *not usually given to find a reference to a specific writing*, shares here [Ign. *Eph.* 5.2] my point of view [that the saying in question is derived from Mt]" (ibid., 1:87, n. 4; emphasis added); also when he states that the Committee, "*despite its leaning*, still gives preference here [Ign. *Eph.* 17.1] to the Matthean text" (ibid., 1:92, n. 16; emphasis added); see also ibid., 3:156, 163 and on non-gospel related material see ibid., 2:155.

[28] Massaux, *Influence*, 1:70; even then, however, in this particular case he goes on to suggest that perhaps it may have been a composition of the author of the epistle himself. The Oxford Committee was of the view that this saying did not derive from Jesus tradition at all, but was a dramatic rendition of what came before it; see *NTAF* 21. Examples of when Massaux clearly considers oral tradition as a source (among other possibilities) of Jesus tradition in the Apostolic Fathers include his discussion of (references in parentheses are to volume and page numbers of Massaux's *Influence*, followed by a short summary of Massaux's conclusions): *1 Clem.* 2.1 (1:33–34; a logion which either "existed in a collection of logia or was transmitted through oral tradition"); *1 Clem.* 13.1b–2 (1:7–12; the source is a catechism that was based on Matthew, perhaps with sentences incorporated into it from oral tradition); *1 Clem.* 15.1–2 (1:19–21; oral tradition as a source "not probable"); *2 Clem.* 3.5 (2:7; "not probable"); *Did.* 8.1–2 (3:154–55, 175: the Lord's Prayer in the *Didache* not dependent on an oral catechism but on Mt); *Did.* 9.5 (3:156: not cited as an independent [oral] saying of the Lord, but from Mt 7:6). In discussing *Did.* 16.4 Massaux mentions "a theme that existed in the first days of Christianity" but does not specify the nature of this source, either oral or written (3:170–71).

ence of *1 Clem.* 23.3–4 on the Gospels and the OT, he concludes, "we have no choice but to admit that this is an apocryphal writing."[29]

The above results stem directly from Massaux's method of investigation: one of his basic presuppositions is that the Gospel of Matthew, as we know it, would have been available to the Apostolic Fathers as they wrote. This is clearly stated in the quote given above – why look for other sources, in this case that might have been used by Polycarp, when "the text of Mt. was within reach"? Whether or not the Gospel of Matthew was available to any given writer, however, should be determined by a careful analysis of the evidence, and cannot be simply assumed.

Another element in Massaux's method that led him to over-emphasize Matthew as a source was his starting point: he sought texts within early Christian literature that showed evidence of literary contact with the Gospel of Matthew. By "literary contact" he meant a "sufficiently striking verbal concurrence" to suggest already that some relationship existed between Matthew and these texts.[30] More often than not, Massaux found upon further analysis that these texts that bore a *resemblance* to Matthew did in fact have some degree of literary *dependence* on Matthew. His approach was thus guided, as described by F. Neirynck, by a "principle of simplicity."[31] If a resemblance to Matthew implied for him a probable dependence on Matthew, it should cause little wonder that he had no interest in positing "unknown" extra-canonical sources (such as apocryphal gospels, oral tradition, Q or M) for the Matthean-like Jesus tradition he encountered.[32] To be fair to Massaux, and as noted by A. J. Bellinzoni, he took the above approach "at a time when Roman Catholic scholarship outside Germany had taken little note of Form Criticism, and before the development of Redac-

---

[29] Ibid., 1:28; for other occasions in which Massaux clearly considers apocryphal writings as a possible source, see his treatment of Ign. *Smyrn.* 3.2 (1:98–99; mentions ancient witnesses but does not come to a conclusion); *2 Clem.* 9.11 (2:9–10, "literarily dependent on the gospels of Mt. and Lk."); *2 Clem.* 11.2–3 (2:11; "This passage can be considered only as a reference to an apocryphon"); *2 Clem.* 4.5 (2:12–13; dependent on an apocryphon at least in part); *2 Clem.* 5:2–4 (2:13–14: an apocryphal source, the author of which may have used Mt and Lk); *2 Clem.* 8.5 (2:14–15: possibly a combination of an apocryphal source with Lk).

[30] Ibid., 1:xxi–xxii, quote taken from p. xxi. Massaux clarified, however, that "These literary contacts do not exhaust the literary influence of the gospel; one can expect, without properly so-called literary contact, the use of typically Matthean vocabulary, themes, and ideas (ibid., 1:xxii). Unfortunately Massaux's discussion of his method in this work was very brief, limited to the two pages already cited.

[31] Neirynck, "Preface to the Reprint," 1:xix.

[32] Neirynck, "Preface to the Reprint," 1:xix; cf. Gregory, *Reception of Luke and Acts*, 8.

tion Criticism."[33] This, as we will see, is one of the main dividing lines between his work and that of Koester.

2.3.2 Helmut Koester

In his *Synoptische Überlieferung*, Koester's assessment of the work of the Oxford Committee differs substantially from that of Massaux. In a number of cases Koester cites the work of the Committee approvingly when it posits oral tradition rather than written gospels,[34] or apocryphal rather than canonical tradition (whether written or oral),[35] as the sources used by the Apostolic Fathers. In certain cases Koester even goes beyond the conclusions of the Committee in positing an oral source, where the Committee had either left open the question of the oral or written nature of the source,[36] or had concluded that a written gospel had influenced the Apostolic Father in question at least indirectly.[37] In general, then (and in contrast to Massaux), Koester goes further down the road traveled by the members of the Oxford Committee, in that he reduces even more the num-

---

[33] Bellinzoni, "Gospel of Matthew," 200; cf. idem, "Luke in the Apostolic Fathers," 52.

[34] See, e.g., Koester, *Synoptische Überlieferung*, 10, 203–7 (cf. *NTAF*, 28–31), where specifically *liturgical* oral tradition is in view; ibid., 16, where Koester supports the alternative of *oral* catechetical material that the Oxford Committee holds as one of two alternatives (oral or written) in *NTAF*, 61.

[35] See, e.g., Koester, *Synoptische Überlieferung*, 72–73, on the Committee's suggestion (*NTAF*, 130) that *2 Clem.* 3.2 is derived from a source other than the canonical Gospels: while the Committee had left open whether this is to be viewed as written or oral, Koester decides in favor of the latter; ibid., 78, where Koester takes up the Committee's suggestion that *2 Clem.* 9.11 seems to be "a fusion of the structure of Luke with the phrasing of Matthew" (*NTAF*, 134) as part of his argument that the source of this material is a written collection of Jesus sayings in which Luke and Matthew have been harmonized (the Committee had left open whether the source was oral or written); see also Koester, ibid., 69, 172, 174, 213, 217, 236, where he sides with the Committee on similar issues.

[36] See, e.g., Koester's frequent references in *Synoptische Überliefung*, 124–58 to the discussion of *Barnabas* in *NTAF* 1–3, 17–22. While the Committee generally concludes against Barnabas' use of canonical Gospels and in favor of his use of sources parallel to them (sources that have been influenced by the OT), Koester himself concludes that Barnabas depends primarily upon an oral "school-tradition" that had arisen from Christian reflection upon the OT.

[37] See, e.g., Koester's treatment of *2 Clem.* 6.7b, where he concludes in disagreement with the Committee that "Dennoch möchte ich meinen, daß diese Gemeinsamkeit von 2. Clem. und Mt. nicht auf literarischer Abhängigkeit beruht [and here he makes reference to *NTAF*, 130], sondern auf dem Zugrundeliegen der gleichen jüdisch-urchristlichen Terminologie" (*Synoptische Überlieferung*, 107).

ber of cases in which the Apostolic Fathers were directly dependent upon the canonical Gospels, and appeals more often to the use of oral tradition.[38]

Just as we saw above that method is at the root of Massaux's essential disagreement with the Committee, so also here it is clear that method is what separates Koester from Massaux. According to Koester's own assessment, his work differs from that of Massaux in two fundamental areas:[39] the first is in his understanding of the role played by written (both canonical and non-canonical) and oral sources in the first two centuries of the Christian era. Koester worked with the sound basic presupposition that the oral tradition that informed the Gospels did not die out abruptly once the latter were committed to writing.[40] The traditional Jesus material that was incorporated into the Gospels found its primary *Sitz im Leben* within the ritual and teaching activities of early Christian communities, where it continued to circulate freely and inform not only the Apostolic Fathers but many other early Christian writings as well.[41] The oral use of this material was so prevalent that there would have been no need to appeal to written gospels, and furthermore the written form of the latter would have lent them no additional authority during this period.[42] In certain cases Koester also points to the introductory formulas that preface some of the sayings of Jesus in the Apostolic Fathers, noting that they imply an appeal to oral tradition rather than written documents.[43] Koester argues that it was not until

---

[38] Cf. C. F. D. Moule, Review of Koester *Synoptische Überlieferung, JTS* n.s. 9 (1958): 369.

[39] Massaux's volume did not reach Koester until he had already completed work on his *Synoptische Überlieferung* (see Koester, ibid., 2, n. 1), so unfortunately the latter does not contain a critique of Massaux's views. Koester does, however, provide both a basic critique of Massaux and an assessment of how their work differed in his "Written Gospels."

[40] Koester, *Synoptische Überlieferung*, 1–3.

[41] See Koester, "Written Gospels," 293–95, 297; cf. Moule, Review of Koester, 368–70. Koester also allowed for the possibility that the Apostolic Fathers counted with non-canonical written documents (such as Q, or apocryphal gospels) among their sources of Jesus tradition. This is already true in his *Synoptische Überlieferung*, but received more attention in his later works; see his own remarks to this effect in his "Written Gospels," 297, and see his *Ancient*. For the most part, however, Koester emphasized oral tradition as the source used by the Apostolic Fathers in his *Synoptische Überlieferung*.

[42] Koester, "Written Gospels," 294–95.

[43] E.g., in his treatment of *1 Clem.* 13.1–2 and 46.7–8, Koester notes that the introductory formulas contain two words that point to the oral nature of what follows: the writer's use of the aorist rather than the present tense of λέγω, and his use of the verb μνημονεύειν, which is a technical term for the handing on of oral tradition (Koester, *Synoptische Überlieferung*, 4–6); we will return to this below.

Justin Martyr that we find the use of oral tradition *replaced* by almost complete reliance upon written gospels.[44]

The second fundamental area in which Koester differs from Massaux is in using form and redaction criticism to evaluate the Apostolic Fathers' quotations of Jesus tradition. The above-mentioned form-critical presupposition that Jesus tradition found its *Sitz im Leben* in the life of early Christian communities leads Koester to reverse the burden of proof regarding the still-commonly held view (in the 1950s) that the Apostolic Fathers made wide use of written gospels: "Unless it can be proven otherwise, it must be assumed that authors who referred to and quoted such [traditional Jesus] materials were dependent on these life situations of the church and did not quote from written documents."[45] For Koester the use of any written gospel now had to be demonstrated, for which he applied the following criterion:

> How can we know when written documents are the source for such quotations and allusions? Redaction criticism is the answer. Whenever one observes words or pbrases [*sic*] that derive from the author or redactor of a gospel writing, the existence of a written source must be assumed.[46]

In sum, in the above two studies Massaux and Koester arrived at very different conclusions regarding the source of the Jesus tradition used by the Apostolic Fathers. Viewed in terms of their conclusions regarding the latter's possible dependence upon the canonical Gospels, Massaux's study can be classified as maximalist, and Koester's as minimalist.[47] While Massaux concluded in favor of an extensive reliance upon the canonical Gospels, especially Matthew, Koester argued for the use (for the most part) of independent oral tradition, tradition that was earlier than, and in many

---

[44] In comparing the situation between the Apostolic Fathers and Justin, Koester states, "Ein ganz anderes Bild bietet sich schon wenige Jahrzehnte später bei Justin, bei dem bereits im großen Maße die Evangelien 'verwendet' werden. Die Quellen der synoptischen Tradition sind bei Justin fast ausschließlich unsere Evangelien, die Geschichte der Tradition ist bei Justin mithin erstmalig eine Geschichte der Auslegung unserer Evangelien" (*Synoptische Überlieferung*, 267; cf. idem, 2–3). Cf. Koester's argument in *Ancient*, 37–40, that "Justin saw the written gospels as a more reliable record of the words and deeds of Jesus and ... advertised them as replacement of the established, but less trustworthy oral traditions about Jesus ..." (quote from p. 37). Koester recognizes, however, that Justin does not *always* quote from the written Gospels, see his full discussion in *Ancient*, 360–402.

[45] Koester, "Written Gospels," 297.

[46] Ibid., 297; Koester made this statement in this 1994 article in the context of discussing his methodological approach in his earlier *Synoptische Überlieferung*; in the latter we find the similar statement, "so hängt die Frage der Benutzung davon ab, ob sich in den angeführten Stücken Redaktionsarbeit eines Evangelisten findet" (p. 3).

[47] Bellinzoni, "Luke in the Apostolic Fathers," 51.

cases fed into, what became the written Gospels. The work of these two scholars has provided the starting point for many studies, which while adding various nuances, have essentially sought to support one or the other of these two basic views.

2.4 Furthering Koester's Conclusions: Donald A. Hagner (1985)

In an important article published in 1985, Donald A. Hagner gives as his purpose "to examine the extent to which the Apostolic Fathers drew upon the written Gospels or the gospel tradition, the way in which such material is utilized, and the esteem in which it is held." [48] Like Koester, Hagner stresses the importance of taking oral tradition into account in explaining the particular shape the Jesus tradition is given in the Apostolic Fathers. [49] Also like Koester, he recognizes the importance of specialized elements within the introductory formulas (where these are found) in pointing to an oral source. [50]

While clarifying that the Apostolic Fathers probably drew on a multiplicity of sources, both written and oral, [51] Hagner finds stronger evidence for dependence on oral tradition than on the written Gospels in *1 Clement* (13.2; 46.8), Polycarp's *Epistle to the Philippians* (2.3), and the *Didache*

---

[48] Hagner, "Sayings," 233–34. As its title indicates ("Sayings of Jesus in the Apostolic Fathers and Justin Martyr"), in this article Hagner also deals with the Jesus tradition in Justin Martyr, which we will set aside here as outside the scope of our study. Hagner had already dealt with the sayings of Jesus in the Apostolic Fathers in his earlier monograph, *Clement of Rome*. While dealing primarily with *1 Clement*, this latter volume also includes a valuable treatment of the use of the NT in the Apostolic Fathers as a whole (ibid., 272–312), which Hagner provides as a contextual framework for understanding the dynamics present in Clement's work. We will focus in what follows primarily on the 1985 article as containing Hagner's more mature thought, while referencing his monograph where appropriate.

[49] Hagner, "Sayings," 250–52, 255–57; and see his more extended treatment of oral tradition in *Clement of Rome*, 303–11.

[50] Hagner, "Sayings," 234; idem, *Clement of Rome*, 272–77, 306–7. As Koester had done, Hagner points to the importance in this regard of the words that introduce Jesus' sayings in *1 Clem.* 13.1–2 and 46.7–8, and also Poly. *Phil.* 2.3 if the latter were found not to be dependent on Clement ("Sayings," 235–38; idem, *Clement of Rome*, 142–43 [Hagner cites Koester's treatment of the topic on p. 143 n. 1], 151, 164, 272–73, 279); cf. also Hagner's treatment of the introductory formulae for Poly. *Phil.* 6.1; 7.2; *Did.* 8.2; 9.5; *Barn.* 4.14; *2 Clem.* 2.4; 13.4, among others (*Clement of Rome*, 273–76, 279).

[51] E.g., he states that "because of the probable overlapping of oral tradition and certain written sources, it may well be that some of the early Christian writers are simultaneously dependent on both written sources and oral tradition" ("Sayings," 252); cf. his *Clement of Rome*, 282–87 and see further below.

(8.1–2).[52] In other cases he finds the evidence for dependence on oral tradition *as* convincing as that for dependence on the Gospels (e.g., Ign. *Poly.* 2.1–2; Ign. *Smyrn.* 1.1; Poly. *Phil.* 7.2; *Did.* 9.5; *Barn.* 5.9).[53] Only when discussing *2 Clement* does Hagner find evidence that is best explained by dependence on the written Gospels, though in the case of certain Jesus sayings there he still leaves open the possibility of an oral-traditional a source.[54]

Overall, Hagner concludes that oral tradition is the most likely source for most of the Jesus tradition in the Apostolic Fathers prior to *2 Clement*. He sets this conclusion in context as follows:

> The situation from the end of the first century to the middle of the second is that the gospel tradition concerning the words and works of Jesus exists side by side in the form of oral tradition and written Gospels. ... [A] transition was slowly taking place. Oral tradition and the Gospels were both available, and the latter were slow in assuming the status of canonicity. But as the decades of the second century pass the probability increases that writers such as 2 Clement and Justin are dependent at least to some extent upon the written Gospels.[55]

That both Koester[56] and Hagner conclude that oral tradition was the source of a large part of the Jesus tradition in the Apostolic Fathers should not be allowed to mask the fact that these two scholars represent conflicting, even incompatible perspectives on the manner in which oral traditions were preserved and passed on in antiquity. Whereas Koester's view is shaped by his form-critical assumption that the oral transmission of Jesus' sayings was characterized by a high level of instability,[57] Hagner, coming from a per-

---

[52] See Hagner, "Sayings," 234–38, 241.

[53] Ibid., 239–42; Hagner also concludes this regarding a number of passages in the *Shepherd* of Hermas, too numerous to add to the list above (see ibid., 243–44).

[54] Ibid., 244–46.

[55] Ibid., 258, and see also ibid., 239: "The data of Clement taken together are best explained as the result of dependence upon oral tradition similar to, but separate from, the written Synoptic Gospels"; ibid., 240: "Other possible allusions can be mentioned [in Ignatius], but in every instance it is impossible to deny the possibility that oral tradition rather than dependence upon the Gospels may explain the words"; ibid., 241–42: "Although the Didache contains an abundance of material similar, and related in some way, to the Gospels, it is very interesting that the case for dependence upon the Gospels is so particularly weak. The phenomena can be readily explained as the result of dependence upon oral tradition"; ibid., 243–44: noting that Hermas probably knew the written Gospels, Hagner stresses the significance of the fact that "tradition can adequately account for the data examined."

[56] Koester, *Synoptische Überlieferung*; and see also his *Ancient*, 66–71.

[57] So, e.g., Koester in his "The Extracanonical Sayings of the Lord as Products of the Christian Community" (*Semeia* 44 [1988]: 57–77; Ger. orig. in *ZNW* 48 [1957]: 220–37, same year as *Synoptische Überlieferung*) finds it likely that (what he identifies as) the oral catechetical material in *1 Clem.* 13.2, was initially made up of "one or two sayings

spective that has been greatly influenced by the work of B. Gerhardsson,[58] views the oral transmission of Jesus' sayings as a fairly stable process.[59] Accordingly, these two scholars differ considerably in their assessment of how the oral tradition of Jesus' sayings in the Apostolic Fathers might be of use to the historian. For Koester, these sayings are of very little value in determining what Jesus might have actually said, but are still valuable for the historian: he argues that by identifying their *Sitz im Leben* within the early church one can learn something about the history of early Christianity.[60] Hagner's view is very different: for him the basic similarity between the oral tradition of Jesus' sayings in the Apostolic Fathers and that of its parallels in the canonical Gospels implies that both serve the historian as

---

... whether these were Jewish proverbs or authentic sayings of Jesus – and that subsequently more sayings were added, including finally a complete new saying constructed by analogy to the form and content of the other sayings. ... *In the formation of these early Christian catechisms, it made no difference where the materials came from or whether they were authentic or spurious. ... No doubt we could select a few authentic words of Jesus* [from the catechism represented in *1 Clem.* 13.2 and from others like it] – *with various degrees of success. But that is a question which the early church did not ask.* For the early church, it was important to possess a canon of virtues authorized by being spoken by the risen Lord" (pp. 61–62; emphasis added). Koester gives a similar example from *Did.* 1.3: while Jesus taught "Love your enemies," this was changed to read what we find in the *Didache*: "Pray for your enemies." Though Polycarp in *Phil.* 2.3 "comes close" to quoting Jesus' teaching as found in Mt 5:44 ("Love your enemies and pray for those who persecute you"), he does not do so. Koester surmises, "Only those sentences that are useful for his practical advice on prayer are repeated. This clearly shows how Jesus' radicalization of the commandment of loving one's enemies was rendered innocuous by being transformed into an admonition for prayer" (ibid., 62). Noting that *Did.* 1.3 continues, "...and fast for your persecutors," Koester concludes, "No parallel exists to this command in the texts of the canonical Gospels. The need to enforce the rules of fasting in addition to those for prayer produced a new formulation by analogy to a traditional saying of Jesus" (ibid., 63). Though Koester's argument is not implausible, one must wonder why one is held to the form of one saying as found in the Gospels: Jesus probably taught about one's relationship to one's enemies on more than one occasion, and may have spoken about praying and fasting for one's enemies and persecutors in so many words. Oral tradition can accommodate similar sayings of Jesus uttered on separate occasions. The assumption that only the Matthean form contains material that finds its *Sitz im Leben* in Jesus' own proclamation seems to go against the very point of Koester's article under examination. Koester also argues that "the church adopted Jewish rules according to its needs and transformed them into sayings of Jesus" (ibid., 66, see also ibid., 64–65) – yet Jesus *as a Jewish teacher* almost certainly adopted and taught Jewish rules.

[58] Esp. as developed in Gerhardsson, *Memory*; idem, *Tradition*; and the essays reprinted in idem, *Reliability*. For a brief overview of Gerhardsson's work see sec. 1.4.2 above.

[59] See Hagner, "Sayings," 249–59; idem, *Clement of Rome*, 303–4, fuller treatment in ibid., 303–12; idem, foreword to Gerhardsson, *Reliability*, vii–xvi, esp. pp. x–xvi.

[60] Koester, "Extracanonical," esp. pp. 74–76.

reliable witnesses to what Jesus himself said.[61] If one were to follow these two very different lines of argument to their logical conclusion, in reality these scholars posit different sources for the Jesus tradition in the Apostolic Fathers (not just the form of the tradition but also its content): while for Koester much of the tradition originated in early church communities, for Hagner the tradition originated for the most part with Jesus himself.

We will not attempt at this point to mediate between Koester and Hagner, nor argue for the viability of one view over the other. Rather in the chapters that follow we will attempt to (a) provide a solid foundation for understanding the workings of oral tradition in antiquity, and (b) see in what way this might inform a study of the Jesus tradition in the Apostolic Fathers as *oral* tradition. We will then revisit the question of origins in our conclusions. For the present we must return to our survey.

2.5 Refining Massaux's Method: Wolf-Dietrich Köhler (1987)

One of the most important works written in support of Massaux's perspective is that of Wolf-Dietrich Köhler, *Die Rezeption des Matthäusevangeliums in der Zeit vor Irenäus*.[62] In this work Köhler is fully conscious of the divergent options offered by the methods of Koester and Massaux, and sets out to bring methodological precision to the discussion.[63] He recognizes that Koester's method is superior to that of Massaux, but also notes the limitations of the former. As Köhler rightly indicates, Koester's redaction-critical criterion only functions properly as a *positive* tool: the presence of redactional elements from a written gospel in the work of any given Apostolic Father may be used to argue that the latter used that gospel, but the absence of such redactional elements does not necessarily imply that said gospel was *not* used.[64] Köhler urges that it is possible to recognize on other grounds whether or not an apparent allusion or quotation was derived from a written gospel, even in the *absence* of said redactional elements. Towards this end he develops a number of interrelated criteria, focusing on such things as whether or not Matthew (or another gospel) is explicitly referred to as the source; the degree of similarity in expression (wording) or ideas (material content) between the allusion or quotation and the Matthean text vs. other texts; the presence of other Matthean-type material (or material from another gospel) elsewhere in the

---

[61] See Hagner, "Sayings," 249–59, esp. pp. 255–57, 259.

[62] Tübingen: Mohr Siebeck, 1987.

[63] Köhler, *Rezeption*, 2–16; on what follows cf. esp. Gregory, *Reception of Luke and Acts*, 8–15 = Gregory and Tuckett, "Reflections on Method," 71–76.

[64] Köhler, *Rezeption*, 4–5.

writing under consideration; and the degree of divergence of all of these quotations and allusions from the text of Matthew.[65] Köhler then details how these interdependent criteria are to be applied so as to determine the level of probability that any given passage is dependent on Matthew.[66] In his conclusions, he classifies both the specific passages he has considered, and each writing in which they are found as a whole, according to the degree to which they show evidence of a reception of Matthew. This he does according to the following six categories: (1) probable, (2) possible to probable, (3) possible but not conclusive, (4) possible but not apparent, (5) improbable, and (6) reception of Matthew is excluded.[67]

What of the place of oral tradition in Köhler's study? In comparing the work of Köhler to that of Massaux, William Schoedel finds an important shift of emphasis in the work of the former, in that he is more open than Massaux – at least in theory – to the possibility that the Apostolic Fathers may have used oral tradition rather than written sources.[68] It is questionable, however, whether this shift of emphasis goes far enough. While Köhler may theoretically leave open the possibility of oral tradition as a source, in practice he never opts for it over other explanations, leaning instead toward Matthew whenever this is feasible. In his own words, he concludes that,

Berücksichtigt man nur die einigermaßen sicher zu datierenden Schriften, so ergibt sich immerhin doch, daß ab der Zeit Justins generell mit der Kenntnis des Mt gerechnet werden kann; vor Justin ist für alle Schriften/Verfasser Mt-Kenntnis und -Benutzung zumindest möglich; *nie war die Aufnahme vorsynoptischer mündlicher Tradition wahrscheinlich zu machen.*[69]

That he *never* found it necessary to appeal to oral tradition as a source puts Köhler squarely within Massaux's camp. This is clear to Köhler himself: specifically relating his findings to the positions of Massaux and Koester, Köhler continues,

---

[65] Ibid., 12–13.

[66] Ibid., 13–14.

[67] Ibid., 539–71; 1) Wahrscheinlich, 2) möglich bis wahrscheinlich, 3) möglich, aber nicht zwingend, 4) möglich, aber nicht naheliegend, 5) unwahrscheinlich, and 6) auszuschließen (for these categories see ibid., 539).

[68] Schoedel, Review of Massaux and Köhler, 563. Köhler does allow in theory that the sources of Jesus tradition that fed into Matthew's gospel continued to circulate after the latter became a finished product, and may have been the source for Matthean-like tradition in other Christian writers (*Rezeption*, 14–15). But he also sets himself up to opt for a dependence on Matthew rather than on Matthew's sources when he adds to the development of his criteria that even documents in close proximity both geographically and in time to Matthew quite possibly depend on Matthew rather than Matthew's sources; cf. the comments in Gregory, *Reception of Luke and Acts*, 10–11.

[69] Köhler, *Rezeption*, 525; emphasis added.

Eingezeichnet in ein Koordinatensystem, dessen Achsen durch die Positionen von KÖSTER (Überlieferung) und MASSAUX (Influence) gekennzeichnet sind, ergibt sich für die frühe Zeit der Rezeption des Mt eine Einordnung der erhobenen Befunde zumeist deutlich näher an MASSAUX als an KÖSTER, nie näher an KÖSTER als an MASSAUX und immerhin in einigen Fällen direkt an oder sogar auf der Linie der MASSAUXschen Position.[70]

Köhler's agreement with Massaux extends, unfortunately, to the basic methodological weakness noted earlier in this chapter: Massaux over-emphasized Matthew as a source due to his starting point, which was seeking texts within early Christian literature that showed evidence of literary contact with the Gospel of Matthew. In reviewing the work of both Köhler and Massaux, William Schoedel notes that one of the central methodological problems involved in taking any of the written Gospels as one's starting point is that "such an approach already tends to narrow the range of possibilities and to hide the significance of materials that cannot be explained in terms of dependence on Matthew or any written Gospel."[71] Schoedel continues with a specific example:

In the case of Ignatius, ... should we begin with the two or three passages for which dependence on distinctively Matthean themes seems a strong possibility and bring along as much other material as possible in the light of this presumed relationship? Or should we begin with the numerous passages for which dependence on Matthew or any written Gospel seems unlikely or unnecessary and argue that in the problematic passages Ignatius and Matthew were in touch with the same special tradition? The second possibility has little chance of coming into clear view in a study that proceeds along the lines laid down by [Massaux and Köhler].[72]

In conclusion, Köhler's work represents an advance over that of Massaux in the greater level of nuance that he brings to methodological theory. When it comes to applying this theory, however, Köhler's repeated choice to err on the side of Massaux's conclusions detracts to a certain extent from the value of his work as a whole.[73] It is no wonder that both Massaux and Köhler decide in favor of a use of Matthew by the Apostolic Fathers, since the beginning point for both of their studies is material similar to Matthew.

---

[70] Ibid., 525.

[71] Schoedel, Review of Massaux and Köhler, 564.

[72] Ibid., 564.

[73] Cf. the remarks by Schoedel, "the formal conclusions of [Köhler's] study strike me as somewhat simplified in the light of many of the details of the argument itself" (ibid., 563).

2.6 Applying and Refining Koester's Method: Tuckett and Gregory

The rationale behind treating the work of Tuckett and Gregory together in this section is that they both make Koester's redactional criterion central to their method. The criterion, as articulated by Koester, is that the presence of words or phrases that resulted from the redaction of one of the evangelists implies a written source.[74] Tuckett and Gregory each apply and refine this criterion in their own way, as will become clear in what follows.

2.6.1 C. M. Tuckett (1989)

In 1989 C. M. Tuckett published an important essay on the use of Jesus tradition by the Apostolic Fathers entitled "The Synoptic Tradition in the *Didache*."[75] The essay is essentially a rigorous application of Koester's redactional criterion to a number of passages in the *Didache* and their synoptic parallels. While fully endorsing Koester's criterion, Tuckett notes a number of problem areas in its application: (a) the presence of the same redactional feature in two documents does not necessarily imply dependence, as a redactional feature may have been incorporated into the tradition independently by two redactors; (b) even if dependence between two texts is established, this may not be direct, as "the later document may be several stages removed from the earlier one";[76] (c) one especially cannot be fully certain of the line between tradition and redaction when working with parallels in Q material: when Luke differs from Matthew, not only is it possible that either one preserves the reading closest to the "original," but one must also account for the possible existence of various editions of Q, "so that one might have to think in terms of a Q^{mt} and a Q^{lk}."[77] Despite the above difficulties with its application, Tuckett endorses Koester's criterion as "the only one which ultimately can determine whether a text like the *Didache* presupposes the finished gospels or whether it uses traditions which lie behind the gospels."[78]

---

[74] On Koester's redactional criterion, see the discussion of his work in sec. 2.3.2 above.

[75] Tuckett, "Synoptic Tradition" (first published in 1989 in *The New Testament in Early Christianity: La réception des écrits néotestamentaires dans le christianisme primitif* [ed. J.-M. Sevrin; BETL 86; Leuven: Leuven University Press and Peeters], 197–230 and repr. in Didache *in Modern Research* [ed. Draper] in 1996; references below are to the reprint).

[76] Ibid., 95.

[77] Ibid., 112–13; see, e.g., his application of this caveat in his discussion of the parallel to *Did.* 1:4b in Mt 5:41, in ibid., 123–24.

[78] Ibid., 95.

A rather ironic aspect of Tuckett's work (given that Massaux and Koester represent contrasting positions) is that while he employs Koester's criterion as his main tool, the conclusions of his essay are intended to support the general thrust of Massaux's argument, "that the *Didache* presupposes the finished form of the synoptic gospels, or [at] least that of Matthew."[79] Tuckett's overall conclusion is that the parallels between the *Didache* and the Synoptics are "best explained if the *Didache* presupposes the finished gospels of Matthew and Luke."[80] He finds the latter to be true of all the sections of the *Didache* that he examines, sections with parallels in the single, double, and triple gospel tradition.

Tuckett's essay is remarkable for the thoroughness and care he brings to bear on every aspect of the discussion. It represents perhaps the best exponent, in spite of its relative brevity and its specific focus on the *Didache*, of the view that the Apostolic Fathers prior to *2 Clement* made use of the finished Gospels (position also held by Massaux and Köhler).[81] What Tuckett's essay lacks, however, is serious consideration of the possibility that the Didachist depended on oral rather than written sources;[82] his discussion takes place entirely within the literary default setting.[83] Chapter 7 below will further develop this line of thinking as part of an in-depth interaction with Tuckett's essay. Here, however, it is necessary to move on.

2.6.2 Andrew Gregory (2003)

Three of the works we have surveyed thus far, those by Massaux, Köhler and Tuckett, are concerned with the use of Matthew in early Christian literature. In contrast, Andrew Gregory's monograph on *The Reception of Luke and Acts in the Period before Irenaeus* is dedicated to answering the question of "whether it is possible to show that other Christian texts have *used Luke* and/or *Acts*." This question in turn depends for Gregory on the more specific one of "whether it is possible to prove either direct literary dependence or the indirect appropriation and use of either *Luke* or *Acts* in another writing."[84] As many before him, Gregory is fully aware of the two

---

[79] Ibid., 93, with an explicit reference to Massaux in n. 4; the "at" added in brackets to the above quote is in the original 1989 essay, but was left out of the text prepared for republication in 1996 (see n. 75 on p. 54 above).

[80] Ibid., 128.

[81] There is widespread agreement that *2 Clement* presupposes the written Gospels, a near consensus that will be challenged in ch. 9 below.

[82] As recognized by Tuckett himself in a later essay, see his "*Didache* and the Synoptics," 513.

[83] See sec. 1.1 above.

[84] Both quotes are from Gregory, *Reception of Luke and Acts*, 5 (emphasis in original). These two questions should not be confused, as Gregory cautions, with the question of whether or not an author *knew of* the work of another. To quote Gregory from another

divergent approaches taken by Massaux and Koester. Following a detailed analysis of the strengths and weaknesses of both of these approaches, and of the methodological advances which Köhler's more developed criteria had brought to that of Massaux, Gregory concludes that the methods adopted by Massaux and Köhler are unsatisfactory for his own purposes, given their inherent bias towards maximalist conclusions.[85] He acknowledges that Koester's redaction-critical criterion also has its weaknesses, in that it will lead to minimalist conclusions, but chooses to adopt it for his own work as leading to the only results that are assured.[86] Given the purposes of his study, his reasoning is sound when he states that "a small sample of quite secure evidence may be of more value than a larger sample of less secure evidence."[87] In keeping with the topic of the present study, in what follows we will focus only upon the material in Gregory's volume that relates to Jesus tradition in the Apostolic Fathers.[88]

The body of Gregory's work, like Tuckett's essay, is a sober, thorough application of Koester's redactional criterion. In keeping with this approach, one of his basic presuppositions is that "*Luke*-like material need not provide evidence of the knowledge and use of *Luke*" – the point of the criterion is that such knowledge and use must be *demonstrated*.[89] In seeking to do the latter, however, Gregory is repeatedly brought up against the shortcomings of his chosen method (and of other methods) for dealing with the relevant material. One of the main difficulties in applying Koester's redaction-critical criterion is that it presupposes the possibility of identifying the redactional work of an evangelist in any given set of parallels. As Gregory shows, however, one is often not able to conclude decisively that any given feature of a passage is the result of Luke's redactional work, even if it is unique to Luke among its synoptic parallels. If such a feature is found, e.g., in Lukan single tradition, it is certainly possible that it is the

---

source, "Not only is it impossible to demonstrate knowledge of a text unless it is used, but also the inability of subsequent scholarship to demonstrate the use of one text in another does not mean that non-use, let alone ignorance, has been proved" (Gregory and Tuckett, "Reflections on Method," 62; I cite the somewhat better articulated statement in the article as the work of Gregory since primary responsibility for the essay rested with him [see ibid., 61 n. 1]; cf. the similar statements in Gregory, *Reception of Luke and Acts*, 5).

[85] Gregory, *Reception of Luke and Acts*, 7–15; though in his work he also notes "parallels to *Luke* that meet the level of evidence required by Köhler, but which do not meet Koester's criterion of the presence of redactional work by an Evangelist," as important to those readers who take more of a maximalist approach (ibid., 13).

[86] Ibid., 12.

[87] Ibid., 13.

[88] See also Gregory's rearticulation of several of the following methodological issues in "Looking for Luke," esp. 402–10.

[89] Gregory, *Reception of Luke and Acts*, 74.

redactional work of Luke. But it may just as well owe its presence there not to the redactional work of Luke but to its prior presence in Luke's written or oral sources (L or Q^{Lk} or other). If the latter were to be the case, the presence of said feature in the writings of an Apostolic Father may be due to his use of an older source held in common with Luke, and used independently of the Gospel of Luke itself.[90] Gregory finds that in certain instances this alternative explanation better fits the evidence.[91] Something similar to the above could also be argued regarding features particular to Luke in the double tradition (common to Matthew and Luke). In these cases, e.g., the form found in Luke may be closer to Q, while the parallel in Matthew may reflect Matthean editorial changes, or the difference between them may be due to Matthew and Luke following difference recensions of Q. In these cases what appears to be the redactional work of Luke actually reflects where Luke is being faithful to his sources. These apparent "Lukan editorial features," if found in another early Christian writing, might thus owe their existence in the latter to the author's dependence on Q or Q^{Lk}, rather than to dependence on Luke. The above becomes less of a problem with material in the triple tradition, since the text of Mark is available for comparison: passages in which Luke seems to depend on Mark, and yet has altered Mark's text, are likely candidates for identifying Lukan redactional activity.[92] Overall, however, and especially when working with single or double tradition, one is faced with LkR as only one option among many for explaining the form of the material as it has come down to us, and in many cases it may not be the best option.

Even if one were able to ascertain with some confidence that a given feature in Luke is the result of LkR, Gregory notes that there is a second difficulty in applying Koester's redaction-critical criterion. This has to do with the ambiguity of the relationship between (the supposed) "precursor" texts and "receptor" texts. It is difficult to conclude with any certainty that the presence of any given Lukan redactional feature in a supposed receptor text is due to dependence on Luke. As noted above, Tuckett had argued that two redactors working independently may have added the same feature to the tradition, and Gregory cites Tuckett approvingly on this point.[93] This would imply, obviously, that any given feature could have been added in-

---

[90] Ibid., 6–7.

[91] This is Gregory's conclusion, e.g., regarding the hypothesis that Ignatius is dependent on Lk 24:36–43 in Ing. *Smyrn.* 3.2 (ibid., 70–75, 113; idem, "Looking for Luke," 405).

[92] Though even then one must take into account that the form of Mark we have today may not be that which was available to Matthew and Luke (Gregory, *Reception of Luke and Acts*, 13–14 and n. 49).

[93] Tuckett, "Synoptic Tradition," 95; Gregory, *Reception of Luke and Acts*, 13.

dependently both by Luke and by the writer of the supposed receptor text. It would also imply, not so obviously, that any given feature could have been added independently by Luke and by the writer of a third source, the writer of the supposed receptor text being dependent on the latter rather than on Luke. In either case, Luke would not be the precursor text for the supposed receptor text. The above arguments become even more plausible with the recognition that many more sources, both written and oral, were available to authors in the first and second century than those which have survived the accidents of history to be available to scholars today.[94] Gregory notes that the finds at Qumran and Nag Hammadi have greatly broadened scholars' understanding both of the Judaism of the period and of early Jesus traditions, and adds, "even now we are aware that more texts existed than are now extant, and this raises the possibility that we rush too quickly to posit literary relationships between texts that we do know rather than remaining open to the possibility that what looks like (say) *Luke* may in fact come from another text altogether."[95]

Given the goals of his study, Gregory is more concerned with ascertaining whether or not he can show conclusively in any given instance that the Apostolic Fathers used our canonical Luke than he is with identifying precisely what other sources they may have used.[96] As for the former, Gregory's findings are for the most part negative. Only in the case of *2 Clement* did he conclude with some certainty that there was evidence of dependence

---

[94] Gregory cites M. Hengel, who "observes that 85% of second-century Christian writings known by their titles have been lost, and that the real loss is likely to be substantially higher" (Gregory, *Reception of Luke and Acts*, 17 n. 58, referring to M. Hengel, *The Four Gospels and the One Gospel of Jesus Christ: An Investigation of the Collection and Origin of the Canonical Gospels* [trans. J. Bowden; London: SCM/Harrisburg: Trinity Press International, 2000], 55); Gregory further notes that "the figure of 85% was calculated by C. Markschies on the basis of Harnack's *Geschichte der altchristlichen Literatur bis Eusebius*" (loc. cit.).

[95] Gregory, *Reception of Luke and Acts*, 75; see also his full discussion of the need to take into account non-extant texts and oral tradition as sources for the documents that have come down to us, in ibid., 15–20.

[96] Nor, I suspect, would he consider that the latter quest would have much hope of success. A sampling of other sources which Gregory considers (in his *Reception of Luke and Acts*) in attempting to account for the form of the Jesus material as found in the Apostolic Fathers include a harmony of the Synoptics, or a harmony made up of both synoptic and non-synoptic material (pp. 141, 147–48); a non-synoptic source with some overlap with synoptic material (p. 141), the hypothetical document Q (including different form of Q which might have been available to each evangelist, i.e., Q^{Mt} and Q^{Lk}; p. 120); other non-canonical sources which might have had a closer affinity to a given extant canonical source than to others (e.g., closer to Mt than to Lk; p. 144); oral tradition (p. 145); apocryphal sources (e.g., the *Gospel of Thomas*; p. 145); and short proverbial utterances (p. 147), among others.

upon Luke, due to what he identified as fairly clear indicators of LkR.[97] Even then, however, out of the numerous sayings of Jesus preserved in *2 Clement*, he found this to be true only of a single saying, that found in *2 Clem.* 9.11. That this saying also contained evidence of MattR led Gregory to conclude that its source was probably a harmony made up of at least these two gospels.[98] Gregory did not conclude decisively in any other case that any of the Apostolic Fathers contained evidence of dependence on Luke.[99]

Gregory is to be commended for the rigor with which he applies Koester's criterion. It is important to note that his conclusion regarding the lack (for the most part) of decisive evidence for the use of Luke in the Apostolic Fathers does not imply that said dependence is *excluded*. It may mean no more than that the nature of our ancient sources imposes serious limitations upon what can be accomplished even following the best method.[100] It should also, however, be kept in mind when the long-held view of the widespread use of the canonical Gospels by the Apostolic Fathers comes up for reconsideration. Specifically as it relates to Luke's gospel, there is no conclusive evidence for such use.

---

[97] Ibid., 136–149, 172.

[98] Ibid., 147–48.

[99] Regarding the *Didache*, Gregory notes that while it seems to show a familiarity either with Matthew or with special Matthean material, the direction of dependence could go either from Matthew to the *Didache* or from the *Didache* to Matthew. He finds none of the arguments for the Didachist's dependence on Luke to be conclusive. Positing that an argument for the Didachist's dependence on Luke might be made if it could first be shown both that (a) *Did.* 16.1 presupposes Lk 12:35, and that (b) the form of Lk 12:35 is due to LkR, he goes on to show that neither of the latter are certain (ibid., 118–21, 171). *1 Clement*, while apparently drawing at least in part upon synoptic *tradition* (probably a collection of sayings) cannot be shown to have been acquainted with any given synoptic gospel (ibid., 125–29, 172). Certain material in Ignatius might appear at first sight to show a familiarity with Luke (cf. *Smyrn.* 3.2–3 and Lk 24:36–43), but it is more probable that Ignatius did not derive the material in question from Luke, but rather that both Ignatius and Luke derived it from a common source, either written or oral (ibid., 69–75, 113). While Polycarp may evince a knowledge of either synoptic tradition or the Synoptic Gospels in general, what is most important for Gregory – whether or not he specifically knew Luke – cannot be ascertained (ibid., 129–36, 172). Finally, the interpretation of Papias' well-known statements preserved in Eus. *Hist. Eccl.* 3.39.15–16 as referring to our canonical Matthew and Mark is problematic, while theories to the effect that Papias knew Luke and John remain conjectural; the possibility that Papias echoes Luke's preface and may cite words of Jesus from Lk 10:18 remains unproven (ibid., 33–38). See also Gregory's conclusions in ibid., 293–98.

[100] As suggested in ibid., 124, 171–72, 293.

2.7 Coming Full Circle (2005)

The year 2005 saw the publication of a two-volume set of studies entitled *The New Testament and the Apostolic Fathers*, to mark the centenary of the similarly titled work by the Oxford Committee, discussed at the beginning of this survey. These volumes, edited by A. Gregory and C. M. Tuckett, revisit the whole question of the relationship between the Apostolic Fathers and the writings that later became the NT.[101] It would be difficult to give a summary of the volumes themselves, since they contain rather disparate essays by various authors. Though the first volume contains an essay by the editors on methodological concerns,[102] not all the essays in the volume subscribe to the recommended method, which adds to the element of diversity.[103] In addition, while overall a remarkable level of consistency is maintained between the findings of the Oxford Committee in 1905 and the various articles in these volumes, at times contributors to the latter also differ in finding both a greater[104] and a lesser[105] degree of use of NT documents by the Apostolic Father they examine.[106] In light of the above, perhaps the best approach is to give a very brief summary of the findings of the articles most relevant to the present study:

1 Clement: in his article on *1 Clement*, A. Gregory considers not only the canonical Gospels, but also oral, catechetical, and other pre-canonical sources of synoptic tradition, among others. He concludes that Clement

---

[101] Tuckett and Gregory, eds., *Reception* and *Trajectories*.

[102] Gregory and Tuckett, "Reflections on Method."

[103] E.g., the method applied by W. Petersen in his essay entitled "Textual Traditions Examined: What the Text of the Apostolic Fathers tells us about the Text of the New Testament in the Second Century" (in *Reception*, 29–46). Of the majority of essays that *do* subscribe to the recommended method, not all do so with equal success; one of the strengths of Tuckett's work, both in the essays referred to above and the essay included in the volumes under discussion (see below), is his mastery of issues related to the study of the Gospels. The latter is not necessarily true of all of the contributors to these two volumes.

[104] E.g., A. Gregory and C. M. Tuckett, "*2 Clement* and the Writings that later formed the New Testament," and J. Verheyden, "The *Shepherd of Hermas* and the writings that later formed the New Testament," in *Reception*, 251–92 and 293–329, respectively.

[105] E.g., P. Foster, "The Epistles of Ignatius of Antioch and the Writings that later formed the New Testament," in *Reception*, 159–86, esp. 185–86; M. W. Holmes, "Polycarp's *Letter to the Philippians* and the Writings that later formed de New Testament," in *Reception*, 187–227, esp. 226.

[106] See Gregory and Tuckett, Introduction and Overview, in both *Reception* and *Trajectories*, 1–5.

"appears ... to have drawn on Jesus traditions, but not in the form preserved in the synoptic gospels."[107]

Ignatius: Paul Foster concludes primarily based on the parallels between *Smyrn*. 1.1 and Mt 3:15 that "it is most likely that Ignatius knew Matthew' gospel," though he does not wish to rule out Koester's suggestion that this knowledge was indirect. In the case of other Ignatian passages he suggests that perhaps they presuppose Q "or oral tradition that fed into that document."[108]

Polycarp: in his study of Polycarp's *Epistle to the Philippians*, Michael Holmes adopts the method followed by A. Gregory in his monograph discussed above,[109] and his overall conclusions are similar to the latter's: "It is possible that Polycarp made use of one or more of the gospels of Matthew, Mark, and/or Luke; but there is no evidence to demonstrate that he did, nor is it possible to demonstrate that he did not know or use any of these three writings."[110]

Barnabas: J. Carleton-Paget finds it likely that, in the case of materials related to the passion, the author of *Barnabas* used "common passion traditions" rather than what became the canonical Gospels, and that a similar

---

[107] Gregory, "*1 Clement* and the Writings that later formed the New Testament," in *Reception*, 157, and see his fuller remarks on p. 139; in the body of his essay Gregory concludes regarding *1 Clem*.13.2 that Clement probably makes use of "a collection of sayings that is independent of and earlier than the broadly similar sayings of Jesus that are preserved also in Matthew and/or Luke" (pp. 133–34); regarding *1 Clem*. 46.8 that it *may* (speculatively) refer to a time when this particular Jesus tradition was a "free-floating logion," apparently oral (p. 137); regarding *1 Clem*. 24.5 that "it is unclear whether Clement echoes that parable [of the sower, found in all three synoptics] at all, either consciously or unconsciously" (p. 138); regarding *1 Clem*. 15.2 that one cannot be certain of the source (p. 139).

[108] Foster, "Ignatius and the Writings," 185.

[109] Gregory, *Reception of Luke and Acts*.

[110] Holmes, "Polycarp and the Writings," 197. Regarding Poly. *Phil*. 2.3a (par. *1 Clem*. 13.2; Mt 5:7; 6:14; 7:1–2; Lk 6:37–38) Holmes considers numerous options that have been raised (including direct dependence on *1 Clem*.; dependence on *1 Clem*. corrected against the written Gospels, citation of *1 Clem*. from memory affected by a reading of Mt and Lk, use of later conflated sources, use of a document similar to Q, and dependence on oral tradition), and concludes: "Clearly both Polycarp and *1 Clement* partake of a similar stream of tradition, but it does not seem possible, in view of the current state of the evidence, to indicate the relationship or connections any more precisely" (p. 193); regarding *Phil*. 2.3b, he considers oral tradition as an option, and concludes that "knowledge of Matthew and Luke is possible, but not demonstrable" (p. 194); regarding *Phil*. 6.2a he finds that a dependence on Mt or Lk is not probable (p. 194); regarding *Phil*. 7.2 he finds no "necessary link" between it and the synoptics, so that it may be dependent on a different source altogether (p. 196); regarding *Phil*. 12.3 he follows the Oxford Committee in noting "the similarities without drawing any conclusions, due to the uncertainty of the evidence" (p. 197).

explanation may apply to other material as well.[111] Overall he arrives at the conclusion that, even in cases where an Apostolic Father appears to know a NT book,[112] "it will never be unambiguously clear whether he acquired such knowledge from an actual reading of the NT document in which the relevant NT passage is found or from knowledge of a source."[113] He notes, however, that it would also be very difficult to prove that the author of *Barnabas* did *not* know the Gospels (speaking specifically of the Gospel of Matthew).[114]

2 Clement: C. M. Tuckett, in considering the parallels to gospel material in *2 Clement*,[115] finds fairly clear evidence that the Jesus tradition used by "Clement" presupposes the finished form of Matthew and Luke. A number of the passages that lead to this conclusion also appear to reflect a conflation of these two gospels, so that Tuckett suggests that "Clement" might have depended upon a harmony of Matthew and Luke for at least some of the tradition.[116] Other sayings, however, appear to derive from non-canonical sources, specifically non-extant gospels.[117]

Shepherd *of Hermas*: in his study of the *Shepherd* of Hermas, J. Verheyden identifies material which in his opinion presupposes MattR and which also agrees with the content and structure of its Matthean paral-

---

[111] Carleton-Paget, "*Barnabas* and the Writings," 238–39.

[112] Carleton-Paget finds this knowledge "quite possible" (in stating that Köhler's judgment that it was "gut möglich" is "not unreasonable") in the case of *Barn.* 4.14//Mt 22:10 (ibid., 233, 239, 249). He qualifies this, however, by stating, "if we are right to assume that *Barnabas* betrays knowledge of Matthew at this point, is it not strange that the author did not use him more frequently, given the fact that he and the first gospel could be seen to have anti-Jewish views in common?" (p. 239).

[113] Ibid., 230; on *Barn.* 5.9f (pp. 233–34); 5.12 (pp. 234–35); 7.3–5 (p. 235); 7.9b (pp. 235–36); 12.10 (p. 236); and 15.9 (pp. 236–37).

[114] Ibid., 239.

[115] Tuckett was responsible for the portion of the article on *2 Clement* that dealt with Jesus tradition, while Gregory was responsible for discussing parallels to the rest of the NT (Gregory and Tuckett, "*2 Clement* and the Writings," 252, n. 5).

[116] The passages Tuckett examines in arriving at this conclusion are many; see ibid., 254–78, and note esp. Tuckett's conclusions on pp. 277–78.

[117] E.g., Tuckett considers that *2 Clem.* 4.5a might have derived from a "Jewish" "gospel," such as the *Gospel of the Nazaraeans* as proposed by P. Vielhauer, that 5.2–4 *may* reflect an "apocryphal" gospel such as (speculatively) the *Gospel of Peter*, while he concludes from his discussion of 12.2 that it provides evidence that "'Clement' had access to other sources [than the Synoptic Gospels] of information about the words of Jesus, one of which may then be the so-called *Gospel according to the Egyptians*" (ibid., 262–63, 264–66, 272–73). For a brief discussion of *2 Clement* also found in these two volumes, that arrives at similar conclusions to Tuckett's, see H. Koester, "Gospels and Gospel Traditions in the Second Century," in *Trajectories*, 31–32.

lels.[118] Drawing from this that "elements from traditions that went back to Matthew" circulated in the community of Hermas, Verheyden concludes that the most plausible explanation for the presence of these elements in the *Shepherd* is that Hermas used Matthew.[119]

Martyrdom of Polycarp: in their two studies devoted to the *Martyrdom of Polycarp*, B. Dehanschutter[120] and M. Holmes[121] arrive at conclusions that are quite similar to each other. In sum, while there are numerous cases of possible dependence of the *Martyrdom* on the Gospels or gospel tradition, it is not possible to demonstrate dependence on any particular gospel.[122]

Looking back on these brief summaries, an element that might be said to characterize them all is the care with which the various authors draw their conclusions. There is very little dogmatic assertion, and much openness to the ambiguity of the sources. As for their treatment of oral tradition, again we find that it is given little consideration on its own. Oral tradition is seen in some cases as the main source of the Jesus or gospel tradition in certain Apostolic Fathers. But the very question being brought to the texts – "To what extent were the documents that later became the NT used by the Apostolic Fathers?" – dictates that oral tradition is given little attention in its own right. Often oral tradition is simply left open as a viable option alongside the use of a gospel, but pursued no further.

Before concluding, we will look at two additional essays in these volumes, one by W. L. Petersen and one by A. J. Bellinzoni, that are directly related to this topic. The essay by Petersen is notable in that it epitomizes the approach that privileges literacy over orality. Petersen's essay is a plea to those who would work with identifying the source(s) of the Jesus tradition in the Apostolic Fathers, to address seriously a preliminary question: "what textual parallels are there for the recognizable passages in the Apos-

---

[118] Verheyden's article is primarily a history of research, in which he sets out the divergent views of and conclusions reached by various scholars on the issue of Hermas' use of gospel tradition (Verheyden, "*Hermas* and the Writings," 296–322). He only actually analyzes one set of parallels in detail – those in Matthew and 1 Corinthians to Herm. *Man.* IV (Herm. 29–32) – urging that his findings might provide a vantage point from which to reassess the conclusions of other scholars (ibid., 322–29). His own conclusions reached in the study, therefore, are based on an analysis of minimal primary data.

[119] Ibid., 327–29, quote from p. 327.

[120] B. Dehandschutter, "The New Testament and the *Martyrdom of Polycarp*," in *Trajectories*, 395–405.

[121] M. W. Holmes, "The *Martyrdom of Polycarp* and the New Testament Passion Narratives," in *Trajectories*, 407–32.

[122] These essays on the *Martyrdom of Polycarp* were included in the two-volume set under consideration, NTAF, even though there was no corresponding treatment of the same in *NTAF*. Neither *NTAF* nor NTAF included a discussion of the relationship between the gospel tradition and the fragments of Papias.

tolic Fathers, and what do these parallels tell us about the *textual complexion* of the documents – whatever they may have been – that were known to the Apostolic Fathers?"[123] This very question, in my opinion, predisposes Petersen to view said sources as written documents. This is evident, e.g., when he states,

> ... in the overwhelming majority of cases, those passages in the Apostolic Fathers which offer recognizable parallels with our present-day New Testament display a text that is very different from what we now find in our modern critical editions of the New Testament.[124]

In speaking of the source of these sayings as "a text," Petersen does not seriously consider the possibility of an *oral* source, but is working under the assumption that the Apostolic Fathers witness to a form of the *written* text different from that of our critical editions of the NT. This in turn is based on his argument that, at the time of the Apostolic Fathers, the text of the documents that later were to comprise the NT "was still very much in flux and subject to change."[125] For him, since "there is a *complete* lack of *any* empirical evidence from the first century," one should not speak, e.g., of the use of "Matthew" by an Apostolic Father.[126]

> While one might be able to speak of the use of 'tradition' which later coalesced, and eventually became part of the fixed text that *today* bears the title 'The Gospel according to Matthew' (that is, *our* Matthew, of the 'great uncials' and of our modern, critically reconstructed text), one cannot speak with any degree of certainty about the form of *our* 'Matthew' in the first half of the second century.[127]

Thus for Petersen it is a mistake to argue, e.g., that deviations from our critically reconstructed text of Matthew in the text of *Barnabas* are due to the latter quoting the text of Matthew freely from memory, or adapting it to suit the moment. To argue the latter is to miss entirely the most likely explanation: that "Barnabas" "simply had a *different* text from ours, one which he quoted *accurately!*"[128] But here we must ask if a *better* explanation is not offered by *Barnabas'* dependence on oral tradition for the sayings in question. Petersen raises the possibility of oral tradition only in his critique of another scholar who does not take it into account,[129] but he himself does no better in the essay under consideration.

---

[123] Petersen, "Textual Traditions," 45; emphasis in the original.

[124] Ibid., 34; original text is in italics.

[125] Ibid., 40.

[126] Ibid., 41; emphasis in the original.

[127] Ibid., 41; emphasis in the original.

[128] Ibid., 42–45, quote from p. 42 n. 43; emphasis in the original.

[129] See Petersen's critique of W. R. Inge's contribution to *NTAF* on Ignatius, in ibid., 31, n. 12. Oral tradition is mentioned in other places in Petersen's essay, but only in quotations from the work of other scholars (p. 32), in noting the options considered by other

The essay by Bellinzoni, entitled "The Gospel of Luke in the Apostolic Fathers," is noteworthy for making a significant contribution to the ongoing discussion on method.[130] Building in large part on his earlier essays on the use of Matthew and Luke in the second century,[131] Bellinzoni begins by making two important points: (1) One must take into account the textual history of both the NT documents and the Apostolic Fathers. What scholars have available to compare today are only later witnesses to the earlier documents, and one must account for textual corruption that has taken place in both corpora.[132] (2) One must also consider the date and place of origin of the various documents being compared. Bellinzoni acknowledges that this is a difficult task, that often involves scholars in circular reasoning, but it must be done to the best of one's ability if one is going to attempt to trace lines of development within the tradition.[133] Where Bellinzoni makes his most important contribution, however, is in refining the criteria for determining what constitutes "use" of a gospel by any given Apostolic Father, building into his method certain features (his criteria of *accessibility* and *rate of recurrence*, see below) that in many other treatments are only occasionally brought to bear on the discussion. The three criteria he advocates are as follows:

Accessibility: this criterion asks whether or not the Apostolic Father would have had access to the document which he is held to use in his writ-

---

scholars (p. 34 n. 22), or as a possibility that Petersen sets aside in favor of another (p. 43, "we are dealing with a *tradition* – almost certainly *written* …"; emphasis in the original). Nowhere is oral tradition given serious consideration in its own right.

[130] Bellinzoni, "Luke in the Apostolic Fathers."

[131] Bellinzoni, "Gospel of Matthew"; idem, "The Gospel of Luke in the Second Century CE," in *Literary Studies in Luke-Acts: Essays in Honor of Joseph B. Tyson* (ed. R. P. Thompson and T. E. Phillips; Macon: Mercer University Press, 1998), 59–76. In the present book a discussion of these two earlier works by Bellinzoni was set aside in favor of a treatment of his 2005 essay on Luke, both because in the latter he has refined the method of his earlier essays, and because in it he deals specifically with Luke *in the Apostolic Fathers*, whereas in his earlier essay on Luke he dealt with later writers.

[132] Bellinzoni, "Gospel of Matthew," 197–98; idem, "Luke in the Second Century," 59; idem, "Luke in the Apostolic Fathers," 47–48. This insight is not new, and Bellinzoni indicates his primary indebtedness to Koester, "Text of the Synoptic." See also W. L. Petersen, "The Genesis of the Gospels," in *New Testament Textual Criticism and Exegesis: Festschrift J. Delobel* (ed. A. Denaux; BETL 161; Leuven: Leuven University Press and Peeters, 2002), 33–65; idem, "Textual Traditions." For a comparison of the types of textual corruption in the two corpora see B. D. Ehrman, "Textual Traditions Compared: The New Testament and the Apostolic Fathers," in *Reception* (ed. Gregory and Tuckett), 9–27.

[133] Bellinzoni, "Gospel of Matthew," 198–99; idem, "Luke in the Second Century," 59; idem, "Luke in the Apostolic Fathers," 48–50.

ings; here the dates and places of origin of the documents in question are of crucial importance.[134]

Textual Distinctiveness: this is essentially Koester's redactional criterion; one must identify redactional features in the supposed precursor document, and then "look for clear evidence of the presence of those redactional characteristics in our second-century writings." Bellinzoni considers this criterion the most difficult to apply.[135]

Rate of Recurrence: this criterion "asks how often there appear to be parallels between the texts in question." The probability of the use of one document by the writer of another increases in proportion to the number of feasible parallels identified, though the presence of only one isolated parallel does not negate use.[136]

The individual elements that make up Bellinzoni's method are not new, but the clarity with which he articulates them and the care with which he balances them in applying them to the text makes his essay as a whole a significant contribution. From his study Bellinzoni concludes that only in the case of *2 Clement* is there evidence that satisfied all three criteria, but that even in this case (in agreement with Koester and Gregory[137]) "it is likely that *2 Clement* did not use Luke itself, but instead used a post-synoptic harmony that combined elements of Matthew and Luke and, in at least two instances (*2 Clem.* 12. 2, 6) extra-canonical apocryphal tradition."[138] Bellinzoni finds little or no evidence for the use of Luke in *1 Clement*, the *Didache*, Ignatius, Polycarp's *Philippians*,[139] the *Epistle of*

---

[134] Bellinzoni considers this criterion "a *sine qua non* in considering the question of use" ("Luke in the Apostolic Fathers," 51).

[135] Ibid., 51.

[136] Ibid., 51.

[137] Bellinzoni cites Koester, *Synoptische Überlieferung*, 110–11; idem, *Ancient*, 349–60; idem, *Introduction to the New Testament* (2 vols.; Philadelphia: Fortress/Berlin: de Gruyter, 1982), 2:235 [in the rev. ed. of the latter volume, New York and Berlin: de Gruyter, 2000, Koester repeats this opinion on p. 242]; Gregory, *Reception of Luke and Acts*, 136–49.

[138] Bellinzoni, "Luke in the Apostolic Fathers," 65.

[139] Here Bellinzoni considers that Poly. *Phil.* 2.3 is possibly dependent on Lk 6:38, but finds the overall evidence of Polycarp's dependence on Luke "decidedly 'underwhelming'" (ibid., 59–60). Later in the same essay he mentions "at most one example of use" of Luke by Polycarp, which we may assume is the parallel mentioned, but clarifies again, "Polycarp's second letter may reflect use of the Gospel of Luke, but even that is not entirely clear, and I very much doubt it" (66–67). Bellinzoni continues to allow for the remote possibility that Polycarp used Luke (as Koester before him, see his *Synoptische Überlieferung*, 117) only because he accepts P. N. Harrison's thesis that Poly. *Phil.* is a conflation of two documents, the first written between A.D. 110–117, and the second two or three decades later (ibid., 59; idem, "Luke in the Second Century," 60 and n. 4; see P. N. Harrison, *Polycarp's Two Epistles to the Philippians* [Cambridge: Cam-

Barnabas, or the *Shepherd* of Hermas.[140] Instead, these writers used "pre-synoptic oral and/or written tradition." He continues,

This literature from the first half of the second century reflects use not of the Synoptic Gospels but of the same tradition that underlies the Synoptic Gospels. The source of that tradition was individual Christian communities, which, based on their practical needs, handed down and made use of synoptic-like oral and written tradition.[141]

The above words provide an appropriate end to our survey, in that they point in the direction we have chosen to follow. If indeed "the literature of the first half of the second century" found its sources of Jesus tradition in community-based oral (and written) synoptic-like material, then the discussion of these sources needs to move on from an almost single focus on the use or non-use of the Gospels, to look seriously at oral tradition in its own right.

2.8 Conclusions

One of the overarching motifs traceable through the past century of scholarship on Jesus tradition in the Apostolic Fathers is a coming to terms with the ambiguity inherent in the nature of the available sources. Certainly there have been those, and here I refer especially to Massaux and Köhler, who have sought to play down this ambiguity, choosing to narrow down the sources of this tradition whenever possible to surviving written sources, especially (what would become) our canonical Matthew. Others have rightly criticized the work of these scholars, pointing out that their approach and method predetermine in large part what they will find in the sources. A more responsible approach searches for concrete evidence for the use of any given gospel prior to concluding that said use has taken place. A tool that has been widely used toward this end is the redactional criterion developed by H. Koester and refined by such scholars as C. M. Tuckett and A. Gregory (while others such as A. J. Bellinzoni have incorporated it into a fuller method).

Whether one can arrive at conclusive evidence for the use or non-use of the Gospels in all of the Apostolic Fathers by using the redactional crite-

---

bridge University Press, 1936]). This thesis allows Bellinzoni to meet his criterion of *accessibility*. In my opinion Harrison's thesis has been accepted all too readily in subsequent scholarship, and does not stand up under scrutiny; see sec. 5.2 below.

[140] Bellinzoni, "Luke in the Apostolic Fathers," 53–65, also idem, "Luke in the Second Century," 60 and n. 3.

[141] Bellinzoni, "Luke in the Apostolic Fathers," 66. He arrives at almost identical conclusions following his study of the use of Matthew by the Apostolic Fathers, see his "Gospel of Matthew," 254.

rion continues to be debated. Two conclusions seem fairly certain: (a) There is no evidence to suggest that any of the Apostolic Fathers used the Gospel of Mark directly; and (b) what little evidence has been found for the use of Luke in the Apostolic Fathers does not prove to be conclusive when subjected to close scrutiny. When it comes to the use of Matthew by the Apostolic Fathers that predate *2 Clement*, however, scholarship continues to be divided between those who find clear evidence of MattR in certain Fathers (e.g., Tuckett in the *Didache*,[142] Foster in Ignatius[143]) and those who find grounds for interpreting the evidence differently (e.g., Milavec on the *Didache*,[144] Bellinzoni on Ignatius[145]). The ambiguity of our sources is highlighted not only by this scholarly impasse, but also by the fact that the inability to demonstrate conclusively that the Apostolic Fathers used the canonical Gospels does not negate such use. Existing methods are simply inadequate for the task at hand.

Compounding this situation of ambiguity is the comparative lack of attention given to the very good possibility that the Apostolic Fathers relied primarily on oral tradition as their source. For the most part, scholars engaged in the task of determining the sources of Jesus tradition in the Apostolic Fathers approach their work without sufficiently challenging the literary mindset that is the scholarly default setting.[146] So they often focus upon which extant written documents provide the best explanation for the form of the Jesus tradition found in the Apostolic Fathers. This is understandable given the goals of a number of the studies surveyed above: it is to be expected that scholars seeking to determine the extent to which any given gospel was used in early Christian literature will approach the material precisely in order to ascertain whether or not any given saying in the Apostolic Fathers depends on the form of its parallels as found in the same gospel. For the most part this enquiry leads said scholars only as far as needed to find an answer to their specific question. To conclude in the negative, however, that a given saying does not depend on a particular gospel, does not necessarily lead to a positive determination on where it *did* originate, whether in a non-canonical written source or, more importantly for our purposes here, in oral tradition.

When it comes to considering the possibility of oral sources for the Jesus tradition in the Apostolic Fathers, a number of scholars – perhaps even

---

[142] Tuckett, "Tradition in the *Didache*"; idem, "*Didache* and the Synoptics"; idem, "*Didache* and the Writings."

[143] Foster, "Ignatius and the Writings."

[144] Milavec, "Synoptic Tradition" = *Didache: Faith, Hope, and Life*, 693–739; idem, "Rejoinder."

[145] Bellinzoni, "Gospel of Matthew."

[146] See sec. 1.1 above, and Dunn, "Altering," esp. 139–40.

unconsciously – incorporate this possibility into their discussion only as a last resort, as a catch-all for those sayings that cannot be explained in some other (preferred?) way. Among the minority of scholars who have sought to give oral tradition equal consideration as other sources, it is the rare scholar who has approached the issue based on any sophisticated theory of orality. Most make only an occasional reference to studies in the field of orality in support of this or that determination on sources. Finally, even among those who consider oral tradition as *the main source* of Jesus tradition in the Apostolic Fathers, and here we refer specifically to H. Koester and D. Hagner, one finds widely diverging views regarding the way oral tradition functioned in antiquity. As concluded above, in the case of these two scholars these diverging views extend to the sources for the Jesus tradition in question: for Koester much of the tradition originated in early church communities, while for Hagner the tradition originated for the most part with Jesus himself. One cannot afford simply to ignore the very different implications of these otherwise superficially similar positions. What is sorely needed is a study of the Jesus tradition in the Apostolic Fathers that not only takes seriously the possibility of oral tradition as a source, but that intentionally approaches the material from the perspective of recent theoretical studies on how oral tradition functioned in antiquity. Such a study might provide a vantage point from which to reevaluate the relationship between the Apostolic Fathers and the written Gospels, and from which to draw wider conclusions regarding the origin of the Jesus or gospel material in question. The chapters that follow seek to address this need.

Chapter 3

Method: Orality and Oral Tradition

As noted in chapter one, this study seeks to reevaluate the Jesus tradition in the Apostolic Fathers from the vantage point of developments in the study of orality and literacy in antiquity that have taken place over the last four decades.[1] In keeping with this goal, its method is geared specifically toward recognizing orally derived materials in written texts, utilizing an approach that is informed by these developments.

The bulk of this chapter will be dedicated to a description of these developments in the study of orality and literacy and the method that will be followed in applying them in the present work. Before launching into that topic, however, two preliminary matters need to be addressed in order to provide important theoretical underpinnings: first, under the sub-title "Orality in Oral-Derived Texts (The Jesus Tradition as it has Come Down to Us)," we will address the very basic question of the *possibility* of identifying orally-derived materials in written texts. Next, under the sub-title "Orality and Literacy in the Ancient Mediterranean World," we will seek to establish the centrality of orally based communication in the first-century milieu in which Christianity was born and spread. This will pave the way for our main discussion of method, that will take place under the sub-title, "Markers of Orality: Identifying Oral Indicators in a Written Medium." Certain issues raised by the discussion of method will be addressed in two sections at the close of the chapter, "The Limits of Comparative Study: Recognizing the Uniqueness of a Tradition," and "Giving Scribality a Fair Hearing ... in Light of Orality."

3.1 Orality in Oral-Derived Texts

One of the obvious difficulties one faces in working with Jesus tradition as *oral* tradition is that in the form it has come down to us it is no longer

---

[1] These developments were addressed briefly in secs. 1.1 and 1.2 above, and will be described more fully in sec. 3.3 below, under the sub-title "Markers of Orality: Oral Indicators in a Written Medium."

"oral" in the most basic sense of the term.[2] Every portion of Jesus tradition that will be discussed in this study is found in a *written* source. To differentiate between sources, however, on the basis of whether they are spoken or written, is to create superficial categories that do not do justice to the complex relationship between orality and writing in antiquity. As helpfully articulated by Egbert Bakker, one can make more meaningful distinctions based both on the *conception of the discourses* found in various writings and on the *conception of their writing*.[3]

Bakker portrays the conception of a discourse and of its writing via the following graph:[4]

Graph 1: Conception of Language and of Writing as Parallel Continua

(a) Conception of a discourse: oral ⟵——————⟶ literate

(b) Conception of its writing: transcription ⟵——————⟶ composition

In this graph continuum 'a' relates to the origin of the discourse itself, whether its conception followed norms that govern spoken interaction or norms that govern literate communication. As Bakker states, "Speaking and writing are different activities and call for different strategies in the presentation and comprehension of a discourse."[5] Even if they are encountered in written form, the products of orality can thus be distinguished from those of literacy by the different set(s) of norms adhered to in their conception. Continuum 'b' relates to the dynamics surrounding the writing of a discourse: was it a spoken discourse that was transcribed, or a discourse that was composed directly in writing? If a discourse was oral in its conception, and is then transcribed, it falls in the category of oral-derived literature.[6] Oral-derived literature will not evince the characteristics usually associated with written discourse simply because spoken phonemes have been replaced with written graphemes.[7] On the contrary, even in its transcribed form, oral-derived discourse will retain certain features that are peculiar to its oral conception, while losing others. As rightly stated by

---

[2] We have already dealt briefly with this issue in sec. 1.3 above, under the subtitle "Problems."

[3] E. J. Bakker, *Poetry in Speech: Orality and Homeric Discourse* (Myth and Poetics; Ithaca and London: Cornell University Press, 1997), 7–9; idem, "How Oral," 29–47.

[4] Graph adapted from Bakker, "How Oral," 31.

[5] Bakker, "How Oral," 30.

[6] J. A. Draper, "Jesus' 'Covenantal Discourse' on the Plain (Luke 6:12–7:17) as Oral Performance: Pointers to 'Q' as Multiple Oral Performance," in *Oral Performance* (ed. Horsley), 73–74.

[7] Bakker, "How Oral," 31–32.

Jonathan Draper, "Oral texts written down do not lose their most characteristic features, although clearly the paralinguistic features will be lost – gesture, intonation, pause, pitch and so on."[8] Likewise, a discourse composed
in writing and adhering to the cultural norms for such activity will remain
a literate composition even if delivered orally (a contemporary example
might be a paper read at a symposium) – it will (most likely) not sound
like everyday spoken language.[9] That something is "oral" thus need not
imply that it is the opposite of "written," but rather "writing runs the gamut
of the whole oral-literate continuum."[10]

It is important to note the reality Bakker sought to capture by using
continua in the above graph. The continua reflect that most discourses will
contain varying ratios of both oral and literate characteristics, so that most
discourses will be found at some point along the continua between the two
extremes.[11] Important to note also for our present purposes is that the
closer a text is placed to the left extreme of the continua, the more it must
be studied not as a written composition but as the spoken word that preceded its transcription.[12]

If the above represents a viable argument, then it is possible to identify
the oral origin of an ancient writing, or oral sources within ancient written
records, based on markers of orality that became incorporated via transcription into the written medium. One must hasten to clarify, however,
that this process of identifying either an oral origin for a given writing, or
oral sources within it, involves levels of likelihood rather than certainty.
There are a number of factors that militate against certainty: the most obvious, as mentioned above, is that the material in question is only available
to the researcher in writing, not in oral form. As we have seen, however,
and as will become clearer in what follows, this is less of an impediment
than might at first be supposed. More problematic is the possibility that the
author of a written composition (to the right of continuum 'b' in the above
graph) may have consciously or unconsciously imitated the oral mode of
delivery.[13] Once a given tradition became associated with a particular type
of spoken language (not only in terms of the content of the tradition it

---

[8] Draper, "Covenantal Discourse," 74.

[9] Bakker, "How Oral," 30, and cf. ibid., 33.

[10] Ibid., 31. On the relationship between oral tradition and oral-derived texts see further Foley, *Immanent Art*; idem, *Singer*, esp. pp. 60–98.

[11] Ibid., 30–31; see also idem, *Poetry in Speech*, 9.

[12] Bakker, "How Oral," 32, 37; cf. R. Thomas on ancient Greece, "the written histories from Greece were largely derived from oral tradition, so ... we need to pay attention
not merely to the written texts but to the nature of the oral sources they reflect and the
possible influence of one on the other" (*Oral Tradition and Written Record in Classical
Athens* [CSOLC 18; Cambridge: Cambridge University Press, 1989], 2).

[13] See Ong, *Orality and Literacy*, 26.

transmitted, but also in terms of a certain meter, catch phrases, etc.), it would be natural for one familiar with that tradition to incorporate the distinctive characteristics of said language into a written composition (to the right of continuum 'b' in the above graph) in order to elicit a response from the reader similar to what was expected of what was up to then exclusively a listening audience.[14] This is further complicated, in terms of tracing the oral or written origins of any given material, by the fact that the distinction between "readers" and "listening audience" would have been blurred in antiquity. This is not only because writings of all kinds were not read silently but out loud[15] – creating in effect a new "listening audience" for written materials – but also because writings in antiquity often served more as aids to memory than as direct sources of discourse.[16] It follows that "even after an oral tradition is written down, it may continue to function almost entirely in oral performance and produce new forms and versions which may get written down again."[17]

---

[14] See Foley, "Bard's Audience," 93–94. This is a central point in D. M. Carr, *Writing on the Tablet of the Heart: Origins of Scripture and Literature* (Oxford: Oxford University Press, 2005). For the application of this idea see also, e.g., Stephen A. Nimis' argument regarding the presence of "ring composition" in Longus' *Daphnis and Chloe* ("Cycles and Sequence in Longus' *Daphnis and Chloe*," in *Speaking Volumes: Orality and Literacy in the Greek and Roman World,* [ed. J. Watson; MnS 218; Leiden: Brill, 2001], 185–98), C. Eyre and J. Baines on the role of formulae in written language ("Interactions between Orality and Literacy in Ancient Egypt," in *Literacy and Society* [ed. K. Schousboe and M. Trolle Larsen; Copenhagen: Akademisk Forlag, 1989], 91–119), and J. Brody on the setting in writing of oral traditions by indigenous authors among the Tojolabal Maya ("Incipient Literacy: From Involvement to Integration in Tojolabal Maya," *OrTr* 3 [1988]: 315–52). There is also the other side of the coin, in that a writer who does not manage to fully replicate the oral characteristics of a genre may betray the chirographic base of his or her own enterprise; see Merritt Sale, "Virgil's Formularity and *Pius Aeneas*," in *Signs of Orality* (ed. Mackay), 199–220.

[15] Though this topic will be addressed further below, for the specific point made here see Sale, "Virgil's Formularity," 213–14; Kelber, "Jesus and Tradition," 153; Draper, "Covenantal Discourse," 73, 75.

[16] Carr, *Writing on the Tablet*, 4–7, 27–30, 71–77, 95–99, 132–33, 177–86, 287–88, and passim; idem, "Torah on the Heart: Literary Jewish Textuality within Its Ancient near Eastern Context," *OrTr* 25 (2010): 18–39. In this sense "literacy was the handmaid of memory, rather than its rival" (M. C. A. Macdonald, "Literacy in an Oral Environment," in *Writing and Ancient Near Eastern Society: Papers in Honour of Alan R. Millard* [eds. P. Bienkowski, C. Mee and E. Slater; LHB/OTS 426. New York and London: T&T Clark, 2005], 69).

[17] Draper, "Covenantal Discourse," 73; see also Kelber, "Jesus and Tradition," 141; idem, "The Authority of The Word in St. John's Gospel: Charismatic Speech, Narrative Text, Logocentric Metaphysics," *OrTr* 2.1 [FS for W. J. Ong] (1987): 122. For a summary statement of what a number of authors have proposed along these lines see R. Finnegan, "Response from an Africanist Scholar," *OrTr* 25 (2010): 10.

Finally, it is also possible that the markers of orality that exist in a document are derivative rather than original to it; i.e., the oral origin or sources detectable in writing 'A' may be characteristics of a writing 'B' upon which writing 'A' depends, rather than of writing 'A' itself.[18]

Having noted the above difficulties, however, there is no reason why they should preclude the kinds of questions the present study seeks to bring to the texts. These difficulties simply serve to draw attention on the one hand to the nature of historical research in general, which always involves levels of likelihood rather than certainty, and on the other hand to the nature of the sources under consideration, which are ambiguous at best. Final judgment on the viability of the questions raised in the present study should be withheld until it has become clear whether or not they serve to enhance our understanding of the ancient texts under consideration.

3.2 Orality and Literacy in the Ancient Mediterranean World

To set out to identify orally conceived materials within written documents from late Western antiquity is fully warranted in light of dynamics associated with orality and literacy in the society of the time. Though literacy was present in these societies to a limited extent, they functioned primarily on the basis of orality. In the first and second centuries the vast majority of the population of the Roman Empire was unable to read or write.[19] Rates of literacy would have differed from one region of the Empire to another, and varied further within the latter based on categories such as gender and urban vs. rural location. In general terms, however, while in a few select Greek cities the rate of literacy among adult males may have risen as high as 30–40% between 400 and 100 B.C., by the first century A.D. even there it had decreased considerably, and the rate for the general population might not have reached even 10–15%.[20] Among Jews in Israel the percentage of

---

[18] These problems are compounded when one is working with fragments, such as isolated pieces of Jesus tradition in the present case. Working with complete documents, especially of epic proportions such as Homer's *Iliad* or *Odyssey*, or the Old English *Beowulf*, or in the case of Jesus tradition, documents such as the Gospel of Mark, would give one much more material upon which to base a judgment.

[19] The choice to speak in terms of "read or write" is following W. V. Harris, *Ancient Literacy* (Cambridge, Mass. and London: Harvard University Press, 1989), 3–5, to avoid misleading rates of literacy calculated on the basis of the ability of a person only to sign his or her name (as in the studies noted in ibid., 4, n. 3), or only to read but not write (ibid., 4, n. 4).

[20] Harris, *Ancient Literacy*, 327–30. H. Y. Gamble arrives at a similar conclusion, though he questions some of Harris' details, in *Books and Readers in the Early Church:*

literacy during this period would have been much lower, probably not much higher than 3%.

On the above see Bar-Ilan, "Illiteracy in Israel," 46–61, esp. 56; generally corroborated by Hezser, *Jewish Literacy*, who, however, leaves open the possibility that the literacy rate might have been slightly higher than 3% (p. 496); see also Jaffee, *Torah in the Mouth*, 15–16, 22. Synagogues would have been important centers of education in this period (see Riesner, *Jesus als Lehrer*, 123–53), but *education* need not imply *literacy*.

A. Millard posits a higher level of literacy in Palestine than do Bar-Ilan and Hezser, but his evidence is questionable at best (*Reading and Writing*, 154–58). For example, Millard appeals to the talmudic reference to Simeon ben Shetach "about 100 BC that all children should go to school (*y. Ket.* 8.32c)" in support of his contention that "In theory, every Jewish male was expected to [read from the Scriptures in synagogue services]" (p. 157), citing as his source E. Schürer, *The History of the Jewish People in the Age of Jesus Christ (175 B.C. – A.D. 135)* (3vols.; rev. and ed. by G. Vermes, et al.; Edinburgh: T&T Clark, 1973–87), 2.417–21, 450. Millard fails to mention, however, that Schürer himself considers the tradition regarding ben Shetach "a later legend ... of little significance" (Schürer, *History*, 2.418). Millard also appeals in support of his view to Josephus *C. Ap.* 2.178 and Philo *Legat.* 210, but both of these texts refer to *memorization* rather than writing and reading: "should anyone of our nation be questioned about the laws, *he should repeat them all the more readily than his own name*. The result, then, of our thorough grounding in the laws from the first dawn of intelligence is that *we have them, as it were, engraven on our souls*" (Jos. *C. Ap.* 2.178 [Thackeray, LCL]; emphasis added); "Holding that the laws are oracles vouschafed by God and having been trained in this doctrine from their earliest years, *they carry the likeness of the commandments enshrined in their souls*" (Philo, *Legat.* 210 [Colson, LCL]; emphasis added). Rote memorization of the Torah under the guidance of a literate instructor does not equate to literacy. The same could be said of other passages mentioned by Schürer (loc. cit.) in Josephus (e.g., *C. Ap.* 1.60) and Philo (e.g., *Legat.* 115) not mentioned by Millard.

Also not mentioned by Millard, however, Josephus does refer specifically to reading when he states that the Law orders that children "shall be taught to read [lit. "taught letters": γράμματα παιδεύειν], and shall learn both the laws and the deeds of their forefathers" (*C. Ap.* 2.204; Thackeray, LCL). This reference to "letters" would imply widespread education beyond memorization, but as noted by A. Baumgarten, this is not presented as a description of current practice, but as an ideal set forth by the Law, and is probably exaggerated ("The Torah as Public Document in Judaism," *SR* 14 [1985]: 19; idem, *The Flourishing of Jewish Sects in the Maccabean Era: An Interpretation* [SJSJ 55; Leiden: Brill, 1997], 121–22). Elsewhere Josephus refers specifically to a priest reciting the laws to the whole assembly, including women and children, so that the laws are "graven on their hearts *through the hearing*" (not through the reading), context within which one is to understand his further statement, "Let your children also begin by learning the laws ..." (Jos. *Ant.* 4.209–11; Thackeray, LCL; emphasis added); this refers to learning through hearing, not literacy. (The above critique of Millard's use of texts also applies to H. Gamble, as he appeals to some of the same texts in stating that, "According to Josephus, in first-century Judaism it was a duty, indeed a religious commandment, that Jewish children be taught to read" [*Books and Readers*, 7 and n. 21].) Josephus and Philo

A History of Early Christian Texts (New Haven and London: Yale University Press, 1995), 2–10.

themselves obviously belong to the literate minority, in which light one should understand Josephus' reference to his own training in literacy in *Vita* 9. Millard himself (ibid.,
158) recognizes that the Synoptics differentiate between a minority of Jewish teachers
who could read ("Have you never read ..."; Mt 12:3, 5; 19:4; 21:16, 42; 22:31; Mk 2:25;
12:10, 26; Lk 6:3; 10:26) and the wider population that could not ("You have heard that
it was said ..."; Mt 5:21, 27, 33, 38, 43; and see also Jn 12:34). The remainder of
Millard's discussion in support of widespread literacy in Palestine actually applies to a
small minority of the population (ibid., 158–84), in spite of his statement to the contrary
(ibid., 181–82); while we cannot substantiate this claim in detail here, the reader is referred to the full texts of Bar-Ilan, "Illiteracy in Israel," Hezser, *Jewish Literacy*, and Jaffee, *Torah in the Mouth*. For a study of a small Palestinian community in which literacy
would have been relatively high, see P. S. Alexander, "Literacy among Jews in Second
Temple Palestine: Reflections on the Evidence from Qumran," in *Hamlet on a Hill: Semitic and Greek Studies Presented to Professor T. Muraoka on the Occasion of his Sixty-
Fifth Birthday* (ed. M. F. J. Baasten and W. Th. van Peursen; OLA 118; Leuven: Peeters
and Department of Oriental Studies, 2003), 3–24.

   L. Hurtado also argues in favor of a much higher level of literacy in first century Palestine in his article "Greco-Roman Textuality," 93–97. Hurtado is right in stating that by
this time literacy had greatly impacted Jewish culture in Palestine for centuries, and also
rightly notes that the culture of first century Palestine was not "dominated by pre-literate
('primary') orality" (pp. 95, 96), to my knowledge a view no one currently holds. His
argument, however, that there was *widespread literacy* in Palestine in the first century
suffers from both (1) anachronisms and (2) an overly generous definition of literacy: (1)
Two examples of anachronisms are found in Hurtado's use of the work of A. Demsky and
M. Bar-Ilan, "Writing in Ancient Israel and Early Judaism," in *Mikra: Text, Translation,
Reading, and Interpretation of the Hebrew Bible in Ancient Judaism and Early Christianity* (ed. M. J. Mulder and H. Sysling; CRINT 2:1; Assen: Van Gorcum/ Philadelphia: Fortress, 1988), 1–38. In arguing that there was widespread literacy in first-century Palestine
Hurtado cites Demsky's p. 15, which is about literacy at the time of the Israelite monar-
chy, thus far too early to be applicable, and Bar-Ilan's p. 37, which relates to the rabbinic
period, thus far too late ("Greco-Roman Textuality," 96, n. 14). As Bar-Ilan notes elsewhere, the sources on literacy in first-century Palestine itself are scarce, so that one must
rely on an indirect method of inquiry ("Illiteracy in Israel," 46–47). Using this method,
Bar-Ilan sets literacy in Roman Palestine at roughly 3% (as noted above), which was still
relatively high, when compared for example with the 0.5% in ancient Egypt (ibid., 55–
56; see also ibid., p. 59, n. 29). (2) Hurtado's overly generous, or maximalist definition
of literacy can be seen in his adoption of "limited-competency" literacy as a standard
(p. 95, n. 9). In adopting this standard Hurtado (loc. cit.) rejects that held by W. V. Harris, which includes both reading and writing (*Ancient Literacy*, 3–5), in favor of one that
includes the ability of a person only to sign his or her name, or only to read but not write
(as in the studies noted in Harris, *Ancient Literacy*, 4, nn. 3–4). Hurtado's maximalist
standard is of little help, however, in assessing the impact of literacy on the early Jesus
tradition: the ability to sign one's name is the equivalent of learning to draw a picture,
and is no guide to levels of literacy, and one would need not only *reading* traditionists,
but also traditionists who could *write* any Jesus tradition before it could be read. With
this in mind, Harris' narrower definition is more applicable for such an assessment, in
that it requires writing. (Hurtado [ibid., p. 96, n. 15] also refers to the texts in Josephus
mentioned in the above critique of Millard, and the same criticism applies in his case.)

The above rates of literacy are not given for the purpose of dwelling on the low attainment of literacy in these societies, but in order to draw attention to the high rate of orality. Even with the presence of a limited degree of literacy, these societies continued to function as oral societies, in which the spoken word was given preference over the written.[21] This requires some explanation.

From a strictly technological viewpoint, the presence of the technology of writing within a society did not imply its use in any given specific context.[22] Different contexts within ancient society (geographical, occupational, socio-economic, among many others) demanded different levels of literacy from its members.[23] So, e.g., most farmers would have had very little use for writing (which is one of the primary explanations for the low levels of literacy among the Jews in Israel, who were predominantly farmers[24]). For the vast majority of daily activities members of rural communities would have made use of the spoken word in face-to-face interaction. For the very few activities that necessitated writing (contracts, letters, petitions) they would have had to hire a scribe, which may have implied travel to a large urban center.[25] In effect, then, increased distance from a city or large town implied a higher dependence on orality, while urban centers were islands of literacy within a largely oral culture.

Within those islands of literacy, different contexts demanded different uses of literacy skills by those who had acquired them. Those who could read and write did not utilize this training in every situation in life, but

---

[21] This informs our understanding of the well-known statement by Papias, that he preferred "a living and abiding voice" over "what came out of books" (in Eusebius, *Hist. Eccl.*, 3.39.4). Oral communication was considered in some ways as *more reliable* than what was written. For a full discussion see Byrskog, *Story as History*, 109–16. Of importance in the wider discussion of literacy and orality in antiquity is also one's definition of "literacy"; e.g., if one defines literacy not in modern terms, but as "an oral-written mastery of a body of texts" reserved for a social elite (Carr, *Writing on the Tablet*, quote from p. 13, and see also pp. 287–88).

[22] So according to M. Cole and H. Keyssar, "the general causal impact of literate knowledge is not unidirectional from technology to activity. Activities provide greater and lesser opportunities for particular literate technologies to be effective. ... [T]he interplay of socio-economic and literate/technological forces represents a classical case of dialectical interacting systems that are always incipiently in a process of change" ("The Concept of Literacy in Print and Film," Manuscript, Communications Program, University of California, San Diego, 1982, cited in Goody, *Logic*, xv–xvi).

[23] Thomas, *Oral Tradition*, 18; see also Harris, *Ancient Literacy*, 25–42, 66–115, 142–43, 190–93, 248–59, 289–306.

[24] See Bar-Ilan, "Illiteracy in Israel," 48–50.

[25] In Israel most scribes would have been found in Jerusalem, and the few scribes to be found in the villages "differed from them enormously with regard to ... expertise, tasks, remuneration, and status" (Hezser, *Jewish Literacy*, 120).

functioned in many contexts based on the norms of orality, as is to be expected in a culture that depends largely on the latter. So W. Harris notes
that, although the Greek and Roman elites used writing extensively, they
nevertheless "relied on the spoken word for purposes which in some other
cultures have been served by the written word."[26] Harris goes on to give
several examples, "They frequently dictated letters instead of writing them
for themselves; they listened to political news rather than reading it; they
attended recitations and performances, or heard slaves reading, without
having to read literary texts for themselves; and so on."[27] The presence of
literacy in Greco-Roman antiquity thus did not destroy society's proficiency in orality: a vast majority of the population continued to function on
the basis of orality in practically every walk of life, while even those who
could read incorporated it into contexts that could have been served by literacy.[28] In this environment those who had not acquired the ability to read
and write should not be thought of as deficient in literacy but as proficient
in orality,[29] while those who *did* acquire the skills of literacy should not be
imagined to have lost their proficiency in orality in the process.[30]

The above interplay between orality and literacy extended also to the
use of written texts in late Western antiquity: texts were spoken and heard.

---

[26] Harris, *Ancient Literacy*, 35–36.

[27] Ibid., 36; see also ibid., 124–25, 326–27; Thomas, *Oral Tradition*, 1–34 and passim.

[28] On all of the above see Harris, *Ancient Literacy*, 84–88, 125–27, 222–29; Assmann, *Religion and Cultural Memory*, 110–14; Rhoads, "Biblical Performance Criticism," 157–63. While it used to be common to draw a hard and fast distinction between
oral societies and literate societies, scholars have come to recognize this as a false di-
chotomy. In the words of J. M. Foley, "We know now that cultures are not oral or literate; rather they employ a menu or spectrum of communicative strategies, some of them
associated with texts, some with voices, and some with both" ("What's In a Sign," 3). R.
Thomas makes similar comments regarding fifth-fourth century (BC) Greece, "The tendency to see a society (or individual) as either literate or oral is over-simple and misleading. The habits of relying on oral communication (or orality) and literacy are not
mutually exclusive (even though literacy and illiteracy are). ...[T]he evidence for Greece
shows *both* a sophisticated and extensive use of writing in some spheres *and* what is to
us an amazing dominance of the spoken word" (*Literacy and Orality*, 4). See further Finnegan, *Literacy and Orality*, 62; Foley, "Bard's Audience," 95–96; idem, *Homer's Traditional Art*, 3; Thomas, *Oral Tradition*, 1–34 and passim.

[29] A point already made in sec. 1.4.2 above. Though it might be natural from the perspective of a highly literate culture to view a low rate of literacy as a deficiency, this
view says more about the biases of the literate than it does about the reality of life in ancient societies; see Thomas, *Literacy and Orality*, 1–14; Hezser, *Jewish Literacy*, 176–
77; A. Kirk, "Memory Theory and Jesus Research," *HSHJ*, 1.829–30.

[30] For a full discussion see A. Kirk, "Manuscript Tradition as a *Tertium Quid*: Orality
and Memory in Scribal Practices," in *Jesus, the Voice, and the Text* (ed. Thatcher), 215–
34.

Orality had a large role in (a) the process of the production of texts, (b) the manner in which they were read, and (c) the manner in which the majority of the population experienced texts. To explain briefly:

a) The common practice for the composition of written texts in Western antiquity was for the authors to *speak them out loud*, either to themselves if writing in their own hand, or in order to dictate them to a scribe.[31] These texts contained, then, not silent thoughts from the mind of the authors, but material that had been vocalized prior to becoming written.

b) Similarly, most written materials did not function as silent texts. The custom prevalent in late Western antiquity was to *vocalize* texts, i.e. read them out aloud, even when read to oneself.[32] In this light, texts served as intermediaries between speech and speech, between the spoken word of the writer and the spoken word of the reader.

c) Of even more importance for our purposes here, the great majority of the population *experienced* texts via oral/aural means. This was true at two levels: on the one level, as implied in point 'b' above, most people ac-cessed written texts through hearing. This was the case not only with the majority of the population that could not read (whose only option was to *hear* a text read) but also with those who could have read a text for them-selves, and who most often chose to have a text read to them out loud.

---

[31] P. J. Achtemeier notes that, while there are many examples of authors writing in their own hand, the more usual practice was to dictate to a scribe (*"Omne Verbum,"* 14–15); see also Park, *Mark's Memory Resources*, 46–49; Rhoads, "Biblical Performance Criticism," 159–60.

[32] Jaffee, *Torah in the Mouth*, 17–18; Park, *Mark's Memory Resources*, 55–58; Rhoads, "Biblical Performance Criticism," 159–60; Thomas, *Literacy and Orality*, 4, 91–93; idem, *Oral Tradition*, 2, and literature cited in n. 2; W. B. Sedgwick, "Reading and Writing in Classical Antiquity," *ContRev* 135 (1990): 90–91. Achtemeier pressed the (lack of) evidence a little too far in arguing that reading aloud was the *exclusive* practice in Western antiquity: "Reading was therefore oral performance *whenever* it occurred and in whatever circumstances. Late antiquity knew nothing of the 'silent, solitary reader'" (*"Omne Verbum,"* 17, emphasis in the original). According to Achtemeier the wonder-ment caused by Bishop Ambrose's silent reading, as narrated by Augustine (*Confessions* 6.3) shows that even in the fourth century this was unique (ibid., 15–17). In a 1992 article M. Slusser basically accepted Achtemeier's main contention of the exclusivity of the practice of reading aloud, but sought to correct him by arguing that the earliest known reference to silent reading in Western antiquity is found in the catecheses of Cyril of Je-rusalem (ca. A.D. 350), where women are instructed to pray and read in silence, appar-ently in obedience to Paul's injunction in 1 Cor 14:34 (Cyril of Jerusalem, *Procatechesis*, 14; see M. Slusser, "Reading Silently in Antiquity," *JBL* 111 [1992]: 499). F. D. Gilliard's 1993 article, however, successfully challenged the notion that reading aloud was an *exclusive* practice in Western antiquity, showing that silent reading was not so rare as Achtemeier would have it. He had no wish, however, to challenge the view that reading aloud was the *predominant* practice ("More Silent Reading in Antiquity: *Non Omne Verbum Sonabat,"* *JBL* 112 [1993]: 689–94, and see also literature cited there).

There is another level, however, at which written texts were experienced within a context of orality: often written texts *were not even present in the process of their delivery*, i.e., orators, politicians, traditionists and the like depended upon their memory for the delivery of the content of written texts.[33] Written texts thus not only originated with the spoken word (point 'a'), and were written to be read aloud (point 'b'), but also were experienced in a context of orality, often even in the absence of the written text (point 'c').

In conclusion, one can say with Hearon that ancient texts available for scholarly scrutiny today are "written remains" of texts "that began in oral expression and were actualized in performance."[34] Today they may function mainly as artifacts to be read silently and in isolation, but in their original context they were part of a social web of orality and literacy with no clearly defined boundaries between them, in which they "enjoyed an essentially oral cultural life."[35] Both the Jesus tradition and the works of

---

[33] Carr, *Writing on the Tablet*, 4–8; Jaffee, *Torah in the Mouth*, 26–27; Assmann, *Religion and Cultural Memory*, 73–75, 86; Horsley, "A Prophet Like Moses and Elijah," 170–71; Park, *Mark's Memory Resources*, 63–64; Rhoads, "Biblical Performance Criticism," 160. As noted by W. Shiner, "the cultural ideal for the oral delivery was in most cases performance without a text" (*Proclaiming*, 112); for a discussion of the role of memorization in the delivery of texts see ibid., 103–25; idem, "Oral Performance," 51–54. In the case of ancient Greece scholars are increasingly coming to recognize that not only Homer, but also "the rest of Greek literature was heard rather than read, presented and transmitted orally *even if a written text existed*" (Thomas, *Oral Tradition*, 2, emphasis added, see also the literature cited there in n. 2; and see also idem, *Literacy and Orality*, 4).

[34] H. E. Hearon, "The Implications of Orality for Studies of the Biblical Text," in *Performing the Gospel* (ed. Horsley, Draper, and Foley), 6; see also idem, "The Interplay between Written and Spoken Word in the Second Testament as Background to the Emergence of Written Gospels," *OrTr* 25 (2010): 57–74.

[35] Jaffee, *Torah in the Mouth*, 124; idem, "Writing and Rabbinic Oral Tradition," 144; on the interpenetration of orality and literacy see further both works by Jaffee in their entirety, and also L. Alexander, "Living Voice," 231–37, 244–45; D. L. Balch, "The Canon: Adaptable and Stable, Oral and Written: Critical Questions for Kelber and Riesner," *Forum* 7 (1991): 190–92; Carr, *Writing on the Tablet*, 6–7, 27–30, 71–77, 95–99, 132–33, 177–86, 287–88, and passim; Gamble, *Books and Readers*, 28–32; Horsley, "Emergence of the Gospel of Mark," 97–99, 101–4; W. H. Kelber, "The History of the Closure of Biblical Texts," *OrTr* 25 (2010): 116–18; idem, *Oral and Written*, xxi–xxiii; A. Kirk, "Memory, Scribal Media, and the Synoptic Problem," in *New Studies in the Synoptic Problem: Oxford Conference, April 2008: Essays in Honour of Christopher M. Tuckett* (ed. P. Foster et al.; BETL 239; Leuven: Peeters, 2011), 460–66; Park, *Mark's Memory Resources*, 43–70, 60–62; Rhoads, "Biblical Performance Criticism," 159–62; V. K. Robbins, "Writing as a Rhetorical Act in Plutarch and the Gospels," in *Persuasive Artistry: Studies in New Testament Rhetoric in Honor of George A. Kennedy* (ed. D. F. Watson; JSNTSup 50; Sheffield: JSOT Press, 1991), 145–68; idem, "Progymnastic Rhetorical Composition and Pre-Gospel Traditions: A New Approach," in *The Synoptic Gos-*

the Apostolic Fathers – the twin foci of this study – were at home in this context. To understand these texts and the tradition they contain one must view them in terms of the ongoing interplay between orality and literacy that characterized their wider milieu.[36]

3.3 Markers of Orality: Oral Indicators in a Written Medium

The approach to Jesus tradition adopted here arises directly from the above considerations regarding the interplay between orality and literacy in late Western antiquity. This approach focuses on the dynamics surrounding why oral traditions were preserved, how they were retained and transmitted (i.e., their acquisition by a traditionist as well as their performance), the elements of which they were composed, and the impact of their performance upon an audience.[37] In sum, this approach has to do with how oral tradition *functioned* in antiquity.

The method to be applied in this study is most indebted to a line of scholarship that goes back to the pioneering work of Milman Parry, as continued by Albert Lord.[38] Focusing initially on the Homeric epics, and test-

---

pels: Source Criticism and the New Literary Criticism (ed. C. Focant; BETL 110; Leuven: Leuven University Press and Peeters, 1993), 116–31; idem, "Interfaces of Orality," 125–46. The words of W. Kelber and P. Sanders serve well to summarize this point: "If the flourishing discipline of orality-scribality-memory studies has shown anything conclusively, it is that prior to the invention of print technology the verbal arts were an intricate interplay of oral and scribal verbalization, with manuscripts often serving as mere reference points for recitation and memorization" ("Oral Tradition in Judaism, Christianity, and Islam: Introduction," *OrTr* 25 [2010]: 3).

[36] Achtemeier describes the culture of late Western antiquity as one "of high residual orality which nevertheless communicated significantly by means of literary creations" ("*Omne Verbum*," 3). His use of the term "residual orality" is technically correct; see the discussion in Ong, *Presence*, 54–63; for the use of the term itself ("residual orality," "residually oral," "oral residue") see ibid., 57, 58; idem, *Interfaces*, 151; idem, *Orality and Literacy*, 41; cf. Uro, "*Thomas* and Oral," 12–19. However, to speak of a culture with "high residual orality" implies a *literate* culture with oral "leftovers." Late Western antiquity is more accurately thought of, however, as an *oral* society with restricted literacy in which the oral was given *preference* over the written. In this case one can speak of it as a "predominantly oral" culture (see above, p. 1, n. 1). With these comments I do not wish to drive a wedge between "oral" and "literate" cultures, but only to note that if one is to be given preference over the other, orality in this case should win out.

[37] This is in keeping with a relatively recent trend in folkloristic studies as a whole; see Alan Dundes' foreword to Foley's *Theory of Oral Composition*, ix.

[38] As noted in n. 2 on p. 2 above, in 1935 Parry's work was cut short, and was carried on by his assistant, Albert Lord. Of their works, the most relevant to the present work include Parry, *Making*; Lord, *Singer of Tales*; idem, "Memory," idem, "Perspectives"; idem, "Characteristics"; idem, "Nature"; idem, *Singer Resumes*.

ing their theory with fieldwork among living Serbo-Croatian singers of oral epics, together Parry and Lord sought to show that the *Iliad* and the *Odyssey* were the not the product of written composition, but transcriptions of epics that had been composed orally.[39] Noting such phenomena as the recurring combinations of nouns and epithets that fit standard slots, as well as the presence of typical scenes of familiar content and outline that are malleable enough to fit diverse contexts, Parry and Lord further argued that these works were not memorized but *composed in performance*.[40] These basic insights were the foundation of what was to be known variously as the "Parry-Lord Theory," the "Oral-Formulaic Theory," or simply the "Oral Theory," which revolutionized not only the field of Homeric studies, but also a number of other fields relating to ancient literatures and the study of orality and literacy in antiquity.[41] What began as the "Homeric Question" became, especially with the comparative work of Lord, the "Oral Traditional Question."[42]

Of most relevance to the present study is Parry and Lord's basic insight that oral features present in ancient written documents can be identified and studied fruitfully in light of parallels discernible in contemporary oral contexts. Lord himself applied the findings from his research among contemporary Serbo-Croatian epic singers to the comparative study of Old English, Old French, and ancient Greek epics, as well as to the canonical Gospels.[43] Lord's approach served as a model for the work of many other

---

[39] See J. M. Foley, "Oral Tradition and Its Implications," in *A New Companion to Homer* (ed. I. Morris and B. Powell; MnS 163; Leiden: Brill, 1997), 146–51.

[40] This held true for them both in the case of the Homeric works and in that of the Yugoslav poets; for full discussions see Foley, "Oral Tradition and Its Implications," 149–59; idem, *Oral-Formulaic Theory and Research*, 11–17; idem, *Theory of Oral Composition*, 19–56.

[41] The impact of the work of M. Parry is described by J. M. Foley as follows, "it was to become, if one may judge by the amount, intensity, and most of all the quality of debate it has inspired, the twentieth century's single most important critical perspective on Homer and a fundamental theoretical fulcrum in the study and comparison of numerous other ancient, medieval, and even contemporary literatures" (*Oral-Formulaic Theory and Research*, 11–12). This is impact was stated succinctly by J. Russo in the words, "It is inevitable that today no reader of Homer can fail to be in some sense a Parryist" ("The Formula," in *New Companion to Homer* [ed. Morris and Powell], 260). As for the work of A. Lord, as Foley states, "The impact of *The Singer of Tales* (1960) has ... been enormous. Suffice it to say that the book has held its position as the bible of Oral Theory for more than twenty-five years; *it will always be the single most important work in the field, because, simply put, it began the field as we know it*" (Foley, *Theory of Oral Composition*, 41; emphasis added).

[42] Foley, *Theory of Oral Composition*, 36.

[43] Lord, *Singer of Tales*, 198–202 (*Beowulf*); 202–6 (*La Chanson de Roland*); 207–20 (*Digenis Akritas*); idem, "Gospels."

scholars, who conducted studies that eventually encompassed traditions in over one hundred languages. These studies both furthered the work of Parry and Lord, and also provided a corrective to it on several fronts, the details of which lie beyond the purview of this study.[44] Most importantly, the work of Parry and Lord provided the stimulus for a whole generation of scholars to re-assess the inner workings of oral tradition. The work of these scholars, among whom we note especially John Miles Foley,[45] Jack Goody,[46] Eric Havelock,[47] and Walter J. Ong,[48] has transformed our understanding not only of how oral tradition functioned, but also of the wider sphere of the relationship between orality and literacy in antiquity.

One of the key insights arising from the work of these and other scholars is that, though oral traditions differ, and no given one will behave in a manner that is identical to another, they share a core set of common characteristics that sets them apart from written compositions. Identifying these characteristics within written texts points to the likelihood that said texts are oral-derived or contain orally conceived discourse. Walter Ong provides a helpful summary of these characteristics that are common across lines of time and culture in his work *Orality and Literacy*.[49] What follows is built upon a summary of Ong's treatment, updated and revised in conversation with other works.

One can recognize the likely presence of orally conceived discourse within written texts in that the communication will tend to be:

---

[44] Given that the present monograph is chiefly concerned not with the work of Parry and Lord itself, but with that of the scholars that built upon the foundation they laid, this is not the place to take up criticisms of Parry and Lord in detail. For this see discussions in Foley, *Oral-Formulaic Theory and Research*, 11–77 (the latter volume also contains an annotated bibliography of over 1800 books and articles related to the field pioneered by Parry and Lord, pp. 81–680); idem, *Theory of Oral Composition*, 57–93; idem, "Oral Tradition and Its Implications"; Adam Parry, Introduction to M. Parry, *Making*; Russo, "Formula"; M. Sale, "The Oral-Formulaic Theory Today," in *Speaking Volumes* (ed. Watson), 53–80.

[45] Foley, "Oral Theory"; idem, "Tradition-Dependent"; idem, *Oral-Formulaic Theory and Research*; idem, *Theory of Oral Composition*; idem, *Immanent Art*; idem, *Homer's Traditional Art*; idem, "What's In a Sign"; idem, *How to Read*; also his edited volumes: idem, ed., *Oral Traditional Literature*; idem, ed., *Oral Tradition in Literature*; idem, ed., *Comparative Research*; idem, ed., *Teaching*.

[46] Goody and Watt, "Consequences"; Goody, *Domestication*; idem, *Logic*; idem, *Interface*.

[47] Havelock, *Plato*; idem, *Literate Revolution*; idem, *Muse*.

[48] Ong, *Presence*; idem, *Interfaces*; idem, *Orality and Literacy*. Additional authors, as well as other works by the above-named authors, will be referenced in the footnotes that follow.

[49] Ong, *Orality and Literacy*, 37–77. See also the discussion of Ong's summary by Lord, "Characteristics."

3.3.1 Additive Rather than Subordinative

In place of the complex logical constructions with subordinate clauses that one finds in written compositions, in oral-derived texts one will tend to find phrases strung together and linked by additive or purposive connectives (e.g., "and then," "and next" or "for").[50] Certain aspects of meaning that in written composition are conveyed by the more complex linguistic structure, in oral communication are communicated by the existential contexts surrounding discourse.[51] Oral communication adheres to "the idea unit, or tone group, or intonation unit" as its norm, based on the amount of information that can be held in short term memory, rather than the complete sentence which is the norm for written language.[52] Each "idea unit" is added on to the one preceding it, and is enhanced by the one following it, to communicate complex information in a *flow of discourse* rather than a self-contained complex syntactical unit (the latter being more at home in written composition).[53]

3.3.2 Aggregative Rather than Analytic

Similar to the above point, the components of orally based communication tend to be clusters rather than integers – "parallel terms or phrases or clauses, antithetical terms or phrases or clauses, epithets." This dynamic reflects in part the role of formulas in enabling memory.[54]

---

[50] E. Havelock, "Oral Composition in the *Oedipus Tyrannus* of Sophocles," *NLH* 16 (1984): 183; J. A. Draper, "Recovering Oral Performance from Written Text in Q," in *Whoever Hears* (by Horsley with Draper), 190–91; Park, *Mark's Memory Resources*, 79–80.

[51] Ong, *Orality and Literacy*, 37–38.

[52] Bakker, "How Oral," 38–39, and see the Homeric example he gives on pp. 40–41. Bakker clarifies that he does not mean to imply that orally conceived discourse does not contain complete sentences, but rather that "in speech the sentence is not a *norm*. In other words, a written discourse in our sense is badly flawed when it does not attain acceptable sentential syntax; a spoken discourse, on the other hand, may still work when its speaker does *not* arrive at sentential structure. In fact, such a structure may well not be in the speaker's interests at all: it may be too complex to grasp by someone who has to listen on the spot, and who cannot review the construction in its entirety on the printed page" (ibid., 38).

[53] See the examples given by Bakker in "How Oral," 42–43.

[54] Ong, *Orality and Literacy*, 38–39, quote taken from p. 38. Ong further notes, "Oral folk prefer, especially in formal discourse, not the soldier, but the brave soldier; not the princess, but the beautiful princess; not the oak, but the sturdy oak. Oral expression thus carries a load of epithets and other formulary baggage which high literacy rejects as cumbersome and tiresomely redundant because of its aggregative weight" (ibid., p. 38).

3.3.3 Redundant or "Copious"

Redundancy is important within an oral medium, as a hearer may quickly forget something said only once.[55] Repetition and circling back provide a source of continuity for both speaker and hearer in orally based discourse, enabling the latter to move forward in the absence of the linear continuity that accompanies the use of written texts. Redundancy thus enables the hearer to better grasp the information being conveyed, in a manner similar to the re-reading of parts of a text in a chirographic context to re-connect with the flow of the argument.[56] In addition, oft-repeated formulas or patterns may function as a shorthand referent to complex ideas that are transparent to one familiar with the tradition being performed, a "traditional referentiality" that "enables an extremely economical transaction of meaning."[57] Furthermore, what may look like mere redundancy to one accustomed to the norms of written composition may be explained in an oral context by the concept of *goal* or *preview*.[58] As explained by Bakker, "In spoken discourse, something can be said, not as information in its own right, but with an eye on a situation to be reached in due course: a detail may be stated in order to be explained, which will lead the listener to a goal that was indicated earlier."[59]

3.3.4 Conservative or Traditionalist

In primary oral cultures, the process for passing down tradition is heavily geared toward conservation, because knowledge that is not continually re-

---

[55] Draper, "Recovering Oral Performance," 184.

[56] Ong, *Orality and Literacy*, 39–41; Park, *Mark's Memory Resources*, 80–81.

[57] Foley, "What's In a Sign," 6–7, 11 (quote from p. 11). Foley gives the example of Homer's use of "swift-footed Achilleus": "by appealing not to a conventional lexicon but to traditional usage, [it] simply summons the whole of the named figure to center-stage. Achilleus need not be sprinting or even poised to run .... Homer's formulaic names for his *dramatis personae* refer to the tradition at large, economically conjuring the actors, script and résumé in hand" (ibid., 7); cf. the comments on the "artificial" forms of the Homeric style in Bakker, *Poetry in Speech*, 13–14. In the Jesus tradition, "the image of being gathered for a banquet in the kingdom with 'Abraham, Isaac, and Jacob' or that of 'Gehenna' or 'Gomorrah' would evoke a ... wide and deep meaning from Israelite tradition" (R. A. Horsley, "Recent Studies of Oral-Derived Literature and Q," in *Whoever Hears* [by Horsley with Draper], 170).

[58] See Bakker, "How Oral," 43.

[59] Bakker, "How Oral," 43. E. Havelock states similarly, "Though the narrative syntax is paratactic – the basic conjunction being 'and then', and 'next' – the narrative is not linear but turns back on itself in order to assist the memory to reach the end by having it anticipated somehow at the beginning" ("Oral Composition," 183); on redundancy in oral tradition see further Mournet, *Oral Tradition*, 174–79.

cycled orally is lost.[60] The advent of writing in any given culture to a certain extent changes this dynamic, in that written texts provide a more durable repository of at least parts of a tradition (though even texts may be "lost" if they cease to be actualized by their oral use).[61] In cultures that remain predominantly oral,[62] however, the traditioning process remains heavily geared toward conservation, in that members of traditional cultures are oriented towards the past.[63] In these cultures, when traditionists incorporate new elements in performing a tradition, originality does not consist in inventing new stories, but (and more on this below) in grappling with how traditional themes and formulas can best be reshuffled to adapt them to new situations.[64] (This results in our next point below: variability within stability.) Study of the artistic expression that captures the traditionist's originality must go hand in hand with attention to the tradition they have

---

[60] Ong, *Orality and Literacy*, 41–42; idem, *Interfaces*, 151 (where he refers to Havelock, *Plato*, 36–60); Henige, *Oral Historiography*, 5; Park, *Mark's Memory Resources*, 73–78; Thomas, *Literacy and Orality*, 113–17. It is difficult for members of our chirographic societies to value the conservative role of traditionists in primary oral cultures: as Ong notes, conservation of knowledge is now done for the most part in writing, which frees the mind from its need to memorize and opens up mental space for innovation and speculation; value is no longer placed on the "wise old men and women" who repeat the past, but on the young who discover new things (*Orality and Literacy*, 41).

[61] Kelber, *Oral and the Written*, xxiv; Kirk, "Memory, Scribal Media," 460–66; Hearon, "Implications of Orality," 6; see further the discussion of the interpenetration of orality and literacy in antiquity in sec. 3.2 above.

[62] "Predominantly oral" is used here in the sense discussed in sec. 3.2 above, to refer to societies with a literate minority in which people (even those who *belong to* the literate minority) continue to conduct most of the activities of their daily lives on the basis of orality.

[63] B. Schwartz, "Christian Origins: Historical Truth and Social Memory," in *Memory, Tradition, and Text* (ed. Kirk and Thatcher), 46; Assmann, *Religion and Cultural Memory*, 114–15; Kelber, "Works of Memory," 234; Carr, *Writing on the Tablet*, 10-11 and n. 26; J. K. Olick, "Products, Processes, and Practices: A Non-Reificatory Approach to Collective Memory," *BTB* 36 (2006): 13; and see further below under point 3.3.10, entitled "Socially Identified."

[64] Ong, *Orality and Literacy*, 41–42, 58–60, and see also Havelock, *Muse*, 11–13, 54–62. As Andersen notes, the face-to-face context of oral communication necessitates this reshuffling, "It is in the nature of [oral] tradition to be adaptive. It is shaped within a parallelogram of forces, between sender and receiver, between inherited elements and present demands" ("Oral Tradition," 18–20, quote taken from p. 20). As noted by Thomas, the element of improvisation both in Homer and in the Yugoslav bards with whom they worked was overemphasized in Parry and Lord's model. The evidence of the material itself would indicate that at least certain portions were probably worked on beforehand and committed in large part to memory (see her *Literacy and Orality*, 36–44, and literature cited there).

captured in their rendition; it is at this intersection that one will find what the traditionist is communicating.[65]

3.3.5 Both Variable and Stable

One of the hallmarks of the retention and transmission of oral tradition is variability within stability; provisionally stated, without stability, it would not be "tradition,"[66] without variability, it would not be "oral."[67] Tradition-ists have methods for preserving the stability of the tradition, as we will see below under "Mnemonically Constructed," but the obsession with ex-actness in repetition that has become characteristic of chirographic socie-ties is both foreign and impracticable in oral societies. In the words of W. Kelber, "A text outlasts the act of writing, but spoken words exist only in the act of speaking and in the memories of hearers."[68] So in the case of oral tradition there is neither a "single, original, correct saying," nor a fixed model available against which to compare a performance for verbatim rep-lication.[69] As will be noted later in the present chapter, the degree of vari-ability and stability will depend on the type of tradition in question. Those such as liturgical traditions that rely on rote memory will vary little if at all, while traditions that utilize mnemonics more as aids to composition in performance will tend to show stability in meaning with variability in wording.[70]

---

[65] Foley, "What's In a Sign," 12–13, 18–19, 25; see also Kelber, "Jesus and Tradi-tion," 148–51.

[66] See Lord, *Singer of Tales*, 220.

[67] These statements are provisional because, as we will see further below (sec. 3.3.10, entitled "Socially Identified"), the variability of oral tradition is not only associated with its orality, but also with its identity as tradition: tradition must be variable in order to remain viable or relevant; see Foley, "Bard's Audience," 96.

[68] Kelber, "Jesus and Tradition," 147.

[69] Kelber, "Jesus and Tradition," 150–51; elsewhere Kelber states succinctly, "From its very inception, ... and beginning with Jesus the oral performer himself, the so-called Synoptic tradition is constituted by plural originals, and not by original singularity .... The heart and ethos of oral tradition is multiple originality" ("Orality, Scribality, and Oral-Scribal Interfaces: Jesus – Tradition – Gospels: Review and Present State of Re-search," paper presented at the SNTS Annual Meeting, Halle, Germany, 6–9 August 2005). See also idem, *Oral and Written*, 29–30; idem, "Generative Force of Memory," 17; idem, "History of the Closure," 121–22; Finnegan, *Oral Poetry*, 65; Draper, "Cove-nantal Discourse," 72; Dunn, *New Perspective on Jesus*, 50–51; idem, "Remembering Jesus," 195; Lord, *Singer of Tales*, 100–101, who states regarding oral tradition that "each performance is 'an' original, if not 'the' original" (p. 101).

[70] So variability is no enemy of memory: "Mnemonics allow for, indeed thrive on, performative inventiveness in social contextuality" (Kelber, "Generative Force of Mem-ory," 18). On variability within stability see further Bauckham, *Jesus and the Eyewit-nesses*, 259–60, 286–87; idem, "Transmission of the Gospel Traditions," 383–84; idem,

3.3.6 Close to the Human Lifeworld

The ability to create abstract, analytical categories to organize knowledge is dependent on writing. Knowledge in an oral context is conceptualized and communicated in a manner that remains closely related to the familiar, everyday world of human activity. So, e.g., inventories of people, things or skills are embedded in a narrative context, rather than itemized abstractly in lists.[71]

3.3.7 Agonistically Toned

This characteristic derives in part from the previous point, "By keeping knowledge embedded in the human lifeworld, orality situates knowledge within a context of struggle." Oral forms such as riddles and proverbs (or bartering) do not serve simply to communicate neutral ideas, but to engage others in a verbal contest. The agonistic tendency of oral cultures is also evidenced in such things as detailed descriptions of violence and other forms of aggressive physical behavior, and in effusive expressions of praise.[72]

3.3.8 Empathetic and Participatory

Writing creates an objective distance between the knower and that which is known that does not exist in the transmission of oral tradition. In the latter, "learning or knowing means achieving close, empathetic, communal identification with the known."[73] This empathetic identification, according to Havelock, enabled both the traditionist and his or her listeners to remember: "You threw yourself into the situation of Achilles, you identified with

---

"Eyewitnesses and Critical History: A Response to Jens Schröter and Craig Evans," *JSNT* 31 (2008): 229; Dunn, "Altering," 160–69; idem, "Eyewitnesses and the Oral Jesus Tradition," 87, 90, 92–94, 99–100; idem, *Jesus Remembered*, 210–38, 249, passim; idem, *New Perspective on Jesus*, 51–53; idem, "On Faith and History, and Living Tradition: In Response to Robert Morgan and Andrew Gregory," *ExpTim* 116 (2004–05): 17; idem, "Remembering Jesus," 196–97; Finnegan, *Oral Poetry*, 65; Havelock, *Plato*, 92, 147, 185; Iyasere, "African Oral Tradition," 171–72; Kelber, "Jesus and Tradition," 150–51; idem, *Oral and Written*, 28–34; Kirk, "Memory Theory," 829–30; Lord, *Singer of Tales*, 100–101, 220; Milavec, "Synoptic Tradition," 466; Mournet, *Oral Tradition*, 179–190; B. Peabody, *The Winged Word: A Study in the Technique of Ancient Greek Oral Composition as Seen Principally through Hesiod's Works and Days* (Albany: State University of New York Press, 1975), 96; Vansina, *Oral Tradition*, 48–54.

[71] Ong, *Orality and Literacy*, 42–43; Havelock, *Plato*, 176–80; idem, *Muse*, 58–59; Park, *Mark's Memory Resources*, 78–79.

[72] Ong, *Orality and Literacy*, 43–45, 68–71, quote taken from p. 44.

[73] Ong, *Orality and Literacy*, 45–46, quote taken from p. 45, where Ong refers to Havelock, *Plato*, 145–46.

his grief or his anger. You yourself became Achilles and so did the reciter to whom you listened."[74] The participatory aspect can also be seen in the role of the audience in the performance of a tradition: not only the performer, but also the audience must be fluent in the traditional idiom in order to enable the transmission of the tradition with the necessary economy of words. In this process both performer and audience, "leave behind the general-purpose standard language in favor of a highly focused set of linguistic integers that generations of [performers] and audiences have endowed with metonymic meaning – the spoken part standing for the unspoken (and unspeakable) whole."[75] This active role of the audience in an oral context approximates the role of intertextuality in a chirographic context. Our attempts today to identify intertextual echoes in ancient texts and fill in their meanings amounts to building our own fluency in the ancient traditional idiom, and in this sense amounts to joining the ancient audience in their active role.

3.3.9 Mnemonically Constructed

The preservation of the integrity of traditions in an oral context depends on the ability of traditionists to accurately recall them.[76] The latter requires a balance between both (a) *remembering* and (b) *memorizing* in a traditionist's preparation: (a) in the public performance of a tradition, "for the performer and the audience alike, the emphasis is on the *experience* of the performance event."[77] A well-rounded performer of a tradition would not memorize the narrative and imagery-related aspects of a tradition being received (such as the parables within the Jesus tradition), but rather remember with the "mind's eye" his or her experience of them in perform-

---

[74] Havelock, *Plato*, 45; I owe this reference to Dewey, "Oral-Aural Event," 152.

[75] Foley, "Bard's Audience," 101, and see also ibid., 97–105. In the cited passage Foley speaks of a "bard" rather than a "performer," but clarifies in the introduction to the cited article that he means "bard" in a very inclusive sense of all traditional oral performers (p. 93).

[76] Ong argues that in societies with a high degree of orality "*Serious thought is intertwined with memory systems,*" and continues, "In an oral culture, to think through something in non-formulaic, non-patterned, non-mnemonic terms, even if it were possible, would be a waste of time, for such thought, once worked through, could never be recovered with any effectiveness, as it could be with the aid of writing" (*Orality and Literacy*, 34, 35; emphasis his). One should not be too quick, however, to assume the reliability and long-term accuracy of *all* memories in ancient oral societies, an assumption which in the words of Henige is "largely untested and untestable" (*Oral Historiography*, 67). As R. Thomas notes, members of oral societies "do have to have better devices or mechanisms for remembering, which is an entirely different thing" (*Oral Tradition*, 4).

[77] Dewey, "Oral-Aural Event," 151; see also Vansina, *Oral Tradition*, 34–39.

ance.[78] In witnessing the performance of the tradition by another traditionist, these aspects of the tradition would have become imprinted on the visual memory of the receiving traditionist via the imagination in a manner
similar to personal experience. In passing on the tradition, the receiving
traditionist would imitate not only words but also gestures and other elements of body language, as well as emotions, intonation, pauses, rhythm
and the like – all part of the "organic memory" of the received performance that are an integral part of its remembering.[79] (b) The dialogue and
sayings material within the tradition, however, require the exercise of
memorization. Memorized verbal material and remembered images and
gestures interact with each other in the process of recall: verbal cues may
bring an image to memory, while images or gestures serve to evoke related
information.[80] Mnemonic devices aid in every aspect of this process of re-

---

[78] See E. Minchin, "Similes in Homer: Image, Mind's Eye, and Memory," in *Speaking Volumes* (ed. Watson), 26, 38, who refers to A. Paivio's treatment of "pictureable"
material in "The Mind's Eye in Arts and Science," *Poetics* 12 (1983): 6. Minchin also
speaks of the poet offering "a commentary on the scene which runs in the cinema of his
mind's eye" (ibid., 44); cf. Havelock, *Plato*, 187–89; Kirk, "Memory Theory," 830–32;
Vansina, *Oral Tradition*, 43; E. J. Bakker, "Discourse and Performance: Involvement,
Visualization and 'Presence' in Homeric Poetry," *ClAnt* 12 (1993): 17–18, who speaks
(among other things) of epic narrators participating as eyewitnesses in the scenes they
visualize; A. Le Donne, *The Historiographical Jesus: Memory, Typology, and the Son of
David* (Waco, Tex.: Baylor University Press, 2009), 55, who discusses the narrativity of
visual images as both mnemonic and distortive. For a treatment of this phenomenon from
the perspective of cognitive psychology see D. C. Rubin, *Memory in Oral Traditions:
The Cognitive Psychology of Epic, Ballads, and Counting-out Rhymes* (Oxford: Oxford
University Press, 1995), 39–64, esp. pp. 54–56, 59–63. These insights into imagery-
related approaches to preservation of tradition should give one pause in attributing imagery-related elements in the Gospels, such as vivid imagery, irrelevant detail, and point
of view, to the recollective memory of eye witnesses (see Bauckham, *Jesus and the Eyewitnesses*, 332–33, 342–44); they may just as well be the product of mnemonic technique.

[79] Cf. B. Antomarini, "The Acoustical Prehistory of Poetry," *NLH* 35 (2004): 357–58.
On the distinction between "remembering" and "memorizing" cf. Kelber, "Oral-Scribal-
Memorial Arts," 253.

[80] Minchin, "Similes in Homer," 27, 48, 50. A common mnemonic technique in antiquity was the method of loci, in which each element to be remembered was associated
with a different location that could then be traversed with the mind's eye to produce recall; for full treatments see J. P. Small, *Wax Tablets of the Mind: Cognitive Studies of
Memory and Literacy in Classical Antiquity* (London: Routledge, 1997), 81–116; F. A.
Yates, *The Art of Memory* (Chicago: University of Chicago Press, 1966), 1–26; see also
Rubin, *Memory in Oral Traditions*, 46–48; W. H. Kelber, "Incarnations, Remembrances,
and Transformations of the Word," in *Time, Memory, and the Verbal Arts* (ed. Weeks and
Hoogestraat), 115–16. B. Peabody notes, however, that remembering need not imply
memorization: "Bards remember what they experience. The repetition of blocks of verses
that occurs sporadically through the epos is best explained as the memory of passages

call. The most basic mnemonic devices that are found across the various genres of oral tradition involve "alliteration, assonance, rhyme, tonal repetition, parallelism, and rhythm."[81] Other mnemonic devices often encountered include the grouping together of sayings with a common theme, formalized speech patterns, standardized formats for describing items,[82] messages put to music, dramatization, rituals in which the tradition is enacted, and ritualized processes for transmitting the tradition.[83]

3.3.10 Socially Identified

Not all oral traditions are preserved, but only those that remain socially relevant and acceptable.[84] Some traditions that become socially obsolete

---

sung in former times – passages not memorized so that they can be repeated, but just remembered" (*Winged Word*, 214).

[81] Draper, "Recovering Oral Performance," 184; see also J. Assmann, "Form as a Mnemonic Device: Cultural Texts and Cultural Memory," in *Performing the Gospel* (ed. Horsley, Draper, and Foley), 72–73. W. Kelber points to the abundance of "alliteration, appositional equivalence, proverbial and aphoristic diction, contrasts and antitheses, synonymous, antithetical and tautological parallelisms, rhythmic structures, and so forth" in the Jesus tradition, all of which are "earmarks of mnemonics" ("Works of Memory," 233).

[82] On this see especially E. Minchin, "Describing and Narrating in Homer's *Iliad*," in *Signs of Orality* (ed. Mackay), 49–64.

[83] Ong, *Orality and Literacy*, 33–36, 64–65; see also Assmann, *Religion and Cultural Memory*, 105–10, 139–54; idem, "Form as a Mnemonic Device," 70–72; Bauckham, *Jesus and the Eyewitnesses*, 280–87; Draper, "Recovering Oral Performance," 184; Goody and Watt, "Consequences," 31; Kelber, *Oral and Written*, 26–28; idem, "Memory's Desire," 57; A. Kirk, "Social and Cultural Memory," in *Memory, Tradition, and Text* (ed. Kirk and Thatcher), 8–9; E. Minchin, "Rhythm and Regularity in Homeric Composition: Questions in the *Odyssey*," in *Oral Performance and Its Context* (ed. C. J. Mackie; MnS 248; OLAG 5; Leiden: Brill, 2004), 21–48; Olick, "Products, Processes, and Practices," 12; Vansina, *Oral Tradition*, 16, 42–47. On the role of ritual in tradition, S. Byrskog speaks of the Passover in Judaism and the Eucharist in Christianity as, "among other things, commemorative rituals, where gestures, mimicry, movements, behaviour and other paralinguistic means of communication – things that could be seen – interacted with what was communicated by word of mouth" (*Story as History*, 107), and G. M. Keightley describes how rituals such as baptism and the eucharist function as "storehouses of the past," providing a context for the reinforcement of the past in collective memory ("Christian Collective Memory and Paul's Knowledge of Jesus," in *Memory, Tradition, and Text* [ed. Kirk and Thatcher], 136–47, quote from p. 137).

[84] Kelber, *Oral and Written*, 24; Kelber goes on to clarify, "This is not to dismiss the possibility that a group retained words precisely because they were alien or even offensive to its experience. The very oddness of the message could render it unforgettable" (loc. cit.). This "social identification" is basically what is referred to as the "homeostatic" nature of oral traditions by Goody and Watt ("Consequences," 30–35), Ong (*Orality and Literacy*, 46–49), and Park (*Mark's Memory Resources*, 72–73), but I have chosen to follow Kelber (*Oral and Written*, 23–27) in his use of "social identification" as it better cap-

are simply lost, while others are reinterpreted to continue to function in light of present realities.[85] This characteristic of oral traditions balances out the previous one; i.e., that oral traditions are shaped in such a way as to enable memory ("mnemonically constructed") does not imply that all traditions are remembered. It also accounts for one of the types of variability that is discernible within a tradition's stability: in performing a tradition, the goal is not simply or only to reproduce the tradition itself, but also to bring out its relevance for the present. One performance will differ from another in reflecting different circumstances upon which the tradition is brought to bear, and in this way the tradition remains a *living* tradition.[86] The constant interplay between memory and present relevance in the performance of tradition continually generates ongoing syntheses, containing both past and present, without either one canceling out the other.

---

tures the dynamic in question. The term "homeostatic" as used by Goody and Watt is misunderstood by W. Kullmann, who takes them to mean that "in non-literate societies historical traditions do not exist. Older traditions are displaced when they are no longer relevant to present life" (W. Kullmann, "Homer and Historical Memory," in *Signs of Orality* [ed. Mackay], 98). Goody and Watt did not hold, however, that *all* traditions were displaced; some remained, i.e., those that continued to be useful. They were careful to note forces that "may shield at least part of the content of memory from the transmuting influence of the immediate pressures of the present" ("Consequences," 31). See further the discussion of homeostasis in Vansina, *Oral Tradition*, 120–23.

[85] On the above, in addition to Ong, *Orality and Literacy*, 46–49, 66–67, see Bakker, "Discourse and Performance," 2; Foley, "Bard's Audience," 96; Goody and Watt, "Consequences," 28–34; Havelock, "Oral Composition," 194–95; Kelber, "Memory's Desire," 79–80; Thomas, *Literacy and Orality*, 108–9; idem, *Oral Tradition*, 6; Vansina, *Oral Tradition*, 16. It is the tension between this social identification of oral traditions and their conservative or traditionalist nature mentioned earlier that is captured in the words of J. Vansina: oral traditions "are the representation of the past in the present. One cannot deny either the past or the present in them. To attribute their whole content to the evanescent present as some sociologists do, it to mutilate tradition; it is reductionistic. To ignore the impact of the present as some historians have done, is equally reductionistic. Traditions must always be understood as reflecting both past and present in a single breath." But in the final analysis, "All messages have some intent which has to do with the present, otherwise they would not be told in the present and the tradition would die out" (*Oral Tradition*, xii, 92). The social identification of tradition has contributed to the notion that "primitive cultures" did not experience much change over the centuries, but this notion is more a reflection of the non-existence of written materials one could use to compare an earlier form of the culture with a later; for the most part, only what justifies the present form of the society has survived (see Thomas, *Literacy and Orality*, 6–7).

[86] Kelber, "Generative Force of Memory," 21; idem, "Jesus and Tradition," 150; idem, "History of the Closure," 122. Elsewhere Kelber states, in relation to the selectivity of memory, "forgetfulness, far from being an insignificant appendix to tradition, is an essential correlate of remembering" ("Memory's Desire," 79–80). For an example of the same oral tradition presented differently so as to apply to two different audiences that were contemporaries of each other see Iyasere, "African Oral Tradition," 171–72.

The field of study variously termed "social memory," "cultural memory" or "collective memory" provides valuable insights into the symbiotic relationship between inherited tradition from the past and the social forces that act upon the "remembering" community in the present.[87] Maurice Halbwachs (1877–1945), usually regarded as the "father" of the discipline, understood social memory as the joint reconstruction of the past by the members of a group or society in accordance with ideas and concerns of the present.[88] To view memory in terms of "reconstruction," however, is to overemphasize the creative part of memory as it responds to the present context, with a concomitant loss of connection to the past (a tendency reminiscent of the overemphasis on the *Sitz im Leben* within form criticism).[89] As argued by Barry Schwartz, more room should be allowed in our

---

[87] As noted by A. Le Donne, M. Halbwachs (on whom see what follows) made a distinction between "collective memory" and "social memory," reserving the latter for the influence of group ideologies upon individual memories, but the terms "social," "collective" and "cultural" are today used fairly interchangeably in memory studies; see A. Le Donne, "Theological Memory Distortion in the Jesus Tradition: A Study in Social Memory Theory," in *Memory in the Bible and Antiquity: The Fifth Durham-Tübingen Research Symposium (Durham, September 2004)* (ed. L. T. Stuckenbruck, S. C. Barton, and B. G. Wold; WUNT 212; Tübingen: Mohr Siebeck, 2007), 165, n. 6. A. Kirk provides good introductions to the study of social memory in relation to early Christianity (and the relevant literature) in his "Social and Cultural Memory," 1–24 and "Memory Theory," 809–42. For an introduction to the wider literature (prior to 1998), see J. K. Olick and J. Robbins, "Social Memory Studies: From 'Collective Memory' to the Historical Sociology of Mnemonic Practices," *ARS* 24 (1998): 105–40.

[88] So for Halbwachs, "[T]he past does not recur as such ... the past is not preserved but is reconstructed on the basis of the present. ... Collective frameworks are ... the instruments used by the collective memory to reconstruct an image of the past which is in accord, in each epoch, with the predominant thoughts of the society" (*On Collective Memory*, 39–40). In sum, according to Halbwachs "collective memory reconstructs its various recollections to accord with contemporary ideas and preoccupations" (ibid., 224). How individuals and groups preserve memories are for Halbwachs one and the same problem, "the individual remembers by placing himself in the perspective of the group, ...[and] the memory of the group realizes and manifests itself in individual memories" (ibid., 40). For Halbwachs one should not confuse this preservation of memories with a "'resonance' of impressions" that will vary from individual to individual and may perdure for a long time (ibid., 40 n. 3; on the above see also idem, *The Collective Memory*, 44–49, 68–71).

[89] So Dunn critiques the contemporary social-memory school's "emphasis on the *creative*, rather than the *retentive* function of memory" (J. D. G. Dunn, "Social Memory and the Oral Jesus Tradition," in *Memory in the Bible and Antiquity* [ed. Stuckenbruck, Barton, and Wold], 180; emphasis in the original). Similarly A. Le Donne notes that the metaphor of reconstruction, "connotes an entity that has become disjointed and can be reassembled," and posits that the concept of "reinforcement" is more accurate: "In order for images associated with the past to make sense in the present state of mind, the localization process must reinforce memories with plausibility and integrity. Since the actual

understanding of social memory for the shaping of the present by the past, or "the continuity of memory" that is brought about in part by such stabilizing forces as the traditioning processes under consideration in the present book.[90] Schwartz notes that continuity of memory will be more pronounced in traditional societies, such as those that provided the context for early Christianity, than in today's Western culture. This is because "people of traditional societies ... orient themselves to the past and are encompassed by their memories and customs."[91] The traditioning process involved in the creation and transmission of oral tradition serves as a stabilizing factor in the concrete moments of interplay between the individual memories of traditionists on the one hand,[92] and present social forces that inform the performance of the tradition on the other, and finds

---

past cannot be conjured up to verify such reinforcements, the imagination is held in check by the combined memories of the social group of which it is a part" (*Historiographical Jesus*, 47–48). On form criticism and the *Sitz im Leben* see section 1.4.1 above.

[90] Schwartz, "Christian Origins," 45; see also the relevant statement by A. Kirk, "the fact that oral tradition is mnemonically configured is a warning against exaggerating its fluidity or underestimating a community's resolute dedication to remembering its past" ("Memory Theory," 839, see further ibid., 819–38; idem, "Social and Cultural Memory," 14–17; Vansina, *Oral Tradition*, 94–100). As noted by J. Assmann ("Collective Memory and Cultural Identity," *NGC* 65 [1995]: 128–29), Halbwachs considered memories that had crystallized so as to become objectified culture (texts, rites, and relatively stable oral tradition) no longer as memory, but as history. This builds a certain level of instability into Halbwach's very definition of memory. In Assmann's own view, objectified culture (to include stable non-written tradition) and communications standardized by ritual have "the structure of memory," and are essential to social memory (ibid., 128, 131). What is more, for Assmann (and he developed these ideas together with his wife Aleida Assmann) it is precisely the presence of these objectified cultural elements that distinguishes "cultural memory" (*kulturelle Gedächtnis*), essential for the continuity of a community's identity, from "communicative memory" (*kommunikative Gedachtnis*), which is based upon direct communication from those who personally experienced foundational events, contains a strong emotional component, and does not last beyond three generations (*Das kulturelle Gedächtnis*, 32, 50–56, 130–33; idem, *Religion and Cultural Memory*, 3–9, 24–25). As noted by A. Kirk, Assmann's model suffers from a certain ambiguity in dealing with oral tradition: while oral tradition can be considered an objectified cultural artifact – which would place it within cultural memory – it would be already present in the period of communicative memory ("Memory Theory," 840 n. 150).

[91] Schwartz, "Christian Origins," 46; see also the remarks along these lines under sec. 3.3.4 above, "Conservative or Traditionalist," and in Assmann, *Religion and Cultural Memory*, 114–15; Kelber, "Works of Memory," 234; Carr, *Writing on the Tablet*, 10-11 and n. 26; Olick, "Products, Processes, and Practices," 13.

[92] See Assmann's statements regarding the "specialization of the bearers of cultural memory" in his "Collective Memory and Cultural Identity," 131; also idem, *Das kulturelle Gedächtnis*, 49–50; idem, *Religion and Cultural Memory*, 105–6.

expression in the stability within variability that is one of the hallmarks of oral tradition.[93]

From the perspective of social memory studies, then, one can speak with Alan Kirk and Tom Thatcher of oral tradition as "the indissoluble, irreducibly complex artifact of the continual negotiation and semantic interpenetration of present social realities and memorialized pasts."[94] As Werner Kelber notes, the purpose of tradition understood in this way "is not transmission per se, but negotiation between ... a constitutive past and the contingencies of an ever-shifting present."[95] In effect, when viewed in terms of social memory, "the early Jesus traditions are growing out of a tension between two competing aspirations: retaining the words of Jesus so

---

[93] While one could conceivably view oral tradition as a sub-category of social memory studies, many studies on social memory deal with aspects of memory that do not involve a traditioning process, and so have at most only indirect bearing on the study of oral tradition. Here Le Donne's critique is also relevant, that "social memory theorists often confuse literal memory with memory as a metaphor for tradition" (*Historiographical Jesus*, 60, n. 92).

[94] A. Kirk and T. Thatcher, "Jesus Tradition and Social Memory," in *Memory, Tradition, and Text* (ed. Kirk and Thatcher), 33; the entirety of Kirk and Thatcher's essay sheds valuable light on the interplay between past and present in the Jesus tradition. On social memory and the Jesus tradition see further especially Le Donne, *Historiographical Jesus*, esp. 41–64; also Byrskog, "New Quest for the *Sitz im Leben*"; Dunn, "Social Memory"; S. Guijarro, "Cultural Memory and Group Identity in Q," *BTB* 37 (2007): 90–100; Horsley, "A Prophet Like Moses and Elijah," 172–83; C. Keith and T. Thatcher, "The Scar of the Cross: The Violence Ratio and the Earliest Christian Memories of Jesus," in *Jesus, the Voice, and the Text* (ed. Thatcher), 197–214; Kirk, "Memory," 166–72; idem, "Social and Cultural Memory"; idem, "Memory Theory"; idem, "Manuscript Tradition," 215–34; Le Donne, "Theological Memory Distortion"; J. Schröter, *Erinnerung an Jesu Worte: Studien zur Rezeption der Logienüberlieferung in Markus, Q und Thomas* (WMANT 76; Neukirchen-Vluyn: Neukirchener, 1997), 463–66; and essays by A. DeConick, A. J. Dewey, H. Hearon, R. Horsley, G. M. Keightley, A. Kirk, and T. Thatcher, in *Memory, Tradition, and Text* (ed. Kirk and Thatcher). See also the volume by R. Rodriguez, *Structuring Early Christian Memory: Jesus in Tradition, Performance and Text* (LNTS 407; New York and London: T&T Clark, 2010), of which I became aware after I had completed revision of the present manuscript for publication.

[95] Kelber, "Works of Memory," 239, who goes on to clarify that the "past" in this case is not "an objectively constituted past" but one that is itself already a "commemorated past." Cf. Olick, who speaks of memory as "a creation of living beings struggling to make meaning," and "a constitutive feature of sense making through time" ("Products, Processes, and Practices," 8). Assmann speaks of the relationship between past and present in social memory as follows, "Cultural memory ... is fixed in immovable figures of memory and stores of knowledge, but every contemporary context relates to these differently, sometimes by appropriation, sometimes by criticism, sometimes by preservation or transformation" ("Collective Memory and Cultural Identity," 130; see also idem, *Das kulturelle Gedächtnis*, 40–42).

as to transport them into the present, and re-forming these words of the past so as to make them address present circumstances."[96]

3.3.11 Situational Rather than Abstract [97]

Communication in an oral context tends to refer outside itself rather than be self-contained. So, e.g., the syllogism is out of place in oral cultures, since the solution to the problem it poses is to be sought in the logical out-working of the premises it contains.[98] In contrast, the riddle is at home in oral cultures, in that a person will draw on elements outside of the riddle itself (such as canniness and personal experience of the world) in order to solve it.[99]

---

[96] Kelber, "Generative Force of Memory," 21; see also Kirk, "Memory Theory," 816–20. In social memory studies, memory is not a database but a process (Olick and Robbins, "Social Memory Studies," 122), not a passive collection of material to be objectively accessed but "a process of encoding information, storing information, and strategically retrieving information" with "social, psychological, and historical influences at each point" (M. Schudson, "Dynamics of Distortion in Collective Memory," in *Memory Distortion* [ed. D. Schachter; Cambridge, Mass.: Harvard University Press, 1995], 348, cited in Le Donne, *Historiographical Jesus*, 50); on some of the overlap in this regard between the findings of social memory studies and the fields of physical and cognitive psychology of memory see Olick, "Collective Memory," 340–41.

[97] Ong applies this characteristic not just to communication in an oral context, but also to *members of oral cultures*, arguing that they tend to look to experience rather than pure logic to solve intellectual problems. He immediately clarifies, however, that to say that members of an oral culture seem "not to operate with formal deductive procedures," is not the same as saying that "they could not think or that their thinking was not governed by logic, but only that they would not fit their thinking into pure logical forms ... in practical matters no one operates in formally stated syllogisms" (*Orality and Literacy*, 52). J. Goody makes a similar point, "While writing helped to develop new types of formal logical operation, it did so initially by making explicit what was implicit in oral cultures, which were neither pre-logical nor yet alogical except in a very narrow sense of those words" (*Logic*, 182). R. Thomas thus oversimplifies the issue in her criticism, "how can we know ... that there was no logical thought before writing?" (*Literacy and Orality*, 20; cf. ibid., 26). Thomas' argument rings true, however, when she insists that writing and literacy will impact different cultures in different ways depending on their history, a point made throughout her *Literacy and Orality*.

[98] In keeping with their experience of riddles (see below), members of oral cultures will tend to look outside a syllogism to solve the problem it poses: e.g., "*In the Far North, where there is snow, all bears are white. Novaya Zembla is in the Far North and there is always snow there. What color are the bears?* Here is a typical response, 'I don't know. I've seen a black bear. I've never seen any others.... Each locality has its own animals'" (Ong, *Orality and Literacy*, 52–53, quoting from A. R. Luria, *Cognitive Development: Its Cultural and Social Foundations* [ed. M. Cole; trans. M. Lopez-Morillas and L. Solotaroff; Cambridge, Mass. and London: Harvard University Press, 1976], 108–9).

[99] See further Havelock, *Plato*, 180–82; Rubin, *Memory in Oral Traditions*, 60–61. Ong continues to develop this point, arguing that although "all conceptual thinking is to a

The above characteristics of orally conceived discourse, then, will guide the present study in determining the likelihood that the Jesus tradition in the Apostolic Fathers was derived from oral sources. Our basic approach will be to identify the presence or absence of these characteristics in the texts to be considered, as one indicator of whether the discourse in the texts was orally conceived or whether the discourse was composed directly in writing. For each text we will also take into consideration other factors unique to it, which will be noted in the course of the discussion.

Some of the above characteristics will also guide further discussion of individual sayings on such matters as their role within the community and the manner in which they may have been preserved by traditionists. Not all the characteristics described will be equally relevant for the purposes of this study, but we will draw on as many of them as are applicable in examining each saying. They will provide some basic guidelines for studying Jesus' sayings in the Apostolic Fathers specifically *as* oral tradition.

3.4 The Limits of Comparative Study

In applying the above criteria for identifying orality within written records, this study will seek to remain aware of the limits of comparative study. A recent trend in orality studies is to move away from broad statements regarding things that are true of all expressions of "the oral."[100] Instead, the recognition that there are "many different ways of being oral" is leading to an increased focus upon what might be unique characteristics of an expression of orality in any given setting.[101] In assessing oral Jesus tradition, one has to question the value of comparing it directly, for example, to the historical traditions in the *Iliad*, since the latter was first put to writing

---

degree abstract," oral cultures tend to use concepts "in situational, operational frames of reference that are minimally abstract in the sense that they remain close to the living human lifeworld" (*Orality and Literacy*, 49) So, e.g., when shown a drawing of a geometrical shape, members of predominantly oral cultures relate it to a familiar object – a square is identified as a door or a mirror – rather than by the abstract category of shape (ibid., 51, referring to Luria, *Cognitive Development*, 32–39; on all of the above see further Ong, *Orality and Literacy*, 49–57). Here it seems that Ong has crossed over from a discussion of the effects of literacy upon an oral culture to a discussion of the effects of a standard Western *education* upon those who had not experienced it. One can hardly expect that a person who has been brought up in a social setting that places little value on geometry would refer to a square object as a square.

[100] See Finnegan, "Response from an Africanist," 9–11.

[101] Ibid., 9; Finnegan suggests that we might need to begin using "multi-literacies" and "multi-oralities" rather than "literacy" and "orality" (idem, 14–15).

roughly five centuries after the happenings that are its subject matter.[102] In contrast, the period of transmission of the Jesus tradition prior to reaching the earliest Apostolic Fathers was only five-plus decades (possibly much less if, e.g., one dates the *Didache* in the mid-first century[103]), and for the latest between ten and thirteen decades.[104] Given this relatively brief time span, it would have been at least *possible* for the traditionists who passed on the Jesus tradition in the Apostolic Fathers to seek out an eyewitness, or people who were not more than one or two generations removed from an eyewitness, of what Jesus said and did.[105] This is but one example of how the Jesus tradition is very different from the type of historical traditions contained in one other oral-traditional source, but examples could be multiplied.

Another consideration arises from the relatively short period of transmission of the Jesus tradition: one of the key moments at which the integrity of a tradition is put in jeopardy is in its transmission from one traditionist to another.[106] The relatively short period of transmission of the Jesus tradition implies that these moments of transition would also have been relatively few, which has great implications for its integrity.

Along similar lines, though the characteristics of orality described above are meant to apply to oral tradition in general, one must keep in mind that not all oral traditions were created equal. Oral tradition in antiquity served various purposes, and was treated differently in keeping with these purposes. Within the early church, e.g., the form and content of litur-

---

[102] See the similar remarks in Bauckham, "Transmission of the Gospel Traditions," 381. On historical memory in the *Iliad* see Kullmann, "Historical Memory."

[103] As noted above (n. 87 on pp. 24–25), there are scholars who argue for a mid-first-century date for the *Didache*, such as Robinson, *Redating*, 322–27, esp. 327; Milavec, *Didache: Faith, Hope, and Life*, xii–xiii; idem, "When, Why and for Whom."

[104] This is true of the Apostolic Fathers in general unless one were to date *Diognetus*, as some have, to the early fourth century; see Olbricht, "Apostolic Fathers," 85. Of the Apostolic Fathers used in the present study the latest document would be *2 Clement*, which most likely was written between A.D. 100 and 140: W. H. C. Frend tentatively suggests A.D. 100 (*The Rise of Christianity* [Philadelphia: Fortress, 1984], 121,), while Ehrman suggests a date in the middle of the second century (*The Apostolic Fathers*, [LCL 24, 25; 2 vols.; Cambridge, Mass. and London: Harvard University Press, 2003], 1:159–60); most credible reconstructions of *2 Clement*'s date fall within those parameters, see the brief surveys in M. W. Holmes, *The Apostolic Fathers: Greek Texts and English Translations* (3rd ed.; Grand Rapids: Baker Academic, 2007), 133–35 and C. N. Jefford with K. J. Harder and L. D. Amezaga, Jr., *Reading the Apostolic Fathers: An Introduction* (Peabody, Mass.: Hendrickson, 1996), 121–22.

[105] On the relationship between autopsy and orality see the in-depth discussion by Byrskog in *Story as History*, 92–144. Byrskog's whole volume is an important investigation into the role of autopsy in the gospel tradition.

[106] Andersen, "Oral Tradition," 36.

gical tradition was especially tenacious, being guarded with special care due to its central role in transmitting and preserving the identity of the community.[107] The Apostle Paul appeals to this relatively fixed kind of liturgical tradition in relating the institution of the Lord's Supper in 1 Cor 11:23–25, as indicated in part by his use in v. 23 of the technical terms παραλαμβάνειν ("received") and παραδίδοναι ("passed on") to introduce his citation of Jesus' words.[108] The narrative traditions in the Synoptic Gospels provide a contrast to this fixed liturgical tradition, in the great deal of freedom the evangelists exercised in retelling the stories found in their sources (as can be seen in Matthew and Luke's use of Mark). As argued by James Dunn, this freedom in the case of certain narratives most likely reflects the evangelists' knowledge of these stories as retold orally in their own communities, or the refashioning of these stories by the evangelists themselves after the manner of an oral retelling.[109] The stories clearly remain the same stories, and yet the details that have been changed provide

---

[107] See, e.g., Audet, *Didachè*, 172–73, and ch. 7 in the present work on the liturgical tradition in *Did.* 8.2.

[108] See further Bauckham, *Jesus and the Eyewitnesses*, 264–65; Byrskog, "Transmission of the Jesus Tradition," 1482–83; J. D. G. Dunn, *The Theology of Paul the Apostle* (Grand Rapids: Eerdmans, 1998), 186; Gerhardsson, *Memory*, 290; Holtz, "Paul and Oral," 382; J. Jeremias, *The Eucharistic Words of Jesus* (trans. N. Perrin; NTL; London: SCM, 1966), 101; H. Riesenfeld, *The Gospel Tradition: Essays* (trans. E. M. Rowley and R. A. Kraft; Oxford: Blackwell/Philadelphia: Fortress, 1970), 15–18; S. Kim, *Paul and the New Perspective: Second Thoughts on the Origin of Paul's Gospel* (Grand Rapids: Eerdmans, 2002), 205; N. Walter, "Paul and the Early Christian Jesus-Tradition," in *Paul and Jesus: Collected Essays* (ed. A. J. M. Wedderburn; JSNTSup 37; Sheffield: JSOT Press, 1989), 54–55.

[109] See Dunn, *Jesus Remembered*, 210–24, esp. 222–23; idem, "On History, Memory and Eyewitnesses," 485–86; and J. F. McGrath's discussion of the alternatives open to Matthew and Luke as they composed their Gospels, in light of the likelihood that they had not only Mark to work with (assuming Markan priority), but also versions of much of what was found in Mark readily available as oral tradition ("Written Islands in an Oral Stream: Gospel and Oral Traditions," in *Jesus and Paul* [ed. Oropeza, Robertson, and Mohrmann, 3–12]. Cf. also A. Kirk's discussion of the ancient scribe as traditionist in "Manuscript Tradition," 220–25; and Carr, *Writing on the Tablet*, 280–81; Robbins, "Writing as a Rhetorical Act," 151–68; idem, "Progymnastic Rhetorical Composition," 116–46. See too, however, the critique by A. Gregory, who argues that Matthew and Luke may have taken a free approach to literary redaction, rather than taking an "oral" approach to their writing process in "An Oral and Written Gospel? Reflections on Remembering Jesus," *ExpTim* 116 (2004–05): 10–11, and Dunn's response to Gregory in "On Faith and History, and Living Tradition: In Response to Robert Morgan and Andrew Gregory," *ExpTim* 116 (2004–05): 18–19. Gregory addresses this topic at greater length in his article "What Is Literary Dependence?," in *New Studies in the Synoptic Problem* (ed. P. Foster, et al.), 87–114, esp. pp. 95–103.

insight into the overall flexibility within stability that characterized the oral transmission of these narrative traditions within early Christianity.

Based on their community use and setting, one may locate different types of oral traditions within early Christianity along two related continua, the first a scale of "formal" to "informal," and the second a scale of "controlled" to "uncontrolled":[110]

Graph 2: Setting and Control of Oral Tradition as Parallel Continua

(a) Setting of a tradition: formal ⟵⟶ informal
(b) Control upon a tradition: controlled ⟵⟶ uncontrolled

In general terms, the more formal the setting of a tradition (continuum 'a'), the more control will be exercised upon the transmission of that tradition (continuum 'b'), while in informal settings (continuum 'a') less control will be exercised (continuum 'b'). Early Christian liturgical tradition would be located near the left extreme of both continua, the formal setting of the liturgy providing a fairly strict control upon the form and content of the tradition (e.g., the Lord's Prayer in *Did.* 8.2). Near the right extreme of both continua one might find the type of material found in the fragments of Papias regarding Judas Iscariot:

But Judas went about in this world as a great model of impurity. He became so bloated in the flesh that he could not pass through a place that was easily wide enough for a wagon – not even his swollen head could fit. They say that his eyelids swelled to such an extent that he could not see the light at all; and a doctor could not see his eyes even with an optical device, so deeply sunken they were in the surrounding flesh. And his genitals became more disgusting and larger than anyone's; simply by relieving himself, to his wanton shame, he emitted pus and worms that flowed through his entire body. And they say that after he suffered numerous torments and punishments, he died on his own land, and that land has been, until now, desolate and uninhabited because of the stench. Indeed,

---

[110] The line of thinking for what follows arose from my reading of K. Bailey's "Informal," 34–54, and "Middle Eastern," 363–67 (cf. the comments in Bauckham, *Jesus and the Eyewitnesses*, 271–73; idem, "Transmission of the Gospel Traditions," 381). Though weaknesses have been identified in Bailey's work (see T. J. Weeden, "Kenneth Bailey's Theory of Oral Tradition: A Theory Contested by Its Evidence," *JSHJ* 7 [2009]: 3–43, and the reply by J. D. G. Dunn, "Kenneth Bailey's Theory of Oral Tradition: Critiquing Theodore Weeden's Critique," *JSHJ* 7 [2009]: 44–62), the basic idea that traditions transmitted in different contexts, for different purposes, were also preserved with varying degrees of stability, matches the evidence examined in the remainder of the present work. Bailey's use of distinct categories for classifying the reliability of traditions, however, remains problematic, which is why I have used continua in the present work. While one may with some confidence assign certain traditions to either extreme of a set of continua (see below), given the nature of the evidence one can do no more than assign many traditions to an unspecified point in between.

even to this day no one can pass by the place without holding his nose. This was how great an outpouring he made from his flesh on the ground.[111]

Here we have material that most likely originated largely from gossip-like embellishments in an informal and uncontrolled environment.[112] This material was not irrelevant to the identity of the Christian community, but it certainly was not central to it either, and so there was no (or very little) control exercised upon its development. Catechetical material would fall closer to the center of the continua than liturgical material, while still tending toward the left, the constant repetition and rote memorization involved in the catechetical process doing much to ensure its continuity in form and content (possible examples might include *1 Clem.* 13.2 and Poly. *Phil.* 2.3). Most material in the Gospels would fall somewhere near the middle of the continua, the community itself providing control of the main content of the tradition, while allowing for freedom of form, in the process of transmitting the tradition in their gatherings.

Thinking in terms of continua rather than in terms of categories is also helpful in understanding the history of the tradition: in the chapters that follow we will encounter examples of traditions that likely were transmitted initially in an informal controlled manner, and only later were perhaps taken up into a more formally controlled context (e.g., the above-mentioned *1 Clem.* 13.2 and Poly. *Phil.* 2.3). Other cases point to material that was transmitted in an informal controlled manner in certain circles, but in a formal controlled manner in others; e.g., the Lord's Prayer as contained in Lk 11:2–4 (informal controlled) vs. what we find in Mt 6:9–13 and *Did.* 8.2 (formal controlled). Here it is good to heed the critique of Rosalind Thomas regarding the misuse of comparative research: "Oral tradition does not have a single characteristic degree of reliability. ... The longevity and reliability of oral traditions vary immensely according to certain factors, and these one must consider for each kind of tradition separately."[113]

Returning to the idea that oral traditions are not created equal, certain characteristics of orality described in the previous section will apply in different ways to different communities. As an example, the social identifica-

---

[111] Papias 4.2–3 in Ehrman, *Apostolic Fathers*, 2:105–7 (unless otherwise indicated, all citations from the Apostolic Fathers in the present work are from Ehrman); the source of this material is a reconstruction by various editors from the works of Apollinaris of Laodicea (4th cent.); see Holmes, *Apostolic Fathers*, 755.

[112] Cf. Bailey, who describes "the telling of jokes, the reporting of the casual news of the day, the reciting of tragedies in nearby villages and (in the case of inter-communal violence) atrocity stories" as activities taking place in informal settings and characterized by "total flexibility" in the use of materials ("Informal," 45).

[113] Thomas, *Oral Tradition*, 4–5.

tion of tradition (meaning that not all oral traditions are preserved, but only
those that remain socially relevant and acceptable) could be taken to imply
that the tradition is subservient to the community. But, as addressed already in chapter 1 above, traditions are not only shaped but also *shapers* of
communities.[114] In the case of Jesus tradition, the authority of the Lord to
whom it was attributed gave it power to transform social contexts and
shape them after the expectations of its message. One thus must allow for
the possibility that the Jesus tradition would not have been passively preserved only by those whose social location caused it to ring true to them,
but would shape a community after itself that would want to preserve it for
its own sake (the sake of the tradition), in light of its authority.[115]

All of these issues will be addressed as the discussion of individual
passages unfolds in the chapters that follow. While the above issues are
offered for consideration as pertaining to the whole of the Jesus tradition to
be examined, others will also arise that are more pertinent to a particular
passage under consideration, and will be discussed in that context.

3.5 Giving Scribality a Fair Hearing ... in Light of Orality

The choice to focus upon oral tradition as providing the best answer to the
question of the sources of the Jesus tradition in most of the Apostolic Fathers does not imply that other possibilities will be ignored. There are other
viable ways to explain the variability within stability that is the hallmark of
oral transmission, and this study will seek to give a fair hearing to earlier
theories regarding the dependence of the Apostolic Fathers upon the written Gospels.

The theoretical approach that will be given preference in this regard is
the redactional criterion developed by Koester and refined by Tuckett and
Gregory: in Tuckett's words, "if material which owes its origin to the redactional activity of a synoptic evangelist reappears in another work, then
the latter presupposes the finished work of that evangelist."[116]

We will also seek to apply two of Bellinzoni's refined criteria for determining what constitutes "use" of a gospel by any given Apostolic Father, noted in the previous chapter:[117] 1) Accessibility: whether the

---

[114] See above sections 1.6 (sub-titled "Definition of Oral Tradition") and 3.3.10 ("Socially Identified"), and further Schwartz "Christian Origins," 45–46; Kelber, "Works of
Memory," 234; Olick, "Products, Processes, and Practices," 13.

[115] Cf. Kelber's critique of G. Theissen in *Oral and Written*, 24–26.

[116] Tuckett, "Synoptic Tradition," 95; for a fuller discussion see sec. 2.6.1 above.

[117] On what follows see Bellinzoni, "Luke in the Apostolic Fathers," 51, and sec. 2.7
above. We leave out Bellinzoni's criterion of "Textual Distinctiveness" (loc. cit.) as it is

Apostolic Father in question would have had access to the particular document he supposedly used in his writings. Here the dates and places of origin of the documents in question are crucially important.[118] 2) Rate of Recurrence: how often there appear to be parallels between the texts under examination. In applying this criterion, the probability of the use of one document by the writer of another increases in proportion to the number of feasible parallels identified, though the presence of only one isolated parallel does not negate use.

In looking for intertextual relationships among the various relevant writings (canonical as well as apocryphal gospels, the Apostolic Fathers, and others), we will bear in mind that the extant texts available for study do not exactly reflect the original autographs. Bellinzoni is right in stating that one can "never be confident that we are comparing the texts that demand comparison."[119] So one cannot know for sure a) how close the extant gospel and other precursor texts are to their respective autographs, b) how close the extant gospel and other precursor texts are to those upon which the Apostolic Fathers based the apparent quotation or allusion, or c) how close the extant texts of the Apostolic Fathers are to *their* respective autographs.[120] All of this is complicated by the probability that texts that were perceived by an ancient scribe as quoting or alluding to other texts were more likely than others to be intentionally changed by the scribe during the course of textual transmission so as to conform more precisely to the perceived precursor text. This in turn is complicated by the possibility that said precursor text may have itself undergone corruption in the process of its transmission. With all of this is mind, while we will take into consideration any relevant textual variants for the texts under consideration, we will simply have to work with the knowledge that our witnesses are imperfect.

In working with previous scholarship on the possibility that the Apostolic Fathers depended on texts of the Gospels, we may find that previous theories will need to be reformulated in light of the insights provided by studies related to the interplay between orality and literacy. To give an example, we may need to reformulate the idea often put forward by scholars that the Apostolic Fathers quoted certain sayings of Jesus from the canoni-

---

essentially Koester's redactional criterion as refined by Tuckett and Gregory, as described above (secs. 2.6.1 and 2.6.2).

[118] Bellinzoni, "Luke in the Apostolic Fathers," 51.

[119] Ibid., 48.

[120] On the study of Gospel manuscripts in light of the ongoing use of oral tradition in the early church see D. C. Parker, *The Living Text of the Gospels* (Cambridge: Cambridge University Press, 1997) and Kirk, "Manuscript Tradition"; and further Bellinzoni, "Luke in the Apostolic Fathers," 47–48; idem, "Gospel of Matthew," 197–98; Gregory and Tuckett, "Reflections on Method," 62–63; Koester, "Text of the Synoptics."

cal Gospels "loosely and from memory."[121] While some of the passages
that have been viewed in this way[122] are best understood as reflecting the
variability within stability that is characteristic of oral tradition, others are
better viewed as originating from the re-oralization of the written Gospels.[123] It is fairly certain that oral traditions of Jesus' sayings continued to
co-exist with the written Gospels or other written collections of Jesus tradition well into the second half of the second century (at least until the time

---

[121] See, e.g., *NTAF*, 76–81 on Ignatius (read in light of their comments in ibid., 64
and 79, "Ignatius always quotes from memory" and "the indications on the whole favour
the hypothesis that he used our Greek Matthew in something like its present shape"); 84
on Poly. *Phil.* ("The quotations have the appearance of having been made from memory ;
rarely, if ever, from a book"); C. M. Tuckett on the *Didache*'s use of Matthew: "any use
of Matthew's gospel is likely to have been at best via an 'oral' medium of remembering,
recalling, and reproducing largely from memory, perhaps too intermingling any traditions
with similar oral traditions known independently" ("*Didache* and the Synoptics," 513);
see also F. E. Vokes, "The Didache and the Canon of the New Testament," *SE* 3 (1964),
431, 433, 435. For a responsible discussion of the place of possible memory citation of
gospel materials in the Apostolic Fathers see Hagner, *Clement of Rome*, 290–93.

[122] In other cases the sayings in this category were most likely taken from sources independent of our canonical Gospels, such as apocryphal works. Specific examples will be
discussed below.

[123] The term "re-oralization" will be used in this book in reference to the influence of
written texts upon, or the (re)incorporation of written texts into, the oral traditions from
which they derived. Re-oralization is better suited for this purpose than either the term
"feedback," that has an established alternative use in historiography (see Henige, *Oral
Historiography*, 81–87) but has sometimes been used to refer to the phenomenon under
discussion (see Thomas, *Literacy and Orality*, 47), or "secondary orality," which has
been used by NT scholars to refer to the phenomenon under discussion (e.g., D. M.
Smith, *John Among the Gospels* [2nd ed.; Columbia: University of South Carolina Press,
2001], 196; Kelber, *Oral and Written*, 217–18), but also has a history of other usage. The
established usage of "secondary orality" refers to the existence within chirographic societies of a "new orality" dependent at least indirectly upon written sources, what Havelock
refers to as "orality reborn" (*Muse*, 32; see Ong, *Interfaces*, 298–99). (I am indebted to R.
Uro for my awareness of this conflict in terminology regarding "secondary orality"; see
his "*Thomas* and Oral," 10, n. 11). On "reoralization"/"re-oralization" see S. Davis, "The
Reoralization of *The Lady of the Lake*," in *(Re)Oralisierung* (ed. H. L. Tristram; Script
Oralia; Tübingen: Gunter Narr, 1996), 335–60; C. Collins, *Reading the Written Image:
Verbal Play, Interpretation, and the Roots of Iconophobia* (University Park, Pa.: Penn-
sylvania State University Press, 1991), 159; M. Barnes, "Oral Tradition and Hellenistic
Epic: New Directions in Apollonius of Rhodes," *OrTr* 18 (2003): 57; J. S. Kloppenborg,
"Variation in the Reproduction of the Double Tradition and an Oral Q?," *ETL* 83 (2007):
61–63; Byrskog, *Jesus the Only Teacher*, 341–49; idem, "New Quest for the *Sitz im Leben*," 327–36; idem, *Story as History*, 16 and n. 64, 138–44; Byrskog cites its use by
Margaret A. Mills in "Domains of Folkloristic Concern: The Interpretation of Scriptures," in *Text and Tradition: The Hebrew Bible and Folklore* (ed. S. Niditch; SemeiaSt;
Atlanta: Scholars, 1990), 231–41 (where it is associated primarily with the re-oralization
of sacred scriptures).

of Irenaeus).[124] This is almost self-evident in light of what we saw above regarding the interplay of orality and literacy in late Western antiquity. Neither the presence of a limited number of literate people nor the committing of the Gospels to writing changed the fact that most people continued to interact with Jesus tradition within a context of orality. In addition, prior to the struggles over the NT canon, which included the identification of the four canonical Gospels as the authoritative record of what Jesus said and did, in all likelihood Jesus tradition did not derive its authority from its inclusion in written gospels, but from its tie to the person of the Lord Jesus.[125] During said time period, it is reasonable to suppose that written Jesus tradition would have been treated in a manner similar to oral Jesus tradition. This would have been true in a number of ways, which we will consider under the following two main points:

First, from the perspective of Christian traditionists witnessing a performance of any given written gospel (that would later become canonized), the material they were receiving would not have been much different from tradition they had received from strictly oral sources. They were, after all, *hearing* rather than reading the tradition. It is even possible that the performer of the tradition would not have used the written text for the performance itself, but used it in preparation for the performance only as an aid to memorization.[126] Regardless, the traditionist would have delivered the tradition in oral form, so that the distinction between the handing on of oral tradition and the performance of a written gospel would have been merely academic from the perspective of the hearers.

The second point concerns other Christian traditionists receiving the oral performance of a written gospel, who would have appropriated the material and incorporated it into the oral tradition they had already mastered. In passing it on in their turn, it is most likely that they would have

---

[124] C. M. Thomas arrives as this important conclusion in "Word and Deed," and see also Koester, "Written Gospels," 293–95, 297. J. Assmann contends that what dams up the stream of tradition is not the process of writing it down, but rather the closure brought by the act of canonization (*Das kulturelle Gedächtnis*, 93–103; idem, *Religion and Cultural Memory*, 41–42, 117–21).

[125] As noted by H. E. Hearon, for the majority of people who could not read or write the authority of a written text would have been at best "iconic," while "the words themselves took on value only as they were oralized" ("Implications of Orality," 10). This is not to deny that the written Gospels would have gained a certain level of authority within certain circles, under the influence of those who could read them – the authority they were given in later times implies that this was indeed the case. The main point to be made here is that in practice what had authority was the spoken word, as that which was actually encountered in a culture of orality.

[126] See Thomas, *Oral Tradition*, 2; idem, *Literacy and Orality*, 4; Shiner, *Proclaiming*, 103–25; idem, "Oral Performance," 51–54.

handled the tradition received in this way in the same manner they handled oral tradition in general: in short, keeping its central elements stable while treating non-essentials with relative freedom. This amounted to re-oralizing the written tradition, which would have made it virtually indistinguishable in its use from tradition that had never been committed to writing.[127] It may be possible in certain cases, however, to recognize this re-oralized tradition *as such* to the extent that it contains features from the redactional work of an evangelist. Here one faces all of the problems inherent in determining conclusively that the presence of any given feature in a text *is* the redactional work of an evangelist, as noted in the previous chapter in discussing the work of Tuckett and Gregory.[128]

---

[127] This process is referred to by J. P. Meier as follows, "our canonical Gospels not only come from ongoing oral tradition but also generate ongoing oral tradition. ... Inevitably they 'contaminated' and modified the oral tradition that existed before and alongside themselves" (J. P. Meier, *A Marginal Jew: Rethinking the Historical Jesus,* Vol. 1: *The Roots of the Problem and the Person* [ABRL; New York: Doubleday, 1991], 131).

[128] See sections 2.6.1 and 2.6.2 above.

Chapter 4

Identifying Markers and Ways of Orality:
The Explicit Appeal to Jesus Tradition in
1 Clement 13.1c–2

4.1 Introduction

Having explained in the previous chapter the method upon which the present work is based, it is now time to apply this method to the relevant texts. The present chapter will focus upon *1 Clem.* 13.2, though it will also include some reference to Poly. *Phil.* 2.3, given (as can be seen in the synopsis below) that these two passages parallel each other to a great extent. Chapter 5 will contain an extended treatment of Poly. *Phil.* 2.3 in its own right.

The issues involved in studying *1 Clem.* 13.2 and Poly. *Phil.* 2.3 are fairly representative of those one must deal with in considering Jesus tradition in the Apostolic Fathers as a whole: whether known written parallels would have been available to serve as a source to the Apostolic Father in question; whether the similarities and differences among the parallels support or deny the possibility of literary dependence; whether there are characteristics of orality in the Jesus tradition in *1 Clement*, and if so what these might indicate regarding its source. After considering these issues in detail in relation to *1 Clem.* 13.2 and Poly. *Phil.* 2.3 in chapters 4 and 5, the findings from this investigation will serve as a vantage point from which to consider more briefly in chapters 6 to 9 the remaining explicit appeals to Jesus tradition in the Apostolic Fathers.

The discussion in this chapter will proceed as follows: it will begin with an assessment of the evidence for and against *1 Clement*'s dependence on the known written parallels to the Jesus tradition in 13.2, giving special attention to the Synoptic Gospels.[1] Next, it will identify elements within the text under consideration that indicate the author's possible use of oral sources for the Jesus tradition he cites. Finally, it will seek to draw out implications of various points raised in the investigation for the manner in which oral tradition was used, or how it functioned, in the early Chris-

---

[1] The reason for this special attention will be made clear in the course of the following discussion.

tian group to which the author belonged. The overall purpose of this chapter (also applicable to the subsequent chapters) is to begin to demonstrate that the presuppositions of orality better inform the study of the texts under consideration than do the presuppositions of scribality.[2]

We begin our study with the text of *1 Clem.* 13.2 followed by a synopsis of its parallels, including an additional saying from the parallel passage in Pol. *Phil.* 2.3 (listed last in the synopsis) that is not found in *1 Clement*, for comparative purposes.[3] Each saying in the synopsis is identified with a letter, letters 'a' through 'g' for the sayings in *1 Clement* and 'h' for the additional saying from Pol. *Phil.* 2.3. In the remainder of this chapter we will refer to each saying by its corresponding letter in the synopsis, in order to facilitate discussion. Exact verbal parallels to *1 Clem.* 13.2 are underlined in the synopsis for ease of recognition.

1 Clement *13.1c–2*[4]

[1c] μάλιστα μεμνημένοι τῶν λόγων τοῦ κυρίου Ἰησοῦ, οὓς ἐλάλησεν διδάσκων ἐπιείκειαν καὶ μακροθυμίαν. [2] οὕτως γὰρ εἶπεν·

Ἐλεᾶτε, ἵνα ἐλεηθῆτε·[5]
ἀφίετε, ἵνα ἀφεθῇ ὑμῖν·[6]
ὡς ποιεῖτε, οὕτω ποιηθήσεται ὑμῖν·[7]
ὡς δίδοτε, οὕτως δοθήσεται ὑμῖν·

---

[2] On the terms "orality" and "scribality" and the method followed to identify markers of orality within written texts see the discussion on method in ch. 3 above.

[3] Synopsis adapted with modifications from Hagner, *Clement of Rome*, 136.

[4] For ease of reference, I have adapted the following list of MSS witnesses for *1 Clement* with their abbreviations from Ehrman, *Apostolic Fathers*, 1:30: Greek: A = Alexandrinus (5th c.; lacks 57.7–63.4); H = Hierosolymitanus (1056 CE). Versions: L = Latin, an 11th c. MS, ed. by G. Morin (possibly representing a 2nd or 3rd c. trans.); S = Syriac, MS of the NT dated 1169 CE that includes *1* and *2 Clement* after the Pastoral Epistles, ed. by R. Bensly (possibly representing an 8th c. trans.); C = 4th c. Coptic MS in Berlin, ed. by C. Schmidt (lacks 34.6–42.2); C[1] = highly fragmentary 5th c. (?) Coptic MS from Strasbourg, also containing portions of James and John, ed. by F. Rösch (1–26.2).

[5] H reads ἐλεεῖτε, rather than ἐλεᾶτε (as in A); see K. Bihlmeyer, *Die Apostolischen Väter: Neubearbeitung der Funkschen Ausgabe* (3rd ed.; SAQ 2.1.1; Tübingen: Mohr Siebeck, 1970), 42; A. Jaubert, *Clément de Rome: Épître aux Corinthiens* (SC 167; Paris: Cerf, 1971), 122 n.; J. B. Lightfoot, *The Apostolic Fathers: Clement, Ignatius, and Polycarp: Revised Texts with Introductions, Notes, Dissertations, and Translations* (2nd ed.; 2 parts in 5 vols.; London: Macmillan, 1889–90), 1.2:52. L reads *ut perveniatis ad misericordiam* (see Hagner, *Clement of Rome*, 137).

[6] H reads ἄφετε in place of ἀφίετε (as in A); see Bihlmeyer, *Apostolischen Väter*, 42; Jaubert, *Clément de Rome*, 122; Lightfoot, *Apostolic Fathers*, 1.2:52.

[7] C and C[1] add ἀνθρώποις after ὡς ποιεῖτε, (as found in A), and L adds *aliis*; see Bihlmeyer, *Apostolischen Väter*, 42 and Jaubert, *Clément de Rome*, 122.

ὡς κρίνετε, οὕτως κριθήσεσθε· [8]
ὡς χρηστεύεσθε, οὕτως χρηστευθήσεται ὑμῖν· [9]
ᾧ μέτρῳ μετρεῖτε, ἐν αὐτῷ μετρηθήσεται ὑμῖν. [10]

a) *1 Clem.* 13.2:   ἐλεᾶτε   ἵνα ἐλεηθῆτε
   Pol. *Phil.* 2.3c: ἐλεᾶτε   ἵνα ἐλεηθῆτε
   Mt 5:7:   μακάριοι οἱ ἐλεήμονες   ὅτι αὐτοὶ ἐλεηθήσονται
   Lk 6:36:   γίνεσθε οἰκτίρμονες   καθὼς [καὶ] ὁ πατὴρ ὑμῶν
                                                              οἰκτίρμων ἐστίν
   Lk 6:37c: ἀπολύετε   καὶ ἀπολυθήσεσθε
   Cl. *Strom.* 2.91.2: [11]   ἐλεᾶτε, φησὶν ὁ κύριος,   ἵνα ἐλεηθῆτε

b) *1 Clem.* 13.2:   ἀφίετε   ἵνα ἀφεθῇ   ὑμῖν
   Pol. *Phil.* 2.3b: ἀφίετε   καὶ ἀφεθήσεται ὑμῖν
   Mt 6:14:   Ἐὰν γὰρ ἀφῆτε τοῖς ἀνθρώποις //   ἀφήσει καὶ ὑμῖν
                        τὰ παραπτώματα αὐτῶν //   ὁ πατὴρ ὑμῶν ὁ οὐράνιος
   Mk 11:25:   ἀφίετε εἴ τι ἔχετε // ἵνα καὶ ὁ πατὴρ ὑμῶν ὁ ἐν τοῖς
                        κατά τινος //   οὐρανοῖς ἀφῇ ὑμῖν τὰ
                                                          παραπτώματα ὑμῶν
   Lk 6:37c: ἀπολύετε   καὶ ἀπολυθήσεσθε [12]
   Didasc. 2.21:   ἄφετε   καὶ ἀφεθήσεται ὑμῖν [13]
   Ps.Mac. *Hom.* 37.3:   ἄφετε   καὶ ἀφεθήσεται ὑμῖν [14]

---

[8] A reads κρίνεται for κρίνετε (see Lightfoot, *Apostolic Fathers*, 1.2:52). H changes the order of the sayings: the saying ᾧ μέτρῳ μετρεῖτε, ἐν αὐτῷ μετρηθήσεται ὑμῖν, that in the other MSS appears two lines below, is inserted in H before this line (ὡς κρίνετε, οὕτως κριθήσεσθε), so that the order in H (using the a-f of the synopsis below) becomes a b c d g e f; see Bihlmeyer, *Apostolischen Väter*, 42 and Jaubert, *Clément de Rome*, 122; also Hagner, *Clement of Rome*, 137 n. 4.

[9] A reads χρηστεύεσθαι for χρηστεύεσθε (see Lightfoot, *Apostolic Fathers*, 1.2:52), and L completely omits this saying (see Hagner, *Clement of Rome*, 137 n. 7).

[10] Following the texts of Ehrman, *Apostolic Fathers*, 1:58; Jaubert, *Clément de Rome*, 122, and Bihlmeyer, *Apostolischen Väter*, 42 in reading ἐν αὐτῷ, as supported by L (*in eadem*) S C and C¹, in place of ἐν αὐτῇ found in A and οὕτω found in H.

[11] The shorter "Cl. *Strom.*" is used in place of "Clem. Alex. *Strom.*" to fit it within the limited space available in the diagram. Here and below, the Greek text of Clement of Alexandria is that of Cl. Mondésert, in P. T. Camelot and Cl. Mondésert, *Clément d'Alexandrie: Les Stromates: Stromate II* (SC 38; Paris: Cerf, 1954), 104; the text of the *Didascalia* in this synopsis and below is from F. X. Funk, ed., *Didascalia et Constitutiones Apostolorum* (2 vols; Paderbornae: Libraria Ferdinandi Schoeningh, 1905), 1.79, 135.

[12] Cf. also the Lord's Prayer: καὶ ἄφες ἡμῖν τὰ ὀφειλήματα ἡμῶν, ὡς καὶ ἡμεῖς ἀφήκαμεν τοῖς ὀφειλέταις ἡμῶν (Mt 6:12); καὶ ἄφες ἡμῖν τὰς ἁμαρτίας ἡμῶν, καὶ γὰρ αὐτοὶ ἀφίομεν παντὶ ὀφείλοντι ἡμῖν (Lk 11:4).

[13] Note that in this same verse the *Didascalia* contains another reference to the words of Jesus: ἄφες ἡμῖν τὰ ὀφειλήματα ἡμῶν, ὡς καὶ ἡμεῖς ἀφήκαμεν τοῖς ὀφειλέταις ἡμῶν ("He also taught us by his prayer to say to God, 'Forgive us our debts, as we forgive our debtors'"), which with the exception of ἀφίεμεν in place of ἀφήκαμεν is identical to Mt 6:12.

[14] Text of Pseudo-Macarius taken from *NTAF*, 59.

c) *1 Clem.* 13.2:   <u>ὡς ποιεῖτε</u>, <u>οὕτω ποιηθήσεται</u> <u>ὑμῖν</u>
  Mt 7.12a: πάντα οὖν ὅσα ἐὰν θέλητε ἵνα <u>ποιῶσιν</u> <u>ὑμῖν</u> οἱ ἄνθρωποι, <u>οὕτως</u> καὶ
        <u>ὑμεῖς</u> <u>ποιεῖτε</u> αὐτοῖς
  Lk 6:31: καὶ καθὼς θέλετε ἵνα <u>ποιῶσιν</u> <u>ὑμῖν</u> οἱ ἄνθρωποι <u>ποιεῖτε</u> αὐτοῖς ὁμοίως
  Cl. *Strom.* 2.91.2: <u>ὡς ποιεῖτε</u>, <u>οὕτως ποιηθήσεται</u> <u>ὑμῖν</u>

d) *1 Clem.* 13.2:   <u>ὡς δίδοτε</u>, <u>οὕτως δοθήσεται ὑμῖν</u>
  Lk 6:38a: <u>δίδοτε</u>, καὶ <u>δοθήσεται ὑμῖν</u>
  Cl. *Strom.* 2.91.2: <u>ὡς δίδοτε</u>, <u>οὕτως δοθήσεται ὑμῖν</u>
  Didasc. 2.21:   <u>δίδοτε</u>, καὶ <u>δοθήσεται ὑμῖν</u>

e) *1 Clem.* 13.2:   <u>ὡς κρίνετε</u>,   <u>οὕτως κριθήσεσθε</u>
  Pol. *Phil.* 2.3a: μὴ <u>κρίνετε</u>   ἵνα μὴ <u>κριθῆτε</u>
  Mt 7:1:   μὴ <u>κρίνετε</u>,   ἵνα μὴ <u>κριθῆτε</u>
  Mt 7:2a: ἐν ᾧ γὰρ κρίματι <u>κρίνετε</u>   <u>κριθήσεσθε</u>
  Lk 6:37a: καὶ μὴ <u>κρίνετε</u>,   καὶ οὐ μὴ <u>κριθῆτε</u>
  Lk 6:37b: καὶ μὴ καταδικάζετε   καὶ οὐ μὴ καταδικασθῆτε
  Cl. *Strom.* 2.91.2:   <u>ὡς κρίνετε</u>,   <u>οὕτως κριθήσεσθε</u>
  Didasc. 2.42:   ᾧ κρίματι <u>κρίνετε</u>   <u>κριθήσεσθε</u>
              καὶ ὡς καταδικάζετε   καταδικασθήσεσθε

f) *1 Clem.* 13.2:   <u>ὡς χρηστεύεσθε</u>, <u>οὕτως χρηστευθήσεται ὑμῖν</u>
  Lk 6:35c: ὅτι αὐτὸς [ὁ ὕψιστος] <u>χρηστός</u> ἐστιν ἐπὶ τοὺς ἀχαρίστους καὶ πονηρούς
  Cl. *Strom.* 2.91.2: <u>ὡς χρηστεύεσθε</u>, <u>οὕτως χρηστευθήσεται ὑμῖν</u>

g) *1 Clem.* 13.2:   <u>ᾧ μέτρῳ μετρεῖτε</u>, ἐν αὐτῷ <u>μετρηθήσεται ὑμῖν</u>
  Pol. *Phil.* 2.3d: <u>ᾧ μέτρῳ μετρεῖτε</u>   ἀντιμετρηθήσεται <u>ὑμῖν</u>
  Mt 7:2b: ἐν ᾧ <u>μέτρῳ μετρεῖτε</u>   <u>μετρηθήσεται ὑμῖν</u>
  Mk 4:24c: ἐν ᾧ <u>μέτρῳ μετρεῖτε</u>   <u>μετρηθήσεται ὑμῖν</u> καὶ προστεθήσεται <u>ὑμῖν</u>
  Luke 6:38c: ᾧ γὰρ <u>μέτρῳ μετρεῖτε</u>   ἀντιμετρηθήσεται <u>ὑμῖν</u>
  Cl. *Strom.* 2.91.2: <u>ᾧ μέτρῳ μετρεῖτε</u>   ἀντιμετρηθήσεται <u>ὑμῖν</u>

h) Pol. *Phil.* 2.3e: καὶ ὅτι
              μακάριοι οἱ πτωχοὶ καὶ οἱ διωκόμενοι ἕνεκεν δικαιοσύνης
  Mt 5:3:   μακάριοι οἱ πτωχοὶ τῷ πνεύματι,
  Mt 5:10:   μακάριοι οἱ   δεδιωγμένοι ἕνεκεν δικαιοσύνης
  Lk 6:20b: μακάριοι οἱ πτωχοί,

  Pol. *Phil.* 2.3e: ὅτι αὐτῶν ἐστιν ἡ βασιλεία τοῦ θεοῦ
  Mt 5:3:   ὅτι αὐτῶν ἐστιν ἡ βασιλεία τῶν οὐρανῶν
  Mt 5:10:   ὅτι αὐτῶν ἐστιν ἡ βασιλεία τῶν οὐρανῶν
  Lk 6:20b: ὅτι ὑμετέρα ἐστὶν ἡ βασιλεία τοῦ θεοῦ

The issue of whether or not the documents represented in the above synopsis could have served as a source for *1 Clement* (Bellinzoni's criterion of accessibility[15]) is simplified by their date of composition. Based on this

---

[15] See discussion in section 3.5 above, and Bellinzoni, "Luke in the Apostolic Fathers," 51.

criterion, one can divide these documents into two groups: (a) documents other than the canonical Gospels; and (b) the canonical Gospels:

(a) The non-gospel documents included in the above synopsis were written too late to be the source for the sayings of Jesus in *1 Clement*. It is most likely that *1 Clement* was written sometime within the years A.D. 70–100, possibly somewhat later.[16] Thus Clement of Alexandria's *Stromateis*,

---

[16] Though there used to be a near-consensus for an A.D. 95–96 date, this has dissolved, and there is currently no new consensus in its place. The date 95–96 was mostly based on understanding Clement's words in 1.1, that the church at Rome had just experienced "sudden" or "unexpected and repeated misfortunes and calamities" (τὰς αἰφνιδίους καὶ ἐπαλλήλους γενομένας ἡμῖν συμφορὰς καὶ περιπτώσεις), as referring to imperial persecution suffered near the end of Domitian's reign. L. L. Welborn has shown, however, based on lexical, historical, and literary considerations, that this interpretation is mistaken (L. L. Welborn, "The Preface to 1 Clement: The Rhetorical Situation and the Traditional Date," in *Encounters with Hellenism: Studies on the First Letter of Clement* [ed. C. Breytenbach and L. L. Welborn; AGJU 53; Leiden: Brill, 2004], 197–216). Other criteria for dating the epistle, both external and internal, are open to diverse interpretations; see J. J. Ayán Calvo, *Clemente de Roma: Carta a los Corintios, Homilía Anónima (Secunda Clementis)* (FPat 4; Madrid: Ciudad Nueva, 1994), 25–27; A. Gregory, "I Clement: An Introduction," *ExpTim* 117. 6 (2006): 223–30 (repr. in *The Writings of the Apostolic Fathers* [ed. P. Foster; T&TCBS; London and New York: T&T Clark, 2007], 21–31), 28–29 in repr. ed; K. Erlemann, "Die Datierung des Ersten Klemensbriefes–Anfragen an eine Communis Opinio," *NTS* 44 (1998): 591–607; Hagner, *Clement of Rome*, 4–6; T. J. Herron, "The Most Probable Date of the First Epistle of Clement to the Corinthians," in *StPatr* 21 (1989): 106–21; Jaubert, *Clément de Rome*, 15–20; A. Lindemann, *Die Clemensbriefe* (HNT:AV 1; Tübingen: Mohr Siebeck, 1992), 12–13; idem, "The First Epistle of Clement," in *The Apostolic Fathers: An Introduction* (ed. W. Pratscher; Waco, Tex.: Baylor University Press, 2010), 64–65; H. E. Lona, *Der erste Clemensbrief: Übersetzt und erklärt* (KAV 2; Göttingen: Vandenhoeck & Ruprecht, 1998), 75–78. For our purposes here it is sufficient to set a rough date, which is possible based on external criteria alone: evidence for a *terminus ad quem* is provided by the influence of *1 Clement* on Polycarp's *Epistle to the Philippians* (see W. R. Schoedel, *Polycarp, Martyrdom of Polycarp, Fragments of Papias* [ApFa 5; Camden: Thomas Nelson & Sons, 1967], 5), which was written ca. A.D. 107 (see discussion in ch. 5 below). In addition, according to Eusebius, both Hegesippus and Dionysius of Corinth refer to an epistle written by a Clement, and Dionysius adds that it was regularly read in the churches (Euseb. *Hist. Eccl.* 4.22.1; 4.23.11). The latter makes it fairly safe to conclude that these references are to the letter we know as *1 Clement*. Though there are problems with pinpointing the exact dates of the writings of Hegesippus and Dionysius, their witness means at least that *1 Clement* could not have been written after the middle of the 2nd century. A *terminus a quo* for the writing of *1 Clement* is provided by the author's use of NT documents. In a recent article that serves well as a guide to the current *status quaestionis*, A. Gregory concluded that the author of *1 Clement* certainly used 1 Corinthians, and possibly used Romans and Hebrews ("*1 Clement* and the Writings," 144–55; see also Lona, *Erste Clemensbrief*, 49–51, 52–55; A. Lindemann, "Paul's Influence on 'Clement' and Ignatius," in *Trajectories* [ed. Gregory and Tuckett], 9–16). This implies that the letter could not have been written prior to A.D. 55. Based on external criteria alone, then, one

the *Didascalia*, and the *Homilies* of Pseudo-Macarius would have been composed too late – late 2nd, early 3rd, and 4th to 5th centuries respectively[17] – to be a source for *1 Clement*. Further, none of these three documents witness to a separate document that might have informed both them and *1 Clement*. Clement of Alexandria was familiar with *1 Clement*, and is clearly dependent upon the latter.[18] The *Didascalia*, in turn, does not show any particular affinity with the form of the sayings found in *1 Clement*, certainly not to the extent that one would posit a literary dependence of both documents upon a common source. As for Pseudo-Macarius, the single parallel to saying 'b' is identical to the form in the *Didascalia*, so what has been said of the latter applies to it as well.[19]

(b) One cannot discount the possibility of *1 Clement*'s dependence on the Gospels based on dating alone. In all likelihood *1 Clement* is roughly contemporary with or a little later than the Synoptic Gospels, so that one must at least consider the possibility that Clement used the Synoptics as sources.[20] Dependence or independence must be ascertained on the basis of an analysis of the parallels. We begin this analysis by seeking to learn as much as possible about the source(s) of the sayings in question via an examination of a number of aspects such as wording, structure, location (of parallels within the Gospels) and the like. This will be followed by an application of the redactional criterion – ascertaining the presence (or ab-

---

can date *1 Clement* to roughly A.D. 55–112, while considerations in the above secondary literature narrow down this date to a probable A.D. 70–100.

[17] These dates are well known; see, e.g., the articles on the respective authors in *ODCC*.

[18] This is the consensus view, and need not be argued further here; see Hagner, *Clement of Rome*, 140, and literature cited there; and further Carlyle in *NTAF*, 60; Gregory, "*1 Clement* and the Writings," 131, n. 10; Lindemann, *Clemensbriefe*, 54; Lona, *Erste Clemensbrief*, 93–104. In the passages laid out in the above synopsis, the Alexandrian Clement cites *1 Clement* verbatim, with the exception of one letter in saying 'c' (οὕτως in place of οὕτω) and a more weighty difference in saying 'g,' which in the *Stromateis* reads ἀντιμετρηθήσεται ὑμῖν in place of *1 Clement*'s ἐν αὐτῷ μετρηθήσεται ὑμῖν. It bears noting that the ἀντιμετρηθήσεται of the *Stromateis* is found also in the parallels in Luke 6:38c and Pol. *Phil.* 2.3d. Perhaps Clement of Alexandria (either intentionally or unintentionally) modified the wording in light of his familiarity with the Gospel of Luke; other possibilities beyond this hypothesis, as well as the implications of the change, remain unclear.

[19] Further study might reveal that Pseudo-Macarius was dependent on the *Didascalia*, or that together they point to a third source; but neither of them witnesses to the sources of *1 Clement*.

[20] We will not here join in the debate over the date of composition of the Gospels. Even if one could be fairly certain of said date, the uncertainty over the date of *1 Clement* would remain, so that it would be unwise to decide the issue of dependence based solely on hypotheses regarding dates.

sence) of redactional elements from the Evangelists in *1 Clem.* 13.2 – which will constitute our main criterion for this enquiry.

4.2 Comparing the Jesus Tradition in *1 Clem.* 13.2 to its Gospel Parallels

Most scholars agree that there is no literary relationship between *1 Clem.* 13.2 and the canonical Gospels,[21] and the gospel parallels in the above synopsis provide no reason to posit otherwise. None of the Gospels contains a verbatim parallel to any of the sayings in *1 Clem.* 13.2. The wording of some is so different that they are parallels only at the level of ideas. Taking saying 'a' as an example, while the idea of showing mercy to others is expressed in *1 Clem.* 13.2 by the imperative form of ἐλεάω (to have mercy on), in Lk 6:36 it is expressed with the imperative of the verb γίνομαι and the adjective οἰκτίρμων (merciful, compassionate).[22] The weaker parallel in Lk 6:37c (also listed under 'b'[23]) contains the imperative of ἀπολύω, which in this context implies the idea of mercy in forgiving personal injury or insult.[24] In short, for saying 'a,' as well as for other sayings such as 'b,' 'c,' and 'f,' the gospel parallels show hardly any verbal

---

[21] Some, however, have held that *1 Clem.* 13.2 is a "loose" or imperfect quotation of the Gospels from memory: Lightfoot, *Apostolic Fathers*, 1.2:52; G. Schneider, *Clemens von Rom: Brief an die Korinther* (FonC; Freiburg: Herder, 1994), 23 (who also considers that the sayings may have been collected in testimonia or florilegium). M. Hengel conjectures that Clement "knew all three Synoptic Gospels but deliberately quoted them freely because he did not want yet to tie 'the word of the Lord Jesus to a fixed wording' but to allow it to have an indirect effect. The fact that it was there in different versions gave him the freedom to shape his own. The written text which he knew was only an aid to memory" (*Four Gospels*, 128–29). Hengel's conjecture, though plausible, is not based on any particular evidence. For O. Knoch, Clement depended at least secondarily upon the Gospels (Knoch, *Eigenart und Bedeutung der Eschatologie im theologischen Aufriß des ersten Clemensbriefes: Eine auslegungsgeschichtliche Untersuchung* [Theophaneia; Bonn: Peter Hanstein, 1964], 70); Hagner notes similar positions in O. Gebhart and A. Harnack, T. Zahn, F. X. Funk, and Ph. Bryennios (*Clement of Rome*, 147). H. B. Green argued (unconvincingly) that an unknown person composed the "cento" in *1 Clem.* 13.2 in dependence upon Mt, and Clement used it in that form ("Matthew, Clement and Luke: Their Sequence and Relationship," *JTS* n.s. 40 [1989]: 1–25, esp. 2–7).

[22] See BDAG, 314, 700.

[23] Since the idea contained in Lk 6:37c reflects elements both of saying 'a' *and* 'b' in *1 Clem.* 13.2, it would have been rather arbitrary to list it as a parallel only to one or the other of the Clementine sayings.

[24] See I. H. Marshall, *The Gospel of Luke: A Commentary on the Greek Text* (NIGTC; Grand Rapids: Eerdmans, 1978), 266; J. A. Fitzmyer, *The Gospel According to Luke I–IX: A New Translation with Introduction and Commentary* (AB 28; New York: Doubleday, 1981), 641; cf. BDAG, 117–18.

similarity at all to the sayings in *1 Clem*, even though they communicate a very similar meaning.

In addition, there is insufficient reason to posit a literary relationship between *1 Clement* and the Gospels even for those sayings that most closely parallel each other. The Clementine sayings with closest parallels in the Gospels are 'd,' 'e,' and 'g,' in that at least the form of the verbs in *1 Clem*. 13.2 is reflected verbatim in one or more of the Synoptics: for 'd' we find δίδοτε and δοθήσεται in Lk 6:38a; for 'e' κρίνετε in Mt 7:1 and Lk 6:37a, and both κρίνετε and κριθήσεσθε in Mt 7:2a; while for 'g' all of ᾧ μέτρῳ μετρεῖτε μετρηθήσεται ὑμῖν is found in Mt 7:2b and Mk 4:24c. It must be noted, however, that these gospel passages are quite different from their Clementine parallels in other regards. Saying 'e,' in spite of the similar verbs in its gospel parallels, in *1 Clem*. is expressed as a positive construction (ὡς κρίνετε, οὕτως κριθήσεσθε), while in Mt 7:1 and Lk 6:37 it is expressed as a negative construction with μή (μὴ κρίνετε, ἵνα μὴ κριθῆτε κτλ). In addition, the one gospel parallel that contains the same exact form of the verbs as saying 'e' in *1 Clement* (κρίνετε and κριθήσεσθε) also contains much additional material not found in *1 Clement* (ὡς κρίνετε, οὕτως κριθήσεσθε in *1 Clement* vs. ἐν ᾧ γὰρ κρίματι κρίνετε κριθήσεσθε in Mt 7:2a), which does away with any idea of an exact parallelism. In all of the sayings noted, the differences in other parts of the same sayings – adverbs, conjunctions and prepositions – are such that a literary relationship between the documents seems highly unlikely.

In sum, there is no indication of a literary relationship between *1 Clem*. 13.2 and its gospel parallels included in the above synopsis.

4.3 Searching for the Redactional Footprints of the Evangelists

All of the above would become moot, however, if *1 Clement* showed evidence of the redactional work of the Evangelists. In what follows, then, we will apply the redactional criterion: i.e., if *1 Clem*. 13.2 contains words or phrases that originated in the redaction of one of the evangelists this would imply that Clement depended – at least indirectly – upon the writing of that evangelist.[25]

Considering first the *Gospel of Mark*, it only contains parallels to two of the sayings in *1 Clem*. 13.2 ('b' and 'g'). Of these two, only the parallel to saying 'g' in Mk 4:24c contains the kind of similarity to *1 Clement* that

---

[25] See discussion of this criterion in secs. 2.3.2, 2.6.1 and 2.6.2 above, under the contributions of Koester, Tuckett and Gregory.

might indicate a dependence of the latter upon the former.[26] To set out the gospel parallels to saying 'g' again:

1 Clem. 13.2:   ᾧ μέτρῳ μετρεῖτε, ἐν αὐτῷ μετρηθήσεται ὑμῖν
Mt 7:2b: ἐν ᾧ μέτρῳ μετρεῖτε   μετρηθήσεται ὑμῖν
Mk 4:24c: ἐν ᾧ μέτρῳ μετρεῖτε μετρηθήσεται ὑμῖν καὶ προστεθήσεται ὑμῖν
Luke 6:38c: ᾧ γὰρ μέτρῳ μετρεῖτε   ἀντιμετρηθήσεται ὑμῖν

Assuming that Matthew and Luke used the Gospel of Mark in writing their gospels,[27] one might posit that Mark was responsible for the basic form of the saying, and was then followed closely by Matthew (though with the omission of καὶ προστεθήσεται ὑμῖν), and to a lesser extent by Luke and Clement. This theory, however, immediately runs into problems. First, the saying in question was probably also present in Q (a topic to be taken up again below).[28] This would suggest not only that Matthew and Luke are probably not dependent upon Mark for this saying, but also that the elements of the saying that Mk 4:24 shares with its Synoptic parallels probably represent pre-Markan tradition (whether the καὶ προστεθήσεται ὑμῖν found only in Mark is a Markan creation[29] or pre-Markan tradition is debatable, but has no bearing upon the present study, since it does not reappear in *1 Clement*). Second, that none of the three parallels – in Matthew, Luke or *1 Clement* – is dependent upon Mark for this saying is further confirmed by the fact that it reflects a widely used axiom in early Judaism.[30] M. McNamara gives the form of the axiom as found in rabbinic

---

[26] The other parallel, Mk 11:25 (saying 'b'), has little verbal similarity to *1 Clem.* 13.2 beyond their common use of the verb ἀφίημι (and even then the form of the verb is different in the two writings in the second half of the saying; ἀφεθῇ in *1 Clem.* vs. ἀφῇ in Mk), and there is no good reason to posit that the simple occurrence of this verb is either redactional in Mk or a reflection of *1 Clement*'s dependence on Mk.

[27] See sec. 1.7 above entitled "Presuppositions and Assumptions."

[28] This is the opinion of most scholars; see the results of the International Q Project in J. M. Robinson, P. Hoffmann, and J. S. Kloppenborg, eds., *The Critical Edition of Q* (Hermeneia: Supplements; Minneapolis: Fortress, 2000), 74–75 as well as the survey of opinions in J. S. Kloppenborg, *Q Parallels: Synopsis, Critical Notes, and Concordance* (FF; Sonoma: Polebridge, 1988), 34 (including only one differing opinion: B. S. Easton includes it in "L" in his *The Gospel According to St. Luke* [New York: Scribner's Sons, 1926], 89).

[29] As suggested, e.g., by J. Marcus, *Mark 1–8: A New Translation with Introduction and Commentary* (AB 27; New York: Doubleday, 2000), 315.

[30] A fact often noted by commentators; see, e.g., R. A. Guelich, *Mark 1–8:26* (WBC 34A; Dallas: Word, 1989), 232; J. Lambrecht, *"Eh bien! Moi je vous dis": Le discourse-programme de Jésus (Mt 5–7 ; Lc 6,20–49)* (LD 125; Paris: Cerf, 1986), 219–20; ; W. L. Lane, *The Gospel According to Mark* (NICNT; Grand Rapids: Eerdmans, 1974), 167; Marcus, *Mark 1–8*, 321; H. D. Betz, *The Sermon on the Mount: A Commentary on the Sermon on the Mount, Including the Sermon on the Plain (Matthew 5:3–7:27 and Luke 6:20–49)* (Hermeneia; Minneapolis: Fortress, 1995), 491 and n. 531; W. F. Albright and

sources as, "with what measure a man measures, in that same they (i.e. God) measure to him," and clarifies, "i.e., the impersonal plural is used where the NT has the passive [μετρηθήσεται, ἀντιμετρηθήσεται]."[31] Given, then, that this saying was widely available in a form that mirrors that of Mk 4:24c, there is no further reason to hold (especially in light of the variations between them) that Matthew or Luke or Clement derived it from Mark.[32] Based on the above we conclude that it is highly unlikely that the form of saying 'g' as reflected in *1 Clem.* 13.2 is either dependent on the redactional hand of Mark or on that of the other Evangelists.

Turning to the *Gospel of Matthew*, its parallel for saying 'e' has potential to yield results for the redactional criterion:[33]

1 Clem. 13.2:	ὡς κρίνετε, οὕτως κριθήσεσθε
Mt 7:1:	μὴ κρίνετε, ἵνα μὴ κριθῆτε
Mt 7:2a:	ἐν ᾧ γὰρ κρίματι κρίνετε κριθήσεσθε

C. S. Mann, *Matthew* (AB 26; Garden City: Doubleday, 1971), 84; D. A. Hagner, *Matthew 1–13* (WBC 33A; Dallas: Word, 1993), 169; J. Nolland, *The Gospel of Matthew: A Commentary on the Greek Text* (NIGTC; Grand Rapids: Eerdmans, 2005), 318–19; E. Schweizer, *The Good News According to Matthew* (Atlanta: John Knox, 1975), 167; D. L. Bock, *Luke 1: 1:1–9:50* (BECNT 3A; Grand Rapids: Baker 1994), 608; J. Nolland, *Luke 1–9:20* (WBC 35A; Dallas: Word, 1989), 301. W. D. Davies and D. C. Allison list a number of Jewish parallels (*Mek.* on Ex 13:19, 21; 14:25; 15:3, 5, 8; 17:14; *m. Soṭah* 1.7; *t. Soṭah* 3.1; *Tg. Ps.-J.* on Gen 38:26; *b. Šabb.* 105b; *b. Sanh.* 100a; *b. Soṭah* 8b; see further Str-B 1:444–46), and point to similar sayings in Sir 16.14; *T. Zeb.* 5.3; *2 En.* 44.5; and *Tg. Isa.* on 27:8 ("in the measure you were measuring with they will measure you..."); see their *A Critical and Exegetical Commentary on the Gospel according to Saint Matthew* (3 vols.; ICC; Edinburgh: T&T Clark, 1988–97), 1:670. For discussions of the parallels in (a) the targumim, see M. McNamara, *The New Testament and the Palestinian Targum to the Pentateuch* (2nd printing, with supplement containing additions and corrections; AnBib 27A; Rome: Pontifical Biblical Institute, 1978), 138–42; I. A. Massey, *Interpreting the Sermon on the Mount in the Light of Jewish Tradition as Evidenced in the Palestinian Targums of the Pentateuch: Selected Themes* (SBEC 25; Lewiston: E. Mellen, 1991), 74–89; (b) other Jewish sources, see H. P. Rüger, "Mit welchen Mass ihr messt, wird euch gemessen werden," *ZNW* 60 (1969): 174–82; (c) non-Jewish sources, see B. Couroyer, "'De la mesure dont vous mesurez il vous sera mesuré,'" *RB* 77 (1970): 366–70; (d) in general, see P. S. Alexander, "Jesus and the Golden Rule," in *Hillel and Jesus: Comparative Studies of Two Major Religious Leaders* (ed. J. H. Charlesworth and L. L. Johns; Minneapolis: Fortress, 1997), 371–88.

[31] McNamara, *Palestinian Targum*, 139.

[32] I do not wish to imply that Matthew or Luke or Clement, or for that matter Mark, simply took the saying from Jewish sources; the tradition that Jesus himself used the saying is reliable, as (a) it is attested in multiple sources (Mk; Q; *1 Clem*), and (b) (as noted by Davies and Allison, *Matthew*, 1:670) "the criterion of coherency is satisfied, for Jesus' eschatological paraenesis took up the law of reciprocity (see e.g. Mt 10.32–3 = Lk 12.8–9)."

[33] *1 Clement* and Matthew come closest to each other in wording in saying 'g,' but we have already concluded that Clement did not depend upon Matthew for this saying.

The negative construction with μή found in Mt 7:1 (and its parallel Lk 6:37) is transposed in Mt 7:2a into a positive statement, and in this sense comes closer to the form of the saying in *1 Clement*. Even with the possibility that Mt 7:2a is the result of Matthean redaction,[34] however, the person responsible for the source behind *1 Clem.* 13.2 appears to have chosen the positive construction of the saying to reflect a stylized pattern rather than due to dependence on Matthew.[35] This can be seen clearly when viewing the whole Clementine citation of Jesus material on its own:

Ἐλεᾶτε,	ἵνα ἐλεηθῆτε
ἀφίετε,	ἵνα ἀφεθῇ ὑμῖν
ὡς ποιεῖτε,	οὕτω ποιηθήσεται ὑμῖν
ὡς δίδοτε,	οὕτως δοθήσεται ὑμῖν
ὡς κρίνετε,	οὕτως κριθήσεσθε
ὡς χρηστεύεσθε,	οὕτως χρηστευθήσεται ὑμῖν
ᾧ μέτρῳ μετρεῖτε,	ἐν αὐτῷ μετρηθήσεται ὑμῖν.

Here we can see that the form of each saying has been crafted to suit the whole (more on this below), so there is little reason to hold that the author was dependent for the positive construction of one of them (saying 'e') upon Matthew (especially given the *dissimilarities* in other aspects of the saying, as noted above). As for the remainder of the sayings under consideration, there is nothing else that might suggest that Clement was dependent upon the final form of Matthew's gospel.[36]

In general the *Lukan* parallels are no closer in wording to the sayings in *1 Clement* than we found to be the case with those in Mark and Matthew. On the contrary, in sayings 'a,' 'b,' 'e' and 'g' Matthew is closer than Luke, while in sayings 'c' and 'f' the parallelism in Luke is mostly at the level of ideas, not wording. This leaves only two Lukan parallels, those for sayings 'd' and 'g,' which show the kind of affinity to *1 Clement* that might suggest dependence. We already concluded above that 'g' in *1 Clement* did not depend on Luke or any of the Gospels. As for saying 'd,' it has a clear Lukan parallel, but no parallel in the other Synoptics:

1 Clem. 13.2:	ὡς δίδοτε, οὕτως δοθήσεται ὑμῖν
Lk 6:38a:	δίδοτε, καὶ δοθήσεται ὑμῖν

---

[34] As suggested, e.g., by Davies and Allison, *Matthew*, 1:669, who consider it a redactional elaboration of 7:1.

[35] This is one of the reasons Massaux decides against Clement's direct dependence upon Matthew; see his *Influence*, 1:12.

[36] Massaux would agree that Clement was not *directly* dependent upon Mt in these sayings, but finds evidence that "Clement drew from a source whose author was inspired by Mt ... a 'catechism' summarizing the teaching of Christ ... [that] came in large part from Matthew's Sermon on the Mount" (*Influence*, 1:12). As we will see below, there are better explanations for the similarities between *1 Clem.* 13.2 and Matthew.

Here, however, the insight from our discussion of the Matthean parallel to saying 'e' also applies: the form of each saying as found in *1 Clement* has been crafted to suit the whole, which leaves little reason to hold that the author was dependent upon Luke for the form of the single saying 'd.'

In sum, the application of the redactional criterion to the Jesus material in *1 Clem.* 13.2 and its parallels does not provide any substantial evidence that would lead one to conclude that *1 Clement* is dependent upon the finished form of any of the written Gospels.

4.4 Tracing the Sources of the Tradition in *1 Clement* 13.2

Although scholars for the most part agree that the Gospels were not the source for *1 Clem.* 13.2,[37] they disagree considerably in identifying an alternative source: suggested options have included an unknown gospel,[38] a written[39] or oral catechism or collection of *logia*,[40] and oral tradition that

---

[37] See, however, scholars mentioned in n. 37 on p. 118 above.

[38] As held most prominently by A. Resch, who posited that *1 Clem.* 13.2 and a number of its parallels derived from a single Synoptic *Grundschrift* tied to a Hebrew *Urevangelium* (see Resch, *Agrapha: Aussercanonische Evangelienfragmente* [TU 5; Leipzig: Hinrichs, 1889], 137; idem, *Die Logia Jesu* [Leipzig: Hinrichs, 1898], 25). For a critique, including a summary of a response by J. H. Ropes (in *Die Sprüche Jesu* [TU 14; Leipzig: Hinrichs, 1896], 6) see Hagner, *Clement of Rome*, 145–46. Henry Wotton, in his edition of *1 Clement* published in 1718, held that Clement was here dependent on the *Gospel of the Nazaraeans*; see J. Donaldson, *The Apostolical Fathers: A Critical Account of their Genuine Writings and of their Doctrines* (London: Macmillan, 1874), 185.

[39] V. H. Stanton, *The Gospels as Historical Documents* (3 vols.; Cambridge: Cambridge University Press, 1903–20), 1.7; W. K. L. Clarke, ed., *The First Epistle of Clement to the Corinthians* (London: SPCK, 1937), 33 (Clarke oddly states that "remembering" in *1 Clem.* 13.2 "does not suit ... an oral tradition" [loc. cit.]; cf. the comments by Hagner [*Clement of Rome*, 148–49]); B. H. Streeter, in *The Four Gospels: A Study in Origins* (2nd rev. ed.; London: Macmillan, 1930), finds in *1 Clem.* 13.2 "evidence of the existence in the Church of Rome of a discourse document to some extent parallel to the Great Sermon in Matthew and Luke" (pp. 239–40); similar to Resch (see immediately preceding note), R. Glover suggests that not only *1 Clem.* 13.2 and Pol. *Phil.* 2.3, but also Justin *I Apol.* 15.9, *Did.* 1.3 (and perhaps *1 Clem.* 46.2) and the Gospel parallels to all of these all point back to a written Aramaic document, which he terms "the Terse Source" (R. Glover, "Patristic Quotations and Gospel Sources," *NTS* 31 [1985]: 240–43, 247–48).

[40] Oral: Koester suggests an oral yet fixed local catechism (*Synoptische Überlieferung*, 13–16; *Ancient*, 67–68; *From Jesus to the Gospels: Interpreting the New Testament in Its Context* [Minneapolis: Fortress, 2007], 27); E. J. Goodspeed seems to lean toward oral catechetical teaching (*A History of Early Christian Literature* [rev. and enl. by R. M. Grant; Chicago: University of Chicago Press, 1966], 9–10); Knoch ("Kenntnis," 170) suggests a collection of Jesus traditions ("Herrenwortsammlung") used in catechet-

circulated in the churches.[41] A number of scholars simply suggest a written or oral source other than (and perhaps earlier than) the canonical Gospels, without further specifying its nature.[42] We now turn, then, to consider what

---

ical, paraenetic and missionary settings. Oral and/or written catechism or collection of *logia*: Jaubert, *Clément de Rome*, 52; Carlyle and the Oxford Committee favor "a citation from some written or unwritten form of 'Catechesis' as to our Lord's teaching, current in the Roman Church, perhaps a local form which may go back to a time before our Gospels existed" (*NTAF*, 13). It is not clear why A. Lindemann considers the fact that *1 Clem.* 13.2 is "formulated very carefully" as evidence for a written source, "perhaps related to the Q source" ("The Apostolic Fathers and the Synoptic Problem," in *New Studies in the Synoptic Problem* [ed. P. Foster et al.], 693); one can expect that mnemonic techniques would result in carefully formulated tradition, which would tend to support an oral source. Elsewhere Lindemann leaves the issue open ("First Epistle of Clement," 58–59. Massaux holds that, with the exception of 'd' and 'f,' the sayings in *1 Clem.* 13.2 are from a oral "catechism" which "came in large part from Matthew's Sermon on the Mount" (*Influence*, 1:12). In 1964 R. M. Grant followed Koester in favoring an oral over a written source (*The Apostolic Fathers: An Introduction* [ApFa 1; New York: Nelson, 1964], 40), but a year later left both possibilities open (*The Formation of the New Testament* [New York: Harper & Row, 1965], 79–80; idem, in *First and Second Clement* [by R. M. Grant and H. H. Graham; AF 2; New York: Nelson, 1965], 36).

[41] Hagner, *Clement of Rome*, 145–51, esp. 151; idem, "Sayings," 236–37 (Ayán Calvo, *Clemente*, 35 follows Hagner); E. Best, "1 Peter and the Gospel Tradition," *NTS* 16 (1969–70): 112–13; A. Louth refers to "the tradition of our Lord's sayings that lies behind the Synoptic Gospels" (*Early Christian Writings: The Apostolic Fathers* [trans. M. Staniforth; rev. trans., intros., and new editorial material by A. Louth; London: Penguin, 1987], 21; L. E. Wright speaks of "an oral compendium of the gospel ethic" (*Alterations of the Words of Jesus: As Quoted in the Literature of the Second Century* [HHM 25; Cambridge: Harvard University Press, 1952], 78); Donaldson, *Apostolical Fathers*, 185–86 leans toward oral tradition; also Stanton, "Jesus Traditions," 573; M. Thompson, *Clothed with Christ: The Example and Teaching of Jesus in Romans 12.1–15:13* (JSNTSup 59; Sheffield: JSOT Press, 1991), 45–46; D. Ruiz Bueno, *Padres Apostólicos: Edición Bilingüe Completa* (2nd ed.; BAC; Madrid: Editorial Católica, 1967), 142; H. A. Credner, *Beiträge zur Einleitung in die biblischen Schriften* (Halle, 1832), 27, cited in Massaux, *Influence*, 1:8 n. 3. Massaux, even though he is ever assigning a Matthean origin for Jesus sayings in the Apostolic Fathers (see sec. 2.3.1 above), suggests that the two maxims without parallel in Mt ('d' and 'f') were inserted into their Clementine context from living oral tradition (*Influence*, 1:12); M. J. Smith finds oral tradition likely, but also leaves open the possibility of Clement's loose quotation of a written gospel from memory ("The Gospels in Early Christian Literature," in *The Content and Setting of the Gospel Tradition* [ed. M. Harding and A. Nobbs; Grand Rapids: Eerdmans, 2010], 201).

[42] So Gregory, "a collection of sayings that is independent of and earlier than the broadly similar sayings of Jesus that are preserved also in Matthew and/or Luke" ("*1 Clement* and the Writings," 133–34), though in *Reception of Luke and Acts* he states that "their rhythmic structure together with the introductory formula might be taken to suggest an oral rather than a written source" (p. 128); also R. Knopf, *Die Lehre der zwölf Apostel, die zwei Clemensbriefe* (HNT: AV 1; Tübingen: Mohr Siebeck, 1920), 64; W. Sanday, *The Gospels in the Second Century: An Examination of the Critical Part of a Work Entitled 'Supernatural Religion'* (London: Macmillan, 1876), 64–66; C. C.

an examination of the gospel parallels to *1 Clem.* 13.2 might reveal regarding Clement's source.

As will become clear in what follows, there is evidence to suggest that the source of the sayings of Jesus in *1 Clem.* 13.2 was oral tradition. The discussion leading up to this conclusion will proceed as follows: first, by comparing the distribution of the parallels to *1 Clem.* 13.2 in the Synoptic Gospels it will narrow down Clement's source to Q-related tradition. Next, by comparing Matthew and Luke's use of sources, it will investigate what might have been the contents of the relevant portion of Q. This will feed into a hypothesis regarding the oral-traditional source(s) used by Q, and the proposition that portions of what is usually considered a written Q may have been oral tradition. All of this will be used to consider the possibility that the oral source(s) of Q may also stand behind *1 Clem.* 13.2, possibility that will be supported by appeal to other indicators of orality within the clementine material.[43]

4.4.1 Distribution of the Synoptic Parallels to 1 Clem. 13.2

The placement of the parallels to *1 Clem.* 13.2 in each gospel is significant in the discussion of sources.[44] As noted above, Mark contains only two

---

Richardson, "The Letter of the Church of Rome to the Church of Corinth, Commonly Called Clement's First Letter," in *Early Christian Fathers* (ed. C. C. Richardson; LCC 1; Philadelphia: Westminster, 1953), 50 n. 39; A. von Harnack, "Das Schreiben der römischen Kirche an die korinthische aus der Zeit Domitians (I. Clemensbrief)," in *Encounters with Hellenism: Studies on the First Letter of Clement* (ed. C. Breytenbach and L. L. Welborn; AGJU 53; Leiden: Brill, 2004), 92; E. Jacquier, in *Le Nouveau Testament dans l'eglise chrétienne* (3rd ed.; 2 vols.; Paris: Gabalda, 1911–13), considers a number of possibilities, concluding that the issue remains open (1.40–43). R. Roukema notes the scholarly consensus that *1 Clem.* is not dependent on the Gospels, but does not advance a personal opinion ("Jesus Tradition in Early Patristic Writings," in *HSHJ*, 3.2126–27).

[43] Having laid out the arguments in favor of an oral-traditional source for the sayings in *1 Clem.* 13.2, the chapter will then conclude with some suggestions as to how *1 Clement* might inform our understanding of how oral tradition functioned in antiquity.

[44] The *order* of the sayings in each Gospel (following the designations 'a' through 'f' used above) provides no further guidance:

1 Clem. 13.2	a – b – c – d – e – f – g
Matthew	a – b – e – g – c
Mark	g – b
Luke	c – f – a – e – a – b – d – g

('a' is listed twice for Lk because the latter contains two parallels to this saying, separated by a parallel to saying 'e.') The considerable variation in order, especially between *1 Clement* and Mark and Luke, provides little upon which to construct an argument based on order. The order in Matthew does not vary as much, but it is difficult to attach much significance to this fact, in the absence of other factors that might tie the sayings in *1 Clem.* 13.2 to this Gospel.

parallels to the sayings in *1 Clem.* 13.2, one to saying 'b' in Mk 11:25 and one to saying 'g' in 4:24. These sayings are located quite far apart from each other in their Markan context, a distance of 318 verses. Though in part an argument from silence, since Mark contains just two parallels to the Clementine sayings that are separated widely from each other in the gospel, one can conclude not only that the tradition that stands behind Mark apparently did not contain most of the sayings collected in *1 Clem.* 13.2, but also that the two it *did* contain were not in close relationship with each other.[45] It is thus likely that *1 Clem.* 13.2 is derived from a stream of tradition that was quite independent from that which informed Mark's gospel.

The parallels to *1 Clem.* 13.2 in Matthew and Luke are contained within material that according to current majority opinion derived from Q, specifically the Q-sermon that was largely incorporated by the evangelists into Matthew's Sermon on the Mount and Luke's Sermon on the Plain (Q 6:20–23, 27–49; Mt 5:1–7:29; Lk 6:20–49). In Matthew the sayings are found at 5:7; 6:14; 7:1–2a, 2b, and 7:12a. This distribution – note especially the distance of 86 verses that separates the first saying in 5:7 from the last in 7:12 – is commonly considered to have resulted from the manner in which the evangelist used his Q material. It is widely held that in Q the sayings under consideration were arranged much closer to their present configuration in Luke than to what we find in Matthew.[46]

In Luke the sayings are found at 6:31, 36, 37a, b, 38a–b, c, only six verses separating the first parallel from the last. What is more, if one sets aside Lk 6:31, not only are all of the parallels to *1 Clem.* 13.2 found in consecutive verses (Lk 6:36–38), but there is also no intervening material between them.[47] Luke 6:36–38 reads as follows:

[36] Be merciful, just as your Father is merciful. [37] And do not judge, and you will not be judged; and do not condemn, and you will not be condemned; pardon, and you will be pardoned. [38] Give, and it will be given to you. A good measure, pressed down, shaken

---

[45] This conclusion is strengthened by the observation that the context preceding Mk 11:25 has to do with Jesus' teaching on the exercise of faith in prayer, while the maxim in 4:24 relates to the way in which one hears and responds to Jesus' parables (on the latter see R. T. France, *The Gospel of Mark: A Commentary on the Greek Text* [NIGTC; Grand Rapids: Eerdmans, 2002], 211). Thus in Mark the sayings are separate not just with regard to textual placement but also with regard to content.

[46] That Luke rather than Matthew reflects the original order of Q for the verses under consideration has been established by V. Taylor, "The Order of Q," *JTS* n.s. 4 (1953): 27–31; idem, "The Original Order of Q," in *New Testament Essays* (Grand Rapids: Eerdmans, 1972), 98–104.

[47] The material in v. 38b, "A good measure, pressed down, shaken together, overflowing, they will pour into your lap," is an expansion upon, and thus part of the saying in v. 38a, so it does not constitute separate material that intervenes between the parallels to *1 Clem.* 13.2.

together, overflowing, they will pour into your lap. For what measure you measure out will be measured out to you.

The above passage combines two important elements that suggest a close relationship between its sources and those of *1 Clem.* 13.2: not only does it contain a parallel to all but two of the Clementine sayings (the exceptions are saying 'c,' paralleled in Lk 6:31, and saying 'f'[48]), but also here – as in *1 Clem.* 13.2 – all the parallels are grouped closely together. It follows that an investigation into the sources of Lk/Q 6:36–38 might shed considerable light on the sources of *1 Clem.* 13.2.

4.4.2 Luke 6:36–38, Matthew 7:1–2, and the Contents of Q 6:36–38

The evidence to be considered points to the likelihood that Luke derived the form of the sayings in his gospel – including saying 'd,' that is unique to his gospel among the Synoptics – not from Q but from a separate, and probably oral, source. This arises from three premises, addressed in turn below: (a) the sayings that parallel *1 Clem.* 13.2 in Luke existed prior to Q within an independent block of tradition, irrespective of whether or not all of this block was later incorporated into Q; (b) Matthew 7:1–2 is probably closer to what was found in Q than Luke 6:37–38; and (c) the sayings as found not only in Lk 6:36–38 but also in *1 Clem.* 13.2 and other parallels bear the marks of orally transmitted tradition.

(a) Dale Allison has established our first point as part of a detailed study entitled *The Jesus Tradition in Q.*[49] Allison begins the section of his

---

[48] Though, as will be argued below, for saying 'f' a parallel is implicit in Lk 6:35 – it is certainly significant that this verse prefaces the block of verses under consideration, and would form one unit with them to include all of Lk 6:35–38.

[49] Harrisburg: Trinity Press International, 1997. Intrinsic to an argument for a pre-Lukan source is the understanding that the material in question is not of Lukan creation, as argued by a number of scholars: not only does the un-Lukan terminology contained in vv. 37b and 38 point to a pre-Lukan source (so U. Luz, *Matthew 1–7: A Commentary* [ed. H. Koester; trans. J. E. Crouch; Hermeneia; Minneapolis: Fortress, 2007] 349; E. Schweizer, *The Good News according to Luke* [trans. D. E. Green; Atlanta: John Knox, 1984], 125, who also entertains the possibility that the vv. in question were in Q and were omitted by Matthew), but also the imagery of Lk 6:38b is on the whole "so obviously Palestinian that the question of Lucan creation does not arise, despite the omission of anything corresponding from Mt" (Marshall, *Luke*, 267; similarly H. Schürmann, *Das Lukasevangelium*, 1: *Kommentar zu Kap. 1, 1 – 9, 50* (HTKNT; Freiburg: Herder, 1969], 363; D. R. Catchpole, *The Quest for Q* [Edinburgh: T&T Clark, 1993], 121–22). Other scholars have questioned the presence of all of Lk 6:37–38 in Q. Nolland finds "a question mark over the original unity of the section (was the section on giving added from another tradition for the sake of the note of plentifulness in God's dealings which it adds?)" (*Luke 1–9:20*, 301). There also are those who hold the opposite to that being argues here: Bovon, without offering any kind of supporting argument, asserts that "condemn not, and you will not be condemned" in Lk 6:37b is "a redactional paraphrase that

argument that most concerns us by showing, based upon a number of structural and other formal resemblances, that a relationship existed between
1 Clem. 13.2 and Q 6:27–38. He notes,

> Not only does the content [of *1 Clem.* 13.2] overlap with portions of Q 6:27–36, 37–38,
> but there are formal resemblances. The pairing of the first two commands (both have an
> imperative + ἵνα) recalls the pairing of imperatives in Q 6:27–30 and 37–38. The string
> of four similar sentences (3–6, all with ὡς ... οὕτως) is analogous to the groups of four in
> the very same Q texts. That the final unit, with its introductory dative (ᾧ μέτρῳ), breaks
> the parallelism of the preceding commands puts one in mind of Q 6:38, which similarly
> breaks the parallelism of its passage – and with the very same saying, that about getting
> back the measure one gives.[50]

Allison then proceeds to marshal significant evidence that suggests that
prior to its incorporation into Q, the material that comprises 6:27–38 circulated as an independent, cohesive block of tradition, to which *1 Clem.* 13.2
is a witness.[51] His argument rests not only upon the noted resemblances
between *1 Clem.* 13.2 and Q 6:27–38, but also upon showing that Paul,[52]
Polycarp (*Phil.* 2.2–3, analyzed below)[53] and the Didachist (*Did.* 1:3–5)
must have known a block of Jesus tradition very similar in content to
1 Clem. 13.2 and Q 6:27–38.[54]

---

removes any misunderstanding of the sense of κρίνω ("to sentence," "to judge," "to condemn" ...)" in the saying that precedes it (6:37a). Likewise he holds that "Verse 37c
["Forgive, and you will be forgiven"] is a further instruction from Luke that restates the
preceding prohibition in the positive," and further, "Verse 38a is symmetrical to v. 37c,
and takes up a pressing Lukan concern: generosity" while Lk 6:38b is a "Lukan insertion." He concludes that "Luke has thus interfered rather strongly with his source [Q],
and has created an artful small composition: two negative imperatives, two positive imperatives, a promise, and a statement" (*Luke 1: A Commentary on the Gospel of Luke
1:1–9:50* [ed. H. Koester; trans. C. M. Thomas; Hermeneia; Minneapolis: Fortress,
2002], 241–42). Why all of this should be Lukan interference with his sources and not
pre-Lukan material is not sufficiently explained. If material contains indicators of pre-
Lukan or non-Lukan origin (as is argued here), it is just as reasonable to assume that
Luke included this material from his sources because it matched his concerns, than that
he created it based on his concerns. Fitzmyer, also without supporting his opinion in any
way, holds that in Lk 6:37bc, 38a, "Luke has fashioned a few verses of his own" (Fitzmyer, *Luke I–IX*, 627, 628, 641, quote from p. 628).

[50] Allison, *Jesus Tradition*, 85; for Allison's full discussion see ibid., pp. 84–89.

[51] Allison, *Jesus Tradition*, 84–85.

[52] Allison notes the parallels between Rom 2:1 and Q 6:37; Rom 12:14 and Q 6:28;
Rom 12:17 and Q 6:27–36; Rom 12:21 and Q 6:27–36; 1 Cor 4:12 and Q 6:28; 1 Thess
4:12 and Q 6:27–36 (*Jesus Tradition*, 86).

[53] Allison points out parallels between Poly. *Phil.* 2.2–3 and Q 6:27–30, 36–38 (*Jesus
Tradition*, 88).

[54] Allison points out parallels between *Did.* 1:3–5 and Q 6:27–30, 32–36 as well as
Mt 5:39, 41–42, 44–48 (*Jesus Tradition*, 89–90). For Allison's full discussion of all these
parallels see ibid., 80–92. In another publication Allison draws out the thematic unity of

Allison has put together a very cogent argument, which we need not replicate here, as his findings are supported by the independent research of a number of scholars.[55] His study suffices to establish that the sayings within what is often identified as Q 6:37–38 (// *1 Clem.* 13.2) existed independently of Q within a cohesive block of tradition. Allison's study does not sufficiently show, however, that these sayings actually became a part of Q. It is possible that Luke derived what is commonly identified as Q 6:37–38, where all but one of the Lukan parallels to *1 Clem.* 13.2 are located, directly from the independent block of tradition that Allison has identified rather than from Q. We now turn to examine this possibility.

(b) Based upon the current shape of Matthew and Luke's shared tradition and upon what can be ascertained regarding each evangelist's use of his sources, and assuming also that this portion of Q as known to Matthew and Luke was a written document,[56] it seems likely (as will be argued below) that the contents of Q 6:37–38 may have been closer to Mt 7:1–2 than to Lk 6:37–38.

We have already noted that the sayings that parallel *1 Clem.* 13.2 in Matthew and Luke are all contained within Matthew's Sermon on the Mount (SM) and Luke's Sermon on the Plain (SP). In the view of most Q

Q 6:27–38 as a rewriting of the holiness code in Lev 19; see his "Q's New Exodus and the Historical Jesus," in *The Sayings Source Q and the Historical Jesus* (ed. A. Lindemann; BETL 118; Leuven: Leuven University Press and Peeters, 2001), 411–16.

[55] Among others, Allison cites J. D. G. Dunn, *Romans 1–8* (WBC 38A; Dallas: Word, 1988), 80 on Rom 2:1; Thompson, *Clothed*, 97–98, 100–102, 161–73 on Rom 2:1; 12:14, 17 and 21; Knoch, "Kenntnis," 170 and Massaux, *Influence*, 2:29 on *1 Clem.* 13.2 and Poly. *Phil.* 2.3; see further Allison's "The Pauline Epistles and the Synoptic Gospels: The Pattern of the Parallels," *NTS* 28 (1982): 1–32; Draper, "Jesus Tradition," 72–91; Dunn, *Jesus Remembered*, 586–88; Schürmann, *Lukasevangelium*, 1.385–86; D. Lührmann, "Liebet eure Feinde (Lk 6,27–36/Mt 5,39–48)," *ZTK* 69 (1972): 412–58; J. Piper, *'Love Your Enemies': Jesus' Love Command* (SNTSMS 38: Cambridge: Cambridge University Press, 1979), 134–36; J. M. Robinson, "ΛΟΓΟΙ ΣΟΦΩΝ: On the *Gattung* of Q," in *The Sayings Gospel Q: Collected Essays* (ed. C. Heil and J. Verheyden; BETL 189; Leuven: Leuven University Press and Peeters, 2005), 57, n. 47; and the essays by R. Bauckham, P. Davids, G. Maier, and D. Wenham in *Jesus Tradition* (ed. Wenham). Though some (e.g., Lührmann and Piper) do not include vv. 37–38 in this block of tradition, Allison argues that since *1 Clem.* 13.2 contains parallels to Q 6:31 and 37–38, vv. 27–36 were already associated with vv. 37–38 in the tradition (see Allison, "Pauline Epistles," 11–12, 31 n. 115; idem, *Jesus Tradition*, 85). Cf. Koester, *Ancient*, 52–55. J. M. Robinson would enlarge the block of tradition to include all of the Sermon on the Plain (Lk 6:20b–49), which he posits, "may have existed not only prior to Q, but also side-by-side with Q" ("Early Collections of Jesus' Sayings," in his *The Sayings Gospel Q*, 172).

[56] Below we will consider the possibility that the portion of Q under consideration was known to Matthew and Luke as oral tradition rather than as a written document, possibility that would greatly impact the discussion that follows.

scholars, Luke did better at preserving the sermon as it was found in Q than did Matthew.

Two scholars often noted in the literature who hold a view that differs considerably from that proposed in this study are H. D. Betz and Hans-Theo Wrege:

(1) Betz argues in several publications that the SM and the SP are redactional in nature, and that they existed as complete units independent of each other (though elaborated from the same sayings material) in Q^{Mt} and Q^{Lk}, in which form both Matthew and Luke incorporated them into their Gospels, largely without modification (Betz, *Essays on the Sermon on the Mount* [Philadelphia: Fortress, 1985], esp. 18, 89, 90; idem, "The Sermon on the Mount and Q: Some Aspects of the Problem," in *Gospel Origins and Christian Beginnings: In Honor of James M. Robinson* [ed. J. E. Goehring et al.; ForFasc; Sonoma, CA: Polebridge, 1990], 19–34; idem, "The Sermon on the Mount in Matthew's Interpretation," in *The Future of Early Christianity: Essays in Honor of Helmut Koester* [ed. B. A. Pearson; Minneapolis: Fortress, 1991], 258–75; idem, "The Sermon on the Mount: In Defense of a Hypothesis," *BR* 36 [1991]: 74–80; *Sermon on the Mount* [Hermeneia], esp. 42–44 but also passim). See, however, the appropriate and detailed critiques of Betz's theory in C. E. Carlston, "Betz on the Sermon on the Mount," *CBQ* 50 (1988): 47–57; G. N. Stanton, *A Gospel for a New People: Studies in Matthew* (Edinburgh: T&T Clark, 1992), 309–25; Allison, *Jesus Tradition*, 67–77; K. R. Snodgrass, "A Response to Hans Dieter Betz on the Sermon on the Mount," *BR* 36 (1991): 88–94; also Luz, *Matthew 1–7*, 176 n. 22.

(2) In *Die Überlieferungsgeschichte der Bergpredigt* (WUNT 9; Tübingen: Mohr Siebeck, 1968) Wrege argues that the variations between the logia in the SM and the SP are due to the varied use of oral tradition within the communities of the evangelists, and from this vantage point launches an attack against the existence of Q as a written document (this is in line with his *Doktorvater*'s view, J. Jeremias, in *New Testament Theology*, Vol. 1: *The Proclamation of Jesus* [trans. J. Bowden; NTL; London: SCM, 1971], 37–41, who cites him approvingly [ibid., p. 38 n.4]). Choosing to base an argument against the existence of Q from a comparison of the SM to the SP is, however, methodologically faulty. Whether or not there is a literary relationship between the Synoptics, and from there whether or not there was a written Q, must be determined by a careful consideration of all the variables that go into the current discussion of the synoptic problem, and based on an examination of the entirety of the documents involved. In my view (which reflects the majority opinion) solutions other than the Two Source Hypothesis raise more questions than they answer. As this relates to the SM and the SP, one can only discuss their relationship to each other in light of a wider theory that accounts for every aspect of the relationship between all of Matthew and all of Luke. In addition, one cannot focus (as does Wrege) simply upon the wording of the various parallels between the SM and the SP. One must also consider, e.g., the remarkable agreement in order not just between the SM and the SP, but also between the contexts in which they are placed within their respective Gospels. See further the reviews of Wrege's work by C. E. Carlston (*JAAR* 38 [1970]: 104–6) and H. K. McArthur (*JBL* 88 [1969]: 91–92).

On the whole topic of the contours of Q and the relationship between the SM and the SP one would do well to heed Hengel's remarks on the many uncertainties that remain regarding Matthew and Luke's sources, on the plurality of sources probably used by each, and even of the possibility that the later Matthew used the earlier Luke (*Four Gospels*, 169–207). For a balanced and thorough discussion on the existence of Q see C. M. Tuckett, *Q and the History of Early Christianity: Studies on Q* (Edinburgh: T&T Clark, 1996), 1–39. For other differing opinions see further Luz, *Matthew 1–7*, 175–76.

Matthew, however, has also followed Q's order, as can be seen in the following chart developed by Graham Stanton:

	Lk 6	*Mt 5, 7*
Introduction	20a	5:1–2
Beatitudes	20b–23	5:3–12
Woes	24–26	
Love of enemy	27–36	5:38–47
Golden Rule	31	7:12
Judge not	37–38	7:1–2
The blind guide	39	
Teacher and disciple	40	
Speck and log	41–42	7:3–5
The tree and its fruit	43–45	7:16–20
Lord, Lord	46	7:21
House on the rock	47–49	7:24–27 [57]

But for one exception – the Golden Rule in Q 6:31//Mt 7:12 – there is overall a remarkable agreement in order between the SP and the SM (of course Matthew has also interpolated considerable material from elsewhere in Q, as well as from Mark and M, into his SM – most notably all of Mt 6).[58] Matthew also contains, at times in reworked form, the vast majority of material found in Luke's SP. Matthew has included most of this material in his SM, though he has also relocated a small amount of it elsewhere in his gospel.[59] In sum, while Luke has better preserved the structural integrity of the material, both Luke and Matthew have incorporated almost the entirety of Q's sermon into their gospels, and largely followed Q's order.

In light of this overall pattern in Matthew's use of Q's sermon material, the exceptional cases in which his gospel does not contain material found in the SP are worthy of attention. These cases are two: Matthew contains neither an equivalent to the woes in Luke 6:24–26, nor parallels to four of

---

[57] Chart taken with slight modifications from Stanton, *Gospel for a New People*, 287; an almost identical chart can be found in Lambrecht, *"Eh bien,"* 31.

[58] As noted by U. Luz, this breaks the pattern of Matthew's use of his sources: his usual *modus operandi* at the large scale is to follow Mark's order, and insert Q material with no regard for the Q order (on a smaller scale he often maintains the Q order in excerpting Q material). In the case of the SM//SP, however, Matthew has followed the order of his main source Q, since he had no Markan framework to follow; see Luz, "Matthew and Q," in idem, *Studies in Matthew* (Grand Rapids: Eerdmans, 2005), 39–53, esp. 45–50.

[59] Q 6:39//Mt 15:14 (a rather weak parallel); Q 6:40//Mt 10:24–25 (reworked); Q 6:44–45 has a parallel in the SM (Mt 7:16–17) but also one that is in some ways closer in wording in Mt 12:33–35. We cannot go into detail on these parallels here, but ample discussion is available in the major commentaries.

the sayings in Q 6:36–38.[60] While the first of these cases has no material bearing on the present argument,[61] the second is of crucial importance, in

---

[60] Another two items that catch the eye are explainable in terms of Matthean redaction: (a) As already noted, Matthew has transplanted the Golden Rule from its place in the SP (Q 6:31) to a later place in the SM. Following the pattern of the parallels, one would expect to find this saying in the range of Mt 5:42–46. By removing the Golden Rule from its Q context of love of enemies and placing it in its present context in Mt 7:12, and adding "for this is the law and the prophets," Matthew "points back to Jesus' fulfillment of the law and the prophets in 5:17 and creates a bracket around the main section of the Sermon on the Mount" (Luz, *Matthew 1–7*, 362; see also Schweizer, *Matthew*, 172). (b) Though the Matthean parallels to the sayings in Q 6:27–30 are all grouped together in the SM (Mt 5:39–44) within this block of text the order of the sayings varies greatly from its Q counterpart, as can be seen in the following chart (blank spaces represent missing parallels):

Q 6	Mt 5
	43
27a	44a
27b	
28a	
28b	44b
	39a
29a	39b
29b	40
	41
30a	42a
30b	42b

The reordering and reworking of these sayings in Mt 5:39–44 correspond to the structure of the antithesis-form that Matthew took from his M source and imposed upon the material in 5:21–48; i.e., he has inserted each saying from Q 6:27–30 beneath its corresponding antithesis, and couched it in language that reflects his customary usage (for a full discussion see Luz, *Matthew 1–7*, 226–32, 270–82).

[61] Explaining the presence of the woes in the SP and their absence in the SM has occasioned much debate, which need not be resolved here. Explanations have included: (1) the woes were in Q, and Matthew chose not to include them (e.g., H. W. Bartsch, "Feldrede und Bergpredigt: Redaktionsarbeit in Luk 6," *TZ* 16 [1960]: 10–11; Schürmann, *Lukasevangelium*, 335–36, 339; H. Frankenmölle, "Die Makarismen [Mt 5,1–12; Lk 6,20–23]: Motive und Umfang der redaktionellen Komposition," *BZ* 15 [1971]: 52–75; Fitzmyer, *Luke I–IX*, 627, 628; G. Schneider, *Das Evangelium nach Lukas* [2nd ed.; 2 vols.; ÖTKNT 3.1–2; Gütersloh and Würzburg: Mohn, 1984], 1.151; Nolland, *Luke 1–9:20*, 280); (2) the woes were in Q^{Lk}, to which Matthew did not have access (e.g., Marshall, *Luke*, 245 [who does not speak of Q^{Mt} and Q^{Lk}, but of "different recensions" of Q]; this view is also implicit in Betz's contention that the SM and the SP were the work of presynoptic authors/redactors, and that Matthew and Luke took their form of the sermon largely unchanged from Q^{Mt} and Q^{Lk}: "If one accepts this conclusion, very definite reasons will have to be given for any characteristic difference between the SM and the SP that is attributed to the evangelists' redaction rather than to their sources" [Betz, *Sermon on the Mount* [Hermeneia], 44]); (3) the woes were in a non-Q source, whether written or

that it concerns Lk 6:36–38 – or so-called Q 6:36–38 – where we find all but one of the parallels to *1 Clem.* 13.2 presently under examination.

The relevant texts from Luke and Matthew are as follows:

Lk 6:37–38	*Mt 7:1–2*
37a: Καὶ μὴ κρίνετε, καὶ οὐ μὴ κριθῆτε·	7:1: Μὴ κρίνετε, ἵνα μὴ κριθῆτε·
37b: καὶ μὴ καταδικάζετε, καὶ οὐ μὴ καταδικασθῆτε.	7:2a: ἐν ᾧ γὰρ κρίματι κρίνετε κριθήσεσθε,
37c: ἀπολύετε, καὶ ἀπολυθήσεσθε·	
38a: δίδοτε, καὶ δοθήσεται ὑμῖν·	
38b: μέτρον καλόν πεπιεσμένον σεσαλευμένον ὑπερεκχυννόμενον δώσουσιν εἰς τὸν κόλπον ὑμῶν·	
38c: ᾧ γὰρ μέτρῳ μετρεῖτε ἀντιμετρηθήσεται ὑμῖν.	7:2b: καὶ ἐν ᾧ μέτρῳ μετρεῖτε μετρηθήσεται ὑμῖν.

While the first pair and the last pair of lines in both texts closely parallel each other, this parallelism does not extend to the intervening lines. The saying in Mt 7:2a contains an idea that is quite independent of Lk 6:37b–38b. In effect, Mt 7:2a is a reformulation of Mt 7:1 in terms of Mt 7:2b, expresing the judgment language contained in the former in terms of the reciprocity idea in the latter, and does not provide a parallel to any part of

---

oral, available to Luke but not to Matthew (e.g., D. Lührmann, *Die Redaktion der Logienquelle: Anhang: Zur weiteren Überlieferung der Logienquelle* [WMANT 33; Neukirchen-Vluyn: Neukirchener, 1969], 54); and (4) Luke created the woes as part of his redactional activity (e.g., J. Dupont, *Les béatitudes*, Vol. 1: *Le problème littéraire* [2nd ed.; Paris: Gabalda, 1958], 299–342 [who in light of linguistic parallels between the SM and the SP argues that Lk was influenced by SM materials not found in the SP]; P.-E. Jacquemin, "Les béatitudes selon saint Luc: Lc 6,17.20–26," *AsSeign* 37 [1971]: 80–91; Bovon, *Luke 1*, 223; Lambrecht, "*Eh bien,*" 64–73, 211, 220). The complexity of the debate is captured well in the words of C. H. Dodd, "if either evangelist be supposed to depend on the other, or both upon some hypothetical source, something much more radical than a mere 'editing' of borrowed material is to be taken into account" in light of each of the Matthean and Lukan beatitudes (and woes) being "a distinct and characteristic literary product, related to different established forms of composition" ("The Beatitudes," in *Mélanges bibliques rédigés en l'honneur de André Robert* [TICP 4; Paris: Bloud & Gay, 1955], 410). It is important for the present discussion to note the possibility, if either explanation (2) or (3) above were correct, that Luke's SP contains tradition from beyond "Q" as commonly understood (in brief: material common to Matthew and Luke but not found in Mark). This importance resides in the precedent it would set within the context of the SP//SM for what we will argue below: that Luke did not create the material in 6:37–38 that has no parallel in Matthew, but derived it from an extra-Q source.

Lk 6:37b–38b. Elsewhere in Matthew we find only one parallel to the four non-underlined sayings in Lk 6:37b, c and 38a, b: the saying in Mt 6:14 that is similar in meaning to Lk 6:37c:

Lk 6:37c	*Mt 6:14*
ἀπολύετε,	Ἐὰν γὰρ ἀφῆτε τοῖς ἀνθρώποις τὰ παραπτώματα αὐτῶν,
καὶ ἀπολυθήσεσθε·	ἀφήσει καὶ ὑμῖν ὁ πατὴρ ὑμῶν ὁ οὐράνιος

Despite the similarity of these two sayings, upon closer inspection one must conclude that Matthew's source for 6:14 was not a hypothetical Q 6:37c but rather Mark 11:25.[62] This becomes clear not only (i) in light of the relationship between Q's sermon and Mt 6, but also (ii) in light of the wider relationship between the Gospel of Mark and the SM.

(i) Given the pattern of Matthew's use of Q's sermon in his SM, it is unlikely that he drew any connection between Q 6:37 (as usually reconstructed) and his own text on forgiveness in Mt 6:14, as suggested by the following considerations: Matthew 6 contains no other material from Q's sermon, and Mt 6:14 in particular is surrounded by a large block of M material (6:1–18) into which Matthew has inserted material on prayer, including the Lord's Prayer in Mt 6:9–13. As will be argued further below, though the Lord's Prayer in Matthew has a clear parallel in Q 11:1–4, Matthew did not derive the content of his prayer from Q but from liturgical tradition in use within his community.[63] This means that Matthew leaves Q as a source after Mt 5:48, and does not return to it until Mt 6:19ff (//Q 12:33–34; 11:34–36; etc.).[64] Based upon this pattern of Matthew's use of sources, it is unlikely that Matthew would allude to a single verse from Q's sermon in this large block of text derived from elsewhere. This becomes even less likely in light of the next point.

(ii) Both the content of Mk 11 and the pattern of Matthew's use of Mark in the SM suggest that Matthew based the material in Mt 6:14–15 at

---

[62] As suggested, e.g., by A. Plummer, *An Exegetical Commentary on the Gospel According to S. Matthew* (London: Elliot Stock, 1909), 104; R. H. Gundry, *Matthew: A Commentary on His Handbook for a Mixed Church under Persecution* (2nd ed.; Grand Rapids: Eerdmans, 1994), 109; Davies and Allison, *Matthew*, 1:616; it is considered also by W. C. Allen, *A Critical and Exegetical Commentary on the Gospel according to S. Matthew* (ICC; Edinburgh: T&T Clark, 1912), 60–61.

[63] There are those who would disagree with this assessment, who hold that the source of Mt 6:9–13 was Q 11:2–4; see, e.g., Lambrecht, *"Eh bien,"* 124–29. See further the discussion of *Did.* 8.2 and its parallels in Mt 6 and Lk 11, in ch. 7 below.

[64] Here I agree with G. Strecker, *The Sermon on the Mount: An Exegetical Commentary* (trans. O. C. J. Dean; Nashville: Abingdon, 1988), 143. Whether Matthew returns to his Q source starting with 6:19 or not until 6:20 is debatable, but immaterial to our argument here.

least in part on Mk 11:25.[65] The relationship between the material in Mt 6 and Mk 11:25 follows the pattern of Matthew's use of Mark elsewhere in the SM. Just as *Jesus' teaching* in the SM culminates, in Mt 7:28–29, with a summary phrase about *Jesus' teaching* derived from Mk 1:21–22,

Mk 1:21–22	*Mt 7:28–29*
[21] when the sabbath came, he entered the synagogue and taught. [22] They were astounded at his teaching, for he taught them as one having authority, and not as the scribes.	[28] Now when Jesus had finished saying these things, the crowds were astounded at his teaching, [29] for he taught them as one having authority, and not as their scribes.

so also *Jesus' prayer* culminates, in Mt 6:14–15, with a summary phrase *regarding prayer* modeled after Mk 11:25:

Mk 11:25	*Mt 6:14–15*
[25] And as you stand praying, forgive if you hold anything against anyone, in order that your father who is in heaven may also forgive you your wrongdoings	[14] For if you forgive others their wrongdoings, your heavenly Father will also forgive you. [15] But if you do not forgive others, neither will your father forgive your wrongdoings

Furthermore, as established by K. Stendahl, two linguistic peculiarities contained in Mt 6:14–15 and Mk 11:25 all but guarantee a close relationship between them: (a) the presence of τὰ παραπτώματα in both texts, a *hapax legomenon* both in Matthew and Mark, and (b) the presence of ὁ πατὴρ ὑμῶν ὁ ἐν τοῖς οὐρανοῖς in Mk 11:25, the only Markan occurrence of this phrase, while Matthew reads "our Father in heaven" not only in 6:14–15 but also in the introduction to the Lord's Prayer in 6:9.[66] These linguistic peculiarities were probably what led Matthew to incorporate Markan tradition at this particular point in his gospel, most likely reworking the tradition on forgiveness that accompanied the version of the Lord's

---

[65] It is also possible that Matthew knew the basic content of Mt 6:14–15 from tradition, and reworked it and placed it here under the influence of his reading of Mk 11:25.

[66] For a complete discussion of these and other factors that tie the material in Mt 6 both to Mk 11:25 and to other material in Mk 11, see K. Stendahl, "Prayer and Forgiveness: The Lord's Prayer," *SEÅ* 22–23 (1957–58): 75–86, repr. in idem, *Meanings: The Bible as Document and as Guide* (Philadelphia: Fortress, 1984), 115–25. Further support for this connection would have been provided by Mk 11:26 if it were authentic, since it is almost identical to Mt 6:15. The presence of 11:26 in Mk, however, is almost certainly due to later scribal assimilation to the text of Mt, as it is not attested in the earliest texts of Mk; see B. M. Metzger, *A Textual Commentary on the Greek New Testament* (2nd ed.; Stuttgart: Deutsche Bibelgesellschaft/New York: American Bible Society, 1994), 93 (even so, Mk 11:25–26 and Mt 6:14–15 were obviously related in the mind of the scribe!) and the commentaries.

Prayer found in his source to fit the Markan material.[67] In light of these considerations, it becomes clear that Mt 6:14 is not Matthew's redactional elaboration of Q 6:37c. This conclusion, together with the lack of any other Matthean parallel to Lk 6:37c, raises the possibility that Matthew did not know the saying in its Lukan form, or at least did not encounter it as a hypothetical Q 6:37c. This in turn lends further support to our contention that the sayings found in Lk 6:37b–38b were not a part of Q.

What then *was* in Q for the sayings under consideration? It is likely that either Matthew or Luke reflects the original form of Q: if there was nothing in Q between 6:37a and Q 6:38c it is unlikely that both Matthew and Luke would independently insert material between the two halves of an otherwise compact doublet, while if there was material in Q between 6:37a and Q 6:38c that is not reflected in either Matthew or Luke it is unlikely that they both would have independently changed it beyond recognition. It follows that if, has has been argued above, Lk 6:37b–38b was not in Q, then Q must have contained something very close or identical to Mt 7:2a, and Mt 7:1–2 as a whole is close to the original text of Q. The presence of v. 2a in Matthew is then to be explained not in terms of Matthew's redactional activity,[68] but in terms of his dependence upon his Q source.[69]

---

[67] This would remain true even if, or especially if, Mark in this verse is echoing the Lord's Prayer (as suggested by J. Marcus, *Mark 8–16: A New Translation with Introduction and Commentary* [AYB 27A; New Haven and London: Yale University Press, 2009], 787. Assuming that Matthew used Mark's Gospel, he would naturally recognize the allusion and associate his own section on the Prayer with this section in Mark. This assumes that the Lord's Prayer was widely used in the liturgy, as will be argued in ch. 7 below regarding the Prayer in the *Didache*.

[68] As held, e.g., by J. Lambrecht, *The Sermon on the Mount: Proclamation and Exhortation* (GNS 14; Wilmington: Glazier, 1985), 178–79; idem, *"Eh bien,"* 174, 209; J. D. Crossan, *In Fragments: The Aphorisms of Jesus* (San Francisco: Harper & Row, 1983), 180; and see further the survey of opinion in Kloppenborg, *Q Parallels*, 34.

[69] So A. Harnack, *New Testament Studies,* Vol. 2: *The Sayings of Jesus: The Second Source of St, Matthew and St. Luke* (trans. J. R. Wilkinson; CTL; New York: G. P. Putnam's Sons/London: Williams & Norgate, 1908), 8–10; Strecker, *Sermon on the Mount*, 143; and see further the survey of opinion in Kloppenborg, *Q Parallels*, 34. In addition to the considerations already noted, Mt 7:2a contains no typically Matthean vocabulary to suggest that it is a Matthean creation (see Luz, *Matthew 1–7*, 349) and Matthew did not need to add 7:2a as an explanatory elaboration relating Mt 7:1 to Mt 7:2b, since in ancient Judaism the language of "measuring" (7:2b) was commonly related to the language of "judging" (7:1) in dealing with the eschatological judgment (see Davies and Allison, *Matthew*, 1:670). S. Schulz has argued that the similarity in pattern between Mt 7:2a and 7:2b implies that 7:2a was present in Q, but was left out of his Gospel by Luke (*Q: Die Spruchquelle der Evangelisten* [Zürich: Theologischer Verlag, 1972], 146; I owe this reference to Bovon, *Luke 1*, 241 n. 72). It is of course possible that Luke derived the basic content of Lk 6:37–38 from Q^{Lk}, and Matthew derived the basic content of Mt 7:1–2 from Q^{Mt} (Harnack considers this a possibility in his *Sayings of Jesus*, 9–10; U. Luz

c) Having dealt so far with two considerations – that the sayings in Lk 6:37–38 were part of a cohesive block of tradition that existed prior to Q, and that these sayings in all likelihood were never incorporated into a written Q known by Matthew and Luke – we now turn to our third consideration: that the source of the sayings in Luke was probably oral rather than written.

Allison, in the above-mentioned study that deals with the preformed block of tradition that encompassed all of Lk 6:26–38, notes that it contains indicators of orality. Allison observes, "the materials now gathered in the central section of the SP were traditionally associated with certain patterns that presumably reflect the handling of tradition in an oral environment."[70] The hypothesis that this unit of tradition circulated in oral form best explains the great variability in language among the various parallels that Allison adduces in arguing for its existence, which were noted in our discussion.

This great variability in language is evident not only when one compares the texts of Matthew and Luke to their extra-gospel parallels, but extends also to the intra-Synoptic relationship between Matthew and Luke themselves. To facilitate discussion, the text of Lk 6:27–38 is given here with its Matthean parallels, with matching language underlined for ease of identification:

Mt 5:43–45, 39b–42; 7:12; 5:46–48; 7:1–2	Lk 6:27–38
[5:43–45] Ἠκούσατε ὅτι ἐρρέθη· ἀγαπήσεις τὸν πλησίον σου καὶ μισήσεις τὸν ἐχθρόν σου. [44] ἐγὼ δὲ λέγω ὑμῖν· ἀγαπᾶτε τοὺς ἐχθροὺς ὑμῶν	[27] Ἀλλὰ ὑμῖν λέγω τοῖς ἀκούουσιν· ἀγαπᾶτε τοὺς ἐχθροὺς ὑμῶν, καλῶς ποιεῖτε τοῖς μισοῦσιν ὑμᾶς,
καὶ προσεύχεσθε ὑπὲρ τῶν διωκόντων ὑμᾶς,	[28] εὐλογεῖτε τοὺς καταρωμένους ὑμᾶς, προσεύχεσθε περὶ τῶν

views this as "the least unlikely explanation" [*Matthew 1–7*, 349] and this is the basic argument of H. D. Betz in several publications, as indicated in a previous footnote; see his *Essays*, esp. 18, 89, 90; "Sermon on the Mount and Q"; "Matthew's Interpretation"; "Defense of a Hypothesis"; *Sermon on the Mount* [Hermeneia], esp. 42–44). However, as noted in ch. 1 above, and argued further below, this kind of explanation stretches the viability of the Two Source Hypothesis as an explanation for the Synoptic Problem. One would have to argue first that the non-Marcan material Matthew has in common with Luke points to the existence of *a common source* Q, and second that the places in which Matthew and Luke differ within this material points to the existence of *two separate* (though related) *sources*. If pushed too far, the second argument begins to cancel out the first, even if in making the second argument one speaks of two or more "recensions" rather than two or more "documents."

[70] Allison, *Jesus Tradition*, 91, see also ibid., pp. 77–92.

Mt 5:43–45, 39b–42; 7:12; 5:46–48; 7:1–2	Lk 6:27–38
⁴⁵ὅπως γένησθε υἱοὶ τοῦ πατρὸς ὑμῶν τοῦ ἐν οὐρανοῖς, ὅτι τὸν ἥλιον αὐτοῦ ἀνατέλλει ἐπὶ πονηροὺς καὶ ἀγαθοὺς καὶ βρέχει ἐπὶ δικαίους καὶ ἀδίκους. [5:39b–42] ³⁹ᵇἀλλ’ ὅστις <u>σε</u> ῥαπίζει εἰς <u>τὴν</u> δεξιὰν <u>σιαγόνα</u> [σου], στρέψον αὐτῷ <u>καὶ τὴν ἄλλην·</u> ⁴⁰<u>καὶ</u> τῷ θέλοντί σοι κριθῆναι <u>καὶ τὸν χιτῶνά σου</u> λαβεῖν, ἄφες αὐτῷ <u>καὶ τὸ ἱμάτιον·</u> ⁴¹καὶ ὅστις σε ἀγγαρεύσει μίλιον ἕν, ὕπαγε μετ’ αὐτοῦ δύο. ⁴²τῷ <u>αἰτοῦντί σε</u> δός, <u>καὶ</u> τὸν θέλοντα <u>ἀπὸ</u> σοῦ δανίσασθαι <u>μὴ</u> ἀποστραφῇς. [7:12] Πάντα οὖν ὅσα ἐὰν <u>θέλητε ἵνα ποιῶσιν ὑμῖν οἱ ἄνθρωποι</u>, οὕτως καὶ ὑμεῖς <u>ποιεῖτε αὐτοῖς·</u> οὗτος γάρ ἐστιν ὁ νόμος καὶ οἱ προφῆται. [5:46–48] ⁴⁶ἐὰν γὰρ <u>ἀγαπήσητε</u> <u>τοὺς ἀγαπῶντας ὑμᾶς,</u> τίνα μισθὸν ἔχετε; οὐχὶ καὶ οἱ τελῶναι τὸ αὐτὸ ποιοῦσιν; ⁴⁷καὶ ἐὰν ἀσπάσησθε τοὺς ἀδελφοὺς ὑμῶν μόνον, τί περισσὸν ποιεῖτε; οὐχὶ <u>καὶ οἱ</u> ἐθνικοὶ <u>τὸ αὐτὸ ποιοῦσιν;</u> καὶ ἁμαρτωλοὶ ἁμαρτωλοῖς δανίζουσιν ἵνα ἀπολάβωσιν τὰ ἴσα. ⁴⁸<u>ἔσεσθε οὖν</u> ὑμεῖς τέλειοι ὡς <u>ὁ πατὴρ ὑμῶν</u> ὁ οὐράνιος τέλειός <u>ἐστιν.</u> [7:1–2] ¹<u>Μὴ κρίνετε, ἵνα μὴ κριθῆτε·</u> ²ἐν ᾧ γὰρ κρίματι κρίνετε κριθήσεσθε,	ἐπηρεαζόντων <u>ὑμᾶς.</u> τῷ τύπτοντί σε ἐπὶ <u>τὴν σιαγόνα</u> πάρεχε <u>καὶ τὴν ἄλλην,</u> <u>καὶ ἀπὸ τοῦ αἴροντός</u> <u>σου τὸ ἱμάτιον</u> <u>καὶ τὸν χιτῶνα</u> μὴ κωλύσῃς. ³⁰παντὶ <u>αἰτοῦντί σε</u> δίδου, <u>καὶ ἀπὸ</u> τοῦ αἴροντος τὰ σὰ <u>μὴ</u> ἀπαίτει. ³¹Καὶ καθὼς <u>θέλετε ἵνα ποιῶσιν ὑμῖν οἱ ἄνθρωποι</u> <u>ποιεῖτε αὐτοῖς</u> ὁμοίως. ³²καὶ εἰ <u>ἀγαπᾶτε</u> <u>τοὺς ἀγαπῶντας ὑμᾶς,</u> ποία ὑμῖν χάρις ἐστίν; καὶ γὰρ οἱ ἁμαρτωλοὶ τοὺς ἀγαπῶντας αὐτοὺς ἀγαπῶσιν. ³³καὶ [γὰρ] ἐὰν ἀγαθοποιῆτε τοὺς ἀγαθοποιοῦντας ὑμᾶς, ποία ὑμῖν χάρις ἐστίν; <u>καὶ οἱ</u> ἁμαρτωλοὶ <u>τὸ αὐτὸ ποιοῦσιν.</u> ³⁴καὶ ἐὰν δανίσητε παρ’ ὧν ἐλπίζετε λαβεῖν, ποία ὑμῖν χάρις [ἐστίν]; ³⁵πλὴν ἀγαπᾶτε τοὺς ἐχθροὺς ὑμῶν καὶ ἀγαθοποιεῖτε καὶ δανίζετε μηδὲν ἀπελπίζοντες· καὶ ἔσται ὁ μισθὸς ὑμῶν πολύς, καὶ <u>ἔσεσθε</u> υἱοὶ ὑψίστου, ὅτι αὐτὸς χρηστός ἐστιν ἐπὶ τοὺς ἀχαρίστους καὶ πονηρούς. ³⁶Γίνεσθε οἰκτίρμονες καθὼς [καὶ] <u>ὁ πατὴρ ὑμῶν</u> οἰκτίρμων <u>ἐστιν.</u> ³⁷<u>Καὶ μὴ κρίνετε, καὶ οὐ μὴ κριθῆτε·</u> καὶ μὴ καταδικάζετε, καὶ οὐ μη καταδικασθῆτε.

Mt 5:43–45, 39b–42; 7:12;	*Lk 6:27–38*
5:46–48; 7:1–2	

Mt 5:43–45, 39b–42; 7:12; 5:46–48; 7:1–2

ἀπολύετε, καὶ ἀπολυθήσεσθε·
38 δίδοτε, καὶ δοθήσεται ὑμῖν·
μέτρον καλὸν
πεπιεσμένον σεσαλευμένον
ὑπερεκχυννόμενον δώσουσιν
εἰς τὸν κόλπον ὑμῶν·

καὶ ἐν ᾧ μέτρῳ μετρεῖτε   ᾧ γὰρ μέτρῳ μετρεῖτε
μετρηθήσεται ὑμῖν.   ἀντιμετρηθήσεται ὑμῖν.

Variability within stability is one of the hallmarks of oral tradition,[71] and here both are clearly evident. In spite of their basic similarity in meaning, the extensive variations in wording between these portions of Matthew and Luke make it highly unlikely that the Evangelists copied the sayings from the same written document. With no intent of denying that Matthew and Luke knew a Q in written form that approximated in large part the current scholarly reconstruction(s), one must also allow for the possibility that they knew certain portions of Q as oral tradition, perhaps including the one presently under consideration. As James Dunn notes specifically of Lk 6:27–35 and its Matthean parallels,

> If the tradition used here was ... typical of the material common to Matthew and Luke which provides the basis for the whole Q hypothesis, then it is doubtful whether the Q hypothesis would ever have emerged – that is, the hypothesis of Q as a written document known to and used as such by Matthew and Luke. The level of verbal agreement [between Lk 6:27–30, 32–35 and its parallels] is just too low to support the hypothesis of a literary document underlying both.[72]

As Dunn rightly states elsewhere, although one could argue that Matthew and Luke copied the sayings from different written documents, this presents its own problems:

> The alternative suggestion that there were several editions of Q (Matthew copying from one, Luke from another) smacks of desperation, since the suggestion undermines the argument for the existence of a Q document in the first place. ... Similarly with the suggestion that Matthew was free in his editing of Q (= Luke) or vice-versa.[73]

The above statement is part of Dunn's effort to alter the scholarly default setting away from hypotheses of textual origins that focus exclusively on written sources and toward the acknowledgment that the documents under

---

[71] See sec. 3.3.5 above, under the subtitle "Both Variable and Stable" and literature cited there.

[72] Dunn, "Q¹ as Oral," 49.

[73] Dunn, *Jesus Remembered*, 233–34; Dunn makes these statements in reference to a number of what are usually considered Q passages from the Sermon on the Mount/Plain, including some of the verses under consideration here.

consideration were created in a world that functioned in most respects at the level of orality.[74] The traditional approach has been to argue that Matthew and Luke freely edited written documents, or used different recensions of Q. It is just as likely, however, and perhaps more so, that the many variations between Matthew and Luke reflect the variability within stability that is characteristic of oral transmission of tradition; i.e., they knew this portion of Q in oral form.[75] The Synoptic Problem is *both* a literary *and* an oral problem.

Dunn is not alone in exploring the theory of an oral Q behind the Sermon on the Plain. Richard Horsley and Jonathan Draper have also developed various aspects of this theory in a number of publications, paying special attention to the presence of elements that witness to the imprint of oral performance upon the material.[76] Basic to Draper and Horsley's approach is the insight that, contrary to the standard form-critical view, the oral Jesus tradition was not preserved and transmitted in the form of isolated or "floating" sayings but rather in the form of "speeches" or "discourses."[77] "Study of oral-derived text ... shows that it can have a high

---

[74] See discussion of Dunn's "Altering" in sec. 1.1 above, and Dunn, "Q[1] as Oral," 46–47.

[75] To cite Dunn's own conclusion, "These are all teachings remembered as teachings of Jesus in the way that oral tradition preserves such teaching: the character and emphasis of the saying is retained through stable words and phrases, while the point is elaborated in ways the reteller judged appropriate to the occasion" (*Jesus Remembered*, 234; see also idem, *Beginning*, 117–20). J. S. Kloppenborg rightly notes that the theory of Matthew and Luke's reliance upon an oral Q is but one way to explain the variability (within stability) of the material under consideration; see his "Variation in the Reproduction," 53–80, esp. p. 79. An explanation in terms of an oral Q is to be preferred, however, in that Kloppenborg's appeal to a form of at least indirect literary dependence in light of the "widespread practice of rhetorical paraphrase of sources, or the practice of authors revising their own works following private oral performances" (ibid., 79–80) cannot account for all the evidence examined in the present chapter.

[76] Even though Horsley and Draper have published essays on the topic separately, they are treated together here both because of their joint publication, *Whoever Hears You Hears Me*, and because of the similarity in their approach. In mentioned volume see the essays by R. A. Horsley: "The Oral Communication Environment of Q" (pp. 123–49); "Recent Studies of Oral-Derived Literature and Q" (pp. 150–74); "The Covenant Renewal Discourse: Q 6:20–49" (pp. 195–227); "The Renewal Movement and the Prophet Performers of Q" (pp. 292–310); and by J. A. Draper: "Recovering Oral Performance from Written Text in Q" (pp. 175–94). See also Draper, "Covenantal Discourse"; Horsley, "Performance and Tradition: The Covenant Speech in Q," in *Oral Performance* (ed. Horsley), 43–70.

[77] Draper, "Covenantal Discourse," 71; idem, "Recovering Oral Performance," 185; Horsley, "Oral-Derived Literature," 166–67; idem, "Covenant Renewal," 195–97, 213–14; idem, "The Contours of Q," in *Whoever Hears* (by Horsley with Draper), 83–93; cf. Lord, "Gospels," 59, and Byrskog's statements regarding the early Christian recollection

level of sophistication and most characteristically is [transmitted and] performed in coherent discourses associated with particular contexts."[78] Draper and Horsley argue that the Sermon on the Mount/Plain, or what they prefer to call "Jesus' covenantal discourse," is an example of such a coherent discourse. In support of this contention, both authors apply Dell Hymes' model of "measured verse" (which focuses on the narrative flow of the whole),[79] and Draper also applies Marcel Jousse's model of "rhythmography" (which focuses upon "the performative balance of small units within the overall structure")[80] to an analysis the oral-performative features of the covenantal discourse (Sermon on the Mount/Plain) in Q.[81] These two models serve to bring out clearly the oral patterning and structure of the covenantal discourse as a whole, as well as the coherent internal oral structuring of its constituent scenes, all of which is characterized by balance

---

of Jesus tradition in "episodes" ("Eyewitness Testimony and Oral Tradition," 46; idem, "Transmission of the Jesus Tradition," 1472–73).

[78] Draper, "Covenantal Discourse," quote from p. 74, addition in brackets from p. 76. Draper continues, "Even a proverb, which comes closest to disembodied currency, depends for its meaning on a specific cultural context since it is 'tied to its interactional setting', and often depends on an underlying assumed narrative" (ibid., 76, Draper's citation is of J. Penfield, *Communicating with Quotes: The Igbo Case* [Westport, Conn.: Greenwood, 1983], 2); see also Draper, "Recovering Oral Performance," 185.

[79] Draper, "Covenantal Discourse," 79; idem, "Recovering Oral Performance," 186–94; Horsley, "Oral-Derived Literature," 167–68; idem, "Covenant Renewal," 210–17; applying the work of D. Hymes, *"In Vain I Tried to Tell You": Essays in Native American Ethnopoetics* (Philadelphia: University of Pennsylvania Press, 1999); idem, "Ways of Speaking," in *Explorations in the Ethnography of Speaking* (ed. Richard Bauman and Joel Sherzer; 2nd ed., Cambridge: Cambridge University Press, 1989), 433–51, 473–74; idem, "Ethnopoetics, Oral-Formulaic Theory, and Editing Texts," *OrTr* 9 (1994): 330–70. On the application of Hyme's theory to the study of oral-derived texts see further Foley, *Singer*, 17–28.

[80] Draper, "Covenantal Discourse," 79; idem, "Recovering Oral Performance," 186–94; applying the work of M. Jousse, *The Oral Style* (trans. E. Sienaert and R. Whitaker; New York: Garland, 1990 [Fr. orig. 1925]); idem, *The Anthropology of Geste and Rhythm: Studies in the Anthropological Laws of Human Expression and Their Application in the Galilean Oral Style Tradition* (ed. and trans. E. Sienaert and J. Conolly; Durban: Center for Oral Studies, University of Natal, 1997 [Fr. orig. 1931–51]), as well as Jousse's translator and exponent E. Sienaert, "Marcel Jousse: The Oral Style and the Anthropology of Gesture," *OrTr* 5 (1990): 91–106; idem, "On the Rhythmographic Representation of an Oral-Style Text" (unpublished paper); E. Sinaert and J. Conolly, "Marcel Jousse on 'Oral Style', 'Memory', and the 'Counting Necklace'," in *Orality, Memory, and the Past: Listening to the Voices of Black Clergy under Colonialism and Apartheid* (ed. P. Dennis; Pietermaritzburg: Cluster, 2000), 65–84.

[81] This amounts to an examination of Lk 6:12–7:17. "Luke 6:12–7:17 seems to be presenting the covenantal discourse in its simplest form, in contrast to the much expanded and developed performances of Matthew 5–7 and the *Didache* 1–6" (Draper, "Covenantal Discourse," 76).

and parallelism.[82] Draper also notes other elements that point to an oral mode of performance, such as repetition in balanced couplets for emphasis and a careful balancing of stanzas according to content.[83] Based on Draper and Horsley's analysis, it seems clear that the discourse/Sermon in Q bears all the marks of an oral-derived text that originated as a scribal transcription of a performed event.[84]

Indicators of orality are also visible specifically within Lk/(Q?) 6:36–38, a carefully crafted composition. Luke 6:36 functions as the heading for the complex of sayings that follows, and serves to ground all the sayings upon the nature of God himself:[85]

γίνεσθε οἰκτίρμονες
    καθὼς [καὶ] ὁ πατὴρ ὑμῶν
    οἰκτίρμων ἐστίν

The next four lines are made up of two identically-constructed negative imperatives followed by subjunctive passive clauses with οὐ μή, "the most definite form of negation regarding the future"[86] (v. 37a–b):

Καὶ μὴ κρίνετε,
    καὶ οὐ μὴ κριθῆτε·
καὶ μὴ καταδικάζετε,
    καὶ οὐ μὴ καταδικασθῆτε.

Next come four lines made up of almost-identically constructed positive imperatives followed by future passive indicatives (vv. 37c–38a):

ἀπολύετε,
    καὶ ἀπολυθήσεσθε·
δίδοτε,
    καὶ δοθήσεται ὑμῖν·

---

[82] Ibid., 80–85, 86–91.

[83] Ibid., 85–86.

[84] On orality and the full text of Q see further the remaining articles in Horsley with Draper, *Whoever Hears You Hears Me*, and Horsley, ed., *Oral Performance*, as well as Kelber, "Jesus and Tradition," 153–57.

[85] It is clear that Matthew has made this verse (Q 6:36) the conclusion of his preceding material, changing the language of "mercy" to that of "perfection," and inserting all of his chapter 6 in between this verse and what followed in Q at Mt 7:1–2. I am of the opinion that in Q, however, it contained the original language of "mercy," and functioned as the heading of the verses that follow on withholding judgment (Mt 7:1–2//Q6:37–38; in this I agree with Tuckett, *Q and the History*, 431–32, though not with his position that Lk 6:37–38 reflects what was in Q), and as Horsley notes, also functioned to "link the covenant teaching of 6:27–35 to that of 6:38–42 and [tie] it to the beatitudes of 6:20–23 that have pronounced God's free grace to those who did not think they deserved it by calling the hearers to imitate God's mercy" ("Covenant Renewal Discourse," 212–13).

[86] See BDF, 184 (sec. 365).

Though this final ὑμῖν (required by δοθήσεται) breaks up the flow of identical constructions, it finds an echo in the final ὑμῖν at the end of the construction as a whole, ἀντιμετρηθήσεται ὑμῖν (v. 36). Next in sequence we find a series of rhythmic and rhyming lines, that rhyme even with their concluding ὑμῶν (v. 38b):

μέτρον καλόν
    πεπιεσμένον
    σεσαλευμένον
    ὑπερεκχυννόμενον
δώσουσιν εἰς τὸν κόλπον ὑμῶν·

This is capped off by the well-known maxim in v. 38c that sums up the whole collection of sayings, and ties them all back to the heading in v. 36:

ᾧ γὰρ μέτρῳ μετρεῖτε
    ἀντιμετρηθήσεται ὑμῖν.

Implicit in each of these verses is the idea not just of reciprocity, but of *divine* reciprocity, contained in the use throughout of the divine passive. The final two lines (38c) put this in general terms: God will measure out to you after the manner in which you have measured out to others. The presupposition set by the previous lines, "Give, and it will be given to you. A good measure, pressed down, shaken together, overflowing, they will pour into your lap" (38a–b) is based on v. 36: you will be "compassionate, even as your Father is compassionate."

The collection crafted in this manner bears the marks of tradition that has been retained and transmitted orally: the pairing of identical verb constructions in 37a–b, 37b–38a, the common theme (of divine reciprocity) that unifies the sayings, the punch line made up of a well-known proverb in 38c, the rhyme and rhythm throughout, and the visual imagery in 38b, all are standard tools in the oral retention and transmission of tradition. This, together with the variability within stability that characterizes this material's relationship to its parallels, and the indicators of orality present in the larger block that provided the source for all of Lk 6:26–38 (noted above), makes it likely that Luke derived these sayings from an oral source. It is probable also that in this source the sayings were already structured after the manner in which we find them in Luke's gospel, as this structure was an integral part of the mnemotechnical approach of the traditionist.

In conclusion, in investigating the sources of the sayings that parallel *1 Clem.* 13.2 in the Gospels we have found multiple indicators of an oral source. It is fairly clear that Matthew and Luke bear witness to a block of oral tradition that stood behind what is commonly identified as Q 6:27–38, though we cannot be certain whether or not this ever became part of a written Q. If Matthew and Luke had access to this source in oral form, this in itself would explain the variability within stability prevalent throughout the material. In this case the presence of the sayings in Lk 6:37b–38b not found in Matthew could be attributed to different performances of the same tradition. If Matthew and Luke knew Q 6:27–38 as part of a written document, it is nevertheless likely that the sayings that parallel *1 Clem.* 13.2 in Lk 6:37b–38b derived not from this written Q but from a separate oral source. Assuming, based on our discussion, that Luke rather than Matthew diverged from his Q source, it seems likely that Luke had access to a collection of Jesus' sayings from a different source (L) that included Lk 6:37b–38b (not attested in Matthew) as well as the essential wording of Q 6:35–37a and probably (but not certainly) Q 6:38c. If this were the case, it stands to reason that Luke would have inserted vv. 6:37b–38b after Q 6:37a and before Q 6:38c, triggered by the presence of v. 6:37a in Q. The indicators of orality present throughout Lk 6:36–38 make it likely that this is an oral-derived text; i.e., Luke's source for this material was oral tradition.

4.5 The Gospel Sources and *1 Clem.* 13.2

Having noted the close relationship that exists between *1 Clem.* 13.2 and Lk 6:36–38, our subsequent detailed discussion of the sources of Lk 6:36–38 in relation to Matthew and the proposed shape of Q has brought us to the very context out of which the sayings in *1 Clem.* 13.2 also arose: the living stream of oral tradition that circulated in and among the early Christian communities. That this is the case arises in part from our argument above: as mentioned in discussing Dale Allison's work, the sayings in *1 Clem.* 13.2 and Lk 6:27–38, along with Jesus tradition contained in texts from Paul, Polycarp and the *Didache*, together bear witness to a preformed discourse of Jesus tradition that predated Q.[87] In addition, we have tentatively concluded that the collection of sayings in Lk 6:36–38, which includes all but one of the parallels to *1 Clem.* 13.2, was an oral-derived text that in its oral form had a shape very close to what we find in the present text of Luke. That these sayings circulated together in the early oral Jesus tradition, and are found together in *1 Clement*, makes it likely – in the absence of strong reasons to posit a literary source for the clementine material – that oral tradition was also the source for Clement's citation.

The hypothesis of an oral-traditional source for *1 Clem.* 13.2 is further strengthened by a number of considerations, some quite similar to those we

---

[87] In addition to the above discussion, see Allison, *Jesus Tradition*, 80–92.

covered in the case of Lk 6:36–38. Negatively, we already concluded at the beginning of this chapter that there is no reason to posit a literary dependence of *1 Clem.* 13.2 upon any of the written Gospels. Here we must add that, even if Q 6:27–38 did become a written document, it is also clear that this written Q was not Clement's source: the arguments against the literary dependence of *1 Clem.* 13.2 upon Matthew or Luke – covered above – also hold for its dependence upon Q.[88] Positively, the collection of sayings in *1 Clem.* 13.2 can be identified as deriving from an oral source based on (a) the introductory formula with which they are prefaced, and (b) a series of indicators of orality.

(a) Up to this point our discussion of *1 Clem.* 13 has focused upon the sayings of Jesus in v. 2, but the introductory material in vv. 1–2a is also relevant to the issue of sources. In these verses the author prefaces his quotation of Jesus' sayings with the words μάλιστα μεμνημένοι τῶν λόγων τοῦ κυρίου Ἰησοῦ, οὓς ἐλάλησεν διδάσκων ἐπιείκειαν καὶ μακροθυμίαν. οὕτως γὰρ εἶπεν. A similar introductory formula is found later in *1 Clem.* 46.7b–8, μνήσθητε τῶν λόγων τοῦ κυρίου Ἰησοῦ. εἶπεν γάρ.[89] This citation formula, the most ancient of its kind,[90] contains two especially noteworthy elements: the verb μνημονεύειν (or in *1 Clem.* 46.7b the similar μιμνήσκομαι[91]) and the aorist εἶπεν.[92] The appeal to the use of memory to recall sayings spoken in the past places the introductory formula within the

---

[88] As rightly noted by Allison, *Jesus Tradition*, 85.

[89] In ch. 6 below we will discuss the sayings in *1 Clem.* 46.8 that are introduced by this formula. As H. Koester has shown, this introductory formula is clearly distinguishable in Clement from other much briefer and simpler formulas that preface the written OT Scriptures: γέγραπται (4.1; 14.4; 17.3; 29.2; 36.3; 39.3; 46.2; 48.2; 50.4, 6), or λέγει ἡ γραφή (34.6; 35.7; 42.5; cf. 23.3), or simply λέγει (15.2; 21.2; 26.2; 30.4; 34.8; cf. 34.3); see Koester, *Synoptische Überlieferung*, 4–6. Within OT citations Clement may use the aorist εἶπεν, but only for quoting *a speaker* within the passage; to give one example among the many Koester offers (p. 5), in using εἶπεν ὁ θεός when citing Gen 13:14–16 in *1 Clem.* 10.4 (see also *1 Clem.* 18.1; 53.2). Based on the contrast between these citation formulas Koester concludes in part, "Da 1 Clem. seine beiden Herrenworte mit εἶπεν einleitet, kann man wenigstens sagen: er zitiert sie nicht als γραφή" (p. 5). Jesus' words certainly had authority, as indicated by the greater detail and solemnity of the citation formula with which they are introduced (ibid., 5). This authority, however, resided not in their status as written Scripture but in the Lordly identity of the one by whom they had been spoken (τοῦ κυρίου Ἰησοῦ); see ibid., 23 and also Harnack, "Schreiben der römischen Kirche," 92.

[90] Harnack, "Schreiben der römischen Kirche," 92.

[91] On the use of the latter cf. Lk 24:6, 2 Pet 3:2 and Jude 17.

[92] As argued by J. Robinson, the plural λόγοι in the introductory formula may also be significant in pointing to the source of what follows as a collection of sayings of Jesus, similar to what we know of Q ("*Gattung* of Q," 59–65). This, however, says nothing of this source being written or oral, which is our concern here.

context of the early Christian process of preserving and transmitting say-ings of Jesus.[93]

Noteworthy parallels to this citation formula are found in other writ-ings: Acts 20:35 reads, μνημονεύειν τε τῶν λόγων τοῦ κυρίου Ἰησοῦ ὅτι αὐτὸς εἶπεν, and Poly. *Phil.* 2.3, μνημονεύοντες δὲ ὧν εἶπεν ὁ κύριος διδάσκων.[94] As in *1 Clem.* 13.1c–2 and 46.7–8, in both of these parallels we find language for "remembering" (μνημονεύειν) as well as the aorist εἶπεν. In the case of the passage in Acts 20:35, that the words of the Lord which follow the introductory formula (μακάριόν ἐστιν μᾶλλον διδόναι ἢ λαμβάνειν) are not preserved in any of the canonical Gospels, and are prover-bial in form, would further suggest dependence on oral tradition.[95]

Of the parallels provided in J. D. Crossan, ed., *Sayings Parallels: A Workbook for the Jesus Tradition* (FF; Philadephia: Fortress, 1986), 110, W. D. Stroker, *Extracanonical Sayings of Jesus* (SBLRBS 18; Atlanta: Scholars, 1989), 227–28, and J. Jeremias, *Un-known Sayings of Jesus* (1st ed; New York: Macmillan, 1957), the closest to the saying as found in the NA[27] text of Acts are the following (the text from NA[27] is provided for com-parison):

Acts 20:35	μακάριόν ἐστιν μᾶλλον διδόναι ἢ λαμβάνειν
Acts 20:35 sy[p]	μακάριος ὁ διδοὺς μᾶλλον ἢ ὁ λαμβάνων
Apostolic Constitutions 4.2	μακάριον ... τὸν διδόντα ἥπερ τὸν λαμβάνοντα
1Clem. 2.1	ἥδιον διδόντες ἢ λαμβάνοντες·

The saying as found in *1 Clement* remains closer in content to that of Acts, since the em-phasis remains on the action, while the textual variant in sy[p] and the saying as found in the *Apostolic Constitutions* remain closer to the saying as found in Acts *in form* (beati-tude; structure) but focus upon the person rather than the action. It is clear that the *Apos-tolic Constitutions*, which date to the late fourth century, cannot be the source of the

---

[93] See the similar statements in R. Cameron, ed., *The Other Gospels: Non-Canonical Gospel Texts* (Philadelphia: Westminster, 1982), 55–56 (and on what follows see also ibid., pp. 91–124); idem, *Sayings Traditions in the Apocryphon of James* (HTS 34; Phila-delphia: Fortress, 1984; repr., Cambridge, Mass.: Harvard University Press, 2004), 92–93, on the opening scene of the *Apocryphon of James*, which reads "Now the twelve dis-ciples [were] sitting all together at [the same time] and remembering what the Savior had said to each one of them, whether secretly or openly, they were setting it down in books. [And] I was writing what was in [my book] ... (2.7–16; trans. is that of Cameron, *Sayings Traditions*, 91, without his Coptic inserts).

[94] Polycarp *Phil.* 2.3 will be discussed fully in ch. 5 below. Cf. also the well-known use of "remember" language by Papias in the fragments preserved in Eusebius, *Hist. Eccl.* 3.39.3–4, 15–16, in which this terminology is applied specifically to the collection of orally transmitted materials about Jesus, which Papias was about to commit to writing.

[95] See Koester, *Synoptische Überlieferung*, 6; Hagner, *Clement of Rome*, 151, 258, 273, 306–7; Cameron, *Sayings Traditions*, 93; among commentators on Acts see W. Neil, *The Acts of the Apostles* (NCB; London: Marshall, Morgan & Scott/Grand Rapids: Eerd-mans, 1981), 215; R. I. Pervo, *Dating Acts: Between the Evangelists and the Apologists* (Santa Rosa, Calif.: Polebridge, 2006), 228–29; idem, *Acts: A Commentary* (ed. H. W. Attridge; Hermeneia; Minneapolis: Fortress, 2009), 528.

saying in Acts (see C. N. Jefford, "Apostolic Constitutions and Canons," *ABD* 1:312; B. Chilton, "Apostolic Constitutions," *ERPWLA* 37; G. D. Dragas, "Apostolic Constitutions," *EEC* 92), though the reverse may be the case. The textual variant and the parallels may attest to a stream of oral tradition that ran parallel to that which informed Luke in Acts 20:35, or simply a different performance of the same one.

One must also consider the possibility that Luke appropriated the saying from his Greco-Roman context and placed it on the lips of Jesus. This view was expressed by Haenchen (*Acts of the Apostles*, 594–95, n. 5 [who also discusses a number of parallels]), and was followed by J. Jeremias in the 3rd edition of his *Unbekannte Jesusworte* (with O. Hofius; Gütersloh: Gerd Mohn, 1963), 37; E.T.: *Unknown Sayings of Jesus* (2nd Eng. ed.; London: SPCK, 1964), 32–33, who cites Haenchen after expressing this view (p. 37 n. 149; E.T. p. 33 n. 1). The latter is a radical change from the first edition of Jeremias' *Unbekannte Jesusworte* (ATANT 16; Zürich: Zwingli-Verlag, 1948 [pp. 67–69]), where he had argued at length that it was "ein echtes Jesuswort!" See also C. K. Barrett, "Sayings of Jesus in the Acts of the Apostles," in *À cause de l'Évangile: Études sur les Synoptiques et les Actes offertes au P. Jacques Dupont, O.S.B. à l'occasion de son 70ᵉ anniversaire* (LD 123; Paris: Saint-André/Cerf, 1985), 681–708 (who follows Jeremias' change of opinion, see pp. 686–87, and to whom I owe my awareness of the latter). Said appropriation is, however, not likely: first of all, though we cannot here go into detail, it bears noting that the main textual witness in support of Haenchen's argument was a rather doubtful reconstruction of what Thucydides *would* have written *if* he had provided a positive statement similar to Acts 20:35, instead of the negative statement he actually gives (see the argument by J. J. Kilgallen, "Acts 20:35 and Thucydides 2.97.4," in *JBL* 112 [1993]: 312–14). In addition, that the saying had parallels in the ancient world need not imply that Jesus did not use it; rather the opposite is to be expected. D. J. Williams is convincing when he argues, "The use of the emphatic pronoun [αὐτός], the Lord Jesus *himself* said ... rules out the view that the apostle was simply giving the sense of some of our Lord's sayings and not directly quoting. It also tells against the view that this was a Greek proverb taken over by the church and attributed falsely to Jesus, though parallels have been found in Greek literature" (*Acts* [NIBCNT 5; Peabody, Mass.: Hendrickson, 1990], 358, word in italics was in bold in original). Other considerations tell against a source in the Greco-Roman context: Sirach 4:31 shows that the basic idea behind the saying circulated also in Jewish circles, μὴ ἔστω ἡ χείρ σου ἐκτεταμένη εἰς τὸ λαβεῖν, καὶ ἐν τῷ διδόναι συνεσταλμένη, and the *form* is also distinctively Jewish, "Blessed is ..." (on this latter point see Williams, *Acts*, 358; I. H. Marshall, *The Acts of the Apostles* [TNTC; Grand Rapids: Eerdmans, 1980], 336). Witherington points out that the parallel in Sirach as well as "the sapiental form of the saying" may provide evidence that the saying as found in Acts originated in Jesus' teaching, "for Jesus' teaching often took such a form and was indebted to early Jewish sapiental traditions" (*Acts of the Apostles*, 626, and points for further support of this view to his own *Jesus the Sage: The Pilgrimage of Wisdom* [Minneapolis: Fortress, 1994], 147–208). On all of the above see also Barrett, *Acts of the Apostles*, 2.983–84; H. Conzelmann, *Acts of the Apostles: A Commentary on the Acts of the Apostles* (ed. E. J. Epp and C. R. Matthews; trans. J. Limburg, A. T. Kraabel, and D. H. Juel; Hermeneia; Philadelphia: Fortress, 1987), 176.

All of this leads to the conclusion that the language the author of *1 Clement* uses to introduce the sayings of Jesus in 13.1c–2a is fairly standard terminology indicating his use of oral traditional sources.[96]

(b) There are also a number of indicators of orality in *1 Clem.* 13.2. The sayings in Clement on the whole are shorter than in their gospel parallels,[97] and each saying is presented in stylized form, in two clauses: either an imperative followed by a ἵνα clause, or a ὡς clause followed by a οὕτω/ς clause – a pattern broken only minimally by the last saying, that echoes elements of the others (ὡς and ᾧ; οὕτω/ς and αὐτῷ; ὑμῖν and ὑμῖν).

As for their content, all of the sayings in *1 Clem.* 13.2 have been shorn of any elements that would tie them to a narrative context (if these elements were present in the tradition in the first place). In addition, each saying in *1 Clement* has been shaped as a variation upon the golden rule. Here, however, it is not "do unto others as you would have them do unto you" but implicitly "do unto others as you would have *God* do to you." That this is the meaning of the passive in the second clause of each saying (the divine passive[98]) is made clear by the wider context of the passage.[99] It is

---

[96] On all of the above see also Hagner, *Clement of Rome*, 151, 258, 306–7, and esp. 272–73; idem, "Sayings," 235; Koester, *Ancient*, 66, 18; Lona, *Erste Clemensbrief*, 214. B. Dehandschutter dismisses this possibility by reading both *1 Clem.* 13.1–2 and 46.7–8 in light of 53.1, which reads, "For you know the sacred Scriptures, loved ones – and know them quite well – and you have gazed into the sayings [τὰ λόγια] of God. And so we write these things simply as a reminder [πρὸς ἀνάμνησιν]." Dehandschutter posits, "The reminder of the words of Jesus in *1 Clem.* 13,1–2 and 46,7–8 seems to us to be read in the light of 53,1, i.e. it gives no indication of a reference to *oral* tradition (of Jesus-sayings)"; B. Dehandschutter, "Polycarp's Epistle to the Philippians: An Early Example of 'Reception,'" in *The New Testament in Early Christianity: La Réception des écrits Néotestamentaires dans le Christianisme Primitif* (ed. J.-M. Sevrin; BETL 86; Leuven: Leuven University Press and Peeters, 1989), 275–91; repr. in idem, *Polycarpiana: Studies on Martyrdom and Persecution in Early Christianity: Collected Essays* (ed. J. Leemans; BETL 205; Leuven: Leuven University Press and Peeters, 2007), 153–71 (p. 165, emphasis in original, and see further ibid., 169; references here and below are to the reprint). Precisely what one does *not* find in *1 Clem.* 53.1, however, is a combination of the verb "to remember" with the aorist εἶπεν, while the context (52.2–3; 53.3–4) clearly indicates that the reference here is to the Hebrew Scriptures. In light of Koester's argument (see n. 89 on p. 140 above) the citation formulas in 13.2 and 46.7–8 are thus to be clearly differentiated from the language in 53.1 in that the former do not refer to written Scripture in the same manner as the latter.

[97] The only cases in which the sayings in *1 Clement* are not shorter than their parallels in the Gospels are those in which the sayings in the Gospels have also been given the briefest of forms, so that the sayings in *1 Clement* and the Gospels are *equally* brief.

[98] See BDF 72 (sec. 130.1).

[99] Most of the material from *1 Clem.* 6.1 through 15.7 has to do with divine reward or retribution in response to human action, and the introduction to 13.2, "We should espe-

possible to read a number of the other gospel parallels to the sayings in
1 Clem. 13.2 as implying a *human* response, in light of the golden rule
(saying 'c') as found in Matthew and Luke: "In everything you will *that
men* (οἱ ἄνθρωποι) do to you, so you do to them" (Mt 7:12); "And just as
you will *that men* (οἱ ἄνθρωποι) do to you, so likewise do to them" (Lk
6:31). The same saying in *1 Clem.* 13.2, however, should be read, "As you
do, so it will be done (οὕτω ποιηθήσεται) to you" – implicit – "by God."
The contrast, then, between the sayings in *1 Clem.* 13.2 and certain of its
parallels is more than stylistic or structural, but extends also to include the
overall thrust of their content. The sayings in *1 Clem.* 13.2 have been gathered together for the purpose of giving instruction on how one must behave, in an overall spirit of gentleness and patience,[100] if one is to expect
favorable treatment from God.

There is thus a clear contrast between the sayings as found in the Gospels and the sayings in *1 Clement*: when seen in light of the variety in format, application, context and content of the former, the latter appear as a
very uniform string of sound-alike maxims that are very similar in meaning. This uniformity of the Clementine sayings is probably a reflection of
the oral context in which they were gathered and transmitted. A popular
method among traditionists was to group sayings together based on common elements, as an aid to memorization and recall.[101] In the case of the
sayings in *1 Clem.* 13.2, a traditionist (or line of traditionists) probably
grouped the sayings together because of their similar content ("behave in x
manner, and you will be treated in x way") as an aid to their recollection.
This process is probably what also led to the standardization of the style
and format of the sayings, as brief sound-alike maxims related topically to
one another and strung together would be easier to memorize and deliver
in an oral performance.

Finally, as mentioned previously in this chapter, a mnemotechnic approach has almost certainly determined the structure and arrangement of
the sayings in *1 Clem.* 13.2. In keeping with the needs for retaining and
reciting oral material, we find a very rhythmic, echoing structure,

... τε, ἵνα	... θῆτε
... τε, ἵνα	... θῇ ὑμῖν
ὡς ... τε, οὕτω	... ται ὑμῖν
ὡς ... τε, οὕτως	... ται ὑμῖν

---

cially remember the words of our Lord Jesus Christ ..." applies the words of the Lord to
this same theme.

[100] As also made clear by the introduction to the sayings in 13.2, "the words the Lord
Jesus spoke when teaching about gentleness and patience ...."

[101] See sec. 3.3.9 above, entitled "Mnemonically Constructed," and Minchin, "Describing," 49–64.

ὡς ... τε, οὕτως ... σθε
ὡς ... σθε, οὕτως ... ται ὑμῖν
ᾧ ... τε, ἐν αὐτῷ ...ται ὑμῖν

That this structure probably arose from the needs associated with the retention and transmission of oral material further informs our previous discussion of the differences between *1 Clem.* 13.2 and its parallels.[102] Since the structure would have determined the traditionist's choice of conjunctions, pronouns and adverbs (to attain noted rhythm and cadence), the latter owe their very existence in the sayings in *1 Clement* to a particular mnemotechnic approach. This serves to highlight the futility of focusing on this type of differences when comparing the material to its parallels. In a setting of oral retention and transmission of tradition differences such as these are to be expected, and are part and parcel of the traditionists' approach to the material.

It is doubtful whether sufficient evidence could ever be marshaled to conclude with certainty whether the source behind *1 Clem.* 13.2 was an oral Q, Q^{Lk} in oral form, pre-Q oral tradition, or a stream of oral tradition that paralleled Q. This question, however, becomes moot when dealing with orality: the search for a precise oral source that would match verbatim what we find in a written document betrays a bias towards textuality. Oral sources only become available (in this case to Clement, Matthew, Luke, or the editor of Q) in performance; there is no such thing as an original performance or an original text,[103] and no given performance is identical with another.[104] In this situation it becomes difficult to even define the locus of a "source": is it the mind of a certain traditionist who has preserved a particular version of the tradition, or a particular core or "common" version of the tradition that is then given various forms from one performance to the other, or the speicific performance of one traditionist? One clearly cannot speak of "*a* source" in the same way that one would speak of a particular written source on a tangible sheet of papyrus. It is more appropriate to re-think our categories and envision a living, malleable river of tradition from which Q, Luke and Clement have all drawn. The variability in the material currently under consideration makes this image of a river appropriate, while the stability makes it clear that it is the same river – variability within stability, characteristic of the essence of oral tradition.

---

[102] Many have identified a mnemotechnic stamp on this material, and concluded as a result that it may derive from oral sources; see, e.g., Jaubert, *Clément de Rome*, 52, 123 n. 1; Massaux, *Influence*, 1:12.

[103] Draper, "Covenantal Discourse," 71–98, esp. 72.

[104] C. Thomas' words are appropriate here, "In the case of oral tradition, one can never demonstrate exactly what circulated, but only that certain stories were told more than once, in more than one way" ("Word and Deed," 135).

4.6 *1 Clement* 13.2, Oral Tradition, and Orality in Antiquity

We turn now to consider the implications of our thesis that the sayings in question derived from oral tradition for our understanding of the material. One implication is that verbal similarity, which becomes all-important in a study of literary dependence, is of little to no import in the study of oral sources. We saw above, e.g., that in the case of saying 'a' the Lukan parallels to *1 Clem.* 13.2 have no verbal similarity whatsoever, but are similar at the level of *ideas*. In a strictly textual-based study the suggestion of a parallel between these texts might be dismissed as contrived, in that with literary dependence one would expect similarity at the level of *language* and *form* and not just of meaning. In transmitting oral tradition within an informal controlled context, however, there is a degree of freedom for the traditionist to determine the form and the language of the material while remaining true to its meaning. This freedom extends to the process of shaping, for example, oral catechetical material in order to aid its remembrance. As noted above, the tradition in *1 Clem.* 13.2 most likely owes its shape to mnemonic concerns, probably to facilitate its use in a catechetical setting. (Once the catechetical material became fixed, however, it would thereafter retain its form and content fairly tenaciously as long as it continued in that role, due to the process of rote memorization by the catechumens.) Thus saying 'a' in *1 Clement* may derive from an oral reworking of tradition that also informed its Matthean and Lukan parallels, in spite of the lack of verbal and formal similarity.

A similar dynamic is discernible in the case of saying 'f,' which in *1 Clement* reads, "as you show kindness, so will kindness be shown to you" (ὡς χρηστεύεσθε, οὕτως χρηστευθήσεται ὑμῖν). It has often been noted that this saying has no parallel in the Gospels, and strictly speaking this is correct.[105] Luke 6:35c, however, provides a parallel in meaning if not in wording, if one takes into account the Lukan context of the saying. Luke 6:27–38 presents Jesus giving a number of injunctions (among which are found all the other Lukan parallels to *1 Clem.* 13.2 – see further below) centered upon the divine example (vv. 35b–36). The commands to love, be good to, and lend to one's enemies without expecting anything in return (vv. 27–35a) are given with the promise of receiving a great reward, "and you will be children of the Most High, because he is kind to those who are unthankful and evil" (v. 35b). Similarly, the commands to refrain from judging and condemning and instead be generous and forgiving (vv. 37–38), can be summed up by the introductory "Be compassionate even as

---

[105] So, e.g., Koester: "there is no parallel at all in the Synoptic Gospels" ("Extracanonical," 61); Hagner, "completely without parallel in the Synoptics" (*Clement of Rome*, 137); see also Lindemann, *Clemensbriefe*, 54; Lona, *Erste Clemensbrief*, 214.

your Father is compassionate" (γίνεσθε οἰκτίρμονες καθὼς καὶ ὁ πατὴρ ὑμῶν οἰκτίρμων ἐστίν; v. 36).[106] Since, then, the injunctions contained in the whole passage are predicated upon the divine example, the statement that God "is kind (χρηστός) to those who are unthankful and evil" (v. 35b) implies an injunction to "be kind, as you have been shown kindness." This injunction is contained in the commands to love, be good, and lend, in that these commands spring from the divine kindness, even though explicit χρηστός or χρηστεύομαι language is not used in the commands themselves. The parallelism between this implied injunction and saying 'f' as found in *1 Clem.* 13.2 is not perfect: while in *1 Clement* the hearers' expectations are made dependent upon the hearers' prior action ("as you show kindness, so will kindness be shown to you"), the implied parallel in Lk 6 makes the action of the hearers dependent on the prior experience of *divine* action ("be kind as you have been shown kindness"). Not because of this, however, should the hypothetical implied saying and parallelism be dismissed. The parallelism would be of a similar nature to that found in another of the Lukan parallels: whereas in *1 Clem.* 13.2 all of the sayings are structured conditionally, "do *x* and you can expect *x*" or "as you do *x* so will *x* be done to you," the parallel to saying 'a' in Lk 6:36 shows the reverse dynamic: "because you have experienced *x* [from God], do *x*" ("Be merciful, just as your Father is merciful"). The hypothetical implied parallel to saying 'f' would thus share in the same type of parallelism that exists between the forms of saying 'a' as found in *1 Clem.* 13.2 and Lk 6:36. That this hypothetical parallel is located in v. 35 is no coincidence: together with v. 36 it points to the existence of a doublet of sayings, marked by an appeal to the divine example, that in Luke's source together headed up the complex of sayings under discussion in vv. 37–38.

The above comments on saying 'f' may appear to have taken the discussion on a tangent, but in reality they have brought us to the heart of the matter, in that they serve to highlight the insight to be gained by studying these sayings *as oral tradition*. If there is, as argued above, a parallel to saying 'f' implicit in Lk 6, then saying 'f' as recorded in *1 Clem.* 13.2 possibly arose from the reworking of the same stream of tradition upon which Luke is dependent. On the occasion of a new performance of the tradition, or perhaps in the transmission of the material from one traditionist to another, it would have been a simple matter to incorporate the implied injunction to be kind into the list of commandments spoken by Jesus. A hypothesis that would account well for the material as reflected both in Luke and in *1 Clement* is that a new traditionist, upon receiving the oral traditional material from another, gave it his or her preferred mnemotech-

---

[106] Translations such as the NIV that introduce vv. 37 and following with a new heading that marks them off from v. 36 hinder this flow of the text.

nic structure as reflected in *1 Clem.* 13.2. The material was reworked while still in oral form so as to conform to the pattern noted above, "do *x* and you can expect *x*" or "as you do *x* so will *x* be done to you." It was also standardized to facilitate recollection, the first two sayings in the form of an imperative with a ἵνα clause, the remaining sayings in the basic form of ὡς ... οὕτως comparisons (with small variations).[107] In this process, just as the saying that in Luke was given the form "because you have experienced *x* [from God], do *x*" (Lk 6:36; mentioned above) was reworked to conform to this overall pattern, so also the mention of God's kindness became the source for saying 'f,' also in conformity to this overall pattern. This reworking of the material by the traditionist reflects the process by which traditional material was retained and transmitted: it relied on mnemotechnic devices that enabled the faithful passing down of essential meaning, while allowing for flexibility in format.[108]

The above is not the only possible explanation for the shape in which we find this material in *1 Clement* and Luke. It is a *plausible* explanation, however, that would also provide an answer to a question that we have not yet raised: i.e., why there is no apparent parallel to saying 'f' in Lk 6:31–38, when we do find there parallels to all of the other sayings in *1 Clem.* 13.2. Certainly there is no compelling reason why every saying *must* be represented in both contexts, but one may be excused for looking for the remaining parallel if all of the others are present. The answer of course is that there is no readily apparent parallel to saying 'f' in Lk 6:31–38 only because it is not explicit, but implicit, if the above argument be accepted.

If the hypothesis being offered here is correct, then saying 'f' did not originate in the creativity of the early church (a common form-critical view regarding the origin of Jesus tradition).[109] Rather it arose from the very nature of the tradition as dynamic, combining fluid and fixed elements in the memory and performance of the traditionist(s). Tradition was shaped differently not only upon appropriation by each new traditionist, but also in the process of each new performance, all the while retaining its basic message. In one performance an implicit component might be left as such, while in others, given the demands of the situation or audience, the im-

---

[107] See Hagner, *Clement of Rome*, 137.

[108] The opposite may also have been the case: the traditionists responsible for the material that became available to Luke may have reworked the sayings so that an explicit parallel to saying 'f' dropped out; the above is offered, however, as a plausible scenario of how this particular tradition may have been handled while in oral form.

[109] See the discussion of form criticism in sec. 1.4.1 above.

plicit might be made explicit; and an implicit element made explicit might remain so in subsequent retellings.[110]

Finally, *1 Clem.* 13.2 provides an illustration of the socially identified nature of oral tradition: not all oral traditions are preserved, but only those that remain socially relevant. One of the ways in which oral tradition retains its social relevance is through reinterpretation, bringing out the applicability of the tradition to the present. If, as argued above, Clement is citing Jesus' words from the oral-traditional discourse that circulated among the churches, he has applied them in a way that is not envisioned in this source. In the pre-Q discourse examined above, the sayings function within a context of covenant renewal.[111] In that context, the injunctions to be merciful, not judge, not condemn, forgive, and give generously (Lk 6:36–38) relate to every-day social realities having to do with the oppression of the poor and powerless by the rich and powerful (Lk 6:20–35).[112] In *1 Clement*, however, the sayings are applied to a situation of inner-church schism brought about by jealousy and envy over leadership (*1 Clem.* 1.1–6.4). This had brough about the deposition of some of the older presbyters within the church by younger members (44.1–6), and the author is calling the latter to repentance and obedience (7.1–13.1). It is in this context that we find Clement's citation of the words of Jesus, where they are explicitly referred to as Jesus' teaching regarding "gentleness and patience" (13.1b).

4.7 Conclusions

The sayings of Jesus contained in *1 Clem.* 13.2 almost certainly derived from an oral-traditional source. This conclusion is supported by external as well as internal evidence: externally, not only is there no conclusive evidence to indicate that Clement depended on any known written sources, but also a consideration of *1 Clem.* 13.2 and its parallels points to the existence of a block of oral tradition that predated not only the Synoptics but also Q, and that circulated fairly widely in early Christianity. The discussion in this chapter provided good reason to hold that Clement derived the

---

[110] The above reflects the presupposition, held for the sake of argument, that the block of material that fed into what became Lk 6:31–38 is earlier than that found in *1 Clem.* 13.2; but what has been said would also hold true – in reverse order – if the contrary were the case. The traditionist who compiled *1 Clem.* 13.2 as we know it may have reworked a source in which saying 'f' was explicit, to make it implicit.

[111] See Horsley, "Covenant Renewal"; idem, "Performance and Tradition"; Draper, "Covenantal Discourse."

[112] See J. B. Green, *The Gospel of Luke* (NICNT; Grand Rapids: Eerdmans, 1997), 260–75.

sayings in 13.2 from this block of tradition. In addition, it argued that perhaps this block of tradition, rather than Q, was also the source for the parallel sayings in Luke. Internally, the conclusion that *1 Clem.* 13.2 derived from oral tradition is based upon indicators of orally-conceived discourse such as the stylized form of the sayings, their rhythmic pattern, and their rhyming endings (described above as "a very uniform string of sound-alike maxims that are very similar in meaning"), all of which indicates that a mnemonic structure has been superimposed on the material. The introductory words that preface *1 Clem.* 13.2 (μεμνημένοι τῶν λόγων τοῦ κυρίου Ἰησοῦ, οὓς ἐλάλησεν) also support the conclusion that they derived from oral tradition.

That the sayings of Jesus in *1 Clem.* 13.2 are oral tradition set in writing makes them the suitable object of study in seeking to understand both the characteristics of oral tradition and how it might have functioned in Christian antiquity. The transmission of oral tradition is not characterized by verbatim similarity, as is the case of literary dependence between texts, but by variability within stability. By focusing upon the variability, one can identify how oral tradition was shaped in any given performance to address specific needs within a community, thus maintaining its relevance, or how a traditionist might have applied mnemonic techniques to a tradition (with the implied freedom to chance its wording and/or structure) in order to facilitate its recall and performance. The flexibility of the tradition allows for a traditionist to emphasize certain elements and leave out others, making explicit in certain performances elements that in others might remain implicit. By focusing on the stability one can ascertain the continuity in transmission implied by the word "tradition." In certain cases this continuity finds expression at the level of meaning, while the tradition is couched in an almost completely different wording.

The overall goal for this chapter, as stated in its introduction, was to begin to demonstrate that the presuppositions of orality better inform the study of the texts under consideration than those of scribality. In light of the conclusions drawn above, hopefully this goal has been attained. We will continue to pursue the same goal in the chapters that follow, while focusing on other texts.

Chapter 5

The Explicit Appeal to Jesus Tradition in Polycarp's *Epistle to the Philippians* 2.3

5.1 Introduction

Having examined *1 Clem.* 13.2 in the previous chapter, we now turn to consider its close parallel in Polycarp's *Epistle to the Philippians* 2.3. As in chapter 4, in this chapter we will also seek to 1) identify elements within the text that might indicate the author's use of oral sources for the Jesus tradition he cites, and 2) draw out implications for the manner in which oral tradition was used, or how it functioned, in the early Christian group to which the author belonged.

Repeating the procedure followed in the previous chapter, our discussion of Pol. *Phil.* 2.3 is prefaced below by the text followed by a synopsis of its parallels, this time in their Philippian order. To facilitate discussion and avoid confusion, the letters a–g used in the previous chapter for the parallels from *1 Clement* will be retained, placed before the pertinent Clementine saying (when applicable), while roman numerals will be used for the Philippian sayings. The discussion in this chapter will refer to the roman numerals unless the Clementine saying has no parallel in Polycarp, in which case the letters associated with *1 Clement* will be used.[1]

Polycarp Philippians *2.3*

μνημονεύοντες δὲ ὧν εἶπεν ὁ κύριος διδάσκων·
    Μὴ κρίνετε ἵνα μὴ κριθῆτε·
      ἀφίετε καὶ ἀφεθήσεται ὑμῖν·
    ἐλεᾶτε ἵνα ἐλεηθῆτε·
      ᾧ μέτρῳ μετρεῖτε ἀντιμετρηθήσεται ὑμῖν·
    καὶ ὅτι μακάριοι οἱ πτωχοὶ καὶ οἱ διωκόμενοι ἕνεκεν δικαιοσύνης
      ὅτι αὐτῶν ἐστὶν ἡ βασιλεία τοῦ θεοῦ.

---

[1] For text-critical issues related to the texts that follow, see notes to the synopsis in section 4.1 above.

I) Pol. *Phil.* 2.3:   <u>μὴ κρίνετε</u>   <u>ἵνα μὴ κριθῆτε</u>
e) *1 Clem.* 13.2:   ὡς <u>κρίνετε</u>,   οὕτως <u>κριθήσεσθε</u>
    Mt 7:1:   <u>μὴ κρίνετε</u>   <u>ἵνα μὴ κριθῆτε</u>
    Mt 7:2a: ἐν ᾧ γὰρ κρίματι <u>κρίνετε</u>   <u>κριθήσεσθε</u>
    Lk 6:37a: καὶ <u>μὴ κρίνετε</u>   καὶ οὐ <u>μὴ κριθῆτε</u>
    Lk 6:37b: καὶ μὴ καταδικάζετε   καὶ οὐ μὴ καταδικασθῆτε
    Cl. *Strom.* 2.91.2:   ὡς <u>κρίνετε</u>,   οὕτως <u>κριθήσεσθε</u>
    Didasc. 2.42:   ᾧ κρίματι <u>κρίνετε</u>   <u>κριθήσεσθε</u>
                        καὶ ὡς καταδικάζετε   καταδικασθήσεσθε

II) Pol. *Phil.* 2.3b: <u>ἀφίετε</u>   <u>καὶ ἀφεθήσεται ὑμῖν</u>
b) *1 Clem.* 13.2:   <u>ἀφίετε</u>   <u>ἵνα ἀφεθῇ   ὑμῖν</u>
    Mt 6:14:   Ἐὰν γὰρ <u>ἀφῆτε</u> τοῖς ἀνθρώποις //   <u>ἀφήσει καὶ ὑμῖν</u>
                        τὰ παραπτώματα αὐτῶν   //   ὁ πατὴρ ὑμῶν ὁ οὐράνιος
    Mk 11:25:   <u>ἀφίετε</u> εἴ τι ἔχετε   // <u>ἵνα καὶ</u> ὁ πατὴρ <u>ὑμῶν</u> ὁ ἐν τοῖς
                        κατά τινος   //   οὐρανοῖς <u>ἀφῇ ὑμῖν</u> τὰ
                                                            παραπτώματα ὑμῶν
    Lk 6:37c: ἀπολύετε   <u>καὶ ἀπολυθήσεσθε</u>
    Didasc. 2.21:   <u>ἄφετε</u>   <u>καὶ ἀφεθήσεται ὑμῖν</u>
    Ps.Mac. *Hom.* 37.3:   <u>ἄφετε</u>   <u>καὶ ἀφεθήσεται ὑμῖν</u>

III) Pol. *Phil.* 2.3:   <u>ἐλεᾶτε</u>   <u>ἵνα ἐλεηθῆτε</u>
a) *1 Clem.* 13.2:   <u>ἐλεᾶτε</u>   <u>ἵνα ἐλεηθῆτε</u>
    Mt 5:7:   μακάριοι οἱ <u>ἐλεήμονες</u>   ὅτι αὐτοὶ <u>ἐλεηθήσονται</u>
    Lk 6:36:   γίνεσθε οἰκτίρμονες   καθὼς [καὶ] ὁ πατὴρ ὑμῶν
                                                            οἰκτίρμων ἐστίν
    Lk 6:37c: ἀπολύετε   καὶ ἀπολυθήσεσθε
    Cl. *Strom.* 2.91.2:   <u>ἐλεᾶτε</u>, φησὶν ὁ κύριος,   <u>ἵνα ἐλεηθῆτε</u>

IV) Pol. *Phil.* 2.3:   <u>ᾧ μέτρῳ μετρεῖτε ἀντιμετρηθήσεται ὑμῖν</u>
g) *1 Clem.* 13.2:   <u>ᾧ μέτρῳ μετρεῖτε</u>, ἐν αὐτῷ <u>μετρηθήσεται ὑμῖν</u>
    Mt 7:2b: ἐν <u>ᾧ μέτρῳ μετρεῖτε μετρηθήσεται ὑμῖν</u>
    Mk 4:24c: ἐν <u>ᾧ μέτρῳ μετρεῖτε   μετρηθήσεται ὑμῖν</u> καὶ προστεθήσεται <u>ὑμῖν</u>
    Luke 6:38c: <u>ᾧ</u> γὰρ <u>μέτρῳ μετρεῖτε ἀντιμετρηθήσεται ὑμῖν</u>
    Cl. *Strom.* 2.91.2: <u>ᾧ μέτρῳ μετρεῖτε ἀντιμετρηθήσεται ὑμῖν</u>

V) Pol. *Phil.* 2.3: καὶ ὅτι

                        <u>μακάριοι οἱ πτωχοὶ</u> καὶ οἱ <u>διωκόμενοι ἕνεκεν δικαιοσύνης</u>
    Mt 5:3:   <u>μακάριοι οἱ πτωχοὶ</u> τῷ πνεύματι,
    Mt 5:10:   <u>μακάριοι οἱ</u>   <u>δεδιωγμένοι ἕνεκεν δικαιοσύνης</u>
    Lk 6:20b: <u>μακάριοι οἱ πτωχοί</u>

    Pol. *Phil.* 2.3:   <u>ὅτι αὐτῶν   ἐστὶν ἡ βασιλεία τοῦ θεοῦ</u>
    Mt 5:3:   <u>ὅτι αὐτῶν   ἐστιν ἡ βασιλεία τῶν οὐρανῶν</u>
    Mt 5:10:   <u>ὅτι αὐτῶν   ἐστιν ἡ βασιλεία τῶν οὐρανῶν</u>
    Lk 6:20b: <u>ὅτι ὑμετέρα ἐστὶν ἡ βασιλεία τοῦ θεοῦ</u>

5.2 The Date of Polycarp's Letter

Before one can address whether there are sufficient grounds for positing a literary relationship between Pol. *Phil.* 2.3 and the documents represented in the above synopsis, one must first settle the issue of the dating of *Philippians*. Currently there is a widespread misperception among scholars, arising from a work by P. N. Harrison, that *Philippians* is a composite document, made up of two letters written ca. A.D. 117 and 135.[2] Clearly this has ramifications for whether or not Polycarp had access to the documents in question: such a late date as A.D. 135 for part of *Philippians* would increase the likelihood that the Gospels, for example, would have reached Polycarp before writing that part of the letter. Due to the importance of this issue we will address it in some detail in what follows.

Traditionally *Philippians* has been dated shortly after the death of Ignatius of Antioch in Rome, which according to Eusebius (*Hist. Eccl.* 3.36) took place during the reign of Trajan, or sometime between A.D. 98 and 117.[3] This date is based on evidence internal to the correspondence of Polycarp and Ignatius: from Ignatius' letters we learn that his route to Rome led through Smyrna, where he met Polycarp, and that he wrote letters both to the church in Smyrna and to Polycarp.[4] Polycarp would thus have been aware of Ignatius' impending martyrdom. Polycarp's language in *Phil.* 9.1–2a can be read to imply both that Ignatius was recently alive, and that Polycarp assumed that he had been martyred:

[1] Therefore I urge all of you to obey the word of righteousness and to practice all endurance, which you also observed with your own eyes not only in *the most fortunate Ignatius*, Zosimus, and Rufus, but also in others who lived among you, and in Paul himself and the other apostles. [2] You should be convinced that none of them acted in vain, but in faith and righteousness, and that *they are in the place they deserved, with the Lord, with whom they also suffered.*

While this traditional dating of *Philippians* has seen various challengers since the 18th century,[5] current scholarship has been most affected by the

---

[2] P. N. Harrison, *Polycarp's Two Epistles to the Philippians* (Cambridge: Cambridge University Press, 1936); we will not refer to the details of his argument here, as this will be done below, in supporting the argument that his theory is a misperception of the evidence.

[3] I am indebted for the brief history of scholarship that follows especially to W. R. Schoedel, "Polycarp of Smyrna and Ignatius of Antioch," *ANRW* 2.27.1:276–85, and also to Harrison, *Polycarp*, 27–72, and Hartog, *Polycarp*, 3–16. This indebtedness remains throughout, even though I have chosen not to clutter the footnotes with every reference I owe to them.

[4] See Ign. *Eph.* 21.1; *Magn.* 15.1; *Trall.* 12.1; *Rom.* 10.1 as well as Ign. *Smyrn.* intro.; 12.1; *Poly.* intro.; 8.1.

[5] See Schoedel, "Polycarp and Ignatius," 276–85.

theory proposed in 1936 by P. N. Harrison in his work *Polycarp's Two Epistles to the Philippians.*[6] The focus of Harrison's argument is the apparent contrast between Poly. *Phil.* 9.1–2a, quoted above, and 13.2c, where Polycarp requests that the Philippians let him know what they had learned "more definitely about Ignatius himself and those who *are with him.*" In Harrison's view, while in 9.2 Polycarp seems to assume that Ignatius is already dead, in 13.2 he seems to assume that he is still alive, so chapters 9 and 13 could not have been written at the same time.[7] Based on this and a number of other considerations Harrison argues that *Philippians* is composed of two letters, both written by Polycarp, that have been conflated: while Polycarp wrote chapter 13 (and possibly 14) shortly after the death of Ignatius, or around the year A.D. 117 (give or take several years), as a cover letter to accompany a collection of Ignatius' epistles,[8] he wrote chapters 1–12 as a separate letter toward the end of Hadrian's reign, or ca. A.D. 135–137.[9] Harrison's thesis has received such wide acceptance over the past seventy-five years that it has now become the majority view.[10]

---

[6] Harrison was not the first to challenge this reading of the evidence in Polycarp, but he merits special attention here, as he has exerted more influence that any other scholar upon Polycarp studies over the last century.

[7] Harrison bases his argument upon the previous work of Johannes Dallaeus, *De Scriptis quae sub Dionysii Aeropagitae et Ignatii Antiocheni nominibus circumferuntur* (Geneva: Antonii & Tournes, 1666), 2.425–29.

[8] Harrison, *Polycarp*, 15: "not long before the end of Trajan's reign" (A.D. 115–117?), or possibly "several years later."

[9] Harrison, *Polycarp*, 243; "within a year or so of A.D. 135–137" (ibid., 315), or perhaps A.D. 133 (ibid., 268).

[10] See, e.g., B. Altaner, *Patrology* (trans. H. C. Graef; Freiburg: Herder/London: Nelson, 1960), 111; J. Bapt. Bauer, *Die Polykarpbriefe* (KAV 5; Göttingen: Vandenhoeck & Ruprecht, 1995), 18–21, 62–63; Bellinzoni, "Gospel of Matthew," 207–9; Berding, *Polycarp*, 15–24; P. T. Camelot, *Ignace d'Antioche, Polycarpe de Smyrne: Lettres, Martyre de Polycarpe* (4th ed.; SC 10 bis; Paris: Cerf, 1998), 165–66; H. R. Drobner, *The Fathers of the Church: A Comprehensive Introduction* (trans. S. S. Schatzmann; Peabody, Mass.: Hendrickson, 2007), 52; Ehrman, *Apostolic Fathers*, 1:327–29; F. X. Glimm, "The Letter of St. Polycarp to the Philippians," in *The Apostolic Fathers* (ed. F. X. Glimm, J. M.-F. Marique, and G. Walsh; FC 1; New York: Cima, 1947), 131–33; R. Hvalvik, "All Those Who in Every Place Call on the Name of Our Lord Jesus Christ: The Unity of the Pauline Churches," in *The Formation of the Early Church* (ed. J. Ådna; WUNT 183; Tübingen: Mohr Siebeck, 2005), 139; J. A. Kleist, *The Didache, The Epistle of Barnabas, The Epistles and the Martyrdom of St. Polycarp, The Fragments of Papias, The Epistle to Diognetus* (ACW 6; Westminster: Newman, 1948), 71; O. Knoch, "Petrus und Paulus in den Schriften der apostolischen Väter," in *Kontinuität und Einheit: Für Franz Mußner* (ed. P.-G. Müller and W. Stenger; Freiburg: Herder, 1981), 251 and n. 31; idem, "Kenntnis," 169–70; Koester, *Synoptische Überlieferung*, 122–23; idem, *Introduction to the New Testament,* Vol. 2: *History and Literature of Early Christianity* (2nd ed.; New York and Berlin: de Gruyter, 2000), 309; idem, *Ancient*, 19, n. 3; K. Lake, Review of Harrison,

In spite of its wide acceptance, Harrison's thesis rests upon very slim evidence. Even among those who have accepted Harrison's overall thesis of two letters, few have extended acceptance to every aspect of his argument. Most scholars have been especially reticent to accept such a late date as A.D. 135–137 for the hypothetical second letter (this is ironic, given that much of Harrison's argument for conflation in *Philippians* depends on his ability to show that it presupposes a much later date than the "first"). What is more, scholars over the past seven-plus decades have shown that most of the elements of Harrison's argument for conflation in *Philippians* are unfounded: his appeal to analogies of conflation in other early Christian literature;[11] his contention that the main reason Polycarp wrote *Phil.* 1–12 was to deal with the crisis occasioned by Marcion in Philippi;[12] his arguments based on Polycarp's age,[13] Polycarp's multiple references to books that were included in the NT canon,[14] and multiple allusions to Igna-

---

Polycarp, *JBL* 56 (1937): 72–75; J. Quasten, *Patrology* (ed. A. di Berardino; 4 vols.; Westminster: Christian Classics, 1983–86), 1:79–80.

[11] Harrison, *Polycarp*, 20–24; A. C. Headlam asks rather wryly, "But what support is given to one guess, by the fact that some people have made similar guesses about other books?" and concludes, "I should say none" ("The Epistle of Polycarp to the Philippians [Review of Harrison, *Polycarp*]," *CQR* 141 [1945]: 4); see further Hartog, *Polycarp*, 151.

[12] Harrison, *Polycarp*, 169–206, see also ibid., 13–14, 267–68, 313–14; on this Harrison is followed unhesitatingly by Kleist, *Didache*, 72, 192. C. M. Nielsen's suggestion that the heretic combated in *Phil.* is in fact Marcion, and that we find no condemnation of Marcion's use of the OT because on this Polycarp was in agreement with him, amounts to no more than speculation ("Polycarp and Marcion: A Note," *TS* 47 [1986]: 297–99). Against this view see: L. W. Barnard, "The Problem of St. Polycarp's Epistle to the Philippians," in idem, *Studies in the Apostolic Fathers and their Background* (Oxford: Blackwell, 1966), 34–35; Berding, *Polycarp*, 21–23; ; C. J. Cadoux, Review of Harrison, *Polycarp*, *JTS* 38 (1937): 268–69; Hartog, *Polycarp*, 94, 151–52; H. O. Maier, "Purity and Danger in Polycarp's Epistle to the Philippians: The Sin of Valens in Social Perspective," *JECS* 1 (1993): 230–31; idem, Review of J. B. Bauer, *Die Polykarpbriefe*, *JTS* n.s. 47 (1996): 642–45; Schoedel, *Polycarp, Martyrdom, Papias*, 23–26. For works that preceded Harrison yet contain refutations of his argument, see W. Bauer, *Die Briefe des Ignatius von Antiochia und der Polykarpbrief* (HNT: AV 2; Tübingen: Mohr Siebeck, 1920), 291–92; Lightfoot, *Apostolic Fathers*, 2.1:584–87; idem, *Essays on the Work Entitled Supernatural Religion* (London and New York: Macmillan, 1889), 116–20.

[13] Harrison, *Polycarp*, 13–16, 170–71, 268–83, 316; against this view see Hartog, *Polycarp*, 153–54; Lightfoot, *Apostolic Fathers*, 2.1:583; and similarly idem, *Essays*, 121.

[14] Harrison, *Polycarp*, 16, 231–66 (esp. 250); 285–310, 315. Harrison (ibid., 306) lists as NT books that Polycarp likely knew "beyond reasonable doubt" Mt, Lk, Acts, the Pauline Epistles, the Pastorals, 1 Pet, 1 Jn, as well as the non-canonical books of *1 Clement* and "a collection of Ignatian epistles"; and "with some probability" Heb, Jas, Jude and "possibly also" 2 and 3 Jn and Mk, as well as "each of our seven Ignatians." Against this view see Cadoux, Review, 269; Hagner, "Sayings," 235–37, 240; idem, *Clement of Rome*, 142–43; Hartog, *Polycarp*, 152, 170–97; Holmes, "Polycarp and the Writings,"

tius;[15] and his preferred reading of Poly. *Phil.* 1.1 that implies that Ignatius had visited the Philippians some twenty years earlier.[16]

All that remains of Harrison's argument after deleting the above elements is a single, questionable tenet: that the present tense of a Latin verb in *Phil.* 13.2c is the only possible reading. That this portion of the verse survives only in Latin translation constitutes the root of the problem. The text reads, *et de ipso Ignatio et de his, qui cum eo sunt, quod certius agnoveritis, significate* ("And let us know what you have learned more definitely about Ignatius himself and *those who are with him*"). While the Latin is clearly in the present tense, J. Pearson, J. B. Lightfoot, and Theodore Zahn have argued that *qui cum eo sunt* ("those who are with him") was probably an a-temporal phrase in the original Greek, given that in other cases the same translator adds a tense in rendering a-temporal Greek phrases into Latin.[17] This would imply that the discrepancy that Harrison finds between chapters 9 and 13 rests upon a mistranslation, and this single remaining basis upon which one might posit the conflation of two letters in *Philippians* is more imagined than real.

In fairness to Harrison, he never intended for his theory of two letters to rest solely on the apparent discrepancy between chapters 9 and 13, even

---

187–227, esp. 225–27. Certain scholars who have followed Harrison's conflation theory also argue for Polycarp's use of Mt and Lk, and it is hard to avoid the suspicion that the presupposition of a later dating has influenced their decision regarding this use; see, e.g., Koester, *Introduction to the NT*, 2:308–9, who in dependence upon Harrison dates Polycarp's *Philippians* "after the year 130"; idem, "Apocryphal and Canonical Gospels," *HTR* 73 (1980): 105–30 (repr. pages 3–23 in idem, *Jesus to the Gospels*, 3–23), 109 n. 13 in original, 6 n. 13 in repr.: "A.D. 140"; Cameron, *Sayings Traditions*, 113 (originally a dissertation written under Koester and others).

[15] Harrison, *Polycarp*, 132, 160, 163–65, 316; against this view see Hartog, *Polycarp*, 152–53; Schoedel, *Polycarp, Martyrdom, Papias*, 38; idem, "Polycarp and Ignatius," 281.

[16] Harrison, *Polycarp*, 155–62. Against this view see esp. W. R. Schoedel, "Polycarp's Witness to Ignatius of Antioch," *VC* 41 (1987): 1–10, and also idem, *Polycarp, Martyrdom, Papias*, 9, 40; Barnard, "Problem of Polycarp," 33; Cadoux, Review, 268; Holmes, "Polycarp and the Writings" 187 n. 3.

[17] J. Pearson, *Vindiciae epistolarum S. Ignatii* (Cambridge: Hayes, 1672), 2.72; repr. *Ss. Patrum qui temporibus apostolicis floruerunt opera*, 2nd ed. (Antwerp: Huguetaronum, 1698). Zahn suggested that the original Greek read καὶ περὶ αὐτοῦ τοῦ Ἰγνατίου καὶ περὶ τῶν μετ᾽ αὐτοῦ or σὺν αὐτῷ (see Schoedel, "Polycarp and Ignatius," 278 n. 21); Lightfoot suggested either τοῖς σὺν αὐτῷ or τοῖς μετ᾽ αὐτοῦ (*Apostolic Fathers*, 2.1:578), but favored τοῖς σὺν αὐτῷ, since "in the opening of this epistle ... τοῖς σὺν αὐτῷ is translated in the same way 'qui cum eo sunt,' and thus has been wrongly rendered as a present" (ibid., 2.3:349); see Lightfoot's full discussion in ibid., 2.1:588–89 = idem, *Essays*, 111–13, where he notes other instances in which the Latin translator of *Phil.* has provided a temporal translation of a-temporal Greek verbs.

if it has come down to that.[18] Rather ironically, many of the scholars who have removed every one of the other supports for Harrison's argument over the last seven and a half decades continue to appeal to his work as if he had succeeded in what he had set out to do.[19] Those who continue to appeal to Harrison in support of the theory of two letters in Polycarp's *Philippians* in reality are appealing to a single factor: the apparent discrepancy between *Philippians* 9 and 13.[20] Harrison himself was reticent to do this; he was willing to admit that one could adopt an a-temporal retro-translation of *Phil.* 13.2 "*if* on other grounds it seems ... preferable."[21] Given all of the above, an a-temporal retro-translation does seem preferable. Since the theory of conflation is so complex, and rests upon so many tenets shown to be false, the theory of a mistranslation that would retain the integrity of the letter is much to be preferred. It is thus time to abandon the theory of two conflated letters in *Philippians*, or at least to recognize that it is a possible but unlikely and unproven hypothesis.

The following study of *Philippians* will proceed, then, based on the presupposition of the letter's integrity.[22] Viewed as a single letter, one can date it based on the internal evidence discussed above to the year of Ignatius' martyrdom. A small amount of uncertainty still remains, in that the

---

[18] Harrison intended for his argument to be cumulative. To use his own imagery, he wished to build a "bundle" of twigs: "It may happen that a twig may be withdrawn here or there from the bundle, and snapped across impatient knees, whereas the bundle itself does not even bend" (*Polycarp*, 75). The present monograph does not provide the last word on the matter, but it does seem in light of the above discussion that Harrison's bundle is made up of a single twig – the apparent contradiction between *Phil.* 9 and 13.

[19] Harrison's approach assumed that there was no single historical situation "into which the whole of the Epistle may be fitted naturally" (*Polycarp*, 31). Much of the force of his argument was meant to derive from internal evidence in the "second letter" that indicated (in his view) that it was written decades after the "first." It follows that the above theories that seek to modify Harrison's proposal by assigning an earlier date to the "second letter" end up destroying its very foundations.

[20] See the similar statements in M. Holmes, "Polycarp of Smyrna, *Letter to the Philippians*," *ExpTim* 118.2 (2006): 53–63, repr. in *Writings of the Apostolic Fathers* (ed. Foster), 108–25 (pp. 121, 123; references here and below are to the reprint).

[21] Harrison, *Polycarp*, 36, emphasis in the original.

[22] Others who argue for the integrity of *Philippians* include Dehandschutter, "Polycarp's Epistle," 156–57; idem, "The Epistle of Polycarp," in *Apostolic Fathers* (ed. Pratscher), 120–22; Hartog, *Polycarp*, 148–69; Holmes, "Polycarp, *Letter to the Philippians*," 120–23; Louth, *Apostolic Fathers*, 116; H. Paulsen, *Die Briefe des Ignatius von Antiochia und der Brief des Polykarp von Smyrna* (Zweite, neubearbeitete Auflage der Auslegung von Walter Bauer. HNT 18: AV 2; Tübingen: Mohr Siebeck, 1985);112; Schoedel, *Polycarp, Martyrdom, Papias*, 4, 29, 37–39; idem, "Polycarp and Ignatius," 277–83.

precise date of Ignatius' martyrdom is not known, but one can at least date
the letter fairly confidently to ca. A.D. 107.[23]

5.3 Poly. *Phil.* 2.3 in Relation to its Parallels

We turn now to consider whether there is sufficient reason to posit a literary relationship between Polycarp's *Philippians* and the documents represented in the synopsis at the beginning of this chapter. On the basis of a
date ca. A.D. 107 for the letter, the same documents that were set aside in
the previous chapter as not providing a source for the sayings of Jesus in

---

[23] Scholars almost unanimously date Ignatius' martyrdom to the reign of Trajan
(A.D. 98–117), as chronicled by Eusebius (*Hist. Eccl.* 3.36); see esp. C. Trevett, *A Study
of Ignatius of Antioch in Syria and Asia* (SBEC 29; Lewiston: Mellen, 1992), 3–9; also B.
Dehandschutter, "Ignatian Epistles," *RPP* 6:406–7; G. F. Snyder, "Ignatius of Antioch,"
EEC 559–60; Lightfoot, *Apostolic Fathers*, 2.1:30; 2.2:398–434, 477 n. 1. That the
younger Pliny (governor of Bithynia) in his correspondence with Trajan mentions other
Christian martyrdoms within this period, and close to the cities to which Ignatius writes,
tends to support this general date (*Ep.* 10.96–97); see Trevett, *Study of Ignatius,* 4; Ehrman, *Apostolic Fathers*, 1:205. It used to be assumed that one could date Ignatius' death
precisely to the year 107 based on Eusebius' *Chronicon*, who speaks of it after mentioning the 221st Olympiad, coinciding with the tenth year of Trajan's reign (for the text see
Lightfoot, *Apostolic Fathers*, 2.2:449; Harrison, *Polycarp*, 211). Harnack showed, however (and Lightfoot followed him on this), that in arranging his material in the *Chronicon*
after a round date (tenth year of Trajan) rather than opposite a specific year, Eusebius
was indicating uncertainty regarding the specific date, assigning it to a rough period of
time (see Harrison, *Polycarp*, 211; Lightfoot, *Apostolic Fathers*, 2.2:449). One may use
Eusebius' rough reckoning, however, allowing for five years before and after the tenth
year of Trajan, to establish a working date of ca. A.D. 102–112. This traditional date has
been contested recently by the work of R. M. Hübner, "Thesen zur Echtheit und Datierung der sieben Briefe des Ignatius von Antiochen," *ZAC/JAC* 1 (1997): 44–72 and T.
Lechner, *Ignatius adversus Valentinianos? Chronologische und theologiegeschichtliche
Studien zu den Briefen des Ignatius von Antiochien* (VCSup 47; Leiden: Brill, 1999), both
of whom attribute Ignatius' letters to a forger engaged in anti-Valentinian polemic, who
wrote ca. A.D. 165–175. If Hübner and Lechner are correct (and there is good reason to
judge that they are not) the date of Ignatius' martyrdom, to which is tied the date of Polycarp's *Philippians*, can only vaguely be assigned to A.D. 105–135; see P. Foster, "The
Epistles of Ignatius of Antioch," *ExpTim* 117.12 (2006): 487–95; 118.1 (2006): 2–11
(repr. in *Writings of the Apostolic Fathers* [ed. Foster], 81–107), 88 (references here and
below are to the reprint); Drobner, *Fathers of the Church*, 50. But see in response to
Hübner and Lechner: M. J. Edwards, "Ignatius and the Second Century: An Answer to R.
Hübner," *ZAC/JAC* 2 (1998): 214–26; A. Lindemann, "Antwort auf die 'Thesen zur
Echtheit und Datierung der sieben Briefe des Ignatius von Antiochen,'" *ZAC/JAC* 1
(1997): 185–94; G. Schöllgen, "Die Ignatianen als pseudepigraphisches Briefcorpus:
Anmerkung zu den Thesen von Reinhard M. Hübner," *ZAC/JAC* 2 (1998): 16–25; H. J.
Vogt, "Bemerkungen zur Echtheit der Ignatiusbriefe," *ZAC/JAC* 3 (1999): 50–63.

1 Clement can also be set aside in the case of *Philippians*. Clement of Alexandria's *Stromateis*, the *Didascalia*, and Pseudo-Macarius' *Homilies* were composed too late (late 2nd, early 3rd, and 4th to 5th centuries respectively) to provide a source for the sayings of Jesus in *Philippians*.

It is also unlikely that any of these three documents witnesses to a nonextant written source from which both they and *Philippians* independently derived these sayings. Clement of Alexandria (as noted in chapter 4) is dependent upon *1 Clement* for the Jesus tradition under consideration.[24] The *Didascalia*'s form of saying I is closer to both Mt 7:2a and Lk 6:37 than to the form of the saying in *Philippians* (which is closer to Mt 7:1 than to Mt 7:2a), so there is little reason to posit that the *Didascalia* and *Philippians* together witness to a non-canonical written source. Saying II in *Philippians* is closer both to the *Didascalia* and to Ps.-Macarius than to the form of the saying in any of the other documents, as can be seen in the following partial reproduction from the synopsis at the beginning of this chapter:

II) Pol. *Phil.* 2.3b:	ἀφίετε		καὶ ἀφεθήσεται ὑμῖν
b) *1 Clem.* 13.2:	ἀφίετε		ἵνα ἀφεθῇ ὑμῖν
Mt 6:14:	Ἐὰν γὰρ ἀφῆτε τοῖς ἀνθρώποις//		ἀφήσει καὶ ὑμῖν
	τὰ παραπτώματα αὐτῶν	//	ὁ πατὴρ ὑμῶν ὁ οὐράνιος
Mk 11:25:	ἀφίετε εἴ τι ἔχετε	//	ἵνα καὶ ὁ πατὴρ ὑμῶν ὁ ἐν τοῖς
	κατά τινος	//	οὐρανοῖς ἀφῇ ὑμῖν τὰ
			παραπτώματα ὑμῶν
Lk 6:37c:	ἀπολύετε		καὶ ἀπολυθήσεσθε
Didasc. 2.21:	ἄφετε		καὶ ἀφεθήσεται ὑμῖν
Ps.Mac. *Hom.* 37.3:	ἄφετε		καὶ ἀφεθήσεται ὑμῖν

The proverbial nature of this saying makes it difficult, however, to argue that the above similarity between the *Didascalia*, Ps.-Macarius, and *Philippians* is due to common literary dependence upon a fourth source. If one could point to the existence of a collection of sayings similar to what we find in *Philippians* in either the *Didascalia* or Ps.-Macarius, and this collection of sayings also contained close parallels to *Philippians*, then perhaps one could argue for a common literary dependence. Saying II in the *Didascalia* and Ps.-Macarius, however, is not found in proximity to any other parallel to the Philippian sayings under consideration. While any number of theories could be advanced to explain the presence of this saying in all these sources, it is probably an instance of a proverb that became well known, and (given its presence in a number of sources) circulated rather widely among the churches.

---

[24] On the relationship between *1 Clement* and Clem. Alex. *Stromateis* see sec. 4.1 above, and Hagner, *Clement of Rome*, 140; Carlyle in *NTAF*, 60; Gregory, "*1 Clement* and the Writings," 131, n. 10; Lindemann, *Clemensbriefe*, 54; Lona, *Erste Clemensbrief*, 93–104.

In sum, from our discussion so far we may conclude that Clement of Alexandria, Ps.-Macarius and the *Didascalia* were not the source for the sayings of Jesus in Poly. *Phil.* 2.3. We may also conclude that there is insufficient evidence to indicate that Poly. *Phil.* 2.3 and any of these three other writings together bear witness to a non-extant document that was their common source.

We will now consider the relationship between the sayings in Polycarp's *Philippians* and their parallels in *1 Clement*. The evidence that Polycarp knew *1 Clement* is fairly conclusive,[25] but this need not imply that Polycarp is dependent on Clement for the Jesus tradition under consideration. On the contrary, in what follows we will argue that a number of indications make clear that Polycarp derived this Jesus tradition from elsewhere (not only saying V that is not paralleled in *1 Clement*, but also sayings I–IV that closely parallel sayings in *1 Clem.* 13.2).[26] In order to facilitate this task, we reproduce in full the sayings in *1 Clem.* 13.2 from our synopsis in chapter 3, following the Clementine order and the designation 'a'– 'h' used there, and adding the identifiers I–V for the Philippian sayings. Close or exact parallels are underlined:

a) *1 Clem.* 13.2:   <u>ἐλεᾶτε ἵνα ἐλεηθῆτε</u>
III) Pol. *Phil.* 2.3:   <u>ἐλεᾶτε ἵνα ἐλεηθῆτε</u>

b) *1 Clem.* 13.2:   <u>ἀφίετε</u> ἵνα ἀφεθῇ   <u>ὑμῖν</u>
II) Pol. *Phil.* 2.3:   <u>ἀφίετε</u> καὶ <u>ἀφεθήσεται ὑμῖν</u>

c) *1 Clem.* 13.2:   ὡς ποιεῖτε, οὕτω ποιηθήσεται ὑμῖν

d) *1 Clem.* 13.2:   ὡς δίδοτε, οὕτως δοθήσεται ὑμῖν

e) *1 Clem.* 13.2:   ὡς <u>κρίνετε</u>, οὕτως <u>κριθήσεσθε</u>
I) Pol. *Phil.* 2.3:   μὴ <u>κρίνετε</u> ἵνα μὴ <u>κριθῆτε</u>

f) *1 Clem.* 13.2:   ὡς χρηστεύεσθε, οὕτως χρηστευθήσεται ὑμῖν

g) *1 Clem.* 13.2:   <u>ᾧ μέτρῳ μετρεῖτε, ἐν αὐτῷ μετρηθήσεται ὑμῖν</u>
IV) Pol. *Phil.* 2.3:   <u>ᾧ μέτρῳ μετρεῖτε</u>   ἀντιμετρηθήσεται ὑμῖν

h) No par. in *1 Clem.*
V) Pol. *Phil.* 2.3e: καὶ ὅτι μακάριοι οἱ πτωχοὶ καὶ οἱ διωκόμενοι ἕνεκεν δι καιοσύνης ὅτι αὐτῶν ἐστὶν ἡ βασιλεία τοῦ θεοῦ

As can be seen from this synopsis, the similarities between the parallels of the first seven sayings are significant but not extensive. Saying 'a'/III in

---

[25] See Lightfoot, *Apostolic Fathers*, 1.1:149–52, whose conclusions have been accepted by a majority of scholars since his time; also Lona, *Erste Clemensbrief*, 90–92.

[26] *Pace* Lightfoot, *Apostolic Fathers*, 1.2:52; 2.3:325, n. 17; Berding, *Polycarp*, 54.

Pol. *Phil.* 2.3 is the only one that finds a verbatim parallel in *1 Clem.* 13.2. When compared with *1 Clem.* 13.2, the other sayings in Pol. *Phil.* 2.3 show the same variability in adverbs, conjunctions, prepositions, and verb forms as was noted in the previous chapter between *1 Clement* and its gospel parallels. In addition, it is important to note that the order of the sayings in Polycarp differs from that in *1 Clement*. To use the designations 'a' through 'h' of the Clementine sayings, the order of the sayings is as follows:

1 Clem. 13.2　　a – b – c – d – e – f – g
Pol. *Phil.* 2.3　　e – b – a – g – h

Polycarp *Phil.* 2.3 clearly does not contain a straightforward quote from *1 Clem.* 13.2 such as we find, e.g., in Clement of Alexandria's use of the same material. Here we again partially reproduce the synopsis from chapter 3 to draw out the similarities:

a) *1 Clem.* 13.2:　　ἐλεᾶτε　　　　　　　　ἵνα ἐλεηθῆτε
　　Cl. *Strom.* 2.91.2:　ἐλεᾶτε, φησὶν ὁ κύριος, ἵνα ἐλεηθῆτε

b) *1 Clem.* 13.2:　　ἀφίετε ἵνα ἀφεθῇ ὑμῖν
　　Cl. *Strom.* 2.91.2:　ἀφίετε ἵνα ἀφεθῇ ὑμῖν

c) *1 Clem.* 13.2:　　ὡς ποιεῖτε, οὕτω　ποιηθήσεται ὑμῖν
　　Cl. *Strom.* 2.91.2:　ὡς ποιεῖτε, οὕτως ποιηθήσεται ὑμῖν

d) *1 Clem.* 13.2:　　ὡς δίδοτε, οὕτως δοθήσεται ὑμῖν
　　Cl. *Strom.* 2.91.2:　ὡς δίδοτε, οὕτως δοθήσεται ὑμῖν

e) *1 Clem.* 13.2:　　ὡς κρίνετε, οὕτως κριθήσεσθε
　　Cl. *Strom.* 2.91.2:　ὡς κρίνετε, οὕτως κριθήσεσθε

f) *1 Clem.* 13.2:　　ὡς χρηστεύεσθε, οὕτως χρηστευθήσεται ὑμῖν
　　Cl. *Strom.* 2.91.2:　ὡς χρηστεύεσθε, οὕτως χρηστευθήσεται ὑμῖν

g) *1 Clem.* 13.2:　　ᾧ μέτρῳ μετρεῖτε, ἐν αὐτῷ μετρηθήσεται ὑμῖν
　　Cl. *Strom.* 2.91.2:　ᾧ μέτρῳ μετρεῖτε　　　ἀντιμετρηθήσεται ὑμῖν

There is a stark contrast between the above two synopses, in that the parallels between *1 Clement* and the *Stromateis* contain all of the hallmarks of literary dependency that one does *not* find in examining the same set of parallels between *1 Clement* and *Philippians*. In comparing *1 Clement* to the *Stromateis* we find not variability within stability, but outright stability, with the variation of only one letter in saying 'c' (οὕτως vs. οὕτω), and ἀντιμετρηθήσεται in place of ἐν αὐτῷ μετρηθήσεται in saying 'g.'[27] Clement of Alexandria clearly depends upon *1 Clement* for the collection of sayings under consideration, but the same cannot be said for Polycarp's relationship to *1 Clement*. If anything, after comparing the two synopses

---

[27] The additional φησὶν ὁ κύριος in saying 'a' is not a variation in the saying itself.

one would conclude that there is no compelling reason to hold that Poly-carp depended for these sayings on *1 Clement*.[28] Further support for this provisional conclusion will emerge in the discussion that follows.

As we turn next to consider the relationship between the sayings in Polycarp and their gospel parallels, it is best to approach the material in two blocks, taking sayings I–IV together as one block separate from saying V. The appropriateness of this approach is suggested by the wording of our text (Pol. *Phil.* 2.3), which is introduced by the words, μνημονεύοντες δὲ ὧν εἶπεν ὁ κύριος διδάσκων, with saying V both connected to this intro-duction and distinguished from sayings I–IV by a connecting καὶ ὅτι: "re-membering what the Lord said when he taught ...," "and that [he also said] ..." Alternatively, the ὅτι here need not be translated as "that," but could be functioning as a marker of direct discourse. Regardless of how one chooses to translate it, the καὶ ὅτι suggests that Polycarp himself treated sayings I–IV and V as two blocks of material, which raises the possibility that he derived them from separate sources.

Sayings I–IV: We begin with a brief description of the gospel parallels to sayings I–IV. When compared to Poly. *Phil.* 2.3 most of the gospel par-allels show the same variability within stability that we encountered in our discussion of *1 Clem.* 13.2. For sayings I and IV some of the parallels show a similar variability in adverbs, particles, conjunctions, and verb tenses, while for sayings II and III the wording is almost completely dif-ferent, and the parallelism is based on a shared verb and/or a common idea. With two of the parallels, however, we encounter a new element not pre-sent in our discussion of *1 Clem.* 13.2: that of verbatim, word-for-word correspondence. Saying I in Pol. *Phil.* 2.3 – μὴ κρίνετε ἵνα μὴ κριθῆτε – is paralleled verbatim by Mt 7:1, and saying IV – ᾧ μέτρῳ μετρεῖτε ἀντιμετρηθήσεται ὑμῖν – is paralleled verbatim by Lk 6:38c (the latter is not contradicted by the presence of the γάρ in the Lukan passage, as it is post-positive).

Most of the explanations that have been offered to account for the shape of sayings I–IV in *Philippians* can be divided into two main camps: those in the majority position hold that Polycarp is dependent on *1 Clem.* 13.2, but corrects the Clementine sayings to bring them into closer align-ment with the written Gospels (mostly Mathew, but also Luke).[29] A minor-

---

[28] Cf. P. V. M. Benecke's careful assessment in *NTAF*, "It is possible that [Poly-carp's] language, including the form of citation..., may have been influenced by Clement. Polycarp does not, however, quote Clement directly, as he omits some of Clement's most characteristic phrases" (p. 102); see also Lindemann, "Apostolic Fathers and the Synoptic Problem," 709 and n. 84.

[29] Harrison, *Polycarp*, 286–87; Hartog, *Polycarp*, 180–81, 191, 195; Dehandschutter, "Polycarp's Epistle," 165–66 (reprint); Koester, *Synoptische Überlieferung*, 118, 120–21;

ity of scholars holds that Polycarp was dependent neither on *1 Clement* nor on the Gospels, but derived the sayings from a separate source (such as an early catechism,[30] oral tradition,[31] or a document written in Hebrew or Aramaic, of which Clement and Polycarp contain independent transla-tions[32]). In what follows we will argue in favor of the minority position

---

idem, *Introduction to the NT*, 2:309; idem, *Ancient*, 20; idem, "Text of the Synoptic," 44 (reprint); Bellinzoni, "Gospel of Matthew," 207–9; Bauer, *Polykarpbriefe*, 44–45; Schoedel, *Polycarp, Martyrdom, Papias*, 12; Berding, *Polycarp*, 54, 56–57, 58–59; J. D. Hernando, "Irenaeus and the Apostolic Fathers: An Inquiry into the Development of the New Testament Canon" (Ph.D. Dissertation; Madison, N.J.: Drew University, 1990), 193 nn. 235, 236; P. Vielhauer, *Geschichte der urchristlichen Literatur: Einleitung in das Neue Testament, die Apokryphen und die Apostolischen Väter* (2nd corrected ed.; Berlin and New York: de Gruyter, 1978), 564.

[30] Massaux, *Influence*, 2:29–30. Barnard *may* represent this position when he states, "In Chs. I–xii he [Polycarp] appears to know Matthew, Luke, Acts, the Pauline Epistles, I Peter and I Clement as well as certain of the Ignatian Epistles" ("Problem of Polycarp," 35–36). This quote is problematic, however, as it is not clear whether he is giving P. N. Harrison's view (in *Polycarp*) or his own – in further discussion in ibid., 36–37 he ap-pears to say that Polycarp may not cite as many NT texts as Harrison thought. The matter may be clarified by Barnard's statement (ibid., 3): "these writers had inherited a body of Christian facts and doctrines which had long been in use in the Church's catechetical, homiletic and paraenetic teaching and liturgical worship; and in addition collections of *verba Christi*, which had been brought together in the earliest period of the Church, were known to them." Then he gives in a footnote the examples of Ign. *Ad Smyrn.* 3.2; Poly. *Phil.* 2.3; 7.2; Papias fragment (in Eus. *H.E.* 3.39); Barn. 4.14. So perhaps Barnard leans toward an early catechism, or another source, be it oral or written.

[31] Hagner, *Clement of Rome*, 142–43, 279, 306–7; idem, "Sayings," 236; J. Knox, *Marcion and the New Testament: An Essay in the Early History of the Canon* (Chicago: University of Chicago Press, 1942), 143 (I owe this reference to Hagner, *Clement of Rome*, 143, n. 2); Köhler, *Rezeption*, 107–8. Lindemann favors oral tradition close to Q, but leaves open the possibility that it was written ("Apostolic Fathers and the Synoptic Problem," 708–10). Sanday prefers "a mixed hypothesis": "It would be natural to sup-pose, and all that we know of the type of doctrine in the early Church would lead us to believe, that the Sermon on the Mount would be one of the most familiar parts of Chris-tian teaching, that it would be largely committed to memory and quoted from memory. ... Perhaps a mixed hypothesis would be best. It is probable that memory has been to some extent at work (the form of the quotation naturally suggests this) and is to account for some of Polycarp's variations; at the same time I cannot but think that there has been somewhere a written version different from our Gospels to which he and Clement have had access." (*Gospels*, 85–86). P. V. M. Benecke in *NTAF* posits an oral *or* written source: "Polycarp assumes that a body of teaching, oral or written, similar to the Sermon on the Mount, was familiar to the Philippian Church. ... In detail he agrees almost equally with Matthew and Luke, but not completely with either" (p. 102). M. Holmes remains undecided ("Polycarp and the Writings," 193, 197).

[32] Translated presumably not by Clement and Polycarp but by their sources. The most notable proponent of this position is A. Resch, who included a discussion of our texts from Clement and Polycarp in his wider discussion of a Hebrew *Urevangelium*; see his

that Polycarp derived these sayings from oral tradition. Our approach will be to outline the argument of the majority position – that he derived them from a combination of Clement, Matthew and Luke – and show in which ways the argument for oral tradition better explains the Philippian material.

The most cogent line of argument for the majority position runs as follows: we know from other evidence that Polycarp was thoroughly acquainted with *1 Clement*. It is safe to assume, then, that when one finds a block of Jesus material in Poly. *Phil.* 2.3 that is similar in many respects to the block of Jesus material in *1 Clem.* 13.2, and both blocks are prefaced by similar introductory formulae, that Polycarp is dependent on Clement. Polycarp does not quote Clement directly, however, but corrects the wording of Clement's sayings to correspond more closely to the wording of the written Gospels. Polycarp is not necessarily reading Clement or the Gospels as he writes, but rather since he knows both Clement and the Gospels well, his remembrance of the Gospels' wording causes him to follow at times Matthew and at other times Luke in citing Clement.[33] That the Gospels have influenced Polycarp (the majority would argue) is clear especially in that Polycarp's form of saying I differs from Clement, and yet reflects Mt 7:1 verbatim (μὴ κρίνετε ἵνα μὴ κριθῆτε), and saying IV also differs from Clement, but reflects Lk 6:38c verbatim (ᾧ μέτρῳ μετρεῖτε ἀντιμετρηθήσεται ὑμῖν). This view finds support (so the argument goes) from Polycarp's clear dependence upon Matthew for saying V (which we will treat separately below), a saying not found in Clement.[34]

Agrapha: Evangelienfragmente, 140; idem, *Logia Jesu*, 25. More recently Glover has argued a form of this theory for an Aramaic source ("Patristic Quotations," 240–43). This proposal has not met with much scholarly approval and will not be considered further here.

[33] In fairness to the majority opinion we offer as representative the more likely views of Harrison and Koester rather than those of, e.g., Cameron and Berding. The idea of an unconscious correction based on memory, argued by Koester (*Synoptische Überlieferung*, 117–18) and held as a possibility by Harrison (*Polycarp*, 286–87) is much to be preferred over the notion that Polycarp deliberately corrected the sayings in Clement to conform to the written Gospels, as argued by Cameron (*Sayings Traditions*, 113–14) and Berding (*Polycarp*, 6–7). On the latter view, why in saying IV would Polycarp "correct" Clement's μετρηθήσεται ὑμῖν to conform to Luke's ἀντιμετρηθήσεται ὑμῖν, when Matthew's reading μετρηθήσεται ὑμῖν already matches Clement? Why would he intentionally correct Clement to conform to Luke, if this also involved "correcting" Matthew's reading, and yet he had just corrected saying I in Clement to conform to Matthew? The idea that he unintentionally misquoted Clement by conforming parts of Clement's sayings to his remembrance of the Gospels, here Matthew there Luke, is a stronger position, even if we will argue below that a different understanding altogether is to be preferred.

[34] Variations on this argument can be found in Harrison, *Polycarp*, 286 and Koester, *Synoptische Überlieferung*, 112, 117–21 (who cites approvingly from Harrison). These two authors are cited and followed by Hartog, *Polycarp*, 180–81, 191, 195; Dehandschut-

This argument regarding the relationships between Poly. *Phil.* 2.3 and its parallels is fairly cogent, and the theory that Polycarp depended on a combination of *1 Clement*, Matthew and Luke for the Jesus sayings under consideration remains a viable option. The argument, however, is not without its problems. As stated previously in this chapter, one cannot simply assume that Polycarp is dependent on *1 Clement* at this particular juncture simply because he was familiar with Clement's epistle. On the contrary, the almost complete lack of verbatim correspondence between *1 Clem.* 13.2 and Poly. *Phil.* 2.3 (only saying 'a'/III is identical in both), the absence of three out of the seven Clementine sayings in *Philippians*, and the completely different order of the sayings would suggest that Polycarp was *not* dependent on Clement. More importantly, however, the argument that Polycarp depended on a combination of Clement and the Gospels for these sayings does not take fully into account the form of the material in *Philippians*.

That Polycarp is most likely using a single source that is neither Clement nor the Gospels is suggested by the arrangement and wording of the sayings in *Philippians*, in an order, and with a rhythm and structure, all their own:

Μὴ κρίνετε ἵνα μὴ κριθῆτε·
  ἀφίετε καὶ ἀφεθήσεται ὑμῖν·
ἐλεᾶτε ἵνα ἐλεηθῆτε·
  ᾧ μέτρῳ μετρεῖτε ἀντιμετρηθήσεται ὑμῖν·

É. Massaux's description of this "quatrain" and his conclusions regarding the implications of its rhyme and rhythm are well stated:

The first and third sentences contain an intentional subordinate introduced by ἵνα and end with an identical rhyme in -θῆτε. The second and fourth sentences end also with a rhyme in -θήσεται ὑμῖν. Now, Polycarp does not usually write in this particular style. It can, therefore, be assumed that this text was already present in a mnemotechnic form and that he borrowed it.[35]

Two things are important to note in this quote from Massaux: first, *Philippians* 2.3 is not Polycarp. Here is one place where those who argue that Polycarp is revising Clement after Matthew and Luke stumble: that this material is not characteristic of Polycarp's manner of writing, and shows every indication of being a pre-formed unit that Polycarp incorporated into his epistle, clearly undermines the idea that Polycarp composed it based on his remembrance of a mixture of three sources.

---

ter, "Polycarp's Epistle," 165–66; Bellinzoni, "Gospel of Matthew," 207–9; Bauer, *Polykarpbriefe*, 44–45; Berding, *Polycarp*, 54, 56–57, 58–59.
  [35] Massaux, *Influence*, 2:29, and see also ibid., 2:30.

Second, and just as important for the present study, the structure, rhythm and rhyme of the quatrain in *Philippians* almost certainly are the result of mnemonic technique. Massaux himself betrays a bias toward textuality when he traces the origin of this material to a "primitive catechism ... whose point of departure was the Matthean Sermon on the Mount."[36] It is ironic that Massaux is able to recognize that the sayings in Pol. *Phil.* 2.3 are worded and structured so as to enable remembrance, but feels the need to identify a written source for them rather than a source that relies on this remembrance. One must keep in mind, however, that *Philippians* originated in a society in which a majority of people could not read or write, and within a church context that mostly heard and spoke rather than read and wrote the Jesus tradition. Given this social and ecclesiastical context, in seeking to identify the source of *mnemonically constructed materials*, one should prefer or default in favor of an oral rather than a written source.

It is significant in this regard that the words of Jesus in Poly. *Phil.* 2.3 are prefaced by an introductory formula similar to the one in *1 Clem.* 13.1–2, discussed in the previous chapter: Clement's formula reads, μάλιστα μεμνημένοι τῶν λόγων τοῦ κυρίου Ἰησοῦ, οὓς ἐλάλησεν διδάσκων ἐπιείκειαν καὶ μακροθυμίαν. ² οὕτως γὰρ εἶπεν ..., while Popycarp's reads, μνημονεύοντες δὲ ὧν εἶπεν ὁ κύριος διδάσκων. Those who hold that Polycarp is dependent upon Clement for the Jesus sayings argue that Polycarp quotes Clement's introductory formula as well.[37] It is important to note, however, that there are substantial differences between the two formulae. In essence the similarities boil down to the verb for "remembering," the aorist εἶπεν, and the context of the sayings in the teaching activity of the Lord (διδάσκων); beyond this the similarities end. Based on the previous considerations, if we set aside the presupposition that Polycarp is quoting *1 Clement*, then what we have in the introductory statement in Pol. *Phil.* 2.3 is best understood as standardized language for appealing to the oral tradition of Jesus' sayings, along similar lines as the formulae discussed in chapter 4 above from *1 Clem.* 13.1–2, 46.7b–8 and Acts 20:35.[38]

---

[36] Massaux, *Influence*, 2:29–30; he had already concluded this in regard to the material in *1 Clem.* 13.2 (ibid., 1:10–12), and here suggests that Polycarp had access to a more developed form of the same catechism. As noted in discussing the history of scholarship on Jesus tradition and the Apostolic Fathers, Massaux's method has a built-in bias in favor of finding Matthew in the sources he investigates (see section 2.3.1 above).

[37] See, e.g., Koester, *Synoptische Überlieferung*, 112. Koester reaches this conclusion based on three considerations: the shared words for "remembering" and "said," that (in his view) Polycarp is *citing* the collection of sayings from *1 Clem.* 13.2, and the general knowledge of *1 Clement* Polycarp evinces in his epistle. In the present work, however, all three of these considerations are being called into question.

[38] See previous discussion (pp. 140–43 above) on the verb for "remembering" and the aorist tense of λέγω in *1 Clem.* 13.1 and other passages as pointing to a source in oral

That Polycarp derived these sayings as a pre-formed quatrain from the oral tradition of Jesus' sayings coheres well with the discussion in chapter four above regarding the sources for *1 Clem.* 13.2. There we noted that Dale Allison has identified a cohesive block of tradition that circulated independently prior to its incorporation into Q, comprising all of what later became Q 6:27–38.[39] His argument rests upon the resemblances not only between *1 Clem.* 13.2 and Q 6:27–38, but also between the latter and passages in Paul,[40] the Didachist (*Did.* 1:3–5)[41] and – most important to our purposes here – Poly. *Phil.* 2.2–3.[42] We then went on to argue that within that larger block of tradition, the sayings in Luke 6:36–38 probably circulated in a form fairly close to the one they now have in Luke, as suggested by the indicators of orality that can be identified in those verses. We concluded that the differences between *1 Clem.* 13.2 and its gospel parallels may be attributed to the dependence of the three writers upon different performances of the same tradition.

A similar explanation best accounts for the shape of Poly. *Phil.* 2.3 in relation to its parallels in Clement and the Gospels. We already gave good reason to hold that Polycarp did not depend upon Clement for the quatrain, nor did he compose it himself, but derived it in its present Philippian shape preformed from the tradition. Here we must add that there is little reason to suppose that the written Gospels influenced the quatrain prior to it becoming a source for Polycarp. As noted above, we find the kind of variability in conjunctions, particles, adverbs and verb tenses in comparing Poly. *Phil.* 2.3 to its parallels as one would expect to find in various performances of a tradition. That for saying I these variables coincide with the shape of the saying in Matthew, while for saying IV they coincide with the shape of the saying in Luke, is best explained by the common use by Matthew, Luke and the composer of the quatrain upon the same tradition. (As noted in the previous chapter, there is nothing particularly Matthean or Lukan, i.e. no evidence of redactional activity, in these particular parallels.) The composer of the quatrain reflected in *Philippians* chose a particular combination of variable elements in response to the mnemotechnic needs of oral composition. As we saw in chapter 4, the same can be said for the performer of the tradition that stands behind Lk 6:36–38. The use of these traditions by Polycarp and Luke led to the verbatim correspondence in saying

---

tradition, and literature cited there; related specifically to Poly. *Phil.* 2.3 see Hagner, *Clement of Rome*, 142–43.

[39] Allison, *Jesus Tradition*, 84–85.

[40] Rom 2:1//Q 6:37; Rom 12:14//Q 6:28; Rom 12:17//Q 6:27–36; Rom 12:21//Q 6:27–36; 1 Cor 4:12//Q 6:28; 1 Thess 4:12//Q 6:27–36; see Allison, *Jesus Tradition*, 86.

[41] *Did.* 1:3–5//Q 6:27–30, 32–36; see Allison, *Jesus Tradition*, 89–90.

[42] *Phil.* 2.2–3//Q 6:27–30, 36–38; see Allison, *Jesus Tradition*, 88.

IV, as a result of the exigencies of rhyme and rhythm in an oral-compositional context, rather than resulting from the literary dependence of Polycarp upon Luke. That likewise the form of saying I in *Philippians* is attributable to the exigencies of oral composition, in order to set up a rhythm and rhyme consonant with saying III, makes literary dependence upon Matthew for this saying very unlikely. The correspondence between saying I in *Philippians* and Matthew is also best explained as resulting from the independent use of a common oral tradition.

Saying V: Polycarp appends a fifth saying to the four we have just considered: (καὶ ὅτι) μακάριοι οἱ πτωχοὶ καὶ οἱ διωκόμενοι ἕνεκεν δικαιοσύνης ὅτι αὐτῶν ἐστιν ἡ βασιλεία τοῦ θεοῦ. Its gospel parallels, reproduced from the synopsis at the beginning of the present chapter, are as follows:

Pol. *Phil.* 2.3e: καὶ ὅτι
          μακάριοι οἱ πτωχοὶ καὶ οἱ διωκόμενοι ἕνεκεν δικαιοσύνης
Mt 5:3:   μακάριοι οἱ πτωχοὶ τῷ πνεύματι,
Mt 5:10:   μακάριοι οἱ   δεδιωγμένοι ἕνεκεν δικαιοσύνης
Lk 6:20b: μακάριοι οἱ πτωχοί

Pol. *Phil.* 2.3e: ὅτι αὐτῶν   ἐστιν ἡ βασιλεία τοῦ θεοῦ
Mt 5:3:   ὅτι αὐτῶν   ἐστιν ἡ βασιλεία τῶν οὐρανῶν
Mt 5:10:   ὅτι αὐτῶν   ἐστιν ἡ βασιλεία τῶν οὐρανῶν
Lk 6:20b: ὅτι ὑμετέρα ἐστὶν ἡ βασιλεία τοῦ θεοῦ

The vast majority of scholars hold that Polycarp, having conflated the two beatitudes found in Mt 5:3 and 5:10, is thus dependent on Matthew for this saying.[43] Some scholars hold a variation on this view: while Polycarp is primarily dependent upon Matthew, he is also dependent upon Luke, in that he follows Luke in leaving out Matthew's qualifier τῷ πνεύματι for οἱ πτωχοί, and uses the Lukan phrase ἡ βασιλεία τοῦ θεοῦ in place of Matthew's ἡ βασιλεία τῶν οὐρανῶν.[44]

---

[43] Massaux, *Influence*, 2:31; Dehandschutter, "Polycarp's Epistle," 166–67; Hernando, "Irenaeus and the Apostolic Fathers," 193, nn. 235, 236; Knoch, "Kenntnis," 171.

[44] Lightfoot, *Apostolic Fathers*, 2.3:326 n. 2; Koester, *Synoptische Überlieferung*, 118, 120–21; Berding, *Polycarp*, 58–59; Köhler, *Rezeption*, 99–100; M. E. Boring, *The Continuing Voice of Jesus: Christian Prophecy and the Gospel Tradition* (Louisville: Westminster/John Knox, 1991), 195. Schoedel, (*Polycarp, Martyrdom, Papias*, 12) considers dependence on Luke as well as Matthew a possibility. Hartog states, in explaining the absence of τῷ πνεύματι in Polycarp, "Although *Phil* 2.3 contains a conflation of he exact vocabulary of Matthew 5:3 and 10, the abridging of Matthew's "poor in spirit" (resembling Luke's mere "poor") is puzzling. If we remember that Polycarp applied the Matthean material to the Philippians' exact situation of material poverty due to Valens' theft, the deletion is explicable. Polycarp may have redacted Matthew (perhaps using the Lukan version) to reflect the situation in Philippi: the congregation had been left materially poor" (*Polycarp*, 193; see also pp. 182, 195). This explanation, however, does not

These arguments for Polycarp's dependence on the Gospels would gain cumulative weight if it could be shown that Polycarp depended on the Gospels for sayings I–IV. Conversely, they lose some of their force if one concludes that Polycarp derived sayings I–IV from oral tradition, which his where we stand in the present discussion. In addition, and as previously noted, for sayings I–IV Polycarp appears to have cited his source verbatim: the structure and cadence of the quatrain suggest a pre-formed source that Polycarp incorporated as a whole into his letter. One should not be hasty in assuming, therefore, that Polycarp would conflate other Jesus traditions he is citing. If he knew saying V as two separate beatitudes from Matthew, given his treatment of sayings I–IV one would expect him to leave their structure as *two* beatitudes intact. Based on these considerations, while it remains possible that Polycarp is dependent upon the written Gospels for saying V, the burden of proof rests with those who would argue in favor of this position.[45]

Polycarp's dependence upon the written Gospels is not the only way to understand the relationship between the parallels under consideration, and leaves a number of questions unanswered. Considering first the possibility that Polycarp is dependent upon Matthew, the differences between Polycarp and Matthew should not be minimized. In applying the redactional criterion, as already noted above, two elements unique to Matthew in the gospel parallels are absent from Polycarp: in place of the characteristically Matthean ἡ βασιλεία τῶν οὐρανῶν in Polycarp we find the ἡ βασιλεία τοῦ θεου common in Mark and Luke (and reflected in the Lukan parallel). In addition, we do not find in Polycarp the Matthean qualifier τῷ πνεύματι for οἱ πτωχοί. In spite of these considerations, one may still argue that Polycarp is dependent on Matthew rather than on pre-Matthean Synoptic tradition due to Polycarp's phrase καὶ οἱ διωκόμενοι ἕνεκεν δικαιοσύνης, paralleled in the Gospels only by Matthew's μακάριοι οἱ δεδιωγμένοι ἕνεκεν δικαιοσύνης (Mt 5:10). That Polycarp uses the present passive διωκόμενοι where Matthew uses the perfect passive δεδιωγμένοι is easily explainable on the basis of a citation from memory, if there were sufficient reason based upon other considerations to suppose that Polycarp is citing Matthew. The strongest argument for Polycarp's de-

---

suit the use of saying V in Polycarp. The saying reads, μακάριοι οἱ πτωχοὶ καὶ οἱ διωκόμενοι ἕνεκεν δικαιοσύνης ὅτι αὐτῶν ἐστιν ἡ βασιλεία τοῦ θεοῦ. Here the ἕνεκεν δικαιοσύνης is best understood as applying not only to οἱ διωκόμενοι but also to οἱ πτωχοί; i.e., those who are poor *on account of righteousness* or for *doing what is right* are blessed, not simply those who have had their property stolen.

[45] Cf. Holmes' cautious conclusion: "given that we are dealing with 'Sermon' material, which almost certainly circulated in oral form ... it is difficult to be so certain: knowledge of Matthew and Luke is possible, but not demonstrable" ("Polycarp and the Writings," 194).

pendence upon Matthew for saying V comes from the contention that the presence of the word δικαιοσύνης reflects dependence upon Matthean redaction. U. Luz views this as the only Matthean beatitude that is undoubtedly redactional, due to the presence of δικαιοσύνης and the very Matthean τῶν οὐρανῶν.[46] If Polycarp had also included τῶν οὐρανῶν in his form of the saying, there would then be a very strong argument in favor of his dependence on Matthew. With only δικαιοσύνης appearing in Poycarp, however, there may be a better way to interpret the evidence.

That δικαιοσύνης is an important theme in Matthew does not preclude the possibility that the oral Jesus tradition contained a beatitude independent of Matthew specifically addressed to those who suffered on account of doing what is right (δικαιοσύνης). Evidence for the existence of such a saying may be found in 1 Peter 3:14a that reads, ἀλλ' εἰ καὶ πάσχοιτε διὰ δικαιοσύνην, μακάριοι. As a number of scholars have noted, it is likely that this Petrine saying echoes Jesus tradition that is not dependent on Matthew.[47] If this is the case, 1 Peter 3:14a would provide evidence that the

---

[46] Luz, *Matthew 1–7*, 186.

[47] In Hagner's opinion this phrase in 1 Peter is "almost certainly a reflection of the same logion as contained in the oral tradition" ("Righteousness in Matthew's Theology," in *Worship, Theology and Ministry in the Early Church: Essays in Honor of Ralph P. Martin* [ed. M. J. Wilkins and T. Paige; JSNTSup 87; Sheffield: JSOT Press, 1992], 114); see also E. Best, "in our present instance [1 Pet 3:14//Mt 5:10] Matthew received [the saying] in the tradition and that the author of 1 Peter knew this tradition, whence he derived it" ("1 Peter," 109); similarly J. R. Michaels, though not committing to an oral or a written source: "The 'impartiality' of the allusions (as between Matthew and Luke) suggests that Peter is drawing not on the finished Gospels but on pre-Synoptic tradition (i.e., the Q material in some form)" (*1 Peter* [WBC 49; Waco: Word, 1988], xli; see also ibid., 185); K. H. Schelkle, *Die Petrusbriefe, der Judasbrief* (HTKNT 13.2; Freiburg: Herder, 1970), 100. The traditional approach to explaining the similarities between 1 Peter and other NT documents was to assume that the author of 1 Peter knew and cited these documents, assumption still found recently in relation to 1 Pet 3:14//Mt 5:10 in, e.g., P. H. Davids, *The First Epistle of Peter* (NICNT; Grand Rapids: Eerdmans, 1990), 130; P. J. Achtemeier, *1 Peter: A Commentary on First Peter* (ed. E. J. Epp; Hermeneia; Minneapolis: Fortress, 1996), 231. This assumption has been challenged over the past several decades based on more nuanced studies of the relationship between early Christian sources. D. G. Horrell's conclusion may sum up the current state of the discussion, "the author [of 1 Peter] was familiar with this Gospel material, though we do not know in exactly what form" (*1 Peter* [NTG; London and New York: T&T Clark, 2008], 36). J. H. Elliot is right when he states that, "literary affinity must be distinguished from literary dependence" ("The Rehabilitation of an Exegetical Step-Child: 1 Peter in Recent Research," *JBL* 95 [1976]: 243–54). Elliott's own position is that "The textual affinities demonstrate only commonality of tradition but not authenticity of either sources or Petrine redaction" (ibid., 248); see further Elliott's more recent discussion in his *1 Peter: A New Translation with Introduction and Commentary* (AB 37B; New York: Doubleday, 2000), 20–40, esp. 24–25, 28, and literature cited there.

Matthean form of the saying had parallels elsewhere in the Jesus tradition, which in turn would dissolve much of the remaining basis for the argument that Polycarp depends on Matthew for this saying. That Polycarp derived saying V complete with the δικαιοσύνης from a source other than Matthew would then explain the absence in Polycarp of the characteristically Matthean ἡ βασιλεία τῶν οὐρανῶν as well as Matthew's τῷ πνεύματι.

Once one has concluded that there is little reason to hold that Polycarp is dependent on Matthew, even less grounds exist for positing his dependence on Luke. As already noted, scholars raise the possibility of dependence on Luke primarily to account for Polycarp's deviations from Matthew. If Polycarp is not dependent on Matthew, then his ἡ βασιλεία τοῦ θεου was not chosen from Luke over Matthew's ἡ βασιλεία τῶν οὐρανῶν, but in all likelihood was present in the tradition, given that everywhere else it is the standard form.[48] Likewise, there is no reason to argue for Polycarp's dependence on Luke by appeal to the argument from shared silence that neither Polycarp nor Luke contain Matthew's τῷ πνεύματι.[49] It was not in Luke or Polycarp's sources, and either Matthew found it in his, or added it in.

Having concluded that Polycarp probably did not derive saying V from Matthew and/or Luke, it remains for us to consider what other source might be suggested. Among the many possibilities that could be raised (a catechism, an unknown gospel, a sayings source such as Q), the most likely source in light of our discussion of sayings I–IV is oral tradition. As already noted in our previous discussion, the καὶ ὅτι with which Polycarp introduces saying V functions both to set it apart from the preceding four sayings and to link it to them. Here we must add that the καὶ ὅτι also serves to apply the introductory formula of sayings I–IV to saying V: μνημονεύοντες δὲ ὧν εἶπεν ὁ κύριος διδάσκων: [sayings I–IV] ... καὶ ὅτι

---

[48] As is well known, the expression βασιλεία τῶν οὐρανῶν is only found in Matthew. Elsewhere in the Synoptics, Acts, the Gospel of John, the Pauline literature, and the Apostolic Fathers, the form is always βασιλεία τοῦ θεοῦ with an occasional βασιλεία τοῦ Χριστοῦ. Even Matthew reads βασιλεία τοῦ θεοῦ in 12:28; 19:24; 21:31, 43. On kingdom of God language in early Christianity see the following essays in *The Kingdom of God in 20th-Century Interpretation* (ed. W. Willis; Peabody, Mass.: Hendrickson, 1987): J. R. Michaels, "The Kingdom of God and the Historical Jesus," 109–18; R. Farmer, "The Kingdom of God in the Gospel of Matthew," 119–30; M. E. Boring, "The Kingdom of God in Mark," 131–45; R. Hodgson, Jr., "The Kingdom of God in the School of St. John," 163–74; R. O'Toole, "The Kingdom of God in Luke-Acts," 147–62; K. P. Donfried, "The Kingdom of God in Paul," 175–90; E. Ferguson, "The Kingdom of God in Early Patristic Literature," 191–208.

[49] Also arguing against Polycarp's literary dependence on Luke is the absence in Polycarp of the specification ὑμετέρα found in the parallel in Lk 6:20, as well as the absence in Luke of a parallel to the beatitude regarding οἱ δεδιωγμένοι ἕνεκεν δικαιοσύνης.

[saying V]. At the risk of belaboring the obvious, the καὶ ὅτι before saying V thus implies, "and here is another thing also to be remembered of what Jesus said when he taught ...." We may be able to infer, then, that if the introductory formula was a standard means of appealing to oral tradition, not only sayings I–IV but also saying V is included within the oral tradition that is being cited.[50]

One final element to discuss regarding saying V is that, when compared to its Matthean parallels, it brings together two beatitudes that hold out the promise of the kingdom.[51] It is important to recall from our discussion in chapter 3 that the bringing together of sayings that share a common subject matter is a common device for organizing material in an oral milieu.[52] It may be that saying V provides an example of this device, and that it contains two separate sayings that were paired based on their similar subject matter as kingdom beatitudes. It is also possible that the saying was transmitted as a single unit in the tradition, much like we find it in Polycarp, and that Matthew has separated it into two beatitudes to cohere with the single-beatitude structure of Mt 5:3–10 – this, however, would not explain why Matthew did not separate 5:11 into distinct beatitudes: μακάριοί ἐστε ὅταν ὀνειδίσωσιν ὑμᾶς καὶ διώξωσιν καὶ εἴπωσιν πᾶν πονηρὸν καθ' ὑμῶν ψευδόμενοι ἕνεκεν ἐμοῦ. Given the presupposition of an oral milieu for these sayings, one need not opt conclusively for either of these possibilities. It is just as likely that different performances of the tradition contained beatitudes for οἱ πτωχοί and beatitudes for οἱ δεδιωγμένοι ἕνεκεν δικαιοσύνης, sometimes together, and sometimes apart, depending on the traditionist and on the occasion of the performance.

In sum, when Polycarp prefaces the block of sayings in *Phil.* 2.3 with a formula containing the verb "remembering" and the aorist tense of λέγω he is not quoting Clement, but rather like Clement he was drawing the readers' attention to material that was living oral tradition. Polycarp may have derived from Clement the idea of quoting a comparatively lengthy collection of Jesus sayings in his letter, and even of using an introductory formula along the lines of what we find in both writings, but of this there is no way to be certain. Most importantly, however, for sayings I–IV Polycarp either intentionally or unintentionally did not use the block of tradition found in Clement (of which he would have been aware, given his

---

[50] This latter point is also made by Massaux, *Influence*, 2:31.

[51] Those who assume that Polycarp knew Matthew hold that he chose these two out of all the Matthean beatitudes because of this promise they have in common (Lightfoot, *Apostolic Fathers*, 2.3:326; Hartog, *Polycarp*, 193–94), or that these two sayings present a summary of the beatitudes, apparently based on their position as first and last of the beatitudes (Massaux, *Influence*, 2:31).

[52] See sec. 3.3.2 above, under the subtitle "Aggregative Rather than Analytic."

familiarity with *1 Clement* as a whole). Instead he appealed to a similar but different block of oral tradition, to which he appended an additional saying also from the tradition. In all probability he used oral traditional material other than that found in *1 Clement* because he knew it by memory, as tradition that was in living use within his own community. It is thus not likely that he was attempting to provide any kind of corrective for the sayings in *1 Clement*.[53]

5.4 Assessing Where We Stand

Having examined a number of aspects of *1 Clem.* 13.2 and Poly. *Phil.* 2.3 and their parallels in detail, and before moving on to consider our next passage from the Apostolic Fathers, we pause to consider what might be learned from our work with these passages.

Clearly in dealing with this type of material one works in the realm of hypotheses and probabilities, not in the realm of certainty. However, the suggestions made above regarding the relationships (or lack thereof) between *1 Clement*, Polycarp's *Philippians* and the written Gospels fit well with what we have come to know of the process of writing in antiquity. The mental picture we may find easy to conjure up, of Polycarp sitting at his desk, with copies of *1 Clement*, Matthew and Luke open before him as he writes, though *possible*, more likely represents an anachronism derived from our literate worldview.[54] This picture is certainly not impossible, but it is very improbable. It is more likely that, in a culture in which orality was still highly valued, orally transmitted material would have been freely used in the process of composition.[55] We saw in our previous chapter that this is very likely the case with *1 Clement*, and given what we have seen above it is also probably true of Polycarp's *Philippians*.

That Poly. *Phil.* 3.2 was derived from oral tradition is suggested by external considerations such as the lack of verbatim correspondence between it and any of its parallels, which one would expect to find in literary dependence. A source in oral tradition is also suggested by internal considerations such as the rhyme and rhythm of the collection of sayings as a whole: the particular wording and structure of the material almost certainly

---

[53] In the unlikely event that he was correcting the sayings found in *1 Clement*, it may be an instance of the respect in antiquity – in Papias' well-known words – for "a living and abiding voice" over "what came out of books" (Papias, in Eusebius, *Hist. Eccl.*, 3.39.4).

[54] See Beaton, "How Matthew Writes," 116; S. L. Mattila, "A Question Too Often Neglected," *NTS* 41 (1995): 202, 213–17.

[55] Cf. Jaubert, *Clément de Rome*, 52–53.

reflect mnemonic concerns to aid in the retention and performance of oral tradition. This structure and wording, which in all likelihood was imposed upon it independently of any of the parallel documents considered in the above discussion, suggest that Polycarp derived the material from an oral source, regardless of whether or not he knew *1 Clement* or any of the Gospels. In addition, an oral source is suggested by the words that introduce the sayings: μνημονεύοντες δὲ ὧν εἶπεν ὁ κύριος διδάσκων.

Specifically regarding the Jesus tradition in Pol. *Phil.* 2.3, and mirroring what we found in examining *1 Clem.* 13.2, our findings confirm the insight that oral tradition in general, and Jesus tradition in particular, is characterized by variability within stability.[56] In what we have seen from studying these two texts and their parallels, the variability is present in a number of rather insignificant details – adverbs, particles, conjunctions, verb tenses, ordering of words and sayings – and does not compromise the basic meaning of the sayings under discussion.

The most substantive of the differences we have encountered is not reflected in changes undergone by any given Jesus saying in *1 Clement* or Polycarp's *Philippians*, but rather is found in the contrast between the rendition of saying III in *1 Clem.* 13.2, Mt 5:7 and Pol. *Phil.* 2.3 on the one hand, and Lk 6:36 on the other. While the saying as found in the first three could be considered a variation on the "Golden Rule"[57] (as is true of all the sayings considered so far in *1 Clem.* 13 and Pol. *Phil.* 2), the Lukan form of the saying shifts the motivation for human action so that it rests upon the divine example: "Be merciful, just as your Father is merciful." The parallel from Luke 6:36, within its Lukan context, is part of a redefinition of the Golden Rule. Lk 6:27–31 portrays Jesus first as making the Rule binding upon his hearers in a rather one-sided way: they were not to use the Rule as a justification for responding in kind to those who had mistreated them, but rather in humility and longsuffering behave towards those who had mistreated them in the way they themselves would like to be treated. Then in Lk 6:32–36 Jesus challenges the validity of the Rule – his followers were not to treat others in a given way expecting to receive the same in return,[58] but were to treat others in the way they themselves were treated *by God:* "because he [God] is good to the ungrateful and wicked. Be merciful, just as your father is merci-

---

[56] See subsection 3.3.5 above, under the subtitle "Both Variable and Stable" and literature cited there.

[57] Cf. "Show mercy, that you may be shown mercy" (Clementine saying 'a') to the "Golden Rule" "Do to others as you would have them do to you," which is also the Lukan parallel to Clementine saying 'c.'

[58] This is clear especially from v. 35, "love those who hate you, and do good [to them], and *lend money without expecting to get it back*" – here not only is the expectation absent of being lent money as they had lent money (the "Golden Rule"), but even of having the money returned that they had lent out.

ful" (Lk 6:35c–36). In place of the Golden Rule – do to others as you would have them do to you – the Lukan Jesus sets up a new rule: do to others as has been done to you by the One Perfect Role Model.[59]

The above comments provide a platform from which to make an observation about Jesus tradition in general: one cannot afford to be dogmatic when speaking of the meaning of isolated sayings (such as the Jesus sayings in the Apostolic Fathers), since one does not have access to the wider context of the tradition that might lead to a more informed opinion. The Gospels, as large repositories of tradition, contain sufficient information for one to be able to nuance one saying of Jesus with another in its wider context. For example, the difference in meaning noted above between the Matthean and Lukan parallels to saying III extends only as far as the saying itself, but is reconciled in the wider context of the Gospels. Though thirty one verses removed from the Matthean parallel to saying III (μακάριοι οἱ ἐλεήμονες ὅτι αὐτοὶ ἐλεηθήσονται; Mt 5:7), Mt 5:38–48 ties human behavior to the divine example in terms very similar to those noted above in Lk 6:27–36, with the overall conclusion, "Therefore be perfect, as your Father in heaven in perfect" (Mt 5:48). The larger contexts of Mt 5 and of Lk 6 thus both contain variations upon the Golden Rule as well as injunctions to go beyond it, basing one's behavior upon the divine example. The Lukan Jesus, then, is not a maverick after all – Matthew conveys the same message, just not in a saying that parallels the one found in Luke. In contrast to what we have just seen of tradition in the Gospels, independent sayings cited in letters, such as those we have just considered in *1 Clement* and Polycarp's *Philippians*, do not allow one the luxury of studying their meaning in light of their wider traditional context.

As we turn in the following chapters to examine other sayings of Jesus in the Apostolic Fathers, we will not consider them in near as much detail as those examined so far; rather our findings above will be assumed in what follows, and referred to briefly as appropriate.

---

[59] In the following verse, Lk 6:37, three sayings serve to set up the expectation that God will respond in keeping with the Golden Rule, by treating people as they have treated others. This expectation is then exploded by v. 38, in which the divine generosity is shown to go *beyond* human expectation, surpassing what would be expected from the reciprocity inherent in the Rule. Verses 39–49 then reinforce in various ways the injunction to follow the divine example.

Chapter 6

Seeking Consistency
Looking for Indicators of Orality in *1 Clement* 46.7b–8

6.1 Introduction

The choice to begin with the study of *1 Clem.* 13.2 and Poly. *Phil.* 2.3 in the previous chapters was based on certain unique characteristics of these texts. Their comparative length, together with the extent to which they parallel each other, combined to make them the ideal test case for the application of the theory on orality and literacy that undergirds the present study.[1]

In the following chapters we set out to ascertain to what extent the findings of the previous chapters are corroborated by applying the same theory to five additional texts that also contain explicit appeals to Jesus tradition: *1 Clem.* 46.7b–8, *Did.* 8.2 and 9.5, Ign. *Smyrn.* 3.2a, and Poly. *Phil.* 7.2b. The discussion of the previous chapter will be presupposed here and in future chapters, so that we will enter into considerably less detail. We begin in this chapter with *1 Clem.* 46.7b–8.

*1 Clem*ent *46.7b–8*

... μνήσθητε τῶν λόγων 'Ιησοῦ τοῦ κυρίου ἡμῶν. [8] εἶπεν γάρ· οὐαὶ τῷ ἀνθρώπῳ ἐκείνῳ· καλὸν ἦν αὐτῷ, εἰ οὐκ ἐγεννήθη, ἢ ἕνα τῶν ἐκλεκτῶν μου σκανδαλίσαι· κρεῖττον ἦν αὐτῷ περιτεθῆναι μύλον καὶ καταποντισθῆναι εἰς τὴν θάλασσαν, ἢ ἕνα τῶν ἐκλεκτῶν μου διαστρέψαι.[2]

Remember the words of Jesus our Lord, [8] for he said, "Woe to that person! It would have been good for him not to be born, rather than cause one of my chosen to stumble. Better for him to have a millstone put on him and be drowned in the sea than to have corrupted one of my chosen."

---

[1] See secs. 4.7 and 5.4 above for brief summaries of the findings of the previous two chapters, that will be presupposed in the present and the following chapters.

[2] For a list of MSS witnesses for *1 Clement* and their abbreviations see n. 4 on p. 108 above.

1 Cl. 46.8b: <u>οὐαὶ</u> <u>τῷ ἀνθρώπῳ ἐκείνῳ</u>
Mk 14:21b: <u>οὐαὶ</u> δὲ <u>τῷ ἀνθρώπῳ ἐκείνῳ</u> δι᾽ οὗ ὁ υἱὸς τοῦ ἀνθρώπου παραδίδοται
Mt 26:24b: <u>οὐαὶ</u> δὲ <u>τῷ ἀνθρώπῳ ἐκείνῳ</u> δι᾽ οὗ ὁ υἱὸς τοῦ ἀνθρώπου παραδίδοται
Lk 22:22b: πλὴν <u>οὐαὶ</u> <u>τῷ ἀνθρώπῳ ἐκείνῳ</u> δι᾽ οὗ παραδίδοται.
Mt 18:7b–c: ἀνάγκη γὰρ ἐλθεῖν τὰ σκάνδαλα
            πλὴν <u>οὐαὶ</u> <u>τῷ ἀνθρώπῳ</u>   δι᾽ οὗ τὸ σκάνδαλον ἔρχεται
Lk 17:1b–c: ἀνένδεκτόν ἐστιν τοῦ τὰ σκάνδαλα μὴ ἐλθεῖν,
            πλὴν <u>οὐαὶ</u>   δι᾽ οὗ   ἔρχεται
Cl.*Str.*3.18.107: <u>οὐαὶ</u> <u>τῷ ἀνθρώπῳ ἐκείνῳ</u> φησὶν ὁ κύριος·

1 Cl. 46.8c: <u>καλὸν ἦν αὐτῷ εἰ οὐκ ἐγεννήθη, ἢ ἕνα τῶν ἐκλεκτῶν μου σκανδαλίσαι</u>
Mk 14:21c: <u>καλὸν</u>   <u>αὐτῷ εἰ οὐκ ἐγεννήθη</u> ὁ ἄνθρωπος ἐκεῖνος
Mt 26:24c: <u>καλὸν ἦν αὐτῷ εἰ οὐκ ἐγεννήθη</u> ὁ ἄνθρωπος ἐκεῖνος
Cl.*Str.*3.18[3]: <u>καλὸν ἦν αὐτῷ εἰ</u> μή <u>ἐγεννήθη, ἢ ἕνα τῶν ἐκλεκτῶν μου σκανδαλίσαι</u>

1 Cl. 46.8d: <u>κρεῖττον ἦν αὐτῷ περιτεθῆναι μύλον</u>
Mk 9:42b: καλόν ἐστιν <u>αὐτῷ</u> μᾶλλον εἰ περίκειται <u>μύλος</u> ὀνικὸς
                                                περὶ τὸν τράχηλον αὐτοῦ
Mt 18:6b: συμφέρει <u>αὐτῷ</u> ἵνα κρεμασθῇ <u>μύλος</u> ὀνικὸς
                                                περὶ τὸν τράχηλον αὐτοῦ
Lk 17:2a: λυσιτελεῖ <u>αὐτῷ</u> εἰ λίθος <u>μυλικὸς</u> περίκειται
                                                περὶ τὸν τράχηλον αὐτοῦ
Cl.*Str.* 3.18: <u>κρεῖττον ἦν αὐτῷ περιτεθῆναι μύλον</u>

1 Cl. 46.8e: <u>καὶ καταποντισθῆναι</u>   <u>εἰς τὴν θάλασσαν</u>
Mk 9:42b: <u>καὶ</u> βέβληται   <u>εἰς τὴν θάλασσαν</u>
Mt 18:6b: <u>καὶ καταποντισθῇ</u> ἐν τῷ πελάγει <u>τῆς θαλάσσης</u>
Lk 17:2a: <u>καὶ</u> ἔρριπται   <u>εἰς τὴν θάλασσαν</u>
Cl.*Str.* 3.18: <u>καὶ καταποντισθῆναι</u>   <u>εἰς</u>   <u>θάλασσαν</u>

1 Clem. 46.8f: <u>ἢ ἕνα τῶν ἐκλεκτῶν μου διαστρέψαι</u>
Mk 9:42a: καὶ ὃς ἂν σκανδαλίσῃ <u>ἕνα τῶν</u> μικρῶν τούτων
                                τῶν πιστευόντων εἰς ἐμέ
Mt 18:6a: Ὃς δ᾽ ἂν σκανδαλίσῃ <u>ἕνα τῶν</u> μικρῶν τούτων
                                τῶν πιστευόντων εἰς ἐμέ
Lk 17:2b: <u>ἢ</u> ἵνα   σκανδαλίσῃ   <u>τῶν</u> μικρῶν τούτων <u>ἕνα</u>
Cl.*Str.* 3.18: <u>ἢ ἕνα τῶν ἐκλεκτῶν μου διαστρέψαι</u> [4]

Textual notes: *1 Cl.* 46.8c, καλὸν ἦν αὐτῷ εἰ οὐκ ἐγεννήθη, ἢ ἕνα τῶν ἐκλεκτῶν μου
σκανδαλίσαι: here we follow Ehrman, Funk as revised by Bihlmeyer, Holmes, Jaubert,
and Lightfoot in reading οὐκ ἐγεννήθη, supported by A, against the μή ἐγεννήθη in H C
and Clem. Alex.; see Ehrman, *Apostolic Fathers*, 1:118; Bihlmeyer, *Apostolischen Väter*,

---

[3] Text here (and in remainder of synopsis under similar notations) is that of Clem.
Stom. 3.18.107; the full reference did not fit within the width of the synopsis.

[4] Greek text of Clement of Alexandria *Stromateis* iii taken from PG 8:1209c. Other
partial parallels to the saying(s) of Jesus in *1 Clem.* 46.8 appear in Christian literature
that is either too late or too clearly dependent upon the Gospels to include in our treatment here; for a discussion see Hagner, *Clement of Rome*, 156–59.

60; Holmes, *Apostolic Fathers*, 106; Jaubert, *Clément de Rome*, 176 n.; Lightfoot, *Apostolic Fathers*, 1.2:142. Koester prefers μή ἐγεννήθη as the *lectio difficilior* (*Synoptische Überlieferung*, 17, n. 1).

1 Clem. 46.8f: ἢ ἕνα τῶν ἐκλεκτῶν μου διαστρέψαι: Again we follow the texts of Ehrman (1:118, 119, n. 86), Holmes (p. 108), Funk and Bihlmeyer (p. 60), Jaubert (p. 176), and Lightfoot (1.2:141) (see previous paragraph) supported by L S C and Clem. Alex. (ἐκλεκτῶν μου διαστρέψαι), against A and H that both read μικρῶν μου σκανδαλίσαι. For a detailed discussion and defense of this textual decision see Lightfoot, *Apostolic Fathers*, 1.2:141–42. Lightfoot's argument, in brief, is that a) this is the more difficult reading, differing the most from its gospel parallels, and is thus to be preferred; b) it is the reading Clement of Alexandria found in *1 Clement*, as shown by his quotation; c) the very next words in *1 Clem.* 46.9 are τὸ σχίσμα ὑμῶν πολλοὺς διέστρεψεν: this is in keeping with Clement of Rome's common practice of picking up and commenting on a leading word in what he has cited. See also the additional comments and literature in Hagner, *Clement of Rome*, 155–56. As Hagner notes, Latin and Coptic MSS discovered since the time of Lightfoot's death further support the latter's argument (ibid., 155, n. 1).

Mark 9:42a: καὶ ὃς ἂν σκανδαλίσῃ ἕνα τῶν μικρῶν τούτων τῶν πιστευόντων εἰς ἐμέ: The εἰς ἐμε in Mk 9:42 remains a contested reading. The editorial committee of the NA[27] includes the text, but within brackets, because even though it has very strong external support (A B L W Θ Ψ *f*[1] *f*[13] syr[s] cop[sa] *al*), it is missing from the texts of ℵ D and Δ, and in the judgment of the committee might have been added to the text of Mk by a scribe harmonizing it with the text of Mt 18.6 (see Metzger, *Textual Commentary*, 86). In my judgment the brackets are unnecessary, not only because of the strength of the external support, but also because of the tendencies apparent in the textual dependence of Mt upon Mk; on this see n. 14 on p. 185 below.

We begin our examination by considering the extent to which *1 Clem.* 46.8 may be dependent on any of the above parallels. Similarly to what was noted in chapter 4 regarding *1 Clem.* 13.2, the almost verbatim parallel to *1 Clem.* 46.8 in Clement of Alexandria can be attributed to the latter's dependence on the Roman Clement.[5] We can therefore simply dispense with any notion of dependence in the opposite direction, as with the idea that both Clements derived their material from a third source independently of each other.[6] This leaves to consider only the parallels in the Gospels.

---

[5] *Almost* verbatim because Clem. *Strom.* 3.18.107 reads εἰ μή ἐγεννήθη rather than εἰ οὐκ ἐγεννήθη, and εἰς θάλασσαν rather than εἰς τὴν θάλασσαν as found in *1 Clem.* 46.8, otherwise the texts are identical (the additional φησὶν ὁ κύριος in Clem. *Strom.* 3.18.107 mirrors the first line of the Alexandrian Clement's parallel to *1 Clem.* 13.2; as we saw when discussing the latter, neither occurrence of φησὶν ὁ κύριος is relevant for this study, in that they are not part of the Jesus tradition being cited).

[6] See discussion in sec. 4.1 above, and also Hagner, *Clement of Rome*, 156; Lightfoot, *Apostolic Fathers*, 1.2:141; Lona, *Erste Clemensbrief*, 497.

6.2 The Relationship of *1 Clem.* 46.8 to its Gospel Parallels

In turning to consider the possibility that Clement of Rome depended upon the canonical Gospels, one is faced with a very complex set of relationships among the parallels. To bring some clarity to this complexity, the discussion that follows will take place in three steps: (1) we will begin by describing the relationship between *1 Clement* and its parallels from the perspective of overall structure and general components, and (2) will then go on to a more detailed examination of order and wording. In all of this we will seek to draw out implications for the history of the material, seeking to understand especially how it all relates to the history of the tradition behind *1 Clem.* 46.8. The discussion to that point will serve to inform the next step, (3) the possibility that Clement might have been dependent upon one or more of the Gospels for the sayings under consideration. As in the previous chapters, our main criterion in this enquiry will be the redactional one: the presence (or absence) of redactional elements from the Evangelists in *1 Clem.* 46.8. Having completed these three steps, a concluding section will seek to relate the findings of our examination of *1 Clem.* 46.8 and its parallels to the theories regarding orality that undergird the present study.

6.2.1 The Structure and Components of 1 Clem. *46.8 and its Parallels*

An important structural element of *1 Clem.* 46.8 is its basic two-part composition: a woe-saying (οὐαί) coupled with a millstone-saying. Each of the Synoptics contains parallels to both of these parts, but there is much divergence between *1 Clem.* 46.8 and its gospel parallels in terms of structure, placement, overall theme of the sayings, and wording, divergence that is also discernible when comparing the gospel parallels to each other.

The *Markan* passages included in the above synopsis, Mk 9:42 and 14:21, are somewhat problematic as parallels to *1 Clem.* 46.8. While in *1 Clem.* 46.8 the woe-saying and the millstone-saying are a continuous whole, in Mark they occur as two separate sayings, and in contexts that are considerably removed from each other (Mk 14:21 and 9:42). In addition, while the Markan woe-saying targets the one who would betray the Son of Man (δι' οὗ ὁ υἱὸς τοῦ ἀνθρώπου παραδίδοται), the Clementine saying targets one who would cause one of the Lord's chosen to stumble (ἢ ἕνα τῶν ἐκλεκτῶν μου σκανδαλίσαι). Though in these respects the Markan woe-saying is quite dissimilar to *1 Clem.* 46.8, it functions as a parallel to the latter because a portion of it shows an almost verbatim linguistic similarity to the Clementine saying: οὐαὶ τῷ ἀνθρώπῳ ἐκείνῳ ... καλὸν αὐτῷ εἰ οὐκ ἐγεννήθη. This linguistic similarity may be sufficient to suggest that the woe-sayings in Mk 14:21 and *1 Clem.* 46.8 are linked in the history of the tradition, even if the Markan stream and that which eventually reached Clement may have parted ways early on.

In contrast to the woe-saying, the Markan millstone-saying shows very little linguistic similarity to *1 Clem.* 46.8:

1 Clem. 46.8:	κρεῖττον ἦν αὐτῷ περιτεθῆναι μύλον
Mk 9:42:	καλόν ἐστιν αὐτῷ μᾶλλον εἰ περίκειται μύλος ὀνικὸς περὶ τὸν τράχηλον αὐτοῦ

1 Clem. 46.8:	καὶ καταποντισθῆναι εἰς τὴν θάλασσαν
Mk 9:42:	καὶ βέβληται εἰς τὴν θάλασσαν

1 Clem. 46.8:	ἢ ἕνα τῶν ἐκλεκτῶν μου διαστρέψαι
Mk 9:42:	καὶ ὃς ἂν σκανδαλίσῃ ἕνα τῶν μικρῶν τούτων τῶν πιστευόντων εἰς ἐμέ

In spite of the linguistic dissimilarity, the two forms of the saying are so similar in meaning that they probably go back to the same saying in the history of the tradition.[7] We will focus further on this possibility after we have surveyed the parallels in the other gospels.

In *Matthew* we find something similar to Mark, but with an added level of complexity. Like Mark, Matthew contains a woe-saying in a context considerably removed from the millstone-saying (Mt 26:24 and 18:6). In this woe-saying Matthew has followed Mark (14:21) almost to the letter, differing only in that Matthew reads ἦν after καλόν, while Mark does not.[8] In this regard Matthew is linguistically even closer than Mark is to *1 Clement*, since *1 Clem.* 46.8 also reads ἦν after καλόν (to be discussed further below). In following closely the text of Mark, this Matthean woe-saying likewise differs from *1 Clem.* 46.8 in that it targets the one who would betray the Son of Man, rather than one who would cause one of the Lord's chosen to stumble.

Matthew differs from Mark, however, in containing a second woe-saying that in the Matthean context follows immediately after the mill-stone-saying (Mt 18:7). As will be further argued below, it is important that Matthew is similar to *1 Clement* in this regard: they both have a woe-saying paired directly with a millstone-saying, though in Matthew the order of woe- and millstone-saying is reversed (Mt: millstone–woe; *1 Clem.* woe–millstone). The two Matthean woe-sayings relate to their parallel in *1 Clem.* 46.8 in a rather complex way: we already noted that the woe-saying found in a context far removed from the millstone-saying (Mt

---

[7] Further support for this statement will be given below.

[8] Mk 14:21:   οὐαὶ δὲ τῷ ἀνθρώπῳ ἐκείνῳ δι' οὗ ὁ υἱὸς τοῦ ἀνθρώπου παραδίδοται
   Mt 26:24:   οὐαὶ δὲ τῷ ἀνθρώπῳ ἐκείνῳ δι' οὗ ὁ υἱὸς τοῦ ἀνθρώπου παραδίδοται

   Mk 14:21:   καλὸν   αὐτῷ εἰ οὐκ ἐγεννήθη ὁ ἄνθρωπος ἐκεῖνος
   Mt 26:24:   καλὸν ἦν αὐτῷ εἰ οὐκ ἐγεννήθη ὁ ἄνθρωπος ἐκεῖνος

26:24, following Mk 14:21) shows significant *linguistic* similarity to *1 Clem.* 46.8,[9] while differing with it regarding the *target of the woe-saying*. With the woe-saying in Mt 18:7, which follows immediately after the millstone-saying, we find the reverse: it is *linguistically* very different from *1 Clem.* 46.8, especially in that it contains no equivalent to "it would have been good for him not to be born,"[10] but it is similar to *1 Clement* in having one who causes others to stumble as the *target of its woe-saying* (Mt 18:7: δι᾽ οὗ τὸ σκάνδαλον ἔρχεται; *1 Clem.* 46.8: ἢ ἕνα τῶν ἐκλεκτῶν μου σκανδαλίσαι).

The Matthean millstone-saying at times follows its parallel in Mark verbatim (as highlighted by double underlining in what follows), and like its Markan parallel shows limited linguistic similarity to *1 Clem.* 46.8:

1 Cl. 46.8:	κρεῖττον ἦν αὐτῷ περιτεθῆναι μύλον
Mk 9:42:	καλόν ἐστιν αὐτῷ μᾶλλον εἰ
	περίκειται μύλος ὀνικὸς περὶ τὸν τράχηλον αὐτοῦ
Matt 18:6:	συμφέρει αὐτῷ ἵνα
	κρεμασθῇ μύλος ὀνικὸς περὶ τὸν τράχηλον αὐτοῦ

1 Cl. 46.8:	καὶ καταποντισθῆναι	εἰς τὴν θάλασσαν
Mk 9:42:	καὶ βέβληται	εἰς τὴν θάλασσαν
Matt 18:6:	καὶ καταποντισθῇ ἐν τῷ πελάγει τῆς θαλάσσης	

1 Clem. 46.8:   ἢ ἕνα τῶν ἐκλεκτῶν μου διαστρέψαι
Mark 9:42: καὶ ὃς ἂν σκανδαλίσῃ ἕνα τῶν μικρῶν τούτων τῶν πιστευόντων εἰς ἐμέ
Matt 18:6: Ὃς δ᾽ ἂν σκανδαλίσῃ ἕνα τῶν μικρῶν τούτων τῶν πιστευόντων εἰς ἐμέ

As with the saying in Mark, the Matthean and Clementine forms are so similar in meaning that they probably go back to the same saying in the history of the tradition. As noted, Matthew follows Mark to a considerable extent, and is no closer to *1 Clement* than to Mark when it differs from the latter, but for one notable exception: Matthew reads καταποντισθῇ in place of Mark's βέβληται, and thus is closer to *1 Clement*'s καταποντισθῆναι. We will address this further below, when discussing the possible presence of redactional material from the Evangelists in *1 Clem.* 46.8.

---

[9] *1 Clem.* 46.8: οὐαὶ   τῷ ἀνθρώπῳ ἐκείνῳ
Mk 14:21: οὐαὶ δὲ τῷ ἀνθρώπῳ ἐκείνῳ δι᾽ οὗ ὁ υἱὸς τοῦ ἀνθρώπου παραδίδοται
Mt 26:24: οὐαὶ δὲ τῷ ἀνθρώπῳ ἐκείνῳ δι᾽ οὗ ὁ υἱὸς τοῦ ἀνθρώπου παραδίδοται

1 Clem. 46.8: καλὸν ἦν αὐτῷ εἰ οὐκ ἐγεννήθη, ἢ ἕνα τῶν ἐκλεκτῶν μου σκανδαλίσαι
Mk 14:21:   καλὸν   αὐτῷ εἰ οὐκ ἐγεννήθη ὁ ἄνθρωπος ἐκεῖνος
Mt 26:24:   καλὸν ἦν αὐτῷ εἰ οὐκ ἐγεννήθη ὁ ἄνθρωπος ἐκεῖνος

[10] *1 Clem.* 46.8a: οὐαὶ τῷ ἀνθρώπῳ ἐκείνῳ καλὸν ἦν αὐτῷ εἰ οὐκ ἐγεννήθη,
                    ἢ ἕνα τῶν ἐκλεκτῶν μου σκανδαλίσαι
   Mt 18:7b–c: ἀνάγκη γὰρ ἐλθεῖν τὰ σκάνδαλα
                πλὴν οὐαὶ τῷ ἀνθρώπῳ δι᾽ οὗ τὸ σκάνδαλον ἔρχεται

Treatment of the parallels in *Luke* was reserved for last because their place in the puzzle is best seen after all of the above has been put in place. Unlike Mark and Matthew, Luke does not contain a woe-saying (that parallels *1 Clem.* 46.8) in a context considerably removed from the millstone-saying. Like Matthew, however, Luke 17:1 does contain a woe-saying in the immediate context of the millstone-saying. The order of the Lukan sayings agrees with *1 Clement* against Matthew in placing the woe-saying first, followed by the millstone-saying. Luke's woe-saying contains important linguistic and other similarities to Mt 18:7 (see further below), the second Matthean woe-saying treated above. Given this similarity to its Matthean parallel, it should come as no surprise that Lk 17:1 also relates to its parallels in the synopsis most like Mt 18:7: not only is it (a) found in the immediate context of the Lukan millstone-saying (Lk 17:2); but it also (b) targets not one who would betray the Son of Man, but one who would cause others to stumble; (c) shows very little *linguistic* similarity to *1 Clem.* 46.8 (and like Mt 18:7 has no equivalent to "it would have been good for him not to be born"); and (d) is very similar *in meaning* to *1 Clem.* 46.8.

What emerges from the above analysis is that, while all of the parallels probably intersected at some point in the history of the tradition, it is likely that Matthew and Luke had access to a stream of tradition both separate from Mark and with a closer affinity to the tradition that informed *1 Clement*. This conclusion arises from the consideration that both Matthew and Luke are closer than their shared source Mark to *1 Clement* in certain respects: most importantly, they both contain a woe-saying that – as in *1 Clement* – is directly attached to a millstone-saying, while Mark does not, and they also both share language of "scandal" with *1 Clement*, while Mark does not. That the double tradition was *oral* tradition would explain the various aspects of variability that we noted above not only between Matthew and Luke, but also between both of them and *1 Clement*, a variability that is expressed within the overall stability of shared components and meaning. We will expand on these conclusions after we have examined the gospel parallels to *1 Clem.* 46.8 in greater detail.

6.2.2 The Order and Wording of the Gospel Parallels to 1 Clem. 46.8

We turn next to compare the details of *1 Clem.* 46.8's gospel parallels to each other in order to identify overall patterns of relatedness that might further aid our understanding of Clement's sources. To better understand how the gospel parallels relate to each other in the history of their tradition, and for ease of reference, we set them out below in a synopsis divided into eight parts, following their Markan order. Single underlining indicates agreements between Mark and the other two Synoptics, while double underlining indicates agreements between Matthew and Luke with no Markan parallel. To better draw out linguistic relationships, the different woe-sayings are listed separately, first those in Mk 14:21//Mt 26:24//Lk 22:22 (lines 1–3) followed by the woe-sayings in Mt 18:7/Lk 17:1 (lines 4–5); lines 6–8 contain the millstone-sayings in all three Synoptics:

1. Mk 14:21a: ὅτι ὁ μὲν υἱὸς τοῦ ἀνθρώπου ὑπάγει καθὼς γέγραπται περὶ αὐτοῦ,
   Mt 26:24a: ὁ μὲν υἱὸς τοῦ ἀνθρώπου ὑπάγει καθὼς γέγραπται περὶ αὐτοῦ,
   Lk 22:22a: ὅτι ὁ υἱὸς μὲν τοῦ ἀνθρώπου κατὰ τὸ ὡρισμένον πορεύεται

2. Mk 14:21b: οὐαὶ δὲ τῷ ἀνθρώπῳ ἐκείνῳ δι' οὗ ὁ υἱὸς τοῦ ἀνθρώπου παραδίδοται
   Mt 26:24b: οὐαὶ δὲ τῷ ἀνθρώπῳ ἐκείνῳ δι' οὗ ὁ υἱὸς τοῦ ἀνθρώπου παραδίδοται
   Lk 22:22b: πλὴν οὐαὶ τῷ ἀνθρώπῳ ἐκείνῳ δι' οὗ παραδίδοται

3. Mk 14:21c: καλὸν αὐτῷ εἰ οὐκ ἐγεννήθη ὁ ἄνθρωπος ἐκεῖνος
   Mt 26:24: καλὸν ἦν αὐτῷ εἰ οὐκ ἐγεννήθη ὁ ἄνθρωπος ἐκεῖνος

4. Mt 18:7a–b: Οὐαὶ τῷ κόσμῳ ἀπὸ τῶν σκανδάλων·
   ἀνάγκη γὰρ ἐλθεῖν τὰ σκάνδαλα
   Lk 17:1b: ἀνένδεκτόν ἐστιν τοῦ τὰ σκάνδαλα μὴ ἐλθεῖν,

5. Matt 18:7c: πλὴν οὐαὶ τῷ ἀνθρώπῳ δι' οὗ τὸ σκάνδαλον ἔρχεται
   Lk 17:1c: πλὴν οὐαὶ δι' οὗ ἔρχεται

6. Mk 9:42a: ὃς ἂν σκανδαλίσῃ ἕνα τῶν μικρῶν τούτων τῶν πιστευόντων εἰς ἐμέ
   Mt 18:6a: ὃς δ' ἂν σκανδαλίσῃ ἕνα τῶν μικρῶν τούτων τῶν πιστευόντων εἰς ἐμέ
   Luke 17:2c: ἢ ἵνα σκανδαλίσῃ τῶν μικρῶν τούτων ἕνα

7. Mk 9:42b: καλόν ἐστιν αὐτῷ μᾶλλον εἰ
   περίκειται μύλος ὀνικὸς περὶ τὸν τράχηλον αὐτοῦ
   Matt 18:6b: συμφέρει αὐτῷ ἵνα
   κρεμασθῇ μύλος ὀνικὸς περὶ τὸν τράχηλον αὐτοῦ
   Lk 17:2a: λυσιτελεῖ αὐτῷ εἰ
   λίθος μυλικὸς περίκειται περὶ τὸν τράχηλον αὐτοῦ

8. Mk 9:42c: καὶ βέβληται εἰς τὴν θάλασσαν
   Matt 18:6c: καὶ καταποντισθῇ ἐν τῷ πελάγει τῆς θαλάσσης
   Lk 17:2b: καὶ ἔρριπται εἰς τὴν θάλασσαν

From the above it is fairly clear that Matthew and Luke have followed a common source other than Mark for the material in their woe-saying(s) in parts 4–5. In the opinion of a majority of scholars this source was Q,[11] but

---

[11] See Robinson et al., *Critical Edition of Q*, 472–77 (on Mt 18:6–7//Lk 17:1–2 as Q). Most commentators speak of a combination of Q and Markan influence in Mt 18:6–7 and Lk 17:1–2; see, e.g., Davies and Allison, *Matthew*, 2:761–64; D. A. Hagner, *Matthew 14–28* (WBC 33B; Dallas: Word, 1995), 520–21; U. Luz, *Matthew 8–20: A Commentary* (ed. H. Koester; trans. J. E. Crouch; Hermeneia; Minneapolis: Fortress, 2001), 423, 431; Schweizer, *Matthew*, 364–65; J. A. Fitzmyer, *The Gospel According to Luke X–XXIV: A*

in light of the discussion above and that follows it may be best to refer to it more generically as the "double tradition."[12] A common source is discernible not only in the language shared by Matthew and Luke (ἐλθεῖν τὰ σκάνδαλα πλὴν οὐαὶ ... δι' οὗ ... ἔρχεται) but also in their shared idea of the inevitability that σκάνδαλα should come (Mt 18:7: ἀνάγκη γὰρ ἐλθεῖν τὰ σκάνδαλα; Lk 17:1: ἀνένδεκτόν ἐστιν τοῦ τὰ σκάνδαλα μὴ ἐλθεῖν), both of which – most importantly – have no parallel in Mk 9:42. It is highly probable that some form of the millstone-saying (parts 6–8 above) also existed in this source, since both Matthew and Luke have chosen to pair a millstone-saying with the woe-saying from the double tradition.[13]

It is also very likely that Matthew and Luke had access to this double tradition (Lk 17:1–2//Mt 18:6–7; parts 4–8 above) as *oral* tradition rather than as a written document (such as a written Q). This would explain why, aside from the above-mentioned similarities, the Matthean and Lukan parallels differ considerably from each other in wording and order whenever they depart from the text of Mark. It is clear that both Matthew and Luke follow Mark in part. This can be seen in the phrase ὃς [δ'] ἂν σκανδαλίσῃ ἕνα τῶν μικρῶν τούτων τῶν πιστευόντων εἰς ἐμέ, followed verbatim by Matthew from the text of Mark with the exception of the δ' (which is why

---

New Translation with Introduction and Commentary (AB 28A; New York: Doubleday, 1985), 1136–37; Marshall, *Luke*, 640; Koester, *Synoptische Überlieferung*, 16.

[12] In speaking of the sources for Mt 18:6–7//Lk 17:1–2, J. Ernst suggests either Q or variegated streams of oral tradition (*Das Evangelium nach Lukas* [RNT 3; Regensburg: Pustet, 1977], 477–80). J. Nolland speaks of Mark and an undefined "second source" as sources for Mt 18:6–7 (*Matthew*, 735). Cf. D. L. Bock, who suggests an origin for Lk 17:1–2 in Luke's special source (L), which "may have had points of contact with elements in Matthew" (*Luke 9:51–24:53* [BECNT 3B; Grand Rapids: Baker, 1996], 1381–82, quote taken from p. 1382), and further Albright and Mann, who conclude that "it is far easier to explain similarities and differences on the basis of three independent approaches to the fixed oral tradition" than to explain the parallels in terms of Matthew's dependence on Mark while taking into account the Lukan tradition (*Matthew*, 217). I found the following comment by L. Morris simply unexplainable, given the Lukan parallel under consideration here: "[In v. 7] Matthew tells of Jesus' words denouncing those who lead others into sin, *a passage found only in this Gospel*" (*The Gospel According to Matthew* [PillNTC; Leicester: InterVarsity/Grand Rapids: Eerdmans, 1992], 462; emphasis added).

[13] Fitzmyer argues that Q contained a form of the millstone-saying because the saying as found in Luke 17:2 is located within a larger block of Q material, Lk 17:1b–c and 3b–6 (*Luke X–XXIV*, 1137). His argument is sound, though perhaps the source was not Q but the double tradition in more general terms. Not all would agree with Fitzmyer; others would hold that the hypothetical Q 17:2 was not found in Q, but reflects Matthean and Lukan redaction of Mk 9:42 (see, e.g., F. Neirynck, "The Reconstruction of Q and IQP/CritEd Parallels," in *Q and the Historical Jesus* [ed. Lindemann], 89–92). For additional authors for and against the inclusion of Lk 17:2//Mt 18:6 in Q see Kloppenborg, *Q Parallels*, 182.

it is enclosed in brackets),[14] and that Luke has shortened to ἢ ἵνα σκανδαλίσῃ τῶν μικρῶν τούτων ἕνα. It can also be seen in the phrase μύλος ὀνικὸς περὶ τὸν τράχηλον αὐτοῦ that is shared verbatim by Mark and Matthew, of which Luke also shares the shorter segment περὶ τὸν τράχηλον αὐτοῦ. Where they differ from Mark, however, Matthew and Luke never agree with each other:

Where Mt has followed Mk's μύλος ὀνικός, Lk reads λίθος μυλικός.
Where Lk has followed Mk's εἰς τὴν θάλασσαν, Mt reads ἐν τῷ πελάγει τῆς θαλάσσης.
Where Lk has followed Mk's idiom περίκειται (though changing the order from περίκειται μύλος ὀνικός to λίθος μυλικὸς περίκειται), Mt reads κρεμασθῇ.
Where Mt has followed the Markan order a–b–c for the millstone saying as a whole (parts 6–8), Lk follows the order c–a–b.[15]
Where they both differ from Mk's καλόν ἐστιν ... μᾶλλον ει, Mt reads συμφέρει ... ἵνα and Lk reads λυσιτελεῖ ... ει.
Where they both differ from Mk's βέβληται, Mt reads καταποντισθῇ and Lk reads ἔρριπται.

Within all of the above variability, however, Matthew and Luke never disagree in meaning; the many differences all involve synonyms or details of descriptive language.[16] This is important because not only the differences noted, but also this similarity in meaning, reflect the variability within sta-

---

[14] Koester, apparently working on the basis of a critical text that did not include εἰς ἐμε at Mk 9:42, has Mt adding εἰς ἐμε to the text he inherited from Mk (*Synoptische Überlieferung*, 18). As mentioned on p. 178 above, the εἰς ἐμε in Mk 9:42 remains a contested reading, but it probably should be included in the Markan text not only because of the strong external support, but also because of the dynamics of Matthean dependence upon Mk: Mt follows Mk almost verbatim up to this point in the saying, so one can logically infer that this verbatim dependence also includes the εἰς ἐμε. This argument is not intended to be conclusive, but when considered in light of the external support, for this writer it is persuasive.

[15] If Q 17:1–2 is treated as a written source, then the assumption is that Luke would be more likely than Matthew to preserve the order found in Q, since this is a Lukan characteristic. The consensus among Q scholars that Lk generally better preserves the order of Q provides the rationale for the practice of reconstructing Q using Luke's chapter and verse numeration, though it does not always hold (see Neirynck, "Reconstruction of Q," 56–57, 61–63). If Q is oral at this point, however, it becomes a non-issue: in an oral setting the order would vary as a matter of course, and unless it were a saying that had a very fixed form there would be no such thing as an "original order" *within the tradition* (see discussion on pp. 20, 87, 145 above).

[16] Though less extensive, there are also variations in order and wording between Mt and Lk in parts 4–5: in wording between ἀνάγκη γάρ in Mt 18:7b and ἀνένδεκτόν ἐστιν τοῦ in Lk 17:1b; in order between the ἐλθεῖν τὰ σκάνδαλα in Mt vs. the τὰ σκάνδαλα μὴ ἐλθεῖν in Lk; the positive construction ἀνάγκη γὰρ ἐλθεῖν τὰ σκάνδαλα in Mt vs. the negative construction ἀνένδεκτόν ἐστιν τοῦ τὰ σκάνδαλα μὴ ἐλθεῖν in Lk – more on this below. As with the material in parts 6–8, in the midst of all this variety the meaning of the sayings does not vary among the parallels.

bility that is characteristic of oral tradition.[17] This further supports the contention that the evangelists accessed the double tradition under consideration in oral form.[18]

If we conclude that the double tradition behind Lk 17:1–2//Mt 18:6–7 was oral tradition, then there is little point in arguing over whether Matthew or Luke best preserves their source's wording and/or order. Assuming that Matthew and Luke witnessed separate performances of the double tradition, each one might faithfully represent its content in their writings, yet differ considerably from each other. This adds another level of uncertainty to the already difficult tasks of determining on the one hand to what extent the double tradition might have influenced the language of the Matthean and Lukan millstone-sayings where they depart from Mark, and on the other hand what language the double tradition held in common with Mk 9:42.[19] We will address this topic further below, in discussing the editorial contributions of each evangelist to their gospel's form of the sayings under consideration. For now we simply conclude that both the double tradition and Mark influenced the forms of the millstone-saying that have been preserved in Matthew and Luke.

As noted above, the double tradition contains the idea, reflected in both Matthew and Luke, of the inevitability that σκάνδαλα should come, which has no parallel in Mk 9:42. It is interesting to note, however, that while the other woe-saying under consideration, found in Mk 14:21//Mt 26:24//Lk

---

[17] See subsection 3.3.5 above, under the subtitle "Both Variable and Stable."

[18] One could also speak of an "oral Q," an idea that is not new; see, e.g., Dunn, "Q[1] as Oral" 45–69, where Dunn argues that the material identified by J. Kloppenborg as 'Q[1]' (Q 6:20b–23b, 27–35, 36–45, 46–49; 9:57–60, [61–62]; 10:2–11, 16, [23–24?]; 11:2–4, 9–13; 12:2–7, 11–12; 12:22b–31, 33–34 [13:18–19, 20–21?]; and probably 13:24; 14:26–27; 17:33; 14:34–35) "is best understood as oral tradition" (Dunn's conclusion on p. 69). Dunn is interacting primarily with Kloppenborg's *The Formation of Q: Trajectories in Ancient Wisdom Collections* (Philadelphia: Fortress, 1987) and *Excavating Q: The History and Setting of the Sayings Gospel* (Minneapolis: Fortress, 2000), but also refers to Kloppenborg's "Jesus and the Parables of Jesus in Q," in *The Gospel Behind the Gospels: Current Studies on Q* (ed. R. A. Piper; NovTSup 75; Leiden: Brill, 1995), 275–319, and his *Q Parallels*.

[19] It seems quite likely that Mt departed more from his double-traditional source than did Luke. As noted by F. Neirynck, Matthew uses the three verbs in Mt 18:6 redactionally elsewhere: συμφέρει in 5:29, 30; 19:10, κρεμάννυμι in 22:40, and καταποντίζομαι in 14:30 ("Reconstruction of Q," 90). This would at least *suggest* that the presence of these three verbs in Mt 18:6 is also redactional. In addition, since Mt appears to follow Mk in the phrase μύλος ὀνικὸς περὶ τὸν τράχηλον αὐτοῦ, perhaps the Lukan λίθος μυλικός was found in the double tradition; the fact that the identical τῶν πιστευόντων εἰς ἐμε in Mk and Mt is missing in Lk might also indicate that it was absent in the double tradition. Perhaps Mt is following the double tradition, however, in reading ἐν τῷ πελάγει τῆς θαλάσσης, while the Lukan εἰς τὴν θάλασσαν derives from Mk. All of this is at best hypothetical.

22:22, also lacks the specific idea of the inevitability of σκάνδαλα, it *is* introduced with an element of inevitability:[20]

Mk 14:21a: ὅτι ὁ μὲν υἱὸς τοῦ ἀνθρώπου ὑπάγει καθὼς γέγραπται περὶ αὐτοῦ
Mt 26:24a: ὁ μὲν υἱὸς τοῦ ἀνθρώπου ὑπάγει καθὼς γέγραπται περὶ αὐτοῦ
Lk 22:22a: ὅτι ὁ υἱὸς μὲν τοῦ ἀνθρώπου κατὰ τὸ ὡρισμένον πορεύεται

The nature of the inevitability, and the subject to which it applies, are very different in Mk 14:21//Mt 26:24//Lk 22:22 than in Mt 18:7//Lk 17:1: in Mk 14:21 and parallels, the inevitability has to do with the "going" (ὑπάγει, πορεύεται) and therefore the betraying of the Son of Man, and arises in Mk 14:21//Mt 26:24 from its prefiguring in Scripture (καθὼς γέγραπται), which Luke (17:1) has changed to the more general "as it has been determined" (κατὰ τὸ ὡρισμένον). The similarity, therefore, of Mk 14:21 and parallels to Mt 18:7 and Lk 17:1 in this regard is admittedly superficial – but it does not follow that it is inconsequential. The mere presence of the notion of inevitability in Mk 14:21//Mt 26:24//Lk 22:22 adds another level of relatedness to the gospel parallels under consideration, and further connects these passages not only to Mt 18:7 and Lk 17:1, but also (as will be argued further below) to *1 Clem.* 46.8.

As noted at the beginning of the present section, the purpose of comparing the above gospel parallels to each other was to identify overall patterns of relatedness that might aid our understanding of the sources of *1 Clem.* 46.8. To summarize our findings as they relate to the saying in *1 Clement*, the overall structure of woe-saying paired with millstone-saying that we find in *1 Clem.* 46.8 was apparently found in the double tradition, as reflected in Mt 18:6–7 and Lk 17:1–2. Although the woe-saying in the double tradition is very different in form than the one in *1 Clement* (especially in lacking a parallel to part 3 above, along the lines of "it would be better if he had not been born"), in content the two are similar, in that they both target those who cause others to stumble. That both the double tradition and *1 Clem.* 46.8 pair a woe-saying with a millstone-saying probably indicates that the traditions they represent were fairly closely related at some point in their history.[21] Apparently a form of the woe-saying

---

[20] The Lukan parallel is included in what follows even though it does not provide a true parallel to *1 Clem.* 46:8, and therefore was not included among the parallels in the synopsis at the beginning of the present chapter. Mark and Matthew provide parallels to *1 Clem.* 46:8 because the lines below lead directly into the woe-saying that contains the statement that it would have been better for such a one not to have been born, similar to what we find in *1 Clem.* 46:8. Luke, however, has abbreviated the woe-saying so that rather than leading into a statement that it would have been better for such a one not to have been born, it ends simply in πλὴν οὐαὶ τῷ ἀνθρώπῳ ἐκείνῳ δι' οὗ παραδίδοται.

[21] In arguing for the dependence of Mt 18:6–7 and Lk 17:1–2 on Mark rather than Q, Neirynck finds "nothing extraordinary" in both Mt and Lk combining the woe with the

in *1 Clem.* 46.8 existed unattached to a millstone-saying in the pre-Markan tradition, as suggested by the similar words οὐαὶ τῷ ἀνθρώπῳ ἐκείνῳ ... καλὸν αὐτῷ εἰ οὐκ ἐγεννήθη in *1 Clem.* 46.8 and Mk 14:21.[22] Though it is possible that Jesus said both forms of the woe-saying on separate occasions, the complex web of relationships between *1 Clem.* 46.8 and all its gospel parallels we have examined would appear to indicate that the two forms go back to a single utterance.[23] We also found good reason in the above discussion to hold that the gospel parallels to *1 Clem.* 46.8 were largely derived from oral (pre-Markan and double) tradition. This points further toward the possibility that the contact between the traditions behind *1 Clem.* 46.8 and the pre-gospel traditions behind its parallels took place in

---

millstone, and supports this view in part with the further argument that Lk and Mt follow a different order in these sayings ("Reconstruction of Q," 90). With all due respect to Neirynck, I do find the pairing of the woe and millstone in Mt and Lk significant, and find in it sufficient evidence of a common source (the double tradition). The issue of order is of no consequence. Not only does Matthew often depart from the order of Q, but also, if the source accessed by the Evangelists for the material in Lk 17:1–2//Mt 18:6–7 was oral tradition (as argued above), the variation in order would represent the variability within stability that one would expect to find in such a source. It is even more significant, as noted above, that the woe and millstone are paired not only in Mt and Lk, pointing to a common source in the double tradition, but also in *1 Clement*. Given that in other respects the sayings in the double tradition differ significantly from those in *1 Clement*, one should hesitate to argue for the direct dependence of *1 Clement* on this source. The common pairing of woe with millstone, however, would at least suggest an influence of one upon the other in the history of their tradition. Returning to the possibility that the double tradition under consideration represents an "oral Q," cf. the discussion by Koester, who posits a special relationship between the Logia in *1 Clem.* 46.8 and Q, but also holds that the dependence of the former upon the latter was indirect (*Synoptische Überlieferung*, 16–19).

[22] Though in the pre-Markan tradition it targeted the one who would betray the Son of Man (Mk 14:21 followed by Mt 26:24) rather than one who would cause one of the Lord's chosen to stumble (*1 Clem.* 46.8).

[23] One could argue that since the saying, "it would have been better for [x] not to have been born" was not uncommon in the Judaism of Jesus' time, it is likely that he used the saying on more than one occasion. We already noted above that a similar saying appears, e.g., in the *Similitudes of Enoch* 38.2. Similar sayings also show up elsewhere in early Christian literature: e.g., in the *Shepherd* of Hermas, αἱρετώτερον ἦν αὐτοῖς τὸ μὴ γεννηθῆναι (Herm. *Vis.* IV.2.6 [Herm. 23.6], not identified explicitly as Jesus tradition) is applied to those who heard the words of the Lady (the church) and disobeyed them; on other occurrences of similar sayings in early Christian literature see Hagner, *Clement of Rome*, 156–59. One could thus argue that *1 Clem.* 46.8 reflected an occasion in which Jesus used the same saying with a more general referent. The quotation in *1 Clem.* 46.8, however, appears to be dependent on Jesus' saying regarding Judas beyond the simple καλὸν ἦν αὐτῷ εἰ οὐκ ἐγεννήθη, to include also the specificity of οὐαὶ τῷ ἀνθρώπῳ ἐκείνῳ. This would tend to support that the first part of *1 Clem.* 46.8 is derived from Jesus' saying regarding Judas.

an oral-traditional context. Two main factors probably contributed to the conflation of the woe-saying related to the pre-Marcan tradition with the woe- and millstone-saying related to the double tradition,[24] leading to the combined form of both sayings as found in *1 Clem.* 46.8: the presence of a woe-saying in both traditions would have attracted them to each other during the oral stage, and the idea of inevitability (of either σκάνδαλα or that the Son of Man ὑπάγει), also found in both traditions, might have facilitated their identification with each other in the mind of the traditionist.

The findings of our inquiry up to this point clearly lessen the possibility of direct dependence of *1 Clem.* 46.8 upon the written Gospels. The possibility of direct dependence is further contradicted by the many smaller differences (within the larger areas of similarity and dissimilarity already considered above) that exist between *1 Clem.* 46.8 and its gospel parallels, as we will see in what follows. In considering these differences, there will be some inevitable overlap with our earlier discussion that was limited to the relationships among the gospel parallels.

In the texts on causing others to stumble we find differing terminology: in *1 Clement* those who are caused to stumble are described as "my [the Lord's] chosen" (τῶν ἐκλεκτῶν μου),[25] in Mk 9:42 and Mt 18:6 as "one of these little ones who believes in me" (ἕνα τῶν μικρῶν τούτων τῶν πιστευόντων εἰς ἐμέ), and in Lk 17:2 more briefly as "one of these little ones" (τῶν μικρῶν τούτων ἕνα). Given that all three Synoptic parallels contain "one of these little ones" as a common denominator, they have more in common with each other than any one of them has with *1 Clem.*

---

[24] The choice of the wording "related to" in both cases is intentional, in that we simply cannot know in what venue Clement's source (assuming it was not Clement himself) encountered the pre-Markan and double-tradition-related material under consideration.

[25] L. E. Wright argues that Clement was here citing the finished from of the Synoptics (most probably Mt [implicit]) from memory, and in so doing deliberately chose to replace the Synoptic μικρῶν with ἐκλεκτῶν for dogmatic purposes: to "vindicate the sacred and divinely ordered office of the bishop and the other spiritually selected officials … [whom] Clement contends, 'God has chosen (ἐκλέλεκται) for his priesthood and ministry' (xliii)" (*Alterations*, 59–60). I disagree with this assessment on a number of points: (a) as argued throughout this chapter, there is no good reason to hold that Clement knew the finished form of the Gospels; (b) in keeping with this, Clement is not citing the Gospels from memory, but (as also argued throughout this chapter) is appealing to oral tradition; (c) I agree with Koester that one cannot assume that the ἐκλεκτῶν in 46.8 refers to church leadership; and it follows that (d) (also with Koester) this choice of wording is not dogmatically motivated on Clement's part (see Koester, *Synoptische Überlieferung*, 18 n. 3). In my view the presence of ἐκλεκτῶν in 46.8 reflects the vagaries of oral tradition; it may have been used in place of μικρῶν in the tradition upon which Clement depended due to being more readily identifiable with the followers of Jesus. It need not represent a late form of the saying, however, as ἐκλεκτῶν is well attested elsewhere in the Synoptic tradition (e.g., Mt 22:14; Mk 13:20, 22, 27//Mt 24:22, 24, 31; Lk 18:4).

46.8. While the verb σκανδαλίζω is found in all three Synoptics (Mk 9:42//Mt 18:6//Lk 17:2; Mt 18:7//Lk 17:1 also contain the noun σκάνδαλα/ σκάνδαλον) and in *1 Clem.* 46.8, all three Synoptics use the subjunctive aorist form σκανδαλίσῃ in place of *1 Clement*'s σκανδαλίσαι, and only *1 Clem.* 46.8 uses also the synonym διαστρέφω – another instance of the Synoptics agreeing with each other against *1 Clem.* 46.8.[26] Mark 14:21 and Mt 26:24 further differ from *1 Clement* in that they both contain an emphatic "that man" (ὁ ἄνθρωπος ἐκεῖνος) at the end of their woe-saying that is not found in *1 Clem.* 46.8.[27] In addition, while all three Synoptics and *1 Clem.* 46.8 refer to some form of a millstone, where *1 Clement* has simply a millstone (μύλος), Mk 9:42 and Mt 18:6 specify a great millstone of the type worked by a donkey (μύλος ὀνικός), and Lk 17:2 has a "stone belonging to a mill" (λίθος μυλικός).[28] Furthermore, the vocabulary used for "it is better" in the saying "it is better for such a one to have a millstone hung/cast around his neck" also differs in the four texts that contain it: in *1 Clem.* 46.8 it is "better" or "more fitting" (κρεῖττον [ἀγαθός]), in Mk 9:42 it is "good" or "fitting" (καλός), Mt 18:6 reads "it is to his advantage" or "it is helpful" (συμφέρω), and Lk 17:2 "it is better" or "it is to his advantage" (λυσιτελέω). Furthermore, only *1 Clement* does not specify that the millstone is to be attached "around his neck" (περὶ τὸν τράχηλον αὐτοῦ; par. in Mk/Mt/Lk), and all four relevant texts differ in their wording for carrying out the general idea of attaching the millstone: in *1 Clem.* 46.8 we find περιτεθῆναι, in Mt 18:6 κρεμασθῇ, and while Mk and Lk both read περίκειται, they differ in terms of word order (Mk 9:42: περίκειται μύλος ὀνικός; Lk 17:2: λίθος μυλικὸς περίκειται).

In sum, in comparing *1 Clem.* 46.8 to its gospel parallels we encounter a great variety and wealth of differences. If one were to argue that Clement derived his material from any given written gospel, it would be difficult to explain why so few of the words that make up the sayings in any given

---

[26] Koester and Massaux both argue that Clement of Rome has here changed the reading σκανδαλίσαι he found in his sources to διαστρέψαι, anticipating and preparing for the next phrase in his letter, τὸ σχίσμα ὑμῶν πολλοὺς διέστρεψεν (46.9a); see Koester, *Synoptische Überlieferung*, 17 n. 1; Massaux, *Influence*, 24. As noted in a previous footnote, however, J. B. Lightfoot argues convincingly that the reverse is the case: Clement has included the word διέστρεψεν in the phrase immediately following the διαστρέψαι of 46.8 because it is his habit to take up a word and comment on it in a subsequent phrase (*Apostolic Fathers*, 1.2:141, and see the full list of examples Lightfoot includes in ibid., 1.2:142). It follows that διαστρέψαι was probably found in Clement's source. For further discussion see Hagner, *Clement of Rome*, 155–56.

[27] Jeremias does not view the ἐκεῖνος as emphatic, but as the result of the mistranslation of "a pleonastically placed Aramaic or Hebrew demonstrative pronoun" (*Eucharistic Words*, 183–84).

[28] See BDAG, s.v. μύλος (p. 661), μυλικός (p. 660).

gospel are reflected in their Clementine parallel. What is more, most of the words *1 Clem.* 46.8 has in common with its gospel parallels are either the minimum of words necessary to communicate the same saying (e.g., some form of μύλος and some basic version of εἰς τὴν θάλασσαν), or represent a brief saying that would have retained its shape in the process of oral transmission (e.g., οὐαὶ τῷ ἀνθρώπῳ ἐκείνῳ, καλὸν ἦν αὐτῷ εἰ οὐκ ἐγεννήθη). In other words, everything that one would expect to change in the process of oral transmission has changed, while what one would expect to remain stable also has done so. All of this would suggest that the material in *1 Clem.* 46.8 was derived from the oral tradition of Jesus' sayings rather than the written Gospels.[29]

6.2.3 Seeking the Redactional Footprints of the Evangelists

The above conclusion would be contradicted, however, if there were evidence of a different sort that showed a literary dependence of *1 Clem.* 46.8 upon its gospel parallels. We turn, then, to apply our main criterion for confirming this possibility: whether any redactional elements from any of the gospel writers are discernible in the saying(s) as found in *1 Clem.* 46.8.

It is fairly clear that none of the elements that *1 Clem.* 46.8 shares with *Mark* are the result of Markan redaction. In the millstone-saying, the words shared by *1 Clement* and Mk 9:42 (as noted above) reflect the bare minimum necessary for the saying to communicate the same meaning in both contexts: μύλος, εἰς τὴν θάλασσαν, ἕνα τῶν, with an additional pronoun and conjunction (αὐτῷ, καί). The only way, then, that the elements Mk 9:42 shares with *1 Clem.* 46.8 could be the result of Mark's redactional activity is if the whole saying was a Markan creation. This possibility is contradicted, however, by the presence of a similar saying in the double tradition behind Lk 17:1–2//Mt 18:6–7, as noted in our discussion above. Clearly, then, Mk 9:42 does not contribute any Markan redactional elements to its parallel in *1 Clem.* 46.8.[30]

---

[29] C. N. Jefford articulates something similar to the above as follows, "For those who would argue that our author has made use of a specific canonical gospel in these two citations [*1 Clem.* 13.2 and 46.8], one is hard pressed to argue why so little has been used in this process. It seems much more likely that we find here specific citations of a free-floating tradition of teachings that have been attributed to Jesus prior to their inclusion into any particular literary work" (*The Apostolic Fathers and the New Testament* [Peabody, Mass.: Hendrickson, 2006], 130).

[30] What is more, it is doubtful that one could identify *any* Markan redactional elements in Mk 9:42. E. Best suggests that Mark derived all of 9:35–50, with the possible exception of the last clause in v. 50, from pre-Markan oral tradition; see Best, "Mark's Preservation of the Tradition," in *L'Évangile selon Marc: Tradition et rédaction* (ed. M. Sabbe; BETL 34; Leuven: Leuven University Press/Gembloux: Duculot, 1974), 28–29 and n. 26. Best's argument is strengthened by D. Allison's contention that Paul knew and

Mark's editorial hand is not responsible either for the form of the woe-saying in Mk 14:21, that shares some words verbatim with *1 Clem.* 46.8: οὐαὶ ... τῷ ἀνθρώπῳ ἐκείνῳ ... καλόν ... αὐτῷ εἰ οὐκ ἐγεννήθη. Matthew Black, Maurice Casey and others have argued convincingly for the pre-Markan origin of the material in Mark 14:21 based on constructions (μέν ... δέ) and terms (ὑπάγει) that are uncharacteristic of Mark, and a vocabulary that as a whole reflects a Semitic tone (e.g., again ὑπάγει used of dying, and καλόν used as comparative).[31] In addition, the most striking part

---

alluded to the pre-Markan block of tradition standing behind Mk 9:33–50; see Allison, "Pauline Epistles," 13–15. Cf. M. Thompson's conclusion, following a detailed discussion, that Paul probably knew the Jesus tradition behind Mk 9:42 (*Clothed*, 161–73).

[31] See M. Black, *An Aramaic Approach to the Gospels and Acts* (3rd ed.; Peabody, Mass.: Hendrickson, 1998), 117, 302–3; M. Casey, *Aramaic Sources of Mark's Gospel* (SNTSMS 102; Cambridge: Cambridge University Press, 1998), 233–36 (also Casey's *The Solution to the 'Son of Man' Problem* [LNTS 343; London: T&T Clark, 2007], 134–36); C. E. B. Cranfield, *The Gospel According to St. Mark: An Introduction and Commentary* (3rd impr.; CGTC; Cambridge: Cambridge University Press, 1966), 423–24; Jeremias, *Eucharistic Words*, 183–84; J. Marcus, *The Way of the Lord: Christological Exegesis of the Old Testament in the Gospel of Mark* (Louisville: Westminster/John Knox, 1992; reprint, SNTW. Edinburgh: T&T Clark, 1993), 189; J. H. Moulton and W. F. Howard, *A Grammar of New Testament Greek,* Vol. 2: *Accidence and Word-Formation with an Appendix on Semitisms in the New Testament* (Edinburgh: T&T Clark, 1928), 448; Moulton, *Grammar of New Testament Greek,* Vol. 4: *Style*, by Nigel Turner; (Edinburgh: T&T Clark, 1976), 14, 22; V. Taylor, *The Gospel according to St. Mark: The Greek Text with Introduction, Notes, and Indexes* (2nd ed.; London: Macmillan, 1966), 541–42; M. D. Hooker, *The Son of Man in Mark* (Montreal: McGill University Press, 1967), 159–61. Cranfield suggests that perhaps all of Mk 14:18–21 constitutes "an independent unit of tradition which has been inserted between *v.* 17 and *v.* 22 by Mark" (*Mark*, 423); see also the similar statement by M. Casey on all of Mk 14:12–26, who in addition argues that this Aramaic source was a written document (*Aramaic Sources*, 250–51); cf. C. S. Mann, who concludes that "this verse [Mk 14:21] was once part of a collection of testimonies about Judas and was later attracted to this place in the narrative" (*Mark* [AB 27; Garden City: Doubleday, 1986], 459). V. K. Robbins holds that Mk 14:21a (ὅτι ὁ μὲν υἱὸς τοῦ ἀνθρώπου ὑπάγει καθὼς γέγραπται περὶ αὐτοῦ) is redactional, while Mark found the contents of Mk 14:21b–c already extant in the tradition ("Last Meal: Preparation, Betrayal, and Absence," in *The Passion in Mark: Studies on Mark 14–16* [ed. W. H. Kelber; Philadelphia: Fortress, 1976], 33–34), but this is contradicted by the findings of Black and Casey in the works cited above (loc. cit.), that are partially based on the Aramaic behind the ὑπάγει in Mk 14:21a. C. Colpe argues for an Aramaic original behind Mk 14:21, but urges without much basis that the title "Son of Man" is secondary, this verse representing a "Second Stage" in which the church added "Son of Man" to a variety of sayings of Jesus that originally did not contain it ("ὁ υἱὸς τοῦ ἀνθρώπου," *TDNT* 8:443–49, esp. 446). Others assign all of Mk 14:21 to Markan creativity, but without giving much of a reason; see, e.g., C. Breytenbach, "Vormarkinische Logientradition: Parallelen in der urchristlichen Briefliteratur," in *The Four Gospels 1992: Festschrift Frans Neirynck* (ed. F. Van Segbroeck et al.; 3 vols.; BETL 100; Leuven: Leuven University Press and Peeters, 1992), 2:746; Crossan, *In Fragments*, 146.

of the material that *1 Clem.* 46.8 and Mk 14:21 hold in common, καλόν ... αὐτῷ εἰ οὐκ ἐγεννήθη, is attested by similar sayings in other Jewish texts; e.g., *1 Enoch* 38.2 reads, "when the Righteous One shall appear ..., where will the dwelling of the sinners be, and where the resting place of those who denied the name of the Lord of the Spirits? It would have been better for them not to have been born."[32] It follows that the core of Mk 14:21, as a familiar woe-saying, would have retained its shape in the process of oral transmission. From all of the above we surmise that the saying as found in Mk 14:21 most likely predates the gospel, and derived its constitutive elements from a pre-Markan oral milieu rather than from Markan redaction. Given that no Markan redactional elements are discernible either in Mk 9:42 or in Mk 14:21, it is impossible to pinpoint any features in *1 Clem.* 46.8 that are the result of Markan redaction, or that in any way presuppose the finished form of Mark's gospel.[33] This does not discount the possibility of "Markan" influence upon *1 Clem.* 46.8 at some level, but there is no reason to argue that such influence came from a complete Gospel of Mark rather than from pre-Markan tradition (and so "Marcan" only in the most general terms).

Where Mark held out very little in terms of editorial elements that might have been incorporated into *1 Clement,* Luke holds out nothing. Whenever Luke differs from Mark in the passages under consideration, these differences are not reflected in *1 Clem.* 46.8. It follows that the similarities between *1 Clem.* 46.8 and its Lukan parallels have resulted from Luke's dependence on Mark, and are not reflective of Luke's hand. We can therefore conclude that *1 Clem.* 46.8 in no way reflects Luke's editorial activity.[34]

Though I disagree with N. Perrin's contention that the early church created the Jesus saying in Mk 14:21 for apologetic purposes, it is important to note that he includes it among those "Son of Man" sayings in Mark "which show little or no trace of Markan redaction or composition" (*A Modern Pilgrimage in New Testament Christology* [Philadelphia: Fortress, 1974], 86).

[32] Trans. is that of E. Isaac, "1 (Ethiopic Apocalypse of) Enoch," *OTP* 1:30; cf. *2 Enoch* 41:2: "How blessed is he who has not been born ..." (trans. F. I. Andersen, "2 [Slavonic Apocalypse of] Enoch," *OTP* 1:167); see C. A. Evans, *Mark 8:27–16:20* (WBC 34B; Nashville: Nelson, 2001), 378.

[33] I know of no author who presents a cogent argument for Clement of Rome's knowledge of Mark's gospel, which raises serious questions for the traditional view that Mark composed his gospel at Rome while a disciple of the Apostle Peter (a tradition attributed to Clement of Alexandria by Eusebius in *Hist. Eccl.* 2.15; 6.14); see the comments by R. Brown in R. E. Brown and J. P. Meier, *Antioch and Rome: New Testament Cradles of Catholic Christianity* (New York: Paulist, 1983), 198.

[34] A. Gregory, in his important study on *The Reception of Luke and Acts in the Period before Irenaeus,* also briefly dismisses the possibility that Clement was dependent

At first sight there seems to be a distinct possibility that *1 Clem.* 46.8 reflects *Matthean* editorial activity. We already noted above that in the woe-saying of Mt 26:24, Matthew agrees with Clement in reading καλὸν ἦν αὐτῷ against Mark's shorter καλὸν αὐτῷ (Mk 14:21c), and that in the millstone saying Mt 18:6 reads καταποντισθῇ, which parallels Clement's καταποντισθῆναι to a remarkable degree when compared to Mark's βέβληται.

The main proponent of the view that the above indicates Clement's literary dependence upon Matthew is É. Massaux, who bases his argument primarily upon the presence of the verb καταποντίζω in both texts.[35] His argument, however, is not convincing. Although καταποντίζω is, as Massaux states, "peculiar to Mt. in the entire New Testament (Mt. 14.30; 18:6)," it is neither (against what he also states) "rare" outside of Matthew, nor "characteristic" of the latter.[36] As rightly noted by A. Gregory, "this shared terminology is hardly compelling; the word is also used by contemporary authors such as Plutarch and Josephus, and its presence here need imply only that 1 Clement and Matthew drew on shared tradition."[37]

Massaux also bases his argument for the dependence of *1 Clement* upon Matthew to a lesser extent upon the presence of the verb ἦν after καλόν in Mt 26:24 and *1 Clem.* 46.8.[38] The presence of this verb in both texts, however, allows for a number of explanations. It is important to note that the text of Mk 14:21 itself reads ἦν after καλόν in many important manuscripts (ℵ, A, C, D, Θ, Ψ, 0116, *f*[1.13], Majority text, a, f, k, vg[cl], sy[p.h]), so that the Markan reading *without* the ἦν is far from conclusive.[39] Given the presence of ἦν in many Markan manuscripts, its presence in Matthew may simply result from the latter's dependence upon an early manuscript of Mark that

---

on Luke in *1 Clem.* 46.8, and simply refers the reader to other secondary literature (p. 125 and n. 40).

[35] Massaux, *Influence*, 1:23.

[36] *Pace* Massaux, *Influence*, 1:23 – two occurrences do not usually suffice to classify a term as "characteristic." Massaux has, however, convinced some: O. Knoch, e.g., arrives at the conclusion that *1 Clem.* 46.8 shows a knowledge of the finished text of Matthew largely based on Massaux's arguments (including the presence of the verb ἦν after καλόν; see below), which he cites approvingly (*Eigenart und Bedeutung*, 71; for Knoch it is also very probable that Clement knew the finished form of Luke, see ibid., 72). W.-D. Köhler also mentions the two occurrences of καταποντίζομαι in Matthew, and argues that it might indicate the dependence of *1 Clement* on the latter (*Rezeption*, 63 and n. 1), but classifies *1 Clem.* 46.8 under the category of passages for which dependence upon Matthew is only "possible" (ibid., 60–64).

[37] Gregory, "*1 Clement* and the Writings," 136, who references BDAG, ad loc.

[38] Massaux, *Influence*, 1:22.

[39] Manuscripts without ἦν include B, L, W, 892, 2427, it, vg[st]; see NA[27], ad loc. This reading is to be preferred on standard text-critical grounds, because it is the most difficult and thus considered the most primitive; see Hagner, *Clement of Rome*, 153, n. 1.

contained it as well, in which case it would not represent Matthew's redactional activity.[40] One could assume for the sake of argument, however, that the earliest text of Mark did not contain ἦν and that Matthew used a manuscript with such a reading, so that the ἦν in Matthew is redactional. Even if such were the case, the fact that scribes also added ἦν to their manuscripts *of Mark* should give one pause before making too much of the presence of the verb in *1 Clement*. Though some of the occurrences of ἦν in the Markan manuscripts may be attributed to scribal harmonization with the text of Matthew, others would have likely resulted from scribes improving upon Mark's style, either intentionally or otherwise. If scribes could improve upon the text of Mark by supplying the verb ἦν without being dependent on Matthew, there is no reason why Clement could not also have added ἦν to his source(s) if it (they) did not contain it, without deriving it from the text of Matthew.[41] In short, to argue that the presence of ἦν in *1 Clem*. 46.8 can only be attributed to Matthean redaction, and therefore that Clement was here dependent on Matthew, would go far beyond what the evidence can support.[42]

We conclude, in light of our application of the redactional criterion above, that the evidence is insufficient to show that the saying(s) in *1 Clem*. 46.8 depended directly or indirectly upon the finished form of any of the Synoptics.

6.3 *1 Clement* 46.8, Oral Tradition, and Orality in Antiquity

Everything considered so far in this chapter has tended to support the contention that the sayings of Jesus in *1 Clem*. 46.8 derived from oral tradition. We noted that the material in the gospel parallels to *1 Clem*. 46.8 probably derived from oral tradition (a combination of oral pre-Markan tradition and oral double tradition), which increases the likelihood that it would have been available to Clement also in this form. We also noted that the type of variability within stability that is characteristic of the relationship between *1 Clem*. 46.8 and its parallels suggests developments within related streams of oral tradition (more closely related in the case of the double tradition

---

[40] Here it is good remember Bellinzoni's comment, cited on p. 103 above: we can "never be confident that we are comparing the texts that demand comparison" ("Luke in the Apostolic Fathers," 48).

[41] There is also the possibility that a later scribe added ἦν to the text of *1 Clem*. 46.8 under the influence of a text of Mark or Matthew, and that it has only survived in this form. Such hypotheses could be multiplied, but we are dealing in such cases with unknowns.

[42] Cf. the comments in Gregory, "*1 Clement* and the Writings," 136.

behind Matthew and Luke than in the case of the pre-Markan tradition). Even the redactional criterion applied in the previous section supports this contention, if only to a small degree. The redactional criterion is a *positive* one, and if one uses it as a *negative* one it amounts to an argument from silence; i.e., the absence of elements that reflect the redactional work of the Evangelists does not amount to proof that Clement did not know of or use any given gospel, but all the same it does make it more likely. By increasing the likelihood that Clement was dependent on a source other than the Gospels, this in turn increases, however slightly, the chances that this other source was oral tradition.

To these considerations in favor of an oral source we may add one more: the formula with which Clement introduces the Jesus tradition in 46.8: μνήσθητε τῶν λόγων τοῦ κυρίου Ἰησοῦ. εἶπεν .... This formula is very similar to those used to introduce Jesus tradition in both *1 Clem.* 13.1c–2 and Poly. *Phil.* 2.3, discussed at some length in the two previous chapters. There is no need to go into great detail again, but two points should be noted: (a) here as there, the use of μνήσθητε together with the aorist εἶπεν suggests that Clement is quoting oral tradition;[43] (b) that Clement uses this standardized introductory language *both times* he explicitly cites Jesus tradition in his epistle, but uses it nowhere else, ties both citations together (*1 Clem.* 13.1–2 and 46.8) and sets them apart as unique within the epistle. Thus the conclusion reached in chapter 4 above regarding the oral provenance of the material in *1 Clem.* 13.1–2 tends to reinforce the same conclusion regarding the material in 46.8.[44]

---

[43] See discussion in secs. 4.5 and 5.3 above on the introductory words in *1 Clem.* 13.1–2, μάλιστα μεμνημένοι τῶν λόγων τοῦ κυρίου Ἰησοῦ, οὓς ἐλάλησεν διδάσκων ἐπιείκειαν καὶ μακροθυμίαν. οὕτως γὰρ εἶπεν, and Poly. *Phil.* 2.3, μνημονεύοντες δὲ ὧν εἶπεν ὁ κύριος διδάσκων.

[44] A number of scholars have concluded, or at least suggested, that the saying(s) of Jesus in *1 Clem.* 46.8 derived from an oral source. Hagner argues that Clement quotes an oral tradition (*Clement of Rome*, 162–64) opinion also held by Stanton ("Jesus Traditions," 573) and Ehrman (*Apostolic Fathers*, 1:26), while offered as a possibility by M. W. Holmes ("Clement of Rome," *DLNTD* 235) and A. Jaubert (*Clément de Rome*, 52 [cf. pp. 53, 58]: "il semble que Clément se réfère à une collection de *logia* soit oraux, soit consignés par écrit, non à un évangile précis"). In R. Knopf's view, while it is possible that Clement freely combined Synoptic tradition, it is more probable that he cited "außerkanonische Ueberlieferung," but Knopf does not specify whether he considers this to be oral or written (*Lehre, Clemensbriefe*, 122). A. J. Carlyle in *NTAF* suggest that a faulty quotation from memory is "not impossible," but considers just as probable that it is a quotation from catechetical material, not specifying whether written or oral (p. 62). G. Schneider's position is unclear: in his view Clement did not use the Gospels, but either quoted freely ("frei zitiert," does this imply "from oral tradition"?) or used collected Testimonia or Florilegium (*Clemens von Rom*, 23; similarly A. von Harnack states that "Wahrscheinlich sind nicht unsre Evangelien zitiert, sondern eine andere Quelle"

The remainder of this chapter will focus upon a number of characteristics of orality reflected in the Jesus tradition contained in *1 Clem.* 46.8. This will serve to simultaneously pursue two objectives: (1) to provide further support for the contention that *1 Clem.* 46.8 received its present shape in an oral-traditional context, while also (2) drawing out what one may learn from the Jesus tradition in *1 Clem.* 46.8 regarding the inner workings of oral tradition as transmitted within this segment of the early church. We will focus here upon the most important five characteristics of orality as reflected in *1 Clem.* 46.8:

(1) The contents of *1 Clem.* 46.8 probably reflect oral tradition's tendency to be *mnemonically constructed*, which among other things involves the grouping together of sayings with a common theme as an aid to memorization.[45] As argued above in light of what we reconstructed of the history of its parallels, the saying as it appears in *1 Clem.* 46.8 is most likely a conflation of two separate sayings of Jesus. These sayings were probably brought together by a traditionist because of their common theme: an action or behavior is regarded as so damnable that it would be preferable for the person engaging in it to not exist at all (either never having been born, or ending their life at once). Initially the two sayings may have been simply grouped together, their common theme serving as an aide to initial retention and as a mental "tag" for retrieval during a performance. Since in the tradition these two sayings would have thus been closely associated with each other, it is easy to see how they might have become conflated, possibly at the point of the passing on of the material from one traditionist to another.

(2) The saying in *1 Clem.* 46.8 provides an example of oral tradition as *socially identified*; i.e., traditions may become disengaged from their

---

("Schreiben der römischen Kirche," 99). Others suggest a gospel source: Hengel posits that Clement may show "knowledge of all three Synoptics," in combining elements from a woe-saying and the millstone saying that within the Gospels come from different contexts (*Four Gospels*, 129). Lightfoot considers oral tradition as an option among others, but appears to favor quotation from the canonical Gospels, which in his view "presents no difficulties" in light of the changes Clement (also) makes to his sources in quoting the Old Testament (*Apostolic Fathers*, 1.2:141). R. M. Grant's position varied: in 1964 he was unclear regarding Clement's source for 46.8, but apparently leaned toward oral tradition (*Apostolic Fathers*, 40–41). In 1965, in Grant and Graham, *First and Second Clement*, Grant followed Koester in holding that Clement does not quote from the written Gospels, but left open the question of an oral or written source, suggesting also "memory quotation" (p. 77). In the same year, however, in *Formation*, he viewed the passage under consideration as evidence for the existence in Rome of "a gospel-like book ... of the teaching of Jesus ... much like our gospels, especially Matthew and Luke" (pp. 80–81). Roukema notes scholars for and against Clement's dependence either on the Gospels or oral tradition, but does not advance a personal opinion ("Jesus Tradition," 2127).

[45] See sec. 3.3.9 above, under the subtitle "Mnemonically Constructed."

original ties to the past in order to reflect the values of the present.[46] This can be seen in that the original referent of the warning of Jesus as found in Mk 14:21 and Mt 26:24 (cf. Lk 22:22), specifically the one who was to *betray the Son of Man*, has been replaced in the conflated saying in *1 Clem.* 46.8 with a general referent to any who would *cause the Lord's chosen to stumble*.[47] The saying has thus been appropriated to serve the ongoing life of the church, rather than continuing to reflect a (perhaps now less relevant) specific situation in the past.[48]

(3) *1 Clement* 46.8 provides an example of the *redundancy* that characterizes oral tradition.[49] Though some material was left out in conflating the two sayings, the phrases ἢ ἕνα τῶν ἐκλεκτῶν μου σκανδαλίσαι and ἢ ἕνα τῶν ἐκλεκτῶν μου διαστρέψαι have both been retained, and are clearly redundant. This does not imply that the repetition of the material was insignificant to the traditionist, as it serves to point out the urgency of the warning and the importance of caring for the Lord's "chosen ones." The above simply serves to make the point that this type of redundancy is char-

---

[46] See sec. 3.3.10 above, under the subtitle "Socially Identified."

[47] It is possible that a traditionist found justification for this generalized application of Jesus' words as found in *1 Clem.* 46.8a–b in the second of the conflated sayings, *1 Clem.* 46.8c–d, "Better for him to have a millstone put on him and be drowned in the sea than to have corrupted one of my chosen." Perhaps in the traditionist's view, Jesus had here made a general statement very similar in nature to his saying about Judas, but in this case about any who would place a stumbling block before "one of these little ones," and this provided the grounds for generalizing the first statement as well, in order to make it more relevant to the church. A more likely hypothesis, however, is that the two sayings were made to coalesce quite unintentionally, drawn together by the shared elements noted above. We remain, however, in the realm of hypotheses.

[48] This interpretation of the evidence is stronger than the alternative suggested by Adela Yarbro Collins, that "Mark took a saying that dealt with the relation of members of the community among themselves and transformed it into a saying about the one who 'handed over' Jesus" (*Mark: A Commentary* [ed. H. W. Attridge; Hermeneia; Minneapolis: Fortress, 2007], 652). As Collins herself notes, it is striking that Mark would do what she suggests, and yet "shift the lion's share of the blame onto the Jewish leaders later in the passion narrative" (loc. cit.). That the latter is emphasized in Mark lends credence to the argument that the blame placed on Judas in the dominical saying in question was original to the material, and the application to the community concerns secondary: why would Mark create a saying that stood so at odds with what he stresses later in his gospel? A number of reasons were already noted above for holding that Mark found the contents of Mk 14:21 in the tradition, including the absence of any Markan redactional features. This lends further support to the position argued here, in that if Mark had transformed the saying after the manner suggested by Yarbro Collins one would expect to find his imprint upon it. For arguments in favor of the authenticity of the saying in Mk 14:21 as related to the betrayal by Judas see S. Kim, *The "Son of Man" as the Son of God* (WUNT 30; Tübingen: Mohr Siebeck, 1983), 45–46; Robbins, "Last Meal," 29–34, esp. pp. 33–34.

[49] See sec. 3.3.3 above, under the subtitle "Redundant or 'Copious.'"

acteristic of an oral setting, and points to the possible oral context in which the two sayings were conflated.

(4) One aspect of the *stability* within variability that characterizes oral tradition can be seen in the almost identical wording of the two phrases οὐαὶ τῷ ἀνθρώπῳ ἐκείνῳ[50] and καλὸν [ἦν] αὐτῷ, εἰ οὐκ ἐγεννήθη in *1 Clem.* 46.8, Mark 14:21, and Matt 26:24.[51] While in Matthew and Mark this exact correspondence is attributable to the literary use of the latter by the former, its independent presence in *1 Clement* is probably an example of how short, memorable sayings can achieve fixity within oral tradition, retaining their shape while variations take place around them.

(5) Finally, the variants in the millstone-saying among the parallels we have been considering provide an ideal example of the types of variations that can be expected in material that is *remembered* as opposed to *memorized*.[52] In chapter 3 we noted that well-rounded traditionists did not need to memorize the imagery-related aspects of a tradition, but only to remember them with their "mind's eye."[53] The visual aspects of the tradition under consideration would have become imprinted on the memory of the traditionist via the imagination in a manner similar to a personal experience of seeing. During a performance of the tradition the traditionist could then simply visualize a man being cast into the sea with a millstone attached to his neck, and describe what she or he saw, using whatever words came to mind at the time – words which would obviously include some form or variation of "man," "millstone," "around the neck," "cast," and "sea." This mnemonic technique may go a long way toward explaining the variations between the forms of the sayings we have considered: these are not memorized sayings, but remembered scenes pictured and described. In view of the latter, one could expect them to be given new linguistic shape by the traditionist in each performance, while remaining consistent in the visual scene they describe.

This would still be true of Matthew and Luke's use of Mark, even though in their cases one is not dealing only with oral tradition (from the double tradition) but also with their handling of their written source Mark. As people working intimately with the Jesus tradition, Matthew and Luke shared the role of the traditionist to some extent, though to what extent it shaped their approach is impossible to know. That it did influence their approach to *some* extent is clear from the evidence in the Gospels, as was already noted when con-

---

[50] The "δέ" in the texts of Mark and Matthew, being post-positive, can be left out as not intrinsic to the saying.

[51] See subsection 3.3.5 above, under the subtitle "Both Variable and Stable."

[52] See subsection 3.3.5 above, under the subtitle "Both Variable and Stable."

[53] In addition to discussion in ch. 3 above (see previous note), see especially Minchin, "Similes in Homer," 26, 38; Paivio, "Mind's Eye," 6. Minchin words are apropos: the poet offers "a commentary on the scene which runs in the cinema of his mind's eye" ("Similes in Homer," 44).

sidering the gospel parallels in the present chapter. For example, when intermingling oral tradition from the double tradition (Mt 18:6–7//Lk 17:1–2) with material now contained in Mk 9:42, Matthew and Luke approached their material "in oral mode" (to borrow a phrase from Dunn, "Q[1] as Oral," 50): they treated the text of Mark with some liberty, so that the resulting text of Matthew and Luke reflect the variability within stability that one would expect from oral rather than written tradition (cf. the comments in Carr, *Writing on the Tablet*, 280–81; Kelber, "History of the Closure," 122; Kirk, "Manuscript Tradition," 220–25; Mattila, "Question Too Often Neglected," 199– 217). This treatment of a written source based on what is expected of oral sources amounts to a re-oralization of the written source, even if it is only temporarily so as to commit it to writing again in a new gospel (see discussion of re-oralization in ch. 3 above, pp. 98–100, esp. n. 367). As mentioned in ch. 3 above, orality and literacy is a two-way street, and each influences the other. To whatever extent the practices of transmitting oral tradition impacted how Matthew and Luke handled the material they inherited in written form from Mark, as well as from whatever portions of Q, M and L were available to them in written form, to that extent we are witnessing a form of re-oralization of written traditions.

Chapter 7

Liturgical Tradition in the *Didache*
The Lord's Prayer in *Did.* 8.2

7.1 Introduction

In turning to study Jesus tradition in the *Didache* a few prefatory comments are in order. As is commonly recognized, the work is a compilation of materials derived from various sources, though the identity of these sources remains a topic of debate.[1] The *Didache*'s contents suggest that it was used as a church order: chapters 1–6 contain moral teaching based on the Jewish Two Ways tradition, chapters 7–15 give instructions on the liturgy and the ministry, and chapter 16 provides an eschatological conclusion to the work.[2]

There are those who argue that the compilation and arrangement of the materials that make up the *Didache* took place over an extended period of time and involved a number of editors, revisions and additions.[3] In this chapter, however, position will be taken with those who consider that the book was given its present shape by a single editor – whom we will call the Didachist – who brought together its rather disparate contents from a variety of sources over a relatively short period of time (though minor glosses may have been added later).[4]

Parallels to the synoptic tradition abound in the *Didache*, which in chapters 1–6 are mostly circumscribed to an insertion of synoptic-like material in 1.3–2.1, but in the remainder of the document are interspersed throughout. Of these parallels only two, however, are explicitly identified as Jesus tradition: the Lord's Prayer in 8.2, which is the topic of the pre-

---

[1] For a survey of various approaches that have been taken in seeking to understand the sources of the *Didache* see J. A. Draper, "The Didache in Modern Research: An Overview," in *Didache in Modern Research* (ed. Draper), 1–42.

[2] W. Rordorf, "Didache," *RPP* 4:54–55; A. Tuilier, "Didache," *TRE* 8:731.

[3] Representatives of this view include S. Giet, *L'énigme de la Didachè* (PFLUS 149; Paris: Ophrys, 1970); Kraft, *Barnabas and the Didache*.

[4] Niederwimmer, *Didache*; similarly, S. Giet (*L'énigme de la Didachè*), W. Rordorf and A. Tuilier (*Doctrine*) propose a model in which a single redactor was responsible for chs. 1–13, and a second redactor for chs. 14–15 and possibly 16; see summary of their views in Niederwimmer, *Didache*, 43.

sent chapter, and an isolated saying in 9.5, to be treated later in chapter 8. We turn, then, to examine the Lord's Prayer in *Did.* 8.2, beginning with our customary text and synopsis.

Didache 8.2

... μηδὲ προσεύχεσθε ὡς οἱ ὑποκριταί ἀλλ' ὡς ἐκέλευσεν ὁ κύριος ἐν τῷ εὐαγγελίῳ αὐτοῦ οὕτω προσεύχεσθε·
Πάτερ ἡμῶν ὁ ἐν τῷ οὐρανῷ
     ἁγιασθήτω τὸ ὄνομά σου
     ἐλθέτω ἡ βασιλεία σου
     γενηθήτω τὸ θέλημά σου ὡς ἐν οὐρανῷ καὶ ἐπὶ γῆς·
τὸν ἄρτον ἡμῶν τὸν ἐπιούσιον δὸς ἡμῖν σήμερον
καὶ ἄφες ἡμῖν τὴν ὀφειλὴν ἡμῶν ὡς καὶ ἡμεῖς ἀφίεμεν τοῖς ὀφειλέταις ἡμῶν
καὶ μὴ εἰσενέγκῃς ἡμᾶς εἰς πειρασμόν ἀλλὰ ῥῦσαι ἡμᾶς ἀπὸ τοῦ πονηροῦ·
ὅτι σοῦ ἐστιν ἡ δύναμις καὶ ἡ δόξα εἰς τοὺς αἰῶνας.

Did. 8.2:	μηδὲ <u>προσεύχεσθε</u>	<u>ὡς οἱ ὑποκριταί</u>
Mt 6:5:	Καὶ ὅταν <u>προσεύχησθε</u>, οὐκ ἔσεσθε <u>ὡς οἱ ὑποκριταί</u>	

Did. 8.2:	ἀλλ' ὡς ἐκέλευσεν ὁ κύριος ἐν τῷ εὐαγγελίῳ αὐτοῦ <u>οὕτω προσεύχεσθε</u>
Mt 6:9:	<u>οὕτως οὖν προσεύχεσθε</u> ὑμεῖς
Lk 11:2:	ὅταν <u>προσεύχησθε λέγετε</u>

Did. 8.2:	<u>Πάτερ ἡμῶν ὁ ἐν τῷ</u> <u>οὐρανῷ</u> <u>ἁγιασθήτω τὸ ὄνομά σου</u>
Mt 6:9:	<u>Πάτερ ἡμῶν ὁ ἐν τοῖς οὐρανοῖς</u> <u>ἁγιασθήτω τὸ ὄνομά σου</u>
Lk 11:2:	<u>Πάτερ</u> <u>ἁγιασθήτω τὸ ὄνομά σου</u>

Did. 8.2:	<u>ἐλθέτω ἡ βασιλεία σου γενηθήτω τὸ θέλημά σου ὡς ἐν οὐρανῷ καὶ ἐπὶ γῆς·</u>
Mt 6:10:	<u>ἐλθέτω ἡ βασιλεία σου γενηθήτω τὸ θέλημά σου ὡς ἐν οὐρανῷ καὶ ἐπὶ γῆς·</u>
Lk 11:2:	<u>ἐλθέτω ἡ βασιλεία σου</u>

Did. 8.2:	<u>τὸν ἄρτον ἡμῶν τὸν ἐπιούσιον δὸς ἡμῖν σήμερον</u>
Mt 6:11:	<u>τὸν ἄρτον ἡμῶν τὸν ἐπιούσιον δὸς ἡμῖν σήμερον</u>
Lk 11:3:	<u>τὸν ἄρτον ἡμῶν τὸν ἐπιούσιον δίδου ἡμῖν</u> τὸ καθ' ἡμέραν

Did. 8.2:	<u>καὶ ἄφες ἡμῖν τὴν ὀφειλὴν ἡμῶν</u>
Mt 6:12a:	<u>καὶ ἄφες ἡμῖν τὰ ὀφειλήματα ἡμῶν</u>
Lk 11:4:	<u>καὶ ἄφες ἡμῖν τὰς ἁμαρτίας ἡμῶν</u>

Did. 8.2:	<u>ὡς καὶ ἡμεῖς ἀφίεμεν τοῖς ὀφειλέταις ἡμῶν</u>
Mt 6:12b:	<u>ὡς καὶ ἡμεῖς ἀφήκαμεν τοῖς ὀφειλέταις ἡμῶν</u>
Lk 11:4:	<u>καὶ γὰρ αὐτοὶ ἀφίομεν παντὶ ὀφείλοντι ἡμῖν</u>

Did. 8.2:	<u>καὶ μὴ εἰσενέγκῃς ἡμᾶς εἰς πειρασμόν ἀλλὰ ῥῦσαι ἡμᾶς ἀπὸ τοῦ πονηροῦ</u>
Mt 6:13:	<u>καὶ μὴ εἰσενέγκῃς ἡμᾶς εἰς πειρασμόν ἀλλὰ ῥῦσαι ἡμᾶς ἀπὸ τοῦ πονηροῦ</u>
Lk 11:4:	<u>καὶ μὴ εἰσενέγκῃς ἡμᾶς εἰς πειρασμόν</u>

Did. 8.2: ὅτι σοῦ ἐστιν   ἡ δύναμις καὶ ἡ δόξα εἰς τοὺς αἰῶνας
In some later MSS only:
(Mat 6:13x): [ὅτι σοῦ ἐστιν ἡ βασιλεία ἡ δύναμις καὶ ἡ δόξα εἰς τοὺς αἰῶνας]

7.2 The *Didache* and the Gospels

In seeking to ascertain whether or not the Gospels were the source of the prayer in the *Didache*, one can confidently set aside the shorter version of the prayer as reflected in Luke. The prayer in the *Didache* clearly is closer to the longer Matthean version, not sharing any of the gaps (when compared to Matthew) of the Lukan prayer. In addition, when the prayer in the *Didache* deviates from Matthew it never follows Luke's wording.

Matthew offers more in terms of the possibility of a literary dependence, in that the prayers in Matthew and the *Didache* are almost identical. The prayer in the *Didache* differs from Matthew's prayer only in reading the singular τῷ οὐρανῷ instead of Matthew's τοῖς οὐρανοῖς (Mt 6:9), τὴν ὀφειλήν in place of τὰ ὀφειλήματα (Mt 6:12a), the present ἀφίεμεν instead of the past ἀφήκαμεν (Mt 6:12b),[5] and most substantially, the *Didache*'s prayer concludes with a doxology – ὅτι σοῦ ἐστιν ἡ δύναμις καὶ ἡ δόξα εἰς τοὺς αἰῶνας – which is only found in some later MSS of Matthew (with variations).[6] Beyond these mostly minor differences, the prayers in the *Didache* and Matthew are exactly alike.

As is to be expected, given the extensive agreement between the prayers in Matthew and the *Didache*, scholars are in full accord that there is some kind of close relationship between the two texts. The nature of this relationship, however, is a topic of ongoing debate. The debate does not center upon the text of the Lord's Prayer itself, but upon the wider relationship between the *Didache* as a whole and the entire Gospel of Matthew. Those who find, based upon wider considerations, that the *Didache* is dependent upon Matthew, or that Matthew is dependent upon the *Didache*, or that both are informed independently of each other by the same (or closely related) pre-Matthean/ pre-*Didache* tradition, tend to explain the relationship between the texts of the Lord's Prayer in the two documents along the same lines.

It is helpful, then, to approach the problem of the relationship between the texts of the Lord's Prayer in Matthew and the *Didache* based on the wider issue of the relationship between the two documents. Taken in isola-

---

[5] Though the best witnesses to the text of Matthew contain the aorist ἀφήκαμεν, many Greek MSS and most ancient versions have the present ἀφίεμεν or ἀφίομεν (see Metzger, *Textual Commentary*, 13).

[6] See Metzger, *Textual Commentary*, 13–14; more on this below.

tion, the texts of the prayer do not provide enough information upon which to base a decision. It would be impossible within the parameters of this study, however, to compare all of the implicit Jesus tradition that has been identified in the *Didache* to its Matthean and other Synoptic parallels.[7] In lieu of that approach, the bulk of the discussion that follows will take the form of an interaction with one of the best studies conducted to date on the topic of the Jesus tradition in the *Didache*. In the process of interacting with the premises and conclusions of the author, in conversation with other literature on the topic, we will offer our own perspective on the sources of the Jesus tradition in the *Didache*, including the Lord's Prayer.

7.2.1 C. M. Tuckett and Jesus Tradion in the Didache

In Chapter 2 above we briefly summarized C. M. Tuckett's essay entitled "The Synoptic Tradition in the *Didache*,"[8] study that will be the focus in what follows. The essay is essentially an application of Koester's redactional criterion to Jesus tradition in the *Didache*; to state the criterion in Tuckett's words, "if material which owes its origin to the redactional activity of a synoptic evangelist reappears in another work, then the latter presupposes the finished work of that evangelist."[9]

Presupposing the Two Source hypothesis as the solution of the Synoptic Problem (which implies Markan priority),[10] Tuckett is careful in his work to distinguish between where the *Didache* finds parallels in the single tradition as distinct from double tradition or triple tradition. What follows is a brief summary of his arguments and conclusions for each of these categories of parallels:

a) *Single Tradition (Matthew or Luke)*: Tuckett argues that scholars have been mistaken in viewing a number of these passages as witnessing to the independent use of an earlier source by the *Didache* and one of the evangelists. He counters this view by examining a series of passages in the *Didache* with parallels in Matthew and Luke: noting that scholars have identified certain elements within these parallels as the product of Matthean redaction (MattR) or Lukan redaction (LkR), he then points out

---

[7] Jefford lists 32 different texts in the *Didache* with parallels in the Synoptics plus one with a parallel to the Jesus saying in Acts 20:35 (*Sayings of Jesus*, 160–61).

[8] See section 2.6.1 on Tuckett, "Tradition in the *Didache*." Tuckett's essay was first published in *New Testament in Early Christianity* (ed. Sevrin) in 1989 and reprinted in Didache *in Modern Research* (ed. Draper) in 1996. References below are to the reprint. See the high praise for Tuckett's article in Rordorf, "Does the Didache," 400; Gregory, *Reception of Luke and Acts*, 117; Draper, "Jesus Tradition," 75; Henderson, "Style-Switching," 179.

[9] Tuckett, "Tradition in the *Didache*," 95.

[10] Ibid., 96, n. 14.

that these redactional elements are also present in the text of the *Didache*.[11] He concludes that these provide evidence of the *Didache*'s use of the finished form of Matthew, and possibly Luke.

b) *Double Tradition (Mark//Matthew; Mark//Luke; Q, or Matthew// Luke)*: Tuckett singles out as especially significant those passages in the *Didache* which he views as possibly containing features which represent MattR or LkR either of Mark or of Q. For Tuckett not all of these need imply literary dependence, as features may have been added independently by two redactors.[12] For the most part, however, he treats them as evidence of the *Didache*'s use of either Matthew or Luke.[13] In considering the parallels between *Did.* 16 and the tradition held in common between Mark and Matthew,[14] Tuckett makes a point that is important for his argument: his findings indicate that the *Didache* used sections of Matthew that were derived from Mark and show MattR, which serves to counter the argument that the *Didache* is here dependent only on special Matthean tradition; i.e., material that predates the Gospels and does not derive from the Gospels themselves.[15]

c) *Triple Tradition (Mark//Matthew//Luke)*: Tuckett also identifies passages in the *Didache* with parallels in the triple tradition, and argues that in certain cases features present in the *Didache* are derived from MattR of Mark, and thus presuppose the *Didache*'s use of Matthew.[16]

---

[11] On Matthean redaction see ibid., 101–2; and see his discussion of *Did.* 16.3–5 and Mt 24:10–12 and also Mt 7:15; 10:23; 24:24; *Did.* 16.6 and Mt 24:30a, 31; in ibid., 101–4, esp. nn. 43, 48. On Lukan redaction see ibid., 109–10, esp. n. 78, on *Did.* 16.1a and Lk 12:35, which in Tuckett's opinion did not belong to Q.

[12] A point already mentioned in ch. 2 above; see, e.g., Tuckett's treatment of the parallel to *Did.* 1.4a in Mt 5:48, where he views the presence of τέλειος in Matthew as the result of MattR, and in the *Didache* as the result of the redactional work of the Didachist (ibid., 123).

[13] For examples of parallels to the double tradition where Tuckett finds the *Didache* dependent on MattR or LkR see ibid., 98–101, 104–5, 107, 113–22, 125–27 on *Did.* 16.8 (Mk 13:26//Mt 24:30); 11.7 (Mk 3:28//Mt 12:31) and 1.2b (Q 6:31 [Mt 7:12//Lk 6:31]; the Matthean parallel is mistakenly given as 7:15 in both the 1989 and the 1996 forms of the essay); 1.3a (Mt 5:44//Lk 6:27–28); 1.3b (Mt 5:45–47//Lk 6:32–33, 35); 1.4d–5a (Mt 5:42//Lk 6:30).

[14] The most important texts he examines along these lines (ibid., 96–101) include *Did.* 16.4 (Mk 13:22//Mt24:24; Mk 13:19//Mt 24:21); 16.5 (Mk 13:13//Mt 24:13; 10:22); and 16.8 (Mk 13:26//Mt 24:30); see also his treatment of 11.7 (Mk 3:28//Mt 12:31) in ibid., 104–5.

[15] Ibid., 96.

[16] E.g., *Did.* 13.1 (Mk 6:8//Mt 10:10//Lk 10:7); 1.2 (Mk 12:29–31//Mt 22:37–40//Lk 10:26–27); see ibid., 105–7. Tuckett does not find any cases of the *Didache*'s use of material in the triple tradition that would presuppose LkR of Mk; though the complex parallels to *Did.* 16.1 include all three of the Synoptics (he considers its relationship to Mk

Overall, Tuckett concludes that the parallels between the *Didache* and the Synoptics, including material with parallels in the single, double, and triple tradition, are "best explained if the *Didache* presupposes the finished gospels of Matthew and Luke."[17]

7.2.2 A Critique of C. M. Tuckett's Approach

To his credit, Tuckett is very careful in wording his conclusions: he speaks of the dependence of the *Didache* upon the finished forms of Matthew and Luke as what "best explains" the parallels he has examined. It remains questionable, however, whether this dependence is indeed the best explanation. Since it is not possible within the parameters of our present investigation to go into a detailed examination of each of the passages that Tuckett considers, we will limit our interaction with his arguments to three general points, the first to set his discussion in perspective and the other two to address the reliability of his methods:

7.2.2.1 The Didache *and the Gospel of Luke*

While one must leave open the possibility that the *Didache* presupposes the finished form of Luke's gospel, Tuckett's arguments to this effect are not very substantive.[18] He only finds evidence of the *Didache*'s use of Luke in three passages: *Did.* 16.1 (par. Lk 12:35), 1.3b (Lk 6:32–33) and 1.4d–5a (Lk 6:30).[19] Tuckett himself is constrained to add some form of qualifying statement in treating each of these passages to the effect that dependence upon Luke is not certain.[20] At issue is both whether the ele-

---

13:33, 35; Mt 24:42, 44; Lk 12:35 in ibid., 108–10) these are rather scattered in the tradition, and thus do not constitute true "triple tradition."

[17] Ibid., 128.

[18] Tuckett concludes his section on the synoptic parallels to *Did.* 1:3–5a with the words, "this section of the *Didache* appears on a number of occasions to presuppose the redactional activity of both evangelists, *perhaps Luke more clearly than Matthew*. This suggests very strongly that the *Didache* here presupposes the gospels of Matthew and Luke in their finished forms" (ibid., 127–28; emphasis added). Gregory's critique is appropriate here, "such a conclusion appears somewhat more definite than his rather more cautious preceding discussion [ibid., 110–28] might be thought to support" (*Reception of Luke and Acts*, 124). The same might be said for Tuckett's overall conclusion that the *Didache* is dependent on the finished form of Luke (ibid., 128): the cases of LkR he identifies in the Lukan parallels he considers are simply not clear enough to warrant such a conclusion.

[19] See Tuckett, "Tradition in the *Didache*," 110, 116–22 (esp. pp. 120–22), 125–27.

[20] On *Did.* 16.1 and Lk 12:35, that the form of the latter is due to LkR "is not certain in view of the very limited extent of the evidence available" but "seems perhaps the least problematic solution" (ibid., 110); on *Did.* 1.3b and Lk 6:32f, "The *Didache* shares some of the same language but not the framework of thought ... he takes over the Lukan rhe-

ments shared by Luke and the *Didache* actually arose from Lukan redaction, and whether an explanation other than the *Didache*'s dependence on Luke better accounts for the evidence.

In his monograph on the use of Luke and Acts in early Christian literature, Andrew Gregory does not find Tuckett's arguments for the presence of material derived from Lukan redaction in the *Didache* particularly compelling, and urges that it is just as likely that both the Didachist and Luke independently drew on similar sources.[21] The conclusion that Gregory reaches in his own study is that "while it is possible that the *Didache*, or parts of it, may have drawn on *Luke* rather than on sources which were known also to its author, nevertheless it is not possible to adduce the *Didache* as a firm witness to the reception and use of *Luke*."[22] Based on Gregory's findings, it becomes apparent that Tuckett's case for the use of the Gospels in the *Didache* is limited to his argument for the use of Matthew, to be considered next.[23]

7.2.2.2 The Didache *and the Gospel of Matthew*

The arguments against the *Didache*'s use of Matthew fall into two categories, having to do with (a) the possible direction of dependence, and (b) whether the relationship between the two documents is best understood as literary:

---

torical question but fails to see its significance" (ibid., 121–22); on *Did.* 1.4d–5a and Lk 6:30, "Both [clauses being considered] are probably LkR in Luke, though one cannot build too much on this here: Luke's aim is to generalize the idea of giving, but the *Didache* has exactly the same idea and hence the παντί and the present imperative δίδου could just as easily be seen as independent redaction of the tradition by the Didachist" (ibid., 126).

[21] Gregory, *Reception of Luke and Acts*, 117–24.

[22] Ibid., 124.

[23] In revisiting the topic of the relationship between the *Didache* and the gospels in a later essay, Tuckett states that, "There are possible links between the *Didache* and Luke but these are less extensive than those with Matthew. The discussion here will therefore be focused primarily on the relationship between the *Didache* and Matthew" ("*Didache* and the Synoptics," 509). Perhaps Tuckett's decision to leave the dependence of the *Didache* upon Luke out of consideration is also due in part to his recognition at the time of writing that his argument for said dependence is much weaker than his argument for the *Didache*'s dependence upon Matthew. In a later article Tuckett sets out to argue that the *Didache* seems to presuppose the redactional work of a gospel writer, "at least in relation to the gospel of Matthew," though he still does see some evidence that it also presupposes the gospel of Luke ("*Didache* and the Writings," 87, 111–12, 122–23, 124–25, 126–27). I was surprised to note that in the latter article, published two years after Gregory's monograph, Tuckett does not take into account Gregory's arguments regarding the difficulty of determining the presence of Lukan redactional features in the *Didache*, only referring to Gregory as one who has "been agnostic" (p. 111).

(a) When Tuckett sets out to show that the relationship between the *Di-dache* and Matthew is one of literary dependence, the results of his inves-tigation are partly predetermined by the prior decision regarding which of the two documents came first.[24] While his opinion that Matthew predates the *Didache* is the most common view, it is not the only one. A number of studies have explored the alternative possibility that the *Didache* (or rele-vant parts of it) may have been written before the Gospel of Matthew, which would reverse the order of the literary dependence Tuckett advo-cates.[25]

---

[24] Cf. Rordorf, "Does the Didache," 395–96.

[25] See, Gregory, *Reception of Luke and Acts*, 117 n. 4; Draper, "First-Fruits," 224–25; idem, "Do the Didache and Matthew Reflect an 'Irrevocable Parting of the Ways' with Judaism?," in *Matthew and the Didache* (ed. Van de Sandt), 217–41 (Draper con-cludes that the *Didache* witnesses to an earlier stage of development in the separation between Christianity and Judaism than witnessed to by Matthew); idem, "Jesus Tradi-tion," 75 n. 15 (where Draper brings up this possibility specifically as an objection against Tuckett's essay). In an article written sixteen years after the one under considera-tion, Tuckett himself recognizes the possibility that Matthew may be dependent on the *Didache*: "Certainly if the *Didache* is to be dated very early, as some would argue, then it may have been written before some *or all* of the NT documents themselves were pro-duced." (Tuckett, "*Didache* and the Writings," 86, n. 19; emphasis added). A. Garrow has given the topic book-length treatment in his *Matthew's Dependence*, though unfortu-nately Garrow's approach suffers from too much emphasis on the prior supposition that the multiple sources evident within the *Didache* imply a history of multiple redactions by multiple editors over an extended period of time; see Garrow, *Matthew's Dependence.*, 6–8, 244–52, and passim. This theory of multiple redactions by multiple editors was de-veloped by R. Kraft using the concept of "evolved literature" (Kraft, *Barnabas and the Didache*) and by S. Giet using the similar "living literature" (Giet, *L'énigme de la Di-dachè*); see Draper, "Didache in Modern Research," 19–22. For Garrow, the scenario that must be reconstructed in order for the *Didache* to be dependent on Matthew is "incredi-ble"; as he states, for this to be possible "the various creators of the whole traditions that ultimately became incorporated into the *Didache* [were required], separately and in each case, to refer to fragments of Matthew's Gospel in the process of creating these whole and self-contained traditions. Not only that but they must also be supposed to have se-lected fragments that are often widely dispersed in Matthew's Gospel and closely con-flated with material from other sources. ... As a result, therefore, it is necessary to imagine a queue of indirect contributors, lining up over a period of time to draw inspira-tion from Matthew's Gospel," whose work "was gathered by direct contributors who have a similar surgeon's instinct for selecting from the gospel material that is 'from Mat-thew's special material or from the synoptic traditions at points where Matthew's distinc-tive rendering is preferred' [this latter statement is a quote taken by Garrow from Court, "Didache and Matthew," 111]" (Garrow, *Matthew's Dependence*, 245–46). As noted by Tuckett, however, the presence of numerous sources in the *Didache* does not necessarily imply that they were incorporated into the *Didache* at different times (see Tuckett, "*Di-dache* and the Writings," 84–85 and n. 9; idem, "Tradition in the *Didache*," 111, 128 n. 142). A single person may have incorporated the many allusions to Matthean-like ma-terial into the *Didache* in the process of compiling and editing the diverse sources that

If one were to determine that the *Didache* antedates Matthew, this would necessitate rethinking several elements of Tuckett's argument. It would imply that the so-called "Matthean redactional features" he identifies in the *Didache* originated not in MattR but in the editorial work or the sources of the Didachist. The presence of these features in Matthew might then be attributed either to Matthew's dependence on the *Didache*, or what is more likely, to Matthew's use of sources he held in common with the *Didache*, whether written or oral.[26] One would also have to rethink how to account for the features in the *Didache* that in Tuckett's view show MattR of Mark (an important component of his argument). These could be viewed as examples of Matthew redacting Mark under the influence either of the *Didache* or of sources he held in common with the *Didache*, in which case the apparent objectivity provided by Tuckett's appeal to material in the *Didache* that originated in MattR of Mark would prove illusory.[27]

In sum, whether Matthew or the *Didache* came first is a topic of continued debate, and will condition in large part the results of an investigation into any literary relationship that might exist between the two documents.

(b) It is questionable, however, whether any theory of *literary* dependence can do justice to the relationship between Matthew and the *Didache*. The tendency in scholarship over the past two decades has been to move away from arguments for a literary relationship between the two documents, and toward a growing consensus that the similarities between them

---

make up the latter. Thus it is not necessary to posit the "incredible" picture that Garrow paints in order to hold, as does Tuckett, that there is Matthean influence in every section of the *Didache*. In sum, there are other explanations for the similarity between certain portions of the *Didache* and Matthew than the assumption of the dependence of the former upon the latter.

[26] Note the conclusion of A. Milavec, "no degree of verbal similarity can, in and of itself, be used to conclude that the framers of the *Didache* knew and/or cited the written Gospel. In every case, it is quite possible that both Matthew and the *Didache* relied upon free-floating sayings that they both incorporated into their material in different ways" ("Synoptic Tradition," 455 = *Didache: Faith, Hope, and Life*, 704).

[27] In a later article (on which see further below) Tuckett seeks to reassert the importance of material that Matthew shares with Mark. Commenting on the relationship between *Did.* 16.8, Mt 24:30 and Mk 13:26, he concludes, "Thus, insofar as *Did.* 16 agrees with Matthew here, the *Didache* is showing an agreement with what is basically Markan material, but Markan material mediated through the prism of Matthew's redaction. ... This suggests that the *Didache* here presupposes Matthew's redaction of Mark and hence (applying the criterion mentioned earlier [that of Koester]) presupposes Matthew's finished gospel" ("*Didache* and the Synoptics," 517–18). But what if the "redactional material" in Matthew was Markan material mediated through the prism of the *Didache*? Tuckett does not consider this possibility, which would involve the priority of composition of the *Didache* over Matthew's gospel.

are best explained as arising from their shared historical and cultural milieu.[28] Approaching the documents from the perspective of this growing consensus clarifies a number of issues:

Firstly, that the two documents are not related at the literary level would explain why there are no clear-cut cases of Matthean redactional features in the *Didache*. In his essay Tuckett succeeds in showing that certain passages in the *Didache* resemble passages in Matthew that may contain Matthean redactional features, but every feature Tuckett brings forward as an example of MattR in the *Didache* has been explained along different lines in a whole series of studies.[29] Not that Tuckett is obviously wrong and these studies are clearly right – the nature of the material under consideration does not allow for such cut and dry conclusions. To posit that the *Didache* is not literarily dependent on Matthew, however, provides a sensible solution to the problem of the absence of clear-cut MattR in the *Didache*.

Secondly, as Tuckett himself notes, his argument for the use of Matthew in the *Didache* depends on viewing such use as limited to "free allusion" rather than direct quotation.[30] He urges that, "It is thus inappropriate

---

[28] Kloppenborg, "Use of the Synoptics," 106; see especially van de Sandt and Flusser, *Didache*, and the introductions to van de Sandt, ed., *Matthew and the Didache* (by H. van de Sandt, 1–9) and van de Sandt and Zangenberg, eds., *Matthew, James, and Didache* (by H. van de Sandt and J. K. Zangenberg, 1–9). Though the studies in the two edited volumes just mentioned arrive at varied conclusions, they are all valuable in illustrating the array of issues that go into making a determination regarding the relationship between Matthew and the *Didache* (as well as James).

[29] The following all conclude that the *Didache* is independent of the final form of Matthew: Audet, *Didachè*, 166–86; Draper, "Jesus Tradition"; Glover, "Didache's Quotations"; Hagner, "Sayings," 240–42; Kloppenborg, "Didache 16"; idem, "Use of the Synoptics"; Koester, *Synoptische Überlieferung*, 159–216 (though Koester does hold that *Did.* 1.3–2.1 presupposes the Gospels of Matthew and Luke, perhaps available to the redactor of the *Didache* in the form of a sayings collection; see ibid., 217–39); Louth, *Apostolic Fathers*, 189; Niederwimmer, *Didache*, 42–52 and passim; Rordorf, "Transmission textuelle"; idem, "Does the Didache"; Rordorf and Tuilier, *Doctrine*, 83–91, 231–32; H. van de Sandt, "Two Windows on a Developing Jewish-Christian Reproof Practice: Matt 18:15–17 and *Did.* 15:3," in *Matthew and the Didache* (ed. van de Sandt), 173–92; van de Sandt and Flusser, *Didache*; A. Tuilier, "Les charismatiques itinérants dans la Didachè et dans l'Évangile de Matthieu," in *Matthew and the Didache* (ed. van de Sandt), 157–72.

[30] Tuckett, "Tradition in the *Didache*," 94, 96 n. 19; 102, 109; though not mentioned above, this applies also to Tuckett's understanding of the *Didache*'s use of Luke. Tuckett's argument, that one could not prove that Paul used the OT if all one had to go on were direct quotations from the latter, stumbles (as has been pointed out by Draper in "Jesus Tradition," 75 n. 15) on the fact that while we are sure that Paul had the Hebrew Scriptures available to him, the same cannot be said regarding the Didachist's access to Matthew (ibid., 94 n. 11; Tuckett cites approvingly from Wengst, *Didache*, 30: "Nach

to judge the *Didache*'s use of synoptic tradition as if it were a case of explicit quotation and to expect exact agreement between the quoted version and the source used."[31] This is, however, to beg the question. If the *Didache* is utilizing material from a written document one should expect a fairly high degree of verbal agreement.[32] Tuckett's notion of free allusion in itself raises the question of whether there might not be a better explanation for the similarities under discussion than Matthew's supposed dependence upon the *Didache*.[33]

Thirdly, if one cannot appeal to clear cases of MattR in the *Didache* or extensive verbal agreement to support the idea of the *Didache*'s dependence on Matthew, one would expect to find other indications of literary dependence, such as a common argument or context for the parallels – but this is not the case. Though addressing the issue of the Didachist's use of Luke as well as of Matthew, the critique of Ian Henderson is especially appropriate,

The individuality which asserts itself whenever the *Didache* resembles the synoptics is so pronounced that Tuckett must remind the reader at least eight times about the freedom with which the *Didache* appropriates material which is in synoptic styles ....[34] [I]s it

---

diesem Argumentationsmuster müßte man etwa Paulus die Benutzung des AT absprechen").

[31] Tuckett, "Tradition in the *Didache*," 94.

[32] As noted in chs. 4 and 5 above (p. 112, n. 32; pp. 161–62) regarding Clement of Alexandria's use of *1 Clem.* 13.2 in the *Stromateis* (2.91.2).

[33] It is unfortunate that Tuckett does not expand upon the statements which follow his main treatment of the Didachist's use of synoptic tradition after the manner of "free allusion": "Hence disagreements between the *Didache* and the gospels in, for example, the context and application of synoptic tradition need not imply that the *Didache* cannot have known the gospels. Indeed it can be argued that precisely such freedom in the use of synoptic tradition is to be expected if the *Didache* is using our gospels as, in some sense, authoritative texts" ("Tradition in the *Didache*," 94). There is nothing objectionable in the first statement, but the second needs further clarification. Tuckett's reference to Vokes' article "Didache and Canon" in a footnote is not very helpful, in that Vokes makes a series of assertions in this regard, but hardly mounts a cogent argument. The value of this article by Vokes, and of a number of his other works, is diminished by his insistence on viewing the *Didache* as a very late work (a pseudepigraphon composed toward the end of the second or the beginning of the third centuries, based in part on the mistaken view that the *Didache* depends on *Barnabas*). As Vokes explicitly notes in the article cited, this would date the *Didache* to the time when it had become common to quote from the written gospels, which adds an element of circularity to his argument: the *Didache* quotes Matthew at a time when it was common to do so, so why object to it? As noted above, however, removing the presupposition of a late date for the *Didache* affects this picture considerably.

[34] Here Henderson makes reference to Tuckett's original 1989 article, pp. 226, 198–99 and n. 11, 201 n. 19, 207–8, 211 n. 68, 212 and n. 71, 222 n. 108 ("Style-Switching," 182).

credible that someone who through direct access to Matthew and/or Luke was able to retain distinct impressions of Matthean or Lukan redactional choices would sometimes reproduce those impressions stylistically, but almost never reflect an understanding of the Matthean or Lukan argument?[35]

In other words, the *Didache* contains much material that *sounds* like Matthew, but apparently does not *come* from Matthew. The *Didache* and Matthew sound alike because they share a common idiom and a common tradition, as documents that arose out of a shared milieu.

Fourthly, while the compiler of the *Didache* indicates explicitly that he is quoting various sources on a number of occasions (1.6; 9.5; 14.3; 16.7),[36] he never does so in the context of materials that according to Tuckett derive from Matthew.[37] One cannot put much weight on an argument from silence, but the most obvious explanation for why the compiler gives no indication that he is citing Matthew is that he is not doing so.[38]

Fifth and finally, the Didachist is open to incorporating large blocks of material into his text, as shown by his use of the Two Ways tradition that comprises most of *Did.* 1–6. Yet nowhere in the *Didache* does one find a direct quote or a cohesive block of tradition from Matthew, but only – if one is to believe that the compiler used Matthew at all – allusive phrases interspersed in the text.[39] This raises the obvious question of why the Didachist did not use more of Matthew, if it was indeed at his disposal. Focusing upon Tuckett's argument for the *Didache*'s dependence on Matthew 24, A. Milavec points out that his scenario presupposes that those who wrote the *Didache* only knew a few lines from the chapter, since this is all that they included. He asks, "how can one explain why the framers of the *Didache* seemingly ignored 98 percent of Matthew in order to reconstruct

---

[35] Henderson, "Style-Switching," 182, 183; I am indebted to Henderson's article for this and the following two points (points 3–5). Along similar lines, Draper concludes that the overall pattern of parallelism between the *Didache* and the first and third gospels, "might at first suggest a knowledge of Matthew and Luke, in which the Synoptic Gospels are harmonized on the basis of Matthew," but continues, "this must be considered unlikely. The context, order and wording of the sayings is independent and cannot be derived from either" (Draper, "Tradition in the *Didache*," 90).

[36] Tuckett notes this as well, in the context of arguing that the *Didache*'s approach to the gospel material is that of "free allusion" rather than "citation" or "quotation" ("Tradition in the *Didache*," 94), but does not dwell on its significance.

[37] *Didache* 9.5 is not an exception, as Tuckett states, though it "is verbally identical with Mt 7:6 ... Mt 7:6 is not clearly MattR and the saying looks very like a stock proverb" (ibid., 108).

[38] See Henderson, "Style-Switching," 182–84, 205–7, esp. 205: "the *Didache* can quote. It certainly is able to make stylistically marked and/or verbatim quotations and explicit allusions. Indeed, the few explicit quotations in the text use a style of quotation which is strongly marked and which is particular to the *Didache*."

[39] Ibid., 205.

their own divergent end times scenario based upon a mere 2 percent?"[40] The most likely answer is that they did not ignore the remainder of Matthew, but simply did not know Matthew's gospel when they compiled and edited the *Didache*.

In conclusion, even if none of the above five considerations is conclusive by itself, taken together they greatly decrease the likelihood that the *Didache* is dependent on a written Matthew. If the *Didache* and Matthew grew out of a closely related milieu, a shared background and overall commonality of tradition and idiom better explain the resemblances between them than does a theory of literary dependence. Just as importantly, a shared milieu would also go a long way in explaining the *differences* between the Jesus tradition in the *Didache* and Matthew, which are very difficult to account for if one follows a theory of literary dependence.[41]

7.2.2.3 The Didache *and Oral Tradition*

In his essay Tuckett does not seriously consider the possibility that the source of the Jesus tradition in the *Didache* may have been *oral tradition*.

---

[40] Milavec, "Rejoinder," 521. Milavec then asks, if the compilers of the *Didache* only knew "some scattered sayings from Matthew," how can one explain that they did not take the trouble to find and use the remainder of the work? "Since only 2 percent of Matt 24 shows up in *Did.* 16, would Tuckett have us imagine that their quest [to find the remainder] failed? And, if they failed, would this not raise the possibility (nay, even the probability) that their failure might be due to the fact that none of the canonical gospels yet existed?" (ibid., 522). Milavec then goes on to outline his reasons for holding that the *Didache* was composed at a very early date, which he would put ca. A.D. 50 (ibid., 522–23; Milavec argues for this dating in other works: *Didache: Faith, Hope, and Life*, xii–xiii; idem, "When, Why, and for Whom," 63–84). This brings us back to our second point of interaction with Tuckett's essay above: the issue of the dating of the documents has a considerable impact on arguments regarding the use of one document in another.

[41] Henderson's assessment is again appropriate, "the more confidently we conclude with Tuckett that the *Didache* in all of its parts reflects the finished text of canonical Matthew, and perhaps Luke, the more strikingly limited and erratic the influence of these books appears to be. The individual verses and contexts of Matthew and Luke that are most likely to have influenced the language of the *Didache* seem *ex hypothesi* to have left no mark beyond the particular phrase in question" (Henderson, "Style-Switching," 181). Tuckett responds to a similar critique in a later article, arguing from the analogy of the use of Mark by Luke and Matthew, "Clearly Matthew and Luke have 'used' and rewritten Mark's gospel in ways that at times involve some reapplication and change of meaning and/or reference" ("*Didache* and the Synoptics," 512). The extent and nature of the similarities between Mark and Matthew and Luke, however, are such that the predominant scholarly view is rightly that the latter two are based upon the former. In the case of the *Didache* and Matthew, however, the extent of similarities is so small, and how to explain the similarities so controversial, that precisely the issue is whether or not there is any literary dependence.

This is due in part to his method being based upon the presuppositions of scribality, as will become clear in what follows.

As noted in chapter 2, in his essay Tuckett identifies several problem areas in the application of Koester's redactional criterion: (a) the presence of the same redactional feature in two documents does not necessarily imply dependence, since a redactional feature may be incorporated into the tradition independently by two redactors; (b) even if a dependence between two texts is established, this may not be direct, as "the later document may be several stages removed from the earlier one";[42] (c) the line between tradition and redaction is not always clear when working with parallels in Q material: when Luke differs from Matthew, not only is it possible that either one preserves the reading closest to the original, but one must also account for the possible existence of various editions of Q (Q^{MT} and a Q^{LK}).[43] These insights are helpful, but they leave no room for orality. The very language of "redactional features" and "redactors" implies written documents and their editors, as opposed to variations in oral performance. Likewise the language of "dependence between two texts" even "several stages removed" does not take into account the role oral tradition might play in disseminating traditions that surface in separate written documents. In addition, in previous chapters we touched upon the inadequacy of explanations that are based upon the hypothesis of several different editions of a written Q, and noted that perhaps different performances of the same oral tradition may better explain the variable and stable elements among "Q parallels" in Matthew and Luke.[44] Finally, to speak of either Matthew or Luke preserving a reading closer to the "original" is out of place when discussing tradition that was transmitted for a period of time only in oral form: in an oral milieu, after the initial utterance there is no longer an "original" against which one can compare the performance of a tradition, even if the stable elements of the tradition may safeguard the basic reliability of its content.[45] In sum, not only is Tuckett's method geared toward written sources, but also the presuppositions upon which it is based may exclude the possibility of concluding in favor of an oral source.

Aaron Milavec has raised similar concerns regarding Tuckett's essay in an article entitled "Synoptic Tradition in the *Didache* Revisited."[46] According to Milavec, Tuckett considers "sources" exclusively in terms of

---

[42] Tuckett, "Tradition in the *Didache*," 95.

[43] Ibid., 112–13 and see sec. 2.6.1 above.

[44] See secs. 1.1, 1.7, 4.4.4, and n. 18 on p. 186 above.

[45] See discussion in secs. 1.4.2, 3.3.5 (and literature cited there), and 4.5 above.

[46] Milavec, "Synoptic Tradition," repr. in idem, *Didache: Faith, Hope, and Life*, 693–739.

written sources,[47] and in seeking to determine when the *Didache* is dependent on Matthew and when on Luke, and the *degree* to which it is indebted to either, does not consider whether literary dependence is *likely*. Milavec states,

> Tuckett never takes into account the possibility that the *Didache* was created in "a culture of high residual orality" wherein "oral sources" (attached to respected persons) were routinely given greater weight and were immeasurably more serviceable than "written sources." Moreover, Tuckett does not seem to allow that "oral sources" had a certain measure of socially maintained stability but not the frozen rigidity of a written text.[48]

In short, in Milavec's view Tuckett's method inherently favors textuality at the expense of orality.[49]

In a follow-up article entitled "The *Didache* and the Synoptics Once More: A Response to Aaron Milavec," Tuckett acknowledges that he had given no serious consideration in his earlier essay to the possibility that the Jesus tradition in the *Didache* might stem from oral sources.[50] In this follow-up article he nuances his argument by stating that in the earlier essay he never indicated a *direct* or *literary* dependence of the *Didache* on Matthew (or Luke). He posits that during the period in which oral and written traditions coexisted, there would have been an intermingling of both, leading to the written Gospels generating their own oral tradition (the phenomenon referred to in the present work as re-oralization[51]).[52] Tuckett concludes, "any use of Matthew's gospel is likely to have been at best via an 'oral' medium of remembering, recalling, and reproducing largely from memory, perhaps too intermingling any traditions with similar oral traditions known independently."[53]

---

[47] This tendency is probably encouraged by the use of redaction criticism, which in its formative stages was most successfully applied to the study of the appropriation of Mark by Matthew and Luke (see N. Perrin, *What is Redaction Criticism?* [GBSNTS; Philadelphia: Fortress, 1969], 1–39). Since in dealing with the Synoptic Problem there is an extant written source against which to compare two other written documents, the application of the method might predispose the interpreter to think in terms of comparing extant written sources. It is to Koester's credit that, although he applies redaction criticism in analyzing the Jesus tradition in the Apostolic Fathers, he does not allow it to bias him against orality (see discussion of Koester in sec. 2.3.2 above).

[48] Within this quote Milavec cites Achtemeier, "*Omne Verbum*," 3, 9–11, 27, and Ong, *Presence*, 52–53, 231–34; quote taken from Milavec, "Synoptic Tradition," 466.

[49] Milavec, "Synoptic Tradition," 466–71.

[50] See Tuckett, "*Didache* and the Synoptics," 513: "It is true that in my earlier essay ["Tradition in the *Didache*"] I did not explicitly refer to the possibility of oral tradition as such."

[51] See sec. 3.5 above.

[52] Tuckett, "*Didache* and the Synoptics," 513, and see also his later "*Didache* and the Writings," 88 and n. 25.

[53] Tuckett, "*Didache* and the Synoptics," 513.

While these clarifications strengthen Tuckett's argument in one way, they weaken it in another. They strengthen it in that they do away with the anachronistic caricature of the ancient scribe sitting with open scrolls, choosing a little piece of this document and a little piece of that in composing his own writing.[54] They weaken it, however, in that once Tuckett has dispensed with the idea of dependence on a written document, and turned to oral tradition as the source for the Jesus tradition in the *Didache*, he no longer has a firm basis for arguing that the *Didache* presupposes a written Matthew. If he could show that there are clearly identifiable Matthean redactional features in the *Didache*, which cannot be understood in any other way, Tuckett would have an argument. In the absence of these features, however, positing an oral milieu for the Jesus tradition in the *Didache* obviates the need for the Gospel of Matthew as a source.

Taking a step back to see where all of the above has led, the following becomes clear: an argument for the *Didache*'s use of the finished work of Matthew that rests on the presupposition that the Matthean material has become extremely fragmented as well as re-oralized, circumscribed to only a small portion of the material in the document from which it came, and recognizable as Matthean only because it contains a few scattered features that possibly originated in MattR, stretches the evidence beyond what it can support. While it is still possible that the *Didache* is dependent on Matthew, the evidence is anything but compelling. A better explanation for the similarities in light of the present discussion is that the so-called MattR features in the *Didache* were part of the oral tradition that informed both the *Didache* and Matthew during their composition. That the Jesus tradition incorporated into the *Didache* was most likely in oral form is one of the important results of the exchange between Tuckett and Milavec (though for Tuckett this includes material re-oralized from the gospels of Matthew and Luke).[55] In what follows we will bring our interaction with Tuckett's article to a close by exploring how the manner in which oral tradition functioned in antiquity is itself enough to explain the form of the Jesus material as found in the *Didache*, with no need to appeal to a re-oralized Matthew.

7.2.2.4 Conclusion

In fairness to Tuckett, we must preface the comments that follow with an already-mentioned qualifier: he left open in his essay the possibility that a

---

[54] See comments in sec. 6.3 above, and also Beaton, "How Matthew Writes," 116; Mattila, "Question Too Often Neglected," 202, 213–17.

[55] This is one of Milavec's basic premises in most of his work on the *Didache*; for Tuckett see "*Didache* and the Synoptics," 512–14.

redactional feature could be added to the tradition by two redactors work-ing independently.[56] If we may adapt that thought somewhat, rather than thinking of redactors, when working with oral tradition it is more appropri-ate to think of traditionists or performers of the tradition. While oral tradi-tion emphasizes conservation of the tradition, each performance of the tradition will also incorporate new elements, what we have previously re-ferred to as the "variability within stability" characteristic of oral tradi-tion.[57] Originality in this process does not involve inventing new material, but grappling with how the tradition can best be introduced in a unique way into a new situation.[58] Tuckett identified certain features in the *Di-dache* that are also found in its Matthean parallels, where they possibly originated in MattR. If these features, however, were also widely available in the surrounding milieu, they could have been incorporated into the tradi-tion during any given performance, tradition that in turn became a source for Matthew and the *Didache*. This would be an example of the variability that accompanies the stability of the tradition. The above scenario is all the more likely when contrasting the fragments of Matthean-like material in the *Didache* with what Milavec calls the "great omissions" – the large sec-tions of Matthew not found in the *Didache* that surround the so-called MattR features.[59] Especially in those sections in which the *Didache* seems most indebted to Matthew, one would expect to find much more continuity with the basic content of Matthew as a whole, or at least with the content of the appropriate sections of Matthew – the preponderance of stability within some variability that is characteristic of literary dependence – if the *Didache* were indeed dependent here on a traditionist's performance of a finished Matthew.[60]

The above discussion is certainly not enough to refute Tuckett's con-clusions, nor was that its aim. Hopefully it has served, however, to show that in spite of the methodological rigor that Tuckett brings to his study, the evidence allows for other interpretations. In the final analysis, Tuckett does not give orality its fair due. He only calls upon oral tradition to allow for the possibility that re-oralized Matthean tradition may have reached the Didachist in oral form. Appealing to oral tradition in this way becomes

---

[56] See Tuckett, "Tradition in the *Didache*," 95.

[57] The dynamic Milavec alluded to in one of the above quotes, in speaking of oral tradition as characterized by "a certain measure of socially maintained stability but not the frozen rigidity of a written text" ("Synoptic Tradition," 466); see further sec. 3.3.5 above, under the subtitle "Both Variable and Stable" (and literature cited there), and ad-ditional references to this idea in chs. 4–6 above (secs. 4.2, 4.6, 5.3, 5.4, 6.2.2, 6.3).

[58] See sec. 3.3.4 above, under the subtitle "Conservative or Traditionalist."

[59] Milavec, "Rejoinder," 520–22.

[60] See, e.g., the discussion of the relationship between *Did.* 16 and Mt 24 in Milavec, "Rejoinder," 520–22, already mentioned above.

only a means toward the end of continuing to hold that the *Didache* was dependent at least indirectly upon the Gospels. In the remainder of this chapter, however, we will argue that the use of oral tradition *independently* of the Gospels offers a better explanation both for the presence of Jesus tradition as reflected in the *Didache* (specifically the Lord's Prayer), and for the similarities and differences between this tradition and its parallels in the Gospels.

7.3 The Lord's Prayer in the *Didache*

As we turn in the remainder of this chapter to focus specifically upon the Lord's Prayer in the *Didache*, our treatment is based in large part on the foregoing discussion. As noted at the beginning of the chapter, viewed in isolation the text of the Lord's Prayer in the *Didache* does not provide enough information upon which to base a decision regarding its relation to the Gospels or other sources. Approaching the issue with the understanding that the *Didache* and Matthew grew out of a closely related milieu, however, and that those who composed the two documents shared a common Jesus tradition and a common idiom, leads naturally to the conclusions that follow.

First, a word on the introductory formula: the prayer in the *Didache* is prefaced by the phrase ὡς ἐκέλευσεν ὁ κύριος ἐν τῷ εὐαγγελίῳ αὐτου (8.2). Scholars continue to debate whether the Didachist uses τὸ εὐαγγέλιον here and elsewhere (11.3; 15.3, 4) to mean the oral proclamation of the good news regarding Jesus, or a gospel such as the Gospel of Matthew. Here again, one's view regarding the overall relationship of the *Didache* to Matthew tends to determine one's opinion as to the referent of τὸ εὐαγγέλιον. Graham Stanton, for example, argues that, "these references confirm that τὸ εὐαγγέλιον was used to refer to a gospel writing, almost certainly Matthew," based in part on his perception that "few scholars doubt that the Didache is dependent on Matthew."[61] As already noted,

---

[61] G. N. Stanton, "Matthew: βίβλος, εὐαγγέλιον, or βίος?" in *Four Gospels 1992* (ed. van Segbroeck et al.), 2:1192–93; partially repr. in idem, *Jesus and Gospel* (Cambridge: Cambridge University Press, 2004), 53–59, (quote from p. 55); also W. R. Farmer, *The Gospel of Jesus: The Pastoral Relevance of the Synoptic Problem* (Louisville: Westminster/John Knox, 1994), 43; A. Harnack, "Gospel: History of the Conception in the Earliest Church," in idem, *The Constitution and Law of the Church in the First Two Centuries* (London: Williams & Norgate/New York: Putnam's Sons, 1910), 313; J. A. Kelhoffer, "'How Soon a Book' Revisited: *EYAΓΓEΛION* as a Reference to 'Gospel' Materials in the First Half of the Second Century," *ZNW* 95 (2004): 17–22; Massaux, *Influence*, 3:145, 155; Schröter, "Jesus and the Canon," 112; Smith, "Gospels in Early Christian Literature," 186.

however, the current scholarly tendency is to move away from the theory that the *Didache* is dependent on Matthew.[62] If the Didachist did not know Matthew's gospel, and he and Matthew used a common Jesus tradition that was available to them within their shared milieu, then there is little reason to hold that τὸ εὐαγγέλιον is used of a written gospel, and it is likely that it refers to the oral tradition of Jesus' sayings.[63]

One other element of the introductory lines in *Did.* 8.2 might lead one to suppose the author's awareness of Matthew's finished text: the Didachist's exhortation not to pray "like the hypocrites" (ὡς οἱ ὑποκριταί). Though this exhortation is not identified as Jesus tradition in the *Didache*, it does echo Jesus' similar statement in the context leading up to the Lord's Prayer in Matthew 6:9–13, "do not be like the hypocrites" (οὐκ ἔσεσθε ὡς οἱ ὑποκριταί; Mt 6:5). On the presupposition, however, that the Jesus tradition available to Matthew was also available to the Didachist, all these similarities need imply is that those who did not pray after the prescribed manner in these writers' milieu were referred to as "the hypocrites."[64] There is no compelling reason to hold that the *Didache* derived this reference to "the hypocrites" from Matthew.[65]

Turning to the prayer itself, it almost certainly had an established history of oral use prior to being committed to writing by Matthew and the Didachist.[66] One can assume that the prayer first circulated orally for a certain period of time as part of the early Jesus tradition.[67] It also had a tradi-

---

[62] For scholars who hold that the *Didache* is independent of Matthew see n. 29 on p. 210 above.

[63] Koester, *Synoptische Überlieferung*, 203–9, esp. 209; van de Sandt and Flusser, *Didache*, 50; Milavec, "When, Why and for Whom," 80, n. 45.

[64] For extensive discussions of the identity of the "hypocrites" in the *Didache* see J. A. Draper, "Christian Self-Definition against the 'Hypocrites' in *Didache* 8," in *Didache in Modern Research* (ed. Draper), 223–43; M. Del Verme, *Didache and Judaism: Jewish Roots of an Ancient Christian-Jewish Work* (New York and London: T&T Clark International, 2004), 143–88.

[65] *Pace* Massaux, *Influence*, 3:154–55; Kelhoffer, "'How Soon a Book' Revisited," 18–19. In arguing against Luz's view that the reference to "the hypocrites" and other contextual elements are due to the Didachist's knowledge of Matthew, that he recalls by memory, H. D. Betz states, "If the *Didache* was familiar with the pre-Matthean Lord's Prayer, which Matthew also took over from his church tradition, then why does *Didache* need Matthew's text, even if only by memory, to know the Lord's Prayer? Would it not be logical to conclude that both *Didache* and Matthew knew the prayer from their respective church traditions?" (*Sermon on the Mount* [Hermeneia], 371, n. 328).

[66] Betz, *Sermon on the Mount* [Hermeneia], 370; Dunn, *Jesus Remembered*, 227.

[67] As D. Juel states, "Few interpreters would deny that the Lord's Prayer in substantial form derives from Jesus of Nazareth" ("The Lord's Prayer in the Gospels of Matthew and Luke," in *The Lord's Prayer: Perspectives for Reclaiming Christian Prayer* [ed. D. L. Migliore; Grand Rapids: Eerdmans, 1993], 57); see the similar statements in O. Cullmann, *Prayer in the New Testament* (OBT; Minneapolis: Fortress, 1995), 38; Jeremias,

tional life of its own, however, within the early Christian liturgy.[68] The (oral) liturgical use of the prayer in the Didachist's community can be deduced from its doxological ending, ὅτι σοῦ ἐστιν ἡ δύναμις καὶ ἡ δόξα εἰς τοὺς αἰῶνας (*Did.* 8.2),[69] and from the exhortation that follows, "Pray this way three times a day" (*Did.* 8.3).[70] Originally the Matthean prayer did not include a doxology, as is clear from its absence in the earliest manuscripts and the early commentaries by Tertullian, Origen and Cyprian.[71]

New Testament Theology, 1:193. As the prayer that Jesus taught his disciples to pray (Mt 6:6, 9; Lk 11:1–2; *Did.* 8.2a), it was preserved by constant use within the early Jesus community.

[68] This is widely recognized; see, e.g., Betz, *Sermon on the Mount* [Hermeneia], 370; R. E. Brown, "The Pater Noster as an Eschatological Prayer," in idem, *New Testament Essays* (Garden City: Image Books/Doubleday, 1968), 279–81; F. H. Chase, *The Lord's Prayer in the Early Church* (TS 3; Cambridge: Cambridge University Press, 1891), 12–13; Cullmann, *Prayer*, 38; Dunn, *Jesus Remembered*, 226–28; K. Froehlich, "The Lord's Prayer in Patristic Literature," in *Lord's Prayer* (ed. Migliore), 73, 74, passim; J. Jeremias, *The Prayers of Jesus* (SBT, 2nd Ser. 6; London: SCM, 1967), 84–85; E. LaVerdiere, "The Lord's Prayer in Literary Context," in *Scripture and Prayer: A Celebration for Carroll Stuhlmueller, CP* (ed. C. Osiek and D. Senior; Wilmington: Michael Glazier, 1988), 107, 110; J. Luzarraga, *El Padrenuestro desde el arameo* (AnBib 171; Roma: Pontificio Istituto Biblico, 2008), 12–13; J. Schröter, "Jesus and the Canon: The Early Jesus Traditions in the Context of the Origins of the New Testament Canon," in *Performing the Gospel* (ed. Horsley, Draper, and Foley), 114.

[69] See also the doxological endings to the eucharistic prayers in *Did.* 9.2, 3, 4. As argued separately by Lohmeyer and Chase, the similarity between the doxologies associated with the Eucharist and that which ends the Lord's Prayer in the *Didache* implies that the Lord's Prayer was probably used in the eucharistic liturgy, and that it was here where it probably received its doxological ending (E. Lohmeyer, *"Our Father": An Introduction to the Lord's Prayer* [trans. J. Bowden; New York: Harper & Row, 1965], 143–44; Chase, *Lord's Prayer*, 173). This is a more likely hypothesis than that which attributes the doxology to the redactional work of the Didachist; *pace* S. Sabugal, *El Padrenuestro en la interpretación catequética antigua y moderna* (NAl 79; Salamanca: Sígueme, 1986), 33.

[70] Van de Sandt and Flusser, *Didache*, 50, 294 n. 78; Hagner, "Sayings," 241; Lohmeyer, *Our Father*, 243–46; T. W. Manson, "The Lord's Prayer," *BJRL* 38 (1955–56): 99–113 (also 436–48), esp. 99–108; Rordorf "Does the Didache," 422; Froehlich, "Lord's Prayer," 73–74. Ironically, A. Tuilier appeals to the presence of the doxology in the Didache as proof that the Didachist *did* use Matthew, arguing that the Didachist must have used a MSS of Matthew that included the doxology; see his "Probléme Synoptique," 114. In S. Sabugal's opinion the *Didache* did not depend directly on Matthew (given the variations between the two prayers and the doxological ending in the *Didache*), but is tied directly to Matthean *tradition* that followed after Matthew's redaction of the prayer; see his *Abbá ...: La oración del Señor* (2nd ed.; BNE; Madrid: Caparrós, 2007), 146, n. 8. The hypothesis that both Matthew and the Didachist derived the prayer from the liturgy in use within their communities does away with the need for such an explanation.

[71] The doxology is lacking in ℵ B D, most of the Old Latin, and *f*¹; see Metzger, *Textual Commentary*, 14. For a brief overview of patristic commentaries on the Lord's

That a number of other important manuscripts of Matthew do include a doxology in a variety of forms, however, shows that it too was used liturgically from early times.[72] It is safe to conclude, then, that the Lord's Prayer had a well-established use in the oral liturgy of the early church before either the Gospel of Matthew or the *Didache* were written.

It follows that it is very likely that both Matthew and the Didachist derived the text of the prayer from its oral-liturgical use, rather than either being dependent on the other, or both deriving it from a different written source.[73] Given that the Lord's Prayer functioned as an oral text within the *Didache*'s community, where it was recited three times a day (*Did.* 8.3), there is no reason to suppose that the Didachist would have turned to the Gospel of Matthew or a different written source for the text of the prayer.[74] On the assumption that Matthew and the *Didache* arose out of the same milieu, something similar can be concluded about the prayer in Matthew, though in this case it is not as clear. The prayer was probably first used in the liturgy of the Jewish-Christian synagogue,[75] out of which the communities of Matthew and the *Didache* both arose. It is reasonable to assume that Matthew derived the prayer from this context.[76] That both Matthew and the Didachist derived the prayer from a shared liturgical use would explain the extensive similarities between their prayers, and just as importantly, it would also explain the differences.

Prayer see Froehlich, "Lord's Prayer," 71–73; for a more extensive treatment see Sabugal, *Padrenuestro*.

[72] It is found in MSS K L W Δ Θ Π *f*[13] and the "majority text"; Metzger, *Textual Commentary*, 13–14. On the implications of the doxology for the liturgical use of the prayer see Brown, "Pater Noster," 279; van de Sandt and Flusser, *Didache*, 294 n. 78; Chase, *Lord's Prayer*, 176; for a detailed discussion on the textual history of the doxology see Parker, *Living Text*, 54–60; on doxologies in early Christianity see M. Black, "The Doxology to the *Pater Noster* with a note on Matthew 6.13b," in *A Tribute to Geza Vermes: Essays on Jewish and Christian Literature and History* (ed. P. R. Davies and R. T. White; JSOTSup 100; Sheffield: JSOT Press, 1990), 327–32.

[73] Cullmann, *Prayer*, 39; Dunn, *Jesus Remembered*, 227 and n. 229; Lindemann, "Apostolic Fathers and the Synoptic Problem," 697; Lohmeyer, *Our Father*, 294–96; Luzarraga, *Padrenuestro*, 12–13. Using a literary paradigm to explain the relationship between the prayers in Matthew and the *Didache* necessitates complex, and ultimately unsatisfactory, arguments; see survey and conclusions in J. S. Subramanian, "The Lord's Prayer in the Gospel of Matthew," in *Resourcing New Testament Studies: Literary, Historical, and Theological Essays in Honor of David L. Dungan* (ed. A. J. McNicol, D. B. Peabody, and J. S. Subramanian; New York and London: T&T Clark, 2009), 109–14.

[74] Draper, "Jesus Tradition," 86; Hagner, "Sayings," 241; Rordorf and Tuilier, *Doctrine*, 86–87; van de Sandt and Flusser, *Didache*, 294–95; and *pace* Wengst, *Didache*, 26–27.

[75] Chase, *Lord's Prayer*, 12–14; cf. Froehlich, "Lord's Prayer," 73.

[76] Brown, "Pater Noster," 279.

The variations between the prayers in Matthew and in the *Didache* are easily explainable on the hypothesis that the source for both writings was the oral liturgy. Firstly, it explains the major difference between the two prayers, which is the presence of the doxology in the *Didache*, lacking in Matthew. This variation probably is due to the different genre of the two writings. The doxology reflects the Jewish practice of daily prayer, and undoubtedly would have been a part of the Lord's Prayer in the early Christian liturgy.[77] The *Didache* is oriented toward the liturgy: it is a church manual intended to provide guidance in liturgical practice, and so it logically includes the doxology. The absence of the doxology in Matthew may simply be a result of the gospel *not* being liturgically oriented. As van de Sandt and Flusser explain, "When the original function of the doxology in the Lord's Prayer was that of response by the worshiping congregation, it might have been taken as not belonging to the Lord's Prayer itself and was, consequently, not incorporated in the gospel."[78]

Secondly, the minor differences between the prayer in Matthew and in the *Didache* are also understandable if the prayer derived from the oral liturgy.[79] To list these differences briefly, the *Didache* reads τῷ οὐρανῷ for Matthew's τοῖς οὐρανοῖς (Mt 6:9), τὴν ὀφειλήν in place of τὰ ὀφειλήματα (Mt 6:12a), and ἀφίεμεν instead of ἀφήκαμεν (Mt 6:12b).[80] As J.-P. Audet convincingly argues, supposing that Matthew's form of the prayer was used in the community of the *Didache*, and the Didachist had incorporated it into his writing, it is highly unlikely that he would modify it in such insignificant ways, especially given that the *Didache* was intended as a guide for liturgical practice.[81] It is more likely that the Didachist is citing the established oral liturgical tradition current in the

---

[77] For further discussion of the relationship of the Christian doxology to Jewish daily prayer, and the forms of the doxology in early Christian writings, see Lohmeyer, *Our Father*, 230–35.

[78] Van de Sandt and Flusser, *Didache*, 294; cf. Jeremias, *Prayers of Jesus*, 106–7. J. Jeremias notes that Jewish custom included two forms of prayer endings, a fixed conclusion and a "seal" or "freely formulated conclusion," and that perhaps the Lord's Prayer originally was an example of the latter, but with time became associated with a standard doxological ending (Jeremias, *New Testament Theology*, 1:202–3). Building on this insight, Cullmann suggests that, "The reason why the old manuscripts [of Matthew] omit the doxology may be that Jesus did not have to add it, since it was more or less a matter of course" (*Prayer*, 68).

[79] E. Lohmeyer represents the position taken here when he states, "These peculiarities [the differences between the prayers] probably indicate that the Didache took over its text not from St. Matthew's Gospel, but from an oral tradition which may well have come from the same district and the same group of communities as that of Matthew" (*Our Father*, 16); see also Froehlich, "Lord's Prayer," 73; Luzarraga, *Padrenuestro*, 13.

[80] These differences were already noted at the beginning of the present chapter.

[81] Audet, *Didachè*, 172–73, esp. p. 173, n. 1.

milieu in which he wrote, a tradition that was strong enough to survive in the form reflected in the *Didache* even after Matthew gained recognition as an authoritative gospel.[82] Orality allowed for such variations, as H. D. Betz explains, "It is characteristic of liturgical material in general that textual fixation occurs at a later stage in the transmission of these texts, while in the oral stage variability within limits is the rule. ... When they were written down, [the] variant forms of the prayer became textually fixed."[83]

In sum, if the prayers in Matthew and the *Didache* derived (independently of each other) from the oral liturgy, this provides a simple explanation for both the major and the minor differences between them.

An important implication of the oral liturgical milieu out of which the prayers in Matthew and the *Didache* arose is that neither of the two texts is the "original" from which the other deviates.[84] This is a basic tenet not only in the study of oral tradition,[85] but also in liturgical studies. Joseph Heinemann articulates the tenet well:

... we must lay down as a fundamental axiom for liturgical studies which would examine developmentally the texts of the various prayers that from the first no single 'original' text of any particular prayer was created, but that originally numerous diverse texts and versions existed side by side. It follows, then, that the widely accepted goal of the philological method – viz., to discover or to reconstruct the one 'original' text of a particular composition by examining and comparing the extant textual variants one with another – is out of place in the field of liturgical studies.[86]

It is not appropriate, then, to speak in terms of the *Didache* correcting Matthew's form of the prayer, or vice versa. Each form of the prayer functioned in its own right as an authoritative guide for the liturgical practice of a community. In this particular case we have to do with two communi-

---

[82] Idem., 173.

[83] Betz, *Sermon on the Mount* [Hermeneia], 370.

[84] An insight that grows naturally out of current trends in biblical studies, but noted already over a century ago (1891) by Frederic Chase ("Lord's Prayer," 12). This insight also applies to the Lukan version of the prayer (Lk 11:2–4); see Lohmeyer, *Our Father*, 30–31, and for a detailed discussion see J. H. Charlesworth, "A Caveat on Textual Transmission and the Meaning of *Abba*: A Study of the Lord's Prayer," in *The Lord's Prayer and Other Prayer Texts from the Greco-Roman Era* (ed. J. H. Charlesworth with M. Harding and M. Kiley; Valley Forge, Pa.: Trinity Press International, 1994), 1–5, 10.

[85] See above, secs. 1.4.2, 3.3.5 (and literature cited there) and 4.5.

[86] J. Heinemann, *Prayer in the Talmud: Forms and Patterns* (SJ 9; Berlin and New York: de Gruyter, 1977), 43, cited in Betz, *Sermon on the Mount* [Hermeneia], 370, n. 320; see also P. F. Bradshaw's wider discussion on how to approach the study of liturgical material in *The Search for the Origins of Christian Worship: Sources and Methods for the Study of Early Liturgy* (2nd ed.; Oxford: Oxford University Press, 2002).

ties that were closely related to each other geographically and historically, which explains the overarching similarity between the two prayers.[87]

7.4 Conclusion

The nature of the evidence at hand is such that any conclusions must remain hypothetical. One cannot rule out the possibility that the Didachist knew the Gospel of Matthew, or, for that matter, that Matthew knew the text of the *Didache*. Hopefully the discussion in this chapter has shown, however, that a different explanation for the relationship between the *Didache* and Matthew is preferable.

The hypothesis that the prayers in the *Didache* and Matthew both were derived from the oral liturgy of their closely-related communities provides the best explanation for the form of the prayer in both documents. It accounts for the overarching similarity between the prayers, for the inclusion of a doxology in the *Didache* and its absence in Matthew, and for the other minor differences noted between the two prayers. It also coheres well with the overall explanation adopted in this chapter for the many similarities between the *Didache* and Matthew: that both writings arose from the same cultural and historical – and possibly also the same geographical – milieu. The strength of this explanation is threefold: (1) it accounts not only for the similarities but also for the dissimilarities between the Jesus tradition reflected in both writings; (2) it accounts for the lack of any concrete evidence of literary dependence between the two documents; and (3) it takes fully into consideration the role of orality in the composition of ancient texts.[88]

The main contribution of the above discussion to the present work is in showing that oral-liturgical tradition functions somewhat differently than the non-liturgical oral tradition we have examined so far.[89] The liturgical context provides for the ritual repetition of a relatively fixed form of a tradition, which accounts for the almost verbatim similarity between the Lord's Prayer in the *Didache* and Matthew. That it is not altogether fixed

---

[87] This is only one of many elements that point to the close relationship between the communities of Matthew and the *Didache*; see further the literature cited in nn. 28 and 29 on p. 210 above.

[88] Unfortunately the volume edited by H. Klein, V. Mihoc, and K.-W. Niebuhr in cooperation with Christos Karakolis, *Das Gebet im Neuen Testament: Vierte europäische orthodox-westliche Exegetenkonferenz in Sambata de Sus, 4.-8. August 2007* (WUNT 1.249; Tübingen: Mohr Siebeck, 2009), which includes important essays on the Lord's Prayer in Matthew, Luke and the Jesus tradition, came to my hands too late to be used in this study.

[89] Cf. the preliminary comments to this effect in secs. 3.3.9 and 3.4 above.

is shown by the minor variations between the prayers that were noted in the course of the above discussion. In the case of oral-liturgical tradition it might be best to reverse the phrase often used in this study, and instead of speaking of "variability within stability," to speak of "stability within variability."

Chapter 8

Three Isolated Sayings from the Jesus Tradition

8.1 Introduction

This chapter represents another transition point in our discussion. The previous four chapters dealt with four blocks of tradition: three that contained collections of Jesus sayings (*1 Clem.* 13.2; 46.7–8; Poly. *Phil.* 2.3) and a fourth that contained a fairly lengthy unit of liturgical tradition (the Lord's Prayer in *Did.* 8.2). Now we turn to consider three passages that contain a single isolated saying: *Didache* 9.5, Ignatius' *Letter to the Smyrneans* 3.2a, and Polycarp's *Letter to the Philippians* 7.2c.

The task of analysis is greatly simplified when working with isolated sayings, but any advantage to be gained from this increased simplicity is offset by a loss of substantive results. Analysis is simplified because of the comparative brevity of the sayings, and also because all the sayings that will be examined in this chapter have only one or two parallels to be taken into account in the wider Jesus tradition. As we will see below, however, there is a good possibility that two out of the three sayings circulated as proverbs.[1] In cases in which a saying of Jesus has become a proverb, or in which Jesus uttered an existing proverb that subsequently was incorporated into the Jesus tradition, the oral use of the proverb all but negates the possibility that the Apostolic Fathers would have turned to a written source for the saying.[2] It follows that there is little value in an extended discussion of usage or sources in the case of proverbial sayings, which detracts considerably from the substance of the conclusions that can be drawn from the discussion in the present chapter.

Given the above, the following discussion of the three mentioned sayings will be fairly brief. Our approach for all three sayings will be to evaluate arguments that have been put forward in favor of each saying's dependence on the canonical Gospels, and then present any arguments that speak in favor of an oral-traditional source. The discussion of each saying

---

[1] The exception is Ign. *Smyrn.* 3.2a.

[2] On the use of the proverb in oral cultures see Ong, *Literacy and Orality*, 44; on the use of the proverb in a cross-section of oral societies see the articles in J. Goody, ed., *Literacy in Traditional Societies* (Cambridge: Cambridge University Press, 1968), 124, 139, 145–46, 150, 206, 293.

will be followed by any relevant conclusions, and these conclusions will be gathered and summarized at the end of the chapter.

8.2 *Didache* 9.5

καὶ γὰρ περὶ τούτου εἴρηκεν ὁ κύριος· Μὴ δῶτε τὸ ἅγιον τοῖς κυσί.

For also the Lord has said about this, "Do not give what is holy to the dogs."

Did. 9.5: Μὴ δῶτε τὸ ἅγιον τοῖς κυσί

Mt 7:6:   Μὴ δῶτε τὸ ἅγιον τοῖς κυσίν

Some have argued that the *Didache* is dependent on Matthew for this saying,[3] but there is no compelling evidence to support such a contention. In light of the wider discussion of Jesus tradition in the *Didache* in the previous chapter, it is more likely that Matthew and the Didachist depended upon a common tradition.[4]

Though the saying is worded almost exactly alike in Matthew as in the *Didache* (Matthew reads κυσίν in place of the *Didache*'s κυσί), it is the type of proverbial saying that could easily be retained and passed on verbatim in oral tradition.[5] A number of studies have suggested that the saying is derived from a Jewish proverb of pre-Christian origin, associated with the realm of Temple sacrifices.[6] As H. van de Sandt notes, "The adage 'Holy things (dedicated sacrifices) are not to be redeemed to feed them to dogs' (אין פודין את הקדשים להאכילן לכלבים) was widely disseminated and the extent of this spread is attested to by many references in rabbinic writings until far into the Amoraic period."[7]

Accepting for the sake of argument that the saying may have originated as a Jewish proverb, this need not imply anything regarding its authenticity

---

[3] E.g., Massaux, *Influence*, 3:156.

[4] See ch. 7 above, esp. literature cited in nn. 28 and 29 on p. 210.

[5] As also argued by Hagner ("Sayings," 241) and Tuckett ("Tradition in the *Didache*," 108).

[6] O. Michel traces the origin of the formula to Jewish sacrificial practice, positing that "τὸ ἅγιον" refers to sacrificial meat. Citing LXX and rabbinic usage, he concludes that the gist of the saying is that "What is holy [i.e., animals appointed for sacrifice] is not to be released to be eaten by dogs" (Michel, "κύων, κυνάριον," *TDNT* 3.1101–4 [quote taken from p. 1102]); see further Audet, *Didachè*, 173–74 (who cites Michel); van de Sandt, "Eucharistic Food," 223–46.

[7] Van de Sandt, "Eucharistic Food," 230; van de Sandt gives the text of the following examples: *b. Bek.* 15a; *b. Tem.* 17a; *y. Maʿaś. Š.* 2, 53c; *m. Tem.* 6.5; *t. Tem.* 4.11 (ibid., 230–31 [n. 17], 234, 235). *Pace* Massaux, who states that "the Talmud contains no trace of a proverb of this kind" (*Influence*, 3:156).

as a saying of Jesus.[8] It is to be expected that Jesus, as a Jewish teacher, would *sound* like a Jewish teacher and make use of the Jewish tradition of his day.[9] The old criterion of double dissimilarity used in Historical Jesus studies, according to which Jesus could not have said anything that sounded like the world of which he was a part, has rightly ceased to command much respect in New Testament studies.[10]

What is unique to the saying in the Jesus tradition, however, is its metaphorical application. While the (extant evidence of) Rabbinic usage all has to do with literal meat and literal dogs,[11] the saying as recorded in Matthew and the *Didache* has to do with practices and/or eucharistic elements that were sacred to the community, that should not be shared with unbelievers or Gentiles.[12] The contrast between this metaphorical use of the saying in the Christian community and the literal use it was given in a Jewish context may imply that both occurrences of the saying in Christian sources – Matthew and the *Didache* – go back to the teaching of Jesus. The slightly different application of the saying in Matthew vs. the *Didache* may be viewed as an example of the reapplication of oral tradition to new situations, in keeping with oral tradition's tendency to be socially identified.[13]

In conclusion, there is simply not enough evidence to determine with certainty the origin of the saying in *Did.* 9.5.[14] It remains possible that it was derived from the Gospel of Matthew, though this is not likely. A more probable hypothesis is that the saying formed part of the wider oral Jesus

---

[8] *Pace* J. A. Draper, who argues that the Didachist uses the saying as a Jewish proverb – the "Lord" being the Lord of the OT, not Jesus – and that Matthew may have taken this proverb and placed it on Jesus' lips ("Jesus Tradition," 78).

[9] On Jesus as teacher see especially Byrskog, *Jesus the Only Teacher*; Riesner, *Jesus als Lehrer*.

[10] See, e.g., the critique by M. Hooker, "Wrong Tool," 573–79.

[11] See the examples listed in van de Sandt, "Eucharistic Food," 230–31 [n. 17], 234, 235), noted already in n. 7 on p. 227 above.

[12] In Matthew the meaning of the saying is not altogether clear; it could be an injunction to either: (i) not spend too much time and effort in proclaiming the gospel to the hardhearted, or (ii) not share with outsiders teachings and practices that were the privileged knowledge of Jesus' followers (see Davies and Allison, *Matthew*, 1:676). The meaning in the *Didache* is that only the baptized should partake of the Eucharist. Yet the meanings are not that far apart: one could view the *Didache*'s meaning as a legitimate application of the Matthean option 'ii' above to the eucharistic practice of the church (cf. Davies and Allison, *Matthew*, 1:676).

[13] See sec. 3.3.10 above, under subtitle "Socially Identified." This is in keeping with the arguments raised by Audet (*Didachè*, 174) and Draper ("Jesus Tradition," 78), that the different application of the proverb in Matthew and the *Didache* implies that they are not literarily dependent upon each other.

[14] Also Lindemann's conclusion ("Apostolic Fathers and the Synoptic Problem," 697).

tradition that circulated in the closely related communities of Matthew and the Didachist. From there Matthew incorporated it, along with other M material, into his gospel, and from there also the Didachist incorporated it into his manual (that the Didachist used it in isolation from any other material in the Jesus tradition is probably due to the saying's proverbial nature). If this hypothesis is correct, the saying provides an example (when compared to Matthew 7:6) of the ability of oral tradition to retain short proverb-like sayings verbatim. It also illustrates how oral tradition could be applied to new situations, as a saying spoken by Jesus prior to the institution of the Eucharist was later applied to a Eucharistic setting.

8.3 Ignatius, *Letter to the Smyrneans*, 3.2a

Ἐγὼ γὰρ καὶ μετὰ τὴν ἀνάστασιν ἐν σαρκὶ αὐτὸν οἶδα καὶ πιστεύω ὄντα. ² καὶ ὅτε πρὸς τοὺς περὶ Πέτρον ἦλθεν, ἔφη αὐτοῖς· Λάβετε, ψηλαφήσατέ με καὶ ἴδετε, ὅτι οὐκ εἰμὶ δαιμόνιον ἀσώματον. καὶ εὐθὺς αὐτοῦ ἥψαντο καὶ ἐπίστευσαν ....

(3.1–2a)

For I know and believe that he was in the flesh even after the resurrection. ² And when he came to those who were with Peter, he said to them, "Reach out, touch me and see that I am not a bodiless demon." And immediately they touched him and believed ....

(3.1–2a)

Ign. *Smyrn.* 3.2a: λάβετε, <u>ψηλαφήσατέ με καὶ ἴδετε, ὅτι</u>
                    οὐκ εἰμὶ δαιμόνιον ἀσώματον
Lk 24:39:   <u>ψηλαφήσατέ με καὶ ἴδετε, ὅτι</u>
                    πνεῦμα σάρκα καὶ ὀστέα οὐκ ἔχει καθὼς ἐμὲ θεωρεῖτε ἔχοντα

This is the only explicit appeal to Jesus tradition in Ignatius. In seeking to ascertain its source, two main leads – both equally unfruitful – suggest themselves: (a) what ancient writers have to say in this regard, and (b) dependence upon the Gospel of Luke.

(a) In *de Viris Illustribus*, 16, Jerome identifies the source of Ignatius' quotation as the *Gospel according to the Hebrews* (cf. his *Comm. Isa.* 18, pref.).[15] Based on a number of problems with Jerome's claim, however, it becomes clear that he is relying not on his own reading of Ignatius or of

---

[15] See P. Vielhauer and G. Strecker, "Jewish-Christian Gospels," in *New Testament Apocrypha* (ed. W. Schneemelcher; Cambridge: James Clarke/Louisville: Westminster/John Knox, 1991), 1:143, where the texts from Jerome are provided. For two detailed defenses of Ignatius' dependence upon the *Gospel according to the Hebrews* see C. Maurer, "Ein umstrittenes Zitat bei Ignatius von Antiochien (Smyrn. 3, 2)," *JGGPÖ* 67 [FS J. Bohatec] (1951): 165–70 and P. F. Beatrice, "The 'Gospel according to the Hebrews' in the Apostolic Fathers," *NovT* 48 (2006): 147–95.

the Hebrew Gospel, but on Eusebius' *Ecclesiastical History* 3.36.11.[16] Since Eusebius himself states clearly that he does not know the provenance of the Ignatian saying, while he did have access to the *Gospel according to the Hebrews*, it seems clear that Ignatius did not derive the saying from the latter *Gospel*.[17] Origen provides another option, mentioning that Jesus' saying, "I am not a bodiless demon," is found in a non-canonical "Teaching of Peter" (*de Princ.* 1, prooem. 8).[18] Here one must wrestle with the issue, however, of which document provides the source for which. In the view of P. Vielhauer and G. Strecker, Ignatius was the source for the saying in the "Teaching of Peter," so that Origen sheds no new light on the source of the saying in Ignatius.[19] We conclude that these various ancient Christian writers do not hold the key to ascertaining the origin of the Ignatian saying.

(b) That part of the saying in *Smyrn.* 3.2a is identical to its parallel in Lk 24:39 might suggest that Ignatius was dependent on the third gospel. As argued by W. Schoedel, however, two factors make this dependence unlikely. Firstly, there is virtually no other evidence for the use of Luke by Ignatius. Secondly, the words δαιμονικοῖς and ἀσωμάτοις Ignatius uses in reference to his docetic opponents in *Smyrn.* 2b are otherwise not found in his vocabulary, but do reflect the δαιμόνιον and ἀσώματον in his citation of Jesus' words in 3.2. The whole text of *Smyrn.* 2 reads:

> For he [Jesus Christ] suffered all these things for our sakes, in order that we might be saved; and he truly suffered just as he truly raised himself – not, as certain unbelievers say, that he suffered in appearance only (it is they who exist in appearance only!). Indeed, their fate will be determined by what they think: they will become disembodied [ἀσωμάτοις] and demonic [δαιμονικοῖς].[20]

The most logical explanation for Ignatius' use of the terms δαιμονικοῖς and ἀσωμάτοις in this passage is that they were in the saying in *Smyrn.* 3.2 as he found it the tradition, and he employed them for rhetorical effect in his

---

[16] Not only does Jerome give the wrong letter of Ignatius as the source of his quote (Ign. *Poly.*), he also misquotes Ignatius' words, making Ignatius claim to be a witness to the resurrection: "And I have also seen him in the flesh after the resurrection and believe that he is, and when he came to Peter and to those with Peter ..." (*Vir.* 16), cf. Ignatius: "For I know and believe that he was in the flesh even after the resurrection. And when he came to those who were with Peter ..." (*Smyrn.* 3.2a); for a full discussion see Vielhauer and Strecker, "Jewish-Christian Gospels," 143–45; for a dissenting opinion see Beatrice, "Gospel according to the Hebrews," 154–58.

[17] Vielhauer and Strecker, "Jewish-Christian Gospels," 144.

[18] Ibid., 144.

[19] Ibid., 144–45.

[20] Trans. is that of Holmes, *Apostolic Fathers*, 251.

argument against his opponents in *Smyrn.* 2b.[21] Based on these considerations, we conclude with Schoedel and others that Ignatius is not paraphrasing Luke in his own words, but rather he and Luke both rely on a common tradition.[22]

Setting aside these arguments for dependence upon non-canonical gospels or upon the Gospel of Luke, it is fairly straightforward to find the possibility of an appeal to oral tradition in the Ignatian saying: the section that is identical in both sources is the type of material that could be easily retained verbatim in oral transmission, while the λάβετε at the front of the Ignatian quote but missing from Luke is in keeping with the variability inherent to oral tradition. In spite of their difference in form,[23] the two endings essentially communicate the same idea:[24] the disciples could touch Jesus' physical body, as he was not a disembodied spirit – an additional element of stability in content with variability in form that is at home in oral tradition. These observations regarding the variability within stability of oral tradition as applied to *Smyrn.* 3.2a, while adding nothing new to our study, serve to reinforce some of the findings from previous chapters.

To make a final point before moving on to the next passage, the saying in *Smyrn.* 3.2a may also illustrate the socially identified character of oral tradition.[25] The presence of the terms δαιμόνιον and ἀσώματον in the saying, used by Ignatius in his polemic against his docetic opponents, may owe their presence in the saying to the anti-docetic polemic taking place in the wider Christian community. Perhaps prior to the docetic threat the say-

---

[21] For Schoedel's full argument see his *Ignatius of Antioch: A Commentary on the Letters of Ignatius of Antioch* (ed. H. Koester; Hermeneia; Philadelphia: Fortress, 1985), 225–27; cf. the similar argument in Gregory, *Reception of Luke and Acts*, 72.

[22] Schoedel, *Ignatius of Antioch*, 227, for his full discussion see ibid., 225–27; C. T. Brown, *The Gospel and Ignatius of Antioch* (StBibLit 12; New York: Peter Lang, 2000), 38–39; R. M. Grant, *Ignatius of Antioch* (ApFa 4; Camden: Thomas Nelson & Sons, 1966), 115; Hagner, "Sayings," 239–40; Koester, *Synoptische Überlieferung*, 45–56; Paulsen, *Ignatius und Polykarp*, 92. Along with oral tradition, A. Gregory leaves open the possibility of a written source common to Luke and Ignatius (*Reception of Luke and Acts*, 73–75; see also idem, "Looking for Luke," 405). Lindemann seems to favor pre-Lukan tradition ("Apostolic Fathers and the Synoptic Problem," 706). C. Trevett refers to 3.2 as "a reminiscence of a not entirely canonical post-resurrection story" (*Study of Ignatius*, 157). From this and the complete absence of a consideration of Luke in her discussion of Ignatius' sources (ibid., 15–27), one can gather that she does not consider Luke to be Ignatius' source (ibid., 142 n. 39; cf., 164).

[23] In Vielhauer and Strecker's view, of the two endings, πνεῦμα σάρκα καὶ ὀστέα οὐκ ἔχει καθὼς ἐμὲ θεωρεῖτε ἔχοντα is probably closer to what Jesus actually said, as the grecized δαιμόνιον ἀσώματον "cannot be the translation of a semitic original" ("Jewish-Christian Gospels," 144).

[24] Also noted by Grant, *Ignatius of Antioch*, 115.

[25] See sec. 3.3.10 above, under the subtitle "Socially Identified."

ing was transmitted with a wording closer to that found in Luke, with πνεῦμα instead of δαιμόνιον, and language that drew attention to the presence of σάρκα καὶ ὀστέα instead of the use of ἀσώματον. With the advent of the docetic threat, however, traditionists may have begun to couch the saying in words that – while not changing the saying's basic meaning – more directly served the anti-docetic polemic. A saying closer to the Lukan form probably filled a polemical purpose for the Christian community from very early on, to argue both for the physical reality of Jesus' resurrection and that the resurrected One was identical with Jesus.[26] In the form it has been given in *Smyrn.* 3.2a, however, it serves the newer polemic of Ignatius' day against docetic views.[27]

8.4 Polycarp's *Epistle to the Philippians*, 7.2c

... δεήσεσιν αἰτούμενοι τὸν παντεπόπτην θεὸν μὴ εἰσενεγκεῖν ἡμᾶς εἰς πειρασμόν καθὼς εἶπεν ὁ κύριος· τὸ μὲν πνεῦμα πρόθυμον ἡ δὲ σὰρξ ἀσθενής.

Through our entreaties let us ask the God who sees all things not to bring us into temptation, just as the Lord said, "For the spirit is willing but the flesh is weak."

Pol *Phil.* 7.2c: τὸ μὲν πνεῦμα πρόθυμον ἡ δὲ σὰρξ ἀσθενής
Mk 14:38:   τὸ μὲν πνεῦμα πρόθυμον ἡ δὲ σὰρξ ἀσθενής
Mt 26:41:   τὸ μὲν πνεῦμα πρόθυμον ἡ δὲ σὰρξ ἀσθενής

In spite of the verbatim agreement between the text of *Philippians* and its gospel parallels, it is doubtful that Polycarp is dependent upon the Gospels for the saying. We will first consider the claims for dependence, and then support a different interpretation.

Perhaps the strongest evidence for Poly. *Phil.* 7.2c's dependence upon the Gospels is found in the words immediately preceding Polycarp's citation of the Jesus saying under consideration. The wider passage reads:

---

[26] R. J. Dillon, *From Eye-Witnesses to Ministers of the Word: Tradition and Composition in Luke 24* (AnBib 82; Rome: Biblical Institute Press, 1978), 193–95; J. Dupont, "Les pèlerins d'Emmaüs (Luc, XXIV, 13–35)," in *Miscellanea biblica B. Ubach* (ed. R. M.ª Díaz; SD 1; Montserrat: Abadia di Montserrat, 1953), 373; Marshall, *Luke*, 900; J. Nolland, *Luke 18:35–24:53* (WBC 35C; Dallas: Word, 1993), 1216; A. Plummer, *A Critical and Exegetical Commentary on the Gospel According to S. Luke* (5th ed.; ICC; Edinburgh: T&T Clark, 1906), 559.

[27] As noted by J. Nolland regarding the saying in Lk 24:39, "There really is no sign here of anti-gnostic or anti-docetic polemic" (*Luke 18:35–24:53*, 1213); see also Brown, *Gospel and Ignatius*, 38–39, 192; Dillon, *Eye-Witnesses to Ministers*, 194–95; Marshall, *Luke*, 900; *pace* C. H. Talbert, *Luke and the Gnostics: An Examination of the Lucan Purpose* (Nashville: Abingdon, 1966), 30–32.

... let us be self-controlled with respect to prayer and persevere in fasting, earnestly ask-ing the all-seeing God to lead us not into temptation [μὴ εἰσενεγκεῖν ἡμᾶς εἰς πειρασμόν], because, as the Lord said, "the spirit is indeed willing, but the flesh is weak" [τὸ μὲν πνεῦμα πρόθυμον ἡ δὲ σὰρξ ἀσθενής].[28]

The Synoptic tradition contains two sets of parallels to Polycarp's words μὴ εἰσενεγκεῖν ἡμᾶς εἰς πειρασμόν ("lead us not into temptation"). The first set of parallels is found in the Lord's Prayer in Matthew and Luke: μὴ εἰσενέγκῃς ἡμᾶς εἰς πειρασμόν (identical in Mt 6:13a and Lk11:4b).The second set of parallels is found in the passion narrative in Mark and Mat-thew: "Watch and pray so that you will not fall into temptation" (Mk 14:38: γρηγορεῖτε καὶ προσεύχεσθε, ἵνα μὴ ἔλθητε εἰς πειρασμόν; Mt 26:41: γρηγορεῖτε καὶ προσεύχεσθε, ἵνα μὴ εἰσέλθητε εἰς πειρασμόν). The parallels from the passion narrative are not as close as the parallels from the Lord's Prayer to the wording of Polycarp's exhortation. The par-allels from the passion narrative are significant, however, in that they in-clude parallels both to *Phil.* 7.2b and to *Phil.* 7.2c in the same sentence, "Watch and pray so that you will not fall into temptation, for the spirit is willing but the flesh is weak" (Mk14:38//Mt 26:41; cf. *Phil.* 7.2b, 7.2c). For a number of scholars, the implication is that in quoting Jesus' words in *Phil.* 7.2c, Polycarp had to have known of the wider context of these words within the passion narrative of the Gospel of Matthew.[29] Their choice of Matthew over Mark as the source of the saying is based on their perception that Matthew's text of the Lord's Prayer impacted the wording of the say-ing in Polycarp.[30]

While this argument for Poly. *Phil.* 7.2c's dependence upon the Gos-pels is coherent, it does not ultimately convince when one examines the presuppositions upon which it is based. The argument works well within the old form-critical paradigm, according to which the sayings of Jesus were transmitted in complete isolation from each other, and were later col-

[28] Trans. is that of Holmes, *Apostolic Fathers*, 289.

[29] Noted, though not necessarily argued, by Lightfoot, *Apostolic Fathers*, 2.3:336; further argued by Koester (*Synoptische Überlieferung*, 114–15), and Massaux (*Influence*, 2:31–32); followed by Schoedel (*Polycarp, Martyrdom, Papias*, 26) and Paulsen (*Igna-tius und Polykarp*, 121).

[30] This impact is viewed in two ways: (1) Polycarp is dependent upon the saying in the passion narrative, but modified its wording under the influence of the Lord's Prayer, and since the only Gospel that contains both the parallels in the passion narrative and the parallels in the Lord's Prayer is Matthew, Polycarp must be dependent upon Matthew; see, e.g., Massaux, *Influence*, 2:31–32. (2) In W. Schoedel's words, "The connection of the petition from the Lord's Prayer with the saying about the spirit and the flesh in [Poly. *Phil.* 7.2] is anticipated already in the Gospels (Mark. 14:38; Matt. 26:41). Since this connection appears secondary, it is reasonable to suppose that Polycarp derived it from the written Gospels" (Schoedel, *Polycarp, Martyrdom, Papias*, 26, who cites Koester, *Synoptische Überlieferung*, 114–15).

lected by the evangelists and "strung together like pearls on a string."[31] If there was evidence to show either (a) that Mark (assuming Markan priority) created one of the two phrases "Watch and pray so that you will not fall into temptation" or "for the spirit is willing but the flesh is weak," or (b) that he brought together the two phrases that in pre-Markan tradition were separate, then there would be an argument for Polycarp's dependence upon the Gospels. There is, however, no such evidence, so that the argument for Polycarp's dependence upon Matthew loses its force.

A different alternative arises if, in keeping with the approach taken in this study, one presupposes that the basic unit of pre-Synoptic tradition was the discourse rather than the isolated saying.[32] In this case there is no reason why a complete phrase similar to the one recorded in Mk 14:38//Mt 26:41 could not have formed part of the Gethsemane narrative in the oral tradition, and not just in the written Gospels.[33]

One can assume that the Gethsemane narrative was widely known in the early church based on its close ties to the narratives of the Lord's Supper and of Jesus' arrest. It is very likely that the current place of the Gethsemane narrative in the three Synoptics, sandwiched between the Lord's Supper and Jesus' arrest, was also its place in pre-Markan tradition, as each section of the narrative presupposes the others.[34] The centrality of the

---

[31] Famously developed by Schmidt in *Rahmen*; see S. Neill and T. Wright, *The Interpretation of the New Testament: 1861–1986* (2nd ed.; Oxford and New York: Oxford University Press, 1988), 254; W. Neil, "The Criticism and Theological Use of the Bible 1700–1950," in *The Cambridge History of the Bible,* Vol. 3: *The West from the Reformation to the Present Day* (ed. S. L. Greenslade; Cambridge: Cambridge University Press, 1963), 291.

[32] See sec. 4.4 above.

[33] For a detailed argument in support of the unity of the Markan Gethsemane narrative see R. Feldmeier *Die Krisis des Gottessohnes: Die Gethsemaneerzählung als Schlüssel der Markuspassion* (WUNT 2.21; Tübingen: Mohr Siebeck, 1987), 67–140. The issue of the origin of the Gethsemane account is closely tied to the wider conversation on the existence of a pre-Markan passion narrative as whole. Though there have been dissenting voices (see, e.g., W. H. Kelber, "Mark 14:32–42: Gethsemane: Passion Christology and Discipleship Failure," *ZNW* 63 [1972]: 166–87, and the essays in idem, ed., *The Passion in Mark: Studies on Mark 14–16* [Philadelphia: Fortress, 1976]) the majority of scholars consider that there was a cohesive passion narrative that Mark incorporated with editorial reworking into his gospel; see the surveys by A. Y. Collins, "The Passion Narrative of Mark," in idem, *The Beginning of the Gospel: Probings of Mark in Context* (Minneapolis: Fortress, 1992), 92–118; M. L. Soards, "The Question of a PreMarkan Passion Narrative," *BiBh* 11 (1985): 144–69. Matthew's account basically follows Mark's, with some minor editorial changes; for a detailed discussion see D. P. Senior, *The Passion Narrative according to Matthew: A Redactional Study* (BETL 39; Leuven: Leuven University Press and Peeters, 1975), 110–19.

[34] See (1) R. Gundry's concise statement: "There is no need to think that the episode in Gethsemane did not originally intervene between the Last Supper and Jesus' arrest.

narratives of the Lord's Supper and of the arrest and crucifixion of Jesus within the proclamation of the early church guaranteed their wide dissemination, and it is very probable that along with them the Gethsemane account also became widely known.[35] It follows that Polycarp's knowledge of the Gethsemane account in the oral tradition is sufficient to account for his words in *Phil.* 7.2b–c, without need to posit his dependence upon a written Matthew.[36] In addition, the similarity of the saying to the sixth petition of the Lord's Prayer as recorded in the *Didache* and Matthew need not be taken as evidence of dependence upon the Lord's Prayer in the first gospel. Building upon the discussion in chapter 7 above, the widespread liturgical use of the Lord's Prayer in the early church is enough to account for this similarity:[37] Polycarp prefaced the saying "the spirit is willing but the flesh is weak" with an exhortation to ask God "to lead us not into temptation" because of his knowledge of Jesus' words from the tradition of the passion narrative; the wording he chose for the exhortation was influenced by his familiarity with the sixth petition of the Lord's Prayer as used in the liturgy.

Two further considerations point to the oral provenance of the saying in *Phil.* 7.2c: First, the introductory formula καθὼς εἶπεν ὁ κύριος slightly

---

For the reference to Gethsemane is hardly fabricated, and the story of Jesus' praying there needs the narrative framework provided by the Last Supper and his arrest. It seems likely, then, that the story circulated with them from the start rather than being inserted between them at a later date" (R. H. Gundry, *Mark: A Commentary on His Apology for the Cross* [Grand Rapids: Eerdmans, 1993], 864); and (2) the well-developed argument in E. Trocmé, *The Passion as Liturgy: A Study in the Origin of the Passion Narratives in the Four Gospels* (London: SCM, 1983), 7–46 (one need not agree with his thesis of the liturgical context for the development of the passion narrative to appreciate the various points he makes regarding its unity). On the historicity of the Gethsemane narrative see J. B. Green, "Gethsemane," *EHJ* 224–25, and the full discussion in R. E. Brown, *The Death of the Messiah: From Gethsemane to the Grave: A Commentary on the Passion Narratives in the Four Gospels* (2vols.; ABRL; New York: Doubleday, 1994), 1:146–234. On the Gethsemane narrative's waking/sleeping motif in the context of Jewish tradition regarding the Passover (and its implications for the historicity of the account), see D. Daube, "Two Incidents after the Last Supper," in idem, *The New Testament and Rabbinic Judaism* (London: Athlone, 1956), 332–35.

[35] The relative silence of the early Fathers on the Gethsemane narrative is probably due to the embarrassment it caused in a context seeking to emphasize Christ's divinity; see U. Luz, *Matthew 21–28: A Commentary* (ed. H. Koester; trans. J. E. Crouch; Hermeneia; Minneapolis: Fortress, 2005), 394, 398–400.

[36] M. L. Soards discusses a number of indicators of orality in the Gethsemane account in "Oral Tradition Before, In, and Outside the Canonical Passion Narratives," in *Jesus and the Oral Gospel* (ed. Wansbrough), 334–50, esp. 340–43; see also Feldmeier, *Krisis des Gottessohnes*, 38, 49, 62–63, and passim.

[37] On the liturgical use of the Lord's Prayer in the early church see the discussion in sec. 7.3 above, and literature cited there.

favors an oral over a written source. The use of the aorist εἶπεν, though not accompanied by a word for "remembering" is significant. Had Polycarp used the *present* tense it would tend to imply quotation from a written document. As it is, Polycarp's use of the aorist may indicate that he is appealing to the oral tradition of Jesus' words.[38]

Second, the form and contents of the saying in *Phil.* 7.2c, τὸ μὲν πνεῦμα πρόθυμον ἡ δὲ σὰρξ ἀσθενής ("the spirit is willing but the flesh is weak") also suggest an oral source. As rightly noted by R. T. France, "The classical μὲν ... δέ construction, together with the general nature of the language, suggests a proverbial expression."[39] The saying would have been very useful in the early church as a proverb that "expresses in a nutshell one of the main problems of Christian discipleship (and indeed human nature in general)."[40] In a culture in which the proverb was a standard part not only of speech but also of thought, sayings such as this were often known in great numbers.[41] Polycarp would have had no need to turn to a written source to recall this kind of proverbial saying.

The above discussion might appear to beg the question of the source of the (probably[42]) implicit and explicit references to Jesus tradition in Poly. *Phil.* 7.2b–c, but it is a much more straightforward reading of the evidence – given Polycarp's cultural milieu – than the hypothesis that he is dependent upon the written Gospels. For the twenty-first-century individual, whose only access to Jesus tradition is through written accounts, it may be

---

[38] On the significance of the aorist vs. the present tense see above, pp. 140–43, 166, 171–72, and literature cited there.

[39] R. T. France, *The Gospel of Matthew* (NICNT; Grand Rapids: Eerdmans, 2007), 1006, n. 21; see also idem, *Mark*, 587. It is commonly noted that the saying "sounds like a proverb" (Davies and Allison, *Matthew*, 3:499; J. R. Donahue and D. J. Harrington, *The Gospel of Mark* [SP 2; Collegeville: Liturgical, 2002], 409; D. J. Harrington *The Gospel of Matthew* [SP 1; Collegeville: Liturgical, 1991], 373). Brown (*Death of the Messiah*, 1:198) refers to it as an "aphorism."

[40] France, *Matthew*, 1006. Regarding the basic historicity of the saying on the lips of Jesus, it used to be common to assign its origin to Hellenistic influence upon the early Christian community, possibly mediated by Pauline theology. This changed with the discovery of the Dead Sea Scrolls, which showed that the contrast of spirit and flesh was at home in a Semitic context (See Brown, *Death of the Messiah*, 1:198 and literature cited there). For a detailed discussion of the various backgrounds that have been suggested see J. W. Holleran, *The Synoptic Gethsemane: A Critical Study* (Roma: Pontificia Universitas Gregoriana, Facultas Theologiae, 1973), 39–45.

[41] Ong, *Literacy and Orality*, 44; and see above, pp. 159–60, 226 (and literature cited there).

[42] Polycarp is almost certainly alluding to Jesus' words in the Gethsemane narrative with his exhortation "earnestly asking the all-seeing God to lead us not into temptation" in *Phil.* 7.2b, but this allusion nevertheless remains hypothetical. The next phrase, however, is explicitly identified as Jesus tradition, "as the Lord said, 'the spirit is indeed willing, but the flesh is weak'" (*Phil.* 7.2c).

natural to think of literary dependence when encountering similarity between two written sources. If one approaches the issue, however, from a perspective that seeks to be true to the ancient context of the sources by giving preference to orality over scribality, other explanations come to the fore. If Polycarp was clearly dependent upon a written gospel in other places, this might call for a change in perspective, but Polycarp's knowledge and use of the Gospels remains an open question.[43]

8.5 Conclusions

It is very probable that the sayings considered in this chapter were part of the oral tradition that circulated among the churches. Though there is no way to be certain of their oral-traditional provenance, in a culture proficient in orality there would have been no need to depend on written sources for such brief sayings (especially those in proverbial form).

The main contribution of two of these sayings, *Did.* 9.5 and Ign. *Smyrn.* 3.2a, to the present work is in illustrating the socially identified tendency of oral tradition. In the case of *Did.* 9.5, the saying "Do not give what is holy to the dogs" is applied in the early church to a situation – exclusion from participation in the Eucharist – different, though related, to the situation in which Jesus first used it. This need not imply that the proverb ceased to be applied according to its earlier meaning (there is no evidence for or against this use), but it gained a wider meaning when applied to a new situation.

The passage in Ignatius' *Letter to the Smyrneans* (3.2a), "Reach out, touch me and see that I am not a bodiless demon," also illustrates the reapplication of a saying to a new situation. While in the form and in the setting in which it was originally spoken it provided words of comfort and reassurance to troubled disciples, it was soon taken up in Luke to serve a polemical function in defense of the reality of Jesus' resurrection, and in the form we find it in Ignatius it has been enlisted for a specifically anti-docetic polemic. That for anti-docetic purposes the wording of the saying was slightly modified, without compromising its basic meaning, also illustrates the variability within stability that is characteristic of the ongoing life of oral tradition. This variability is one of the ways oral tradition remains "alive" and able to function within a community in the many ways that it is needed.

---

[43] See ch. 5 above; *pace* the confident statements to the contrary in Jefford with Harder and Amezaga, *Reading*, 81; Massaux, *Influence*, 2:27–33, 51. More appropriate are the guarded statements, e.g., of Hagner, *Clement of Rome*, 279–80; idem, "Sayings," 240.

Finally, the saying in Poly. *Phil.* 7.2 and the words with which it is introduced illustrate the influence that one saying could have upon another. Though the introductory exhortation to ask God "to lead us not into temptation" is not clearly identified as Jesus tradition, its close association with the explicit citation that follows makes it very likely that an implicit appeal to Jesus' words is intended. That the implicit citation reflects a different wording than that of its referent, following instead the wording of the sixth petition of the Lord's Prayer, serves as another example of the variability within stability that characterized the use of the Jesus tradition in the daily life of the early church.

Chapter 9

"Another Scripture says ..."
Jesus tradition in *2 Clement*

9.1 Introduction

Interpreting the sayings of Jesus in *2 Clement* is a complex task. The sheer number of explicit appeals to Jesus tradition – either nine or eleven depending on how one breaks up the sayings[1] – contrasts sharply with the paucity of such appeals in the Apostolic Fathers studied in the previous chapters. This increase in number of appeals carries a corresponding increase in the variety of introductory formulas, in the number of parallels to the sayings cited, and in the number of possible sources from which the sayings might have derived. There are other complicating factors. Certain sayings contain whole lines or multiple lines with no known parallel in the Jesus tradition (5:3–4a; 8.5a). In addition, "Clement" appears to introduce one saying as Scripture, "And also another Scripture says [καὶ ἑτέρα δὲ γραφὴ λέγει]" (2.4), something not encountered in the other Apostolic Fathers considered so far.[2] As is to be expected, scholars disagree on how best to interpret all of this evidence.

The question of whether or not the Jesus sayings in *2 Clement* presuppose the finished form of the canonical Gospels has dominated much of the scholarly discussion, and thus provides a good entry-point for our treatment in this chapter. While scholars have offered various theories, ranging from the direct use of the Gospels (primarily of Matthew and Luke), to the exclusive use of an apocryphal gospel, most scholars find evidence for the indirect use of the Gospels, via either a gospel harmony that drew on Matthew and Luke as well as other sources, or oral tradition that was influenced by the Gospels. We will interact with these views in detail as we treat the individual sayings, to which we now turn.

---

[1] *2 Clement* 6.1–2 and 4.2, 5 can both be viewed as containing either one saying or two; see further below.

[2] The ascription of the document known as *2 Clement* to Clement of Rome dates from the third century, and is widely recognized as false (see Grant and Graham, *First and Second Clement*, 109). Rather than speak in this chapter of "pseudo-Clement," however, we will refer to the author of the document as "Clement."

9.2 The Jesus Tradition in *2 Clement* in Relation to its Parallels

Rather than superimpose an artificial structure on our treatment of the sayings that follow based upon the results of the investigation, we will treat them in the order in which they appear in *2 Clement*, and categorize the sayings according to our findings in the concluding section.[3]

9.2.1 2 Clement 2.4

καὶ ἑτέρα δὲ γραφὴ λέγει, ὅτι οὐκ ἦλθον καλέσαι δικαίους, ἀλλὰ ἁμαρτωλούς·

And also another Scripture says, "I did not come to call the upright, but sinners."

2 Clem. 2.4:	οὐκ ἦλθον καλέσαι δικαίους ἀλλὰ ἁμαρτωλούς
Barn. 5.9:	οὐκ ἦλθεν καλέσαι δικαίους ἀλλὰ ἁμαρτωλούς
Mt 9:13:	οὐ γὰρ ἦλθον καλέσαι δικαίους ἀλλὰ ἁμαρτωλούς
Mk 2:17:	οὐκ ἦλθον καλέσαι δικαίους ἀλλὰ ἁμαρτωλούς
Lk 5:32:	οὐκ ἐλήλυθα καλέσαι δικαίους ἀλλὰ ἁμαρτωλοὺς εἰς μετάνοιαν
Justin, *1 Apol.* 15.8:	οὐκ ἦλθον καλέσαι δικαίους ἀλλὰ ἁμαρτωλοὺς εἰς μετάνοιαν

The inclusion of this saying in the present study that deals with explicit appeals to Jesus' sayings is an exception, though one made on good grounds. On the one hand, the introductory "And also another Scripture says" identifies the words that follow as an explicit quotation. On the other hand, given that the only parallels in extant literature are from the Jesus tradition, it is fairly safe to assume that the author is quoting words of Jesus. Bringing these two considerations together, it is very probable that the author expected his readers to recognize that he was citing a written source of Jesus tradition. In effect, then, the formula "And also another Scripture says" serves to identify the words that follow as a saying of Jesus.

Turning to the saying itself, there is very little variation among its parallels. The forms in *2 Clement* and Mark are identical, while those in *Barnabas* and Matthew are so close to the latter that for all intents and purposes they constitute four matching witnesses to the logion. The third

---

[3] I decided upon this approach after the third complete revision of the contents of the present chapter. I began work on the sayings in *2 Clement* assuming that most of them were derived from a harmony of Matthew and Luke that also included material from other sources. Accordingly, I divided the chapter into two main sections, the first dealing with sayings that presupposed the finished form of the Gospels and the second with the few sayings that did not. When I found that the evidence from the sayings did not support my presuppositions, I completely revised the chapter and structured it in three parts, the first dealing with sayings that certainly presupposed the finished Gospels, the second with those that possibly did so, and the third with those that did not. Further investigation made that arrangement also unworkable, so I again completely revised the chapter to reflect its present structure, chosen so that the arrangement of the sayings does not presuppose any given outcome of the investigation.

person singular ἦλθεν, the only variant in *Barn.* 5.9, is necessary given the context of the sentence in that document, as there it is not part of a quotation but of a narrative in the third person.[4] As noted by Donfried, the γάρ of Matthew functions as a connective; if the connective were missing one would have to change the οὐ to οὐκ, in which case the Matthean rendition would be identical to the parallels in Mark and *2 Clement*.[5] Luke's change of ἦλθον to the perfect ἐλήλυθα and his addition of εἰς μετάνοιαν – which Justin also reflects, probably in direct dependence upon Luke – are thus the only substantive variants in the above parallels. The almost verbatim similarity among all the parallels indicates that this saying was known fairly widely in the early Christian community, perhaps as a proverb.

The recurrence of this proverb in a variety of Christian writings makes it impossible to say anything specific about the source used by "Clement" beyond the basic fact that it was written.[6] Only by going against the plain meaning of the words ἑτέρα δὲ γραφή could one argue that the saying is cited from oral tradition.[7] One might also infer that the reference to ἑτέρα δὲ γραφή implies that "Clement" attributed a certain authority to his source.[8] Perhaps at this juncture in history one of the canonical Gospels would be the best candidate to fit this criterion, but this is unverifiable with the information at our disposal.[9] The evidence is simply insufficient to de-

---

[4] "And when he [the Lord] selected his own apostles who were about to preach his gospel, they were altogether lawless beyond all sin. This was to show *that he did not come to call the upright but sinners*" (*Barn.* 5.9; trans. Ehrman, LCL; emphasis added).

[5] See K. P. Donfried, *The Setting of Second Clement in Early Christianity* (NovTSup 38; Leiden: Brill, 1974), 57.

[6] Cf. Gregory, *Reception of Luke and Acts*, 145–46.

[7] Donfried's argument that the saying is probably derived from oral tradition depends on his view that "The author of 2 Clement uses the phrase γραφή in a rather general way, intending only to lend some authority to his citations" (*Second Clement*, 59, see also pp. 79–81). Donfried's example in support of this view, however, does not provide enough of a basis: he notes that the words in *2 Clem.* 6:8, that are introduced with the statement λέγει δὲ καὶ ἡ γραφὴ ἐν τῷ Ἰεζεκιήλ, contain "only a vague reflection of Ezekiel" (p. 59). That "Clement" did not have the book of Ezekiel open before him as he cited it, however, and therefore was not able to reproduce the contents of his citation verbatim, does not detract from his knowledge that the provenance of his quote was written Scripture, as he indicates with the ἡ γραφή.

[8] Most scholars hold this view; see, e.g., Köhler, *Rezeption*, 136; Koester, *Synoptische Überlieferung*, 71; Hagner, "Sayings," 244; Lindemann, *Clemensbriefe*, 205; Massaux, *Influence*, 2:4–5; W. Pratscher, *Der zweite Clemensbrief* (KAV 3; Göttingen: Vandenhoeck & Ruprecht, 2007), 32, 33, 80; Schröter, "Jesus and the Canon," 112; Smith, "Gospels in Early Christian Literature," 197, 201.

[9] Lindemann ("Apostolic Fathers and the Synoptic Problem," 711), Massaux (*Influence*, 2:3–6) and Warns ("Untersuchungen zum 2. Clemens-Brief" [Inauguraldissertation zur Erlangung der Würde eines Doktors der Theologie; Marburg: Philipps-Universität Marburg, 1985], 279, 284–88) are certain that *2 Clem.* 2.4 was drawn from Matthew;

termine what source "Clement" used: it may have been a canonical gospel, a source dependent on the canonical Gospels such as a gospel harmony, a source "Clement" shared with the Gospels, a non-canonical gospel (such as the *Gospel of the Egyptians*[10]), a writing of an altogether different genre such as the *Epistle of Barnabas*, or perhaps a different option.

9.2.2 2 Clement 3.2

λέγει δὲ καὶ αὐτός· Τὸν ὁμολογήσαντά με ἐνώπιον τῶν ἀνθρώπων, ὁμολογήσω αὐτὸν ἐνώπιον τοῦ πατρός μου.

Indeed, he [Christ] himself says, "Whoever acknowledges me before men, I will acknowledge before my Father"[11]

2 Clem. 3.2:	τὸν ὁμολογήσαντά με ἐνώπιον τῶν ἀνθρώπων
Mt 10:32:	πᾶς οὖν ὅστις ὁμολογήσει ἐν ἐμοὶ ἔμπροσθεν τῶν ἀνθρώπων
Lk 12:8:	πᾶς ὃς ἂν ὁμολογήσῃ ἐν ἐμοὶ ἔμπροσθεν τῶν ἀνθρώπων

2 Clem. 3.2:	ὁμολογήσω αὐτὸν ἐνώπιον τοῦ πατρός μου
Mt 10:32:	ὁμολογήσω κἀγὼ ἐν αὐτῷ ἔμπροσθεν τοῦ πατρός μου
	τοῦ ἐν τοῖς οὐρανοῖς
Lk 12:8:	καὶ ὁ υἱὸς τοῦ ἀνθρώπου
	ὁμολογήσει ἐν αὐτῷ ἔμπροσθεν τῶν ἀγγέλων τοῦ θεοῦ·
Rev 3:5:	ὁμολογήσω τὸ ὄνομα αὐτοῦ ἐνώπιον τοῦ πατρός μου
	καὶ ἐνώπιον τῶν ἀγγέλων αὐτοῦ.

The similarities and dissimilarities between *2 Clem.* 3.2 and its gospel parallels resemble what has been observed in the previous chapters regarding many other sayings in the Apostolic Fathers. There are a number of minor differences in the use of adverbs, pronouns and prepositions (τόν vs. a πᾶς construction; με vs. ἐν ἐμοί; αὐτόν vs. ἐν αὐτῷ; the κἀγώ found only in

---

Köhler also thinks this is very possible (*Rezeption*, 135–36); Kelhoffer refers to *2 Clem.* 2.4 as "a citation of Mark 2.17//Matt 9.13" ("'How Soon a Book' Revisited," 6); Smith finds it "highly probable" that "Clement" depends directly upon Mark or Matthew ("Gospels in Early Christian Literature," 201); for Tuckett, "that *2 Clement* here presupposes the gospel of Matthew" is the "more economical solution" (in Gregory and Tuckett, "*2 Clement* and the Writings," 255). Hagner considers the possibility of a canonical Gospel, along with "some other written collection of the sayings of Jesus" ("Sayings," 244); Bartlet leaves the question open (*NTAF*, 133). Lightfoot suggests that either Matthew or Luke was *2 Clement*'s source, and in referring to the introductory words ἑτέρα δὲ γραφή, states: "Thus the Gospel, treated as a written document, is regarded as Scripture like the Old Testament" (*Apostolic Fathers*, 1.2:215). Lightfoot is followed by Pratscher (*Zweite Clemensbrief*, 32, n. 16), who after considering a number of possibilities leans toward Matthew (ibid., 33, 80).

[10] On the rationale for singling out the *Gospel of the Egyptians* here see sec. 9.2.8 below, on *2 Clem.* 12.2, 6.

[11] Trans. is that of Holmes, *Apostolic Fathers*, 141, as it serves to better bring out the parallelism with the gospel material than Ehrman's trans. in the LCL.

Mt), verb forms (ὁμολογήσαντά vs. ὁμολογήσει and ὁμολογήσῃ), and synonymous terms (ἐνώπιον twice vs. ἔμπροσθεν twice). There are also two
differences of greater substance in the second line of the saying, both cases
of "Clement" and Matthew agreeing against Luke: (a) the first person
ὁμολογήσω ... μου vs. Luke's third person ὁ υἱὸς τοῦ ἀνθρώπου
ὁμολογήσει, and (b) confession taking place before τοῦ πατρός μου (to
which Matthew adds τοῦ ἐν τοῖς οὐρανοῖς) vs. before Luke's τῶν
ἀγγέλων τοῦ θεοῦ.

As noted by Christopher Tuckett, these two more substantive differences are significant in that the Matthean elements that agree with "Clement" against Luke are widely held to have originated in Matthean
redaction.[12] In the opinion of most Q scholars, Luke's ὁ υἱὸς τοῦ
ἀνθρώπου ὁμολογήσει is what stood in Q, and Matthew changed it to the
first person ὁμολογήσω in his gospel. Likewise, Luke's ἔμπροσθεν τῶν
ἀγγέλων τοῦ θεοῦ was probably the reading in Q, since the τοῦ πατρός
μου is a distinctive Matthean theme, and it is difficult to imagine why Luke
would change this fatherhood language to "God's angels" if τοῦ πατρός
μου had been Q's reading. Tuckett articulates well the possible implication
of these insights: "The version in *2 Clement* thus agrees with Matthew at
just those points where Matthew has redacted the tradition. It is thus most
probable that *2 Clement* presupposes the development of the tradition after
it has gone through Matthew's editorial hand, and hence presupposes Matthew's finished gospel."[13]

The above argument for *2 Clement* presupposing the Gospel of Matthew seems sound, but it loses most of its force when one takes into account the additional parallel to *2 Clem.* 3.2b in the Book of Revelation.
Revelation 3:5 (ὁμολογήσω τὸ ὄνομα αὐτοῦ ἐνώπιον τοῦ πατρός μου καὶ
ἐνώπιον τῶν ἀγγέλων αὐτοῦ) is closer than Matthew to the wording of
2 Clement, not only sharing the Matthean similarities with *2 Clement* already noted (ὁμολογήσω and τοῦ πατρός μου), but in addition agreeing
with *2 Clement's* ἐνώπιον against Matthew and Luke's ἔμπροσθεν. The existence of a saying that both (a) circulated independently of the Gospels
and (b) is closer than the Gospels to the wording of *2 Clem.* 3.2b, makes it
unlikely that "Clement" derived this saying from Matthew or a source in-

---

[12] Tuckett, in Gregory and Tuckett, "*2 Clement* and the Writings," 257.

[13] Ibid., 258; others who hold that *2 Clement* presupposes the finished form of Matthew include Koester, *Synoptische Überlieferung*, 71–73; Massaux, *Influence*, 2:6 (directly dependent on Mt.); and Warns, "Untersuchungen," 333–48. Both Köhler
(*Rezeption*, 131–32) and Lindemann ("Apostolic Fathers and the Synoptic Problem,"
712) see it as probable. Pratscher considers it a possibility among others, but leaves it
open (*Zweite Clemensbrief*, 32, 86–87). Lightfoot represents a now outdated readiness to
find direct dependence of the Apostolic Fathers on the Gospels in suggesting that the
quotation is "A free quotation of Matt. X. 32" (*Apostolic Fathers*, 1.2:216).

fluenced by Matthean tradition.[14] It is just as likely, or perhaps more so, that Matthew, *2 Clement* and the author of Revelation all independently drew from similar or related sources of Jesus tradition.[15] Unfortunately neither the saying in *2 Clem.* 3.2 nor its parallels contain enough information to determine whether *2 Clement*'s source was oral or written, though we will revisit this issue in sec. 9.4 below.

9.2.3 2 Clement *4.2, 5*

λέγει γάρ· Οὐ πᾶς ὁ λέγων μοι· Κύριε, κύριε, σωθήσεται, ἀλλ' ὁ ποιῶν τὴν δικαιοσύνην. [5] ... εἶπεν ὁ κύριος· Ἐὰν ἦτε μετ' ἐμοῦ συνηγμένοι ἐν τῷ κόλπῳ μου καὶ μὴ ποιῆτε τὰς ἐντολάς μου, ἀποβαλῶ ὑμᾶς καὶ ἐρῶ ὑμῖν· Ὑπάγετε ἀπ' ἐμοῦ, οὐκ οἶδα ὑμᾶς, πόθεν ἐστέ, ἐργάται ἀνομίας.

For he [the Lord] says, "Not everyone who says to me 'Lord, Lord' will be saved, but only the one who practices righteousness." [5] ... the Lord said,[16] "Even if you were nestled close to my breast but did not do what I commanded, I would cast you away and say to you, 'Leave me! I do not know where you are from, you who do what is lawless.'"

---

[14] As concluded by Donfried, *Second Clement*, 61; Gregory, *Reception of Luke and Acts*, 144–45. The saying in Revelation brings together the witness before the angels of Lk 12:8 and the witness before "my Father" of Mt 10:32, yet there is no reason to view it as dependent on the Gospels or Q. Those who argue for the independence of the saying in Revelation from the Gospels include D. E. Aune, *Revelation 1–5* (WBC 52A; Dallas: Word, 1997), 226; R. Bauckham, "Synoptic Parousia Parables and the Apocalypse," *NTS* 23 (1976–77): 162–76, repr. in idem, *The Climax of Prophecy: Studies on the Book of Revelation* (Edinburgh: T&T Clark, 1993), 92–117 (here pp. 95–96 in repr.); Gregory, *Reception of Luke and Acts*, 145; A. Y. Collins, "The 'Son of Man' Tradition and the Book of Revelation," in *The Messiah: Developments in Earliest Judaism and Christianity: The First Princeton Symposium on Judaism and Christian Origins* (ed. J. H. Charlesworth; Minneapolis: Fortress, 1992), 560; L. A. Vos, *The Synoptic Traditions in the Apocalypse* (Kampen: J. H. Kok, 1965), 87–89. C. J. Hemer apparently leans toward dependence on the Synoptics, but leaves the issue unresolved: "The form of the saying [in Rev. 3:5] might be seen as a combination of Mt. 10.32 with Lk. 12.8, which concludes ἔμπροσθεν τῶν ἀγγέλων τοῦ Θεοῦ. We cannot however infer with certainty here a knowledge of either Gospel or indeed of Q" (*The Letters to the Seven Churches of Asia in Their Local Setting* [BRS; Grand Rapids: Eerdmans/Livonia: Dove, 2001], 149). G. K. Beale refers to Rev. 3:5 as "an allusion to Matt. 10:32," but it is unclear whether he means an allusion to the *Jesus saying* reflected in Mt 10:32 or to the *text* of Mt 10:32 itself (*The Book of Revelation: A Commentary on the Greek Text* [NIGTC; Grand Rapids: Eerdmans, 1999], 280). For two dissenting opinions see Koester, *Synoptische Überlieferung*, 71–73 (who finds *2 Clem.* 3.2 to be dependent on Matthew, but – significantly – does not discuss the parallel in Revelation) and Tuckett, in Gregory and Tuckett, "*2 Clement* and the Writings," 257 n. 23.

[15] This conclusion is also that of Donfried, *Second Clement*, 61; J. V. Bartlet in *NTAF*, 130 (though he does not consider the text from Revelation).

[16] I have changed Ehrman's LCL trans. "the Lord has said" to "the Lord said" in order to set up a clear distinction between the present and aorist, as this will inform the discussion later in the present chapter.

2 *Cl* 4.2:   Oὐ πᾶς ὁ λέγων μοι· Κύριε, κύριε, σωθήσεται,
Mt 7:21:   Oὐ πᾶς ὁ λέγων μοι· Κύριε κύριε,
        εἰσελεύσεται εἰς τὴν βασιλείαν τῶν οὐρανῶν,
Lk 6:46:   Τί δέ με καλεῖτε· Κύριε κύριε,

2 *Cl* 4.2:   ἀλλ' ὁ ποιῶν τὴν δικαιοσύνην
Mt 7:21:   ἀλλ' ὁ ποιῶν τὸ θέλημα τοῦ πατρός μου τοῦ ἐν τοῖς οὐρανοῖς
Lk 6:46:   καὶ οὐ ποιεῖτε ἃ λέγω;

2 *Cl* 4:5:   ἐὰν ἦτε μετ' ἐμοῦ συνηγμένοι ἐν τῷ κόλπῳ μου
"Jewish G."   ἐὰν ἦτε   ἐν τῷ κόλπῳ μου

2 *Cl* 4:5:   καὶ μὴ ποιῆτε τὰς ἐντολάς μου,
"Jewish G."   καὶ τὸ θέλεμα τοῦ πατρός μου τοῦ ἐν οὐρανοῖς μὲ ποιῆτε.

2 *Cl* 4:5:   ἀποβαλῶ ὑμᾶς
"Jewish G."   ἐκ τοῦ κόλπου μου ἀπορρίψω ὑμᾶς.

2 *Cl* 4:5:   καὶ ἐρῶ ὑμῖν·
Mt 7:23:   καὶ τότε ὁμολογήσω αὐτοῖς ὅτι
Lk 13:27:   καὶ ἐρεῖ λέγων ὑμῖν·
Jus.*1Ap*.16.11:   καὶ τότε ἐρῶ αὐτοῖς·

2 *Cl* 4:5:   ὑπάγετε ἀπ' ἐμοῦ, οὐκ οἶδα ὑμᾶς, πόθεν ἐστέ, ἐργάται ἀνομίας.
Ps. 6:9 (LXX): ἀπόστητε ἀπ' ἐμοῦ, πάντες οἱ ἐργαζόμενοι τὴν ἀνομίαν.
Mt 7:23:   οὐδέποτε ἔγνων ὑμᾶς· ἀποχωρεῖτε ἀπ' ἐμοῦ οἱ ἐργαζόμενοι τὴν ἀνομίαν.
Lk 13:27:   οὐκ οἶδα [ὑμᾶς] πόθεν ἐστέ· ἀπόστητε ἀπ' ἐμοῦ πάντες ἐργάται ἀδικίας.
Jus.*1Ap*.16.11:   ἀποχωρεῖτε ἀπ' ἐμοῦ,   ἐργάται τῆς ἀνομίας.

As argued cogently by Karl Donfried, it is very likely that the sayings in
2 Clem. 4.2 and 4.5 formed a single unit in *2 Clement*'s source.[17] This view
is buttressed especially by the two Matthean parallels to the saying(s),
which belong to a single cohesive unit of discourse (parallels to *2 Clem.* 4
in italics):

*Not everyone who says to me "Lord, Lord," will enter into the kingdom of heaven, but
only the one who does the will of my Father in heaven.* Many will say to me in that day,
"Lord, Lord, was it not in your name that we prophesied, and in your name that we cast
out demons, and in your name that we performed many mighty works?" *And then I will
declare to them, "I never knew you, leave me, you who do what is lawless!"* (Mt 7:21–
23).

---

[17] Donfried, *Second Clement*, 62–66. As will be suggested below, this need not imply
that "Clement" followed a single source, but only that in his sources the words of Jesus
in 4.2 and 4.5 formed a cohesive whole. As will be developed further in what follows, he
may have been familiar with more than one source that contained a form of the saying,
which would account for the wording of the saying and for the introductory formulas.

The unity of the parallel material in *2 Clement* has been broken up by the intervening verses 4.3–5a, which are best understood as "Clement's" exegesis of the first part of the saying in 4.2:[18]

So then, brothers, we should acknowledge him by what we do, by loving one another, by not committing adultery or slandering one another or showing envy. We should be restrained, charitable, and good. We should be sympathetic with one another and not be attached to money. By doing such deeds we acknowledge him, not by doing their opposites. And we must not fear people, but God. For this reason, when you do these things, the Lord has said .... (*2 Clem.* 4.3–5a)

As will be argued below, "Clement" probably did not derive the two-part saying in 4.2 and 5 from the Gospel of Matthew. It follows that the existence of these two blocks of material in Mt 7:21–23 and *2 Clem.* 4.2, 5 that closely parallel and yet do not directly depend upon each other, suggests that both Matthew and "Clement" accessed the material as a cohesive unit in the tradition.

Turning to the first part of the saying, in *2 Clem.* 4.2, certain scholars hold that its agreements with Matthew against Luke are indications that it presupposes Matthew's finished gospel.[19] The wording in *2 Clement* is much closer to Matthew than to Luke, sharing verbatim with Matthew the phrases οὐ πᾶς ὁ λέγων μοι· Κύριε, κύριε against Luke's τί δέ με καλεῖτε· Κύριε κύριε, and ἀλλ᾽ ὁ ποιῶν against Luke's καὶ οὐ ποιεῖτε. In addition, most scholars hold that Luke's form of the saying is nearer to what was in Q, and that Matthew's differences with Luke originated in Matthean redaction.[20] All of this could be taken to mean that *2 Clem.* 4.2 presupposes the finished form of Matthew.

The differences between *2 Clem.* 4.2 and Mt 7:21 call into question, however, the idea that "Clement" used Matthew or a source influenced by Matthew: First, "Clement" speaks of righteousness where Matthew refers to the divine will (τὴν δικαιοσύνην vs. τὸ θέλημα τοῦ πατρός μου). Second, and most importantly, the most characteristic elements of Matthean redaction in Matthew's parallel, τὴν βασιλείαν τῶν οὐρανῶν and τοῦ

---

[18] Donfried, *Second Clement*, 62.

[19] See, e.g., Köhler, *Rezeption*, 132–34 ("probable"), who is followed by Lindemann, "Apostolic Fathers and the Synoptic Problem," 713; Koester, *Synoptische Überlieferung*, 80–83; idem, *Ancient*, 356; idem, "Gospels and Gospel Traditions," 27–28; Massaux, *Influence*, 2:7–8; Tuckett in Gregory and Tuckett, "*2 Clement* and the Writings," 258–60; Lightfoot, *Apostolic Fathers*, 1.2:217; Warns, "Untersuchungen," 298–300. Pratscher considers this a possibility but leaves it undecided (*Zweite Clemensbrief*, 33, 92–93).

[20] See Koester, *Synoptische Überlieferung*, 81; idem, *Ancient*, 356; Tuckett in Gregory and Tuckett, "*2 Clement* and the Writings," 259.

πατρός μου τοῦ ἐν τοῖς οὐρανοῖς, are not found in *2 Clement*.²¹ If these Matthean elements were present in *2 Clement* it would make for a very strong argument that *2 Clement* presupposes the finished form of Matthew. As it is, their absence does not negate this argument, but it does weaken it considerably. There is nothing particularly Matthean about the remaining two phrases that *2 Clement* and Matthew do share, οὐ πᾶς ὁ λέγων μοι· Κύριε, κύριε and ἀλλ' ὁ ποιῶν. Both of these phrases could have been in a source common to both authors – whether oral or written – rather than taken by "Clement" from Matthew or a source influenced by Matthew.²²

The parallels to the second part of the saying in *2 Clem.* 4.5 are complex: There is only one known parallel to the first three lines, and its close relationship to the Gospel of Matthew makes it problematic as an independent witness to the saying. The parallel is found in a marginal gloss to Mt 7:5 in MS 1424 ("Jewish G[ospel]" in the above synopsis), prefaced by the words "The Jewish gospel [Τὸ Ἰουδαϊκόν] reads here as follows."²³ Given its nature as a marginal gloss closely associated with the Matthean text, its wording may have been influenced by Mt 7:21, especially in reading τὸ θέλεμα τοῦ πατρός μου τοῦ ἐν οὐρανοῖς in place of the τὰς ἐντολάς μου of the saying in *2 Clement*.²⁴ This diminishes the value of this gloss as an independent witness to the precise wording of the saying under consideration.

The fourth and fifth lines of *2 Clem.* 4.5 are closer to Luke than to Matthew, but this need not imply that they presuppose the finished form of Luke. These lines contain what appears to be Jesus' quotation of Psalm 6:9

---

²¹ As noted by Gregory, *Reception of Luke and Acts*, 141; Tuckett in Gregory and Tuckett, "*2 Clement* and the Writings," 259, who, however, attributes their absence to "Clement's" use of preferred vocabulary.

²² Bartlet in *NTAF* posits a non-canonical written source or oral tradition (p. 131).

²³ The marginal notations in MS 1424 provide one of the most important MSS witnesses to this so-called "Jewish" or "Hebrew" gospel, usually identified as belonging to the *Gospel of the Nazaraeans* (see Vielhauer and Strecker, "Jewish-Christian Gospels," 154–65, esp. 160; H.-J. Klauck, *Apocryphal Gospels: An Introduction* [trans. B. McNeil; London and New York: T&T Clark, 2003], 43–51, esp. 49). MS 1424 "presents the largest number, namely ten of the thirteen Judaikon readings on Mt., and for eight of them it is the sole witness" (Vielhauer and Strecker, "Jewish-Christian Gospels," 149). For a complete list of the glosses from MS 1424 attributed to the *Gospel of the Nazaraeans* see ibid., 160–62; J. K. Elliott, ed., *The Apocryphal New Testament: A Collection of Apocryphal Christian Literature in an English Translation* (Oxford: Clarendon, 1993), 13–14. See also Donfried, *Second Clement*, 63–66; Koester, *Ancient*, 356–57; Tuckett in Gregory and Tuckett, "*2 Clement* and the Writings," 262.

²⁴ Mt 7:21 reads τὸ θέλημα τοῦ πατρός μου τοῦ ἐν τοῖς οὐρανοῖς; see above synopsis where it is given as a parallel to *2 Clem.* 4.2.

(LXX).[25] Though *2 Clem.* 4.5 agrees with Lk 13:27 against the LXX, Matthew, and Justin in reading οὐκ οἶδα [ὑμᾶς] πόθεν ἐστέ, "Clement" almost certainly did not derive the citation directly from the Gospel of Luke, as Luke contains no parallel to the first three lines of *2 Clem.* 4.5 (Ἐὰν ἦτε μετ' ἐμοῦ συνηγμένοι ἐν τῷ κόλπῳ μου καὶ μὴ ποιῆτε τὰς ἐντολάς μου, ἀποβαλῶ ὑμᾶς). The agreement of *2 Clement* and Luke against the other parallels also need not imply the influence of Luke upon *2 Clement*'s sources, as there is no compelling reason to view the phrase as resulting from Lukan redaction.[26] The phrase may just as well have been in sources shared by Luke and "Clement," whether written or oral.[27] In sum, as with the first part of the saying in *2 Clem.* 4.2, there is no conclusive evidence to indicate that the second part in 4.5 presupposes a finished gospel, in this case that of Luke.[28]

9.2.4 2 Clement 5.2–4

λέγει γὰρ ὁ κύριος· Ἔσεσθε ὡς ἀρνία ἐν μέσῳ λύκων. ³ ἀποκριθεὶς δὲ ὁ Πέτρος αὐτῷ λέγει· Ἐὰν οὖν διασπαράξωσιν οἱ λύκοι τὰ ἀρνία; ⁴ εἶπεν ὁ Ἰησοῦς τῷ Πέτρῳ· Μὴ φοβείσθωσαν τὰ ἀρνία τοὺς λύκους μετὰ τὸ ἀποθανεῖν αὐτά· καὶ ὑμεῖς μὴ φοβεῖσθε τοὺς ἀποκτέννοντας ὑμᾶς καὶ μηδὲν ὑμῖν δυναμένους ποιεῖν, ἀλλὰ φοβεῖσθε τὸν μετὰ τὸ ἀποθανεῖν ὑμᾶς ἔχοντα ἐξουσίαν ψυχῆς καὶ σώματος τοῦ βαλεῖν εἰς γέενναν πυρός.

For the Lord says, "You will be like sheep in the midst of wolves." ³ But Peter replied to him, "What if the wolves rip apart the sheep?" ⁴ Jesus said to Peter, "After they are dead, the sheep should fear the wolves no longer. So too you: do not fear those who kill you

---

[25] It is to be expected that the quotation in the Gospels and other parallels would differ in wording from the LXX, since Jesus would not have spoken the words in Greek. Unless those who passed on the tradition of this saying each turned to the wording of the LXX, their renditions of it are bound to differ, especially in the oral stage.

[26] Gregory, *Reception of Luke and Acts*, 142; Köhler, *Rezeption*, 144; for differing views see Koester, *Synoptische Überlieferung*, 84; Massaux, *Influence*, 2:12–13; Roukema, "Jesus Tradition," 2132–33; Tuckett in Gregory and Tuckett, "*2 Clement* and the Writings," 263; Warns, "Untersuchungen," 326–28. A. J. Bellinzoni overreaches when he states that the witness of *2 Clem.* 4.5 "proves" the existence of a Gospel harmony before Justin's time (*Sayings of Jesus*, 25).

[27] As concluded by Donfried, *Second Clement*, 62–68; Gregory, *Reception of Luke and Acts*, 142. Pratscher suggests a source in oral tradition, a sayings-collection, or an apocryphal gospel (*Zweite Clemensbrief*, 35, 98). While it is possible that *2 Clement*'s source was the *Gospel of the Egyptians* (see sec. 9.2.8 below on *2 Clem.* 12.2, 6) as suggested by J. B. Lightfoot and others (Lightfoot, *Apostolic Fathers*, 1.2:218; Grant and Graham, *First and Second Clement*, 115), this possibility remains purely speculative.

[28] For a nuanced discussion of *2 Clem.* 4.2, 5 that arrives at conclusions similar to the above see Gregory, *Reception of Luke and Acts*, 140–42.

and then can do nothing more to you; but fear the one who, after you die, has the power to cast your body and soul into the hell of fire."[29]

2 *Clem.* 5.2:   ἔσεσθε ὡς ἀρνία   ἐν μέσῳ λύκων
Mt 10:16:   ἰδοὺ ἐγὼ ἀποστέλλω ὑμᾶς ὡς πρόβατα ἐν μέσῳ λύκων
Lk 10:3:   ὑπάγετε· ἰδοὺ ἀποστέλλω ὑμᾶς ὡς ἄρνας ἐν μέσῳ λύκων

2 *Clem.* 5.3–4a: ἀποκριθεὶς δὲ ὁ Πέτρος αὐτῷ λέγει· Ἐὰν οὖν διασπαράξωσιν οἱ
λύκοι τὰ ἀρνία; εἶπεν ὁ Ἰησοῦς τῷ Πέτρῳ· Μὴ φοβείσθωσαν
τὰ ἀρνία τοὺς λύκους μετὰ τὸ ἀποθανεῖν αὐτά·

2 *Clem.* 5.4b: καὶ ὑμεῖς μὴ φοβεῖσθε   τοὺς ἀποκτέννοντας ὑμᾶς
Just. *Apol.* 19.7:   μὴ φοβεῖσθε τοὺς ἀναιροῦντας ὑμᾶς
Ps.Clem. *Hom.* 17.5.2:   μὴ φοβηθῆτε ἀπὸ τοῦ ἀποκτέννοντος τὸ σῶμα
Mt 10:28:   καὶ μὴ φοβεῖσθε ἀπὸ τῶν ἀποκτεννόντων τὸ σῶμα,
Lk 12:4:   μὴ φοβηθῆτε ἀπὸ τῶν ἀποκτεινόντων τὸ σῶμα

2 *Clem.* 5.4c: καὶ μηδὲν ὑμῖν δυναμένους   ποιεῖν,
Just. *Apol.* 19.7:   καὶ μετὰ ταῦτα μὴ δυναμένους τι ποιῆσαι (εἶπε),
Ps.Clem. *Hom.* 17.5.2:   τῇ δὲ ψυχῇ μὴ δυναμένων ποιῆσαι·
Mt 10:28:   τὴν δὲ ψυχὴν μὴ δυναμένων ἀποκτεῖναι·
Lk 12:4:   καὶ μετὰ ταῦτα μὴ ἐχόντων περισσότερόν τι ποιῆσαι.

2 *Clem.* 5.4d: ἀλλὰ φοβεῖσθε τὸν μετὰ τὸ ἀποθανεῖν ὑμᾶς ἔχοντα ἐξουσίαν
Just. *Apol.* 19.7:   φοβήθητε δὲ τὸν μετὰ τὸ ἀποθανεῖν δυνάμενον
Ps.Clem. *Hom.* 17.5.2:   φοβήθητε δὲ τὸν δυνάμενον
Mt 10:28:   φοβεῖσθε δὲ μᾶλλον   τὸν δυνάμενον
Lk 12:5:   ὑποδείξω δὲ ὑμῖν τίνα φοβηθῆτε·
φοβήθητε τὸν μετὰ τὸ ἀποκτεῖναι   ἔχοντα ἐξουσίαν

2 *Clem.* 5.4e: ψυχῆς καὶ σώματος τοῦ βαλεῖν εἰς γέενναν πυρός
Just. *Apol.* 19.7: καὶ ψυχὴν καὶ σῶμα   εἰς γέενναν ἐμβαλεῖν.
Ps.Clem. *Hom.* 17.5.2: καὶ ψυχὴν καὶ σῶμα   εἰς τὴν γέενναν τοῦ πυρὸς βαλεῖν.
Mt 10:28:   καὶ ψυχὴν καὶ σῶμα   ἀπολέσαι ἐν γεέννῃ
Lk 12:5:   ἐμβαλεῖν εἰς τὴν γέενναν.

Second Clement 5.2–4 presents many of the same issues as *2 Clem.* 4.2, 5, the last passage considered. It agrees in minor details at times with Matthew (e.g., μὴ φοβεῖσθε vs Lk's μὴ φοβηθῆτε) and at times with Luke (e.g., ἀρνία/ ἄρνας vs. Mt's πρόβατα), at times with both (e.g., ἐν μέσῳ λύκων) and at times with neither (e.g., *2 Clem.*'s ἔσεσθε vs. the Gospels' ἀποστέλλω ὑμᾶς). It also contains a more substantive agreement with Luke against Matthew: *2 Clement* reads φοβεῖσθε τὸν μετὰ τὸ ἀποθανεῖν ὑμᾶς ἔχοντα ἐξουσίαν, much closer to Luke's φοβήθητε τὸν μετὰ τὸ ἀποκτεῖναι ἔχοντα ἐξουσίαν than to Matthew's φοβεῖσθε δὲ μᾶλλον τὸν δυνάμενον. A

---

[29] I have modified the fourth word of this translation from Ehrman's "said" (*Apostolic Fathers*, 1:171) to "says" in order to reflect the present tense of λέγει, as tenses will be important in the discussion below.

major disagreement between *2 Clement* and all the other documents in the
above synopsis is the lengthy block of unique material it contains:
ἀποκριθεὶς δὲ ὁ Πέτρος αὐτῷ λέγει· Ἐὰν οὖν διασπαράξωσιν οἱ λύκοι
τὰ ἀρνία; εἶπεν ὁ Ἰησοῦς τῷ Πέτρῳ· Μὴ φοβείσθωσαν τὰ ἀρνία τοὺς
λύκους μετὰ τὸ ἀποθανεῖν αὐτά.

The noted agreements and disagreements between *2 Clem.* 5.2–4 and its
parallels are such that it would be difficult to argue for a literary relationship among them. There is little reason to hold that "Clement" is here dependent on a harmony of Matthew and Luke,[30] as none of the agreements
between *2 Clement* and the Gospels contain elements that are unquestiona-
bly the redactional work of the evangelists. The words of A. Gregory are
pertinent here, "although parallels both of vocabulary and of content may
easily be seen between *2 Clement* and each of *Matthew* and *Luke*, uncertainty as to the precise content and vocabulary of Q means that it is much
less evident that these parallels contain redactional material from either
evangelist."[31] In addition, the agreements in wording between *2 Clem.* 5.2–
4 and either gospel are rather insignificant, are offset by a higher number
of disagreements, and could be viewed as the bare minimum necessary for
all three sources to communicate the same saying.[32] The lack of a parallel
in Justin and the Pseudo-Clementine *Homilies* to the whole first half of the
saying in *2 Clement*, together with the many differences between them in
the second half, also makes any dependence between them unlikely.

It appears that *2 Clem.* 5.2–4 represents a stream of tradition that was
separate from that of its parallels in the above synopsis. The saying in
2 Clement is a cohesive unit, the unique block of material made up of Peter's question and Jesus' initial answer being of one piece with the rest.[33]
There is no compelling reason to doubt that this is how "Clement" found it

---

[30] *Pace* Bartlet, *NTAF*, 136; Bellinzoni, *Sayings of Jesus*, 111; Koester, *Synoptische
Überlieferung*, 99; idem, "Gospels and Gospel Traditions," 31; Tuckett in Gregory and
Tuckett, "*2 Clement* and the Writings," 265–66; Warns, "Untersuchungen," 330–48. In
Massaux's view *2 Clement*'s dependence on an apocryphal source is likely, but the au-
thor of that source "may have used Mt. and Lk." (*Influence*, 2:14).

[31] Gregory, *Reception of Luke and Acts*, 144; see also Köhler, *Rezeption*, 144–46.

[32] Similarly Donfried, *Second Clement*, 69–70.

[33] The "unique block of material" in question is made up of the words, "But Peter replied to him, 'What if the wolves rip apart the sheep?' Jesus said to Peter, 'After they are
dead, the sheep should fear the wolves no longer.'" As noted by Donfried (*Second Clement*, 68), this unique dialogue "does not appear to be an afterthought ... it appears to fit
into the context smoothly"; similarly Gregory, *Reception of Luke and Acts*, 143. J. Jeremias, however, is of the opinion that the unique material points to "a not strikingly suc-
cessful combination of two separate sayings by means of an artificial connecting link"
(*Unknown Sayings* [2nd Eng. ed.], 38–39).

in his source.[34] In Matthew and Luke, which contain parallels to the first line of *2 Clem.* 5.2–4 as well as the last four, these parallels appear as separate, unconnected sayings (Mt 10:16, 28; Lk 10:3; 12:4–5). Justin Martyr and the Pseudo-Clementine *Homilies* only contain parallels to the last four lines of *2 Clem.* 5.2–4. These considerations lead to the probable conclusion that the saying in *2 Clem.* 5.2–4 was transmitted in three different forms within the tradition: one that reflected the full form of the saying as found in *2 Clement* as a single unit (attested only in *2 Clement*), a second that contained the first and the last four lines of *2 Clem.* 5.2–4, but did not connect them to each other (attested in Mt and Lk), and a third that contained only the last four lines (attested in Justin and Pseudo-Clement).[35] If this assessment is on target, it follows that neither *2 Clem.* 5.2–4 nor its sources were dependent on any of the documents represented in the above synopsis. It is not possible to specify anything further regarding *2 Clement*'s source, including whether it was written or oral.[36]

9.2.5 2 Clement 6.1–2

Λέγει δὲ ὁ κύριος· Οὐδεὶς οἰκέτης δύναται δυσὶ κυρίοις δουλεύειν. ἐὰν ἡμεῖς θέλωμεν καὶ θεῷ δουλεύειν καὶ μαμωνᾷ, ἀσύμφορον ἡμῖν ἐστίν. [2] τί γὰρ τὸ ὄφελος, ἐάν τις τὸν κόσμον ὅλον κερδήσῃ, τὴν δὲ ψυχὴν ζημιωθῇ;

[1a] But the Lord [Jesus] says, [1b] "No household servant can serve as the slave of two masters. [1c] If we wish to serve as slaves of both God and wealth, it is of no gain to us. [2] For what is the advantage of acquiring the whole world while forfeiting your life?"[37]

2 Clem. 6.1b:	Οὐδεὶς οἰκέτης δύναται δυσὶ κυρίοις δουλεύειν
Mt 6:24a:	Οὐδεὶς δύναται δυσὶ κυρίοις δουλεύειν
Lk 16:13a:	Οὐδεὶς οἰκέτης δύναται δυσὶ κυρίοις δουλεύειν
G. Thom. 47:	Οὐ δύναται δοῦλος δυσὶ κυρίοις λατρεύειν *(trans. from Coptic)*[38]

---

[34] Donfried, *Second Clement*, 68; Gregory, *Reception of Luke and Acts*, 143; Lindemann, *Clemensbriefe*, 213.

[35] Koester argues that the saying in *2 Clement* is secondary to the Gospels based on the form-critical rule that names (in this case Peter) are secondary additions to the tradition (*Synoptische Überlieferung*, 98). As noted by E. P. Sanders, however, such a "rule" does not hold, in that names can also drop out of the tradition (*Tendencies*, 10). It follows that one cannot argue on such a basis that one form of the tradition was earlier than the other.

[36] Again there are those who hold that the source was the *Gospel of the Egyptians* (e.g., Lightfoot, *Apostolic Fathers*, 1.2:219; considered by Bartlet in *NTAF*, 136), but see sec. 9.2.8 below on *2 Clem.* 12.2, 6. Others suggest the *Gospel of Peter*; see Lindemann, "Apostolic Fathers and the Synoptic Problem," 715 and literature cited in n. 112.

[37] I have changed the use of quotation marks in Ehrman's translation; for the rationale see below.

[38] Logion 47 of the *Gospel of Thomas* is extant only in Coptic; I have used the Greek translation by the Berliner Arbeitskreis für Koptisch-Gnostische Schriften, found in K. Aland, ed., *Synopsis quattuor Evangeliorum: Locis parallelis evangeliorum apocrypho-*

2 Clem. 6.1c:	ἐὰν ἡμεῖς θέλωμεν καὶ <u>θεῷ δουλεύειν καὶ μαμωνᾷ</u>, ἀσύμφορον ἡμῖν ἐστίν
Mt 6:24c:	οὐ δύνασθε <u>θεῷ δουλεύειν καὶ μαμωνᾷ.</u>
Lk 16:13c:	οὐ δύνασθε <u>θεῷ δουλεύειν καὶ μαμωνᾷ</u>

2 Clem. 6.2:	<u>τί γὰρ</u> τὸ ὄφελος, <u>ἐάν</u> τις
Mt 16:26:	<u>τί γὰρ</u> ὠφεληθήσεται ἄνθρωπος <u>ἐὰν</u>
Mk 8:36:	<u>τί γὰρ</u> ὠφελεῖ ἄνθρωπον κερδῆσαι
Lk 9:25:	<u>τί γὰρ</u> ὠφελεῖ ται ἄνθρωπος κερδήσας
Cl. *Str.* 4.112.3:	<u>τί γὰρ</u> ὄφελος, <u>ἐάν</u>
Jus. *1 Ap.* 15.12	<u>τί γὰρ</u> ὠφελεῖται ἄνθρωπος ἂν

2 Clem. 6.2:	<u>τὸν κόσμον ὅλον κερδήσῃ τὴν δὲ ψυχὴν</u> <u>ζημιωθῇ;</u>
Mt 16:26:	<u>τὸν κόσμον ὅλον κερδήσῃ τὴν δὲ ψυχὴν</u> αὐτοῦ <u>ζημιωθῇ;</u>
Mk 8:36:	<u>τὸν κόσμον ὅλον</u> καὶ <u>ζημιωθῆναι τὴν ψυχὴν</u> αὐτοῦ;
Lk 9:25:	<u>τὸν κόσμον ὅλον</u> ἑαυτὸν δὲ ἀπολέσας ἢ <u>ζημιωθείς;</u>
Cl. *Str.* 4.112.3:	<u>τὸν κόσμον</u> <u>κερδήσῃς,</u> φησί, <u>τὴν δὲ ψυχὴν</u> ἀπολέσῃς;
Jus. *1 Ap.* 15.12	<u>τὸν κόσμον ὅλον κερδήσῃ τὴν δὲ ψυχὴν</u> αὐτοῦ ἀπολέσῃ;

A basic problem confronting the interpreter here is to decide where the cited words of Jesus end and the words of "Clement" begin. Given that 6.1c is worded in the first person plural – "If we [ἡμεῖς] wish to serve as slaves of both God and wealth, it is of no gain to us [ἡμῖν]" – and is constructed quite differently than its gospel parallels, some scholars consider that this phrase is "Clement's" explanatory interjection rather than part of his citation of Jesus' words.[39] On this premise the explicit appeal to Jesus tradition would be limited to 6.1a–b and 6.2. It is probably best, however, to consider the entire passage as a citation of Jesus' words. The presence of a verbatim correspondence not just to *2 Clem.* 6.1b (Οὐδεὶς οἰκέτης δύναται δυσὶ κυρίοις δουλεύειν) but also to *2 Clem.* 6.1c (θεῷ δουλεύειν καὶ μαμωνᾷ) in the *same verse* of the two gospel parallels (Mt 6:24a,c//Lk 16:13a,c) is too much to attribute to chance. It stands to reason that if

---

rum et patrum adhibitis (15th ed., Korrigierter und um die Papyri 101–111 erweiterter Druck 2001; Stuttgart: Deutsche Bibelgesellschaft, 2001), 531. There it is spoken of as a "retranslation" on the assumption that *Thomas* goes back to a Greek *Vorlage* (p. 518). While a great majority of scholars would agree that *Thomas* was originally written in Greek, Nicholas Perrin's carefully argued theory for a Syriac original calls this into question; see his *Thomas and Tatian: The Relationship between the* Gospel of Thomas *and the* Diatessaron (SBL AcBib 5; Atlanta: Society of Biblical Literature/Leiden: Brill, 2002) and *Thomas, the Other Gospel* (London: SPCK/Louisville: Westminster John Knox, 2007). While Perrin is not the first hold this view (on others see the survey in Perrin, *Thomas and Tatian*, 29–43; and also idem, *Thomas, the Other Gospel*, 78 and n. 8), his argument for a Syriac *Vorlage* is persuasive in its wide scope and responsible treatment of the evidence, and will be preferred in the discussion that follows.

[39] So Ehrman, *Apostolic Fathers*, 1:173, where this interpretation is indicated by his use of quotation marks; see also Tuckett, in Gregory and Tuckett, "2 Clement and the Writings," 267, who considers it as a possibility.

"Clement" cites Jesus tradition paralleling the first part of Mt 6:24//Lk 16:13 in *2 Clem.* 6.1b, and follows this immediately with a statement that closely parallels the final lines of Mt 6:24//Lk 16:13 in *2 Clem.* 6.1c, that all of *2 Clem.* 6.1b–c is part of his citation of Jesus tradition that extends through 6.2.[40]

The parallels to *2 Clem.* 6.1 do not provide much evidence upon which to base a decision regarding the source of Jesus' words. Very little can be said regarding the parallel in the *Gospel of Thomas* beyond simply noting its existence. Besides being limited to a single line out of the four under consideration, *Thomas'* language is so different from that of *2 Clement* that there is no reason to hold that there is a literary relationship between them.[41] As for the Synoptic Gospels, Luke 16:13a parallels *2 Clem.* 6.1b verbatim, while Mt 6:24a, lacking the οἰκέτης, does not. It would be difficult, however, to draw any implications from the presence or absence of this single term:[42] there is nothing particularly Lukan about οἰκέτης that would lead one to argue for the presence of Lukan redaction in *2 Clem.* 6.1,[43] and the term may have been in the tradition common to Matthew and Luke (and "Clement") but been left out by the first evangelist.[44] Similarly, nothing can be said with certainty regarding *2 Clem.* 6.1c; its very different shape when compared with Mt 6:24c//Lk 16:13c may indicate that "Clement" is citing tradition, whether written or oral, that he held in common with Matthew and/or Luke, and which has undergone transformation in the process of transmission.

The evidence that *2 Clem.* 6.2 presupposes the finished form of the Gospel of Matthew is stronger but still not conclusive. Though not reflecting Mt 16:26 verbatim, 6.2 is clearly closer to its Matthean parallel than to the other gospels. Most importantly, it shares Matthew's ἐάν + subjunctive (κερδήσῃ, ζημιωθῇ) construction that almost certainly owes its presence in

---

[40] It is also possible that "Clement's" citation of Jesus' words extends beyond 6.2. The passage goes on, "But this age and the age to come are two enemies. This one preaches adultery, depravity, avarice, and deceit, but that one renounces these things. We cannot, therefore, be friends of both. We must renounce this world to obtain that one" (6.3–5). While the citation of Jesus' words may be meant to include some of this additional material, for lack of a more definitive criterion we will limit ourselves to the portion that has identifiable parallels in other known Jesus tradition (6.1–2).

[41] This would be true even if the original language of *Thomas* was Greek, but is perhaps more so if the Coptic is based on a Syriac *Vorlage* (see comments on the work of Nicholas Perrin in n. 38 on pp. 251–52 above).

[42] See Tuckett in Gregory and Tuckett, "*2 Clement* and the Writings," 267.

[43] *Pace* Massaux, *Influence*, 2:14.

[44] Cf. the similar statements in Gregory, *Reception of Luke and Acts*, 145. Lindemann also considers an origin in Matthew and Luke's common source, which for him is Q ("Apostolic Fathers and the Synoptic Problem," 715).

the first gospel to Matthew's redaction of Mark.[45] It is likely that Clement
of Alexandria and Justin Martyr provide independent witness to the influence of the Matthean form of the saying in the early church, as they also
contain an ἐάν + subjunctive construction.[46] In light of the above considerations, it is possible that *2 Clem.* 6.2, while not citing Matthew directly,
presupposes the finished form of Matthew.[47] It is also possible, however,
that the ἐάν + subjunctive construction was found in Matthew and
2 Clement's sources. The entire saying in 6.1–2 is proverbial in nature,
which would lend itself to fairly stable transmission within the oral tradition, and this may be how it became available to "Clement." We will re-
serve judgment on this issue until we have examined the other sayings.

9.2.6 2 Clement 8.5

λέγει γὰρ ὁ κύριος ἐν τῷ εὐαγγελίῳ· Εἰ τὸ μικρὸν οὐκ ἐτηρήσατε, τὸ μέγα τίς
ὑμῖν δώσει; λέγω γὰρ ὑμῖν, ὅτι ὁ πιστὸς ἐν ἐλαχίστῳ καὶ ἐν πολλῷ πιστός ἐστιν.

---

[45] Tuckett, in Gregory and Tuckett, "*2 Clement* and the Writings," 268; also Köhler,
Rezeption, 135.

[46] With variations, the most significant of which is the last word in the saying, both
of them reading ἀπόλλυμι in place of *2 Clement*'s ζημιόω. On the sources of the saying
in Justin Martyr and Clement of Alexandria see Bellinzoni, *Sayings of Jesus*, 89–90;
Tuckett, in Gregory and Tuckett, "*2 Clement* and the Writings," 268.

[47] As concluded by Koester, *Synoptische Überlieferung*, 73–74; Tuckett, in Gregory
and Tuckett, "*2 Clement* and the Writings," 268. For Massaux dependence on Mt is certain (*Influence*, 2:7–8), and while Köhler does not share Massaux's certainty, he still
views dependence on Matthew as the most probable option (*Rezeption*, 135). For Lindemann the source is either Matthew or an apocryphal gospel also cited elsewhere by
"Clement" ("Apostolic Fathers and the Synoptic Problem," 715). J. B. Lightfoot is again
representative of an older readiness to find direct dependence of the Apostolic Fathers on
the Gospels when he suggests that the quotation "may have been derived from either S.
Matthew or S. Mark, though it differs slightly from both" (*Apostolic Fathers*, 1.2:221 and
see n. 13 on p. 243 above). Similarly Bartlet concludes that "Clement knew both Matthew and Luke, or a document based on them" (*NTAF*, 134). One must also leave open
the possibility, however, that the similarities between Matthew and *2 Clement* derive
from their independent use of the same or related written sources. In Gregory's opinion it
is "possible although not certain that the saying in *2 Clement* reflects Matthean tradition,
although an independent form of the saying cannot be ruled out" (*Reception of Luke and
Acts*, 148). Hagner considers that 6.1–2 might witness either to "the fusion of material
from Matthew and Luke" or "material drawn from tradition that has similarities to the
Gospels" ("Sayings," 245). Pratscher leaves the question open (*Zweite Clemensbrief*, 33–
34, 110). We will revisit this issue in the conclusions to the present chapter.

For the Lord says in the gospel, [48] "If you do not keep what is small, who will give you what is great? For I say to you that the one who is faithful in very little is faithful also in much."

2 Clem. 8.5:   εἰ τὸ μικρὸν οὐκ ἐτηρήσατε, τὸ μέγα <u>τίς ὑμῖν δώσει</u>;
Lk 16:11:   εἰ οὖν ἐν τῷ ἀδίκῳ μαμωνᾷ πιστοὶ οὐκ ἐγένεσθε,
                          τὸ ἀληθινὸν <u>τίς ὑμῖν</u> πιστεύσει;
Lk 16:12:   καὶ εἰ ἐν τῷ ἀλλοτρίῳ πιστοὶ οὐκ ἐγένεσθε,
                          τὸ ὑμέτερον <u>τίς ὑμῖν</u> δώσει;

2 Clem. 8.5: λέγω γὰρ ὑμῖν, ὅτι <u>ὁ πιστὸς ἐν ἐλαχίστῳ καὶ ἐν πολλῷ πιστός ἐστιν</u>
Lk 16:10:   <u>ὁ πιστὸς ἐν ἐλαχίστῳ καὶ ἐν πολλῷ πιστός ἐστιν</u>
                     καὶ ὁ ἐν ἐλαχίστῳ ἄδικος καὶ ἐν πολλῷ ἄδικός ἐστιν.
Mt 25:21b, 23b: ἐπὶ ὀλίγα ἧς <u>πιστός</u>, ἐπὶ <u>πολλῶν</u> σε καταστήσω·

There is little reason to hold that this saying presupposes the finished form of the Gospels. Its overall language bears little resemblance to its gospel parallels, though the main idea it conveys is reflected in both Matthew and Luke. The obvious exception is the phrase ὁ πιστὸς ἐν ἐλαχίστῳ καὶ ἐν πολλῷ πιστός ἐστιν, which is paralleled verbatim in Luke 16:10. Though this verbatim correspondence could lead one to suppose that "Clement" was dependent (at least indirectly) upon Luke for the saying, such dependence is difficult to prove for three reasons:[49] First, it is difficult to show that this phrase resulted from Lukan redaction, in that (a) the other gospels contain no true parallels with which one might compare the passage to ascertain the influence of Luke's hand,[50] and (b) there is nothing particularly Lukan in the phrase. Second, the proverbial form of the phrase (ὁ πιστὸς ἐν ἐλαχίστῳ καὶ ἐν πολλῷ πιστός ἐστιν) makes it difficult to argue for any kind of literary dependence. Parallels in early Christian Latin literature suggest that the saying may have circulated as a proverb in the early church, which would account for the verbatim correspondence between *2 Clement* and Luke.[51] Third, the first part of the saying in *2 Clement* has

---

[48] I have changed the upper case "Gospel" in Ehrman's translation to lower case, to avoid predetermining part of the results of our investigation from the outset with the suggestion of a written gospel.

[49] On what follows see Tuckett in Gregory and Tuckett, "*2 Clement* and the Writings," 269.

[50] In Luke the saying under consideration is appended to the parable of the unjust steward (Lk 16:1–8), while in the Matthean parallel it is embedded within the parable of the talents (Mt 25:14–30), so that although the parallels from Matthew and Luke contain the same basic idea, they do not function as true parallels to each other in the synoptic tradition.

[51] Irenaeus, *Adv. Haer.* 2.34.2: et ideo dominus dicebat ingratis existentibus in eum: si in modico fideles non fuistis, quod magnum est, quis dabit vobis?; Hilary, *Epistula seu libellus*, 1: si in modico fideles non fuistis, quod maius est, quis dabit vobis? In A. Jülicher's view it was a common maxim (*Die Gleichnisreden Jesu*, Vol. 2 [Darmstadt:

no Lukan parallel, which makes it very unlikely that "Clement" is citing Lukan tradition.[52] This third point is strengthened by the observation that "Clement" does not take up the second part of the saying in Luke 16:10 (καὶ ὁ ἐν ἐλαχίστῳ ἄδικος καὶ ἐν πολλῷ ἄδικός ἐστιν).[53] In sum, it is almost certain that *2 Clem.* 8.5 is not a direct quotation from Luke, and it is also highly unlikely that it presupposes the finished form of Luke.[54]

The words that introduce the saying in *2 Clem.* 8.5 are potentially relevant to a discussion of sources: λέγει γὰρ ὁ κύριος ἐν τῷ εὐαγγελίῳ ("For the Lord says in the gospel"). What the specification ἐν τῷ εὐαγγελίῳ might imply, however, is not clear. During this period the meaning of the term εὐαγγέλιον was fairly ambiguous: it could mean (a) in general terms either "the good news" proclaimed by Jesus or the oral proclamation about Jesus in the early church,[55] or (b) beginning in this period and more common in later decades, specifically the four written narratives about Jesus' life that became the canonical Gospels.[56] It is not possible to determine conclusively how the use of εὐαγγέλιον in *2 Clement* fits into this overall picture. Based on our argument above, however, if *2 Clement*'s source was written – and it may not have been – this writing was probably not identical with the Gospel of Luke or any of the other canonical gospels.[57] We will take up the topic of the introductory formula again before the conclusion of this chapter.

Wissenschaftliche Buchgesellschaft, 1963], 508, and he is cited and followed by Donfried, *Second Clement*, 72; see also Tuckett, in Gregory and Tuckett, "*2 Clement* and the Writings," 269.

[52] J. V. Bartlet in *NTAF*, 133; Gregory, *Reception of Luke and Acts*, 137.

[53] Gregory, *Reception of Luke and Acts*, 137.

[54] As concluded also by Donfried, *Second Clement*, 72–73; Gregory, *Reception of Luke and Acts*, 137; Köhler, *Rezeption*, 146. Roukema ("Jesus Tradition," 2131–32) and Smith ("Gospels in Early Christian Literature," 202) leave the issue open. For different opinions see Lightfoot, *Apostolic Fathers*, 1.2:227; Warns, "Untersuchungen," 354–57. Massaux suggests an apocryphal source, but one possibly influenced by Luke (*Influence*, 2:15).

[55] Donfried takes the reference to ἐν τῷ εὐαγγελίῳ in 8.5 in this sense, as referring to "the oral message of salvation, rather than as a designation for a written book" (*Second Clement*, 72); also Hagner, "Sayings," 245; Massaux, *Influence*, 2:15.

[56] For discussions on the use of εὐαγγέλιον in the early church see Koester, *Synoptische Überlieferung*, 6–12; idem, *Ancient*, 4–23 and literature cited on p. 1, n. 1 (pp. 7–8, 14–20 deal specifically with the term in the Apostolic Fathers); Stanton, "Matthew: βίβλος, εὐαγγέλιον, or βίος?"; Harnack, "Gospel." The argument that the word εὐαγγέλιον during this period begins to apply to written Gospels can be somewhat circular, in that it depends upon statements such as the one under discussion in *2 Clem.* 8.5 – but precisely the nature and identity of the source referred to is the issue.

[57] Those who argue that εὐαγγέλιον here refers to a written document of some sort, but not the canonical Gospels, include Gregory, *Reception of Luke and Acts*, 137; Kelhoffer, "'How Soon a Book' Revisited," 14–15; Lindemann, *Clemensbriefe*, 224; Pratscher,

9.2.7 2 Clement 9.11

καὶ γὰρ εἶπεν ὁ κύριος· Ἀδελφοί μου οὗτοί εἰσιν οἱ ποιοῦντες τὸ θέλημα τοῦ πατρός μου.

For the Lord also said, "My brothers are those who do the will of my Father."

2 Clem. 9.11:	<u>ἀδελφοί μου οὗτοί εἰσιν οἱ ποιοῦντες τὸ θέλημα τοῦ πατρός μου</u>
Mt 12:50:	ὅστις γὰρ ἂν <u>ποιήσῃ</u> <u>τὸ θέλημα τοῦ πατρός μου</u>
	τοῦ ἐν οὐρανοῖς αὐτός <u>μου ἀδελφὸς</u> καὶ ἀδελφὴ καὶ μήτηρ ἐστίν
Mk 3:35:	ὃς [γὰρ] ἂν <u>ποιήσῃ τὸ θέλημα τοῦ</u> θεοῦ,
	οὗτος <u>ἀδελφός μου</u> καὶ ἀδελφὴ καὶ μήτηρ ἐστίν
Lk 8:21:	μήτηρ μου καὶ <u>ἀδελφοί μου οὗτοί εἰσιν οἱ</u>
	τὸν λόγον τοῦ θεοῦ ἀκούοντες καὶ <u>ποιοῦντες</u>
G.Ebion.:	<u>οὗτοί εἰσιν οἱ ἀδελφοί μου</u> καὶ ἡ μήτηρ καὶ ἀδελφαί
	<u>οἱ ποιοῦντες τὰ θελήματα τοῦ πατρός μου</u> [58]
G.Thom. 99.2:	ὅιδε <u>οἱ ποιοῦντες τὸ θέλημα τοῦ πατρός μου,</u>
	<u>οὗτοί εἰσιν οἱ ἀδελφοί μου</u> καὶ ἡ μήτηρ μου (trans. from Coptic)[59]
Clem. Alex., Ecl.	
Proph. 20.3:	<u>ἀδελφοί μου</u> γάρ, φησὶν ὁ κύριος,
	καὶ συγκληρονόμοι <u>οἱ ποιοῦντες τὸ θέλημα τοῦ πατρός μου</u>

This saying in *2 Clem.* 9.11 contains a number of elements that could be interpreted as pointing to dependence upon the Gospels. *Second Clement* agrees with Matthew's redaction of Mark in the phrase τὸ θέλημα τοῦ πατρός μου, and also agrees with Luke's redaction of Mark both in the phrase ἀδελφοί μου οὗτοί εἰσιν οἱ and in the word ποιοῦντες (though

---

Zweite Clemensbrief, 35, 36, 132; Tuckett, in Gregory and Tuckett, "2 *Clement* and the Writings," 269. *Pace* Donfried, who holds that "Clement" is citing oral tradition (*Second Clement*, 72) and Stanton, who holds that he is citing the Gospel of Luke ("Matthew: βίβλος, εὐαγγέλιον, or βίος?," 1191; idem, *Jesus and Gospel*, 54, 79). Koester considers the possibility that the sayings of Jesus in *2 Clement* derive from a sayings collection that was based upon Mt and Lk, but concludes "It must remain highly unlikely, though by no means impossible, that such a sayings collection was called a 'gospel'" (*Ancient*, 18; similarly in idem, *Synoptische Überlieferung*, 11). Hagner states that "ἐν τῷ εὐαγγελίῳ here probably refers to gospel tradition rather than any specific Gospel" and continues, "the two sayings involve the kind of terse parallelism that could easily be explained as the result of oral transmission" ("Sayings," 244–45). It is quite likely that, if the saying derived from a written source, the differences between it and Luke and its other parallels originated within the context of the oral transmission of the tradition.

[58] Text cited in Epiphanius of Salamis, *Panarion* 30.14.5.

[59] Logion 99 is only extant in Coptic; this Greek translation is by the Berliner Arbeitskreis für Koptisch-Gnostische Schriften, in Aland, *Synopsis quattuor Evangeliorum*, 542. Given that the Greek of this logion is a translation I have chosen to underline with a broken rather than a full line. It is important to note that the Arbeitskreis' choice of Greek wording may have been influenced by the Gospel parallels under the assumption that *Thomas'* Vorlage was Greek. It might look different if one approached the task with the assumption of a Syriac *Vorlage* (see comments on the work of Nicholas Perrin in n. 38 on pp. 251–52 above).

unlike in *2 Clement*, in Luke these two are separated by the intervening words τὸν λόγον τοῦ θεοῦ ἀκούοντες καί). A majority of scholars is of the opinion that these elements in *2 Clem.* 9.11 originated in the redactional work of the evangelists, which implies that *2 Clement* presupposes the finished gospels of Matthew and Luke.[60]

It is also possible, however, that "Clement" is dependent upon a source held in common with Matthew and Luke and that influenced the evangelists' redaction of Mark – in which case *2 Clement* would not presuppose the finished form of the Gospels. That this is the case is suggested by two main considerations: First, by the absence of any "sister" or "mother" language in *2 Clement*. If this language was found in Mark but not in the other source held in common by Matthew, Luke and *2 Clement*, then it is simple enough to explain its presence or absence in the latter three documents: Matthew follows Mark in mentioning both "mother" and "sister," Luke follows Mark to a certain extent in mentioning "mother" but – as in his other source – leaves out "sister" ("sister" would have been implied anyhow in the inclusive ἀδελφοί), and "Clement" mentions neither "mother" nor "sister" because they were not in his source. Otherwise one would have to explain why, if "Clement" is following both Matthew and Luke, or a third source that followed them both, he does not use the "mother" and/or "sister" language shared at least partially by both evangelists.

Secondly, that "Clement" is not dependent upon Matthew and Luke is suggested by the absence in *2 Clement* of key redactional features of the evangelists. In relation to Luke, while *2 Clem.* 9.11 shares the phrase ἀδελφοί μου οὗτοί εἰσιν οἱ and the word ποιοῦντες with Lk 8:21, it does not share Luke's pairing of hearing and doing the word of God, τὸν λόγον τοῦ θεοῦ ἀκούοντες καὶ ποιοῦντες, instead speaking of those who "do the will of my father" (ποιοῦντες τὸ θέλημα τοῦ πατρός μου). The pairing of hearing and doing the word of God is uniquely important in Luke's context, as he has made it the controlling thought for all of 8:4–21 in the way he has rearranged and edited his Markan source.[61] In 8:4–15 Jesus gives and explains the parable of the sower – better thought of in Luke as the "parable of the seed" because of its emphasis on the word/seed[62] – culmi-

---

[60] Donfried, *Second Clement*, 73; Gregory, *Reception of Luke and Acts*, 147–48; Köhler, *Rezeption*, 137–39 ("very possible"); Koester, *Synoptische Überlieferung*, 79; Massaux, *Influence*, 2:910; Tuckett, in Gregory and Tuckett, "2 *Clement* and the Writings," 270, who is followed by Lindemann, "Apostolic Fathers and the Synoptic Problem," 717.

[61] As commonly recognized among commentators; see, e.g., F. Bovon, *Luke 1*, 316; Fitzmyer, *Luke I–IX*, 723; Green, *Luke*, 321–23; Nolland, *Luke 1–9:20*, 370–71.

[62] J. Dupont, "La Parabole du Semeur dans la version de Luc," in *Apophoreta: Festschrift für Ernst Haenchen zu seinem siebzigsten Geburtstag am 10. Dezember 1964* (ed. W. Eltester and F. H. Kettler; BZNW 30; Berlin: Alfred Töpelmann, 1964), 97–98.

nating with the paradigm of true discipleship in 8:15: "as for [the seed] in the good soil, these are those who *upon hearing the word*, hold it fast in a worthy and good heart, and *bear fruit with patience*." The emphasis upon the word is found again in 8:18, "consider therefore *how you hear ....*" When in 8:21, then, we arrive at the statement "My mother and brothers are those who the word of God [both] *hear and do*,"[63] the pairing of hearing and doing is more than an isolated Lukan redactional feature; it is a Lukan emphasis woven into all of 8:4–21.[64] If this important Lukan emphasis were present in the wording of *2 Clem.* 9.11, one could then speak with confidence of a redactional feature pointing to *2 Clement*'s dependence on Luke. Its absence does not negate dependence, but it does put the agreements between *2 Clem.* 9.11 and Lk 8:21 in perspective: these agreements are not particularly Lukan, and may have simply arisen from shared sources.

The same is true, though to a lesser extent, in relation to Matthew. *Second Clement* shares Mt 12:50's τοῦ πατρός μου, but does not share the Matthean qualifier τοῦ ἐν οὐρανοῖς. While both πατὴρ ὁ ἐν (τοῖς) οὐρανοῖς and τοῦ πατρός μου are frequent Matthean redactional features,[65] the former is more truly Matthean than the latter. Outside of Matthew the phrase "Father in heaven" is found in the Synoptics only once, in Mk 11:25 (//Mt 21:14), and the similar phrase "heavenly Father" only once, in Lk 11:13 (//Mt 7:11), while in Matthew they occur twenty times, so that

---

[63] The awkward English is intended to better capture the emphasis in the Greek, τὸν λόγον τοῦ θεοῦ ἀκούοντες καὶ ποιοῦντες.

[64] As J. Fitzmyer notes regarding 8:21 in light of its wider context, "Luke has adapted the criterion of discipleship to suit this section of his Gospel, especially to 8:11b,15 (hearing the word of God and bearing fruit); his emphasis is thus quite different [from Mark's]." (*Luke I–IX*, 725). See also Marshall, "Thus Luke stresses the need to hear the message of Jesus and respond to it ..." (*Luke*, 332); Dupont, "Parabole du Semeur," 97–99, 108; Nolland, *Luke 1–9:20*, 395. In W. C. Robinson, Jr.'s view, Luke's emphasis on hearing and doing in Lk 8:4–21 reflects his concern for asserting the authority of the church's preaching, as well as the danger inherent in rejecting it ("On Preaching the Word of God [Luke 8:4–21]," in *Studies in Luke-Acts: Essays Presented in Honor of Paul Schubert* [ed. L. E. Keck and J. L. Martyn; Nashville: Abingdon, 1966], 131–38, esp. 136).

[65] That these are part of the characteristically Matthean vocabulary is well known, and need not be belabored here. See especially Matthew's use of "doing the will of my/your Father in heaven" in Mt 7:21: Οὐ πᾶς ὁ λέγων μοι· κύριε κύριε, εἰσελεύσεται εἰς τὴν βασιλείαν τῶν οὐρανῶν, ἀλλ' ὁ ποιῶν τὸ θέλημα τοῦ πατρός μου τοῦ ἐν τοῖς οὐρανοῖς and 18:14: οὕτως οὐκ ἔστιν θέλημα ἔμπροσθεν τοῦ πατρὸς ὑμῶν τοῦ ἐν οὐρανοῖς ἵνα ἀπόληται ἓν τῶν μικρῶν τούτων. On Matthew's use of the phrase "Father in heaven" or "heavenly Father" see Allen, *Matthew*, lvi, 44; Luz, *Matthew 1–7*, 34. On the phrase πατήρ μου/ὑμῶν etc. in Matthew see Allen, *Matthew*, lvi; Gundry, *Matthew*, 250; Hagner, *Matthew 1–13*, 101; Luz, *Matthew 1–7*, 35.

the idea these phrases contain is truly Matthean.[66] In contrast, outside of Matthew the phrase τοῦ πατρός μου is found four times in Luke, and – significantly – two of these occurrences are found in the double tradition (material shared by Matthew and Luke not derived from Mark).[67] Since τοῦ πατρός μου is not uncommon in the sources shared by Matthew and Luke, and the more uniquely Matthean qualifier τοῦ ἐν οὐρανοῖς is not reflected in 2 *Clement*, one may tentatively surmise that the similarities between 2 *Clem.* 9.11 and Mt 12:50 arose not from literary dependence between them but from their use of common sources.

The non-canonical parallels to 2 *Clem.* 9.11 contribute no additional evidence to the discussion of sources. Some scholars who hold that 2 *Clement* depends on a harmony of Matthew and Luke make a similar case for Clement of Alexandria, the *Gospel of the Ebionites* and the *Gospel of Thomas*: they point to redactional prints from the evangelists in these three documents similar to those noted above, and on this basis argue that they also depend on a harmony of the Gospels.[68] As argued above, however, the so-called "redactional prints" may have originated not with the evangelists but from shared sources, and one could argue that the same is true of these features in the non-canonical parallels. In addition, the theory that the non-canonical parallels derive from a harmony of Matthew and Luke does not explain all of the elements in the parallels, such as the mention of καὶ ἀδελφαί in the *Gospel of the Ebionites*, found in the Synoptic parallels only in Mark, and Clement of Alexandria's καὶ συγκληρονόμοι, without parallel in any of the other documents. The one line found consistently in all the non-canonical writings under consideration (including 2 *Clement*), with but slight variations in the *Gospel of the Ebionites*, is οἱ ποιοῦντες τὸ θέλημα τοῦ πατρός μου (*G. Ebion.*: οἱ ποιοῦντες τὰ θελήματα τοῦ πατρός μου). This line, which is the core of the saying under consideration, could easily retain this basic form in the context of oral transmission, so that one need not argue for literary dependence upon the Gospels to explain its presence in these writings.

In short, the source behind 2 *Clem.* 9.11 remains an open question. Though we tentatively conclude that there is insufficient reason to hold that it is dependent on a gospels harmony, this does not resolve the issue of

---

[66] Not to suggest that the idea *originated* with Matthew – its common attestation in rabbinic writings would suggest otherwise; see Allen, *Matthew*, 44; Luz, *Matthew 1–7*, 315–16 and nn. 67–68. Matthew uses the phrase "Father in heaven" or "heavenly Father" in 5:16, 45, 48; 6:1, 9, 14, 26, 32; 7:11, 21; 10:32, 33; 12:50; 15:13; 16:17; 18:10, 14, 19, 35; 23:9.

[67] Lk 2:49; 10:22 (//Mt 11:27); 22:29 (cf. Mt 19:28//Lk 22:28–30); 24:49; see also 15:17. It is found 16 times in Matthew (see Davies and Allison, *Matthew*, 1:79).

[68] Donfried, *Second Clement*, 73; Gregory, *Reception of Luke and Acts*, 147–48; Tuckett, in Gregory and Tuckett, "2 *Clement* and the Writings," 270–71.

its source. Nor is there any consensus in this regard among scholars: besides those who hold the theory of a gospels harmony,[69] others have (for
the most part cautiously) suggested a number of alternatives, including direct use of the Gospels,[70] oral tradition,[71] or an apocryphal gospel,[72] while
some scholars simply note the various parallels and leave the source unde-
termined.[73] For now we must move on, though we will revisit the question
of sources below.

9.2.8 2 Clement *12.2, 6*

ἐπερωτηθεὶς γὰρ αὐτὸς ὁ κύριος ὑπό τινος, πότε ἥξει αὐτοῦ ἡ βασιλεία, εἶπεν·
"Ὅταν ἔσται τὰ δύο ἕν, καὶ τὸ ἔξω ὡς τὸ ἔσω, καὶ τὸ ἄρσεν μετὰ τῆς θηλείας οὔτε
ἄρσεν οὔτε θῆλυ. [6] ... ταῦτα ὑμῶν ποιούντων, φησίν, ἐλεύσεται ἡ βασιλεία τοῦ
πατρός μου.

For when the Lord himself was asked by someone when his kingdom would come, he
said, "When the two are one, and the outside like the inside, and the male with the female
is neither male nor female' '... When you do these things,' he says, 'the kingdom of my
Father will come.'"

Clement of Alexandria, *Strom.* 3.92.2

(Therefore Cassianus now says,) "When Salome asked when what she had inquired about
would be known, the Lord said, 'When you have trampled on the garment of shame and
when the two become one and the male with the female (is) neither male nor female.'"

---

[69] Koester, *Synoptische Überlieferung*, 79, followed by Donfried, *Second Clement*,
73, n. 2; Gregory, *Reception of Luke and Acts*, 147–48; Lindemann, "Apostolic Fathers
and the Synoptic Problem," 717; Tuckett, in Gregory and Tuckett, "*2 Clement* and the
Writings," 270–71.

[70] Massaux, *Influence*, 2:9–10, included in his treatment of "Texts [from *2 Clement*]
in Which the Literary Influence of Matthew is Certain" (pp. 3–10); Köhler argues for a
"free quotation" from Mt, with any reference to Lk possible but not necessary (*Rezeption*,
138–39), and he is followed by Lindemann (*Clemensbriefe*, 229). In Hagner's view 9.11
"could be explained as a mixture of Luke 8:21 and Matt 12:49ff," but he also considers
the option of oral tradition ("Sayings," 245).

[71] Hagner considers this as a possibility ("Sayings," 245).

[72] Knopf, *Lehre, Clemensbriefe*, 167; Pratscher, *Zweite Clemensbrief*, 143; Bartlet
leans in this direction after considering 9.11 together with 4.5, 5.2–4, and 8.5 (*NTAF*,
134).

[73] Metzger echoes Bartlet's assessment regarding a fusion of Luke's structure with
the phrasing of Matthew, but does not suggest where this fusion took place (*Canon*, 68;
cf. Bartlet, in *NTAF*, 134: "a fusion of the structure of Luke with the phrasing of Matthew"). Grant and Graham note that the saying "roughly parallel to Matthew 12:50, perhaps mixed with Luke 8:21" (*First and Second Clement*, 120), but go no further in
identifying a source.

Now in the first place we have not this word in the four Gospels that have been handed down to us, but in the Gospel of the Egyptians.[74]

Gos. Thom. 22.4–7

Jesus said to them, "When you make the two into one, and when you make the inner like the outer and the outer like the inner, and the upper like the lower, and when you make male and female into a single one, so that the male will not be male nor the female be female, when you make eyes in place of an eye, a hand in place of a hand, a foot in place of a foot, an image in place of an image, then you will enter [the kingdom]."[75]

2 Clem. 12.2, 6

Ἐπερωτηθεὶς γὰρ αὐτὸς ὁ κύριος ὑπό τινος, πότε ἥξει αὐτοῦ ἡ βασιλεία, εἶπεν· ὅταν ἔσται τὰ δύο ἕν, καὶ τὸ ἔξω ὡς τὸ ἔσω, καὶ τὸ ἄρσεν μετὰ τῆς θηλείας οὔτε ἄρσεν οὔτε θῆλυ. ... ταῦτα ὑμῶν ποιούντων, φησίν, ἐλεύσεται ἡ βασιλεία τοῦ πατρός μου.

Clement of Alexandria, *Strom.* 3.92.2

πυνθανομένης τῆς Σαλώμης πότε γνωσθήσεται τὰ περὶ ὧν ἤρετο, ἔφη ὁ κύριος· ὅταν τὸ τῆς αἰσχύνης ἔνδυμα πατήσητε καὶ ὅταν γένηται τὰ δύο ἕν, καὶ τὸ ἄρρεν μετὰ τῆς θηλείας οὔτε ἄρρεν οὔτε θῆλυ. πρῶτον μὲν οὖν ἐν τοῖς παραδεδομένοις ἡμῖν τέτταρσιν εὐαγγελίοις οὐκ ἔχομεν τὸ ῥητόν, ἀλλ᾽ ἐν τῷ Κατ᾽ Αἰγυπτίους.

Gos. Thom. 22.4–7 *(translation from the Coptic)*[76]

εἶπεν Ἰησοῦς αὐτοῖς· ὅταν ποιήσητε τὰ δύο εἰς ἕν καὶ ποιήσητε τὰ ἔσω ὡς τὰ ἔξω καὶ τὰ ἔξω ὡς τὸ ἔσω καὶ τὰ ἄνω ὡς τὰ κάτω καὶ ἵνα ποιήσητε τὸ ἄρσεν καὶ τὸ θῆλυ εἰς τὸ ἕν ἵνα τὸ ἄρσεν οὐ ποιήσῃ ἄρσεν (καὶ) τὸ θῆλυ οὐ ποιήσῃ θῆλυ ὅταν ποιήσητε ὀφθαλμοὺς ἀντὶ ὀφθαλμοῦ καὶ χεῖρα ἀντὶ χειρὸς καὶ πόδα ἀντὶ ποδός, εἰκόνα ἀντὶ εἰκόνος τότε εἰσελεύσεσθε εἰς [τὴν βασιλείαν].

The similarities between *2 Clem.* 12.2, 6 and its parallels in Clement of Alexandria and the *Gospel of Thomas* suggest that they are somehow related, thought it is highly unlikely that any of the texts depends directly upon the others. In what follows we will point out both the similarities and the differences between the texts, bringing in an additional text from *Thomas* to bear on the discussion. We will see that while the sources for the Jesus tra-

---

[74] Trans. is ed. by R. McL. Wilson, from W. Schneemelcher, "The Gospel of the Egyptians," in *New Testament Apocrypha* (ed. Schneemelcher), 1:211.

[75] Trans. is from M. Meyer, "The Gospel of Thomas with the Greek Gospel of Thomas," in *The Nag Hammadi Scriptures: The International Edition* (ed. M. Meyer; New York: Harper One, 2007), 142–43.

[76] Logion 22 is only extant in Coptic; this Greek retranslation is by the Berliner Arbeitskreis für Koptisch-Gnostische Schriften, in Aland, *Synopsis quattuor Evangeliorum*, 526. As already mentioned in other footnotes, the Arbeitskreis worked under the assumption of a Greek *Vorlage* for *Thomas*, but N. Perrin has developed a convincing argument in favor of a Syriac original (see n. 38 on pp. 251–52 above), that will be presupposed in the discussion that follows.

dition in these texts ultimately remains an open question, all three probably reflect independent contact with a common tradition.

The similarity between the sayings in *2 Clement* and Clement of Alexandria is obvious in one line of text, conflated here with variations indicated by a forward slash: ὅταν γένηται/ἔσται τὰ δύο ἕν, καὶ τὸ ἄρρεν/ἄρσεν μετὰ τῆς θηλείας οὔτε ἄρρεν/ἄρσεν οὔτε θῆλυ. Within this line the similarity of wording is almost verbatim, the only minor differences being *2 Clement*'s indicative future ἔσται in place of Clement of Alexandria's subjunctive aorist γένηται, and the two occurrences of ἄρσεν in *2 Clement* where Clement of Alexandria reads ἄρρεν. Clearly one is dealing with the same saying reflected in both texts.

That this is not a case of direct literary dependence, however, is suggested by the more substantial differences between the two texts. First, the settings for the sayings differ: while the saying in *2 Clement* relates to the coming of the kingdom, in Clement of Alexandria it has to do with attaining knowledge on an unspecified matter.[77] Second, the καὶ τὸ ἔξω ὡς τὸ ἔσω in *2 Clement*'s saying is completely missing from Clement of Alexandria. Third, *2 Clement* contains no reference to Clement of Alexandria's language of trampling on garments of shame, ὅταν τὸ τῆς αἰσχύνης ἔνδυμα πατήσητε. Given these considerations, literary dependence between the two documents is unlikely.

The relationship between *2 Clem.* 12.2, 6 and *Gospel of Thomas* 22.4–7 is difficult to analyze in detail, given that this portion of *Thomas* is extant only in Coptic. A consideration of the content of the saying(s) in both documents, however, leads to conclusions similar to those we arrived at in considering the parallel in Clement of Alexandria. As with the latter, similarities between *2 Clement* and *Thomas* include references to the two becoming one, and the male with the female no longer being male nor female. *Thomas* also shares two elements with *2 Clement* not found in Clement of Alexandria: the reference to the outside becoming like the inside, and a context related to the coming of the kingdom.[78] *Thomas* contains additional elements, however, not found in *2 Clement*: the references to making the inner like the outer, the upper like the lower, eyes in place of

---

[77] Donfried, *Second Clement*, 76. T. Baarda notes, however, that wider references in Clement of Alexandria's *Stromata* may serve to place this saying in the context of a conversation between Salome and Jesus regarding the consummation, so that the unspecified matter in the text under consideration may actually be the coming of the kingdom; see T. Baarda, "2 Clement 12 and the Sayings of Jesus," in *Logia: Les Paroles de Jésus – The Sayings of Jesus: Mémorial Joseph Coppens* (ed. J. Delobel; BETL 59; Leuven: Leuven University Press and Peeters, 1982), 529–56; repr. in *Early Transmission of Words of Jesus: Thomas, Tatian and the Text of the New Testament* (Amsterdam: Vrije Universiteit, 1983), 261–88 (p. 273; references here and below are to the reprint).

[78] Though see comments on Baarda in the immediately preceding note.

an eye, a hand in place of a hand, a foot in place of a foot, and an image in place of an image.

The longer saying in *Thomas* clearly has some affinities, then, with the saying in *2 Clement*, but there is little to indicate that the two documents are related at the literary level. It is certainly possible that either (a) *2 Clement* is dependent on a Greek translation of *Thomas*,[79] and "Clement" left out a considerable portion of the saying as found in his source, or (b) the compiler of *Thomas* depended in part on *2 Clement* for the saying under consideration, supplementing what he found in *2 Clement* for this saying with material from other sources. It is impossible to verify either of these possibilities, however, the basic problem of lack of evidence being compounded further by the limitations of comparing the Greek to the Coptic. It is also much simpler to view the similarities and differences between the parallels as pointing to their independent use either of a common tradition or of divergent traditions that at some point shared a common history, a view that is also more likely.[80]

The likelihood that at least *Thomas* and Clement of Alexandria depend on a common tradition (or traditions with a common history) is bolstered by another text in *Thomas* that we have not yet considered:

Gos. Thom. 37 (partial Greek text from POxy 655 col. i, 17–col. ii, 1)

λέγουσιν αὐτῷ οἱ μαθηταὶ αὐτοῦ· πότε ἡμεῖν ἐμφανὴς ἔσει, καὶ πότε σε ὀψόμεθα; λέγει· ὅταν ἐκδύσησθε καὶ μὴ αἰσχυνθῆτε [- - - οὐδὲ Φοβη]θ[ήσεσθε].

Gos. Thom. 37

His disciples said, "When will you appear to us and when shall we see you?" Jesus said: "When you strip without being ashamed and you take your clothes and put them under your feet like little children and trample them, then [you] will see the child of the living one and you will not be afraid."[81]

This additional text from *Thomas* is important because it both mentions the trampling of garments and uses language of "shame," two elements also found in the parallel under consideration from Clement of Alexandria, "When you have trampled on the garment of shame ..." (*Strom.* 3.92.2). Again, the level of similarity between the saying in *Thomas* and the *Stromateis* is not one that would suggest literary dependence, but the additional parallel strengthens the possibility that they shared a common source, or had access to sources that were connected at some point in the history of their transmission.

---

[79] This statement is based on the assumption that *Thomas*' *Vorlage* was in Syriac rather than Greek (see n. 38 on pp. 251–52 above).

[80] As concluded also by Donfried, *Second Clement*, 76.

[81] Trans. is that of Meyer, "Gospel of Thomas," 144; cf. ibid., 155.

To sum up the discussion so far, though the parallels to *2 Clem.* 12.2, 6 show little evidence of literary interdependence (among themselves or with *2 Clement*), it does seem quite likely that together *2 Clement*, Clement of Alexandria, and the *Gospel of Thomas* attest either to a common source, or to sources that point back to a common history.

Can one go further and identify a possible source for at least some of these parallels? The only likely candidate for such a source, the *Gospel of the Egyptians* mentioned by Clement of Alexandria,[82] turns out to be un-verifiable. Immediately after citing the Jesus saying under consideration, Clement of Alexandria states: "Now in the first place we have not this word in the four Gospels that have been handed down to us, but in the Gospel of the Egyptians [πρῶτον μὲν οὖν ἐν τοῖς παραδεδομένοις ἡμῖν τέτταρσιν εὐαγγελίοις οὐκ ἔχομεν τὸ ῥητόν, ἀλλ' ἐν τῷ Κατ' Αἰγυπτίους]" (*Strom.* 3.92.2). A little further on he refers to the same passage with the words, "the words spoken to Salome, which we have mentioned previously. I fancy the passage comes from the *Gospel according to the Eyptians*."[83] Clement of Alexandria does not, however, *cite* the saying from the *Gospel of the Egyptians*, but from Julius Cassian's *On Self-Control* or *On Celibacy*, as can be gathered from the wider context of *Strom.* 3.92 and his introduction to the saying, "Therefore Cassianus now says ...."[84] Although one cannot be certain, there is little reason to doubt Clement of Alexandria's statement that the *Gospel of the Egyptians* contained a saying similar to the one in *2 Clem.* 12.2, 6. There is no way, however, to ascertain either (a) how close the saying in the *Gospel of the Egyptians* was in wording and content to the saying in Cassian (since neither document is extant), or (b) how much of the saying in Cassian was included in Clement of Alexandria's quotation. It is possible, e.g., that in his writings Cassian cited only part of a saying that in its fullest form was closer to its two parallels in *Thomas*, or that Clement of Alexandria cited only that part of the saying found in Cassian's writings that fit his purposes, so that the full saying in Cassian looked quite different than it has

---

[82] Lightfoot attributes not only the source of *2 Clem.* 12.2, 6 but also that of other passages in *2 Clement* to the *Gospel of the Egyptians* (*Apostolic Fathers*, 1.2:236–38).

[83] *Strom.* 3.63.1; trans. is by J. Ferguson, in *Clement of Alexandria: Stromateis: Books One to Three* (FC 85; Washington, D. C.: Catholic University of America Press, 1991), 295.

[84] In *Strom.* 3.91.1 Clement states, "In such ways Julius Cassian, the founder of Docetism, argues his case. Anyway, in his book *On Self-Control* or *On Celibacy* he says ...," and later "In an effort to defend his godless opinions he adds ...," followed by another quote from Cassian (3.92.1). It is likely, then, that when Clement states "That is why Cassian says ..." in 3.92.2, he is still citing the same work by this author (trans. by Ferguson, *Clement of Alexandria: Stromateis Books One to Three*, 313–14).

come down to us in the *Stromateis*.[85] In short, it is impossible to reconstruct the saying as it was found in the *Gospel of the Egyptians*, so that any argument that this gospel was the source for Cassian, *2 Clement*, or the *Gospel of Thomas* remains purely speculative.[86]

In sum, the most likely hypothesis regarding the sources of *2 Clement*, the *Gospel of Thomas* and the *Stromateis* for the saying under consideration is that all three documents reflect independent contact with various forms of the same tradition. The available evidence is simply insufficient to further specify the identity or nature of *2 Clement*'s sources.

9.2.9 2 Clement *13.4*

λέγει ὁ θεός· Οὐ χάρις ὑμῖν, εἰ ἀγαπᾶτε τοὺς ἀγαπῶντας ὑμᾶς, ἀλλὰ χάρις ὑμῖν, εἰ ἀγαπᾶτε τοὺς ἐχθροὺς καὶ τοὺς μισοῦντας ὑμᾶς·

… God says, "It is no great accomplishment for you to love those who love you; it is great if you love your enemies and those who hate you."[87]

2 Clem. 13.4a: Οὐ χάρις ὑμῖν, εἰ ἀγαπᾶτε τοὺς ἀγαπῶντας ὑμᾶς,
Lk 6:32:   καὶ εἰ ἀγαπᾶτε τοὺς ἀγαπῶντας ὑμᾶς, ποία ὑμῖν χάρις ἐστίν;
Mt 5:46:   ἐὰν γὰρ ἀγαπήσητε τοὺς ἀγαπῶντας ὑμᾶς, τίνα μισθὸν ἔχετε;

2 Clem. 13.4b: ἀλλὰ χάρις ὑμῖν, εἰ
                    ἀγαπᾶτε τοὺς ἐχθροὺς καὶ   τοὺς μισοῦντας ὑμᾶς·
Mt 5:44:   ἀγαπᾶτε τοὺς ἐχθροὺς ὑμῶν
Lk 6:27b: ἀγαπᾶτε τοὺς ἐχθροὺς ὑμῶν, καλῶς ποιεῖτε τοῖς μισοῦσιν ὑμᾶς
Lk 6:35:   πλὴν ἀγαπᾶτε τοὺς ἐχθροὺς ὑμῶν

---

[85] For an analysis of the possible textual history behind the saying(s) in the three relevant documents see Baarda, "2 Clement 12," 269–79, who concludes that all three documents preserve developments of the same saying, of which *2 Clement* preserves the most original form (p. 279). Cf. Donfried, *Second Clement*, 76–77, who argues that *2 Clement* represents the earliest, *Thomas* the middle, and the *Gospel of the Egyptians* the latest stage of the development of a shared tradition.

[86] See the careful treatment of this issue by Schneemelcher in "Gospel of the Egyptians," 212–13. Schneemelcher's statement that *2 Clem.* 12.2 "possibly derives directly from the Gospel of the Egyptians or at least is connected with the traditions handed down in it," is clarified by his general assessment: "Whether the conversation with Salome (and particularly this logion) was originally transmitted in the Gospel of the Egyptians, or stood in a sayings collection, or was disseminated in oral tradition, cannot be said in the present state of our sources" (ibid., 213). There are those, however, for whom the meager evidence available is enough to conclude that *2 Clem.* 12.2 depends on the *Gospel of the Egyptians*; see, e.g., A. Orbe, "Cristo y la iglesia en su matrimonio anterior a los siglos," *EstEcl* 29 (1955): 331, who is followed by Ayán Calvo, *Clemente*, 165, 193, n. 80.

[87] I have modified the second word of this translation from Ehrman's "has said" (*Apostolic Fathers*, 1:185) to "says" in order to reflect the present tense of λέγει, as the tense will be important in the discussion below.

Given that the introductory formula attributes the words to "God" (λέγει ὁ θεός), the inclusion of this saying in the present study might be viewed as an exception. From an examination of his argument, however, it appears that "Clement" is using the attribution to God as a synonym for "Christian teaching."[88] Beginning in 13.1 he has been urging his readers that their behavior should match God's words that they claim to follow, so as not to cause the name of the Lord to be blasphemed by outsiders. In 13.2 he then cites two words of the Lord from Isa 52:5 and an unknown source, "For the Lord says, 'My name is constantly blasphemed among all the Gentiles.' And again he says, 'Woe to the one who causes my name to be blasphemed. How is it blasphemed? When you fail to do what I wish.'"[89] This brings us to the immediate context of our verse, where "Clement" gives the application of these citations:

For when outsiders hear the sayings of God from our mouths, they are astonished at their beauty and greatness. Then when they discover that our actions do not match our words, they turn from astonishment to blasphemy, saying that our faith is some kind of myth and error. For, on the one hand, they hear from us that God says,[90] "It is no great accomplishment for you to love those who love you; it is great if you love your enemies and those who hate you." And when they hear these things, they are astonished by their extraordinary goodness. But then when they see that we fail to love not only those who hate us, but even those who love us, they ridicule us and the name is blasphemed. (*2 Clem.* 13.3–4)

Viewing the citation in 13.4 within this context, it becomes clear that the emphasis is not upon the precise origin of the words – i.e., God the Father as opposed to Jesus – but upon the divine or Christian moral teaching they contain. From the point of view of the "outsiders" or "Gentiles" (τοῖς ἔθνεσιν/τὰ ἔθνη) there is no distinction to be made between words of Jesus and of God, as they both represent divine instruction. The distinction to be made is between putting in practice vs. disobeying those words by which the Christian community represents itself.[91] Viewed in this light, the words

---

[88] This explanation is to be preferred over that which sees 13.4 as a Christological statement in light of 1.1, where "Clement" states, "Brothers, we must think about Jesus Christ as we think about God, as about the judge of the living and the dead." For this latter view see Grant and Graham, *First and Second Clement*, 124; Pratscher, *Zweite Clemensbrief*, 33, 175.

[89] I have changed Ehrman's translation to read the more literal "Gentiles" in place of "outsiders" (see his own note in *Apostolic Fathers*, 1:185), and to include the words "How is it blasphemed? When you fail to do what I wish" as part of the citation of the Lord's words from an unknown source (where they belong most naturally, given that they are in the first person).

[90] On the present tense here see n. 87 on p. 266 above.

[91] See Lindemann, *Clemensbriefe*, 239.

of Jesus in *2 Clem.* 13.4 can be regarded as an explicit appeal to Jesus tradition, which warrants their inclusion in the present study.

Some scholars have argued, based on the similarities between the form of this saying in *2 Clement* and in Luke, that *2 Clement* presupposes the finished form of Luke's gospel.[92] In support of this view, the wording in *2 Clem.* 13.4 is considerably closer to its Lukan than to its Matthean parallel: Luke and "Clement" share the words εἰ ἀγαπᾶτε (against Matthew's ἐὰν γὰρ ἀγαπήσητε) so that the line εἰ ἀγαπᾶτε τοὺς ἀγαπῶντας ὑμᾶς is identical in both documents. They also share references to loving "those who hate you" (Lk τοῖς μισοῦσιν ὑμᾶς; *2 Clem.* τοὺς μισοῦντας ὑμᾶς) and to χάρις, both of which are not found in Matthew. If the elements in Luke that agree with *2 Clem.* 13.4 are seen as the result of Lukan redaction of Q, then it is viable to conclude that *2 Clement* presupposes the finished form of Luke.[93]

The number and variety of differences between the saying in *2 Clement* and Luke call into question, however, the hypothesis that *2 Clem.* 13.4 presupposes Luke's finished gospel. K. P. Donfried offers a convenient summary of these differences:

Those sections of Luke which correspond to 2 Clement are separated by four verses and then in reverse order. We find in 2 Clement both a variation in the order and a regrouping – characteristics which, for example, mark the sayings source behind the Gospel of Thomas. Furthermore, there are differences in the text between Luke and 2 Clement. 2 Clement's οὐ χάρις ὑμῖν is missing in Lk 6:32a. For 2 Clement's ἀλλὰ χάρις ὑμῖν, Lk 6:32 has ποία ὑμῖν χάρις ἐστίν. We also note that this verse in Luke (and Mt. 5:46) is in the form of a question; in 2 Clement it is not. Furthermore, the καλῶς ποιεῖτε of Lk. 6:27 has no equivalent in Clement.[94]

Against those who argue that these differences are due to "Clement" changing the wording of his Lukan source, Donfried continues, "Certainly it is possible that 2 Clement made some alterations for theological reasons. But surely one cannot convincingly explain all the differences on this basis."[95] Donfried rightly concludes that *2 Clement* is quoting not from Luke, or a source dependent on Luke, but from a non-canonical source.[96]

---

[92] See, e.g., Lightfoot, *Apostolic Fathers*, 1.2:243 ("A loose quotation from Luke vi. 32, 35); Koester, *Synoptische Überlieferung*, 75–76; Massaux, *Influence*, 2:15; Tuckett, in Gregory and Tuckett, "*2 Clement* and the Writings," 271. Pratscher considers this option but leaves it open (*Zweite Clemensbrief*, 34, 175–76).

[93] See, e.g., Koester, *Synoptische Überlieferung*, 75–76; Tuckett, in Gregory and Tuckett, "*2 Clement* and the Writings," 271. Tuckett (loc. cit.) admits that the attribution of τοῖς μισοῦσιν ὑμᾶς to Lukan redaction is debatable, but finds that it still points to dependence on Luke, given the other agreements.

[94] Donfried, *Second Clement*, 78.

[95] Ibid., 78, who argues this against Koester, *Synoptische Überlieferung*, 76–77.

[96] Ibid., 78; cf. Gregory, *Reception of Luke and Acts*, 139.

That a saying very similar to *2 Clem*. 13.4 formed part of a block of Jesus tradition that circulated fairly widely in the early church prior to its incorporation into the Gospels (and other writings) further supports the argument that *2 Clement* depends on a non-canonical source. Here we appeal to work from a previous chapter: in our examination of *1 Clem*. 13.2 we dwelt at some length upon the work of Dale Allison and others who argue that prior to its incorporation into Q, the material that comprises Q 6:27–38 circulated as an independent, cohesive block of tradition.[97] That this block of tradition is attested in *1 Clement*, Paul, Polycarp, and the *Didache* shows that it had a fairly wide circulation in the early church.[98] Q 6:27b and 6:32, which go back to this pre-Q block of tradition, parallel both parts of *2 Clem*. 13.4, which implies that this cohesive block of tradition contained a saying very similar to the one in *2 Clement*. Given its widespread availability, it is likely that this block of pre-Q tradition provided the source, at least indirectly, for the saying in *2 Clem*. 13.4. It is not possible to ascertain from the saying itself whether "Clement" accessed it while still in oral form or from a written source.

9.3 Assessing the Evidence from the Jesus Sayings in *2 Clement*

The discussion in this chapter has not resolved all the issues related to the Jesus tradition in *2 Clement*. Among other things, the relationship between *2 Clement* and the canonical Gospels, which was the focus above, remains to some extent an open question. This chapter does, however, make a contribution to the ongoing discussion on *2 Clement*'s sources. In what follows we will summarize our findings and draw out some of their implications for understanding the Jesus tradition in *2 Clement*.

In all, we have found: (1) one saying that definitely does not presuppose the Gospels; (2) six sayings for which there is no compelling reason to hold that they presuppose the Gospels; and (3) two sayings with evidence that could be interpreted either way, as presupposing or not presupposing the finished form of the Gospels. We will briefly summarize our findings in the first two categories in order to revisit the evidence in the third:

1) *Sayings that definitely do not presuppose the Gospels*: the only saying in this category is found in 12.2, 6, which has no gospel parallels and so obviously does not presuppose the Gospels.

---

[97] See Allison, *Jesus Tradition*, 84–89, and sec. 4.4.1 (esp. literature cited in n. 55 on p. 124) above.

[98] See ibid., 80–92.

2) *Sayings for which there is no compelling reason to hold that they presuppose the Gospels*: four of the six sayings in this category, those found in *2 Clem.* 2.4, 5.2–4, 8.5 and 13.4, contain no clear evidence of the evangelists' redactional work. There are additional reasons to hold that these sayings are not dependent upon the Gospels: the proverbial nature of the saying in 2.4 is enough to account for the verbatim similarity among the parallels; 5.2, 4 is significantly different from its gospel parallels, especially given the sizeable block of material it contains – extending for twenty-eight words – with no gospel parallel; similar to 2.4, the section of 8.5 which has gospel parallels is proverbial in nature, which is enough to account for the similarity among the parallels, and the remainder of 8.5 has no true parallel in the Gospels; finally, a saying similar to 13.4 circulated widely as part of an independent, cohesive block of tradition that later became Q 6:27–38 (see Q 6:27b, 32), as attested not only by Matthew and Luke but also by *1 Clement*, Paul, Polycarp, and the *Didache*, so that there is little reason to argue that 13.4 is dependent on the Gospels.

Regarding the other two sayings in this category, found in 3.2 and 4.2, 5, we concluded that they may depend upon a source or sources shared by "Clement" and the evangelists that perhaps influenced the evangelists' redactional work. In the case of 3.2, certain scholars have held that it presupposes the finished form of Matthew. We argued, however, that the existence of a saying in Rev 3:5 that circulated independently of the Gospels, and is closer than the Matthean parallel to the wording of *2 Clement*, makes it unlikely that the saying in *2 Clement* derived from Matthew or a source influenced by Matthew. As for the saying in 4.2, 5, certain scholars hold that 4.2 presupposes the finished form of Matthew, and 4.5 the finished form of Luke. The elements in common between 4.2 and Matthew, however, are not particularly Matthean, and those in common between 4.5 and Luke are not particularly Lukan. In addition, the characteristically Matthean redactional features present in the Matthean parallel to 4.2 are not present in *2 Clement*. That in the case of 4.2, 5 we are dealing with at least one non-canonical source is clear from the block of text it contains with no gospel parallels, that extends to seventeen words. In all likelihood this non-canonical source accounts for the entire saying in 4.2, 5, so that there is no need to appeal to indirect dependence upon the Gospels. In conclusion, the presence of any so-called redactional footprint of the evangelists in *2 Clem.* 3.2 and 4.2, 5 is best viewed as reflecting shared sources rather than literary dependence.

3) All of the above considerations decrease the likelihood that the two remaining sayings in *2 Clem.* 6.1–2 and 9.11 presuppose the finished form of the Gospels. While we found evidence in considering these sayings that might point to indirect dependence on the Gospels, we also indicated that

the evidence could be interpreted otherwise. Given that there is no compelling evidence in the other sayings we have examined for *2 Clement*'s dependence upon the Gospels (Bellinzoni's criterion of "rate of recurrence"[99]), the burden of proof shifts to those who would argue that this is the case with these two remaining sayings.

In the case of 6.2, the question is whether the presence of the ἐάν + subjunctive (κερδήσῃ, ζημιωθῇ) construction that *2 Clement* shares with Mt 16:26 means that *2 Clement* presupposes the finished form of Matthew. The construction almost certainly owes its presence in the first gospel to the evangelist's redaction of Mk 8:36,[100] but this need not imply *2 Clement* was dependent upon Matthew for the same. It is possible that Matthew redacted Mark at this juncture under the influence of sources he shared with *2 Clement*, which would account for the presence of the ἐάν + subjunctive construction in both documents. It is important in this regard to note that (a) we found no evidence of the redactional work of the evangelists in *2 Clem.* 6.1; (b) *2 Clem.* 6.1c is different enough from its gospel parallels to suggest a non-canonical source; and (c) both parts of the saying in 6.1 and 6.2 are proverbial in nature and would retain their basic wording well in transmission, so that one need not appeal to literary dependence in order to account for the similarities among the parallels.[101]

Similarly, while *2 Clem.* 9.11 might possibly reflect Matthew and Luke's redaction of Mark, it is also possible that Matthew, Luke and "Clement" shared a common or similar source(s). Earlier in this chapter we argued that the latter is the case based on the absence in *2 Clement* of certain key elements: not only Markan features found in both Matthew and Luke (the "mother" and "sister" language), but also the typical Matthean feature τοῦ ἐν οὐρανοῖς and, more importantly, Luke's pairing of hearing and doing the word of God, which is Lukes' emphasis in his redaction of the Markan saying within its wider Lukan context. Granted that one cannot place too much weight on an argument from silence, it is still easier to explain the absence of these features in *2 Clement* on the supposition that "Clement" did not use Matthew, Luke, or a source based upon these two gospels, than it would be to explain what criteria an editor followed to create a harmony of Matthew and Luke (later used by *2 Clement*) that is miss-

---

[99] See Bellinzoni, "Luke in the Apostolic Fathers," 51, and sec. 3.5 above.

[100] Tuckett, in Gregory and Tuckett, "*2 Clement* and the Writings," 268; also Köhler, *Rezeption*, 135.

[101] That the parallels from Clement of Alexandria and Justin Martyr also contain an ἐάν + subjunctive construction may point to the influence of the Matthean form of the saying in the early church (as argued by Bellinzoni, *Sayings of Jesus*, 89–90), or may witness also to a source that predates the Gospels. A determination on this issue would involve a thorough analysis of the Jesus tradition in both of these documents, which lies outside of the scope of this study.

ing all these Matthean and Lukan elements. The simplest explanation for
the shape of this saying in *2 Clement* and the Gospels is that it circulated as
a proverb among the churches in the basic form in which we find it in
2 Clement ("My brothers are those who do the will of my Father"), and in
this way was available both to the evangelists and to "Clement." "Clement" cited it in this basic form in his writing, and in this form it influenced
Matthew and Luke in their redaction of their Markan source. That in this
case *2 Clement* would not presuppose the finished form of Matthew and/or
Luke coheres well with the overall paucity of evidence for *2 Clement*'s use
– even indirectly – of the canonical Gospels.

Before moving on it is important to clarify that the above does not imply a complete rejection of the possibility that *2 Clement* presupposes the
finished form of the Gospels. It is still possible that *2 Clem.* 6.2 and 9.11
presuppose the finished form of Matthew and Luke. It is equally as important to recognize, however, that according to the analysis of the sayings of
Jesus in *2 Clement* carried out in this chapter, the argument that *2 Clement*
presupposes the finished form of the Gospels rests on evidence from only
two sayings, evidence that also lends itself to the opposite interpretation.
In sum, it is questionable whether the evidence from these two passages
alone is enough to support the whole hypothesis of *2 Clement*'s indirect
dependence on the Gospels.

We now turn to consider the implications of the above for three of the
main theories that have been proposed regarding the sources of the Jesus
sayings in *2 Clement*. First, we have found no support for the older theory
that a majority of the Jesus sayings in *2 Clement* derived from the *Gospel
of the Egyptians*, based on Clement of Alexandria's statement in the parallel to *2 Clem.* 12.2. In rejecting this theory, current scholarship has rightly
recognized it as purely speculative.[102] Even for the saying in 12.2 itself
there is no clear evidence that would point to such derivation, beyond the
simple presence of a parallel saying in both documents. Second, we have
found no support for the more recent theory put forward by Massaux and
others that *2 Clement* was directly dependent upon the canonical gospels of

---

[102] See discussion in sec. 9.2.8 above in relation to *2 Clem.* 12.2 and Clem. Alex.
Strom. 3.92.2, and see Lightfoot, *Apostolic Fathers*, 1.2:236–38, esp. his statement, "As
several of his quotations [in *2 Clement*] cannot be referred to the canonical Gospels, is
seems not unnatural to assign them to the apocryphal source which in this one instance he
is known to have used [the *Gospel of the Egyptians*]" (p. 238); also Bartlet, *NTAF*, 136:
"it is quite likely that the Egyptian Gospel embodied much matter from earlier Gospels,
… in which case the *Gospel according to the Egyptians* may be the one source cited by
2 Clem. throughout." But see Schneemelcher, "Gospel of the Egyptians," 212–15, especially his statement, "After Köster's penetrating investigation of all the relevant passages
in 2 Clem [Koester, *Synoptische Überlieferung*, 62–111], an assignment to the Gospel of
the Egyptians (apart from 12.2) can no longer be maintained" (p. 213).

Matthew and Luke.[103] Third, we have found no conclusive evidence to support the current widely held opinion advanced by Koester and others that a majority of the sayings in *2 Clement* derived indirectly from the gospels of Matthew and Luke, via a harmony made up of sayings from these two gospels and apocryphal materials (a collection that was also used by Justin).[104]

The evidence points instead in two different directions: on the one hand, *2 Clement* apparently depended upon a source or sources that were close to the sayings tradition that informed Matthew and Luke, whether this be identified as Q or a source influenced by Q, or in more general terms as the "double tradition."[105] Six of the sayings in *2 Clement* point in this direction, as they do not appear dependent upon Matthew or Luke, but rather upon sources either identical with, or related to, sources used by these two gospels (*2 Clem.* 3.2; 6.1–2; 8.5; 9.11; 13.4). On the other hand, in three sayings the presence of material not paralleled in any of the canonical Gospels suggests that *2 Clement* may have depended upon other sources as well: while two of these sayings apparently derived from sources that were fairly removed from those that informed the canonical Gospels, though sharing a common history with them (*2 Clem.* 4.2, 5; 5.2–4), one saying probably derived from a source that had little if any connection with the gospel sources (12.2, 6).

The above need not imply that the explicit appeals to Jesus tradition in *2 Clement* derived from a multiplicity of sources, but there is also no conclusive evidence to indicate use of a single source. The sayings of Jesus in *2 Clement* are many and varied, including not only proverbial sayings (2.4;

---

[103] We thus disagree with Massaux when he states that, "The author of 2 Clement knows the Gospel of Mt. He is literarily dependent on it in many parts of his writing" and when he holds similarly that "The author of 2 Clement certainly knew the Gospel of Lk" (*Influence*, 2:11, 17). See similarly, e.g., Warns, "Untersuchungen," 279, 284–88; Lightfoot, *Apostolic Fathers*, 1.2:215, 216, 221, 243.

[104] Koester, *Synoptische Überlieferung*, 62–111; idem, *Introduction to the NT*, 2:242; idem, *Ancient*, 349–60, especially his conclusion on p. 360: "Clement" "quotes from a collection of sayings of Jesus. Insofar as these sayings have parallels in the Synoptic Gospels, their text reveals a harmonization of Matthean and Lukan elements which occasionally are paralleled elsewhere .... In addition ..., *2 Clement*'s sayings collection included sayings from the free tradition, that is, non-canonical sayings which have also found their way into so-called apocryphal gospels." Koester is followed by A. J. Bellinzoni, "Luke in the Apostolic Fathers," 63–65, 67, and Warns argues something similar ("Untersuchungen," 279–474, esp. 323–24). As Hagner notes, the theory of a single gospels harmony behind all *2 Clement*'s citations "is attractive, but remains beyond proof" (*Clement of Rome*, 282, n. 2). Against Koester, Donfried finds "no evidence for the assertion that Justin and 2 Clement are dependent upon the same gospel harmony" (*Second Clement*, 82).

[105] See the similar conclusions in Donfried, *Second Clement*, 79–82.

3.2; 9.11; 13.4), but also lengthier sayings (4.2, 5; 6.1–2; 8.5) and dialogues (5.2–4; 12.2, 6), ranging in length from six (2.4) to sixty-three words (5.2–4). These sayings are paralleled in a variety of early Christian documents, both canonical and non-canonical, and are prefaced by a variety of introductory formulae. Given this quantity and variety it is logical, even if not provable, to hold that the Jesus tradition in *2 Clement* came from a variety of sources, both written and oral.

This brings us to the last topic to be discussed before concluding this chapter: is there any way to identify the nature of the sources behind *2 Clement*? Our treatment of this topic will include a discussion of the formulae that introduce the sayings of Jesus in *2 Clement*, left to address all together at this juncture rather than with each saying for reasons of logical clarity.

9.4 The Sources of Jesus Tradition in *2 Clement*: Written or Oral?

Hardly anything can be concluded with certainty about the nature of the sources used by *2 Clement*.[106] The sole exception relates to the saying in 2.4 that, as noted above, is prefaced by the statement καὶ ἑτέρα δὲ γραφὴ λέγει which explicitly identifies its source as written.[107] The introductory formulae for the other sayings, which at first might appear to offer insight into the nature of their sources as well, on closer analysis come up empty. This statement will be supported in what follows.

As noted above, the formulae used to introduce the sayings of Jesus in *2 Clement* are many and varied, as can be seen in the following list:

2.4:   καὶ ἑτέρα δὲ γραφὴ λέγει: "and also another Scripture says"
3.2:   λέγει δὲ καὶ αὐτός: "indeed, he himself says"
4.2:   λέγει γάρ: "for he says"
4.5:   εἶπεν ὁ κύριος: "the Lord said"
5.2–4:   λέγει γὰρ ὁ κύριος: "for the Lord says"
6.1–2:   λέγει δὲ ὁ κύριος: "but the Lord says"
8.5:   λέγει γὰρ ὁ κύριος ἐν τῷ εὐαγγελίῳ: "for the Lord says in the gospel"
9.11:   καὶ γὰρ εἶπεν ὁ κύριος: "for the Lord also said"

---

[106] W. Pratscher rightly concludes, "The source of the quotations [of Jesus tradition in *2 Clement*] is nearly impossible to determine. … Not least of the reasons for this fact is the open question of orality and written texts in the second century" ("The Second Epistle of Clement," in *The Apostolic Fathers* [ed. Pratscher], 76 and n. 9)

[107] See further the discussion in sec. 9.2.1 above on the use of ἑτέρα δὲ γραφή in the introductory formula.

12.2: ἐπερωτηθεὶς γὰρ αὐτὸς ὁ κύριος ὑπό τινος, πότε ἥξει αὐτοῦ ἡ βασιλεία,
       εἶπεν: "For when the Lord himself was asked by someone when his kingdom
       would come, he said"
12.6: φησίν: "he says"
13.4: λέγει ὁ θεός: "God says"

In previous chapters we adopted a distinction made by H. Koester and others between the use of εἶπεν vs. λέγει in introductory formulas: the use of
the past tense εἶπεν (often paired with terms for "remembering") implies a
reference to a voice that has spoken in the past, and probably indicates use
of oral tradition. In contrast, the present tense λέγει implies a voice that
speaks in the present from a page to the reader, and thus usually indicates
use of a written source.[108] If one were to apply this distinction to the introductory formulas in *2 Clement*, one would conclude that only three sayings
were derived from oral sources (4.5; 9.11; 12.2) while the remainder came
from written sources.

It is not clear, however, whether this distinction between εἶπεν and
λέγει applies to the sayings in *2 Clement*. In cases examined in previous
chapters, such as *1 Clem.* 13.2, 46.7–8, and Poly. *Phil.* 2.3, the use of εἶπεν
in the introductory formulae was only one element among many that
pointed to the authors' use of an oral source.[109] In contrast, among the sayings in *2 Clement* only the one in 2.4 provides clear evidence beyond the
use of εἶπεν or λέγει regarding the nature of its source, via the explicit
statement καὶ ἑτέρα δὲ γραφὴ λέγει that identifies its source as written.[110]

---

[108] See above, pp. 140–43, 166, 171–72, 235–36, and Koester, *Synoptische Überlieferung*, 4–6, esp. 5; idem, *Ancient*, 18, 66; Cameron, *Sayings Traditions*, 92–93. Donfried's arguments to the contrary in relation to *2 Clement* (*Second Clement*, 81 and n. 4)
involve a misreading of Koester. Donfried holds that Koester is wrong in stating that the
Apostolic Fathers do not use εἶπεν in reference to written texts, and gives *Barn.* 5.5;
6.12; 10.1, 11; *1 Clem.* 10.4 as examples of such use. Each and every one of the texts
Donfried gives as examples, however, supports rather than undermines Koester's argument: Koester had made clear that within OT citations Clement may use the aorist εἶπεν,
but only for quoting *a speaker* within the passage he is citing (*Synoptische Überlieferung*, 4–6, esp. 5), and even gives one of the passages cited by Donfried, *1 Clem.*
10.4, as an example. (Koester does not treat the passages from *Barnabas* that Donfried
cites in that context, as he is dealing with *1 Clement*, but they all meet the same criterion
as *1 Clem.* 10.4.) Donfried also gives *1 Clem.* 13.2 as an example of εἶπεν used to cite an
"amalgamation of several synoptic verses," but as argued in the present work, in 13.2
Clement does not cite written Gospels but oral tradition (see above, ch. 4). In sum, Donfried's comments do not invalidate Koester's argument regarding the use of εἶπεν and
λέγει in the Apostolic Fathers we have examined in the previous chapters, though as we
will see below, Koester's argument may not apply to *2 Clement* on other grounds.

[109] See secs. 4.5 and 5.3 above within the wider context of the discussion in chs. 4
and 5.

[110] See further the full discussion earlier in the present chapter, in sec. 9.2.1 on
2 Clem. 2.4, regarding the use of ἑτέρα δὲ γραφή in the introductory formula.

In this case the distinction between εἶπεν and λέγει holds, as the saying in 2.4 is appropriately introduced with λέγει. The other eight sayings in *2 Clement*, however, lack additional elements that would aid in determining the nature of their source. Given this lack, one should question whether in *2 Clement*, with its variety of introductory formulae, the distinction between the use of εἶπεν and λέγει can be retained. It would certainly be methodologically unsound to make a determination regarding the source of the eight relevant sayings in *2 Clement* based solely upon whether or not they contained εἶπεν or λέγει in their introductory formulae.[111]

9.5 Conclusions

The results of the investigation conducted in this chapter are more negative than positive, in that they say more about what sources were not used in *2 Clement* than about those that were. As in the present work as a whole, what follows pertains only to explicit appeals to Jesus tradition.

It is quite certain that the Jesus tradition in *2 Clement* was not directly dependent on the canonical Gospels, as we have found no evidence whatsoever to support such a position. It is only a little less certain that seven out of the nine sayings examined were not indirectly dependent on the Gospels either, and that their similarity to the Gospels derived from shared sources. One must leave open the possibility that the other two sayings, in *2 Clem.* 6.1–2 and 9.11, presuppose the finished form of Matthew and Luke. Given, however, both that the evidence can (perhaps best) be interpreted otherwise, and that there is no other clear evidence to support such a possibility, the burden of proof rests with those who would argue in its favor.

Regarding the nature of the sources used by "Clement," one can be certain only that the saying in 2.4 derived from a written source. The source(s) for the other sayings may have been oral or written; there is no conclusive evidence either way. This uncertainty would remain even if one could show (contrary to what has been argued above) that *2 Clem.* 6.2 and 9.11 presuppose the finished form of Matthew and Luke (which is doubtful). If these two sayings presupposed the finished form of the Gospels, this need not imply that they derive from a written source, especially since most scholars are in agreement that any influence of Matthew and Luke upon *2 Clement* was at best indirect: it could just as well imply that "Clement" had access to oral tradition that has been impacted by its con-

---

[111] Here I agree with Donfried's conclusions in his *Second Clement*, 81, though I do not agree with his argument; see n. 108 on p. 275 above.

tact with a written Matthew and Luke. This would provide an example of re-oralization, or of tradition that has been committed to writing re-entering the stream of oral tradition, a dynamic quite at home in a culture in which written documents still held a subsidiary role within orality.[112]

Given that the Jesus tradition in *2 Clement* defies classification in terms of sources, it is difficult to assign it a place within the argument developed in the present work. Since it is not clear that the sayings in *2 Clement* derived from oral tradition, they can contribute little of substance to a discussion of the use of oral tradition in Christian antiquity. There is little use in noting that certain sayings *could* have been at home in an oral context because of their proverbial form (3.2; 4.2, 5; 6.1–2; 8.5; 9.11; 13.4) or because (when compared to their parallels) they evince the variability within stability characteristic of oral tradition, including differences in adverbs, pronouns and prepositions, verb forms, and the use of synonymous rather than identical terms (3.2; 4.2, 5; 6.1–2; 8.5; 9.11; 12. 2, 6; 13.4). If nothing else, however, the discussion in this chapter has served to determine whether or not the sayings of Jesus in *2 Clement* can be an integral part of the present work. Arriving at a negative answer is not without its value.

Finally, the discussion in this chapter points again to the problems of working with non-extant sources. In dealing with the triple tradition (parallels shared by Matthew, Mark and Luke), and assuming Markan priority, even when one can identify the redactional work of Matthew or Luke, one cannot be certain whether this redactional work was influenced by other sources at the evangelists' disposal. In working with parallels in the double tradition (shared by Matthew and Luke but not Mark), any argument predicated on the redactional work of one of the evangelists faces the inherent weakness that one cannot verify the actual shape of his source, understood as Q or otherwise. Either evangelist may be more faithful than the other in any given case to his source, and although one can follow patterns and tendencies, in the final analysis judgments in this regard remain hypothetical.

---

[112] On re-oralization see sec. 3.5 above, esp. n. 123 on p. 104; Schröter also notes this possibility regarding Jesus tradition in *2 Clement* in "Jesus and the Canon," 112–13. That the written Matthew has impacted the oral tradition that continues to be in use in the early Christian community is a better explanation for the form of the saying in *2 Clem.* 3.2 than the theory that "Clement" is citing Matthew loosely from memory (an option suggested by Tuckett in Gregory and Tuckett, "*2 Clement* and the Writings," 258).

Chapter 10

Conclusions

Having completed the examination of explicit appeals to Jesus tradition in the Apostolic Fathers,[1] we now turn to assess the outcomes of our investigation. What follows will be divided into three main sections: (1) some implications of the basic insight that the explicit appeals to Jesus tradition in the Apostolic Fathers are appeals to oral tradition; (2) a description of the main characteristics of the oral tradition used by the Apostolic Fathers; and (3) the impact of the findings of the present work upon select wider issues.

10.1 Oral-Traditional Sources in the Apostolic Fathers

The most basic insights resulting from the above investigation relate to the likelihood that the explicit appeals to Jesus tradition in the Apostolic Fathers prior to *2 Clement* derive from an oral-traditional source: this likelihood approaches certainty in the case of *1 Clem.* 13.2 and 46.8, Poly. *Phil.* 2.3 and *Did.* 8.2 (the Lord's Prayer), examined in chapters 4 though 7. It is also very likely in the case of the isolated sayings examined in chapter 8: *Did.* 9.5, Ign. *Smyrn.* 3.2a and Poly. *Phil.* 7.2c. Members of a culture proficient in orality would have no need to depend on written sources for brief sayings such as these.

Our findings on the Jesus tradition in *2 Clement* remain inconclusive: though we found good reason to hold that it does not presuppose the finished form of the Synoptics, beyond that more evidence would be required to decide whether it derived from an oral-traditional or a written source. Our tentative conclusion that it derived from a variety of sources, both oral and written, was based upon three considerations: (1) the many and varied forms of the Jesus tradition in *2 Clement* (short proverbs [2.4; 3.2; 9.11; 13.4]; lengthier sayings [4.2, 5; 6.1–2; 8.5]; dialogues [5.2–4; 12.2, 6] ranging from six [2.4] to sixty-three words [5.2–4] in length); (2) the vari-

---

[1] The fragments traditionally attributed to Papias contain two additional explicit appeals to Jesus tradition, which are covered in "Appendix: The Fragments of Papias" (for reasons given there), following this concluding section.

ety of early Christian documents with parallels to these sayings, both canonical and non-canonical; and (3) the variety of formulae with which the
sayings are introduced. Given this quantity and variety we concluded that
it is logical, even if not provable, to hold that the Jesus tradition in *2 Clement* derived from a variety of written and oral sources.

The oral-traditional provenance of the explicit appeals to Jesus tradition
in the Apostolic Fathers that predate *2 Clement* carries a number of implications, which we will develop in what follows:

(a) We need to revise our mental images of what the process of writing
entailed in Christian antiquity. As noted in the conclusions to chapter 5,
the use of oral-traditional sources by the Apostolic Fathers fits well with
what we have come to know of the process of writing in antiquity. It does
away with the anachronistic mental picture, derived from the Western literate worldview, of the Apostolic Fathers sitting at their desks, with copies
of the gospels of Matthew, Luke and perhaps some non-canonical sources
open before them as they wrote.[2] While this picture is possible, it is very
improbable. It is more likely that the Apostolic Fathers freely used orally-
transmitted tradition in their writings, given their cultural context that relied heavily on orality.

(b) We may need to revisit arguments for the dating and provenance not
only of the writings of the Apostolic Fathers, but also of the canonical
Gospels, that are based largely on the perceived use of one by the other.
For example, the Gospel of Matthew has often been linked to Syria in part
because of the perception that Ignatius is the first to cite from it, and this
supposed citation is also used in arguments for its dating.[3] The present
work has only dealt with explicit appeals to Jesus tradition, so revisiting
arguments for date and provenance based on the Apostolic Fathers' use of
the Gospels would have to include further study of implicit Jesus tradition.
The present study, however, provides a starting point.

(c) Some of the findings of the present study have implications for the
content and/or nature of Q. As argued in chapter 3, it is almost certain that
not only the sayings in *1 Clem.* 13.2 but also its parallels in Lk 6:36–38
derived from oral tradition. This would imply that what is usually held to
be Q 6:36–38 was either (a) not as close to Lk 6:36–38 as is usually be-

---

[2] See comments in sec. 6.3 above, and further Beaton, "How Matthew Writes," 116;
Mattila, "Question Too Often Neglected," 202, 213–17.

[3] E.g., by B. H. Streeter, *The Primitive Church: Studied with Special Reference to the
Origins of the Christian Ministry* (New York: Macmillan, 1929), 64; J. P. Meier in
Brown and Meier, *Antioch and Rome*, 24. Among commentators on Matthew see, e.g., D.
L. Turner, *Matthew* (BECNT; Grand Rapids: Baker Academic, 2007), 13–14; C. L.
Blomberg, *Matthew* (NAC 22; Nashville: Broadman, 1992), 41; B. Witherington, III,
Matthew (SHBC; Macon, Ga.: Smyth & Helwys, 2006), 88–89; on this topic see further
Trevett, *Study of Ignatius*, 22–23.

lieved, but rather closer to the briefer form in the other parallel in Mt 7:1–2, or (2) not part of a written Q at all, but belonging in more general terms to the double (oral) tradition held in common by Matthew and Luke. Relating to the contents of the Sermon on the Mount/Plain as a whole, our findings thus tend to support the arguments of those who hold that the evangelists accessed part at least of the sermon as oral tradition rather than from a written Q. In addition, our discussion of *1 Clem.* 46.8 led to the conclusion that its parallels in Mt 18:6–7 and Lk 17:1–2 are dependent not on a written Q but on oral tradition, also better understood in general terms as double (oral) tradition. This implies that the contents of what is usually held to be Q 17:1–2 may need to be rethought. Overall, our conclusions tend to undermine the idea of a single Q source behind the double tradition, and support the idea that the double tradition represents a plurality of sources, both written and oral.

(d) The findings of our investigation serve to reinforce two basic premises noted in chapter 3 above: first, that oral Jesus tradition co-existed with the written Gospels and other written collections of Jesus tradition well into the second half of the second century (at least until the time of Irenaeus); second, that neither the presence of a literate minority nor the existence of the written Gospels changed the fact that most people continued to interact with Jesus tradition within a context of orality. Both of these basic premises are almost self-evident in light of the interplay of orality and literacy in late Western antiquity discussed in chapter 3, and are further supported by the findings of the present work in relation to the use of oral tradition in the Apostolic Fathers.

10.2 Characteristics of Oral Tradition in the Apostolic Fathers

Another main area impacted by the results of our investigation relates to the characteristics of oral tradition, addressed in chapter 3 above.[4] Of

---

[4] For a full discussion of the characteristics that follow, see ch. 3 above. As noted in ch. 1, there is an element of circularity involved in describing the inner workings of oral tradition in antiquity: one first identifies the oral-traditional provenance of portions of ancient writings based on certain characteristics of the material, and then proceeds to describe the way oral tradition functioned in antiquity based on these characteristics. Throughout the present work we have trusted, however, that comparative research into surviving oral cultures provides enough of a control to assure the validity of the approach upon which this study is based. In dealing with this type of material one works in the realm of hypotheses and probabilities, not in the realm of certainty.

these, four closely interrelated characteristics are consistently true of the oral Jesus tradition in the Apostolic Fathers examined above: [5]

(a) *Conservative or Traditionalist*: conservation is important in passing on tradition within predominantly oral cultures, because knowledge that is not continually recycled orally is lost. While new performances of the tradition will include new elements, originality in this process does not consist in inventing new materials, but in adapting the tradition to new situations.

In the Apostolic Fathers prior to *2 Clement*, i.e. in those whose use of oral tradition we found to be almost certain or very likely, we did not find any sayings that departed in meaning from their parallels in the pre-synoptic tradition (as far as this could be reconstructed).

(b) *Both Variable and Stable*: in the preceding chapters we have often referred to variability within stability as one of the hallmarks of the retention and transmission of oral tradition: without stability, it would not be "tradition," and without variability, it would not be "oral."

The variability is present in *1 Clem.* 13.2, 46.8 and Pol. *Phil.* 2.3, in the use of different adverbs, particles, conjunctions, pronouns and prepositions, verb forms and tenses, and synonymous rather than identical terms, as well as in the order of words and sayings. Variability greatly decreases with the Lord's Prayer in *Did.* 8.2, in keeping with the greater tenacity of oral liturgical tradition. Similarly, variability greatly decreases in short proverbial sayings such as those found in *Did.* 9.5 and Poly. *Phil.* 7.2c (and to a lesser extent in Ign. *Smyrn.* 3.2a).

Variability, however, is balanced out by the overarching stability of the tradition: as noted in the previous point ("Conservative or Traditionalist"), this stability finds expression in a consistent meaning within the variability of form.

(c) *Mnemonically Constructed*: the integrity of a tradition in an oral context depends on the traditionists' ability to accurately recall it, requiring a balance between both (i) *remembering* and (ii) *memorizing*:

(i) *1 Clement* 46.8 and its parallels provide an example of remembering, as shown by the great variability in language related to the visual elements of the millstone-saying: during a performance the traditionist would probably visualize this scene in their mind, describing what they "saw" using words that would include some form of "man," "millstone," "around

---

[5] In addition to the characteristics of orality that will be our focus below, we also noted in analyzing *1 Clem.* 46.8 that it provides an example of the *redundancy* that characterizes oral tradition: in conflating two sayings, the phrases ἢ ἕνα τῶν ἐκλεκτῶν μου σκανδαλίσαι and ἢ ἕνα τῶν ἐκλεκτῶν μου διαστρέψαι have both been retained, and are clearly redundant. We have not included this in the discussion below because in its isolation it is rather insignificant in the wider scheme of the conclusions being drawn.

the neck," "cast," and "sea." Here we would not be dealing with a saying memorized and repeated, then, but with a scene visualized and described.

(ii) Most of the Jesus tradition in the Apostolic Fathers would require memorization, the traditionist making use of a variety of mnemonic techniques. Evidence of such techniques in the texts examined includes rhyme and rhythm (*1 Clem.* 13.2; Pol. *Phil.* 2.3) and the grouping together of sayings with a similar theme (*1 Clem.* 13.2, 46.8; Pol. *Phil.* 2.3). (Unfortunately, other mnemonic techniques such as gestures and other elements of body language, or emotions and intonation, are not recoverable from these written texts.) In addition, memory would have been served by the ritualized processes for transmitting the tradition of the Lord's Prayer in *Did.* 8.2, while with *Did.* 9.5 and Poly. *Phil.* 7.2c it would have been served by the repeated use of brief proverbial sayings.

(d) *Socially Identified*: not all oral traditions are preserved, but only those that remain socially relevant and acceptable. This can be seen in the injunctions to be merciful, not judge, not condemn, forgive, and give generously found in *1 Clem.* 13.2: while in the pre-Q block of tradition that was Clement's source these injunctions related to the every-day social realities of the oppression of the poor and powerless by the rich and powerful (Lk 6:20–35), in *1 Clement* they are applied to a situation of inner-church schism occasioned by jealousy and envy over leadership (*1 Clem.* 1.1–6.4).

Similarly, in *1 Clem.* 46.8 the original referent of the warning of Jesus as found in Mk 14:21 and Mt 26:24 (cf. Lk 22:22) – the one who was to betray the Son of Man – has been replaced by a more general referent: any who would cause the Lord's chosen to stumble. In this way the saying has been appropriated to serve the ongoing life of the church.

The saying "Do not give what is holy to the dogs" that in Matthew is rather general (relating to the overall teachings and practices of the Jesus community) is applied in *Did.* 9.5 to a new situation in the early church: exclusion from participation in the Eucharist. The proverb thus gained a wider meaning when applied to a new situation.

Finally, the passage in Ign. *Smyrn.* 3.2a, "Reach out, touch me and see that I am not a bodiless demon," also reapplies a saying to a new situation: where it once provided words of reassurance to Jesus' troubled disciples, in Ignatius it serves a specifically anti-docetic polemic. That the wording of the saying was slightly modified to serve this anti-docetic purpose, without compromising its basic meaning, also serves to illustrate the oral-traditional characteristic of variability within stability.

10.3 Impact upon Larger Issues

The discussion in the preceding chapters has raised a number of questions that, although tangential to the topic at hand, are of great importance: What, then, of the canonical Gospels? What was the role of the gospel texts in the communities represented by the Apostolic Fathers? Why did the Apostolic Fathers not cite the Gospels directly? What implications does their use of oral tradition have for a four-gospel canon? How reliable was the oral gospel tradition used by the evangelists if it functioned in the manner here described?

One answer to these questions brings us back to the heart of the present work: people within predominantly oral cultures engaged texts in a certain way. If Clement, when wishing to make a point about what Jesus taught regarding gentleness and patience (*1 Clem.* 13.2), cited a seven-part collection of sayings he knew from oral tradition, this does not necessarily say anything about his access, for example, to a written Gospel of Matthew. If he had such access, is it likely that he would have unrolled a scroll of Matthew and searched for the texts he needed? In a predominantly oral society, the answer is no. Clement's church in Rome might well have owned a scroll of Matthew that was read in its corporate worship, or to widen the example, Ignatius might have had a codex of the Gospels on his shelf that was used in the liturgy and worship at Antioch. This need not imply that Clement or Ignatius would have made use of these written texts if they had ready access to what they needed for their writings in their memories.[6]

It follows that to argue that all the explicit appeals to Jesus tradition in the Apostolic Fathers prior to *2 Clement* derive from oral tradition does not detract in any way from the argument that the Gospels were known and used in the communities to which the Apostolic Fathers belonged. These are two separate issues. That the explicit appeals to Jesus tradition in the Apostolic Fathers do not contain proof of their use of the Gospels does, however, carry implications: one cannot use these explicit appeals as proof for or against the authority of the Gospels in the communities to which the Apostolic Fathers belonged, or as evidence for or against an incipient canon that excluded what later became non-canonical gospels. These issues simply must be settled using other kinds of evidence.

As for the oral tradition that informed the canonical Gospels, everything we have seen of the oral tradition in the Apostolic Fathers prior to

---

[6] With the *Didache* it is different, in that as a repository of a large amount of (mostly implicit) Jesus tradition its relationship to the tradition is similar to that of the Gospels. Position was taken in ch. 7 above with those who consider that the *Didache* and Matthew arose out of a closely related milieu, and that they were both informed by the same oral tradition.

2 Clement supports its reliability. This reliability does not consist, however, in capturing Jesus' *ipsissima verba* – a concept at home in today's Western cultures with our wealth of TV cameras and recording equipment – but in faithfully conveying the meaning of what he said.

It would be a mistake to imagine that one could *prove* that the Jesus tradition in the Apostolic Fathers derived from oral sources. To some readers it might appear from certain parts of this book and the above conclusions that this has been my goal, but such is not the case; both the nature of our sources and the interpenetration of orality and literacy in antiquity do not allow for certainty in these matters. One of the central tenets of this book, however, is that if the Jesus tradition in the Apostolic Fathers *can* be understood as stemming from oral sources, then perhaps it is *best* so understood, especially given that a number of indicators point in that direction.

My goal in this book has been, as stated in the introductory chapter, to show that the study of the explicit appeals to Jesus tradition in the Apostolic Fathers is better informed by the presuppositions of orality than by those of scribality. This is true because the presuppositions of orality are better able to account not only for the similarities but also for the dissimilarities between the Jesus tradition in the Apostolic Fathers and its parallels in other writings. They also better account for the lack of any concrete evidence of literary dependence of the Jesus tradition in the Apostolic Fathers upon the documents that contain its parallels. In addition, they take fully into consideration the role of orality in the cultural milieu to which the Apostolic Fathers belonged. I hope that this book, to whatever extent is has shown these various points to be true, will contribute to our growing appreciation of the place of orality in early Christianity.

Appendix

The Fragments of Papias

Any treatment of appeals to Jesus tradition in the Apostolic Fathers would not be complete without a discussion of Papias. The rationale for treating Papias in an appendix rather than the body of the present book is that Papias' actual work – his "Exposition of the Lord's Logia" (Eus. *Hist. Eccl.*, 3.39.15) – has not survived, but only fragments cited in other sources. At issue are not only uncertainties such as whether or not a fragment traditionally attributed to Papias actually came from his writings, or whether writers such as Irenaeus and Eusebius were faithful in transmitting what Papias wrote, though one should not minimize the importance of these two points. One also cannot access the wider context of Papias' writings for information on how he used the Jesus tradition in the known fragments, or how this compares with his use of Jesus tradition in the large percentage of his work that is lost.

Based on the above considerations, including the fragments of Papias in the main body of the present work would have been methodologically suspect for three main reasons: (1) if one cannot be certain that a fragment actually came from Papias' writings, then it is problematic to include it in a study focused upon Jesus tradition specifically in the Apostolic Fathers; (2) even if one could ascertain that any given fragment came from Papias, if uncertainty remains as to the fidelity with which it was transcribed by later writers one still cannot arrive at confident conclusions regarding Jesus tradition *in Papias*; and (3) even if the above two points were not an issue, the lack of contextual information that comes with the fragmentary nature of the material leaves one with too many unknowns to be able to make any confident statements regarding how Papias used the Jesus tradition at his disposal. The above considerations explain the decision to treat the fragments of Papias in this appendix rather than the main body of the present book.

The fragments traditionally attributed to Papias include two explicit appeals to Jesus tradition: fragment 1.1b–5b (from Iren. *Adv. Haer.*, 5.33,3–4) and fragment 13.2 (from George Hamartolos, *Chronicon*).[1] In discussing each of these sayings in turn, we will first deal with issues of

---

[1] The fragments are numbered following Ehrman, *Apostolic Fathers*, 2:92–119.

authenticity and attribution to Papias, followed by a brief treatment of the saying in light of its parallels.

Fragment 1.1b–5 (Iren. *Adv. Haer.* 5.33.3–4)

Thus the elders who saw John, the disciple of the Lord, remembered hearing him say how the Lord used to teach about those times, saying: [2] "The days are coming when the vines will come forth, each with ten thousand boughs; and on a single bough will be ten thousand branches. And indeed, on a single branch will be ten thousand shoots and on every shoot ten thousand clusters; and in every cluster will be ten thousand grapes, and every grape, when pressed, will yield twenty-five measures of wine. [3]And when any of the saints grabs hold of a cluster, another will cry out, 'I am better, take me; bless the Lord through me.' So too a grain of wheat will produce ten thousand heads and every head will have ten thousand grains and every grain will yield ten pounds of pure, exceptionally fine flour. So too the remaining fruits and seeds and vegetation will produce in similar proportions. And all the animals who eat this food drawn from the earth will come to be at peace and harmony with one another, yielding in complete submission to humans."

[4] Papias as well, an ancient man – the one who heard John and was a companion of Polycarp – gives a written account of these things in the fourth of his books. For he wrote five books. And in addition he says: [5] "These things can be believed by those who believe. And the betrayer Judas," he said, "did not believe, but asked, 'How then can the Lord bring forth such produce?' The Lord then replied, 'Those who come into those times will see.'"

The above-mentioned problems that inhere in working with the fragments of Papias are readily apparent in this passage, in that one cannot be certain that Irenaeus attributes the Jesus tradition in vv. 2–3 to Papias.

Does Irenaeus cite Papias for the contents of vv. 2–3, or just for v. 5? Irenaeus states that the tradition in vv. 2–3 derived from "the elders who saw John, the disciple of the Lord" (v. 1), and adds, "Papias as well … the one who heard John … gives a written account of these things" (v. 4). In the most straightforward reading, Irenaeus cites an oral source that went back to "the elders who saw John" for vv. 2–3, corroborates the contents of these verses by appeal to the written witness of Papias, and adds additional material from Papias in v. 5.[2] Since there is no indication, however, that Irenaeus himself had contact with the elders mentioned in v. 1, it is also possible that Papias was his source for the tradition "from the elders."[3] Ac-

---

[2] As argued by T. Zahn, *Forschungen zur Geschichte des neutestamentlichen Kanons und der altkirchlichen Literatur,* Vol. 6: *Apostel und Apostelschüler in der Provinz Asien* (Leipzig: A. Deichert, 1900), 89. J. Chapman overstates his case when he states "This [reading] seems to me quite impossible" ("Papias on the Age of Our Lord," *JTS* 9 [1908]: 57).

[3] See Schoedel, *Polycarp, Martyrdom, Papias,* 94; idem, "Papias," *ANRW* 2. 27.1:243. F. Loofs goes further, arguing that a number of Irenaeus' other appeals to uni-

cording to this second reading Irenaeus' statement in v. 4, "Papias as well … gives a written account," should be understood in light of v. 1 to mean, "not only did they [the elders] witness the fact, but also Papias has consigned their testimony to writing."[4] Though it is not conclusive, a consideration that favors this second interpretation is that in v. 4 Irenaeus describes Papias in the same terms he uses for those who were the source of vv. 2–3: as an "elder" who had heard John. In the absence of conclusive evidence for either of these two readings, and simply for the purpose of continuing the investigation of this material as stemming from the Apostolic Fathers, we opt for the second: that Papias was the source for vv. 2–3.

Assuming for the sake of argument, then, that Irenaeus used Papias as his source for all of vv. 2–3 and 5, what source did Papias use? Irenaeus' claim in v. 1 that the tradition in vv. 2–3 came from John the disciple, who in turn heard it from Jesus, while possible, is unlikely. This unlikelihood stems from four considerations: (1) vv. 2–3 and 5 do not resemble any other known Jesus tradition; (2) the Jesus tradition in vv. 2–3 and 5 appears to be an elaboration of known Jewish sources, (3) another Christian document contains material very similar to vv. 2–3, but does not attribute it to Jesus, and (4) understanding this material as commentary rather than tradition that goes back to Jesus would be in keeping with the nature of Papias' work.

(1) The first point, that the Jesus tradition in the Papias fragment does not resemble any other known Jesus tradition, needs no further elaboration.

(2) Verses 2–3 appear to be a midrashic-type elaboration of Jewish apocalyptic ideas found in *1 Enoch* 10:19 and *2 Baruch* 29:5.[5] *1 Enoch* 10:19 is found in that section of the work known as "The Book of the Watchers," which dates to the mid-third or early-second century BCE.[6] In

---

dentified "elders" are also from Papias (*Theophilus von Antiochien Adversus Marcionem und die anderen theologischen Quellen bei Irenaeus* [TU 46; Leipzig: Heinrichs, 1930], 311–12).

[4] Chapman, "Papias," 57; followed by Schoedel, *Polycarp, Martyrdom, Papias*, 94; idem, "Papias [*ANRW*]," 243.

[5] See esp. Schoedel, *Polycarp, Martyrdom, Papias*, 94–96; also D. E. Aune, "Prolegomena to the Study of Oral Tradition in the Hellenistic World," in *Jesus and the Oral Gospel* (ed. Wansbrough), 82; C. E. Hill, "Papias of Hierapolis," *ExpTim* 117.8 (2006): 309–15; repr. in *Writings of the Apostolic Fathers* (ed. Foster), 42–51 (p. 49, citations here and below are to the reprint); G. W. E. Nickelsburg, *1 Enoch 1: A Commentary on the Book of 1 Enoch, Chapters 1–36; 81–108* (Hermeneia; Minneapolis: Fortress, 2001), 227.

[6] Nickelsburg dates it to the mid-third century (*1 Enoch*, 7); M. A. Knibb dates it to "the end of the third or the beginning of the second century BC" ("The Ethiopic Book of Enoch," in *Outside the Old Testament* [ed. M. de Jonge; CCWJCW 4; Cambridge: Cambridge University Press, 1985], 28).

the midst of a description of the earth cleansed from the wickedness of the watchers and their offspring (10:4–11:2), the passage reads:

Then all the earth will be tilled in righteousness, and all of it will be planted with trees and filled with blessing; and all the trees of joy will be planted on it. They will plant vines on it, and every vine that will be planted on it will yield a thousand jugs of wine; and of every seed that is sown on it, each measure will yield a thousand measures; and each measure of olives will yield ten baths of oil.[7]

The proportions in *1 Enoch* are multiplied in the similar passage in *2 Bar.* 29:5, possibly composed during Papias' lifetime:[8] "The earth will also yield fruits ten thousandfold. And on one vine will be a thousand branches, and one branch will produce a thousand clusters, and one cluster will produce a thousand grapes, and one grape will produce a cor of wine."[9]

Papias 1.5 also has parallels in Jewish eschatological literature. In this verse Jesus replies to Judas' unbelieving question about how the Lord could bring about the fruit described in vv. 2–3 with the words, "Those who come into those times will see." As noted by Charles Hill, "This sounds like the view of *4 Ezra* (7.28; 13.24), in which the Messiah's kingdom is 'seen' only by the last generation of humans, who 'live until those times'. By contrast, the 'millennial reign' of Christ with his saints in the Christian apocalypse written by John (Rev. 20.1–10) is explicitly for those who have already 'died' and 'come to life' as partakers in 'the first resurrection'."[10]

These parallels in Jewish literature in and of themselves are not sufficient to indicate that the tradition in Papias did not derive from Jesus. It is to be expected that Jesus would incorporate elements from his own Jewish milieu into his speech.[11] The above considerations only lead to the prob-

---

[7] Trans. is by Nickelsburg, *1 Enoch 1*, 216.

[8] Scholars date *2 Baruch* generally between A.D. 70 and 135 ("Baruch, II," in *ODCC* 167), and more probably between the last decade of the first century and the second decade of the second (A. F. J. Klijn, "2 [Syriac Apocalypse of] Baruch," in *OTP* 1:616–17; M. E. Stone, "Apocalyptic Literature," in *Jewish Writings of the Second Temple Period: Apocrypha, Pseudepigrapha, Qumran Sectarian Writings, Philo, Josephus* [ed. M. E. Stone; CRINT 3.2; Assen: Van Gorcum/Philadelphia: Fortress, 1984], 410).

[9] Trans. is by Klijn, "2 Baruch," 630. Papias was probably born ca. A.D. 70 and wrote sometime between the late first century and the 4th decade of the second century, probably around A.D. 110; see Schoedel, "Papias [*ANRW*]," 236 and Hill, "Papias," 42, and literature cited there.

[10] Hill, "Papias," 50.

[11] As noted in ch. 8 above (p. 228), the criterion of dissimilarity that has been applied for decades by the form critics to determine what Jesus "could have" and "could not have" said has rightly been discredited; see, e.g., the critique by Hooker, "Wrong Tool," 573–79.

able conclusion that the tradition in Papias did not derive from Jesus when taken in conjunction with the other three points developed here.

(3) There is a parallel in early Christian literature to vv. 2–3 that is not identified as a saying of Jesus, in the mid-third to late fourth century Christian compilation known as the *Apocalypse of Paul*. This parallel pushes the eschatological abundance found in *1 Enoch* 10:19 and *2 Baruch* 29:5 to a level similar to Papias:[12]

And the trees were full of fruit from root (up) to tree-top. From the root of each tree up to its heart there were ten thousand branches with tens of thousands of clusters [and there were ten thousand clusters on each branch] and there were ten thousand dates in each cluster. And it was the same with the vines. Each vine had ten thousand branches, and each branch had on it ten thousand bunches of grapes, and each bunch had ten thousand grapes. And there were other trees there, myriads of myriads of them, and their fruit was in the same proportion (*Apoc. Paul,* 22).[13]

In terms of the abundance described, the saying in Papias is much closer to the later saying in the *Apocalypse of Paul* than to the earlier "leaner" sayings found in *1 Enoch* and *2 Baruch*. Again it is important to emphasize, however, that in the *Apocalypse of Paul* this material is not attributed to Jesus.

That a later document such as the *Apocalypse of Paul* would contain material so similar to the Jesus saying in Papias vv. 2–3, yet not attribute it to Jesus, implies that the saying in Papias may have been a foreign element incorporated at some point into the Jesus tradition. This is more feasible than the alternative, that an extended saying of Jesus would have lost its connection to him in Christian circles; why, then, preserve it? In addition, that the material is not treated as Jesus tradition in the *Apocalypse of Paul* implies that the *Apocalypse* is probably not dependent on Papias, in spite of their similarity. It is more likely that the author of the *Apocalypse* and Papias both derived the saying from a closely related source.

(4) Finally, what can be reconstructed regarding the method of Papias' "Exposition of the Lord's Logia" may shed some light on the source of the material in question: it appears that it was built upon the sequence of a saying of Christ, followed by its interpretation ("which is characteristically

---

[12] The *Apocalypse of Paul* is a composite work, its earliest material dating from the mid-third century, and its final compilation probably ca. 388 (Elliott, *Apocryphal New Testament*, 616–17) or more generally in the late fourth or early fifth century (E. Ferguson, "Vision of Paul," *EEC* 1167).

[13] Trans. is that of H. Duensing and A. de Santos Otero, "Apocalypse of Paul," in *New Testament Apocrypha* (ed. Schneemelcher), 2:726.

millennial"), to which was added a story from oral tradition as an illustration.[14]

If these were the components of Papias' work, it raises the question of whether in the case of vv. 2–3 Irenaeus may have mistaken Papias' interpretation – based on the midrashic elaboration of Jewish themes – for a saying of Jesus. This would be an understandable mistake, especially if Irenaeus did not have the writings of Papias open beside him, but was relying on memory. Here is where access to the actual writings of Papias would be indispensable to the present study; as it is, there is no way to verify this possibility.

One more point may be made regarding v. 5: we know from another fragment of Papias that his writings included apocryphal material regarding Judas. In fragment 4.2–3 we read:

> But Judas went about in this world as a great model of impurity. He became so bloated in the flesh that he could not pass through a place that was easily wide enough for a wagon – not even his swollen head could fit. They say that his eyelids swelled to such an extent that he could not see the light at all; and a doctor could not see his eyes even with an optical device, so deeply sunken they were in the surrounding flesh. And his genitals became more disgusting and larger than anyone's; simply by relieving himself, to his wanton shame, he emitted pus and worms that flowed through his entire body. And they say that after he suffered numerous torments and punishments, he died on his own land, and that land has been, until now, desolate and uninhabited because of the stench. Indeed, even to this day no one can pass by the place without holding his nose. This was how great an outpouring he made from his flesh on the ground.[15]

There is little reason to grant any historical validity to this gossip-like material, but it is valuable in witnessing to a certain type of Judas-related tradition in Papias' writings. The above fragment regarding Judas' death is apparently an attempt to harmonize the narratives of Mt 27:3–10, which has Judas hanging himself, and Acts 1:18, according to which Judas fell and burst open so that his bowels gushed out.[16] Apollinarius, the source of this Papias fragment, explains how Judas could have both hung himself and fallen in the manner described, by positing that he had not died in the hanging narrated in Matthew, but had been taken down and lived on to experience the fall described in Acts.[17] It is in this context that Apollinarius quotes the above tradition from Papias regarding Judas' death.

---

[14] Lightfoot, *Essays*, 156–59, quote from p. 159; see also Schoedel, *Polycarp, Martyrdom, Papias*, 94.

[15] Ehrman, *Apostolic Fathers*, 2:105–7, already cited in sec. 3.4 above; this material has been reconstructed by various editors from the works of Apollinaris of Laodicea (4th cent.); see Holmes, *Apostolic Fathers*, 755.

[16] Schoedel, *Polycarp, Martyrdom, Papias*, 111.

[17] Ibid., 111.

It may be that Papias' fragment 1.5 is to be understood along similar lines to the above, even though its brevity does not offer much to the interpreter. Verse 5, again, reads: "These things can be believed by those who believe. And the betrayer Judas," he said, "did not believe, but asked, 'How then can the Lord bring forth such produce?' The Lord then replied, 'Those who come into those times will see.'" This passage is probably best viewed as another gossip-like tradition (like Papias fragment 4.2–3) regarding Judas, in this case attempting to understand how one of the Twelve could have betrayed the Lord. Fragment 1.5 portrays Judas as the "ideal" doubter, obviously (given the events that were to follow) one who would not be among those to "come into those times." As noted in our discussion in chapter 3, the type of oral tradition represented by both of these fragments on Judas would have been subject to very little control.[18]

We tentatively conclude, in light of the above discussion, that it is very likely that the contents of vv. 2–3 in this fragment of Papias did not originate in oral tradition, but from the literary reworking of Jewish written sources. In addition, it is possible that these verses were not part of the tradition passed on by Papias, but rather of his interpretation of a tradition. There is less to conclude regarding the Jesus tradition in v. 5, but it may have originated as gossip-type material in order to portray Judas as the "ideal" doubter.[19]

Fragment 13.2 (George Hamartolos, *Chronicon*)

εἰπὼν γὰρ ὁ κύριος πρὸς αὐτούς· Δύνασθε πιεῖν τὸ ποτήριον, ὃ ἐγὼ πίνω; καὶ κατανευσάντων προθύμως καὶ συνθεμένων· τὸ ποτήριόν μου, φησίν, πίεσθε, καὶ τὸ βάπτισμα, ὃ ἐγὼ βαπτίζομαι, βαπτισθήσεσθε.

For the Lord said to them, "Are you able to drink the cup that I drink?" And when they eagerly nodded their assent and agreed to do so, he said, "You will drink my cup, and you will be baptized with the baptism that I experience."

Pap 13.2:	εἰπὼν γὰρ ὁ κύριος πρὸς <u>αὐτούς</u>·
Mk 10:38a:	ὁ δὲ Ἰησοῦς εἶπεν <u>αὐτοῖς</u>· οὐκ οἴδατε τί αἰτεῖσθε.
Mt 20:22a:	ἀποκριθεὶς δὲ ὁ Ἰησοῦς <u>εἶπεν</u>· οὐκ οἴδατε τί αἰτεῖσθε.

---

[18] See comments in sec. 3.4 above.

[19] In light of these conclusions, F. F. Bruce may be fully justified when he states, "if this was the kind of thing with which oral tradition provided Papias in addition to the dominical oracles recorded in the 'books' at his disposal, we can only conclude that the stream of genuine oral tradition had dried up almost entirely in his part of the world" (*Tradition Old and New* [Grand Rapids: Zondervan, 1970], 111).

Pap 13.2:   δύνασθε πιεῖν τὸ ποτήριον ὃ ἐγὼ πίνω;
Mk 10:38b: δύνασθε πιεῖν τὸ ποτήριον ὃ ἐγὼ πίνω
              ἢ τὸ βάπτισμα ὃ ἐγὼ βαπτίζομαι βαπτισθῆναι;
Mt 20:22b: δύνασθε πιεῖν τὸ ποτήριον ὃ ἐγὼ μέλλω πίνειν;

Pap 13.2:   καὶ κατανευσάντων προθύμως καὶ συνθεμένων·
Mk 10:39a: οἱ δὲ εἶπαν αὐτῷ· δυνάμεθα. ὁ δὲ Ἰησοῦς εἶπεν αὐτοῖς·
Mt 20:22c: λέγουσιν   αὐτῷ· δυνάμεθα. λέγει αὐτοῖς·

Pap 13.2:   τὸ ποτήριόν μου, φησίν, πίεσθε,
              καὶ τὸ βάπτισμα ὃ ἐγὼ βαπτίζομαι, βαπτισθήσεσθε
Mk 10:39b: τὸ ποτήριον ὃ ἐγὼ πίνω πίεσθε,
              καὶ τὸ βάπτισμα ὃ ἐγὼ βαπτίζομαι, βαπτισθήσεσθε
Mt 20:23a: τὸ μὲν ποτήριόν μου   πίεσθε

Here, again, there is a problem with assigning the Jesus tradition to Papias. The problem becomes apparent in light of the wider context in George's *Chronicon*, that has to do with the fate of John:

> And after Domitian, Nerva reigned for one year. He recalled John from his island and allowed him to live in Ephesus. He alone of the twelve disciples remained alive at that time; and after he composed his Gospel he was found worthy to become a martyr. For Papias, bishop of Hierapolis, an eyewitness of John, asserts in the second book of the Lord's sayings that John was killed by Jews. And so he, along with his brother, clearly fulfilled the prediction of Christ about them and the confession and consent that they gave to it. For the Lord said to them, "Are you able to drink the cup that I drink?" And when they eagerly nodded their assent and agreed to do so, he said, "You will drink my cup, and you will be baptized with the baptism that I experience." And it makes sense that this happened, because God cannot lie. (13.1–2)

As noted by J. B. Lightfoot, in this wider context of the fragment, "The fate which really befell James is attributed to John." Lightfoot derives from this the implication that George "cannot be quoting directly from Papias, for Papias cannot have reported the *martyrdom* of John."[20] Scholars have suggested various theories to solve this problem, which need not detain us here.[21] The above is enough to make the point that one cannot with any degree of confidence attribute the saying under consideration to Papias, since George apparently did not have direct access to his writings and in fact

---

[20] Lightfoot, *Essays*, 211–12. The tradition that John suffered a martyr's death, despite its antiquity, is not reliable, and unfortunately the text under consideration has played a large role in its formation; see esp. the discussion in F.-M. Braun, *Jean le théologien* (3 vols.; EBib; Paris: J. Gabalda, 1959–72), 1:375–88; and also in Davies and Allison, *Matthew*, 3:90–92; R. Schnackenburg, *The Gospel According to St. John* (trans. K. Smyth, et al; 3 vols.; HTCNT; New York: Herder and Herder, 1968, 1990), 1:86–88; Taylor, *Mark*, 442, and literature cited there.

[21] Lightfoot himself solves the problem by suggesting that there was a lacuna in the quotation, and George's reference was to the martyrdom of James, not John (*Essays*, 212). For a survey of other solutions see Schoedel, "Papias [*ANRW*]," 241.

misunderstood what they contained. We will treat the fragment, however, as if it came from Papias in order to move forward with our examination.

The core of the words of Jesus in 13.2 is stable, as reflected in the verbatim parallelism between two of the lines in Papias and Mark (we will leave Matthew's parallel out of the following discussion, on the presupposition that it was dependent on Mark):

Pap 13.2:   δύνασθε πιεῖν τὸ ποτήριον ὃ ἐγὼ πίνω
Mk 10:38b: δύνασθε πιεῖν τὸ ποτήριον ὃ ἐγὼ πίνω
            ἢ τὸ βάπτισμα ὃ ἐγὼ βαπτίζομαι βαπτισθῆναι;

Pap 13.2:   τὸ ποτήριόν μου, φησίν, πίεσθε,
            καὶ τὸ βάπτισμα ὃ ἐγὼ βαπτίζομαι, βαπτισθήσεσθε
Mk 10:39b: τὸ ποτήριον ὃ ἐγὼ πίνω πίεσθε,
            καὶ τὸ βάπτισμα ὃ ἐγὼ βαπτίζομαι, βαπτισθήσεσθε

The tradition that informed the saying in Papias is probably even closer to Mark than this surviving written saying, as it is obvious that the fragment of Papias presupposes the longer form of the Lord's question in Mk 10:38: the καὶ τὸ βάπτισμα ὃ ἐγὼ βαπτίζομαι, βαπτισθήσεσθε of the answer (paralleling Mark verbatim) contains implicitly the δύνασθε ... τὸ βάπτισμα ὃ ἐγὼ βαπτίζομαι βαπτισθῆναι; of the Markan question. (Jesus' οὐκ οἴδατε τί αἰτεῖσθε found in Mark but not in Papias would be out of place in the latter, which did not contain the question that precedes this line in the gospel.)

Where one finds most variability in the tradition is precisely where one would expect it: not in the words of Jesus, but in the reply of the disciples:

Pap 13:2:   καὶ κατανευσάντων προθύμως καὶ συνθεμένων·
Mk 10:39a: οἱ δὲ εἶπαν αὐτῷ· δυνάμεθα.

This variability within stability may indicate that Papias and Mark depended upon a common oral tradition.

Due to the status of the sons of Zebedee in the early church, one would expect the tradition regarding what Jesus said about their fate to become fairly widespread. There is thus no intrinsic reason to doubt that the oral tradition of the Jesus saying under consideration would have been available to both Mark and Papias.

Given that we have treated the fragments of Papias in this appendix only for the sake of completeness, we will not here draw out implications of the above discussion for the present work. It bears noting, however, that the above discussion has confirmed what was said in the introduction to this appendix: one cannot be confident that the explicit sayings of Jesus in the fragments usually attributed to Papias actually were found in his writings. This justifies the choice in the present study to treat these fragments separately in an appendix rather than as an integral part of the book as a whole, given that the book as a whole is devoted specifically to the Jesus tradition in the Apostolic Fathers.

Bibliography

A Committee of the Oxford Society of Historical Theology. *The New Testament in the Apostolic Fathers.* Oxford: Clarendon, 1905.

Abel, Ernest L. "The Psychology of Memory and Rumor Transmission and Their Bearing on Theories of Oral Transmission in Early Christianity." *The Journal of Religion* 51 (1971): 270–81.

Achtemeier, Paul J. *1 Peter: A Commentary on First Peter.* Edited by Eldon Jay Epp. Hermeneia. Minneapolis: Fortress, 1996.

–. *"Omne Verbum Sonat:* The New Testament and the Oral Environment of Late Western Antiquity." *Journal of Biblical Literature* 109 (1990): 3–27.

Aitken, Ellen Bradshaw. *Jesus' Death in Early Christian Memory: The Poetics of the Passion.* Novum Testamentum et Orbis Antiquus 53. Göttingen: Vandenhoeck & Ruprecht/Fribourg: Academic, 2004.

Aland, Kurt. "The Problem of Anonymity and Pseudonymity in Christian Literature of the First Two Centuries." *Journal of Theological Studies* n.s. 12 (1961): 39–49.

Aland, Kurt, ed. *Synopsis quattuor Evangeliorum: Locis parallelis evangeliorum apocryphorum et patrum adhibitis.* Korrigierter und um die Papyri 101–111 erweiterter Druck 2001. 15th ed. Stuttgart: Deutsche Bibelgesellschaft, 2001.

Albright, William Foxwell, and C. S. Mann. *Matthew.* Anchor Bible 26. Garden City: Doubleday, 1971.

Alexander, Elizabeth Shanks. "The Orality of Rabbinic Writing." Pages 38–57 in *The Cambridge Companion to the Talmud and Rabbinic Literature.* Edited by Charlotte Elisheva Fonrobert and Martin S. Jaffee. Cambridge Companions to Religion. Cambridge: Cambridge University Press, 2007.

–. *Transmitting Mishnah: The Shaping Influence of Oral Tradition.* Cambridge: Cambridge University Press, 2006.

Alexander, Loveday C. A. "The Living Voice: Scepticism towards the Written Word in Early Christian and in Graeco-Roman Texts." Pages 221–247 in *The Bible in Three Dimensions: Essays in Celebration of Forty Years of Biblical Studies in the University of Sheffield.* Edited by David J. A. Clines, Stephen E. Fowl and Stanley E. Porter. Journal for the Study of the Old Testament Supplement Series 87. Sheffield: JSOT Press, 1990.

Alexander, Patrick H., John F. Kutsko, James D. Ernest, Shirley A. Decker-Lucke, and David L. Petersen, eds. *The SBL Handbook of Style: For Ancient Near Eastern, Biblical, and Early Christian Studies.* Peabody, Mass.: Hendrickson, 1999.

Alexander, Philip S. "Jesus and the Golden Rule." Pages 363–388 in *Hillel and Jesus: Comparative Studies of Two Major Religious Leaders.* Edited by James H. Charlesworth and Loren L. Johns. Minneapolis: Fortress, 1997.

–. "Literacy among Jews in Second Temple Palestine: Reflections on the Evidence from Qumran." Pages 3–24 in *Hamlet on a Hill: Semitic and Greek Studies Presented to Professor T. Muraoka on the Occasion of his Sixty-Fifth Birthday.* Edited by M. F. J.

Baasten and W. Th. van Peursen. Orientalia Lovaniensia analecta 118. Leuven: Peeters and Department of Oriental Studies, 2003.

–. "Orality in Pharisaic-rabbinic Judaism at the Turn of the Eras." Pages 159–184 in *Jesus and the Oral Gospel Tradition*. Edited by H. Wansbrough. Journal for the Study of the New Testament Supplement Series 64. Sheffield: JSOT Press, 1991.

Allen, Willoughby C. *A Critical and Exegetical Commentary on the Gospel according to S. Matthew*. International Critical Commentary. Edinburgh: T&T Clark, 1912.

Allison, Dale C., Jr. *The Jesus Tradition in Q*. Harrisburg: Trinity Press International, 1997.

–. "Paul and the Missionary Discourse." *Ephemerides theologicae Lovanienses* 61 (1985): 369–75.

–. "The Pauline Epistles and the Synoptic Gospels: The Pattern of the Parallels." *New Testament Studies* 28 (1982): 1–32.

–. "Q's New Exodus and the Historical Jesus." Pages 395–428 in *The Sayings Source Q and the Historical Jesus*. Edited by A. Lindemann. Bibliotheca Ephemeridum Theologicarum Lovaniensium 118. Leuven: Leuven University Press and Peeters, 2001.

Alon, Gedaliah. "Halakah in the Teaching of the Twelve Apostles (*Didache*)." Pages 165–194 in *The Didache in Modern Research*. Edited by Jonathan A. Draper. Arbeiten zur Geschichte des antiken Judentums und des Urchristentums 37. Leiden: Brill, 1996.

Altaner, Berthold. *Patrology*. Translated by Hilda C. Graef. Freiburg: Herder/London: Nelson, 1960.

Amman, É. Review of P. N. Harrison, *Polycarp's Two Epistles to the Philippians*. *Revue des sciences religieuses* 17 (1937): 344–48.

Amodio, Mark C. "Contemporary Critical Approaches and Studies in Oral Tradition." Pages 95–105 in *Teaching Oral Traditions*. Edited by John Miles Foley. New York: Modern Language Association, 1998.

Amphoux, Christian B. "Le style oral dans le Nouveau Testament." *Études Théologiques et Religieuses* 63 (1988): 379–84.

Andersen, F. I. "2 (Slavonic Apocalypse of) Enoch (Late First Century A.D.)." Pages 91–221 in vol. 1 of *The Old Testament Pseudepigrapha*. Edited by James H. Charlesworth. 2 vols. New York: Doubleday, 1983, 1985.

Andersen, Øivind. "Oral Tradition." Pages 17–58 in *Jesus and the Oral Gospel Tradition*. Edited by H. Wansbrough. Journal for the Study of the New Testament Supplement Series 64. Sheffield: JSOT Press, 1991.

Antomarini, Brunella. "The Acoustical Prehistory of Poetry." *New Literary History* 35 (2004): 355–372.

Assmann, Jan. "Collective Memory and Cultural Identity." *New German Critique* 65 (1995): 125–33.

–. "Form as a Mnemonic Device: Cultural Texts and Cultural Memory." Pages 67–82 in *Performing the Gospel: Orality, Memory, and Mark: Essays Dedicated to Werner Kelber*. Edited by Richard A. Horsley, Jonathan A. Draper and John Miles Foley. Minneapolis: Fortress, 2006.

–. *Das kulturelle Gedächtnis: Schrift, Erinnerung und politische Identität in frühen Hochkulturen*. Munich: C. H. Beck, 1992.

–. *Religion and Cultural Memory: Ten Studies*. Translated by Rodney Livingstone. Stanford, Calif.: Stanford University Press, 2006.

Audet, Jean Paul. *La Didachè: Instructions des Apôtres*. Études bibliques. Paris: Librairie Lecoffre, 1958.

–. "Literary and Doctrinal Relationships of the 'Manual of Discipline.'" Pages 129–147 in *The Didache in Modern Research.* Edited by Jonathan A. Draper. Arbeiten zur Geschichte des antiken Judentums und des Urchristentums 37. Leiden: Brill, 1996. E.T. of "Affinités littéraires et doctrinales du 'Manual de Discipline.'" *Revue biblique* 59 (1952): 219–238.

Aune, David E. "Jesus Tradition and the Pauline Letters." Pages 63–86 in *Jesus in Memory: Traditions in Oral and Scribal Practices.* Edited by Werner H. Kelber and Samuel Byrskog. Waco, Tex.: Baylor University Press, 2009.

–. "Oral Tradition and the Aphorisms of Jesus." Pages 211–241 in *Jesus and the Oral Gospel Tradition.* Edited by H. Wansbrough. Journal for the Study of the New Testament Supplement Series 64. Sheffield: JSOT Press, 1991.

–. "Prolegomena to the Study of Oral Tradition in the Hellenistic World." Pages 59–106 in *Jesus and the Oral Gospel Tradition.* Edited by H. Wansbrough. Journal for the Study of the New Testament Supplement Series 64. Sheffield: JSOT Press, 1991.

–. *Revelation 1–5.* Word Biblical Commentary 52A. Dallas: Word, 1997.

Avery-Peck, Alan J. "Oral Tradition (Judaism)." Pages 34–37 in vol. 5 of *The Anchor Bible Dictionary.* Edited by David Noel Freedman. 6 vols. New York: Doubleday, 1992.

Ayán Calvo, Juan José. *Clemente de Roma: Carta a los Corintios; Homilía Anónima (Secunda Clementis).* Fuentes Patrísticas 4. Madrid: Editorial Ciudad Nueva, 1994.

Baarda, Tjitze. "2 Clement 12 and the Sayings of Jesus." Pages 529–56 in *Logia: Les Paroles de Jésus – The Sayings of Jesus: Mémorial Joseph Coppens.* Edited by Joël Delobel. Bibliotheca Ephemeridum Theologicarum Lovaniensium 59. Leuven: Leuven University Press and Peeters, 1982.

Bailey, Kenneth E. "Informal Controlled Oral Tradition and the Synoptic Gospels." *Asia Journal of Theology* 5 (1991): 34–54.

–. "Middle Eastern Oral Tradition and the Synoptic Gospels." *Expository Times* 106 (1994–95): 363–367.

Baird, William. *History of New Testament Research,* Vol. 1: *From Deism to Tübingen.* Minneapolis: Fortress, 1992.

–. *History of New Testament Research,* Vol. 2: *From Jonathan Edwards to Rudolf Bultmann.* Minneapolis: Fortress, 2003.

Bakke, Odd Magne. *"Concord and Peace": A Rhetorical Analysis of the First Letter of Clement with an Emphasis on the Language of Unity and Sedition.* Wissenschaftliche Untersuchungen zum Neuen Testament 2.141. Tübingen: Mohr Siebeck, 2001.

Bakker, Egbert J. "Activation and Preservation: The Interdependence of Text and Performance in an Oral Tradition." *Oral Tradition* 8 (1993): 5–20.

–. "Discourse and Performance: Involvement, Visualization and 'Presence' in Homeric Poetry." *Classical Antiquity* 12 (1993): 1–29.

–. "How Oral is Oral Composition?" Pages 29–47 in *Signs of Orality: The Oral Tradition and its Influence in the Greek and Roman Worlds.* Edited by E. Anne Mackay. Supplements to Mnemosyne 188. Leiden: Brill, 1999.

–. *Poetry in Speech: Orality and Homeric Discourse.* Myth and Poetics. Ithaca and London: Cornell University Press, 1997.

–. "Storytelling in the Future: Truth, Time, and Tense in Homeric Epic." Pages 11–36 in *Written Voices, Spoken Signs: Tradition, Performance, and the Epic Text.* Edited by Egbert J. Bakker and Ahuvia Kahane. Center for Hellenistic Studies Colloquia. Cambridge, Mass.: Harvard University Press, 1997.

–. "The Study of Homeric Discourse." Pages 284–304 in *A New Companion to Homer*. Edited by Ian Morris and Barry Powell. Supplements to Mnemosyne 163. Leiden: Brill, 1997.

Balabanski, Vicky. *Eschatology in the Making: Mark, Matthew and the Didache*. Society for New Testament Studies Monograph Series 97. Cambridge: Cambridge University Press, 1997.

Balch, David L. "The Canon: Adaptable and Stable, Oral and Written: Critical Questions for Kelber and Riesner." *Forum* 7 (1991): 183–205.

Bammel, C. P. Hammond. "Ignatian Problems." *Journal of Theological Studies* n.s. 33 (1982): 62–97.

Bardenhewer, Otto. *Patrology: The Lives and Works of the Fathers of the Church*. Translated by Thomas J. Shahan. Freiburg: Herder, 1908.

Bar-Ilan, Meir. "Illiteracy in the Land of Israel in the First Centuries C.E." Pages 46–61 in *Essays in the Social Scientific Study of Judaism and Jewish Society*. Edited by Simcha Fishbane, Stuart Schoenfeld and Alain Goldschläger. Hoboken: KTAV, 1992.

Barnard, L. W. "The Church in Rome in the First Two Centuries A.D." Pages 131–180 in idem, *Studies in Church History and Patristics*. Analecta Vlatadon 26. Thessaloniki: Patriarchal Institute for Patristic Studies, 1978.

–. "The Dead Sea Scrolls, Barnabas, the *Didache* and the Later History of the 'Two Ways.'" Pages 87–107 in idem, *Studies in the Apostolic Fathers and their Background*. Oxford: Blackwell, 1966.

–. "The Problem of St. Polycarp's Epistle to the Philippians." Pages 31–39 in idem, *Studies in the Apostolic Fathers and their Background*. Oxford: Blackwell, 1966.

Barnes, Michael. "Oral Tradition and Hellenistic Epic: New Directions in Apollonius of Rhodes." *Oral Tradition* 18 (2003): 55–58.

Barr, David. "The Apocalypse of John as Oral Enactment." *Interpretation* 40 (1986): 243–56.

Barrett, C. K. *A Critical and Exegetical Commentary on the Acts of the Apostles*. International Critical Commentary. 2 vols. Edinburgh: T&T Clark, 1994, 1998.

–. *Jesus and the Gospel Tradition*. Philadelphia: Fortress, 1968.

–. "Sayings of Jesus in the Acts of the Apostles." Pages 681–708 in *À cause de l'Évangile: Études sur les Synoptiques et les Actes offertes au P. Jacques Dupont, O.S.B. à l'occasion de son 70ᵉ anniversaire*. Lectio Divina 123. Paris: Saint-André/ Cerf, 1985.

Bartsch, Hans Werner. "Feldrede und Bergpredigt: Redaktionsarbeit in Luk 6," *Theologische Zeitschrift* 16 (1960): 5–18.

Bauckham, Richard. "Eyewitnesses and Critical History: A Response to Jens Schröter and Craig Evans." *Journal for the Study of the New Testament* 31 (2008): 221–35.

–. "The Eyewitnesses in the Gospel of Mark." *Svensk Exegetisk Årsbok* 74 (2009): 19–39.

–. *Jesus and the Eyewitnesses: The Gospels as Eyewitness Testimony*. Grand Rapids: Eerdmans, 2006.

–. "Synoptic Parousia Parables and the Apocalypse." *New Testament Studies* 23 (1976– 77): 162–76. Repr. pages 92–117 in idem, *The Climax of Prophecy: Studies on the Book of Revelation*. Edinburgh: T&T Clark, 1993.

–. "The Transmission of the Gospel Traditions." *Revista Catalana de Teologia* 32 (2008): 377–94.

Bauer, Johannes Bapt. *Die Polykarpbriefe*. Kommentar zu den Apostolischen Vätern 5. Göttingen: Vandenhoeck & Ruprecht, 1995.

Bauer, Walter. *Die Briefe des Ignatius von Antiochia und der Polykarpbrief.* Handbuch zum neuen Testament, Ergänzungsband: Die apostolischen Väter 2. Tübingen: Mohr Siebeck, 1920.

Baum, Armin D. "Matthew's Sources – Oral or Written? A Rabbinic Analogy and Empirical Insights." Pages 1–23 in *Built Upon the Rock: Studies in the Gospel of Matthew.* Edited by Daniel M. Gurtner and John Nolland. Grand Rapids: Eerdmans, 2008.

–. *Der mündliche Faktor und seine Bedeutung für die synoptische Frage: Analogien aus der antiken Literatur, der Experimentalpsychologie, der Oral Poetry-Forschung und dem rabbinischen Traditionswesen.* Texte und Arbeiten zum neutestamentlichen Zeitalter 49. Tübingen: Francke, 2008.

–. „Papias, der Vorzug der Viva Vox und die Evangelienschriften." *New Testament Studies* 44 (1998): 144–51.

Baumgarten, Albert I. "The Torah as Public Document in Judaism." *Studies in Religion/ Sciences Religieuses* 14 (1985): 17–24.

–. *The Flourishing of Jewish Sects in the Maccabean Era: An Interpretation.* Supplements to the Journal for the Study of Judaism 55. Leiden: Brill, 1997.

Beale, G. K. *The Book of Revelation: A Commentary on the Greek Text.* New International Greek Testament Commentary. Grand Rapids: Eerdmans, 1999.

Beaton, Richard. "How Matthew Writes." Pages 116–134 in *The Written Gospel [Festschrift for Graham Stanton].* Edited by Markus Bockmuehl and Donald A. Hagner. Cambridge: Cambridge University Press, 2005.

Beatrice, P. F. "The 'Gospel according to the Hebrews' in the Apostolic Fathers." *Novum Testamentum* 48 (2006): 147–95.

Bellah, Robert N., Richard Madsen, William M. Sullivan, Ann Swidler, and Steven M. Tipton. *Habits of the Heart: Individualism and Commitment in American Life.* Berkeley: University of California Press, 1985.

Bellinzoni, Arthur J. "The Gospel of Luke in the Apostolic Fathers: An Overview." Pages 45–68 in *Trajectories through the New Testament and the Apostolic Fathers.* Edited by Andrew Gregory and Christopher Tuckett. The New Testament and the Apostolic Fathers 2. Oxford: Oxford University Press, 2005.

–. "The Gospel of Luke in the Second Century CE." Pages 59–76 in *Literary Studies in Luke-Acts: Essays in Honor of Joseph B. Tyson.* Edited by Richard P. Thompson and Thomas E. Phillips. Macon: Mercer University Press, 1998.

–. "The Gospel of Matthew in the Second Century." *Second Century* 9 (1992): 197–258.

–. *The Sayings of Jesus in the Writings of Justin Martyr.* Supplements to Novum Testamentum 17. Leiden: Brill, 1967.

Benoit, Pierre. "The Transmission of the Gospel in the First Centuries." Pages 145–168 in *The Gospel as History.* Edited by Vilmos Vajta. Philadelphia: Fortress, 1975.

Berding, Kenneth. *Polycarp and Paul: An Analysis of their Literary and Theological Relationship in Light of Polycarp's Use of Biblical and Extra-Biblical Literature.* Supplements to Vigiliae Christianae 62. Leiden: Brill, 2002.

Berger, Klaus. "Form Criticism, New Testament." Pages 413–17 in vol. 1 of *Dictionary of Biblical Interpretation.* Edited by John H. Hayes. 2 vols. Nashville: Abingdon, 1999.

Best, Ernest. "1 Peter and the Gospel Tradition." *New Testament Studies* 16 (1969–70): 95–113.

–. "Mark's Preservation of the Tradition." Pages 21–34 in *L'Évangile selon Marc: Tradition et rédaction.* Edited by M. Sabbe. Bibliotheca Ephemeridum Theologicarum Lovaniensium 34. Leuven: Leuven University Press/Gembloux: Duculot, 1974.

Betz, Hans Dieter. *Essays on the Sermon on the Mount.* Philadelphia: Fortress, 1985
–. *The Sermon on the Mount: A Commentary on the Sermon on the Mount, Including the
    Sermon on the Plain (Matthew 5:3–7:27 and Luke 6:20–49).* Hermeneia. Minneapo-
    lis: Fortress, 1995.
–. "The Sermon on the Mount and Q: Some Aspects of the Problem." Pages 19–34 in
    Gospel Origins and Christian Beginnings: In Honor of James M. Robinson. Edited
    by James E. Goehring, Charles W. Hedrick, Jack T. Sanders and Hans Dieter Betz.
    Forum Fascicles. Sonoma, Calif.: Polebridge, 1990.
–. "The Sermon on the Mount: In Defense of a Hypothesis." *Biblical Research* 36 (1991):
    74–80.
–. "The Sermon on the Mount in Matthew's Interpretation." Pages 258–275 in *The Future
    of Early Christianity: Essays in Honor of Helmut Koester.* Edited by Birger A. Pear-
    son. Minneapolis: Fortress, 1991.
Betz, Johannes. "The Eucharist in the *Didache*." Pages 244–275 in *The Didache in Mod-
    ern Research.* Edited by Jonathan A. Draper. Arbeiten zur Geschichte des antiken
    Judentums und des Urchristentums 37. Leiden: Brill, 1996.
Bihlmeyer, Karl. *Die Apostolischen Väter: Neubearbeitung der Funkschen Ausgabe.* 3rd
    ed. Sammlung ausgewählter Kirchen- und dogmen-geschichtlicher Quellenschriften
    2.1.1. Tübingen: Mohr Siebeck, 1970.
Black, Matthew. *An Aramaic Approach to the Gospels and Acts.* 3rd ed. Introduction by
    Craig A. Evans. Appendix by Geza Vermes. Peabody, Mass.: Hendrickson, 1998.
–. "The Doxology to the *Pater Noster* with a note on Matthew 6.13b." Pages 327–338 in
    A Tribute to Geza Vermes: Essays on Jewish and Christian Literature and History.
    Edited by Philip R. Davies and Richard T. White. Journal for the Study of the Old
    Testament Supplement Series 100. Sheffield: JSOT Press, 1990.
Bloch, Maurice. "Literacy and Enlightenment." Pages 15–37 in *Literacy and Society.*
    Edited by Karen Schousboe and Mogens Trolle Larsen. Copenhagen: Akademisk
    Forlag, 1989.
Blomberg, Craig L. "Form Criticism." Pages 243–250 in *Dictionary of Jesus and the
    Gospels.* Edited by Joel B. Green, Scot McKnight and I. Howard Marshall. Downers
    Grove: InterVarsity, 1992.
–. *Matthew.* New American Commentary 22. Nashville: Broadman, 1992.
Bock, Darrell L. "Form Criticism." Pages 106–127 in *Interpreting the New Testament:
    Essays on Methods and Issues.* Edited by David Alan Black and David S. Dockery.
    Nashville: Broadman & Holman, 2001.
–. *Luke 1: 1:1–9:50.* Baker Exegetical Commentary on the New Testament 3A. Grand
    Rapids: Baker 1994.
–. *Luke 9:51–24:53.* Baker Exegetical Commentary on the New Testament 3B. Grand
    Rapids: Baker, 1996.
Bockmuehl, Markus. Review of James D. G. Dunn, *Christianity in the Making*, Vol. 1:
    Jesus Remembered. Journal of Theological Studies n.s. 56 (2005): 140–49.
–. *Seeing the Word: Refocusing New Testament Study.* Studies in Theological Interpreta-
    tion. Grand Rapids: Baker Academic, 2006.
Boomershine, Thomas E. "Jesus of Nazareth and the Watershed of Ancient Orality and
    Literacy." Pages 7–36 in *Orality and Textuality in Early Christian Literature.* Edited
    by Joanna Dewey. *Semeia* 65. Atlanta: Society of Biblical Literature/Scholars, 1994.
Boring, M. Eugene. *The Continuing Voice of Jesus: Christian Prophecy and the Gospel
    Tradition.* Louisville: Westminster/John Knox, 1991.

–. "The Kingdom of God in Mark." Pages 131–145 in *The Kingdom of God in 20th-Century Interpretation.* Edited by Wendell Willis. Peabody, Mass.: Hendrickson, 1987.

Botha, Pieter J. J. "Greco-Roman Literacy as Setting for New Testament Writings." *Neotestamentica* 26 (1992): 195–215.

–. "Mark's Story as Oral Traditional Literature: Rethinking the Transmission of Some Traditions about Jesus." *Hervormde Teologiese Studies* 47 (1991): 304–331.

Bovon, François. *Luke 1: A Commentary on the Gospel of Luke 1:1–9:50.* Translated by Christine M. Thomas. Edited by Helmut Koester. Hermeneia. Minneapolis: Fortress, 2002.

–. "The Reception and Use of the Gospel of Luke in the Second Century." Pages 379–400 in *Reading Luke: Interpretation, Reflection, Formation.* Edited by Craig G. Bartholomew, Joel B. Green and Anthony C. Thiselton. Scripture and Hermeneutics 6. Milton Keynes: Paternoster/Grand Rapids: Zondervan, 2005.

Bradshaw, Paul F. *The Search for the Origins of Christian Worship: Sources and Methods for the Study of Early Liturgy.* 2nd ed. Oxford: Oxford University Press, 2002.

Bradshaw, Paul F., Maxwell E. Johnson, and L. Edward Phillips. *The Apostolic Tradition: A Commentary.* Edited by Harold W. Attridge. Hermeneia. Minneapolis: Fortress, 2002.

Braun, F.-M. *Jean le théologien.* 3 vols. (vol. 3 in 2 parts). Études bibliques. Paris: J. Gabalda, 1959–1972.

Brent, Allen. "Ignatius and Polycarp: The Transformation of New Testament Traditions in the Context of Mystery Cults." Pages 325–49 in *Trajectories through the New Testament and the Apostolic Fathers.* Edited by Andrew Gregory and Christopher Tuckett. The New Testament and the Apostolic Fathers 2. Oxford: Oxford University Press, 2005.

–. "The Relations Between Ignatius and the Didascalia." *Second Century* 8 (1991): 129–56.

Breytenbach, Cilliers. "Civic Concord and Cosmic Harmony: Sources of Metaphoric Mapping in 1 Clement 20:3." Pages 182–96 in *Encounters with Hellenism: Studies on the First Letter of Clement.* Edited by Cilliers Breytenbach and Laurence L. Welborn. Arbeiten zur Geschichte des antiken Judentums und des Urchristentums 53. Leiden: Brill, 2004. Repr. from pages 259–73 in *Early Christianity and Classical Culture: Comparative Studies in Honor of Abraham J. Malherbe.* Edited by J. T. Fitzgerald, T. H. Olbricht and L. Michael White. Supplements to Novum Testamentum 110. Leiden: Brill, 2003. Repr. pages 297–311 in idem, *Grace, Reconciliation, Concord: The Death of Christ in Graeco-Roman Metaphors.* Supplements to Novum Testamentum 135. Leiden: Brill, 2010.

–. "Vormarkinische Logientradition: Parallelen in der urchristlichen Briefliteratur." Pages 725–49 in vol. 2 of *The Four Gospels 1992: Festschrift Frans Neirynck.* Edited by F. Van Segbroeck, C. M. Tuckett, G. van Belle and J. Verheyden. Bibliotheca Ephemeridum Theologicarum Lovaniensium 100. 3 vols. Leuven: Leuven University Press and Peeters, 1992.

Brody, Jill. "Incipient Literacy: From Involvement to Integration in Tojolabal Maya." *Oral Tradition* 3 (1988): 315–52.

Brown, Charles Thomas. *The Gospel and Ignatius of Antioch.* Studies in Biblical Literature 12. New York: Peter Lang, 2000.

Brown, Raymond E. *The Death of the Messiah: From Gethsemane to the Grave: A Commentary on the Passion Narratives in the Four Gospels.* Anchor Bible Reference Library. 2 vols. New York: Doubleday, 1994.

–. "The Pater Noster as an Eschatological Prayer." Pages 275–320 in idem, *New Testament Essays*. Garden City: Image Books/Doubleday, 1968.

Brown, Raymond E., and John P. Meier. *Antioch and Rome: New Testament Cradles of Catholic Christianity*. New York: Paulist, 1983.

Bruce, F. F. *The Acts of the Apostles: The Greek Text with Introduction and Commentary*. 3rd rev. and enl. ed. Grand Rapids: Eerdmans/Leicester: Apollos, 1990.

–. *Tradition Old and New*. Grand Rapids: Zondervan, 1970.

Bultmann, Rudolf. *History and Eschatology*. Edinburgh: Edinburgh University Press, 1957.

–. *The History of the Synoptic Tradition*. Translated by John Marsh. Rev. ed. New York and Evanston: Harper & Row, 1968.

–. *Jesus and the Word*. Translated by L. P. Smith and E. H. Lantero. New York: Scribner's Sons, 1934.

–. "The New Approach to the Synoptic Problem." *The Journal of Religion* 6 (1926): 337–362. Repr. pages 35–54 in *Existence and Faith: Shorter Writings of Rudolf Bultmann*. Selected, translated, and introduced by Schubert M. Ogden. Cleveland: World, 1960.

–. "The Study of the Synoptic Gospels." Pages 5–76 in *Form Criticism: Two Essays on New Testament Research*, by Rudolf Bultmann and Karl Kundsin. Translated by Frederick C. Grant. New York: Harper Torchbooks/Harper & Row, 1962.

Butler, B. C. "The Literary Relations of Didache, Ch. XVI." *Journal of Theological Studies* n.s. 11 (1960): 265–83.

–. "The 'Two Ways' in the Didache." *Journal of Theological Studies* n.s. 12 (1961): 27–38.

Byrskog, Samuel. "The Eyewitnesses as Interpreters of the Past: Reflections on Richard Bauckham's, *Jesus and the Eyewitnesses*." *Journal for the Study of the Historical Jesus* 6 (2008): 157–68.

–. Introduction to *Jesus in Memory: Traditions in Oral and Scribal Practices*. Edited by Werner H. Kelber and Samuel Byrskog. Waco, Tex.: Baylor University Press, 2009.

–. *Jesus the Only Teacher: Didactic Authority and Transmission in Ancient Israel, Ancient Judaism and the Matthean Community*. Coniectanea Biblica: New Testament Series 24. Stockholm: Almqvist & Wiksell, 1994.

–. "A New Perspective on the Jesus Tradition: Reflections on James D. G. Dunn's *Jesus Remembered*." Pages 59–78 in *Memories of Jesus: A Critical Appraisal of James D. G. Dunn's* Jesus Remembered. Edited by Robert B. Stewart and Gary R. Habermas. Nashville: B&H Publishing Group, 2010. Revision of article that appeared in *Journal for the Study of the New Testament* 26 (2004): 459–71.

–. "A New Quest for the *Sitz im Leben*: Social Memory, the Jesus Tradition and the Gospel of Matthew." *New Testament Studies* 52 (2006): 319–36.

–. Review of R. Bultmann, *History of the Synoptic Tradition*. *Journal of Biblical Literature* 122 (2003): 549–55.

–. *Story as History – History as Story: The Gospel Tradition in the Context of Ancient Oral History*. Wissenschaftliche Untersuchungen zum Neuen Testament 123. Tübingen: Mohr Siebeck, 2000. Repr. Boston and Leiden: Brill Academic, 2002.

–. "The Transmission of the Jesus Tradition." Pages 1465–94 in vol. 2 of *Handbook for the Study of the Historical Jesus*. Edited by Tom Holmén and Stanley E. Porter. 4 vols. Leiden: Brill, 2011.

–. "When Eyewitness Testimony and Oral Tradition Become Written Text." *Svensk Exegetisk Årsbok* 74 (2009): 41–53.

Cadoux, Cecil John. Review of P. N. Harrison, *Polycarp's Two Epistles to the Philippians*. *Journal of Theological Studies* 38 (1937): 267–70.

Camelot, Pierre Thomas. *Ignace d'Antioche, Polycarpe de Smyrne: Lettres, Martyre de Polycarpe*. 4th ed. (1968) with additions and corrections. Sources Chrétiennes 10. Paris: Cerf, 1998.

Camelot, Pierre Thomas, and Cl. Mondésert. *Clément d'Alexandrie: Les Stromates: Stromate II*. Sources Chrétiennes 38. Paris: Cerf, 1954.

Cameron, Ron. *The Other Gospels: Non-Canonical Gospel Texts*. Philadelphia: Westminster, 1982.

–. *Sayings Traditions in the Apocryphon of James*. Harvard Theological Studies 34. Philadelphia: Fortress, 1984. Repr. Cambridge, Mass.: Harvard University Press, 2004.

Campenhausen, Hans von. *The Formation of the Christian Bible*. Translated by John Austin Baker. London: A. & C. Black/Philadelphia: Fortress, 1972. German original: *Die Enstehung der christlichen Bibel*. Tübingen: Mohr Siebeck, 1968.

Carleton Paget, James. "The *Epistle of Barnabas* and the Writings that later Formed the New Testament." Pages 229–249 in *The Reception of the New Testament in the Apostolic Fathers*. Edited by A. Gregory and C. M. Tuckett. The New Testament and the Apostolic Fathers 1. Oxford: Oxford University Press, 2005.

–. *The Epistle of Barnabas: Outlook and Background*. Wissenschaftliche Untersuchungen zum Neuen Testament 2.64. Tübingen: Mohr Siebeck, 1994.

–. "Jewish Christianity." Pages 731–775 in *The Cambridge History of Judaism,* Vol. 3: *The Early Roman Period*. Edited by William Horbury, W. D. Davies and John Sturdy. Cambridge: Cambridge University Press, 1999.

Carlston, Charles E. "Betz on the Sermon on the Mount." *Catholic Biblical Quarterly* 50 (1988): 47–57.

–. Review of Hans-Theo Wrege, *Die Überlieferungsgeschichte der Bergpredigt. Journal of the American Academy of Religion* 38 (1970): 104–6.

Carlston, Charles E. and Dennis Norlin. "Once More – Statistics and Q." *Harvard Theological Review* 64 (1971): 59–78.

Carr, David M. "Torah on the Heart: Literary Jewish Textuality within Its Ancient near Eastern Context." *Oral Tradition* 25 (2010): 17–40.

–. *Writing on the Tablet of the Heart: Origins of Scripture and Literature*. Oxford: Oxford University Press, 2005.

Casey, M. *Aramaic Sources of Mark's Gospel*. Society for New Testament Studies Monograph Series 102. Cambridge: Cambridge University Press, 1998.

–. *The Solution to the 'Son of Man' Problem*. Library of New Testament Studies (JSNTSup) 343. London: T&T Clark, 2007.

Catchpole, David R. "Jesus and the Community of Israel – The Inaugural Discourse in Q." *Bulletin of the John Rylands University Library of Manchester* 68 (1986): 296–316.

–. *The Quest for Q*. Edinburgh: T&T Clark, 1993.

–. "Source, Form and Redaction Criticism of the New Testament." Pages 167–188 in *Handbook to Exegesis of the New Testament*. Edited by Stanley E. Porter. New Testament Tools and Studies 25. Leiden: Brill, 1997.

Chapman, J. "Papias on the Age of Our Lord." *Journal of Theological Studies* 9 (1908): 42–61.

Charlesworth, James H. "A Caveat on Textual Transmission and the Meaning of *Abba*: A Study of the Lord's Prayer." Pages 1–14 in *The Lord's Prayer and Other Prayer*

Texts from the Greco-Roman Era. Edited by James H. Charlesworth with Mark Harding and Mark Kiley. Valley Forge, Pa.: Trinity Press International, 1994.

Chase, Frederic H. *The Lord's Prayer in the Early Church.* Texts and Studies: Contributions to Biblical and Patristic Literature 3. Cambridge: Cambridge University Press, 1891.

Chilton, Bruce. "Apostolic Constitutions." Pages 37–38 in *Encyclopedia of Religious and Philosophical Writings in Late Antiquity: Pagan, Judaic, Christian.* Editors in Chief Jacob Neusner and Alan J. Avery-Peck. Consulting Editor William Scott Green. Leiden: Brill, 2007.

Clabeaux, John. "The Eucharistic Prayers from *Didache* 9 and 10." Pages 260–266 in *Prayer from Alexander to Constantine: A Critical Anthology.* Edited by Mark Kiley, et al. London and New York: Routledge, 1997.

Clarke, W. K. Lowther, ed. *The First Epistle of Clement to the Corinthians.* London: SPCK, 1937.

Collins, Adela Yarbro. *Mark: A Commentary.* Edited by Harold W. Attridge. Hermeneia. Minneapolis: Fortress, 2007.

–. "The Passion Narrative of Mark." Pages 92–118 in idem, *The Beginning of the Gospel: Probings of Mark in Context.* Minneapolis: Fortress, 1992.

–. "The 'Son of Man' Tradition and the Book of Revelation." Pages 536–568 in *The Messiah: Developments in Earliest Judaism and Christianity: The First Princeton Symposium on Judaism and Christian Origins.* Edited by James H. Charlesworth. Minneapolis: Fortress, 1992.

Collins, Christopher. *Reading the Written Image: Verbal Play, Interpretation, and the Roots of Iconophobia.* University Park, Pa.: Pennsylvania State University Press, 1991.

Colpe, Carsten. "ὁ υἱὸς τοῦ ἀνθρώπου." Pages 400–477 in vol. 8 of *Theological Dictionary of the New Testament.* Edited by Gerhard Kittel and Gerhard Friedrich. Translated by Geoffrey W. Bromiley. 10 vols. Grand Rapids: Eerdmans, 1964–76.

Colson, F. H., G. H. Whitaker and R. Marcus, ed. and trans. *Philo.* 10 vols. and 2 supplementary vols. Loeb Classical Library. Cambridge, Mass.: Harvard University Press/London: Heinemann, 1929–62.

Connolly, R. H. "The *Didache* in Relation to the Epistle of Barnabas." *Journal of Theological Studies* 33 (1932): 237–53.

Connors, R. J. "Greek Rhetoric and the Transition from Orality." *Philosophy and Rhetoric* 19 (1986): 38–65. Repr. pages 91–109 in *Essays on the Rhetoric of the Western World.* Edited by Edward P. J. Corbett, James L. Golden and Goodwin F. Berquist. Dubuque: Kendall/Hunt, 1990.

Conzelmann, Hans. *Acts of the Apostles: A Commentary on the Acts of the Apostles.* Translated by James Limburg, A. Thomas Kraabel and Donald H. Juel. Edited by Eldon Jay Epp and Christopher R. Matthews. Hermeneia. Philadelphia: Fortress, 1987.

Corwin, Virginia. *St. Ignatius and Christianity in Antioch.* Yale Publications in Religion 1. New Haven: Yale University Press, 1960.

Cotelier, J. B. *SS. Patrum qui Temporibus Apostolicis floruerunt, Barnabae, Clementis, Hermae, Ignatii, Polycarpi opera edita et inedita, vera, et suppositicia; una cum Clementis, Ignatii, Polycarpi actis atque martyriis.* 2 vols. Paris: Typis Petri Le Petit, 1672.

Couroyer, B. "'De la mesure dont vous mesurez il vous sera mesuré.'" *Revue Biblique* 77 (1970): 366–70.

Court, J. M. "The Didache and St. Matthew's Gospel." *Scottish Journal of Theology* 34 (1981): 109–20.

Cranfield, C. E. B. *The Gospel According to St. Mark: An Introduction and Commentary.* Third Impression with Additional Supplementary Notes. Cambridge Greek Testament Commentary. Cambridge: Cambridge University Press, 1966.

Cross, F. L., and E. A. Livingstone, eds. *The Oxford Dictionary of the Christian Church.* 3rd ed. revised. Oxford: Oxford University Press, 2005.

Crossan, John Dominic. *In Fragments: The Aphorisms of Jesus.* San Francisco: Harper & Row, 1983.

–, ed. *Sayings Parallels: A Workbook for the Jesus Tradition.* Foundations and Facets. Philadephia: Fortress, 1986.

Culley, Robert C. "Oral Tradition and Biblical Studies." *Oral Tradition* 1 (1986): 30–65.

–. "Oral Tradition and Historicity." Pages 102–16 in *Studies on the Ancient Palestinian World: Presented to Professor F. V. Winnett on the Occasion of his Retirement, 1 July 1971.* Edited by J. W. Wevers and D. B. Redford. Toronto Semitic Texts and Studies 2. Toronto: University of Toronto Press, 1972.

Cullmann, Oscar. *Prayer in the New Testament.* Overtures to Biblical Theology. Minneapolis: Fortress, 1995.

Dahl, Nils Alstrup. "Der Erstgeborene Satans und der Vater des Teufels (Polyk. 7:1 und Joh. 8:44)." Pages 70–84 in *Apophoreta: Festschrift für Ernst Haenchen zu seinem siebzigsten Geburtstag am 10. Dezember 1964.* Edited by W. Eltester and F. H. Kettler. Beihefte zur Zeitschrift für die neutestamentliche Wissenschaft 30. Berlin: Alfred Töpelmann, 1964.

–. "La terre où coulent le lait et le miel selon Barnabé 6. 8–19." Pages 62–70 in *Aux sources de la tradition chrétienne: Mélanges offerts à M. Maurice Goguel à l'occasion de son soixante-dixième anniversaire.* Bibliothèque théologique. Neuchatel and Paris: Delachaux & Niestlé, 1950.

Daube, David. "Two Incidents after the Last Supper." Pages 330–335 in *The New Testament and Rabbinic Judaism.* London: Athlone, 1956. Repr. Peabody, Mass.: Hendrickson, n/d.

Davids, Peter H. *The First Epistle of Peter.* New International Commentary on the New Testament. Grand Rapids: Eerdmans, 1990.

–. "The Gospels and Jewish Tradition: Twenty Years after Gerhardsson." Pages 75–99 in *Gospel Perspectives,* Vol. 1: *Studies of History and Tradition in the Four Gospels.* Edited by R. T. France and David Wenham. Sheffield: JSOT Press, 1980.

–. "James and Jesus." Pages 63–84 in *Gospel Perspectives,* Vol. 5: *The Jesus Tradition Outside the Gospels.* Edited by David Wenham. Sheffield: JSOT Press, 1985.

–. "Tradition and Citation in the Epistle of James." Pages 113–126 in *Scripture, Tradition, and Interpretation: Essays Presented to Everett F. Harrison by His Students and Colleagues in Honor of His Seventy-Fifth Birthday.* Edited by W. Ward Gasque and William Sanford LaSor. Grand Rapids: Eerdmans, 1978.

Davies, John K. "The Reliability of the Oral Tradition." Pages 87–110 in *The Trojan War: Its Historicity and Context.* Edited by Lin Foxhall and John K. Davies. Bristol: Bristol Classical, 1984.

Davies, W. D. "Reflections on a Scandinavian Approach to 'the Gospel Tradition.'" Pages 14–34 in *Neotestamentica et Patristica: Eine Freundesgabe, Herrn Professor Dr. Oscar Cullmann zu seinem 60. Geburtstag überreicht.* Supplements to Novum Testamentum 6. Leiden: Brill, 1962.

Davies, W. D., and D. C. Allison. *A Critical and Exegetical Commentary on the Gospel according to Saint Matthew.* International Critical Commentary. 3 vols. Edinburgh: T&T Clark, 1988–97.

Davis, Sioned. "The Reoralization of *The Lady of the Lake*." Pages 335–360 in *(Re)Oralisierung*. Edited by Hildegard L. Tristram. ScriptOralia. Tübingen: Gunter Narr, 1996.

DeConick, April D. "The Gospel of Thomas." *Expository Times* 118 (2007): 469–79.

–. *Recovering the Original Gospel of Thomas: A History of the Gospel and its Growth*. Library of New Testament Studies 286. Early Christianity in Context. New York: T&T Clark International, 2005.

Deeks, David G. "Papias Revisited." *Expository Times* 88 (1976–77): 296–301, 324–29.

Dehandschutter, Boudewijn. "The Epistle of Polycarp." Pages 117–33 in *The Apostolic Fathers: An Introduction*. Edited by Wilhelm Pratscher. Waco, Tex.: Baylor University Press, 2010.

–. "Ignatian Epistles." Pages 406–407 in vol. 6 of *Religion Past and Present: Encyclopedia of Theology and Religion*. Edited by Hans Dieter Betz, Don S. Browning, Bernd Janowski and Eberhard Jüngel. Leiden: Brill, 2009.

–. "The New Testament and the *Martyrdom of Polycarp*." Pages 395–405 in *Trajectories through the New Testament and the Apostolic Fathers*. Edited by Andrew Gregory and Christopher Tuckett. The New Testament and the Apostolic Fathers 2. Oxford: Oxford University Press, 2005. Repr. pages 131–141 in idem, *Polycarpiana: Studies on Martyrdom and Persecution in Early Christianity: Collected Essays*. Edited by J. Leemans. Bibliotheca Ephemeridum Theologicarum Lovaniensium 205. Leuven: Leuven University Press and Peeters, 2007.

–. "Polycarp's Epistle to the Philippians: An Early Example of 'Reception.'" Pages 275–291 in *The New Testament in Early Christianity/La réception des écrits néotestamentaires dans le christianisme primitif*. Edited by Jean-Marie Sevrin. Bibliotheca Ephemeridum Theologicarum Lovaniensium 86. Leuven: Leuven University Press and Peeters, 1989. Repr. pages 153–171 in idem, *Polycarpiana: Studies on Martyrdom and Persecution in Early Christianity: Collected Essays*. Edited by J. Leemans. Bibliotheca Ephemeridum Theologicarum Lovaniensium 205. Leuven: Leuven University Press and Peeters, 2007.

Del Verme, Marcello. *Didache and Judaism: Jewish Roots of an Ancient Christian-Jewish Work*. New York and London: T&T Clark International, 2004.

Delobel, Joël. "The Lord's Prayer in the Textual Tradition: A Critique of Recent Theories and their View on Marcion's Role." Pages 293–309 in *The New Testament in Early Christianity/La réception des écrits néotestamentaires dans le christianisme primitif*. Edited by Jean-Marie Sevrin. Bibliotheca Ephemeridum Theologicarum Lovaniensium 86. Leuven: Leuven University Press and Peeters, 1989.

Demsky, Aaron, and Meir Bar-Ilan. "Writing in Ancient Israel and Early Judaism." Pages 1–38 in *Mikra: Text, Translation, Reading, and Interpretation of the Hebrew Bible in Ancient Judaism and Early Christianity*. Edited by M. J. Mulder and Harry Sysling. Compendia Rerum Iudaicarum ad Novum Testamentum, Section 2: The Literature of the Jewish People in the Period of the Second Temple and the Talmud, Vol. 1. Assen: Van Gorcum/Philadelphia: Fortress, 1988.

Derrett, J. Duncan M. "Scripture and Norms in the Apostolic Fathers." Pages 649–99 in vol. 27.1 of *Aufstieg und Niedergang der römischen Welt, II: Principat*. Edited by H. Temporini and Wolfgang Haase. Berlin and New York: de Gruyter, 1993.

Dewey, Joanna. "From Oral Stories to Written Text." Pages 20–28 in *Women's Sacred Scriptures*. Edited by Kwok Pui-Lan and Elisabeth Schüssler Fiorenza. Concilium 1998/3. London: SCM/Maryknoll: Orbis, 1998.

–. "The Gospel of Mark as an Oral-Aural Event: Implications for Interpretation." Pages 145–163 in *The New Literary Criticism and the New Testament*. Edited by Edgar V.

McKnight and Elizabeth Struthers Malbon. Journal for the Study of the New Testament Supplement Series 109. Sheffield: JSOT Press, 1994.

–. "The Gospel of Mark as Oral Hermeneutic." Pages 71–87 in *Jesus, the Voice, and the Text: Beyond The Oral and the Written Gospel.* Edited by Tom Thatcher. Waco, Tex.: Baylor University Press, 2008.

–. Introduction to *Orality and Textuality in Early Christian Literature.* Edited by Joanna Dewey. *Semeia* 65. Atlanta: Society of Biblical Literature/Scholars, 1994.

–. "Mark as Aural Narrative: Structures as Clues to Understanding." *Sewanee Theological Review* 36 (1992): 45–56.

–. "Mark as Interwoven Tapestry: Forecasts and Echoes for a Listening Audience." *Catholic Biblical Quarterly* 53 (1991): 221–36.

–. "Oral Methods of Structuring Narrative in Mark." *Interpretation* 43 (1989): 32–44.

–. "The Survival of Mark's Gospel: A Good Story?" *Journal of Biblical Literature* 123 (2004): 495–507.

–. "Textuality in an Oral Culture: A Survey ofthe Pauline Traditions." Pages 37–65 in *Orality and Textuality in Early Christian Literature.* Edited by Joanna Dewey. *Semeia* 65. Atlanta: Society of Biblical Literature/Scholars, 1994.

–, ed. *Orality and Textuality in Early Christian Literature. Semeia* 65. Atlanta: Society of Biblical Literature/Scholars, 1994.

Di Marco, Angelico-Salvatore. "La recezione del Nuovo Testamento nei padri apostolici." Pages 724–62 in vol. 27.1 of *Aufstieg und Niedergang der römischen Welt, II: Principat.* Edited by Wolfgang Haase. Berlin and New York: de Gruyter, 1993.

Dibelius, Martin. *From Tradition to Gospel.* Translated by Bertram Lee Woolf. Library of Theological Translations. Cambridge: James Clarke, 1971.

Dillon, Richard J. *From Eye-Witnesses to Ministers of the Word: Tradition and Composition in Luke 24.* Analecta Biblica 82. Rome: Biblical Institute Press, 1978.

Dodd, C. H. "The Beatitudes." Pages 404–10 in *Mélanges bibliques rédigés en l'honneur de André Robert.* Travaux de l'Institut Catholique de Paris 4. Paris: Bloud & Gay, 1955.

Donahue, John R. and Daniel J. Harrington. *The Gospel of Mark.* Sacra Pagina 2. Collegeville: Liturgical, 2002.

Donahue, P. J. "Jewish Christianity in the Letters of Ignatius of Antioch." *Vigiliae Christianae* 32 (1978): 81–93.

Donaldson, James. *The Apostolical Fathers: A Critical Account of their Genuine Writings and of their Doctrines.* London: Macmillan, 1874.

Donfried, Karl P. "The Kingdom of God in Paul." Pages 175–90 in *The Kingdom of God in 20th-Century Interpretation.* Edited by Wendell Willis. Peabody, Mass.: Hendrickson, 1987.

–. *The Setting of Second Clement in Early Christianity.* Supplements to Novum Testamentum 38. Leiden: Brill, 1974.

Douglas, R. Conrad. "A Jesus Tradition Prayer (Q 11:2b–4; Matt 6:9b–13; Luke 11:2b–4; *Didache* 8.2)." Pages 211–15 in *Prayer from Alexander to Constantine: A Critical Anthology.* Edited by Mark Kiley, et al. London and New York: Routledge, 1997.

Downing, F. Gerald. "A bas les aristos: The Relevance of Higher Literature for the Understanding of the Earliest Christian Writings." *Novum Testamentum* 30 (1988): 212–30.

–. "Word-Processing in the Ancient World: The Social Production and Performance of Q." *Journal for the Study of the New Testament* 64 (1996): 29–48.

Dragas, George D. "Apostolic Constitutions." Pages 92–93 in *Encyclopedia of Early Christianity*. Edited by Everett Ferguson. Garland Reference Library of the Humanities. New York and London: Garland, 1998.

Draper, Jonathan A. "Christian Self-Definition against the 'Hypocrites' in *Didache* 8." Pages 223–43 in *The Didache in Modern Research*. Edited by Jonathan A. Draper. Arbeiten zur Geschichte des antiken Judentums und des Urchristentums 37. Leiden: Brill, 1996.

–. "A Commentary on the Didache in the Light of the Dead Sea Scrolls and Related Documents." Ph.D. Dissertation; Cambridge: University of Cambridge, 1983.

–. "Confessional Western Text-Centered Biblical Interpretation and an Oral or Residual-Oral Context." Pages 59–77 in *"Reading With": An Exploration of the Interface between Critical and Ordinary Readings of the Bible*. Edited by Gerald West and Musa W. Dube. *Semeia* 73. Atlanta: Scholars/Society of Biblical Literature, 1996.

–. "A Continuing Enigma: The 'Yoke of the Lord' in Didache 6.2–3 and Early Jewish-Christian Relations." Pages 106–23 in *The Image of the Judaeo-Christians in Ancient Jewish and Christian Literature*. Edited by Peter J. Tomson and Doris Lambers-Petry. Wissenschaftliche Untersuchungen zum Neuen Testament 158. Tübingen: Mohr Siebeck, 2003.

–. "The Didache in Modern Research: An Overview." Pages 1–42 in *The Didache in Modern Research*. Edited by Jonathan A. Draper. Arbeiten zur Geschichte des antiken Judentums und des Urchristentums 37. Leiden: Brill, 1996.

–. "Do the Didache and Matthew Reflect an 'Irrevocable Parting of the Ways' with Judaism?" Pages 217–41 in *Matthew and the Didache: Two Documents from the Same Jewish-Christian Milieu?* Edited by Huub van de Sandt. Assen: Van Gorcum/Philadelphia: Fortress, 2005.

–. "First-fruits and the Support of Prophets, Teachers, and the Poor in *Didache* 13 in Relation to New Testament Parallels." Pages 223–43 in *Trajectories through the New Testament and the Apostolic Fathers*. Edited by Andrew Gregory and Christopher Tuckett. The New Testament and the Apostolic Fathers 2. Oxford: Oxford University Press, 2005.

–. "The Jesus Tradition in the Didache." Pages 72–91 in *The Didache in Modern Research*. Edited by Jonathan A. Draper. Arbeiten zur Geschichte des antiken Judentums und des Urchristentums 37. Leiden: Brill, 1996. Revised from pages 269–87 in *Gospel Perspectives*, Vol. 5: *The Jesus Tradition Outside the Gospels*. Edited by David Wenham. Sheffield: JSOT Press, 1985.

–. "Jesus' 'Covenantal Discourse' on the Plain (Luke 6:12–7:17) as Oral Performance: Pointers to 'Q' as Multiple Oral Performance." Pages 71–98 in *Oral Performance, Popular Tradition, and Hidden Transcript in Q*. Edited by Richard A. Horsley. SBL Semeia Studies 60. Atlanta: Society of Biblical Literature, 2006.

–. "Lactantius and the Jesus Tradition in the Didache." *Journal of Theological Studies* n.s. 40 (1989): 112–16.

–. "Recovering Oral Performance from Written Text in Q." Pages 175–94 in *Whoever Hears You Hears Me: Prophets, Performance, and Tradition in Q*, by Richard A. Horsley with Jonathan A. Draper. Harrisburg: Trinity Press International, 1999.

–. "Ritual Process and Ritual Symbol in Didache 7–10." *Vigiliae Christianae* 54 (2000): 121–58.

–. "Social Ambiguity and the Production of Text: Prophets, Teachers, Bishops, and Deacons and the Development of the Jesus Tradition in the Community of the *Didache*." Pages 284–312 in *The Didache in Context: Essays on Its Text, History and Transmis-*

sion. Edited by Clayton N. Jefford. Supplements to Novum Testamentum 77. Leiden: Brill, 1995.

–. "Torah and Troublesome Apostles in the *Didache* Community." Pages 340–63 in *The Didache in Modern Research.* Edited by Jonathan A. Draper. Arbeiten zur Geschichte des antiken Judentums und des Urchristentums 37. Leiden: Brill, 1996.

–. "Vice Catalogues as Oral-Mnemonic Cues: A Comparative Study of the Two-Ways Tradition in the *Didache* and Parallels from the Perspective of Oral Tradition." Pages 111–33 in *Jesus, the Voice, and the Text: Beyond The Oral and the Written Gospel.* Edited by Tom Thatcher. Waco, Tex.: Baylor University Press, 2008.

–, ed. *The* Didache *in Modern Research.* Arbeiten zur Geschichte des antiken Judentums und des Urchristentums 37. Leiden: Brill, 1996.

–, ed. *Orality, Literacy, and Colonialism in Antiquity.* SBL Semeia Studies 47. Atlanta: Society of Biblical Literature, 2004.

Drobner, Hubertus R. *The Fathers of the Church: A Comprehensive Introduction.* Translated by Siegfried S. Schatzmann. Peabody, Mass.: Hendrickson, 2007.

Duensing, H., and A. de Santos Otero. "Apocalypse of Paul." Pages 712–48 in *New Testament Apocrypha,* Vol. 2: *Writings Relating to the Apostles: Apocalypses and Related Subjects.* Edited by Wilhelm Schneemelcher. English edition edited by R. McL. Wilson. Rev. ed. Cambridge: James Clarke/Louisville: Westminster/John Knox, 1992.

Dundes, Alan. Foreword to *The Theory of Oral Composition: History and Methodology,* by John Miles Foley. Bloomington and Indianapolis: Indiana University Press, 1988.

Dungan, David L. *The Sayings of Jesus in the Churches of Paul: The Use of the Synoptic Tradition in the Regulation of Early Church Life.* Oxford: Blackwell/Philadelphia: Fortress, 1971.

Dunn, James D. G. *The Acts of the Apostles.* Narrative Commentaries. Valley Forge: Trinity Press International, 1996.

–. "Altering the Default Setting: Re-envisaging the Early Transmission of the Jesus Tradition." *New Testament Studies* 49 (2003): 139–75.

–. *Christianity in the Making,* Vol. 1: *Jesus Remembered.* Grand Rapids: Eerdmans, 2003.

–. *Christianity in the Making,* Vol. 2: *Beginning from Jerusalem.* Grand Rapids: Eerdmans, 2009.

–. "Eyewitnesses and the Oral Jesus Tradition." *Journal for the Study of the Historical Jesus* 6 (2008): 85–105.

–. "Jesus Tradition in Paul." Pages 155–78 in *Studying the Historical Jesus: Evaluations of the State of Current Research.* Edited by Bruce Chilton and Craig A. Evans. New Testament Tools and Studies 19. Leiden: Brill, 1994. Repr. pages 169–89 in *The Christ and the Spirit: Collected Essays of James D. G. Dunn,* Vol. 1: *Christology.* Grand Rapids: Eerdmans, 1998.

–. "John and the Oral Gospel Tradition." Pages 351–79 in *Jesus and the Oral Gospel Tradition.* Edited by H. Wansbrough. Journal for the Study of the New Testament Supplement Series 64. Sheffield: JSOT Press, 1991.

–. "Kenneth Bailey's Theory of Oral Tradition: Critiquing Theodore Weeden's Critique." *Journal for the Study of the Historical Jesus* 7 (2009): 44–62.

–. *A New Perspective on Jesus: What the Quest for the Historical Jesus Missed.* Acadia Studies in Bible and Theology. Grand Rapids: Baker Academic, 2005.

–. "On Faith and History, and Living Tradition: In Response to Robert Morgan and Andrew Gregory." *Expository Times* 116 (2004–05): 13–19.

–. "On History, Memory and Eyewitnesses: In Response to Bengt Holmberg and Samuel Byrskog." *Journal for the Study of the New Testament* 26 (2004): 473–87.
–. "Q¹ as Oral Tradition." Pages 45–69 in *The Written Gospel [Festschrift for Graham Stanton]*. Edited by Markus Bockmuehl and Donald A. Hagner. Cambridge: Cambridge University Press, 2005.
–. "Reappreciating the Oral Jesus Tradition." *Svensk Exegetisk Årsbok* 74 (2009): 1–17.
–. "Remembering Jesus: How the Quest of the Historical Jesus Lost Its Way." Pages 183–205 in vol. 1 of *Handbook for the Study of the Historical Jesus*. Edited by Tom Holmén and Stanley E. Porter. 4 vols. Leiden: Brill, 2011.
–. *Romans 1–8*. Word Biblical Commentary 38A. Dallas: Word, 1988.
–. "Social Memory and the Oral Jesus Tradition." Pages 179–94 in *Memory in the Bible and Antiquity: The Fifth Durham-Tübingen Research Symposium (Durham, September 2004)*. Edited by Loren T. Stuckenbruck, Stephen C. Barton and Benjamin G. Wold. Wissenschaftliche Untersuchungen zum Neuen Testament 212. Tübingen: Mohr Siebeck, 2007.
–. "The Spoken Word versus the Written Word [Review of Werner H. Kelber, *The Oral and the Written Gospel*]." *Interpretation* 40 (1986): 72–75.
–. *The Theology of Paul the Apostle*. Grand Rapids: Eerdmans, 1998.
Dupont, Jacques. *Les béatitudes*, Vol. 1: *Le problème littéraire*. 2nd ed. Paris: Gabalda, 1958.
–. "La Parabole du Semeur dans la version de Luc." Pages 97–108 in *Apophoreta: Festschrift für Ernst Haenchen zu seinem siebzigsten Geburtstag am 10. Dezember 1964*. Edited by W. Eltester and F. H. Kettler. Beihefte zur Zeitschrift für die neutestamentliche Wissenschaft 30. Berlin: Alfred Töpelmann, 1964.
–. "Les pèlerins d'Emmaüs (Luc, XXIV, 13–35)." Pages 349–74 in *Miscellanea biblica B. Ubach*. Edited by Romualdo M.ª Díaz. Scripta et documenta 1. Montserrat: Abadia di Montserrat, 1953.
Easton, Burton Scott. *The Gospel According to St. Luke*. New York: Scribner's Sons, 1926.
Echo-Hawk, Roger C. "Ancient History in the New World: Integrating Oral Traditions and the Archaeological Record in Deep Time." *American Antiquity* 65 (2000): 267–90.
Edwards, M. J. "Ignatius and the Second Century: An Answer to R. Hübner." *Zeitschrift für Antikes Christentum/Journal of Ancient Christianity* 2 (1998): 214–26.
Ehrman, Bart D., ed. *The Apostolic Fathers*. Loeb Classical Library 24, 25. 2 vols. Cambridge, Mass.: Harvard University Press, 2003.
–. "Textual Traditions Compared: The New Testament and the Apostolic Fathers." Pages 9–27 in *The Reception of the New Testament in the Apostolic Fathers*. Edited by A. Gregory and C. M. Tuckett. The New Testament and the Apostolic Fathers 1. Oxford: Oxford University Press, 2005.
Elliott, J. K. "The Nature of the Evidence Available for Reconstructing the Text of the New Testament in the Second Century." Pages 9–18 in *The New Testament Text in Early Christianity: Proceedings of the Lille Colloquium, July 2000/Le texte du Nouveau Testament au début du christianisme: Actes du colloque de Lille, juillet 2000*. Edited by Christian-B. Amphoux and J. Keith Elliott. Histoire du Texte Biblique 6. Lausanne: Zèbre, 2003.
–, ed. *The Apocryphal New Testament: A Collection of Apocryphal Christian Literature in an English Translation*. Oxford: Clarendon, 1993.
Elliott, John H. *1 Peter: A New Translation with Introduction and Commentary*. Anchor Bible 37B. New York: Doubleday, 2000.

–. "The Rehabilitation of an Exegetical Step-Child: 1 Peter in Recent Research." *Journal of Biblical Literature* 95 (1976): 243–54.

Ellis, E. Earle. "The Making of Narratives in the Synoptic Gospels." Pages 310–33 in *Jesus and the Oral Gospel Tradition.* Edited by H. Wansbrough. Journal for the Study of the New Testament Supplement Series 64. Sheffield: JSOT Press, 1991.

–. "Traditions in I Corinthians." *New Testament Studies* 32 (1986): 481–502.

Erlemann, K. "Die Datierung des Ersten Klemensbriefes–Anfragen an eine Communis Opinio." *New Testament Studies* 44 (1998): 591–607.

Ernst, J. *Das Evangelium nach Lukas.* Regensburger Neues Testament 3. Regensburg: Pustet, 1977.

Evans, Craig A. "Form Criticism." Pages 204–8 in *Encyclopedia of the Historical Jesus.* Edited by Craig A. Evans. New York and London: Routledge, 2008.

–. "The Interpretation of Scripture in the New Testament Apocrypha and Gnostic Writings." Pages 430–56 in *A History of Biblical Interpretation,* Vol. 1: *The Ancient Period.* Edited by Alan J. Hauser and Duane F. Watson. Grand Rapids: Eerdmans, 2003.

–. *Mark 8:27–16:20.* Word Biblical Commentary 34B. Nashville: Nelson, 2001.

–. "Source, Form and Redaction Criticism: The 'Traditional' Methods of Synoptic Interpretation." Pages 17–45 in *Approaches to New Testament Study.* Edited by Stanley E. Porter and David Tombs. Journal for the Study of the New Testament Supplement Series 120. Sheffield: Sheffield Academic, 1995.

Everding, H. Edward, Jr. "A Reponse to Arthur J. Bellinzoni." *Second Century* 9 (1992): 259–63.

Eyre, Christopher and John Baines. "Interactions between Orality and Literacy in Ancient Egypt." Pages 91–119 in *Literacy and Society.* Edited by Karen Schousboe and Mogens Trolle Larsen. Copenhagen: Akademisk Forlag, 1989.

Farkasfalvy, Denis. "Matthew's Gospel in the Second Century: Response to Arthur J. Bellinzoni." *Second Century* 9 (1992): 271–75.

Farmer, Ron. "The Kingdom of God in the Gospel of Matthew." Pages 119–30 in *The Kingdom of God in 20th-Century Interpretation.* Edited by Wendell Willis. Peabody, Mass.: Hendrickson, 1987.

Farmer, William R. *The Gospel of Jesus: The Pastoral Relevance of the Synoptic Problem.* Louisville: Westminster/John Knox, 1994.

Farrell, Thomas J. "Early Christian Creeds and Controversies in the Light of the Orality-Literacy Hypothesis." *Oral Tradition* 2 [Festschrift W. J. Ong] (1987): 132–49.

–. "Kelber's Breakthrough." Pages 27–45 in *Orality, Aurality and Biblical Narrative.* Edited by Lou H. Silberman. *Semeia* 39. Decatur: Society of Biblical Literature/ Scholars, 1987.

Feldmeier, Reinhard. *Die Krisis des Gottessohnes: Die Gethsemaneerzählung als Schlüssel der Markuspassion.* Wissenschaftliche Untersuchungen zum Neuen Testament 2.21. Tübingen: Mohr Siebeck, 1987.

Ferguson, Everett. "The Kingdom of God in Early Patristic Literature." Pages 191–208 in *The Kingdom of God in 20th-Century Interpretation.* Edited by Wendell Willis. Peabody, Mass.: Hendrickson, 1987.

–. "Vision of Paul." Page 1167 in *Encyclopedia of Early Christianity.* Edited by Everett Ferguson. Garland Reference Library of the Humanities. New York and London: Garland, 1998.

Ferguson, John. *Clement of Alexandria: Stromateis: Books One to Three.* Fathers of the Church 85. Washington, D. C.: Catholic University of America Press, 1991.

Finnegan, Ruth. *Literacy and Orality: Studies in the Technology of Communication*. Oxford: Blackwell, 1988.

–. *Oral Literature in Africa*. Oxford: Clarendon, 1970.

–. *Oral Poetry: Its Nature, Significance, and Social Context*. Bloomington: Indiana University Press, 1992.

–. "Response from an Africanist Scholar." *Oral Tradition* 25 (2010): 7-16.

Fischer, Joseph Anton. "Die ältesten Ausgaben der Patres Apostolici: Ein Beitrag zu Begriff und Begrenzung der Apostolischen Väter." *Historisches Jahrbuch* 94 (1974): 157–90; 95 (1975): 88–119.

Fitzmyer, Joseph A. *The Acts of the Apostles: A New Translation with Introduction and Commentary*. Anchor Bible 31. New York: Doubleday, 1998.

–. *The Gospel According to Luke I–IX: A New Translation with Introduction and Commentary*. Anchor Bible 28. New York: Doubleday, 1981.

–. *The Gospel According to Luke X–XXIV: A New Translation with Introduction and Commentary*. Anchor Bible 28A. New York: Doubleday, 1985.

Flesseman-Van Leer, Ellen. *Tradition and Scripture in the Early Church*. Van Gorcum's Theologische Bibliotheek 26. Assen: Van Gorcum, 1954.

Foley, John Miles. "The Bard's Audience Is Always More Than a Fiction." Pages 92–108 in *Time, Memory, and the Verbal Arts: Essays on the Thought of Walter Ong*. Edited by Dennis L. Weeks and Jane Hoogestraat. Selinsgrove: Susquehanna University Press/London: Associated University Presses, 1998.

–. *Homer's Traditional Art*. University Park: Pennsylvania State University Press, 1999.

–. *How to Read an Oral Poem*. Urbana: University of Illinois Press, 2002.

–. *Immanent Art: From Structure to Meaning in Traditional Oral Epic*. Bloomington and Indianapolis: Indiana University Press, 1991.

–. "Individual Poet and Epic Tradition: Homer as Legendary Singer." *Arethusa* 31 (1998): 149–78.

–. "Memory in Oral Tradition." Pages 83–96 in *Performing the Gospel: Orality, Memory, and Mark: Essays Dedicated to Werner Kelber*. Edited by Richard A. Horsley, Jonathan A. Draper and John Miles Foley. Minneapolis: Fortress, 2006.

–. *Oral-Formulaic Theory and Research: An Introduction and Annotated Bibliography*. Garland Folklore Bibliographies 6. Garland Reference Library of the Humanities 400. New York: Garland, 1985.

–. "The Oral Theory in Context." Pages 27–122 in *Oral Traditional Literature: A Festschrift for Albert Bates Lord*. Edited by John Miles Foley. Columbus: Slavica, 1981.

–. "Oral Tradition and Its Implications." Pages 146–73 in *A New Companion to Homer*. Edited by Ian Morris and Barry Powell. Supplements to Mnemosyne 163. Leiden: Brill, 1997.

–. "Reading the Oral Traditional Text: Aesthetics of Creation and Response." Pages 185–212 in *Comparative Research on Oral Traditions: A Memorial for Milman Parry*. Edited by John Miles Foley. Columbus: Slavica, 1987.

–. *The Singer of Tales in Performance*. Voices in Performance and Text. Bloomington and Indianapolis: Indiana University Press, 1995.

–. *The Theory of Oral Composition: History and Methodology*. Bloomington and Indianapolis: Indiana University Press, 1988.

–. "Tradition-Dependent and -Independent Features in Oral Literature: A Comparative View of the Formula." Pages 262–81 in *Oral Traditional Literature: A Festschrift for Albert Bates Lord*. Edited by John Miles Foley. Columbus: Slavica, 1981.

–. *Traditional Oral Epic: The Odyssey, Beowulf, and the Serbo-Croatian Return Song*. Berkeley and Los Angeles: University of California Press, 1990.

–. "What's In a Sign?" Pages 1–27 in *Signs of Orality: The Oral Tradition and its Influence in the Greek and Roman Worlds*. Edited by E. Anne Mackay. Supplements to Mnemosyne 188. Leiden: Brill, 1999.

–. "Words in Tradition, Words in Text: A Response." Pages 169–80 in *Orality and Textuality in Early Christian Literature*. Edited by Joanna Dewey. *Semeia* 65. Atlanta: Society of Biblical Literature/Scholars, 1994.

–, ed. *Comparative Research on Oral Traditions: A Memorial for Milman Parry*. Columbus: Slavica, 1987.

–, ed. *Oral-Formulaic Theory: A Folklore Casebook*. Garland Folklore Casebooks 5. New York and London: Garland, 1990.

–, ed. *Oral Tradition in Literature: Interpretation in Context*. Columbia: University of Missouri Press, 1986.

–, ed. *Oral Traditional Literature: A Festschrift for Albert Bates Lord*. Columbus: Slavica, 1981.

–, ed. *Teaching Oral Traditions*. New York: Modern Language Association, 1998.

Foster, Paul. "The Epistles of Ignatius of Antioch." *Expository Times* 117.12 (2006): 487–95; 118.1 (2006): 2–11. Repr. pages 81–107 in *The Writings of the Apostolic Fathers*. Edited by Paul Foster. T&T Clark Biblical Studies. London and New York: T&T Clark, 2007.

–. "The Epistles of Ignatius of Antioch and the Writings that later Formed the New Testament." Pages 159–86 in *The Reception of the New Testament in the Apostolic Fathers*. Edited by A. Gregory and C. M. Tuckett. The New Testament and the Apostolic Fathers 1. Oxford: Oxford University Press, 2005.

France, R. T. *The Gospel of Mark: A Commentary on the Greek Text*. New International Greek Testament Commentary. Grand Rapids: Eerdmans/Carlisle: Paternoster, 2002.

–. *The Gospel of Matthew*. New International Commentary on the New Testament. Grand Rapids: Eerdmans, 2007.

Frankenmölle, H. "Die Makarismen (Mt 5,1–12; Lk 6,20–23): Motive und Umfang der redaktionellen Komposition." *Biblische Zeitschrift* 15 (1971): 52–75.

Frend, W. H. C. *The Rise of Christianity*. Philadelphia: Fortress, 1984.

Froehlich, Karlfried. "The Lord's Prayer in Patristic Literature." Pages 71–87 in *The Lord's Prayer: Perspectives for Reclaiming Christian Prayer*. Edited by Daniel L. Migliore. Grand Rapids: Eerdmans, 1993.

Funk, Franciscus Xaverius, ed. *Didascalia et Constitutiones Apostolorum*. 2 vols. Paderbornae: Libraria Ferdinandi Schoeningh, 1905.

Gamble, Harry. *Books and Readers in the Early Church: A History of Early Christian Texts*. New Haven and London: Yale University Press, 1995.

Garrow, Alan J. P. *The Gospel of Matthew's Dependence on the Didache*. Journal for the Study of the New Testament Supplement Series 254. London and New York: T&T Clark International, 2004.

Gavrilov, A. K. "Techniques of Reading in Classical Antiquity." *Classical Quarterly* 47 (1997): 56–73.

Gentili, B., and G. Cerri. "Written and Oral Communication in Greek Historiographical Thought." Pages 137–55 in *Communication Arts in the Ancient World*. Edited by Eric A. Havelock and Jackson P. Hershbell. Humanistic Studies in the Communication Arts. New York: Hastings House, 1978.

Gerhardsson, Birger. *The Gospel Tradition*. Coniectanea Biblica: New Testament Series 15. Lund: Gleerup, 1986. Repr. pages 497–545 in *The Interrelations of the Gospels*. Edited by David L. Dungan. Bibliotheca Ephemeridum Theologicarum Lovaniensium 45. Leuven: Leuven University Press and Peeters/Macon: Mercer University Press,

1990. Repr. pages 89–143 in idem, *The Reliability of the Gospel Tradition*. Peabody, Mass.: Hendrickson, 2001.

–. "If We Do Not Cut the Parables out of Their Frames." *New Testament Studies* 37 (1991): 321–35.

–. "Illuminating the Kingdom: Narrative Meshalim in the Synoptic Gospels." Pages 266–309 in *Jesus and the Oral Gospel Tradition*. Edited by H. Wansbrough. Journal for the Study of the New Testament Supplement Series 64. Sheffield: JSOT Press, 1991.

–. *Memory and Manuscript: Oral Tradition and Written Transmission in Rabbinic Judaism and Early Christianity*. Translated by Eric J. Sharpe. Acta Seminarii Neotestamentici Upsaliensis 22. Lund: Gleerup/Copenhagen: Munksgaard, 1961. Repr. as idem, *Memory and Manuscript: Oral Tradition and Written Transmission in Rabbinic Judaism and Early Christianity*, with *Tradition and Interpretation in Early Christianity*. Biblical Resource Series. With a foreword by Jacob Neusner. Grand Rapids: Eerdmans/Livonia: Dove, 1998.

–. *The Mighty Acts of Jesus According to Matthew*. Scripta Minora 1978–79 5. Lund: Gleerup, 1979.

–. "The Narrative Meshalim in the Old Testament Books and in the Synoptic Gospels." Pages 289–304 in *To Touch the Text: Biblical and Related Studies in Honor of Joseph A. Fitzmyer*. Edited by Maurya P. Horgan and Paul J. Kobelski. New York: Crossroad, 1989.

–. "Oral Tradition (New Testament)." Pages 498–501 in *A Dictionary of Biblical Interpretation*. Edited by R. J. Coggins and J. L. Houlden. London: SCM/ Philadelphia: Trinity Press International, 1990.

–. *The Origins of the Gospel Tradition*. Philadelphia: Fortress, 1979. Repr. pages 1–58 in idem, *The Reliability of the Gospel Tradition*. Peabody, Mass.: Hendrickson, 2001. Translated from *Evangeliernas Förhistoria*. Lund: Verbum-Håkan Ohlssons, 1977.

–. "The Path of the Gospel Tradition." Pages 75–96 in *The Gospel and the Gospels*. Edited by Peter Stuhlmacher. Translated by John Vriend. Grand Rapids: Eerdmans, 1991. Repr. pages 59–87 in idem, *The Reliability of the Gospel Tradition*. Peabody, Mass.: Hendrickson, 2001. Previously published as "Der Weg der Evangelientradition." Pages 79–102 in *Das Evangelium und die Evangelien: Vorträge vom Tübinger Symposium 1982*. Edited by Peter Stuhlmacher. Wissenschaftliche Untersuchungen zum Neuen Testament 28. Tübingen: Mohr Siebeck, 1983.

–. *The Reliability of the Gospel Tradition*. Foreword by Donald A. Hagner. Peabody, Mass.: Hendrickson, 2001.

–. "The Secret of the Transmission of the Unwritten Jesus Tradition." *New Testament Studies* 51 (2005): 1–18.

–. *The Testing of God's Son (Matt 4:1–11 & PAR): An Analysis of an Early Christian Midrash*. Coniectanea Biblica: New Testament Series 2.1. Lund: Gleerup, 1966.

–. *Tradition and Interpretation in Early Christianity*. Coniectanea Neotestamentica 20. Translated by Eric J. Sharpe. Lund: Gleerup/Copenhagen: Munksgaard, 1964. Repr. in idem, *Memory and Manuscript: Oral Tradition and Written Transmission in Rabbinic Judaism and Early Christianity,* with *Tradition and Interpretation in Early Christianity*. Biblical Resource Series. Foreword by Jacob Neusner. Grand Rapids: Eerdmans/Livonia: Dove, 1998.

Giet, Stanislas. *L'énigme de la Didachè*. Publications de la Faculté des Lettres de l'Université de Strasbourg 149. Paris: Les Editions Ophrys, 1970.

Gilliard, Frank D. "More Silent Reading in Antiquity: *Non Omne Verbum Sonabat*." *Journal of Biblical Literature* 112 (1993): 689–94.

Glimm, Francis X. "The Letter of St. Polycarp to the Philippians." Pages 129–43 in *The Apostolic Fathers*. Edited by Francis X. Glimm, Joseph M.-F. Marique and Gerald Walsh. The Fathers of the Church 1. New York: Cima, 1947.

Glover, Richard. "The Didache's Quotations and the Synoptic Gospels." *New Testament Studies* 5 (1958–59): 12–29.

–. "Patristic Quotations and Gospel Sources." *New Testament Studies* 31 (1985): 234–51.

Goodspeed, Edgar J. *A History of Early Christian Literature*. Revised and enlarged by Robert M. Grant. Chicago: University of Chicago Press, 1966. 1942.

Goody, Jack R. *The Domestication of the Savage Mind*. Themes in the Social Sciences. Cambridge: Cambridge University Press, 1977.

–. *The Interface between the Written and the Oral*. Studies in Literacy, Family, Culture and the State. Cambridge: Cambridge University Press, 1987.

–. *The Logic of Writing and the Organization of Society*. Studies in Literacy, Family, Culture and the State. Cambridge: Cambridge University Press, 1986.

–, ed. *Literacy in Traditional Societies*. Cambridge: Cambridge University Press, 1968.

Goody, Jack R., and Ian Watt. "The Consequences of Literacy." Pages 27–68 in *Literacy in Traditional Societies*. Edited by Jack R. Goody. Cambridge: Cambridge University Press, 1968.

Grant, Robert M. *The Apostolic Fathers: An Introduction*. The Apostolic Fathers 1. New York: Thomas Nelson & Sons, 1964.

–. *The Formation of the New Testament*. New York: Harper & Row, 1965.

–. *Ignatius of Antioch*. The Apostolic Fathers 4. Camden: Thomas Nelson & Sons, 1966.

–. "Polycarp of Smyrna." *Anglican Theological Review* 28 (1946): 137–48.

–. "Scripture and Tradition in Ignatius of Antioch." Pages 37–54 in idem, *After the New Testament*. Philadelphia: Fortress, 1967.

Grant, Robert M. and Holt H. Graham. *First and Second Clement*. The Apostolic Fathers 2. New York: Thomas Nelson & Sons, 1965.

Gray, Bennison. "Repetition in Oral Literature." *Journal of American Folklore* 84 (1971): 289–303.

Green, H. Benedict. "Matthew, Clement and Luke: Their Sequence and Relationship." *Journal of Theological Studies* n.s. 40 (1989): 1–25.

Green, Joel B. "Gethsemane." Pages 224–5 in *Encyclopedia of the Historical Jesus*. Edited by Craig A. Evans. New York and London: Routledge, 2008.

–. *The Gospel of Luke*. New International Commentary on the New Testament. Grand Rapids: Eerdmans, 1997.

Gregory, Andrew F. "1 Clement: An Introduction." *Expository Times* 117.6 (2006): 223–30. Repr. pages 21–31 in *The Writings of the Apostolic Fathers*. Edited by Paul Foster. T&T Clark Biblical Studies. London and New York: T&T Clark, 2007.

–. "*1 Clement* and the Writings that later Formed the New Testament." Pages 129–57 in *The Reception of the New Testament in the Apostolic Fathers*. Edited by A. Gregory and C. M. Tuckett. The New Testament and the Apostolic Fathers 1. Oxford: Oxford University Press, 2005.

–. "Disturbing Trajectories: *1 Clement*, the *Shepherd of Hermas*, and the Development of Early Roman Christianity." Pages 142–66 in *Rome in the Bible and the Early Church*. Edited by Peter Oakes. Carlisle: Paternoster/Grand Rapids: Baker Academic, 2002.

–. "Looking for Luke in the Second Century: A Dialogue with François Bovon." Pages 401–15 in *Reading Luke: Interpretation, Reflection, Formation*. Edited by Craig G. Bartholomew, Joel B. Green and Anthony C. Thiselton. Scripture and Hermeneutics 6. Milton Keynes: Paternoster/Grand Rapids: Zondervan, 2005.

–. "An Oral and Written Gospel? Reflections on Remembering Jesus." *Expository Times* 116 (2004–05): 7–12.

–. *The Reception of Luke and Acts in the Period before Irenaeus: Looking for Luke in the Second Century.* Wissenschaftliche Untersuchungen zum Neuen Testament 2.169. Tübingen: Mohr Siebeck, 2003.

–. Review of Paul Hartog, *Polycarp and the New Testament*, and Kenneth Berding, *Polycarp and Paul. Journal of Theological Studies* n.s. 54 (2003): 738–46.

–. "What Is Literary Dependence?" Pages 87–114 in *New Studies in the Synoptic Problem: Oxford Conference, April 2008: Essays in Honour of Christopher M. Tuckett.* Edited by P. Foster, A. Gregory, J. S. Kloppenborg and J. Verheyden. Leuven: Peeters, 2011.

Gregory, Andrew F., and Christopher M. Tuckett. "2 *Clement* and the Writings that later Formed the New Testament." Pages 251–92 in *The Reception of the New Testament in the Apostolic Fathers.* Edited by A. Gregory and C. M. Tuckett. The New Testament and the Apostolic Fathers 1. Oxford: Oxford University Press, 2005.

–. Introduction and Overview to *The Reception of the New Testament in the Apostolic Fathers* and *Trajectories through the New Testament and the Apostolic Fathers*, edited by Andrew Gregory and Christopher Tuckett. The New Testament and the Apostolic Fathers 1 and 2. Oxford: Oxford University Press, 2005.

–. "Reflections on Method: What Constitutes the Use of the Writings that later Formed the New Testament in the Apostolic Fathers?" Pages 61–82 in *The Reception of the New Testament in the Apostolic Fathers.* Edited by A. Gregory and C. M. Tuckett. The New Testament and the Apostolic Fathers 1. Oxford: Oxford University Press, 2005.

–, eds. *The Reception of the New Testament in the Apostolic Fathers.* The New Testament and the Apostolic Fathers 1. Oxford: Oxford University Press, 2005.

–, eds. *Trajectories through the New Testament and the Apostolic Fathers.* The New Testament and the Apostolic Fathers 2. Oxford: Oxford University Press, 2005.

Grey, Morgan E., Mary Louise Lord, and John Miles Foley. "A Bibliography of Publications by Albert Bates Lord." *Oral Tradition* 25 (2010): 497–504.

Guelich, Robert A. *Mark 1–8:26.* Word Biblical Commentary 34A. Dallas: Word, 1989.

Guijarro, Santiago. "Cultural Memory and Group Identity in Q." *Biblical Theology Bulletin* 37 (2007): 90–100.

Gundry, Robert H. "Further *Verba* on *Verba Christi* in First Peter." *Biblica* 55 (1974): 212–32.

–. *Mark: A Commentary on His Apology for the Cross.* Grand Rapids: Eerdmans, 1993.

–. *Matthew: A Commentary on His Handbook for a Mixed Church under Persecution.* 2nd ed. Grand Rapids: Eerdmans, 1994.

–. "*Verba Christi* in I Peter: Their Implications concerning the Authorship of I Peter and the Authenticity of the Gospel Tradition." *New Testament Studies* 13 (1966–67): 336–50.

Güttgemanns, Erhardt. *Candid Questions Concerning Gospel Form Criticism: A Methodological Sketch of the Fundamental Problematics of Form and Redaction Criticism.* Translated by William G. Doty. Pittsburgh Theological Monograph Series 26. Pittsburgh: Pickwick, 1979.

Haenchen, Ernst. *The Acts of the Apostles: A Commentary.* Translated by R. McL. Wilson, Bernard Noble and Gerald Shinn. Oxford: Blackwell/Philadelphia: Westminster, 1971.

Hagner, Donald A. Foreword to *The Reliability of the Gospel Tradition*, by Birger Gerhardsson. Peabody, Mass.: Hendrickson, 2001.

–. *Matthew 1–13*. Word Biblical Commentary 33A. Dallas, Tex.: Word, 1993.

–. *Matthew 14–28*. Word Biblical Commentary 33B. Dallas, Tex.: Word, 1995.

–. "Righteousness in Matthew's Theology." Pages 101–20 in *Worship, Theology and Ministry in the Early Church: Essays in Honor of Ralph P. Martin*. Edited by Michael J. Wilkins and Terence Paige. Journal for the Study of the New Testament Supplement Series 87. Sheffield: JSOT Press, 1992.

–. "The Sayings of Jesus in the Apostolic Fathers and Justin Martyr." Pages 233–68 in *Gospel Perspectives,* Vol. 5: *The Jesus Tradition Outside the Gospels*. Edited by David Wenham. Sheffield: JSOT Press, 1985.

–. *The Use of the Old and New Testaments in Clement of Rome*. Supplements to Novum Testamentum 34. Leiden: Brill, 1973.

Hainsworth, J. B. "The Fallibility of an Oral Heroic Tradition." Pages 111–35 in *The Trojan War: Its Historicity and Context*. Edited by Lin Foxhall and John K. Davies. Bristol: Bristol Classical Press, 1984.

Halbwachs, Maurice. *Les cadres sociaux de la mémoire*. Bibliothèque de philosophie contemporaine: Les Travaux de L'Année Sociologique. Paris: F. Alcan, 1925.

–. *The Collective Memory*. Translated by Francis J. Ditter, Jr. and Vida Yazdi Ditter. New York: Harper & Row, 1980. French original: *La mémoire collective*. Paris: Presses Universitaires de France, 1950.

–. *On Collective Memory*. Edited, Translated, and with an Introduction by Lewis A. Coser. The Heritage of Sociology. Chicago: University of Chicago Press, 1992. Translated from *Les cadres sociaux de la mémoire*. New ed. Paris: Presses Universitaires de France, 1952; and from *La topographie légendaire des évangiles en terre sainte: Etude de mémoire collective*. Paris: Presses Universitaires de France, 1941.

Halverson, John. "Oral and Written Gospel: A Critique of Werner Kelber." *New Testament Studies* 40 (1994): 180–95.

Halton, Thomas P. *Saint Jerome: On Illustrious Men*. The Fathers of the Church 100. Washington, D. C.: Catholic University of America Press, 1999.

Hanson, R. P. C. *Tradition in the Early Church*. Library of History and Doctrine. Philadelphia: Westminster, 1962.

Harbsmeier, Michael. "Writing and the Other: Travellers' Literacy, or Towards an Archaeology of Orality." Pages 197–228 in *Literacy and Society*. Edited by Karen Schousboe and Mogens Trolle Larsen. Copenhagen: Akademisk Forlag, 1989.

Harnack, Adolf. "Bishop Lightfoot's 'Ignatius and Polycarp.'" *The Expositor,* third series, vol. 2 (1885): 401–14, vol. 3 (1886): 175–92.

–. "Gospel: History of the Conception in the Earliest Church." Pages 275–331 in *The Constitution and Law of the Church in the First Two Centuries*. London: Williams & Norgate/New York: Putnam's Sons, 1910. E.T. of "Evangelium: Geschichte des Begriffs in der ältesten Kirche." Pages 199–239 in *Entstehung und Entwickelung der Kirchenverfassung und des Kirchenrechts in den zwei ersten Jahrhunderten*. Leipzig: Hinrichs, 1910.

–. *Geschichte der altchristlichen Literatur bis Eusebius,* Part 1: *Die Überlieferung und der Bestand*. 2nd expanded ed. 2 books. Leipzig: J. C. Hinrichs, 1958.

–. *Geschichte der altchristlichen Literatur bis Eusebius,* Part 2: *Die Chronologie,* Vol. 1: *Die Chronologie der Literatur bis Irenäus nebst einleitenden Untersuchungen*. 2nd expanded ed. 2 vols. Leipzig: J. C. Hinrichs, 1958.

–. *New Testament Studies*, Vol. 2: *The Sayings of Jesus*. Translated by J. R. Wilkinson. Crown Theological Library. New York: G. P. Putnam's Sons/London: Williams & Norgate, 1908.

–. "Das Schreiben der römischen Kirche an die korinthische aus der Zeit Domitians (I. Clemensbrief)." Pages 1–103 in *Encounters with Hellenism: Studies on the First Letter of Clement.* Edited by Cilliers Breytenbach and Laurence L. Welborn. Arbeiten zur Geschichte des antiken Judentums und des Urchristentums 53. Leiden: Brill, 2004.

Harrington, Daniel J. *The Gospel of Matthew.* Sacra Pagina 1. Collegeville: Liturgical, 1991.

Harris, William V. *Ancient Literacy.* Cambridge, Mass.: Harvard University Press, 1989.

Harrison, P. N. *Polycarp's Two Epistles to the Philippians.* Cambridge: Cambridge University Press, 1936.

Hartin, Patrick J. *James and the Q Sayings of Jesus.* Journal for the Study of the New Testament Supplement Series 47. Sheffield: JSOT Press, 1991.

Hartog, Paul. *Polycarp and the New Testament: The Occasion, Rhetoric, Theme, and Unity of the Epistle to the Philippians an its Allusions to New Testament Literature.* Wissenschaftliche Untersuchungen zum Neuen Testament 2.134. Tübingen: Mohr Siebeck, 2002.

Harvey, John D. *Listening to the Text: Oral Patterning in Paul's Letters.* Evangelical Theological Society Studies Series. With a foreword by Richard N. Longenecker. Grand Rapids: Baker/Leicester: Apollos, 1998.

–. "Orality and Its Implications for Biblical Studies: Recapturing an Ancient Paradigm." *Journal of the Evangelical Theological Society* 45 (2002): 99–109.

Havelock, Eric A. "The Alphabetic Mind: A Gift of Greece to the Modern World." *Oral Tradition* 1 (1986): 134–50.

–. *The Literate Revolution in Greece and Its Cultural Consequences.* Princeton Series of Collected Essays. Princeton: Princeton University Press, 1982.

–. *The Muse Learns to Write: Reflections on Orality and Literacy from Antiquity to the Present.* New Haven and London: Yale University Press, 1986.

–. "Oral Composition in the *Oedipus Tyrannus* of Sophocles." *New Literary History* 16 (1984): 175–97.

–. *Preface to Plato.* Cambridge, Mass.: Belknap Press of Harvard University Press, 1963.

Headlam, Arthur C. "The Epistle of Polycarp to the Philippians [Review of Harrison, *Polycarp's Two Epistles*]." *Church Quarterly Review* 141 (1945): 1–25.

Heard, Richard G. "The APOMNHMONEYMATA in Papias, Justin, and Irenaeus." *New Testament Studies* 1 (1954–55): 122–29.

–. "Papias' Quotations from the New Testament." *New Testament Studies* 1 (1954–55): 130–34.

Hearon, Holly E. "The Implications of 'Orality' for Studies of the Biblical Text." *Oral Tradition* 19 (2004): 96–107.

–. "The Interplay between Written and Spoken Word in the Second Testament as Background to the Emergence of Written Gospels." *Oral Tradition* 25 (2010): 57–74.

Heinemann, Joseph. *Prayer in the Talmud: Forms and Patterns.* Studia Judaica 9. Berlin and New York: de Gruyter, 1977.

Hemer, Colin J. *The Letters to the Seven Churches of Asia in Their Local Setting.* With a new foreword by David E. Aune. Biblical Resource Series. Grand Rapids: Eerdmans/ Livonia: Dove, 2001.

Hemmer, Hippolyte. *Les Péres Apostoliques,* Vol. 2: *Clément de Rome: Épitre aux Corinthiens, Homélie du IIe Siécle.* Paris: Picard, 1909.

Henaut, Barry W. *Oral Tradition and the Gospels: The Problem of Mark 4.* Journal for the Study of the New Testament Supplement Series 82. Sheffield: JSOT Press, 1993.

Henderson, Ian H. "Didache and Orality in Synoptic Comparison." *Journal of Biblical Literature* 111 (1992): 283–306.

–. "Style-Switching in the *Didache:* Fingerprint or Argument?" Pages 177–209 in *The Didache in Context: Essays on Its Text, History and Transmission.* Edited by Clayton N. Jefford. Supplements to Novum Testamentum 77. Leiden: Brill, 1995.

Hengel, Martin. *The Charismatic Leader and His Followers.* Edited by John Riches. Translated by James C. G. Greig. Edinburgh: T&T Clark, 1996.

–. *The Four Gospels and the One Gospel of Jesus Christ: An Investigation of the Collection and Origin of the Canonical Gospels.* Translated by John Bowden. London: SCM/Harrisburg: Trinity Press International, 2000.

Henige, David. "Oral, but Oral What? The Nomenclatures of Orality and Their Implications." *Oral Tradition* 3 (1988): 229–38.

–. *Oral Historiography.* New York: Longman, 1982.

Herder, Johann Gottfried. *Against Pure Reason: Writings on Religion, Language, and History.* Fortress Texts in Modern Theology. Translated, edited, and with an introduction by Marcia Bunge. Minneapolis: Fortress, 1993.

Hernando, James Daniel. "Irenaeus and the Apostolic Fathers: An Inquiry into the Development of the New Testament Canon." Ph.D. Dissertation; Madison, N.J.: Drew University, 1990.

Herron, Thomas J. "The Most Probable Date of the First Epistle of Clement to the Corinthians." Pages 106–21 in *Studia Patristica,* Vol. 21: *Papers presented to the Tenth International Conference on Patristic Studies held in Oxford 1987: Second Century, Tertullian to Nicaea in the West, Clement of Alexandria and Origen, Athanasius.* Edited by Elizabeth A. Livingstone. Leuven: Peeters, 1989.

Hezser, Catherine. *Jewish Literacy in Roman Palestine.* Texts and Studies in Ancient Judaism 81. Tübingen: Mohr Siebeck, 2001.

–. "Oral and Written Communication and Transmission of Knowledge in Ancient Judaism and Christianity." *Oral Tradition* 25 (2010): 75–92.

Hill, Charles E. "Ignatius, 'the Gospel,' and the Gospels." Pages 267–85 in *Trajectories through the New Testament and the Apostolic Fathers.* Edited by Andrew Gregory and Christopher Tuckett. The New Testament and the Apostolic Fathers 2. Oxford: Oxford University Press, 2005.

–. "Papias of Hierapolis." *Expository Times* 117.8 (2006): 309–15. Repr. pages 42–51 in *The Writings of the Apostolic Fathers.* Edited by Paul Foster. T&T Clark Biblical Studies. London and New York: T&T Clark, 2007.

Hodgson, Peter C. Introduction to *The Life of Jesus Critically Examined*, by David Friedrich Strauss. Lives of Jesus Series. Edited by Peter C. Hodgson. Translated by George Eliot. Philadelphia: Fortress, 1974.

Hodgson, Robert, Jr. "The Kingdom of God in the School of St. John." Pages 163–74 in *The Kingdom of God in 20th-Century Interpretation.* Edited by Wendell Willis. Peabody, Mass.: Hendrickson, 1987.

Hollander, Harm W. "The Words of Jesus: From Oral Traditions to Written Record in Paul and Q." *Novum Testamentum* 42 (2000): 340–57.

Holleran, J. Warren. *The Synoptic Gethsemane: A Critical Study.* Roma: Pontificia Universitas Gregoriana, Facultas Theologiae, 1973.

Holmes, Michael W. "Clement of Rome." Pages 233–38 in *Dictionary of the Later New Testament and Its Developments.* Edited by Ralph P. Martin and Peter H. Davids. Downers Grove: InterVarsity, 1997.

–. "Didache, The." Pages 300–302 in *Dictionary of the Later New Testament and Its Developments*. Edited by Ralph P. Martin and Peter H. Davids. Downers Grove: Inter-Varsity, 1997.

–. "The *Martyrdom of Polycarp* and the New Testament Passion Narratives." Pages 407–32 in *Trajectories through the New Testament and the Apostolic Fathers*. Edited by Andrew Gregory and Christopher Tuckett. The New Testament and the Apostolic Fathers 2. Oxford: Oxford University Press, 2005.

–. "Polycarp of Smyrna, *Letter to the Philippians*." *Expository Times* 118.2 (2006): 53–63. Repr. pages 108–25 *The Writings of the Apostolic Fathers*. Edited by Paul Foster. T&T Clark Biblical Studies. London and New York: T&T Clark, 2007.

–. "Polycarp's *Letter to the Philippians* and the Writings that Later Formed the New Testament." Pages 187–227 in *The Reception of the New Testament in the Apostolic Fathers*. Edited by Andrew Gregory and Christopher Tuckett. The New Testament and the Apostolic Fathers 1. Oxford: Oxford University Press, 2005.

–, ed. *The Apostolic Fathers: Greek Texts and English Translations*. 3rd ed. Grand Rapids: Baker Academic, 2007.

Holtz, Traugott. "Paul and the Oral Gospel Tradition." Pages 380–93 in *Jesus and the Oral Gospel Tradition*. Edited by H. Wansbrough. Journal for the Study of the New Testament Supplement Series 64. Sheffield: JSOT Press, 1991.

Hooker, Morna D. "On Using the Wrong Tool." *Theology* 75 (1972): 570–81.

–. *The Son of Man in Mark*. Montreal: McGill University Press, 1967.

Horrell, David G. *1 Peter*. New Testament Guides. London and New York: T&T Clark, 2008.

–. *The Social Ethos of the Corinthian Correspondence: Interests and Ideology from 1 Corinthians to 1 Clement*. Studies of the New Testament and Its World. Edinburgh: T&T Clark, 1996.

Horsley, Richard A. "The Contours of Q." Pages 61–93 in *Whoever Hears You Hears Me: Prophets, Performance, and Tradition in Q*, by Richard A. Horsley with Jonathan A. Draper. Harrisburg: Trinity Press International, 1999.

–. "The Covenant Renewal Discourse: Q 6:20–49." Pages 195–227 in *Whoever Hears You Hears Me: Prophets, Performance, and Tradition in Q*, by Richard A. Horsley with Jonathan A. Draper. Harrisburg: Trinity Press International, 1999.

–. *Hearing the Whole Story: The Politics of Plot in Mark's Gospel*. Louisville: Westminster John Knox, 2001.

–. Introduction to *Performing the Gospel: Orality, Memory, and Mark: Essays Dedicated to Werner Kelber*, edited by Richard A. Horsley, Jonathan A. Draper, and John Miles Foley. Minneapolis: Fortress, 2006.

–. "Oral and Written Aspects of the Emergence of the Gospel of Mark as Scripture," *Oral Tradition* 25 (2010): 93–114.

–. "The Oral Communication Environment of Q." Pages 123–49 in *Whoever Hears You Hears Me: Prophets, Performance, and Tradition in Q*, by Richard A. Horsley with Jonathan A. Draper. Harrisburg: Trinity Press International, 1999.

–. "Oral Performance and Mark: Some Implications of The Oral and the Written Gospel, Twenty-Five Years Later." Pages 45–70 in *Jesus, the Voice, and the Text: Beyond The Oral and the Written Gospel*. Edited by Tom Thatcher. Waco, Tex.: Baylor University Press, 2008.

–. "Oral Tradition in New Testament Studies." *Oral Tradition* 18 (2003): 34–36.

–. "Performance and Tradition: The Covenant Speech in Q." Pages 43–70 in *Oral Performance, Popular Tradition, and Hidden Transcript in Q*. Edited by Richard A. Horsley. SBL Semeia Studies 60. Atlanta: Society of Biblical Literature, 2006.

–. "A Prophet Like Moses and Elijah: Popular Memory and Cultural Patterns in Mark." Pages 166–90 in *Performing the Gospel: Orality, Memory, and Mark: Essays Dedicated to Werner Kelber.* Edited by Richard A. Horsley, Jonathan A. Draper and John Miles Foley. Minneapolis: Fortress, 2006.

–. "Recent Studies of Oral-Derived Literature and Q." Pages 150–74 in *Whoever Hears You Hears Me: Prophets, Performance, and Tradition in Q,* by Richard A. Horsley with Jonathan A. Draper. Harrisburg: Trinity Press International, 1999.

–. "The Renewal Movement and the Prophet Performers of Q." Pages 292–310 in *Whoever Hears You Hears Me: Prophets, Performance, and Tradition in Q,* by Richard A. Horsley with Jonathan A. Draper. Harrisburg: Trinity Press International, 1999.

–, ed. *Oral Performance, Popular Tradition, and Hidden Transcript in Q.* SBL Semeia Studies 60. Atlanta: Society of Biblical Literature, 2006.

Horsley, Richard A., with Jonathan A. Draper. *Whoever Hears You Hears Me: Prophets, Performance, and Tradition in Q.* Harrisburg: Trinity Press International, 1999.

Horsley, Richard A., Jonathan A. Draper, and John Miles Foley, eds. *Performing the Gospel: Orality, Memory, and Mark: Essays Dedicated to Werner Kelber.* Minneapolis: Fortress, 2006.

Hübner, R. M. "Thesen zur Echtheit und Datierung der sieben Briefe des Ignatius von Antiochen." *Zeitschrift für Antikes Christentum/Journal of Ancient Christianity* 1 (1997): 44–72.

Hurtado, Larry W. "Greco-Roman Textuality and the Gospel of Mark: A Critical Assessment of Werner Kelber's *The Oral and the Written Gospel." Bulletin for Biblical Research* 7 (1997): 91–106.

–. "The New Testament in the Second Century: Text, Collections and Canon." Pages 3–27 in *Transmission and Reception: New Testament Text-Critical and Exegetical Studies.* Edited by J. W. Childers and D. C. Parker. Texts and Studies, Third Series 4. Piscataway: Georgias, 2006.

Hvalvik, Reidar. "All Those Who in Every Place Call on the Name of Our Lord Jesus Christ: The Unity of the Pauline Churches." Pages 123–43 in *The Formation of the Early Church.* Edited by Jostein Ådna. Wissenschaftliche Untersuchungen zum Neuen Testament 183. Tübingen: Mohr Siebeck, 2005.

–. *The Struggle for Scripture and Covenant: The Purpose of the Epistle of Barnabas and Jewish-Christian Competition in the Second Century.* Wissenschaftliche Untersuchungen zum Neuen Testament 2.82. Tübingen: Mohr Siebeck, 1996.

Hymes, D. "Ethnopoetics, Oral-Formulaic Theory, and Editing Texts." *Oral Tradition* 9 (1994): 330–70.

–. *"In Vain I Tried to Tell You": Essays in Native American Ethnopoetics.* Philadelphia: University of Pennsylvania Press, 1999.

–. "Ways of Speaking." Pages 433–51 in *Explorations in the Ethnography of Speaking.* Edited by Richard Bauman and Joel Sherzer. 2nd ed. Cambridge: Cambridge University Press, 1989.

Isaac, E. "1 (Ethiopic Apocalypse of) Enoch (Second Century B.C. – First Century A.D.)." Pages 5–89 in vol. 1 of *The Old Testament Pseudepigrapha.* Edited by James H. Charlesworth. 2 vols. New York: Doubleday, 1983, 1985.

Isacson, Mikael. *To Each Their Own Letter: Structure, Themes, and Rhetorical Strategies in the Letters of Ignatius of Antioch.* Coniectanea Biblica: New Testament Series 42. Stockholm: Almqvist & Wiksell International, 2004.

Iverson, Kelly R. "Orality and the Gospels: A Survey of Recent Research." *Currents in Biblical Research* 8 (2009): 71–106.

Iyasere, Solomon O. "African Oral Tradition – Criticism as a Performance a Ritual." Pages 169–74 in *African Literature Today,* No. 11: *Myth and History.* Edited by Eldred Durosimi Jones. London: Heinemann/New York: Africana, 1980.

Jacquemin, Paul-Edmond. "Les béatitudes selon saint Luc: Lc 6,17.20–26," *Assemblées du Seigneur* 37 (1971): 80–91.

Jacquier, E. *Le Nouveau Testament dans l'eglise chrétienne.* 3rd ed. 2 vols. Paris: Gabalda, 1911–13.

Jaffee, Martin S. "Figuring Early Rabbinic Literary Culture: Thoughts Occasioned by Boomershine and Dewey." Pages 67–73 in *Orality and Textuality in Early Christian Literature.* Edited by Joanna Dewey. *Semeia* 65. Atlanta: Society of Biblical Literature/Scholars, 1994.

–. *Torah in the Mouth: Writing and Oral Tradition in Palestinian Judaism 200 BCE – 400 CE.* Oxford: Oxford University Press, 2001.

–. "Writing and Rabbinic Oral Tradition: On Mishnaic Narrative, Lists and Mnemonics." *The Journal of Jewish Thought and Philosophy* 4 (1994): 123–46.

Jaubert, Annie. *Clément de Rome: Épître aux Corinthiens.* Sources Chrétiennes 167. Paris: Cerf, 1971.

Jefford, Clayton N. "Apostolic Constitutions and Canons." Pages 312–13 in vol. 1 of *The Anchor Bible Dictionary.* Edited by David Noel Freedman. 6 vols. New York: Doubleday, 1992.

–. *The Apostolic Fathers and the New Testament.* Peabody, Mass.: Hendrickson, 2006.

–. "Did Ignatius of Antioch Know the *Didache?*" Pages 330–51 in *The Didache in Context: Essays on Its Text, History and Transmission.* Edited by Clayton N. Jefford. Supplements to Novum Testamentum 77. Leiden: Brill, 1995.

–. "The Milieu of Matthew, the Didache, and Ignatius of Antioch: Agreements and Differences." Pages 35–47 in *Matthew and the Didache: Two Documents from the Same Jewish-Christian Milieu?* Edited by Huub van de Sandt. Assen: Van Gorcum/Philadelphia: Fortress, 2005.

–. *The Sayings of Jesus in the Teaching of the Twelve Apostles.* Supplements to Vigiliae Christianae 11. Leiden: Brill, 1989.

–. "Social Locators as a Bridge between the *Didache* and Matthew." Pages 245–64 in *Trajectories through the New Testament and the Apostolic Fathers.* Edited by Andrew Gregory and Christopher Tuckett. The New Testament and the Apostolic Fathers 2. Oxford: Oxford University Press, 2005.

Jefford, Clayton N. with Kenneth J. Harder and Louis D. Amezaga, Jr. *Reading the Apostolic Fathers: An Introduction.* Peabody, Mass.: Hendrickson, 1996.

Jeremias, Joachim. *The Eucharistic Words of Jesus.* Translated by Norman Perrin. New Testament Library. London: SCM, 1966. E.T. of *Die Abendmahlsworte Jesu.* 3rd ed. Göttingen: Vandenhoeck & Ruprecht, 1960, with the author's revisions to July 1964.

–. *New Testament Theology,* Vol. 1: *The Proclamation of Jesus.* Translated by John Bowden. New Testament Library. London: SCM, 1971.

–. *The Prayers of Jesus.* Studies in Biblical Theology, 2nd Series 6. Naperville: Allenson, 1967.

–. *Unbekannte Jesusworte.* Zürich: Zwingli-Verlag, 1948. E.T.: *Unknown Sayings of Jesus.* New York: Macmillan, 1957.

–. *Unbekannte Jesusworte.* 3rd ed. With the assistance of Otfried Hofius. Gütersloh: Gerd Mohn, 1963. E.T.: *Unknown Sayings of Jesus.* 2nd Eng. ed. London: SPCK, 1964.

–. *Unknown Sayings of Jesus.* New York: Macmillan, 1957.

–. *Unknown Sayings of Jesus.* Translated by Reginald Fuller. 2nd English ed. London: SPCK, 1964.

Johnson, Luke Timothy. *The Acts of the Apostles.* Sacra Pagina 5. Collegeville: Liturgical, 1992.

Jonge, Henk Jan de. "On the Origin of the Term 'Apostolic Fathers.'" *Journal of Theological Studies* n.s. 29 (1978): 503–5.

Jousse, Marcel. *The Anthropology of Geste and Rhythm: Studies in the Anthropological Laws of Human Expression and Their Application in the Galilean Oral Style Tradition.* Edited and translated by E. Sienaert and J. Conolly. Durban: Center for Oral Studies, University of Natal, 1997.

–. *The Oral Style.* Translated by E. Sienaert and R. Whitaker. New York: Garland, 1990.

Juel, Donald H. "The Lord's Prayer in the Gospels of Matthew and Luke." Pages 56–70 in *The Lord's Prayer: Perspectives for Reclaiming Christian Prayer.* Edited by Daniel L. Migliore. Grand Rapids: Eerdmans, 1993.

Jülicher, A. *Die Gleichnisreden Jesu.* Vol. 2. Darmstadt: Wissenschaftliche Buchgesellschaft, 1963.

Keck, Leander E. "Oral Traditional Literature and the Gospels: The Seminar." Pages 103–22 in *The Relationships Among the Gospels: An Interdisciplinary Dialogue.* Edited by William O. Walker, Jr. Trinity University Monograph Series in Religion 5. San Antonio. Tex.: Trinity University Press, 1978.

Keightley, Georgia Masters. "Christian Collective Memory and Paul's Knowledge of Jesus." Pages 129–50 in *Memory, Tradition, and Text: Uses of the Past in Early Christianity.* Edited by Alan Kirk and Tom Thatcher. SBL Semeia Studies 52. Atlanta: Society of Biblical Literature, 2005.

Keith, Chris, and Tom Thatcher. "The Scar of the Cross: The Violence Ratio and the Earliest Christian Memories of Jesus." Pages 197–214 in *Jesus, the Voice, and the Text: Beyond the Oral and the Written Gospel.* Edited by Tom Thatcher. Waco, Tex.: Baylor University Press, 2008.

Kelber, Werner H. "The Authority of The Word in St. John's Gospel: Charismatic Speech, Narrative Text, Logocentric Metaphysics." *Oral Tradition* 2.1 [Festschrift for Walter J. Ong] (1987): 108–31.

–. "Biblical Hermeneutics and the Ancient Art of Communication: A Response." Pages 97–105 in *Orality, Aurality and Biblical Narrative.* Edited by Lou H. Silberman. *Semeia* 39. Decatur: Society of Biblical Literature/Scholars, 1987.

–. "The Case of the Gospels: Memory's Desire and the Limits of Historical Criticism." *Oral Tradition* 17 (2002): 55–86.

–. "The Generative Force of Memory: Early Christian Traditions as Process of Remembering." *Biblical Theology Bulletin* 36 (2006): 15–22.

–. "The History of the Closure of Biblical Texts." *Oral Tradition* 25 (2010): 115–40.

–. "Incarnations, Remembrances, and Transformations of the Word." Pages 111–33 in *Time, Memory, and the Verbal Arts: Essays on the Thought of Walter Ong.* Edited by Dennis L. Weeks and Jane Hoogestraat. Selinsgrove: Susquehanna University Press/London: Associated University Presses, 1998.

–. "Jesus and Tradition: Words in Time, Words in Space." Pages 139–67 in *Orality and Textuality in Early Christian Literature.* Edited by Joanna Dewey. *Semeia* 65. Atlanta: Society of Biblical Literature/Scholars, 1994.

–. "Mark 14:32–42: Gethsemane: Passion Christology and Discipleship Failure." *Zeitschrift für die neutestamentliche Wissenschaft* 63 (1972): 166–87.

–. "Mark and Oral Tradition." Pages 7–55 in *Perspectives on Mark's Gospel.* Edited by Norman R. Petersen. *Semeia* 16. Missoula: Society of Biblical Literature/Scholars, 1979.

–. "Modalities of Communication, Cognition, and Physiology of Perception: Orality, Rhetoric, and Scribality." Pages 193–216 in *Orality and Textuality in Early Christian Literature*. Edited by Joanna Dewey. *Semeia* 65. Atlanta: Society of Biblical Literature/Scholars, 1994.

–. "Narrative as Interpretation and Interpretation as Narrative: Hermeneutical Reflections on the Gospels." Pages 107–33 in *Orality, Aurality and Biblical Narrative*. Edited by Lou H. Silberman. *Semeia* 39. Decatur: Society of Biblical Literature/Scholars, 1987.

–. "New Testament Texts: Rhetoric and Discourse." Pages 330–38 in *Teaching Oral Traditions*. Edited by John Miles Foley. New York: Modern Language Association, 1998.

–. *The Oral and the Written Gospel: The Hermeneutics of Speaking and Writing in the Synoptic Tradition, Mark, Paul, and Q*. Philadelphia: Fortress, 1982. Repr. with a new introduction by the author and a foreword by Walter J. Ong, Bloomington and Indianapolis: Indiana University Press, 1997.

–. "The Oral-Scribal-Memorial Arts of Communication in Early Christianity." Pages 235–62 in *Jesus, the Voice, and the Text: Beyond The Oral and the Written Gospel*. Edited by Tom Thatcher. Waco, Tex.: Baylor University Press, 2008.

–. "Oral Tradition (NT)." Pages 30–34 in vol. 5 of *The Anchor Bible Dictionary*. Edited by David Noel Freedman. 6 vols. New York: Doubleday, 1992.

–. "Oral Tradition in Bible and New Testament Studies." *Oral Tradition* 18 (2003): 40–42.

–. "Orality, Scribality, and Oral-Scribal Interfaces: Jesus – Tradition – Gospels: Review and Present State of Research." Paper presented at the SNTS Annual Meeting, Halle, Germany, 6-9 August 2005.

–. "The Works of Memory: Christian Origins as Mnemohistory – A Response." Pages 221–48 in *Memory, Tradition, and Text: Uses of the Past in Early Christianity*. Edited by Alan Kirk and Tom Thatcher. SBL Semeia Studies 52. Atlanta: Society of Biblical Literature, 2005.

–, ed. *The Passion in Mark: Studies on Mark 14–16*. Philadelphia: Fortress, 1976.

Kelber, Werner H., and Samuel Byrskog, eds. *Jesus in Memory: Traditions in Oral and Scribal Practices*. Waco, Tex.: Baylor University Press, 2009.

Kelber, Werner H., and Paula Sanders. "Oral Tradition in Judaism, Christianity, and Islam: Introduction." *Oral Tradition* 25 (2010): 3–6.

Kelhoffer, James A. "'How Soon a Book' Revisited: *ΕΥΑΓΓΕΛΙΟΝ* as a Reference to 'Gospel' Materials in the First Half of the Second Century." *Zeitschrift für die neutestamentliche Wissenschaft* 95 (2004): 1–34.

Kilgallen, John J. "Acts 20:35 and Thucydides 2.97.4." *Journal of Biblical Literature* 112 (1993): 312–4.

Kim, Seyoon. "The Jesus Tradition in 1 Thess 4.13–5.11." *New Testament Studies* 48 (2002): 225–42.

–. *Paul and the New Perspective: Second Thoughts on the Origin of Paul's Gospel*. Grand Rapids: Eerdmans, 2002.

–. *The "Son of Man" as the Son of God*. Wissenschaftliche Untersuchungen zum Neuen Testament 30. Tübingen: Mohr Siebeck, 1983. Repr. Grand Rapids: Eerdmans, 1985.

Kirk, Alan. "Manuscript Tradition as a *Tertium Quid*: Orality and Memory in Scribal Practices." Pages 215–34 in *Jesus, the Voice, and the Text: Beyond the Oral and the Written Gospel*. Edited by Tom Thatcher. Waco, Tex.: Baylor University Press, 2008.

–. "Memory." Pages 155–72 in *Jesus in Memory: Traditions in Oral and Scribal Practices*. Edited by Werner H. Kelber and Samuel Byrskog. Waco, Tex.: Baylor University Press, 2009.

–. "Memory, Scribal Media, and the Synoptic Problem." Pages 459–82 in *New Studies in the Synoptic Problem: Oxford Conference, April 2008: Essays in Honour of Christopher M. Tuckett*. Edited by P. Foster, A. Gregory, J. S. Kloppenborg and J. Verheyden. Bibliotheca Ephemeridum Theologicarum Lovaniensium 239. Leuven: Peeters, 2011.

–. "Memory Theory and Jesus Research." Pages 809–42 in vol. 1 of *Handbook for the Study of the Historical Jesus*. Edited by Tom Holmén and Stanley E. Porter. 4 vols. Leiden: Brill, 2011.

–. "Social and Cultural Memory." Pages 1–24 in *Memory, Tradition, and Text: Uses of the Past in Early Christianity*. Edited by Alan Kirk and Tom Thatcher. SBL Semeia Studies 52. Atlanta: Society of Biblical Literature, 2005.

Kirk, Alan, and Tom Thatcher. "Jesus Tradition and Social Memory." Pages 25–42 in *Memory, Tradition, and Text: Uses of the Past in Early Christianity*. Edited by Alan Kirk and Tom Thatcher. SBL Semeia Studies 52. Atlanta: Society of Biblical Literature, 2005.

–. eds. *Memory, Tradition, and Text: Uses of the Past in Early Christianity*. SBL Semeia Studies 52. Atlanta: Society of Biblical Literature, 2005.

Klauck, Hans-Josef. *Apocryphal Gospels: An Introduction*. Translated by Brian McNeil. London and New York: T&T Clark, 2003.

Klein, Hans, Vasile Mihoc, and Karl-Wilhelm Niebuhr, in cooperation with Christos Karakolis, eds. *Das Gebet im Neuen Testament: Vierte europäische orthodox-westliche Exegetenkonferenz in Sambata de Sus, 4.–8. August 2007*. Wissenschaftliche Untersuchungen zum Neuen Testament 1.249. Tübingen: Mohr Siebeck, 2009.

Kleist, James A. *The Didache, The Epistle of Barnabas, The Epistles and the Martyrdom of Polycarp, The Fragments of Papias, The Epistle to Diognetus*. Ancient Christian Writers 6. Westminster: Newman, 1948.

–. *The Epistles of St. Clement of Rome and St. Ignatius of Antioch*. Ancient Christian Writers 1. Westminster: Newman, 1946.

Klijn, A. F. J. "2 (Syriac Apocalypse of) Baruch: A New Translation and Introduction." Pages 615–52 in vol. 1 of *The Old Testament Pseudepigrapha*. Edited by James H. Charlesworth. 2 vols. New York: Doubleday, 1983, 1985.

Kloppenborg, John S. "*Didache* 1. 1–6. 1, James, Matthew, and the Torah." Pages 193–221 in *Trajectories through the New Testament and the Apostolic Fathers*. Edited by Andrew Gregory and Christopher Tuckett. The New Testament and the Apostolic Fathers 2. Oxford: Oxford University Press, 2005.

–. "Didache 16 6–8 and Special Matthaean Tradition." *Zeitschrift für die neutestamentliche Wissenschaft* 70 (1979): 54–67.

– (Verbin). *Excavating Q: The History and Setting of the Sayings Gospel*. Minneapolis: Fortress, 2000.

–. *The Formation of Q: Trajectories in Ancient Wisdom Collections*. Philadelphia: Fortress, 1987.

–. "Jesus and the Parables of Jesus in Q." Pages 275–319 in *The Gospel Behind the Gospels: Current Studies on Q*. Edited by R. A. Piper. Supplements to Novum Testamentum 75. Leiden: Brill, 1995.

–. *Q Parallels: Synopsis, Critical Notes, and Concordance*. Foundations and Facets. Sonoma, Calif.: Polebridge, 1988.

–. "The Transformation of Moral Exhortation in *Didache* 1–5." Pages 88–109 in *The Didache in Context: Essays on Its Text, History and Transmission*. Edited by Clayton N. Jefford. Supplements to Novum Testamentum 77. Leiden: Brill, 1995.

–. "The Use of the Synoptics or Q in *Did.* 1:3b–2:1." Pages 105–29 in *Matthew and the Didache: Two Documents from the Same Jewish-Christian Milieu?* Edited by Huub van de Sandt. Assen: Van Gorcum/Philadelphia: Fortress, 2005.

–. "Variation in the Reproduction of the Double Tradition and an Oral Q?" *Ephemerides Theologicae Lovanienses* 83 (2007): 53–80.

Knibb, Michael A. "The Ethiopic Book of Enoch." Pages 26–55 in *Outside the Old Testament.* Edited by Marinus de Jonge. Cambridge Commentaries on Writings of the Jewish and Christian World 200 BC to AD 200, 4. Cambridge: Cambridge University Press, 1985.

Knoch, Otto. *Eigenart und Bedeutung der Eschatologie im theologischen Aufriß des ersten Clemensbriefes: Eine auslegungsgeschichtliche Untersuchung.* Theophaneia 17. Bonn: Peter Hanstein, 1964.

–. "Kenntnis und Verwendung des Matthäus-Evangeliums bei den Apostolischen Vätern." Pages 157–77 in *Studien zum Matthäusevangelium: Festschrift für Wilhelm Pesch.* Edited by Ludger Schenke. Stuttgarter Bibelstudien. Stuttgart: Katholisches Bibelwerk, 1988.

–. "Petrus und Paulus in den Schriften der apostolischen Väter." Pages 240–60 in *Kontinuität und Einheit: Für Franz Mußner.* Edited by Paul-Gerhard Müller and Werner Stenger. Freiburg: Herder, 1981.

Knopf, Rudolf. *Die Lehre der zwölf Apostel, die zwei Clemensbriefe.* Handbuch zum Neuen Testament, Ergänzungsband: Die apostolischen Väter 1. Tübingen: Mohr Siebeck, 1920.

Knox, John. *Marcion and the New Testament: An Essay in the Early History of the Canon.* Chicago: University of Chicago Press, 1942.

Koester (Köster), Helmut. *Ancient Christian Gospels: Their History and Development.* London: SCM/Philadelphia: Trinity Press International, 1990.

–. "Apocryphal and Canonical Gospels." *Harvard Theological Review* 73 (1980): 105–30. Repr. pages 3–23 in idem, *From Jesus to the Gospels: Interpreting the New Testament in Its Context.* Minneapolis: Fortress, 2007.

–. "The Extracanonical Sayings of the Lord as Products of the Christian Community." *Semeia* 44 (1988): 57–77. Repr. pages 84–99 in idem, *From Jesus to the Gospels: Interpreting the New Testament in Its Context.* Minneapolis: Fortress, 2007.

–. *From Jesus to the Gospels: Interpreting the New Testament in Its Context.* Minneapolis: Fortress, 2007.

–. "From the Kerygma-Gospel to Written Gospels." *New Testament Studies* 35 (1989): 361–81.

–. "Gospels and Gospel Traditions in the Second Century." Pages 27–44 in *Trajectories through the New Testament and the Apostolic Fathers.* Edited by Andrew Gregory and Christopher Tuckett. The New Testament and the Apostolic Fathers 2. Oxford: Oxford University Press, 2005. Repr. pages 24–38 in idem, *From Jesus to the Gospels: Interpreting the New Testament in Its Context.* Minneapolis: Fortress, 2007.

–. *Introduction to the New Testament,* Vol. 1: *History, Culture, and Religion of the Hellenistic Age.* 2nd ed. New York and Berlin: de Gruyter, 1995.

–. *Introduction to the New Testament,* Vol. 2: *History and Literature of Early Christianity.* 2nd ed. New York and Berlin: de Gruyter, 2000.

–. "One Jesus and Four Primitive Gospels." *Harvard Theological Review* 61 (1968): 203–47. Repr. pages 158–204 in *Trajectories through Early Christianity*, by James M. Robinson and Helmut Koester. Philadephia: Fortress, 1971.

– (Köster). *Synoptische Überlieferung bei den apostolischen Vätern.* Texte und Untersuchungen 65. Berlin: Akademie-Verlag, 1957.

–. "The Text of the Synoptic Gospels in the Second Century." Pages 19–37 in *Gospel Traditions in the Second Century: Origins, Recensions, Text, and Transmission*. Edited by William L. Petersen. Christianity and Judaism in Antiquity 3. Notre Dame: University of Notre Dame Press, 1989. Repr. pages 39–53 in idem, *From Jesus to the Gospels: Interpreting the New Testament in Its Context*. Minneapolis: Fortress, 2007.

–. "Written Gospels or Oral Tradition?" *Journal of Biblical Literature* 113 (1994): 293–97.

Köhler, Wolf-Dietrich. *Die Rezeption des Matthäusevangeliums in der Zeit vor Irenäus*. Wissenschaftliche Untersuchungen zum Neuen Testament 2.24. Tübingen: Mohr Siebeck, 1987.

Kraft, Robert A. *Barnabas and the Didache*. The Apostolic Fathers 3. New York: Thomas Nelson & Sons, 1965.

–. "Didache." Pages 197–98 in vol. 2 of *The Anchor Bible Dictionary*. Edited by David Noel Freedman. 6 vols. New York: Doubleday, 1992.

Kraus, Thomas J. "'Uneducated,' 'Ignorant,' or even 'Illiterate'? Aspects and Background for an Understanding of ἀγράμματοι (and ἰδιῶται) in Acts 4.13." *New Testament Studies* 45 (1999): 434–49. Repr. pages 149–70 in idem, *Ad fontes: Original Manuscripts and Their Significance for Studying Early Christianity: Selected Essays*. Texts and Editions for New Testament Study 3. Leiden: Brill, 2007.

Kullmann, Wolfgang. "Homer and Historical Memory." Pages 95–113 in *Signs of Orality: The Oral Tradition and its Influence in the Greek and Roman Worlds*. Edited by E. Anne Mackay. Supplements to Mnemosyne 188. Leiden: Brill, 1999.

Kümmel, Werner Georg. *The New Testament: The History of the Investigation of its Problems*. Translated by S. MacLean Gilmour and Howard Clark Kee. Nashville: Abingdon, 1972.

Lake, Kirsopp. Review of P. N. Harrison, *Polycarp's Two Epistles to the Philippians*. *Journal of Biblical Literature* 56 (1937): 72–75.

Lake, Kirsopp and J. E. L. Oulton, trans. *Eusebius: The Ecclesiastical History*. 2 vols. Loeb Classical Library 153, 265. Cambridge, Mass: Harvard University Press/ London: Heinemann, 1926, 1932.

Lambrecht, Jan. *"Eh bien! Moi je vous dis": Le discourse-programme de Jésus (Mt 5–7; Lc 6,20–49)*. Lectio Divina 125. Paris: Éditions du Cerf, 1986.

–. *The Sermon on the Mount: Proclamation and Exhortation*. Good News Studies 14. Wilmington: Michael Glazier, 1985.

Lane, William L. *The Gospel According to Mark*. New International Commentary on the New Testament. Grand Rapids: Eerdmans, 1974.

Lardinois, André. "The Wisdom and Wit of Many: The Orality of Greek Proverbial Expressions." Pages 93–107 in *Speaking Volumes: Orality and Literacy in the Greek and Roman World*. Edited by Janet Watson. Supplements to Mnemosyne 218. Leiden: Brill, 2001.

LaVerdiere, Eugene. "The Lord's Prayer in Literary Context." Pages 104–16 in *Scripture and Prayer: A Celebration for Carroll Stuhlmueller, CP*. Edited by Carolyn Osiek and Donald Senior. Wilmington: Michael Glazier, 1988.

Lawlor, H. J. and J. E. L. Oulton, eds. *Eusebius of Caesarea: The Ecclesiastical History and The Martyrs of Palestine*. 2 vols. London: SPCK, 1927.

Lawson, John. *A Theological and Historical Introduction to the Apostolic Fathers*. New York: Macmillan, 1961.

Layton, Bentley. "The Sources, Date and Transmission of *Didache* 1.3b–2.1." *Harvard Theological Review* 61 (1968): 343–83.

Le Donne, Anthony. *The Historiographical Jesus: Memory, Typology, and the Son of David.* Waco, Tex.: Baylor University Press, 2009.

–. "Theological Memory Distortion in the Jesus Tradition: A Study in Social Memory Theory." Pages 163–77 in *Memory in the Bible and Antiquity: The Fifth Durham-Tübingen Research Symposium (Durham, September 2004).* Edited by Loren T. Stuckenbruck, Stephen C. Barton and Benjamin G. Wold. Wissenschaftliche Untersuchungen zum Neuen Testament 212. Tübingen: Mohr Siebeck, 2007.

Lechner, T. *Ignatius adversus Valentinianos? Chronologische und theologiegeschichtliche Studien zu den Briefen des Ignatius von Antiochien.* Supplements to Vigiliae Christianae 47. Leiden: Brill, 1999.

Lessing, Gotthold. "New Hypothesis Concerning the Evangelists Regarded as Merely Human Historians." Pages 65–81 in *Lessing's Theological Writings.* Edited and translated by Henry Chadwick. A Library of Modern Religious Thought. Stanford: Stanford University Press, 1957.

Liberty, Stephen. Review of P. N. Harrison, *Polycarp's Two Epistles to the Philippians. Church Quarterly Review* 124.247 (1937): 141–47.

Lightfoot, J. B. *The Apostolic Fathers: Clement, Ignatius, and Polycarp: Revised Texts with Introductions, Notes, Dissertations, and Translations.* 2nd ed. 2 parts in 5 vols. London: Macmillan, 1889–90.

–. *Essays on the Work Entitled Supernatural Religion.* London and New York: Macmillan, 1889.

Lindemann, Andreas. "Antwort auf die 'Thesen zur Echtheit und Datierung der sieben Briefe des Ignatius von Antiochen.'" *Zeitschrift für Antikes Christentum/Journal of Ancient Christianity* 1 (1997): 185–94.

–. "Apostolic Fathers." Page 335 in vol. 1 of *Religion Past and Present: Encyclopedia of Theology and Religion.* Edited by Hans Dieter Betz, Don S. Browning, Bernd Janowski and Eberhard Jüngel. Leiden: Brill, 2007.

–. "The Apostolic Fathers and the Synoptic Problem." Pages 689–719 in *New Studies in the Synoptic Problem: Oxford Conference, April 2008: Essays in Honour of Christopher M. Tuckett.* Edited by P. Foster, A. Gregory, J. S. Kloppenborg and J. Verheyden. Bibliotheca Ephemeridum Theologicarum Lovaniensium 239. Leuven: Peeters, 2011.

–. *Die Clemensbriefe.* Handbuch zum Neuen Testament 17: Die Apostolischen Väter 1. Tübingen: Mohr Siebeck, 1992.

–. "The First Epistle of Clement." Pages 47–69 in *The Apostolic Fathers: An Introduction.* Edited by Wilhelm Pratscher. Waco, Tex.: Baylor University Press, 2010.

–. "Paul's Influence on 'Clement' and Ignatius." Pages 9–24 in *Trajectories through the New Testament and the Apostolic Fathers.* Edited by Andrew Gregory and Christopher Tuckett. The New Testament and the Apostolic Fathers 2. Oxford: Oxford University Press, 2005.

Löfstedt, Torsten. "A Message for the Last Days: Didache 16.1–8 and the New Testament Traditions." *Estudios Bíblicos* 60 (2002): 351–80.

Lohmeyer, Ernst. *"Our Father": An Introduction to the Lord's Prayer.* Translated by John Bowden. New York: Harper & Row, 1965. German original: *Das Vater-Unser.* Göttingen: Vandenhoeck & Ruprecht, 1952.

Lohr, Charles H. "Oral Techniques in the Gospel of Matthew." *Catholic Biblical Quarterly* 23 (1961): 403–35.

Lona, Horacio E. *Der erste Clemensbrief.* Kommentar zu den Apostolischen Vätern 2. Göttingen: Vandenhoeck & Ruprecht, 1998.

Loofs, F. *Theophilus von Antiochien Adversus Marcionem und die anderen theologischen Quellen bei Irenaeus.* Texte und Untersuchungen 46. Leipzig: Heinrichs, 1930.

Lord, Albert B. "Characteristics of Orality." *Oral Tradition* 2.1 [Festschrift for Walter J. Ong] (1987): 54–72.

–. "The Gospels as Oral Traditional Literature." Pages 33–91 in *The Relationships Among the Gospels: An Interdisciplinary Dialogue.* Edited by William O. Walker, Jr. Trinity University Monograph Series in Religion 5. San Antonio, Tex.: Trinity University Press, 1978.

–. "Memory, Fixity, and Genre in Oral Traditional Poetries." Pages 451–61 in *Oral Traditional Literature: A Festschrift for Albert Bates Lord.* Edited by John Miles Foley. Columbus: Slavica, 1981.

–. "The Merging of Two Worlds: Oral and Written Poetry as Carriers of Ancient Values." Pages 19–64 in *Oral Tradition in Literature: Interpretation in Context.* Edited by John Miles Foley. Columbia: University of Missouri Press, 1986.

–. "The Nature of Oral Poetry." Pages 313–49 in *Comparative Research on Oral Traditions: A Memorial for Milman Parry.* Edited by John Miles Foley. Columbus: Slavica, 1987.

–. "Perspectives on Recent Work on the Oral Traditional Formula." *Oral Tradition* 1 (1986): 467–503.

–. *The Singer of Tales.* Harvard Studies in Comparative Literature 24. Cambridge, Mass.: Harvard University Press, 1960. Repr. New York: Atheneum, 1974.

–. *The Singer Resumes the Tale.* Edited by Mary Louise Lord. Ithaca and London: Cornell University Press, 1995.

Louth, Andrew. *Early Christian Writings: The Apostolic Fathers.* Translated by Maxwell Staniforth. Revised translation, introductions and new editorial material by Andrew Louth. London: Penguin, 1987.

Lührmann, Dieter. "Liebet eure Feinde (Lk 6,27–36/Mt 5,39–48)." *Zeitschrift für Theologie und Kirche* 69 (1972): 412–58.

–. *Die Redaktion der Logienquelle: Anhang: Zur weiteren Überlieferung der Logienquelle.* Wissenschaftliche Monographien zum Alten und Neuen Testament 33. Neukirchen-Vluyn: Neukirchener, 1969.

Lumpp, Randolph F. "Walter Jackson Ong, S.J.: A Selected Bibliography." *Oral Tradition* 2.1 [Festschrift Walter J. Ong] (1987): 19–30.

Luria, A. R. *Cognitive Development: Its Cultural and Social Foundations.* Translated by M. Lopez-Morillas and L. Solotaroff. Edited by M. Cole. Cambridge, Mass.: Harvard University Press, 1976.

Luz, Ulrich. *Matthew 1–7: A Commentary.* Translated by James E. Crouch. Edited by Helmut Koester. Hermeneia. Minneapolis: Fortress, 2007.

–. *Matthew 8–20: A Commentary.* Translated by James E. Crouch. Edited by Helmut Koester. Hermeneia. Minneapolis: Fortress, 2001.

–. *Matthew 21–28: A Commentary.* Translated by James E. Crouch. Edited by Helmut Koester. Hermeneia. Minneapolis: Fortress, 2005.

–. "Matthew and Q." Pages 39–53 in idem, *Studies in Matthew.* Translated by Rosemary Selle. Grand Rapids: Eerdmans, 2005.

Luzarraga, J. *El Padrenuestro desde el arameo.* Analecta Biblica 171. Roma: Editrice Pontificio Istituto Biblico, 2008.

Macdonald, M. C. A. "Literacy in an Oral Environment." Pages 49–118 in *Writing and Ancient Near Eastern Society: Papers in Honour of Alan R. Millard.* Edited by Piotr Bienkowski, Christopher Mee and Elizabeth Slater. Library of Hebrew Bible/Old Testament Studies 426. New York and London: T&T Clark, 2005.

Maier, Gerhard. "Jesustradition im 1. Petrusbrief?" Pages 85–128 in *Gospel Perspectives,* Vol. 5: *The Jesus Tradition Outside the Gospels.* Edited by David Wenham. Sheffield: JSOT Press, 1985.

Maier, Harry O. "The Politics and Rhetoric of Discord and Concord in Paul and Ignatius." Pages 307–24 in *Trajectories through the New Testament and the Apostolic Fathers.* Edited by Andrew Gregory and Christopher Tuckett. The New Testament and the Apostolic Fathers 2. Oxford: Oxford University Press, 2005.

–. "Purity and Danger in Polycarp's Epistle to the Philippians: The Sin of Valens in Social Perspective." *Journal of Early Christian Studies* 1 (1993): 229–47.

–. Review of Johannes Bapt. Bauer, *Die Polykarpbriefe. Journal of Theological Studies* n.s. 47 (1996): 642–45.

–. *The Social Setting of the Ministry as Reflected in the Writings of Hermas, Clement and Ignatius.* Dissertations SR 1. Waterloo: Published for the Canadian Corporation for Studies in Religion/Corporation Canadienne des Sciences Religieuses by Wilfrid Laurier University Press, 1991.

Mann, C. S. *Mark: A New Translation with Introduction and Commentary.* Anchor Bible 27. Garden City: Doubleday, 1986.

Manson, T. W. "The Lord's Prayer." *Bulletin of the John Rylands Library* 38 (1955–56): 99–113, 436–48.

Marcus, Joel. *Mark 1–8: A New Translation with Introduction and Commentary.* Anchor Bible 27. New York: Doubleday, 2000.

–. *Mark 8–16: A New Translation with Introduction and Commentary.* Anchor Yale Bible 27A. New Haven and London: Yale University Press, 2009.

–. *The Way of the Lord: Christological Exegesis of the Old Testament in the Gospel of Mark.* Louisville: Westminster/John Knox, 1992. Repr. Studies in the New Testament and Its World. Edinburgh: T&T Clark, 1993.

Marshall, I. Howard. *The Acts of the Apostles.* Tyndale New Testament Commentaries. Grand Rapids: Eerdmans, 1980.

–. *The Gospel of Luke: A Commentary on the Greek Text.* New International Greek Testament Commentary. Grand Rapids: Eerdmans, 1978.

Massaux, Édouard. *Influence de l'Évangile de saint Matthieu sur la littérature chrétienne avant saint Irénée.* 2nd ed., with new bibliographical supplement 1950–1985 by B. Dehandschutter. Bibliotheca Ephemeridum Theologicarum Lovaniensium 75. Leuven: Leuven University Press and Peeters, 1986 [1st ed. 1950].

–. *The Influence of the Gospel of Saint Matthew on Christian Literature before Saint Irenaeus.* 3 vols. Translated by Norman J. Belval and Suzanne Hecht. Edited and with an introduction and addenda by Arthur J. Bellinzoni. New Gospel Studies 5. Leuven: Peeters/Macon: Mercer University Press, 1990–93.

Massey, Isabel Ann. *Interpreting the Sermon on the Mount in the Light of Jewish Tradition as Evidenced in the Palestinian Targums of the Pentateuch: Selected Themes.* Studies in the Bible and Early Christianity 25. Lewiston: Edwin Mellen, 1991.

Mattila, Sharon Lea. "A Question Too Often Neglected." *New Testament Studies* 41 (1995): 199–217.

Maurer, Christian. *Ignatius von Antiochien und das Johannesevangelium.* Abhandlungen zur Theologie des Alten und Neuen Testaments 18. Zürich: Zwingli-Verlag, 1949.

–. "Ein umstrittenes Zitat bei Ignatius von Antiochien (Smyrn. 3, 2)." *Jahrbuch der Gesellschaft für die Geschichte des Protestantismus in Österreich* 67 [Festschrift für Prof. D. Dr. Dr. Josef Bohatec; ed. Wilhelm Kühnert] (1951): 165–70.

McArthur, Harvey K. Review of Hans-Theo Wrege, *Die Überlieferungsgeschichte der Bergpredigt. Journal of Biblical Literature* 88 (1969): 91–92.

McGrath, James F. "Written Islands in an Oral Stream: Gospel and Oral Traditions." Pages 3–12 in *Jesus and Paul: Global Perspectives in Honor of James D. G. Dunn for His 70th Birthday.* Edited by B. J. Oropeza, C. K. Robertson and Douglas C. Mohrmann. Library of New Testament Studies 414. London and New York: T&T Clark International, 2009.

McIver, Robert K., and Marie Carroll. "Experiments to Develop Criteria for Determining the Existence of Written Sources, and Their Potential Implications for the Synoptic Problem." *Journal of Biblical Literature* 121 (2002): 667–87.

McKnight, Edgar V. *What is Form Criticism?* Guides to Biblical Scholarship: New Testament Series. Philadelphia: Fortress, 1969.

McNamara, Martin. *The New Testament and the Palestinian Targum to the Pentateuch.* Second printing, with supplement containing additions and corrections. Analecta Biblica 27A. Rome: Pontifical Biblical Institute, 1978.

Mees, Michael. "Das Herrenwort aus dem Ersten Clemensbrief, Kap. 46,8, und seine Bedeutung für die Überlieferung der Jesusworte." *Augustinianum* 12 (1972): 233–56.

–. "Die Bedeutung der Sentenzen und ihrer auxesis für die Formung der Jesusworte nach *Didaché* 1,3b–2,1." *Vetera Christianorum* 8 (1971): 55–76.

–. "Schema und Dispositio in ihrer Bedeutung für die Formung der Herrenworte aus dem *1.Clemensbrief*, Kap. 13,2." *Vetera Christianorum* 8 (1971): 257–72.

Meier, John P. *A Marginal Jew: Rethinking the Historical Jesus,* Vol. 1: *The Roots of the Problem and the Person.* Anchor Bible Reference Library. New York: Doubleday, 1991.

–. "Matthew and Ignatius: A Reponse to William R. Schoedel." Pages 178–86 in *Social History of the Matthean Community: Cross-Disciplinary Approaches.* Edited by David L. Balch. Minneapolis: Fortress, 1991.

Metzger, Bruce M. *The Canon of the New Testament: Its Origin, Development, and Significance.* Oxford: Clarendon/New York: Oxford University Press, 1987.

–. "The Fourth Book of Ezra (Late First Century A.D.): With the Four Additional Chapters." Pages 517–59 in vol. 1 of *The Old Testament Pseudepigrapha.* Edited by James H. Charlesworth. 2 vols. New York: Doubleday, 1983, 1985.

–. "Patristic Evidence and the Textual Criticism of the New Testament." *New Testament Studies* 18 (1971–72): 379–400.

–. *A Textual Commentary on the Greek New Testament.* 2nd ed. Stuttgart: Deutsche Bibelgesellschaft/New York: American Bible Society, 1994.

Meyer, Ben F. "Some Consequences of Birger Gerhardsson's Account of the Origins of the Gospel Tradition." Pages 424–40 in *Jesus and the Oral Gospel Tradition.* Edited by H. Wansbrough. Journal for the Study of the New Testament Supplement Series 64. Sheffield: JSOT Press, 1991.

Meyer, Marvin. "The Gospel of Thomas with the Greek Gospel of Thomas." Pages 133–56 in *The Nag Hammadi Scriptures: The International Edition.* Edited by Marvin Meyer. New York: Harper One, 2007.

Michaels, J. Ramsey. *1 Peter.* Word Biblical Commentary 49. Waco, Tex.: Word, 1988.

–. "The Kingdom of God and the Historical Jesus." Pages 109–18 in *The Kingdom of God in 20th-Century Interpretation.* Edited by Wendell Willis. Peabody, Mass.: Hendrickson, 1987.

Michel, Otto. "κύων, κυνάριον." Pages 1101–14 in vol. 3 of *Theological Dictionary of the New Testament.* Edited by Gerhard Kittel and Gerhard Friedrich. Translated by Geoffrey W. Bromiley. 10 vols. Grand Rapids: Eerdmans, 1964–76.

Migne, J.-P., ed. *Patrologia graeca.* 162 vols. Paris, 1857–86.

Milavec, Aaron. *The Didache: Faith, Hope, and Life of the Earliest Christian Communities, 50–70 C.E.* New York and Mahwah: Newman/Paulist, 2003.
–. "A Rejoinder [to "The *Didache* and the Synoptics Once More: A Response to Aaron Milavec," by C. M. Tuckett]." *Journal of Early Christian Studies* 13 (2005): 519–23.
–. "Synoptic Tradition in the *Didache* Revisited." *Journal of Early Christian Studies* 11 (2003): 443–80.
–. "When, Why, and for Whom Was the Didache Created? Insights into the Social and Historical Setting of the Didache Communities." Pages 63–84 in *Matthew and the Didache: Two Documents from the Same Jewish-Christian Milieu?* Edited by Huub van de Sandt. Assen: Van Gorcum/Philadelphia: Fortress, 2005. Revised and expanded version of "A New Paradigm for Recovering the Origins and Use of the *Didache.*" Pages 45–67 in *SBL Seminar Papers, 2003.* SBL Seminar Papers 42. Atlanta: Society of Biblical Literature, 2003.
Millard, Alan. *Reading and Writing in the Time of Jesus.* Biblical Seminar 69. Sheffield: Sheffield Academic, 2000.
Mills, Margaret A. "Domains of Folkloristic Concern: The Interpretation of Scriptures." Pages 231–41 in *Text and Tradition: The Hebrew Bible and Folklore.* Edited by Susan Niditch. SBL Semeia Studies. Atlanta: Scholars, 1990.
Minchin, Elizabeth. "Describing and Narrating in Homer's *Iliad.*" Pages 49–64 in *Signs of Orality: The Oral Tradition and its Influence in the Greek and Roman Worlds.* Edited by E. Anne Mackay. Supplements to Mnemosyne 188. Leiden: Brill, 1999.
–. "The Performance of Lists and Catalogues in the Homeric Epics." Pages 3–20 in *Voice into Text: Orality and Literacy in Ancient Greece.* Edited by Ian Worthington. Supplements to Mnemosyne 157. Leiden: Brill, 1996.
–. "Rhythm and Regularity in Homeric Composition: Questions in the *Odyssey.*" Pages 21–48 in *Oral Performance and Its Context.* Edited by C. J. Mackie. Supplements to Mnemosyne 248. Orality and Literacy in Ancient Greece 5. Leiden: Brill, 2004.
–. "Similes in Homer: Image, Mind's Eye, and Memory." Pages 25–52 in *Speaking Volumes: Orality and Literacy in the Greek and Roman World.* Edited by Janet Watson. Supplements to Mnemosyne 218. Leiden: Brill, 2001.
Morrice, William. *Hidden Sayings of Jesus: Words Attributed to Jesus Outside the Four Gospels.* London: SPCK/Peabody, Mass.: Hendrickson, 1997.
Morris, Leon. *The Gospel According to Matthew.* Pillar New Testament Commentary. Leicester: InterVarsity/Grand Rapids: Eerdmans, 1992.
Moule, C. F. D. Review of H. Köster, *Synoptische Überlieferung bei den apostolischen Vätern, Journal of Theological Studies* n.s. 9 (1958): 368–70.
Moulton, J. H. *A Grammar of New Testament Greek,* Vol. 4: *Style,* by Nigel Turner. Edinburgh: T&T Clark, 1976.
Moulton, J. H., and Wilbert Francis Howard. *A Grammar of New Testament Greek,* Vol. 2: *Accidence and Word-Formation with an Appendix on Semitisms in the New Testament.* Edinburgh: T&T Clark, 1928.
Mournet, Terence C. "The Jesus Tradition as Oral Tradition." Pages 39–61 in *Jesus in Memory: Traditions in Oral and Scribal Practices.* Edited by Werner H. Kelber and Samuel Byrskog. Waco, Tex.: Baylor University Press, 2009.
–. *Oral Tradition and Literary Dependency: Variability and Stability in the Synoptic Tradition and Q.* Wissenschaftliche Untersuchungen zum Neuen Testament 2.195. Tübingen: Mohr Siebeck, 2005.
Nardoni, Enrique. "Interaction of Orality and Textuality: Response to Arthur J. Bellinzoni." *Second Century* 9 (1992): 265–70.

Neil, William. *The Acts of the Apostles*. New Century Bible. Grand Rapids: Eerd-
mans/London: Marshall, Morgan & Scott, 1981.

–. "The Criticism and Theological Use of the Bible 1700–1950." Pages 238–93 in *The
Cambridge History of the Bible*, Vol. 3: *The West from the Reformation to the Present Day*. Edited by S. L. Greenslade. Cambridge: Cambridge University Press, 1963.

Neill, Stephen, and Tom Wright. *The Interpretation of the New Testament: 1861–1986*.
2nd ed. Oxford: Oxford University Press, 1988.

Neirynck, Frans. "Preface to the Reprint." Pages xi–xix in vol. 1 and xiii–xxi in vols. 2
and 3 of *The Influence of the Gospel of Saint Matthew on Christian Literature before
Saint Irenaeus*, by Édouard Massaux. Translated by Norman J. Belval and Suzanne
Hecht. Edited and with an introduction and addenda by Arthur J. Bellinzoni. New
Gospel Studies 5. 3 vols. Leuven: Peeters/Macon: Mercer University Press, 1990–93.

–. *Q-Parallels: Q-Synopsis and IQP/CritEd Parallels*. Studiorum Novi Testamenti
Auxilia 20. Leuven: Leuven University Press and Peeters, 2001.

–. "The Reconstruction of Q and IQP/CritEd Parallels." Pages 53–147 in *The Sayings
Source Q and the Historical Jesus*. Edited by A. Lindemann. Bibliotheca
Ephemeridum Theologicarum Lovaniensium 118. Leuven: Leuven University Press
and Peeters, 2001.

Nickelsburg, George W. E. *1 Enoch 1: A Commentary on the Book of 1 Enoch, Chapters
1–36; 81–108*. Edited by Klaus Baltzer. Hermeneia. Minneapolis: Fortress, 2001.

Niederwimmer, Kurt. *The Didache: A Commentary*. Hermeneia. Edited by Harold W.
Attridge. Translated by Linda M. Maloney. Minneapolis: Fortress, 1998.

–. "Der Didachist und seine Quellen." Pages 15–36 in *The Didache in Context: Essays on
Its Text, History and Transmission*. Edited by Clayton N. Jefford. Supplements to
Novum Testamentum 77. Leiden: Brill, 1995.

Nielsen, Charles M. "Polycarp and Marcion: A Note." *Theological Studies* 47 (1986):
297–9.

Nimis, Stephen A. "Cycles and Sequence in Longus' *Daphnis and Chloe*." Pages 185–98
in *Speaking Volumes: Orality and Literacy in the Greek and Roman World*. Edited by
Janet Watson. Supplements to Mnemosyne 218. Leiden: Brill, 2001.

Nogueira, Carlos. "Oral Tradition: A Definition." *Oral Tradition* 18.2 (2003): 164–65.

Nolland, John. *The Gospel of Matthew: A Commentary on the Greek Text*. New International Greek Testament Commentary. Grand Rapids: Eerdmans/Milton Keynes: Paternoster, 2005.

–. *Luke 1–9:20*. Word Biblical Commentary 35A. Dallas, Tex.: Word, 1989.

–. *Luke 18:35–24:53*. Word Biblical Commentary 35C. Dallas, Tex.: Word, 1993.

Oesterreicher, Wulf. "Types of Orality in Text." Pages 190–214 in *Written Voices, Spoken Signs: Tradition, Performance, and the Epic Text*. Edited by Egbert J. Bakker
and Ahuvia Kahane. Center for Hellenistic Studies Colloquia. Cambridge, Mass.:
Harvard University Press, 1997.

Okpewho, Isidore. *African Oral Literature: Backgrounds, Character and Continuity*.
Bloomington and Indianapolis: Indiana University Press, 1992.

O'Loughlin, Thomas. "The *Didache* as a Source for Picturing the Earliest Christian
Communities: The Case of the Practice of Fasting." Pages 83–112 in *Christian Origins: Worship, Belief and Society*. Edited by Kieran J. O'Mahony. Journal for the
Study of the New Testament Supplement Series 241. London and New York: Sheffield Academic, 2003.

Olbricht, T. H. "Apostolic Fathers." Pages 81–85 in *Dictionary of New Testament Background*. Edited by Craig A. Evans and Stanley E. Porter. Downers Grove: Inter-
Varsity, 2000.

Olick, Jeffrey K. "Collective Memory: The Two Cultures." *Sociological Theory* 17 (1999): 333–48.
–. "Products, Processes, and Practices: A Non-Reificatory Approach to Collective Memory." *Biblical Theology Bulletin* 36 (2006): 5–14.
Olick, Jeffrey K., and Joyce Robbins. "Social Memory Studies: From 'Collective Memory' to the Historical Sociology of Mnemonic Practices." *Annual Review of Sociology* 24 (1998): 105–40.
Ong, Walter J. *Interfaces of the Word: Studies in the Evolution of Consciousness and Culture*. Ithaca and London: Cornell University Press, 1977.
–. *Orality and Literacy: The Technologizing of the Word*. New Accents. London and New York: Methuen, 1982.
–. "Orality-Literacy Studies and the Unity of the Human Race." *Oral Tradition* 2.1 [Festschrift Walter J. Ong] (1987): 271–82.
–. *The Presence of the Word: Some Prolegomena for Cultural and Religious History*. The Terry Lectures. New Haven and London: Yale University Press, 1967.
–. "The Psychodynamics of Oral Memory and Narrative: Some Implications for Biblical Studies." Pages 55–73 in *The Pedagogy of God's Image: Essays on Symbol and the Religious Imagination*. Edited by Robert Masson. College Theological Society Annual Publications 1981. Chico, Calif.: Scholars, 1982.
–. "Text as Interpretation: Mark and After." Pages 7–26 in *Orality, Aurality and Biblical Narrative*. Edited by Lou H. Silberman. *Semeia* 39. Decatur: Society of Biblical Literature/Scholars, 1987.
Orbe, Antonio. "Cristo y la iglesia en su matrimonio anterior a los siglos." *Estudios Eclesiásticos* 29, no. 114 (1955): 299–344.
Osiek, Carolyn. "The Oral World of Early Christianity in Rome: The Case of Hermas." Pages 151–72 in *Judaism and Christianity in First-Century Rome*. Edited by K. P. Donfried and P. Richardson. Grand Rapids: Eerdmans, 1998.
O'Toole, Robert. "The Kingdom of God in Luke-Acts." Pages 147–62 in *The Kingdom of God in 20th-Century Interpretation*. Edited by Wendell Willis. Peabody, Mass.: Hendrickson, 1987.
Paivio, Allan. "The Mind's Eye in Arts and Science." *Poetics* 12 (1983): 1–18.
Park, Yoon-Man. *Mark's Memory Resources and the Controversy Stories (Mark 2:1–3:6): An Application of the Frame Theory of Cognitive Science to the Markan Oral-Aural Narrative*. Linguistic Biblical Studies 2. Leiden: Brill, 2010.
Parker, David C. *The Living Text of the Gospels*. Cambridge and New York: Cambridge University Press, 1997.
Parks, Ward. "Orality and Poetics: Synchrony, Diachrony, and the Axes of Narrative Transmission." Pages 511–32 in *Comparative Research on Oral Traditions: A Memorial for Milman Parry*. Edited by John Miles Foley. Columbus: Slavica, 1987.
Parry, Adam. Introduction to *The Making of Homeric Verse: The Collected Papers of Milman Parry*. Edited by Adam Parry. Oxford: Clarendon, 1971.
Parry, Milman. *The Making of Homeric Verse: The Collected Papers of Milman Parry*. Edited by Adam Parry. Oxford: Clarendon, 1971.
Patterson, Stephen J. "Can You Trust a Gospel? A Review of Richard Bauckham's *Jesus and the Eyewitnesses*." *Journal for the Study of the Historical Jesus* 6 (2008): 194–210.
Patterson, Stephen J., James M. Robinson, and Hans-Gebhard Bethge. *The Fifth Gospel: The Gospel of Thomas Comes of Age*. Harrisburg: Trinity Press International, 1998.
Paulsen, Henning. *Die Briefe des Ignatius von Antiochia und der Brief des Polykarp von Smyrna*. Zweite, neubearbeitete Auflage der Auslegung von Walter Bauer. Handbuch

zum Neuen Testament 18. Die Apostolischen Väter 2. Tübingen: Mohr Siebeck, 1985.

Peabody, Berkley. *The Winged Word: A Study in the Technique of Ancient Greek Oral Composition as Seen Principally through Hesiod's Works and Days.* Albany: State University of New York Press, 1975.

Pearson, J. *Vindiciae epistolarum S. Ignatii.* Cambridge: Hayes, 1672. Repr. *Ss. Patrum qui temporibus apostolicis floruerunt opera.* 2nd ed. Antwerp: Huguetaronum, 1698.

Penfield, J. *Communicating with Quotes: The Igbo Case.* Westport, Conn.: Greenwood, 1983.

Perrin, Nicholas. *Thomas and Tatian: The Relationship between the* Gospel of Thomas *and the* Diatessaron. SBL Academia Biblica 5. Atlanta: Society of Biblical Literature/Leiden: Brill, 2002.

–. *Thomas, the Other Gospel.* London: SPCK/Louisville: Westminster John Knox, 2007.

Perrin, Norman. *A Modern Pilgrimage in New Testament Christology.* Philadelphia: Fortress, 1974.

–. *What is Redaction Criticism?* Guides to Biblical Scholarship: New Testament Series. Philadelphia: Fortress, 1969.

Pervo, Richard I. *Dating Acts: Between the Evangelists and the Apologists.* Santa Rosa, Calif.: Polebridge, 2006.

–. *Acts: A Commentary.* Edited by Harold W. Attridge. Hermeneia. Minneapolis: Fortress, 2009.

Petersen, William L. "The Genesis of the Gospels." Pages 33–65 in *New Testament Textual Criticism and Exegesis: Festschrift J. Delobel.* Edited by A. Denaux. Bibliotheca Ephemeridum Theologicarum Lovaniensium 161. Leuven: Leuven University Press and Peeters, 2002.

–. "Textual Traditions Examined: What the Text of the Apostolic Fathers Tells us about the Text of the New Testament in the Second Century." Pages 29–46 in *The Reception of the New Testament in the Apostolic Fathers.* Edited by Andrew Gregory and Christopher Tuckett. The New Testament and the Apostolic Fathers 1. Oxford: Oxford University Press, 2005.

Peterson, David G. *The Acts of the Apostles.* Pillar New Testament Commentary. Grand Rapids: Eerdmans/Nottingham: Apollos, 2009.

Piper, John. *'Love Your Enemies': Jesus' Love Command.* Society for New Testament Studies Monograph Series 38. Cambridge: Cambridge University Press, 1979.

Plummer, Alfred. *A Critical and Exegetical Commentary on the Gospel According to S. Luke.* 5th ed. International Critical Commentary. Edinburgh: T&T Clark, 1906.

–. *An Exegetical Commentary on the Gospel According to S. Matthew.* London: Elliot Stock, 1909.

Pratscher, Wilhelm. "The Second Epistle of Clement." Pages 71–90 in *The Apostolic Fathers: An Introduction.* Edited by Wilhelm Pratscher. Waco, Tex.: Baylor University Press, 2010.

–. *Der zweite Clemensbrief.* Kommentar zu den Apostolischen Vätern 3. Göttingen: Vandenhoeck & Ruprecht, 2007.

Prigent, Pierre. *Les testimonia dans le christianisme primitif: L'Épître de Barnabé I–XVI et ses sources.* Études bibliques. Paris: Gabalda, 1961.

Prigent, Pierre and Robert A. Kraft. *Épître de Barnabé.* Sources Chrétiennes 172. Paris: Cerf, 1971.

Prostmeier, Ferdinand R. *Der Barnabasbrief.* Kommentar zu den Apostolischen Vätern 8. Göttingen: Vandenhoeck & Ruprecht, 1999.

Quasten, J. *Patrology.* 4 vols. Ed. Angelo di Berardino. Westminster: Christian Classics, 1983–86.

Reimarus, Hermann Samuel. "Concerning the Intention of Jesus and His Teaching." Pages 59–269 in *Reimarus: Fragments.* Edited by Charles H. Talbert. Translated by Ralph S. Fraser. Lives of Jesus Series. Philadelphia: Fortress, 1970.

Renoir, Alain. "Oral-Formulaic Rhetoric and the Interpretation of Written Texts." Pages 103–35 in *Oral Tradition in Literature: Interpretation in Context.* Edited by John Miles Foley. Columbia: University of Missouri Press, 1986.

Resch, Alfred. *Agrapha: Aussercanonische Evangelienfragmente.* Texte und Untersuchungen zur Geschichte der altchristlichen Literatur 5.4. Leipzig: J. C. Hinrichs, 1889.

–. *Die Logia Jesu nach dem griechischen und hebräischen Text wiederhergestellt: Ein Versuch.* Leipzig: J. C. Hinrichs, 1898.

Rhoads, David. "Biblical Performance Criticism: Performance as Research." *Oral Tradition* 25 (2010): 157–98.

Richardson, Cyril C. "An Anonymous Sermon, Commonly Called Clement's Second Letter." Pages 183–202 in *Early Christian Fathers.* Edited by Cyril C. Richardson. Library of Christian Classics 1. Philadelphia: Westminster, 1953.

–. "The Letter of the Church of Rome to the Church of Corinth, Commonly Called Clement's First Letter." Pages 33–73 in *Early Christian Fathers.* Edited by Cyril C. Richardson. Library of Christian Classics 1. Philadelphia: Westminster, 1953.

Richardson, Peter, and Peter Gooch. "Logia of Jesus in 1 Corinthians." Pages 39–62 in *Gospel Perspectives, Vol. 5: The Jesus Tradition Outside the Gospels.* Edited by David Wenham. Sheffield: JSOT Press, 1985.

Richardson, Peter, and John C. Hurd, eds. *From Jesus to Paul: Studies in Honour of Francis Wright Beare.* Waterloo: Wilfrid Laurier University Press, 1984.

Riesenfeld, Harald. *The Gospel Tradition: Essays.* Translated by E. Margaret Rowley and Robert A. Kraft. Foreword by W. D. Davies. Oxford: Blackwell/Philadelphia: Fortress, 1970.

Riesner, Rainer. "From the Messianic Teacher to the Gospels of Jesus Christ." Pages 405–46 in vol. 1 of *Handbook for the Study of the Historical Jesus.* Edited by Tom Holmén and Stanley E. Porter. Leiden: Brill, 2011.

–. *Jesus als Lehrer: Eine Untersuchung zum Ursprung der Evangelien-Überlieferung.* 3rd expanded ed. Wissenschaftliche Untersuchungen zum Neuen Testament 2.7. Tübingen: Mohr Siebeck, 1988.

–. "Jesus as Preacher and Teacher." Pages 185–210 in *Jesus and the Oral Gospel Tradition.* Edited by H. Wansbrough. Journal for the Study of the New Testament Supplement Series 64. Sheffield: JSOT Press, 1991.

–. "Paulus und die Jesus-Überlieferung." Pages 347–65 in *Evangelium, Schriftauslegung, Kirche: Festschrift für Peter Stuhlmacher zum 65. Geburtstag.* Edited by Jostein Ådna, Scott J. Hafemann and Otfried Hofius. Göttingen: Vandenhoeck & Ruprecht, 1997.

Rius-Camps, Josep. *The Four Authentic Letters of Ignatius.* Rome: Pontificium Institutum Orientalium Studiorum, 1980.

Robbins, Vernon K. "Form Criticism: New Testament." Pages 841–44 in vol. 2 of *The Anchor Bible Dictionary.* Edited by David Noel Freedman. 6 vols. New York: Doubleday, 1992.

–. "Interfaces of Orality and Literature in the Gospel of Mark." Pages 125–46 in *Performing the Gospel: Orality, Memory, and Mark: Essays Dedicated to Werner Kel-*

ber. Edited by Richard A. Horsley, Jonathan A. Draper and John Miles Foley. Minneapolis: Fortress, 2006.

–. "Last Meal: Preparation, Betrayal, and Absence." Pages 21–40 in *The Passion in Mark: Studies on Mark 14–16.* Edited by Werner H. Kelber. Philadelphia: Fortress, 1976.

–. "Oral, Rhetorical, and Literary Cultures: A Response." Pages 75–91 in *Orality and Textuality in Early Christian Literature.* Edited by Joanna Dewey. *Semeia* 65. Atlanta: Society of Biblical Literature/Scholars, 1994.

–. "Progymnastic Rhetorical Composition and Pre-Gospel Traditions: A New Approach." Pages 111–47 in *The Synoptic Gospels: Source Criticism and the New Literary Criticism.* Edited by Camille Focant. Bibliotheca Ephemeridum Theologicarum Lovaniensium 110. Leuven: Leuven University Press and Peeters, 1993.

–. "Writing as a Rhetorical Act in Plutarch and the Gospels." Pages 142–68 in *Persuasive Artistry: Studies in New Testament Rhetoric in Honor of George A. Kennedy.* Edited by Duane F. Watson. Journal for the Study of the New Testament Supplement Series 50. Sheffield: JSOT Press, 1991.

Robinson, J. Armitage. *Barnabas, Hermas and the Didache.* Being the Donnellan Lectures delivered before the University of Dublin in 1920. London: SPCK/New York: Macmillan, 1920.

–. "The Epistle of Barnabas and the Didache." *Journal of Theological Studies* 35 (1934): 113–46, 225–48.

–. "The Problem of the Didache." *Journal of Theological Studies* 13 (1912): 339–56.

Robinson, James M. "Early Collections of Jesus' Sayings." Pages 169–75 in *The Sayings Gospel Q: Collected Essays.* Edited by Christopher Heil and Joseph Verheyden. Bibliotheca Ephemeridum Theologicarum Lovaniensium 189. Leuven: Leuven University Press and Peeters, 2005. Repr. from pages 389–94 in *Logia: Les Paroles de Jésus – The Sayings of Jesus: Mémorial Joseph Coppens.* Edited by Joël Delobel. Bibliotheca Ephemeridum Theologicarum Lovaniensium 59. Leuven: Leuven University Press and Peeters, 1982.

–. "ΛΟΓΟΙ ΣΟΦΩΝ: On the *Gattung* of Q." Pages 37–74 in *The Sayings Gospel Q: Collected Essays.* Edited by Christopher Heil and Joseph Verheyden. Bibliotheca Ephemeridum Theologicarum Lovaniensium 189. Leuven: Leuven University Press and Peeters, 2005. Repr. from pages 71–113 in *Trajectories through Early Christianity,* by James M. Robinson and Helmut Koester. Philadelphia: Fortress, 1971.

Robinson, J. M., P. Hoffmann, and J. S. Kloppenborg, eds. *The Critical Edition of Q: Synopsis including the Gospels of Matthew and Luke, Mark and Thomas with English, German, and French Translations of Q and Thomas.* Managing Editor: Milton C. Moreland. Hermeneia: Supplements. Leuven: Peeters/Minneapolis: Fortress, 2000.

Robinson, John A. T. *Redating the New Testament.* London: SCM/Philadelphia: Westminster, 1976.

Robinson, William C., Jr. "On Preaching the Word of God (Luke 8:4–21)." Pages 131–38 in *Studies in Luke-Acts: Essays Presented in Honor of Paul Schubert.* Edited by Leander E. Keck and J. Louis Martyn. Nashville: Abingdon, 1966.

Rodriguez, Rafael. *Structuring Early Christian Memory: Jesus in Tradition, Performance and Text.* Library of New Testament Studies 407. New York and London: T&T Clark, 2010.

Ropes, J. H. *Die Sprüche Jesu.* Texte und Untersuchungen 14. Leipzig: Hinrichs, 1896.

Rordorf, Willy. "An Aspect of the Judeo-Christian Ethic: The Two Ways." Pages 148–64 in *The Didache in Modern Research.* Edited by Jonathan A. Draper. Arbeiten zur Geschichte des antiken Judentums und des Urchristentums 37. Leiden: Brill, 1996.

–. "Baptism according to the *Didache*." Pages 212–22 in *The Didache in Modern Research*. Edited by Jonathan A. Draper. Arbeiten zur Geschichte des antiken Judentums und des Urchristentums 37. Leiden: Brill, 1996.

–. "The *Didache*." Pages 1–23 in *The Eucharist of the Early Christians*, by Willy Rordorf, et al. Translated by M. J. O'Connell. New York: Pueblo, 1978.

–. "Didache." Pages 54–55 in vol. 4 of *Religion Past and Present: Encyclopedia of Theology and Religion*. Edited by Hans Dieter Betz, Don S. Browning, Bernd Janowski and Eberhard Jüngel. Leiden: Brill, 2008.

–. "Does the Didache Contain Jesus Tradition Independently of the Synoptic Gospels?" Pages 394–423 in *Jesus and the Oral Gospel Tradition*. Edited by H. Wansbrough. Journal for the Study of the New Testament Supplement Series 64. Sheffield: JSOT Press, 1991.

–. "Le problème de la transmission textuelle de *Didachè* 1, 3b.–2, 1." Pages 499–513 in *Überlieferungsgeschichtliche Untersuchungen*. Edited by Franz Paschke. Texte und Untersuchungen 125. Berlin: Akademie-Velag, 1981. Repr. pages 139–53 in *Liturgie, foi et vie des premiers Chrétiens: Études Patristiques*. Théologie Historique 75. Paris: Beauchesne, 1986.

Rordorf, Willy and André Tuilier. *La Doctrine des Douze Apôtres (Didaché)*. 2nd rev. and expanded ed. Sources Chrétiennes 248 bis. Paris: Cerf, 1998.

Rosenberg, Bruce A. "The Complexity of Oral Tradition." *Oral Tradition* 2.1 [Festschrift for Walter J. Ong] (1987): 73–90.

Roukema, Riemer. "Jesus Tradition in Early Patristic Writings." Pages 2119–47 in vol. 3 of *Handbook for the Study of the Historical Jesus*. Edited by Tom Holmén and Stanley E. Porter. Leiden: Brill, 2011.

Rubin, David C. *Memory in Oral Traditions: The Cognitive Psychology of Epic, Ballads, and Counting-out Rhymes*. Oxford: Oxford University Press, 1995.

Rüger, H. P. "Mit welchen Mass ihr messt, wird euch gemessen werden." *Zeitschrift für die neutestamentliche Wissenschaft* 60 (1969): 174–82.

Ruiz Bueno, Daniel. *Padres Apostólicos: Edición bilingüe completa*. 2nd ed. Biblioteca de Autores Cristianos. Madrid: Editorial Católica, 1967.

Russo, Joseph. "The Formula." Pages 238–60 in *A New Companion to Homer*. Edited by Ian Morris and Barry Powell. Supplements to Mnemosyne 163. Leiden: Brill, 1997.

Sabbe, M. "The Arrest of Jesus in Jn 18,1–11 and its Relation to the Synoptic Gospels: A Critical Evaluation of A. Dauer's Hypothesis." Pages 203–34 in *L'Évangile de Jean: Sources, rédaction, théologie*. Edited by M. de Jonge. Bibliotheca Ephemeridum Theologicarum Lovaniensium 44. Leuven: Leuven University Press/Gembloux: Duculot, 1977.

Sabugal, Santos. *Abbá ...: La oración del Señor*. 2nd ed. Biblioteca para la Nueva Evangelización. Madrid: Caparrós Editores, 2007.

–. *El Padrenuestro en la interpretación catequética antigua y moderna*. Nueva Alianza 79. Salamanca: Ediciones Sígueme, 1986.

Sale, Mary. "The Oral-Formulaic Theory Today." Pages 53–80 in *Speaking Volumes: Orality and Literacy in the Greek and Roman World*. Edited by Janet Watson. Supplements to Mnemosyne 218. Leiden: Brill, 2001.

Sale, Merritt. "Virgil's Formularity and *Pius Aeneas*." Pages 199–220 in *Signs of Orality: The Oral Tradition and its Influence in the Greek and Roman Worlds*. Edited by E. Anne Mackay. Supplements to Mnemosyne 188. Leiden: Brill, 1999.

Sanday, W. *The Gospels in the Second Century: An Examination of the Critical Part of a Work Entitled 'Supernatural Religion.'* London: Macmillan, 1876.

Sanders, E. P. *The Tendencies of the Synoptic Tradition.* Society for New Testament Studies Monograph Series 9. Cambridge: Cambridge University Press, 1969.

Sanders, E. P. and Margaret Davies. *Studying the Synoptic Gospels.* London: SCM/Philadelphia: Trinity Press International, 1989.

Sandt, Huub van de. "Les charismatiques itinérants dans la Didachè et dans l'Évangile de Matthieu (with an English abstract)." Pages 157–72 in *Matthew and the Didache: Two Documents from the Same Jewish-Christian Milieu?* Edited by Huub van de Sandt. Assen: Van Gorcum/Philadelphia: Fortress, 2005.

–. "'Do Not Give what Is Holy to the Dogs' (Did 9:5d and Matt 7:6a): The Eucharistic Food of the Didache in its Jewish Purity Setting." *Vigiliae Christianae* 56 (2002): 223–46.

–. "The Egyptian Background of the 'Ointment' Prayer in the Eucharistic Rite of the *Didache* (10.8)." Pages 227–45 in *The Wisdom of Egypt: Jewish, Christian, and Gnostic Essays in Honour of Gerard P. Luttikhuizen.* Edited by Anthony Hilhorst and George H. Van Kooten. Ancient Judaism and Early Christianity (AGJU) 59. Leiden: Brill, 2005.

–. "The Gathering of the Church in the Kingdom: The Self-Understanding of the *Didache* Community in the Eucharistic Prayers." Pages 69–88 in *SBL Seminar Papers, 2003.* Society of Biblical Literature Seminar Papers 42. Atlanta: Society of Biblical Literature, 2003.

–. "Matthew and the *Didache*." Pages 123–38 in *Matthew and His Christian Contemporaries.* Edited by David C. Sim and Boris Repschinski. Library of New Testament Studies (JSNTSup) 333. London and New York: T&T Clark, 2008.

–. "Two Windows on a Developing Jewish-Christian Reproof Practice: Matt 18:15–17 and *Did.* 15:3." Pages 173–92 in *Matthew and the Didache: Two Documents from the Same Jewish-Christian Milieu?* Edited by Huub van de Sandt. Assen: Van Gorcum/Philadelphia: Fortress, 2005.

–, ed. *Matthew and the Didache: Two Documents from the Same Jewish-Christian Milieu?* Assen: Van Gorcum/Philadelphia: Fortress, 2005.

Sandt, Huub van de, and David Flusser. *The Didache: Its Jewish Sources and its Place in Early Judaism and Christianity.* Compendia Rerum Iudaicarum ad Novum Testamentum 3.5. Assen: Van Gorcum/Minneapolis: Fortress, 2002.

Sandt, Huub van de, and Jürgen K. Zangenberg, eds. *Matthew, James, and Didache: Three Related Documents in Their Jewish and Christian Settings.* SBL Symposium Series 45. Atlanta: Society of Biblical Literature, 2008.

Schelkle, Karl Hermann. *Die Petrusbriefe, der Judasbrief.* Herders theologischer Kommentar zum Neuen Testament 13.2. Freiburg: Herder, 1970.

Schleiermacher, Friedrich. *Luke: A Critical Study.* Translated and with an Introduction by Connop Thrilwall. With Further Essays, Emendations and Other Apparatus by Terrence N. Tice. Schleiermacher: Studies and Translations 13. Lewiston: Edwin Mellen, 1993.

Schmidt, Karl Ludwig. *Der Rahmen der Geschichte Jesu.* Berlin: Trowitzsch, 1919.

Schnackenburg, Rudolf. *The Gospel According to St. John.* Translated by Kevin Smyth, Cecily Hastings, Francis McDonagh, David Smith, Richard Foley, and G. A. Kon. Herder's Theological Commentary on the New Testament. 3 vols. New York: Herder and Herder, 1968, 1990.

Schneemelcher, Wilhelm. "The Gospel of the Egyptians." Pages 209–15 in *New Testament Apocrypha,* Vol. 1: *Gospels and Related Writings.* Edited by Wilhelm Schneemelcher. English ed. edited by R. McL. Wilson. Rev. ed. Cambridge: James Clarke/Louisville: Westminster/John Knox, 1991.

Schneidau, Herbert N. "'Let the Reader Understand.'" Pages 135–45 in *Orality, Aurality and Biblical Narrative*. Edited by Lou H. Silberman. *Semeia* 39. Decatur: Society of Biblical Literature/Scholars, 1987.

Schneider, Gerhard. *Clemens von Rom: Brief an die Korinther: Übersetzt und eingeleitet*. Fontes Christiani 15. Freiburg: Herder, 1994.

–. *Das Evangelium nach Lukas*. 2nd ed. 2 vols. Ökumenischer Taschenbuch-Kommentar zum Neuen Testament 3.1–2. Gütersloh and Würzburg: Mohn, 1984.

Schoedel, William R. "Ignatius and the Reception of the Gospel of Matthew in Antioch." Pages 129–77 in *Social History of the Matthean Community: Cross-Disciplinary Approaches*. Edited by David L. Balch. Minneapolis: Fortress, 1991.

–. *Ignatius of Antioch: A Commentary on the Letters of Ignatius of Antioch*. Edited by Helmut Koester. Hermeneia. Philadelphia: Fortress, 1985.

–. "Papias." Pages 140–42 in vol. 5 of *The Anchor Bible Dictionary*. Edited by David Noel Freedman. 6 vols. New York: Doubleday, 1992.

–. "Papias." Pages 235–70 in vol. 27.1 of *Aufstieg und Niedergang der römischen Welt, II: Principat*. Edited by H. Temporini and Wolfgang Haase. Berlin and New York: de Gruyter, 1993.

–. *Polycarp, Martyrdom of Polycarp, Fragments of Papias*. The Apostolic Fathers 5. Camden: Thomas Nelson & Sons, 1967.

–. "Polycarp of Smyrna and Ignatius of Antioch." Pages 272–358 in vol. 27.1 of *Aufstieg und Niedergang der römischen Welt, II: Principat*. Edited by Wolfgang Haase. Berlin and New York: de Gruyter, 1993.

–. "Polycarp's Witness to Ignatius of Antioch." *Vigiliae Christianae* 41 (1987): 1–10.

–. Review of É. Massaux, *The Influence of the Gospel of Saint Matthew on Christian Literature before Saint Irenaeus* and W.-D. Köhler, *Die Rezeption des Matthäusevangeliums in der Zeit vor Irenäus*, *Catholic Biblical Quarterly* 51 (1989): 562–64.

–. "Theological Norms and Social Perspectives in Ignatius of Antioch." Pages 30–56 in *Jewish and Christian Self-Definition*, Vol. 1: *The Shaping of Christianity in the Second and Third Centuries*. Edited by E. P. Sanders. Philadelphia: Fortress, 1980.

Schölgen, Georg. "The *Didache* as a Church Order: An Examination of the Purpose for the Composition of the *Didache* and its Consequences for its Interpretation." Pages 43–71 in *The Didache in Modern Research*. Edited by Jonathan A. Draper. Arbeiten zur Geschichte des antiken Judentums und des Urchristentums 37. Leiden: Brill, 1996.

–. "Die Ignatianen als pseudepigraphisches Briefcorpus: Anmerkung zu den Thesen von Reinhard M. Hübner." *Zeitschrift für Antikes Christentum/Journal of Ancient Christianity* 2 (1998): 16–25.

Schröter, Jens. *Erinnerung an Jesu Worte: Studien zur Rezeption der Logienüberlieferung in Markus, Q und Thomas*. Wissenschaftliche Monographien zum Alten und Neuen Testament 76. Neukirchen-Vluyn: Neukirchener, 1997.

–. "Jesus and the Canon: The Early Jesus Traditions in the Context of the Origins of the New Testament Canon." Pages 104–22 in *Performing the Gospel: Orality, Memory, and Mark: Essays Dedicated to Werner Kelber*. Edited by Richard A. Horsley, Jonathan A. Draper and John Miles Foley. Minneapolis: Fortress, 2006.

Schudson, M. "Dynamics of Distortion in Collective Memory." Pages 346–64 in *Memory Distortion*. Edited by D. Schachter. Cambridge, Mass.: Harvard University Press, 1995.

Schulz, Siegfried. *Q: Die Spruchquelle der Evangelisten*. Zurich: Theologischer Verlag, 1972.

Schürer, Emil. *The History of the Jewish People in the Age of Jesus Christ (175 B.C. –
    A.D. 135)*. Revised and edited by Geza Vermes, Fergus Millar, Matthew Black and
    Martin Goodman. 3 vols. Edinburgh: T&T Clark, 1973–87.
Schürmann, Heinz. *Das Lukasevangelium*, Vol. 1: *Kommentar zu Kap. 1, 1 – 9 , 50*.
    Herders Theologischer Kommentar zum Neuen Testament 3.1. Freiburg: Herder,
    1969.
Schwartz, Barry. "Christian Origins: Historical Truth and Social Memory." Pages 43–56
    in *Memory, Tradition, and Text: Uses of the Past in Early Christianity*. Edited by
    Alan Kirk and Tom Thatcher. SBL Semeia Studies 52. Atlanta: Society of Biblical
    Literature, 2005.
Schweizer, Eduard. *The Good News According to Luke*. Translated by David E. Green.
    Atlanta: John Knox, 1984.
–. *The Good News According to Matthew*. Translated by David E. Green. Atlanta: John
    Knox, 1975.
Sedgwick, W. B. "Reading and Writing in Classical Antiquity." *Contemporary Review*
    135 (1990): 90–94.
Sellew, Philip. "Eusebius and the Gospels." Pages 110–38 in *Eusebius, Christianity, and
    Judaism*. Edited by Harold W. Attridge and Gohei Hata. Detroit: Wayne State Uni-
    versity Press, 1992.
Sellin, Gerhard. "Das lebendige Wort und der tote Buchstabe: Aspekte von Mündlichkeit
    und Schriftlichkeit in christlicher und jüdischer Theologie." Pages 11–31 in *Logos
    und Buchstabe: Mündlichkeit und Schriftlichkeit im Judentum und Christentum der
    Antike*. Edited by Gerhard Sellin and François Vouga. Texte und Arbeiten zum
    neutestamentlichen Zeitalter 20. Tübingen: Francke, 1997.
Senior, Donald P. *The Passion Narrative according to Matthew: A Redactional Study*.
    Bibliotheca Ephemeridum Theologicarum Lovaniensium 39. Leuven: Leuven Uni-
    versity Press and Peeters, 1975.
Shiner, Whitney. "Memory Technology and the Composition of Mark." Pages 147–65 in
    *Performing the Gospel: Orality, Memory, and Mark: Essays Dedicated to Werner
    Kelber*. Edited by Richard A. Horsley, Jonathan A. Draper and John Miles Foley.
    Minneapolis: Fortress, 2006.
–. "Oral Performance in the New Testament World." Pages 49–63 in *The Bible in Ancient
    and Modern Media: Story and Performance [Essays in Honor of Thomas E. Boomer-
    shine]*. Edited by Holly E. Hearon and Philip Ruge-Jones. Biblical Performance
    Criticism 1. Eugene, Ore.: Cascade, 2009.
–. *Proclaiming the Gospel: First Century Performance of Mark*. Harrisburg: Trinity Press
    International, 2003.
Sibinga, J. Smit. "Ignatius and Matthew." *Novum Testamentum* 8 (1966): 263–83.
Sienaert, E. "Marcel Jousse: The Oral Style and the Anthropology of Gesture." *Oral Tra-
    dition* 5 (1990): 91–106.
–. "On the Rhythmographic Representation of an Oral-Style Text." (Unpublished paper.)
Sienaert, E., and J. Conolly. "Marcel Jousse on 'Oral Style,' 'Memory,' and the 'Count-
    ing Necklace.'" Pages 65–84 in *Orality, Memory, and the Past: Listening to the
    Voices of Black Clergy under Colonialism and Apartheid*. Edited by P. Dennis.
    Pietermaritzburg: Cluster, 2000.
Silberman, Lou H. "Introduction: Reflections on Orality, Aurality and Perhaps More."
    Pages 1–6 in *Orality, Aurality and Biblical Narrative*. Edited by Lou H. Silberman.
    Semeia 39. Decatur: Society of Biblical Literature/Scholars, 1987.
–, ed. *Orality, Aurality and Biblical Narrative*. *Semeia* 39. Decatur: Society of Biblical
    Literature/Scholars, 1987.

Sim, David C. "Matthew and Ignatius of Antioch." Pages 139–54 in *Matthew and His Christian Contemporaries*. Edited by David C. Sim and Boris Repschinski. Library of New Testament Studies (JSNTSup) 333. London and New York: T&T Clark, 2008.

Slusser, Michael. "Reading Silently in Antiquity." *Journal of Biblical Literature* 111 (1992): 499.

Small, Jocelyn Penny. *Wax Tablets of the Mind: Cognitive Studies of Memory and Literacy in Classical Antiquity*. London: Routledge, 1997.

Smith, D. Moody. *John among the Gospels*. 2nd ed. Columbia: University of South Carolina Press, 2001.

–. "John and the Synoptics: Historical Tradition and the Passion Narrative." Pages 77–91 in *Light in a Spotless Mirror: Reflections on Wisdom Traditions in Judaism and Early Christianity*. Edited by James H. Charlesworth and Michael A. Daise. Faith and Scholarship Colloquies. Harrisburg: Trinity Press International, 2003.

Smith, Murray J. "The Gospels in Early Christian Literature." Pages 181–208 in *The Content and Setting of the Gospel Tradition*. Edited by Mark Harding and Alanna Nobbs. Grand Rapids: Eerdmans, 2010.

Snodgrass, Klyne R. "A Response to Hans Dieter Betz on the Sermon on the Mount." *Biblical Research* 36 (1991): 88–94.

Snyder, Graydon F. "Ignatius of Antioch." Pages 559–60 in *Encyclopedia of Early Christianity*. Edited by Everett Ferguson. Garland Reference Library of the Humanities. New York and London: Garland, 1998.

Soards, Marion L. "Oral Tradition Before, In, and Outside the Canonical Passion Narratives." Pages 334–50 in *Jesus and the Oral Gospel Tradition*. Edited by H. Wansbrough. Journal for the Study of the New Testament Supplement Series 64. Sheffield: JSOT Press, 1991.

–. "The Question of a PreMarkan Passion Narrative." *Bible Bhashyam* 11 (1985): 144–69.

Sparks, Kenton L. "Form Criticism." Pages 111–4 in *Dictionary of Biblical Criticism and Interpretation*. Edited by Stanley E. Porter. London and New York: Routledge, 2007.

Stanton, Graham N. *A Gospel for a New People: Studies in Matthew*. Edinburgh: T&T Clark, 1992.

–. *Jesus and Gospel*. Cambridge: Cambridge University Press, 2004.

–. "Jesus Traditions." Pages 565–79 in *Dictionary of the Later New Testament and Its Developments: A Compendium of Contemporary Biblical Scholarship*. Edited by Ralph P. Martin and Peter H. Davids. Downers Grove: InterVarsity, 1997.

–. "Matthew: βίβλος, εὐαγγέλιον, or βίος?" Pages 1187–201 in vol. 2 of *The Four Gospels 1992: Festschrift Frans Neirynck*. Edited by F. Van Segbroeck, C. M. Tuckett, G. van Belle and J. Verheyden. Bibliotheca Ephemeridum Theologicarum Lovaniensium 100. 3 vols. Leuven: Leuven University Press and Peeters, 1992.

Stanton, V. H. *The Gospels as Historical Documents*. 3 vols. Cambridge: Cambridge University Press, 1903–20.

Stendahl, Krister. "Prayer and Forgiveness: The Lord's Prayer." *Svensk Exegetisk Årsbok* 22–23 (1957–58): 75–86. Repr. pages 115–25 in *Meanings: The Bible as Document and as Guide*. Philadelphia: Fortress, 1984.

Stone, Michael E. "Apocalyptic Literature." Pages 383–441 in *Jewish Writings of the Second Temple Period: Apocrypha, Pseudepigrapha, Qumran Sectarian Writings, Philo, Josephus*. Edited by Michael E. Stone. Compendia Rerum Iudaicarum ad Novum Testamentum 3.2. Assen: Van Gorcum/Philadelphia: Fortress, 1984.

–. *Fourth Ezra: A Commentary on the Book of Fourth Ezra.* Edited by Frank Moore Cross. Hermeneia. Minneapolis: Fortress, 1990.

Strauss, David Friedrich. "Hermann Samuel Reimarus and His Apology." Pages 44–57 in *Reimarus: Fragments*, by Hermann Samuel Reimarus. Edited by Charles H. Talbert. Translated by Ralph S. Fraser. Lives of Jesus Series. Philadelphia: Fortress, 1970.

–. *The Life of Jesus Critically Examined.* Lives of Jesus Series. Edited by Peter C. Hodgson. Translated by George Eliot. Philadelphia: Fortress, 1974.

Strecker, Georg. *The Sermon on the Mount: An Exegetical Commentary.* Translated by O. C. Jr. Dean. Nashville: Abingdon, 1988.

Streeter, Burnett Hillman. *The Four Gospels: A Study in Origins: Treating of the Manuscript Tradition, Sources, Authoriship and Dates.* 2nd rev. ed. London: Macmillan/New York: St. Martin's, 1930.

–. "Prefatory Note." Pages v–vi in *Polycarp's Two Epistles to the Philippians*, by P. N. Harrison. Cambridge: Cambridge University Press, 1936.

–. *The Primitive Church: Studied with Special Reference to the Origins of the Christian Ministry.* The Hewett Lectures, 1928. New York: Macmillan, 1929.

Stroker, William D. *Extracanonical Sayings of Jesus.* SBL Resources for Biblical Study 18. Atlanta: Scholars, 1989.

Subramanian, J. Samuel. "The Lord's Prayer in the Gospel of Matthew." Pages 107–22 in *Resourcing New Testament Studies: Literary, Historical, and Theological Essays in Honor of David L. Dungan.* Edited by Allan J. McNicol, David B. Peabody and J. Samuel Subramanian. New York and London: T&T Clark, 2009.

Suggs, M. Jack. "The Christian Two Ways Tradition: Its Antiquity, Form, and Function." Pages 60–74 in *Studies in New Testament and Early Christian Literature: Essays in Honor of Allen P. Wikgren.* Edited by David E. Aune. Supplements to Novum Testamentum 33. Leiden: Brill, 1972.

–. "The Use of Patristic Evidence in the Search for a Primitive New Testament Text." *New Testament Studies* 4 (1957–58): 139–47.

Syreeni, Kari. "The Sermon on the Mount and the Two Ways Teaching of the Didache." Pages 87–103 in *Matthew and the Didache: Two Documents from the Same Jewish-Christian Milieu?* Edited by Huub van de Sandt. Assen: Van Gorcum/Philadelphia: Fortress, 2005.

Talbert, Charles H. *Luke and the Gnostics: An Examination of the Lucan Purpose.* Nashville: Abingdon, 1966.

–. "Oral and Independent or Literary and Interdependent? A Response to Albert B. Lord." Pages 93–102 in *The Relationships Among the Gospels: An Interdisciplinary Dialogue.* Edited by William O. Walker, Jr. Trinity University Monograph Series in Religion 5. San Antonio, Tex.: Trinity University Press, 1978.

Talmon, Shemaryahu. "Oral Tradition and Written Transmission, or the Heard and the Seen Word in Judaism of the Second Temple Period." Pages 121–58 in *Jesus and the Oral Gospel Tradition.* Edited by H. Wansbrough. Journal for the Study of the New Testament Supplement Series 64. Sheffield: JSOT Press, 1991.

Tannen, Deborah. "The Oral/Literate Continuum in Discourse." Pages 1–16 in *Spoken and Written Language: Exploring Orality and Literacy.* Edited by Deborah Tannen. Norwood, N.J.: Ablex, 1982.

Tarrant, Harold. "Dialogue and Orality in a Post-Platonic Age." Pages 181–97 in *Signs of Orality: The Oral Tradition and its Influence in the Greek and Roman Worlds.* Edited by E. Anne Mackay. Supplements to Mnemosyne 188. Leiden: Brill, 1999.

Taylor, Vincent. *The Formation of the Gospel Tradition: Eight Lectures.* 2nd ed. London: Macmillan, 1935.

–. *The Gospel according to St. Mark: The Greek Text with Introduction, Notes, and In-
    dexes.* 2nd ed. London: Macmillan/New York: St. Martin's, 1966.
–. "The Order of Q." *Journal of Theological Studies* n.s. 4 (1953): 27–31.
–. "The Original Order of Q." Pages 246–69 in *New Testament Essays: Studies in Mem-
    ory of Thomas Walter Manson 1893–1958.* Edited by A. J. B. Higgins. Manchester:
    Manchester University Press, 1959. Repr. pages 95–118 in idem, *New Testament Es-
    says.* Grand Rapids: Eerdmans, 1972.
Thackeray, H. St. J., Ralph Marcus, Allen Wikgren, and Louis H. Feldman, trans. *Works
    of Josephus.* Loeb Classical Library. 10 vols. Cambridge, Mass.: Harvard University
    Press/London: Heinemann, 1926–65.
Thatcher, Tom. *The Riddles of Jesus in John: A Study in Tradition and Folklore.* SBL
    Monograph Series 53. Atlanta: Society of Biblical Literature, 2000.
–, ed. *Jesus, the Voice, and the Text: Beyond The Oral and the Written Gospel.* Waco,
    Tex.: Baylor University Press, 2008.
Thomas, Christine M. "Word and Deed: The *Acts of Peter* and Orality." *Apocrypha* 3
    (1992): 125–64.
Thomas, Rosalind. *Literacy and Orality in Ancient Greece.* Key Themes in Ancient His-
    tory. Cambridge: Cambridge University Press, 1992.
–. *Oral Tradition and Written Record in Classical Athens.* Cambridge Studies in Oral and
    Literate Culture 18. Cambridge: Cambridge University Press, 1989.
Thompson, Michael. *Clothed with Christ: The Example and Teaching of Jesus in Romans
    12.1–15:13.* Journal for the Study of the New Testament Supplement Series 59. Shef-
    field: JSOT Press, 1991.
Tischendorf, Constantin. *Wann wurden unsere Evangelien verfaßt?* 4th ed. Leipzig: J. C.
    Hinrichs'sche Buchhandlung, 1880. E.T.: *When were Our Gospels Written? An Ar-
    gument.* London: Religious Tract Society, 1896.
Tonkin, Elizabeth. *Narrating our Pasts: The Social Construction of Oral History.* Cam-
    bridge Studies in Oral and Literate Culture 22. Cambridge: Cambridge University
    Press, 1992.
Topel, L. John. "The Lukan Version of the Lord's Sermon." *Biblical Theology Bulletin*
    11 (1981): 48–53.
Travis, Stephen H. "Form Criticism." Pages 153–64 in *New Testament Interpretation:
    Essays on Principles and Methods.* Edited by I. Howard Marshall. Grand Rapids:
    Eerdmans, 1977.
Trevett, Christine. "Approaching Matthew from the Second Century: The Under-Used
    Ignatian Correspondence." *Journal for the Study of the New Testament* 20 (1984):
    59–67.
–. *A Study of Ignatius of Antioch in Syria and Asia.* Studies in the Bible and Early Chris-
    tianity 29. Lewiston: Mellen, 1992.
Trocmé, Etienne. *The Passion as Liturgy: A Study in the Origin of the Passion Narratives
    in the Four Gospels.* London: SCM, 1983.
Tsang, Sam. "Are We 'Misreading' Paul?: Oral Phenomena and Their Implication for the
    Exegesis of Paul's Letters." *Oral Tradition* 24 (2009): 205–25.
Tuckett, Christopher M. "The *Didache* and the Synoptics Once More: A Response to
    Aaron Milavec." *Journal of Early Christian Studies* 13 (2005): 509–18.
–. "The *Didache* and the Writings that Later Formed the New Testament." Pages 83–127
    in *The Reception of the New Testament in the Apostolic Fathers.* Edited by Andrew
    Gregory and Christopher Tuckett. The New Testament and the Apostolic Fathers 1.
    Oxford: Oxford University Press, 2005.

–. "Form Criticism." Pages 21–38 in *Jesus in Memory: Traditions in Oral and Scribal Practices*. Edited by Werner H. Kelber and Samuel Byrskog. Waco, Tex.: Baylor University Press, 2009.

–. *Q and the History of Early Christianity: Studies on Q*. Edinburgh: T&T Clark, 1996.

–. "Synoptic Tradition in 1 Thessalonians?" Pages 160–82 in *The Thessalonian Correspondence*. Edited by Raymond F. Collins. Bibliotheca Ephemeridum Theologicarum Lovaniensium 87. Leuven: Leuven University Press and Peeters, 1990.

–. "Synoptic Tradition in the Didache." Pages 92–128 in *The Didache in Modern Research*. Edited by Jonathan A. Draper. Arbeiten zur Geschichte des antiken Judentums und des Urchristentums 37. Leiden: Brill, 1996.

Tuilier, André. "Didache." *Theologische Realenzyklopädie* 8 (1981): 731–6.

–. "La Didaché et le probléme synoptique." Pages 110–30 in *The Didache in Context: Essays on Its Text, History and Transmission*. Edited by Clayton N. Jefford. Supplements to Novum Testamentum 77. Leiden: Brill, 1995.

–. "Les charismatiques itinérants dans la Didachè et dans l'Évangile de Matthieu." Pages 157–72 in *Matthew and the Didache: Two Documents from the Same Jewish-Christian Milieu?* Edited by Huub van de Sandt. Assen: Van Gorcum/Philadelphia: Fortress, 2005.

Turner, David L. *Matthew*. Baker Exegetical Commentary on the New Testament. Grand Rapids: Baker Academic, 2007.

Uro, Risto. "*Thomas* and Oral Gospel Tradition." Pages 8–32 in *Thomas at the Crossroads: Essays on the Gospel of Thomas*. Edited by Risto Uro. Studies in the New Testament and Its World. Edinburgh: T&T Clark, 1998.

Vansina, Jan. *Oral Tradition as History*. Madison: University of Wisconsin Press/ London: Currey, 1985.

Verheyden, Joseph. "Eschatology in the Didache and in the Gospel of Matthew." Pages 193–215 in *Matthew and the Didache: Two Documents from the Same Jewish-Christian Milieu?* Edited by Huub van de Sandt. Assen: Van Gorcum/Philadelphia: Fortress, 2005.

–. "The *Shepherd of Hermas* and the Writings that later Formed the New Testament." Pages 293-329 in *The Reception of the New Testament in the Apostolic Fathers*. Edited by Andrew Gregory and Christopher Tuckett. The New Testament and the Apostolic Fathers 1. Oxford: Oxford University Press, 2005.

Vielhauer, Philipp. *Geschichte der urchristlichen Literatur: Einleitung in das Neue Testament, die Apokryphen und die Apostolischen Väter*. 2nd corrected ed. Berlin and New York: de Gruyter, 1978.

Vielhauer, Philipp and Georg Strecker. "Jewish-Christian Gospels." Pages 134–78 in *New Testament Apocrypha*, Vol. 1: *Gospels and Related Writings*. Edited by Wilhelm Schneemelcher. English ed. edited by R. McL. Wilson. Rev. ed. Cambridge: James Clarke/Louisville: Westminster/John Knox, 1991.

Viviano, B. T. "Hillel and Jesus on Prayer." Pages 427–57 in *Hillel and Jesus: Comparative Studies of Two Major Religious Leaders*. Edited by James H. Charlesworth and Loren L. Johns. Minneapolis: Fortress, 1997.

Vogt, H. J. "Bemerkungen zur Echtheit der Ignatiusbriefe." *Zeitschrift für Antikes Christentum/Journal of Ancient Christianity* 3 (1999): 50–63.

Vokes, Frederick E. "The Didache and the Canon of the New Testament." Pages 427–36 in *Studia Evangelica 3*. Edited by F. L. Cross. Texte und Untersuchungen 88. Berlin: Akademie-Verlag, 1964.

–. "The Didache – Still Debated." *Church Quarterly* 3 (1970): 57–62.

–. "Life and Order in the Early Church: The Didache." Pages 209–33 in vol. 27.1 of *Aufstieg und Niedergang der römischen Welt, II: Principat.* Edited by H. Temporini and Wolfgang Haase. Berlin and New York: de Gruyter, 1993.

Vööbus, Arthur. *Liturgical Traditions in the Didache.* Papers of the Estonian Theological Society in Exile 16. Stockholm: ETSE, 1968.

Vos, Louis Arthur. *The Synoptic Traditions in the Apocalypse.* Kampen: J. H. Kok, 1965.

Wake, W. *The genuine epistles of the Apostolical fathers S. Barnabas, S. Clement, S. Ignatius, S. Polycarp: The Shepherd of Hermas, and the Martyrdoms of St. Ignatius and St. Polycarp ...: Translated and published with a large preliminary discourse.* London: Printed for Richard Sare at Grays-Inn Gate in Holbourn, 1693.

Walls, A. F. "Papias and Oral Tradition." *Vigiliae Christianae* 21 (1967): 137–40.

Walter, Nikolaus. "Paul and the Early Christian Jesus-Tradition." Pages 51–80 in *Paul and Jesus: Collected Essays.* Edited by A. J. M. Wedderburn. Journal for the Study of the New Testament Supplement Series 37. Sheffield: JSOT Press, 1989.

Wansbrough, Henry, ed. *Jesus and the Oral Gospel Tradition.* Journal for the Study of the New Testament Supplement Series 64. Sheffield: JSOT Press, 1991.

Warns, Rüdiger. "Untersuchungen zum 2. Clemens-Brief." Inauguraldissertation zur Erlangung der Würde eines Doktors der Theologie; Marburg: Philipps-Universität Marburg, 1985.

Weeden, Theodore J. "Kenneth Bailey's Theory of Oral Tradition: A Theory Contested by Its Evidence." *Journal for the Study of the Historical Jesus* 7 (2009): 3–43.

Welborn, Laurence L. "The Preface to 1 Clement: The Rhetorical Situation and the Traditional Date." Pages 197–216 in *Encounters with Hellenism: Studies on the First Letter of Clement.* Edited by Cilliers Breytenbach and Laurence L. Welborn. Arbeiten zur Geschichte des antiken Judentums und des Urchristentums 53. Leiden: Brill, 2004.

Wengst, Klaus. *Didache (Apostellehre), Barnabasbrief, Zweiter Clemensbrief, Schrift an Diognet.* Schriften des Urchristentums 2. Darmstadt: Wissenschaftliche Buchgesellschaft, 1984.

Wenham, David, ed. *Gospel Perspectives, Vol. 5: The Jesus Tradition Outside the Gospels.* Sheffield: JSOT Press, 1985.

Westcott, B. F. *A General Survey of the History of the Canon of the New Testament.* 7th ed. London and New York: Macmillan, 1896.

–. *An Introduction to the Study of the Gospels.* 7th ed. London: Macmillan, 1888.

Whitaker, Richard. "Orality and Literacy in the Poetic Traditions of Archaic Greece and Southern Africa." Pages 205–17 in *Voice into Text: Orality and Literacy in Ancient Greece.* Edited by Ian Worthington. Supplements to Mnemosyne 157. Leiden: Brill, 1996.

Williams, David J. *Acts.* New International Biblical Commentary 5. Peabody, Mass.: Hendrickson, 1990.

Willis, Wendell, ed. *The Kingdom of God in 20th-Century Interpretation.* Peabody, Mass.: Hendrickson, 1987.

Witherington, Ben, III. *The Acts of the Apostles: A Socio-Rhetorical Commentary.* Grand Rapids: Eerdmans/Carlisle: Paternoster, 1998.

–. *Jesus the Sage: The Pilgrimage of Wisdom.* Minneapolis: Fortress, 1994.

–. *Matthew.* Smyth & Helwys Bible Commentary. Macon, Ga.: Smyth & Helwys, 2006.

Wrege, Hans-Theo. *Die Überlieferungsgeschichte der Bergpredigt.* Wissenschaftliche Untersuchungen zum Neuen Testament 9. Tübingen: Mohr Siebeck, 1968.

Wright, Leon E. *Alterations of the Words of Jesus: As Quoted in the Literature of the Second Century.* Harvard Historical Monographs 25. Cambridge, Mass.: Harvard University Press, 1952.

Wright, N. T. *Christian Origins and the Question of God,* Vol. 1: *The New Testament and the People of God.* Minneapolis: Fortress, 1992.

–. *Christian Origins and the Question of God,* Vol. 2: *Jesus and the Victory of God.* Minneapolis: Fortress, 1996.

Wright, Stephen I. "Debtors, Laborers and Virgins: The Voice of Jesus and the Voice of Matthew in Three Parables." Pages 13-23 in *Jesus and Paul: Global Perspectives in Honor of James D. G. Dunn for His 70th Birthday.* Edited by B. J. Oropeza, C. K. Robertson and Douglas C. Mohrmann. Library of New Testament Studies 414. London and New York: T&T Clark International, 2009.

Yates, Frances A. *The Art of Memory.* Chicago: University of Chicago Press, 1966.

Zahn, Theodor. *Forschungen zur Geschichte des neutestamentlichen Kanons und der altkirchlichen Literatur,* Vol. 6: *Apostel und Apostelschüler in der Provinz Asien.* Leipzig: A. Deichert, 1900.

–. *Geschichte des neutestamentlichen Kanons.* 2 vols. Erlangen and Leipzig: A. Deichert, 1888–90.

Index of Ancient Sources

1. Hebrew Scriptures and Septuagint

2. New Testament

3. Apostolic Fathers

4. Other Early Christian Literature

5. Rabbinic Literature

6. Other Greco-Roman and Jewish Writings

Index of Modern Authors

Index of Subjects

Wissenschaftliche Untersuchungen zum Neuen Testament

Alphabetical Index of the First and Second Series

Becker, Michael: Wunder und Wundertäter im frührabbinischen Judentum. 2002. *Vol. II/144.*

Becker, Michael and *Markus Öhler* (Ed.): Apo-kalyptik als Herausforderung neutestament-licher Theologie. 2006. *Vol. II/214.*

Bell, Richard H.: Deliver Us from Evil. 2007. *Vol. 216.*

– The Irrevocable Call of God. 2005. *Vol. 184.*

– No One Seeks for God. 1998. *Vol. 106.*

– Provoked to Jealousy. 1994. *Vol. II/63.*

Bennema, Cornelis: The Power of Saving Wisdom. 2002. *Vol. II/148.*

Bergman, Jan: see *Kieffer, René*

Bergmeier, Roland: Das Gesetz im Römerbrief und andere Studien zum Neuen Testament. 2000. *Vol. 121.*

Bernett, Monika: Der Kaiserkult in Judäa unter den Herodiern und Römern. 2007. *Vol. 203.*

Betz, Otto: Jesus, der Messias Israels. 1987. *Vol. 42.*

– Jesus, der Herr der Kirche. 1990. *Vol. 52.*

Beyschlag, Karlmann: Simon Magus und die christliche Gnosis. 1974. *Vol. 16.*

Bieringer, Reimund: see *Koester, Craig.*

Bittner, Wolfgang J.: Jesu Zeichen im Johannes-evangelium. 1987. *Vol. II/26.*

Bjerkelund, Carl J.: Tauta Egeneto. 1987. *Vol. 40.*

Blackburn, Barry Lee: Theios Aner and the Markan Miracle Traditions. 1991. *Vol. II/40.*

Blanton IV, Thomas R.: Constructing a New Covenant. 2007. *Vol. II/233.*

Bock, Darrell L.: Blasphemy and Exaltation in Judaism and the Final Examination of Jesus. 1998. *Vol. II/106.*

– and *Robert L. Webb* (Ed.): Key Events in the Life of the Historical Jesus. 2009. *Vol. 247.*

Bockmuehl, Markus: The Remembered Peter. 2010. *Vol. 262.*

– Revelation and Mystery in Ancient Judaism and Pauline Christianity. 1990. *Vol. II/36.*

Bøe, Sverre: Cross-Bearing in Luke. 2010. *Vol. II/278.*

– Gog and Magog. 2001. *Vol. II/135.*

Böhlig, Alexander: Gnosis und Synkretismus. Vol. 1 1989. *Vol. 47* – Vol. 2 1989. *Vol. 48.*

Böhm, Martina: Samarien und die Samaritai bei Lukas. 1999. *Vol. II/111.*

Börstinghaus, Jens: Sturmfahrt und Schiff-bruch. 2010. *Vol. II/274.*

Böttrich, Christfried: Weltweisheit – Mensch-heitsethik – Urkult. 1992. *Vol. II/50.*

– and *Herzer, Jens* (Ed.): Josephus und das Neue Testament. 2007. *Vol. 209.*

Bolyki, János: Jesu Tischgemeinschaften. 1997. *Vol. II/96.*

Bosman, Philip: Conscience in Philo and Paul. 2003. *Vol. II/166.*

Bovon, François: New Testament and Christian Apocrypha. 2009. *Vol. 237.*

– Studies in Early Christianity. 2003. *Vol. 161.*

Brändl, Martin: Der Agon bei Paulus. 2006. *Vol. II/222.*

Braun, Heike: Geschichte des Gottesvolkes und christliche Identität. 2010. *Vol. II/279.*

Breytenbach, Cilliers: see *Frey, Jörg.*

Broadhead, Edwin K.: Jewish Ways of Follo-wing Jesus Redrawing the Religious Map of Antiquity. 2010. *Vol. 266.*

Brocke, Christoph vom: Thessaloniki – Stadt des Kassander und Gemeinde des Paulus. 2001. *Vol. II/125.*

Brunson, Andrew: Psalm 118 in the Gospel of John. 2003. *Vol. II/158.*

Büchli, Jörg: Der Poimandres – ein paganisier-tes Evangelium. 1987. *Vol. II/27.*

Bühner, Jan A.: Der Gesandte und sein Weg im 4. Evangelium. 1977. *Vol. II/2.*

Burchard, Christoph: Untersuchungen zu Joseph und Aseneth. 1965. *Vol. 8.*

– Studien zur Theologie, Sprache und Umwelt des Neuen Testaments. Ed. by D. Sänger. 1998. *Vol. 107.*

Burnett, Richard: Karl Barth's Theological Exegesis. 2001. *Vol. II/145.*

Byron, John: Slavery Metaphors in Early Judaism and Pauline Christianity. 2003. *Vol. II/162.*

Byrskog, Samuel: Story as History – History as Story. 2000. *Vol. 123.*

Cancik, Hubert (Ed.): Markus-Philologie. 1984. *Vol. 33.*

Capes, David B.: Old Testament Yaweh Texts in Paul's Christology. 1992. *Vol. II/47.*

Caragounis, Chrys C.: The Development of Greek and the New Testament. 2004. *Vol. 167.*

– The Son of Man. 1986. *Vol. 38.*

– see *Fridrichsen, Anton.*

Carleton Paget, James: The Epistle of Barna-bas. 1994. *Vol. II/64.*

– Jews, Christians and Jewish Christians in Antiquity. 2010. *Vol. 251.*

Carson, D.A., O'Brien, Peter T. and *Mark Seifrid* (Ed.): Justification and Variegated Nomism.
Vol. 1: The Complexities of Second Temple Judaism. 2001. *Vol. II/140.*
Vol. 2: The Paradoxes of Paul. 2004. *Vol. II/181.*

Chae, Young Sam: Jesus as the Eschatological Davidic Shepherd. 2006. *Vol. II/216.*

Chapman, David W.: Ancient Jewish and Christian Perceptions of Crucifixion. 2008. *Vol. II/244.*

Chester, Andrew: Messiah and Exaltation. 2007. *Vol. 207.*

Chibici-Revneanu, Nicole: Die Herrlichkeit des Verherrlichten. 2007. *Vol. II/231.*

Ciampa, Roy E.: The Presence and Function of Scripture in Galatians 1 and 2. 1998. *Vol. II/102.*

Classen, Carl Joachim: Rhetorical Criticsm of the New Testament. 2000. *Vol. 128.*

Colpe, Carsten: Griechen – Byzantiner – Semiten – Muslime. 2008. *Vol. 221.*

– Iranier – Aramäer – Hebräer – Hellenen. 2003. *Vol. 154.*

Cook, John G.: Roman Attitudes Towards the Christians. 2010. *Vol. 261.*

Coote, Robert B. (Ed.): see *Weissenrieder, Annette.*

Coppins, Wayne: The Interpretation of Freedom in the Letters of Paul. 2009. *Vol. II/261.*

Crump, David: Jesus the Intercessor. 1992. *Vol. II/49.*

Dahl, Nils Alstrup: Studies in Ephesians. 2000. *Vol. 131.*

Daise, Michael A.: Feasts in John. 2007. *Vol. II/229.*

Deines, Roland: Die Gerechtigkeit der Tora im Reich des Messias. 2004. *Vol. 177.*

– Jüdische Steingefäße und pharisäische Frömmigkeit. 1993. *Vol. II/52.*

– Die Pharisäer. 1997. *Vol. 101.*

Deines, Roland, Jens Herzer and *Karl-Wilhelm Niebuhr* (Ed.): Neues Testament und hellenistisch-jüdische Alltagskultur. III. Internationales Symposium zum Corpus Judaeo-Hellenisticum Novi Testamenti. 21.–24. Mai 2009 in Leipzig. 2011. *Vol. 274.*

– and *Karl-Wilhelm Niebuhr* (Ed.): Philo und das Neue Testament. 2004. *Vol. 172.*

Dennis, John A.: Jesus' Death and the Gathering of True Israel. 2006. *Vol. 217.*

Dettwiler, Andreas and *Jean Zumstein* (Ed.): Kreuzestheologie im Neuen Testament. 2002. *Vol. 151.*

Dickson, John P.: Mission-Commitment in Ancient Judaism and in the Pauline Communities. 2003. *Vol. II/159.*

Dietzfelbinger, Christian: Der Abschied des Kommenden. 1997. *Vol. 95.*

Dimitrov, Ivan Z., James D.G. Dunn, Ulrich Luz and *Karl-Wilhelm Niebuhr* (Ed.): Das Alte Testament als christliche Bibel in orthodoxer und westlicher Sicht. 2004. *Vol. 174.*

Dobbeler, Axel von: Glaube als Teilhabe. 1987. *Vol. II/22.*

Docherty, Susan E.: The Use of the Old Testament in Hebrews. 2009. *Vol. II/260.*

Dochhorn, Jan: Schriftgelehrte Prophetie. 2010. *Vol. 268.*

Downs, David J.: The Offering of the Gentiles. 2008. *Vol. II/248.*

Dryden, J. de Waal: Theology and Ethics in 1 Peter. 2006. *Vol. II/209.*

Dübbers, Michael: Christologie und Existenz im Kolosserbrief. 2005. *Vol. II/191.*

Dunn, James D.G.: The New Perspective on Paul. 2005. *Vol. 185.*

Dunn, James D.G. (Ed.): Jews and Christians. 1992. *Vol. 66.*

– Paul and the Mosaic Law. 1996. *Vol. 89.*

– see *Dimitrov, Ivan Z.*

–, *Hans Klein, Ulrich Luz,* and *Vasile Mihoc* (Ed.): Auslegung der Bibel in orthodoxer und westlicher Perspektive. 2000. *Vol. 130.*

Ebel, Eva: Die Attraktivität früher christlicher Gemeinden. 2004. *Vol. II/178.*

Ebertz, Michael N.: Das Charisma des Gekreuzigten. 1987. *Vol. 45.*

Eckstein, Hans-Joachim: Der Begriff Syneidesis bei Paulus. 1983. *Vol. II/10.*

– Verheißung und Gesetz. 1996. *Vol. 86.*

–, *Christoph Landmesser* and *Hermann Lichtenberger* (Ed.): Eschatologie – Eschatology. The Sixth Durham-Tübingen Research Symposium. 2011. *Vol. 272.*

Ego, Beate: Im Himmel wie auf Erden. 1989. *Vol. II/34.*

Ego, Beate, Armin Lange and *Peter Pilhofer* (Ed.): Gemeinde ohne Tempel – Community without Temple. 1999. *Vol. 118.*

– and *Helmut Merkel* (Ed.): Religiöses Lernen in der biblischen, frühjüdischen und frühchristlichen Überlieferung. 2005. *Vol. 180.*

Eisele, Wilfried: Welcher Thomas? 2010. *Vol. 259.*

Eisen, Ute E.: see *Paulsen, Henning.*

Elledge, C.D.: Life after Death in Early Judaism. 2006. *Vol. II/208.*

Ellis, E. Earle: Prophecy and Hermeneutic in Early Christianity. 1978. *Vol. 18.*

– The Old Testament in Early Christianity. 1991. *Vol. 54.*

Elmer, Ian J.: Paul, Jerusalem and the Judaisers. 2009. *Vol. II/258.*

Endo, Masanobu: Creation and Christology. 2002. *Vol. 149.*

Ennulat, Andreas: Die 'Minor Agreements'. 1994. *Vol. II/62.*

Ensor, Peter W.: Jesus and His 'Works'. 1996. *Vol. II/85.*

Eskola, Timo: Messiah and the Throne. 2001. *Vol. II/142.*

– Theodicy and Predestination in Pauline Soteriology. 1998. *Vol. II/100.*

Farelly, Nicolas: The Disciples in the Fourth Gospel. 2010. *Vol. II/290.*

Fatehi, Mehrdad: The Spirit's Relation to the Risen Lord in Paul. 2000. *Vol. II/128.*

Feldmeier, Reinhard: Die Krisis des Gottessohnes. 1987. *Vol. II/21.*

– Die Christen als Fremde. 1992. *Vol. 64.*

Feldmeier, Reinhard and *Ulrich Heckel* (Ed.): Die Heiden. 1994. *Vol. 70.*

Felsch, Dorit: Die Feste im Johannesevangelium. 2011. *Vol. II/308.*

Finnern, Sönke: Narratologie und biblische Exegese. 2010. *Vol. II/285.*

Fletcher-Louis, Crispin H.T.: Luke-Acts: Angels, Christology and Soteriology. 1997. *Vol. II/94.*

Förster, Niclas: Marcus Magus. 1999. *Vol. 114.*

Forbes, Christopher Brian: Prophecy and Inspired Speech in Early Christianity and its Hellenistic Environment. 1995. *Vol. II/75.*

Fornberg, Tord: see *Fridrichsen, Anton.*

Fossum, Jarl E.: The Name of God and the Angel of the Lord. 1985. *Vol. 36.*

Foster, Paul: Community, Law and Mission in Matthew's Gospel. *Vol. II/177.*

Fotopoulos, John: Food Offered to Idols in Roman Corinth. 2003. *Vol. II/151.*

Frank, Nicole: Der Kolosserbrief im Kontext des paulinischen Erbes. 2009. *Vol. II/271.*

Frenschkowski, Marco: Offenbarung und Epiphanie. Vol. 1 1995. *Vol. II/79* – Vol. 2 1997. *Vol. II/80.*

Frey, Jörg: Eugen Drewermann und die biblische Exegese. 1995. *Vol. II/71.*

– Die johanneische Eschatologie. Vol. I. 1997. *Vol. 96.* – Vol. II. 1998. *Vol. 110.* – Vol. III. 2000. *Vol. 117.*

Frey, Jörg and *Cilliers Breytenbach* (Ed.): Aufgabe und Durchführung einer Theologie des Neuen Testaments. 2007. *Vol. 205.*

– *Jens Herzer, Martina Janßen* and *Clare K. Rothschild* (Ed.): Pseudepigraphie und Verfasserfiktion in frühchristlichen Briefen. 2009. *Vol. 246.*

– *Stefan Krauter* and *Hermann Lichtenberger* (Ed.): Heil und Geschichte. 2009. *Vol. 248.*

– and *Udo Schnelle (Ed.):* Kontexte des Johannesevangeliums. 2004. *Vol. 175.*

– and *Jens Schröter* (Ed.): Deutungen des Todes Jesu im Neuen Testament. 2005. *Vol. 181.*

– Jesus in apokryphen Evangelienüberlieferungen. 2010. *Vol. 254.*

–, *Jan G. van der Watt,* and *Ruben Zimmermann* (Ed.): Imagery in the Gospel of John. 2006. *Vol. 200.*

Freyne, Sean: Galilee and Gospel. 2000. *Vol. 125.*

Fridrichsen, Anton: Exegetical Writings. Edited by C.C. Caragounis and T. Fornberg. 1994. *Vol. 76.*

Gadenz, Pablo T.: Called from the Jews and from the Gentiles. 2009. *Vol. II/267.*

Gäbel, Georg: Die Kulttheologie des Hebräerbriefes. 2006. *Vol. II/212.*

Gäckle, Volker: Die Starken und die Schwachen in Korinth und in Rom. 2005. *Vol. 200.*

Garlington, Don B.: 'The Obedience of Faith'. 1991. *Vol. II/38.*

– Faith, Obedience, and Perseverance. 1994. *Vol. 79.*

Garnet, Paul: Salvation and Atonement in the Qumran Scrolls. 1977. *Vol. II/3.*

Gemünden, Petra von (Ed.): see *Weissenrieder, Annette.*

Gese, Michael: Das Vermächtnis des Apostels. 1997. *Vol. II/99.*

Gheorghita, Radu: The Role of the Septuagint in Hebrews. 2003. *Vol. II/160.*

Gordley, Matthew E.: The Colossian Hymn in Context. 2007. *Vol. II/228.*

– Teaching through Song in Antiquity. 2011. *Vol. II/302.*

Gräbe, Petrus J.: The Power of God in Paul's Letters. 2000, ²2008. *Vol. II/123.*

Gräßer, Erich: Der Alte Bund im Neuen. 1985. *Vol. 35.*

– Forschungen zur Apostelgeschichte. 2001. *Vol. 137.*

Grappe, Christian (Ed.): Le Repas de Dieu / Das Mahl Gottes. 2004. *Vol. 169.*

Gray, Timothy C.: The Temple in the Gospel of Mark. 2008. *Vol. II/242.*

Green, Joel B.: The Death of Jesus. 1988. *Vol. II/33.*

Gregg, Brian Han: The Historical Jesus and the Final Judgment Sayings in Q. 2005. *Vol. II/207.*

Gregory, Andrew: The Reception of Luke and Acts in the Period before Irenaeus. 2003. *Vol. II/169.*

Grindheim, Sigurd: The Crux of Election. 2005. *Vol. II/202.*

Gundry, Robert H.: The Old is Better. 2005. *Vol. 178.*

Gundry Volf, Judith M.: Paul and Perseverance. 1990. *Vol. II/37.*

Häußer, Detlef: Christusbekenntnis und Jesusüberlieferung bei Paulus. 2006. *Vol. 210.*

Hafemann, Scott J.: Suffering and the Spirit.
1986. *Vol. II/19.*
– Paul, Moses, and the History of Israel. 1995.
Vol. 81.
Hahn, Ferdinand: Studien zum Neuen Testa-
ment.
Vol. I: Grundsatzfragen, Jesusforschung,
Evangelien. 2006. *Vol. 191.*
Vol. II: Bekenntnisbildung und Theologie in
urchristlicher Zeit. 2006. *Vol. 192.*
Hahn, Johannes (Ed.): Zerstörungen des Jeru-
salemer Tempels. 2002. *Vol. 147.*
Hamid-Khani, Saeed: Relevation and Conceal-
ment of Christ. 2000. *Vol. II/120.*
Hannah, Darrel D.: Michael and Christ. 1999.
Vol. II/109.
Hardin, Justin K.: Galatians and the Imperial
Cult? 2007. *Vol. II /237.*
Harrison, James R.: Paul and the Imperial
Authorities at Thessolanica and Rome.
2011. *Vol. 273.*
– Paul's Language of Grace in Its Graeco-
Roman Context. 2003. *Vol. II/172.*
Hartman, Lars: Text-Centered New Testament
Studies. Ed. von D. Hellholm. 1997.
Vol. 102.
Hartog, Paul: Polycarp and the New Testament.
2001. *Vol. II/134.*
Hasselbrook, David S.: Studies in New Testa-
ment Lexicography. 2011. *Vol. II/303.*
Hays, Christopher M.: Luke's Wealth Ethics.
2010. *Vol. 275.*
Heckel, Theo K.: Der Innere Mensch. 1993.
Vol. II/53.
– Vom Evangelium des Markus zum vier-
gestaltigen Evangelium. 1999. *Vol. 120.*
Heckel, Ulrich: Kraft in Schwachheit. 1993.
Vol. II/56.
– Der Segen im Neuen Testament. 2002.
Vol. 150.
– see *Feldmeier, Reinhard.*
– see *Hengel, Martin.*
Heemstra, Marius: The Fiscus Judaicus and the
Parting of the Ways. 2010. *Vol. II/277.*
Heiligenthal, Roman: Werke als Zeichen. 1983.
Vol. II/9.
Heininger, Bernhard: Die Inkulturation des
Christentums. 2010. *Vol. 255.*
Heliso, Desta: Pistis and the Righteous One.
2007. *Vol. II/235.*
Hellholm, D.: see *Hartman, Lars.*
Hemer, Colin J.: The Book of Acts in the Setting
of Hellenistic History. 1989. *Vol. 49.*
Henderson, Timothy P.: The Gospel of Peter
and Early Christian Apologetics. 2011.
Vol. II/301.

Hengel, Martin: Jesus und die Evangelien.
Kleine Schriften V. 2007. *Vol. 211.*
– Die johanneische Frage. 1993. *Vol. 67.*
– Judaica et Hellenistica. Kleine Schriften I.
1996. *Vol. 90.*
– Judaica, Hellenistica et Christiana. Kleine
Schriften II. 1999. *Vol. 109.*
– Judentum und Hellenismus. 1969, ³1988.
Vol. 10.
– Paulus und Jakobus. Kleine Schriften III.
2002. *Vol. 141.*
– Studien zur Christologie. Kleine Schriften
IV. 2006. *Vol. 201.*
– Studien zum Urchristentum. Kleine Schrif-
ten VI. 2008. *Vol. 234.*
– Theologische, historische und biographische
Skizzen. Kleine Schriften VII. 2010.
Vol. 253.
– and *Anna Maria Schwemer:* Paulus zwi-
schen Damaskus und Antiochien. 1998.
Vol. 108.
– Der messianische Anspruch Jesu und die
Anfänge der Christologie. 2001. *Vol. 138.*
– Die vier Evangelien und das eine Evange-
lium von Jesus Christus. 2008. *Vol. 224.*
Hengel, Martin and *Ulrich Heckel* (Ed.): Paulus
und das antike Judentum. 1991. *Vol. 58.*
– and *Hermut Löhr* (Ed.): Schriftauslegung
im antiken Judentum und im Urchristentum.
1994. *Vol. 73.*
– and *Anna Maria Schwemer* (Ed.): Königs-
herrschaft Gottes und himmlischer Kult.
1991. *Vol. 55.*
– Die Septuaginta. 1994. *Vol. 72.*
–, *Siegfried Mittmann* and *Anna Maria
Schwemer* (Ed.): La Cité de Dieu / Die Stadt
Gottes. 2000. *Vol. 129.*
Hentschel, Anni: Diakonia im Neuen Testament.
2007. *Vol. 226.*
Hernández Jr., Juan: Scribal Habits and Theo-
logical Influence in the Apocalypse. 2006.
Vol. II/218.
Herrenbrück, Fritz: Jesus und die Zöllner. 1990.
Vol. II/41.
Herzer, Jens: Paulus oder Petrus? 1998.
Vol. 103.
– see *Böttrich, Christfried.*
– see *Deines, Roland.*
– see *Frey, Jörg.*
Hill, Charles E.: From the Lost Teaching of
Polycarp. 2005. *Vol. 186.*
Hoegen-Rohls, Christina: Der nachösterliche
Johannes. 1996. *Vol. II/84.*
Hoffmann, Matthias Reinhard: The Destroyer
and the Lamb. 2005. *Vol. II/203.*
Hofius, Otfried: Katapausis. 1970. *Vol. 11.*

- Der Vorhang vor dem Thron Gottes. 1972. *Vol. 14.*
- Der Christushymnus Philipper 2,6–11. 1976, ²1991. *Vol. 17.*
- Paulusstudien. 1989, ²1994. *Vol. 51.*
- Neutestamentliche Studien. 2000. *Vol. 132.*
- Paulusstudien II. 2002. *Vol. 143.*
- Exegetische Studien. 2008. *Vol. 223.*
- and *Hans-Christian Kammler:* Johannesstudien. 1996. *Vol. 88.*
Holloway, Paul A.: Coping with Prejudice. 2009. *Vol. 244.*
- see *Ahearne-Kroll, Stephen P.*
Holmberg, Bengt (Ed.): Exploring Early Christian Identity. 2008. *Vol. 226.*
- and *Mikael Winninge* (Ed.): Identity Formation in the New Testament. 2008. *Vol. 227.*
Holtz, Traugott: Geschichte und Theologie des Urchristentums. 1991. *Vol. 57.*
Hommel, Hildebrecht: Sebasmata.
  Vol. 1 1983. *Vol. 31.*
  Vol. 2 1984. *Vol. 32.*
Horbury, William: Herodian Judaism and New Testament Study. 2006. *Vol. 193.*
Horn, Friedrich Wilhelm and *Ruben Zimmermann* (Ed.): Jenseits von Indikativ und Imperativ. Vol. 1. 2009. *Vol. 238.*
Horst, Pieter W. van der: Jews and Christians in Their Graeco-Roman Context. 2006. *Vol. 196.*
Hultgård, Anders and *Stig Norin* (Ed): Le Jour de Dieu / Der Tag Gottes. 2009. *Vol. 245.*
Hume, Douglas A.: The Early Christian Community. 2011. *Vol. II/298.*
Hvalvik, Reidar: The Struggle for Scripture and Covenant. 1996. *Vol. II/82.*
Jackson, Ryan: New Creation in Paul's Letters. 2010. *Vol. II/272.*
Janßen, Martina: see *Frey, Jörg.*
Jauhiainen, Marko: The Use of Zechariah in Revelation. 2005. *Vol. II/199.*
Jensen, Morten H.: Herod Antipas in Galilee. 2006; ²2010. *Vol. II/215.*
Johns, Loren L.: The Lamb Christology of the Apocalypse of John. 2003. *Vol. II/167.*
Jossa, Giorgio: Jews or Christians? 2006. *Vol. 202.*
Joubert, Stephan: Paul as Benefactor. 2000. *Vol. II/124.*
Judge, E. A.: The First Christians in the Roman World. 2008. *Vol. 229.*
- Jerusalem and Athens. 2010. *Vol. 265.*
Jungbauer, Harry: „Ehre Vater und Mutter". 2002. *Vol. II/146.*
Kähler, Christoph: Jesu Gleichnisse als Poesie und Therapie. 1995. *Vol. 78.*

Kamlah, Ehrhard: Die Form der katalogischen Paränese im Neuen Testament. 1964. *Vol. 7.*
Kammler, Hans-Christian: Christologie und Eschatologie. 2000. *Vol. 126.*
- Kreuz und Weisheit. 2003. *Vol. 159.*
- see *Hofius, Otfried.*
Karakolis, Christos: see *Alexeev, Anatoly A.*
Karrer, Martin und *Wolfgang Kraus* (Ed.): Die Septuaginta – Texte, Kontexte, Lebenswelten. 2008. *Vol. 219.*
- see *Kraus, Wolfgang.*
Kelhoffer, James A.: The Diet of John the Baptist. 2005. *Vol. 176.*
- Miracle and Mission. 2000. *Vol. II/112.*
- Persecution, Persuasion and Power. 2010. *Vol. 270.*
- see *Ahearne-Kroll, Stephen P.*
Kelley, Nicole: Knowledge and Religious Authority in the Pseudo-Clementines. 2006. *Vol. II/213.*
Kennedy, Joel: The Recapitulation of Israel. 2008. *Vol. II/257.*
Kensky, Meira Z.: Trying Man, Trying God. 2010. *Vol. II/289.*
Kieffer, René and *Jan Bergman* (Ed.): La Main de Dieu / Die Hand Gottes. 1997. *Vol. 94.*
Kierspel, Lars: The Jews and the World in the Fourth Gospel. 2006. *Vol. 220.*
Kim, Seyoon: The Origin of Paul's Gospel. 1981, ²1984. *Vol. II/4.*
- Paul and the New Perspective. 2002. *Vol. 140.*
- "The 'Son of Man'" as the Son of God. 1983. *Vol. 30.*
Klauck, Hans-Josef: Religion und Gesellschaft im frühen Christentum. 2003. *Vol. 152.*
Klein, Hans, Vasile Mihoc und *Karl-Wilhelm Niebuhr* (Ed.): Das Gebet im Neuen Testament. Vierte, europäische orthodox-westliche Exegetenkonferenz in Sambata de Sus, 4. – 8. August 2007. 2009. Vol. 249.
- see Dunn, James D.G.
Kleinknecht, Karl Th.: Der leidende Gerechtfertigte. 1984, ²1988. *Vol. II/13.*
Klinghardt, Matthias: Gesetz und Volk Gottes. 1988. *Vol. II/32.*
Kloppenborg, John S.: The Tenants in the Vineyard. 2006, student edition 2010. *Vol. 195.*
Koch, Michael: Drachenkampf und Sonnenfrau. 2004. *Vol. II/184.*
Koch, Stefan: Rechtliche Regelung von Konflikten im frühen Christentum. 2004. *Vol. II/174.*
Köhler, Wolf-Dietrich: Rezeption des Matthäusevangeliums in der Zeit vor Irenäus. 1987. *Vol. II/24.*

Köhn, Andreas: Der Neutestamentler Ernst
  Lohmeyer. 2004. *Vol. II/180.*
Koester, Craig and *Reimund Bieringer* (Ed.):
  The Resurrection of Jesus in the Gospel of
  John. 2008. *Vol. 222.*
Konradt, Matthias: Israel, Kirche und die Völ-
  ker im Matthäusevangelium. 2007. *Vol. 215.*
Kooten, George H. van: Cosmic Christology
  in Paul and the Pauline School. 2003.
  Vol. II/171.
– Paul's Anthropology in Context. 2008.
  Vol. 232.
Korn, Manfred: Die Geschichte Jesu in ver-
  änderter Zeit. 1993. *Vol. II/51.*
Koskenniemi, Erkki: Apollonios von Tyana
  in der neutestamentlichen Exegese. 1994.
  Vol. II/61.
– The Old Testament Miracle-Workers in
  Early Judaism. 2005. *Vol. II/206.*
Kraus, Thomas J.: Sprache, Stil und historischer
  Ort des zweiten Petrusbriefes. 2001.
  Vol. II/136.
Kraus, Wolfgang: Das Volk Gottes. 1996.
  Vol. 85.
– see *Karrer, Martin.*
– see *Walter, Nikolaus.*
– and *Martin Karrer* (Hrsg.): Die Septua-
  ginta – Texte, Theologien, Einflüsse. 2010.
  Bd. 252.
– and *Karl-Wilhelm Niebuhr* (Ed.): Frühjuden-
  tum und Neues Testament im Horizont Bib-
  lischer Theologie. 2003. *Vol. 162.*
Krauter, Stefan: Studien zu Röm 13,1-7. 2009.
  Vol. 243.
– see *Frey, Jörg.*
Kreplin, Matthias: Das Selbstverständnis Jesu.
  2001. *Vol. II/141.*
Kuhn, Karl G.: Achtzehngebet und Vaterunser
  und der Reim. 1950. *Vol. 1.*
Kvalbein, Hans: see *Ådna, Jostein.*
Kwon, Yon-Gyong: Eschatology in Galatians.
  2004. *Vol. II/183.*
Laansma, Jon: I Will Give You Rest. 1997.
  Vol. II/98.
Labahn, Michael: Offenbarung in Zeichen und
  Wort. 2000. *Vol. II/117.*
Lambers-Petry, Doris: see *Tomson, Peter J.*
Lampe, Peter: Die stadtrömischen Christen
  in den ersten beiden Jahrhunderten. 1987,
  ²1989. *Vol. II/18.*
Landmesser, Christof: Wahrheit als Grundbe-
  griff neutestamentlicher Wissenschaft. 1999.
  Vol. 113.
– Jüngerberufung und Zuwendung zu Gott.
  2000. *Vol. 133.*
– see *Eckstein, Hans-Joachim.*
Lange, Armin: see *Ego, Beate.*

Lau, Andrew: Manifest in Flesh. 1996.
  Vol. II/86.
Lawrence, Louise: An Ethnography of the
  Gospel of Matthew. 2003. *Vol. II/165.*
Lee, Aquila H.I.: From Messiah to Preexistent
  Son. 2005. *Vol. II/192.*
Lee, Pilchan: The New Jerusalem in the Book
  of Relevation. 2000. *Vol. II/129.*
Lee, Sang M.: The Cosmic Drama of Salvation.
  2010. *Vol. II/276.*
Lee, Simon S.: Jesus' Transfiguration and the
  Believers' Transformation. 2009. *Vol. II/265.*
Lichtenberger, Hermann: Das Ich Adams und
  das Ich der Menschheit. 2004. *Vol. 164.*
– see *Avemarie, Friedrich.*
– see *Eckstein, Hans-Joachim.*
– see *Frey, Jörg.*
Lierman, John: The New Testament Moses.
  2004. *Vol. II/173.*
– (Ed.): Challenging Perspectives on the
  Gospel of John. 2006. *Vol. II/219.*
Lieu, Samuel N.C.: Manichaeism in the Later
  Roman Empire and Medieval China. ²1992.
  Vol. 63.
Lindemann, Andreas: Die Evangelien und die
  Apostelgeschichte. 2009. *Vol. 241.*
Lincicum, David: Paul and the Early Jewish
  Encounter with Deuteronomy. 2010.
  Vol. II/284.
Lindgård, Fredrik: Paul's Line of Thought in 2
  Corinthians 4:16–5:10. 2004. *Vol. II/189.*
Livesey, Nina E.: Circumcision as a Malleable
  Symbol. 2010. *Vol. II/295.*
Loader, William R.G.: Jesus' Attitude Towards
  the Law. 1997. *Vol. II/97.*
Löhr, Gebhard: Verherrlichung Gottes durch
  Philosophie. 1997. *Vol. 97.*
Löhr, Hermut: Studien zum frühchristlichen und
  frühjüdischen Gebet. 2003. *Vol. 160.*
– see *Hengel, Martin.*
Löhr, Winrich Alfried: Basilides und seine
  Schule. 1995. *Vol. 83.*
Lorenzen, Stefanie: Das paulinische Eikon-
  Konzept. 2008. *Vol. II/250.*
Luomanen, Petri: Entering the Kingdom of
  Heaven. 1998. *Vol. II/101.*
Luz, Ulrich: see *Alexeev, Anatoly A.*
– see *Dunn, James D.G.*
Mackay, Ian D.: John's Raltionship with Mark.
  2004. *Vol. II/182.*
Mackie, Scott D.: Eschatology and Exhorta-
  tion in the Epistle to the Hebrews. 2006.
  Vol. II/223.
Magda, Ksenija: Paul's Territoriality and Mis-
  sion Strategy. 2009. *Vol. II/266.*
Maier, Gerhard: Mensch und freier Wille. 1971.
  Vol. 12.

– Die Johannesoffenbarung und die Kirche. 1981. *Vol. 25.*

Markschies, Christoph: Valentinus Gnosticus? 1992. *Vol. 65.*

Marshall, Jonathan: Jesus, Patrons, and Benefactors. 2009. *Vol. II/259.*

Marshall, Peter: Enmity in Corinth: Social Conventions in Paul's Relations with the Corinthians. 1987. *Vol. II/23.*

Martin, Dale B.: see *Zangenberg, Jürgen.*

Maston, Jason: Divine and Human Agency in Second Temple Judaism and Paul. 2010. *Vol. II/297.*

Mayer, Annemarie: Sprache der Einheit im Epheserbrief und in der Ökumene. 2002. *Vol. II/150.*

Mayordomo, Moisés: Argumentiert Paulus logisch? 2005. *Vol. 188.*

McDonough, Sean M.: YHWH at Patmos: Rev. 1:4 in its Hellenistic and Early Jewish Setting. 1999. *Vol. II/107.*

McDowell, Markus: Prayers of Jewish Women. 2006. *Vol. II/211.*

McGlynn, Moyna: Divine Judgement and Divine Benevolence in the Book of Wisdom. 2001. *Vol. II/139.*

Meade, David G.: Pseudonymity and Canon. 1986. *Vol. 39.*

Meadors, Edward P.: Jesus the Messianic Herald of Salvation. 1995. *Vol. II/72.*

Meißner, Stefan: Die Heimholung des Ketzers. 1996. *Vol. II/87.*

Mell, Ulrich: Die „anderen" Winzer. 1994. *Vol. 77.*

– see *Sänger, Dieter.*

Mengel, Berthold: Studien zum Philipperbrief. 1982. *Vol. II/8.*

Merkel, Helmut: Die Widersprüche zwischen den Evangelien. 1971. *Vol. 13.*

– see *Ego, Beate.*

Merklein, Helmut: Studien zu Jesus und Paulus. Vol. 1 1987. *Vol. 43.* – Vol. 2 1998. *Vol. 105.*

Merkt, Andreas: see *Nicklas, Tobias*

Metzdorf, Christina: Die Tempelaktion Jesu. 2003. *Vol. II/168.*

Metzler, Karin: Der griechische Begriff des Verzeihens. 1991. *Vol. II/44.*

Metzner, Rainer: Die Rezeption des Matthäusevangeliums im 1. Petrusbrief. 1995. *Vol. II/74.*

– Das Verständnis der Sünde im Johannesevangelium. 2000. *Vol. 122.*

Mihoc, Vasile: see *Dunn, James D.G.*

– see *Klein, Hans.*

Mineshige, Kiyoshi: Besitzverzicht und Almosen bei Lukas. 2003. *Vol. II/163.*

Mittmann, Siegfried: see *Hengel, Martin.*

Mittmann-Richert, Ulrike: Magnifikat und Benediktus. 1996. *Vol. II/90.*

– Der Sühnetod des Gottesknechts. 2008. *Vol. 220.*

Miura, Yuzuru: David in Luke-Acts. 2007. *Vol. II/232.*

Moll, Sebastian: The Arch-Heretic Marcion. 2010. *Vol. 250.*

Morales, Rodrigo J.: The Spirit and the Restorat. 2010. *Vol. 282.*

Mournet, Terence C.: Oral Tradition and Literary Dependency. 2005. *Vol. II/195.*

Mußner, Franz: Jesus von Nazareth im Umfeld Israels und der Urkirche. Ed. von M. Theobald. 1998. *Vol. 111.*

Mutschler, Bernhard: Das Corpus Johanneum bei Irenäus von Lyon. 2005. *Vol. 189.*

– Glaube in den Pastoralbriefen. 2010. *Vol. 256.*

Myers, Susan E.: Spirit Epicleses in the Acts of Thomas. 2010. *Vol. 281.*

Nguyen, V. Henry T.: Christian Identity in Corinth. 2008. *Vol. II/243.*

Nicklas, Tobias, Andreas Merkt und *Joseph Verheyden* (Ed.): Gelitten – Gestorben – Auferstanden. 2010. *Vol. II/273.*

– see *Verheyden, Joseph*

Niebuhr, Karl-Wilhelm: Gesetz and Paränese. 1987. *Vol. II/28.*

– Heidenapostel aus Israel. 1992. *Vol. 62.*

– see *Deines, Roland.*

– see *Dimitrov, Ivan Z.*

– see *Klein, Hans.*

– see *Kraus, Wolfgang.*

Nielsen, Anders E.: "Until it is Fullfilled". 2000. *Vol. II/126.*

Nielsen, Jesper Tang: Die kognitive Dimension des Kreuzes. 2009. *Vol. II/263.*

Nissen, Andreas: Gott und der Nächste im antiken Judentum. 1974. *Vol. 15.*

Noack, Christian: Gottesbewußtsein. 2000. *Vol. II/116.*

Noormann, Rolf: Irenäus als Paulusinterpret. 1994. *Vol. II/66.*

Norin, Stig: see *Hultgård, Anders.*

Novakovic, Lidija: Messiah, the Healer of the Sick. 2003. *Vol. II/170.*

Obermann, Andreas: Die christologische Erfüllung der Schrift im Johannesevangelium. 1996. *Vol. II/83.*

Öhler, Markus: Barnabas. 2003. *Vol. 156.*

– see *Becker, Michael.*

Okure, Teresa: The Johannine Approach to Mission. 1988. *Vol. II/31.*

Onuki, Takashi: Heil und Erlösung. 2004. *Vol. 165.*

Oropeza, B. J.: Paul and Apostasy. 2000. *Vol. II/115.*

Ostmeyer, Karl-Heinrich: Kommunikation mit Gott und Christus. 2006. *Vol. 197.*
- Taute und Typos. 2000. *Vol. II/118.*

Pao, David W.: Acts and the Isaianic New Exodus. 2000. *Vol. II/130.*

Park, Eung Chun: The Mission Discourse in Matthew's Interpretation. 1995. *Vol. II/81.*

Park, Joseph S.: Conceptions of Afterlife in Jewish Insriptions. 2000. *Vol. II/121.*

Parsenios, George L.: Rhetoric and Drama in the Johannine Lawsuit Motif. 2010. *Vol. 258.*

Pate, C. Marvin: The Reverse of the Curse. 2000. *Vol. II/114.*

Paulsen, Henning: Studien zur Literatur und Geschichte des frühen Christentums. Ed. von Ute E. Eisen. 1997. *Vol. 99.*

Pearce, Sarah J.K.: The Land of the Body. 2007. *Vol. 208.*

Peres, Imre: Griechische Grabinschriften und neutestamentliche Eschatologie. 2003. *Vol. 157.*

Perry, Peter S.: The Rhetoric of Digressions. 2009. *Vol. II/268.*

Pierce, Chad T.: Spirits and the Proclamation of Christ. 2011. *Vol. II/305.*

Philip, Finny: The Origins of Pauline Pneumatology. 2005. *Vol. II/194.*

Philonenko, Marc (Ed.): Le Trône de Dieu. 1993. *Vol. 69.*

Pilhofer, Peter: Presbyteron Kreitton. 1990. *Vol. II/39.*
- Philippi. Vol. 1 1995. *Vol. 87.* – Vol. 2 ²2009. *Vol. 119.*
- Die frühen Christen und ihre Welt. 2002. *Vol. 145.*
- see *Becker, Eve-Marie.*
- see *Ego, Beate.*

Pitre, Brant: Jesus, the Tribulation, and the End of the Exile. 2005. *Vol. II/204.*

Plümacher, Eckhard: Geschichte und Geschichten. 2004. *Vol. 170.*

Pöhlmann, Wolfgang: Der Verlorene Sohn und das Haus. 1993. *Vol. 68.*

Poirier, John C.: The Tongues of Angels. 2010. *Vol. II/287.*

Pokorný, Petr and *Josef B. Souček:* Bibelauslegung als Theologie. 1997. *Vol. 100.*
- and *Jan Roskovec* (Ed.): Philosophical Hermeneutics and Biblical Exegesis. 2002. *Vol. 153.*

Popkes, Enno Edzard: Das Menschenbild des Thomasevangeliums. 2007. *Vol. 206.*
- Die Theologie der Liebe Gottes in den johanneischen Schriften. 2005. *Vol. II/197.*

Porter, Stanley E.: The Paul of Acts. 1999. *Vol. 115.*

Prieur, Alexander: Die Verkündigung der Gottesherrschaft. 1996. *Vol. II/89.*

Probst, Hermann: Paulus und der Brief. 1991. *Vol. II/45.*

Puig i Tàrrech, Armand: Jesus: An Uncommon Journey. 2010. *Vol. II/288.*

Rabens, Volker: The Holy Spirit and Ethics in Paul. 2010. *Vol. II/283.*

Räisänen, Heikki: Paul and the Law. 1983, ²1987. *Vol. 29.*

Rehkopf, Friedrich: Die lukanische Sonderquelle. 1959. *Vol. 5.*

Rein, Matthias: Die Heilung des Blindgeborenen (Joh 9). 1995. *Vol. II/73.*

Reinmuth, Eckart: Pseudo-Philo und Lukas. 1994. *Vol. 74.*

Reiser, Marius: Bibelkritik und Auslegung der Heiligen Schrift. 2007. *Vol. 217.*
- Syntax und Stil des Markusevangeliums. 1984. *Vol. II/11.*

Reynolds, Benjamin E.: The Apocalyptic Son of Man in the Gospel of John. 2008. *Vol. II/249.*

Rhodes, James N.: The Epistle of Barnabas and the Deuteronomic Tradition. 2004. *Vol. II/188.*

Richards, E. Randolph: The Secretary in the Letters of Paul. 1991. *Vol. II/42.*

Riesner, Rainer: Jesus als Lehrer. 1981, ³1988. *Vol. II/7.*
- Die Frühzeit des Apostels Paulus. 1994. *Vol. 71.*

Rissi, Mathias: Die Theologie des Hebräerbriefs. 1987. *Vol. 41.*

Röcker, Fritz W.: Belial und Katechon. 2009. *Vol. II/262.*

Röhser, Günter: Metaphorik und Personifikation der Sünde. 1987. *Vol. II/25.*

Rose, Christian: Theologie als Erzählung im Markusevangelium. 2007. *Vol. II/236.*
- Die Wolke der Zeugen. 1994. *Vol. II/60.*

Roskovec, Jan: see *Pokorný, Petr.*

Rothschild, Clare K.: Baptist Traditions and Q. 2005. *Vol. 190.*
- Hebrews as Pseudepigraphon. 2009. *Vol. 235.*
- Luke Acts and the Rhetoric of History. 2004. *Vol. II/175.*
- see *Frey, Jörg.*

Rudolph, David J.: A Jew to the Jews. 2011. *Vol. II/304.*

Rüegger, Hans-Ulrich: Verstehen, was Markus erzählt. 2002. *Vol. II/155.*

Rüger, Hans Peter: Die Weisheitsschrift aus der Kairoer Geniza. 1991. *Vol. 53.*

Ruf, Martin G.: Die heiligen Propheten, eure Apostel und ich. 2011. *Vol. II/300.*
Runesson, Anders: see *Becker, Eve-Marie.*
Sänger, Dieter: Antikes Judentum und die Mysterien. 1980. *Vol. II/5.*
– Die Verkündigung des Gekreuzigten und Israel. 1994. *Vol. 75.*
– see *Burchard, Christoph*
– and *Ulrich Mell* (Ed.): Paulus und Johannes. 2006. *Vol. 198.*
Salier, Willis Hedley: The Rhetorical Impact of the Semeia in the Gospel of John. 2004. *Vol. II/186.*
Salzmann, Jörg Christian: Lehren und Ermahnen. 1994. *Vol. II/59.*
Samuelsson, Gunnar: Crucifixion in Antiquity. 2011. *Vol. II/310.*
Sandnes, Karl Olav: Paul – One of the Prophets? 1991. *Vol. II/43.*
Sato, Migaku: Q und Prophetie. 1988. *Vol. II/29.*
Schäfer, Ruth: Paulus bis zum Apostelkonzil. 2004. *Vol. II/179.*
Schaper, Joachim: Eschatology in the Greek Psalter. 1995. *Vol. II/76.*
Schimanowski, Gottfried: Die himmlische Liturgie in der Apokalypse des Johannes. 2002. *Vol. II/154.*
– Weisheit und Messias. 1985. *Vol. II/17.*
Schlichting, Günter: Ein jüdisches Leben Jesu. 1982. *Vol. 24.*
Schließer, Benjamin: Abraham's Faith in Romans 4. 2007. *Vol. II/224.*
Schnabel, Eckhard J.: Law and Wisdom from Ben Sira to Paul. 1985. *Vol. II/16.*
Schnelle, Udo: see *Frey, Jörg.*
Schröter, Jens: Von Jesus zum Neuen Testament. 2007. *Vol. 204.*
– see *Frey, Jörg.*
Schutter, William L.: Hermeneutic and Composition in I Peter. 1989. *Vol. II/30.*
Schwartz, Daniel R.: Studies in the Jewish Background of Christianity. 1992. *Vol. 60.*
Schwemer, Anna Maria: see *Hengel, Martin*
Scott, Ian W.: Implicit Epistemology in the Letters of Paul. 2005. *Vol. II/205.*
Scott, James M.: Adoption as Sons of God. 1992. *Vol. II/48.*
– Paul and the Nations. 1995. *Vol. 84.*
Shi, Wenhua: Paul's Message of the Cross as Body Language. 2008. *Vol. II/254.*
Shum, Shiu-Lun: Paul's Use of Isaiah in Romans. 2002. *Vol. II/156.*
Siegert, Folker: Drei hellenistisch-jüdische Predigten. Teil I 1980. *Vol. 20* – Teil II 1992. *Vol. 61.*
– Nag-Hammadi-Register. 1982. *Vol. 26.*
– Argumentation bei Paulus. 1985. *Vol. 34.*

– Philon von Alexandrien. 1988. *Vol. 46.*
Siggelkow-Berner, Birke: Die jüdischen Feste im Bellum Judaicum des Flavius Josephus. 2011. *Vol. II/306.*
Simon, Marcel: Le christianisme antique et son contexte religieux I/II. 1981. *Vol. 23.*
Smit, Peter-Ben: Fellowship and Food in the Kingdom. 2008. *Vol. II/234.*
Snodgrass, Klyne: The Parable of the Wicked Tenants. 1983. *Vol. 27.*
Söding, Thomas: Das Wort vom Kreuz. 1997. *Vol. 93.*
– see *Thüsing, Wilhelm.*
Sommer, Urs: Die Passionsgeschichte des Markusevangeliums. 1993. *Vol. II/58.*
Sorensen, Eric: Possession and Exorcism in the New Testament and Early Christianity. 2002. *Vol. II/157.*
Souček, Josef B.: see *Pokorný, Petr.*
Southall, David J.: Rediscovering Righteousness in Romans. 2008. *Vol. 240.*
Spangenberg, Volker: Herrlichkeit des Neuen Bundes. 1993. *Vol. II/55.*
Spanje, T.E. van: Inconsistency in Paul? 1999. *Vol. II/110.*
Speyer, Wolfgang: Frühes Christentum im antiken Strahlungsfeld. Vol. I: 1989. *Vol. 50.*
– Vol. II: 1999. *Vol. 116.*
– Vol. III: 2007. *Vol. 213.*
Spittler, Janet E.: Animals in the Apocryphal Acts of the Apostles. 2008. *Vol. II/247.*
Sprinkle, Preston: Law and Life. 2008. *Vol. II/241.*
Stadelmann, Helge: Ben Sira als Schriftgelehrter. 1980. *Vol. II/6.*
Stein, Hans Joachim: Frühchristliche Mahlfeiern. 2008. *Vol. II/255.*
Stenschke, Christoph W.: Luke's Portrait of Gentiles Prior to Their Coming to Faith. *Vol. II/108.*
Stephens, Mark B.: Annihilation or Renewal? 2011. *Vol. II/307.*
Sterck-Degueldre, Jean-Pierre: Eine Frau namens Lydia. 2004. *Vol. II/176.*
Stettler, Christian: Der Kolosserhymnus. 2000. *Vol. II/131.*
– Das letzte Gericht. 2011. *Vol. II/299.*
Stettler, Hanna: Die Christologie der Pastoralbriefe. 1998. *Vol. II/105.*
Stökl Ben Ezra, Daniel: The Impact of Yom Kippur on Early Christianity. 2003. *Vol. 163.*
Strobel, August: Die Stunde der Wahrheit. 1980. *Vol. 21.*
Stroumsa, Guy G.: Barbarian Philosophy. 1999. *Vol. 112.*
Stuckenbruck, Loren T.: Angel Veneration and Christology. 1995. *Vol. II/70.*

–, *Stephen C. Barton* and *Benjamin G. Wold* (Ed.): Memory in the Bible and Antiquity. 2007. *Vol. 212.*

Stuhlmacher, Peter (Ed.): Das Evangelium und die Evangelien. 1983. *Vol. 28.*

– Biblische Theologie und Evangelium. 2002. *Vol. 146.*

Sung, Chong-Hyon: Vergebung der Sünden. 1993. *Vol. II/57.*

Svendsen, Stefan N.: Allegory Transformed. 2009. *Vol. II/269.*

Tajra, Harry W.: The Trial of St. Paul. 1989. *Vol. II/35.*

– The Martyrdom of St.Paul. 1994. *Vol. II/67.*

Tellbe, Mikael: Christ-Believers in Ephesus. 2009. *Vol. 242.*

Theißen, Gerd: Studien zur Soziologie des Urchristentums. 1979, ³1989. *Vol. 19.*

Theobald, Michael: Studien zum Corpus Iohanneum. 2010. *Vol. 267.*

– Studien zum Römerbrief. 2001. *Vol. 136.*

– see *Mußner, Franz.*

Thornton, Claus-Jürgen: Der Zeuge des Zeugen. 1991. *Vol. 56.*

Thüsing, Wilhelm: Studien zur neutestamentlichen Theologie. Ed. von Thomas Söding. 1995. *Vol. 82.*

Thurén, Lauri: Derhethorizing Paul. 2000. *Vol. 124.*

Thyen, Hartwig: Studien zum Corpus Iohanneum. 2007. *Vol. 214.*

Tibbs, Clint: Religious Experience of the Pneuma. 2007. *Vol. II/230.*

Toit, David S. du: Theios Anthropos. 1997. *Vol. II/91.*

Tolmie, D. Francois: Persuading the Galatians. 2005. *Vol. II/190.*

Tomson, Peter J. and *Doris Lambers-Petry* (Ed.): The Image of the Judaeo-Christians in Ancient Jewish and Christian Literature. 2003. *Vol. 158.*

Toney, Carl N.: Paul's Inclusive Ethic. 2008. *Vol. II/252.*

Trebilco, Paul: The Early Christians in Ephesus from Paul to Ignatius. 2004. *Vol. 166.*

Treloar, Geoffrey R.: Lightfoot the Historian. 1998. *Vol. II/103.*

Troftgruben, Troy M.: A Conclusion Unhindered. 2010. *Vol. II/280.*

Tso, Marcus K.M.: Ethics in the Qumran Community. 2010. *Vol. II/292.*

Tsuji, Manabu: Glaube zwischen Vollkommenheit und Verweltlichung. 1997. *Vol. II/93.*

Twelftree, Graham H.: Jesus the Exorcist. 1993. *Vol. II/54.*

Ulrichs, Karl Friedrich: Christusglaube. 2007. *Vol. II/227.*

Urban, Christina: Das Menschenbild nach dem Johannesevangelium. 2001. *Vol. II/137.*

Vahrenhorst, Martin: Kultische Sprache in den Paulusbriefen. 2008. *Vol. 230.*

Vegge, Ivar: 2 Corinthians – a Letter about Reconciliation. 2008. *Vol. II/239.*

Verheyden, Joseph, Korinna Zamfir and *Tobias Nicklas* (Ed.): Prophets and Prophecy in Jewish and Early Christian Literature. 2010. *Vol. II/286.*

– see *Nicklas, Tobias*

Visotzky, Burton L.: Fathers of the World. 1995. *Vol. 80.*

Vollenweider, Samuel: Horizonte neutestamentlicher Christologie. 2002. *Vol. 144.*

Vos, Johan S.: Die Kunst der Argumentation bei Paulus. 2002. *Vol. 149.*

Waaler, Erik: The *Shema* and The First Commandment in First Corinthians. 2008. *Vol. II/253.*

Wagener, Ulrike: Die Ordnung des „Hauses Gottes". 1994. *Vol. II/65.*

Wagner, J. Ross: see *Wilk, Florian.*

Wahlen, Clinton: Jesus and the Impurity of Spirits in the Synoptic Gospels. 2004. *Vol. II/185.*

Walker, Donald D.: Paul's Offer of Leniency (2 Cor 10:1). 2002. *Vol. II/152.*

Walter, Nikolaus: Praeparatio Evangelica. Ed. von Wolfgang Kraus und Florian Wilk. 1997. *Vol. 98.*

Wander, Bernd: Gottesfürchtige und Sympathisanten. 1998. *Vol. 104.*

Wardle, Timothy: The Jerusalem Temple and Early Christian Identity. 2010. *Vol. II/291.*

Wasserman, Emma: The Death of the Soul in Romans 7. 2008. *Vol. 256.*

Waters, Guy: The End of Deuteronomy in the Epistles of Paul. 2006. *Vol. 221.*

Watt, Jan G. van der: see *Frey, Jörg*

– see *Zimmermann, Ruben*

Watts, Rikki: Isaiah's New Exodus and Mark. 1997. *Vol. II/88.*

Webb, Robert L.: see *Bock, Darrell L.*

Wedderburn, Alexander J.M.: Baptism and Resurrection. 1987. *Vol. 44.*

– Jesus and the Historians. 2010. *Vol. 269.*

Wegner, Uwe: Der Hauptmann von Kafarnaum. 1985. *Vol. II/14.*

Weiß, Hans-Friedrich: Frühes Christentum und Gnosis. 2008. *Vol. 225.*

Weissenrieder, Annette: Images of Illness in the Gospel of Luke. 2003. Vol. II/164.

–, and *Robert B. Coote* (Ed.): The Interface of Orality and Writing. 2010. *Vol. 260.*

–, *Friederike Wendt* and *Petra von Gemünden* (Ed.): Picturing the New Testament. 2005. *Vol. II/193.*

Welck, Christian: Erzählte ‚Zeichen‘. 1994. *Vol. II/69.*

Wendt, Friederike (Ed.): see *Weissenrieder, Annette.*

Wiarda, Timothy: Peter in the Gospels. 2000. *Vol. II/127.*

Wifstrand, Albert: Epochs and Styles. 2005. *Vol. 179.*

Wilk, Florian and *J. Ross Wagner* (Ed.): Between Gospel and Election. 2010. *Vol. 257.*
– see *Walter, Nikolaus.*

Williams, Catrin H.: I am He. 2000. *Vol. II/113.*

Wilson, Todd A.: The Curse of the Law and the Crisis in Galatia. 2007. *Vol. II/225.*

Wilson, Walter T.: Love without Pretense. 1991. *Vol. II/46.*

Winn, Adam: The Purpose of Mark’s Gospel. 2008. *Vol. II/245.*

Winninge, Mikael: see *Holmberg, Bengt.*

Wischmeyer, Oda: Von Ben Sira zu Paulus. 2004. *Vol. 173.*

Wisdom, Jeffrey: Blessing for the Nations and the Curse of the Law. 2001. *Vol. II/133.*

Witmer, Stephen E.: Divine Instruction in Early Christianity. 2008. *Vol. II/246.*

Wold, Benjamin G.: Women, Men, and Angels. 2005. *Vol. II/2001.*

Wolter, Michael: Theologie und Ethos im frühen Christentum. 2009. *Vol. 236.*
– see *Stuckenbruck, Loren T.*

Wright, Archie T.: The Origin of Evil Spirits. 2005. *Vol. II/198.*

Wucherpfennig, Ansgar: Heracleon Philologus. 2002. *Vol. 142.*

Yates, John W.: The Spirit and Creation in Paul. 2008. *Vol. II/251.*

Yeung, Maureen: Faith in Jesus and Paul. 2002. *Vol. II/147.*

Young, Stephen E.: Jesus Tradition in the Apostolic Fathers. 2011. *Vol. II/311.*

Zamfir, Corinna: see *Verheyden, Joseph*

Zangenberg, Jürgen, Harold W. Attridge and *Dale B. Martin* (Ed.): Religion, Ethnicity and Identity in Ancient Galilee. 2007. *Vol. 210.*

Zimmermann, Alfred E.: Die urchristlichen Lehrer. 1984, ²1988. *Vol. II/12.*

Zimmermann, Johannes: Messianische Texte aus Qumran. 1998. *Vol. II/104.*

Zimmermann, Ruben: Christologie der Bilder im Johannesevangelium. 2004. *Vol. 171.*
– Geschlechtermetaphorik und Gottesverhältnis. 2001. *Vol. II/122.*
– (Ed.): Hermeneutik der Gleichnisse Jesu. 2008. *Vol. 231.*
– and *Jan G. van der Watt* (Ed.): Moral Language in the New Testament. Vol. II. 2010. *Vol. II/296.*
– see *Frey, Jörg.*
– see *Horn, Friedrich Wilhelm.*

Zugmann, Michael: „Hellenisten“ in der Apostelgeschichte. 2009. *Vol. II/264.*

Zumstein, Jean: see *Dettwiler, Andreas*

Zwiep, Arie W.: Christ, the Spirit and the Community of God. 2010. *Vol. II/293.*
– Judas and the Choice of Matthias. 2004. *Vol. II/187.*

For a complete catalogue please write to the publisher
Mohr Siebeck • P.O. Box 2030 • D–72010 Tübingen/Germany
Up-to-date information on the internet at www.mohr.de